EQUITY VALUATION, FIXED INCOME

CFA® Program Curriculum
2023 • LEVEL 2 • VOLUME 4

WILEY

ISBN 978-1-953337-08-5 (paper)
ISBN 978-1-953337-32-0 (ebook)

2022

Please visit our website at
www.WileyGlobalFinance.com.

CONTENTS

◙ indicates an optional segment

◙ indicates an optional segment

Fixed Income

◙ indicates an optional segment

How to Use the CFA Program Curriculum

The CFA® Program exams measure your mastery of the core knowledge, skills, and abilities required to succeed as an investment professional. These core competencies are the basis for the Candidate Body of Knowledge (CBOK™). The CBOK consists of four components:

- A broad outline that lists the major CFA Program topic areas (www.cfainstitute.org/programs/cfa/curriculum/cbok)

- Topic area weights that indicate the relative exam weightings of the top-level topic areas (www.cfainstitute.org/programs/cfa/curriculum)

- Learning outcome statements (LOS) that advise candidates about the specific knowledge, skills, and abilities they should acquire from curriculum content covering a topic area: LOS are provided in candidate study sessions and at the beginning of each block of related content and the specific lesson that covers them. We encourage you to review the information about the LOS on our website (www.cfainstitute.org/programs/cfa/curriculum/study-sessions), including the descriptions of LOS "command words" on the candidate resources page at www.cfainstitute.org.

- The CFA Program curriculum that candidates receive upon exam registration

Therefore, the key to your success on the CFA exams is studying and understanding the CBOK. You can learn more about the CBOK on our website: www.cfainstitute.org/programs/cfa/curriculum/cbok.

The entire curriculum, including the practice questions, is the basis for all exam questions and is selected or developed specifically to teach the knowledge, skills, and abilities reflected in the CBOK.

ERRATA

The curriculum development process is rigorous and includes multiple rounds of reviews by content experts. Despite our efforts to produce a curriculum that is free of errors, there are instances where we must make corrections. Curriculum errata are periodically updated and posted by exam level and test date online on the Curriculum Errata webpage (www.cfainstitute.org/en/programs/submit-errata). If you believe you have found an error in the curriculum, you can submit your concerns through our curriculum errata reporting process found at the bottom of the Curriculum Errata webpage.

DESIGNING YOUR PERSONAL STUDY PROGRAM

An orderly, systematic approach to exam preparation is critical. You should dedicate a consistent block of time every week to reading and studying. Review the LOS both before and after you study curriculum content to ensure that you have mastered the applicable content and can demonstrate the knowledge, skills, and abilities described by the LOS and the assigned reading. Use the LOS self-check to track your progress and highlight areas of weakness for later review.

Successful candidates report an average of more than 300 hours preparing for each exam. Your preparation time will vary based on your prior education and experience, and you will likely spend more time on some study sessions than on others.

CFA INSTITUTE LEARNING ECOSYSTEM (LES)

Your exam registration fee includes access to the CFA Program Learning Ecosystem (LES). This digital learning platform provides access, even offline, to all of the curriculum content and practice questions and is organized as a series of short online lessons with associated practice questions. This tool is your one-stop location for all study materials, including practice questions and mock exams, and the primary method by which CFA Institute delivers your curriculum experience. The LES offers candidates additional practice questions to test their knowledge, and some questions in the LES provide a unique interactive experience.

FEEDBACK

Please send any comments or feedback to info@cfainstitute.org, and we will review your suggestions carefully.

Equity Valuation

LEARNING MODULE

1

Free Cash Flow Valuation

by Jerald E. Pinto, PhD, CFA, Elaine Henry, PhD, CFA, Thomas R. Robinson, PhD, CFA, CAIA, and John D. Stowe, PhD, CFA.

Jerald E. Pinto, PhD, CFA, is at CFA Institute (USA). Elaine Henry, PhD, CFA, is at Stevens Institute of Technology (USA). Thomas R. Robinson, PhD, CFA, CAIA, Robinson Global Investment Management LLC, (USA). John D. Stowe, PhD, CFA, is at Ohio University (USA).

LEARNING OUTCOMES

Mastery	The candidate should be able to:
☐	compare the free cash flow to the firm (FCFF) and free cash flow to equity (FCFE) approaches to valuation
☐	explain the ownership perspective implicit in the FCFE approach
☐	explain the appropriate adjustments to net income, earnings before interest and taxes (EBIT), earnings before interest, taxes, depreciation, and amortization (EBITDA), and cash flow from operations (CFO) to calculate FCFF and FCFE
☐	calculate FCFF and FCFE
☐	describe approaches for forecasting FCFF and FCFE
☐	explain how dividends, share repurchases, share issues, and changes in leverage may affect future FCFF and FCFE
☐	compare the FCFE model and dividend discount models
☐	evaluate the use of net income and EBITDA as proxies for cash flow in valuation
☐	explain the use of sensitivity analysis in FCFF and FCFE valuations
☐	explain the single-stage (stable-growth), two-stage, and three-stage FCFF and FCFE models and justify the selection of the appropriate model given a company's characteristics
☐	estimate a company's value using the appropriate free cash flow model(s)
☐	describe approaches for calculating the terminal value in a multistage valuation model; and
☐	evaluate whether a stock is overvalued, fairly valued, or undervalued based on a free cash flow valuation model

1   INTRODUCTION

☐ | compare the free cash flow to the firm (FCFF) and free cash flow to equity (FCFE) approaches to valuation
☐ | explain the ownership perspective implicit in the FCFE approach

Discounted cash flow (DCF) valuation views the intrinsic value of a security as the present value of its expected future cash flows. When applied to dividends, the DCF model is the discounted dividend approach or dividend discount model (DDM). Our coverage extends DCF analysis to value a company and its equity securities by valuing free cash flow to the firm (FCFF) and free cash flow to equity (FCFE). Whereas dividends are the cash flows actually paid to stockholders, free cash flows are the cash flows *available* for distribution to shareholders.

Unlike dividends, FCFF and FCFE are not readily available data. Analysts need to compute these quantities from available financial information, which requires a clear understanding of free cash flows and the ability to interpret and use the information correctly. Forecasting future free cash flows is a rich and demanding exercise. The analyst's understanding of a company's financial statements, its operations, its financing, and its industry can pay real "dividends" as he or she addresses that task. Many analysts consider free cash flow models to be more useful than DDMs in practice. Free cash flows provide an economically sound basis for valuation.

A study of professional analysts substantiates the importance of free cash flow valuation (Pinto, Robinson, Stowe 2019). When valuing individual equities, 92.8% of analysts use market multiples and 78.8% use a discounted cash flow approach. When using discounted cash flow analysis, 20.5% of analysts use a residual income approach, 35.1% use a dividend discount model, and 86.9% use a discounted free cash flow model. Of those using discounted free cash flow models, FCFF models are used roughly twice as frequently as FCFE models. Analysts often use more than one method to value equities, and it is clear that free cash flow analysis is in near universal use.

Analysts like to use free cash flow as the return (either FCFF or FCFE) whenever one or more of the following conditions is present:

- The company does not pay dividends.

- The company pays dividends, but the dividends paid differ significantly from the company's capacity to pay dividends.

- Free cash flows align with profitability within a reasonable forecast period with which the analyst is comfortable.

- The investor takes a "control" perspective. With control comes discretion over the uses of free cash flow. If an investor can take control of the company (or expects another investor to do so), dividends may be changed substantially; for example, they may be set at a level approximating the company's capacity to pay dividends. Such an investor can also apply free cash flows to uses such as servicing the debt incurred in an acquisition.

Common equity can be valued directly by finding the present value of FCFE or indirectly by first using an FCFF model to estimate the value of the firm and then subtracting the value of non-common-stock capital (usually debt) to arrive at an estimate of the value of equity. The purpose of the coverage in the subsequent sections is to develop the background required to use the FCFF or FCFE approaches to value a company's equity.

In the next section, we define the concepts of free cash flow to the firm and free cash flow to equity and then present the two valuation models based on discounting of FCFF and FCFE. We also explore the constant-growth models for valuing FCFF and FCFE, which are special cases of the general models. The subsequent sections turn to the vital task of calculating and forecasting FCFF and FCFE. They also explain multistage free cash flow valuation models and present some of the issues associated with their application. Analysts usually value operating assets and non-operating assets separately and then combine them to find the total value of the firm, an approach described in the last section on this topic.

FCFF and FCFE Valuation Approaches

The purpose of this section is to provide a conceptual understanding of free cash flows and the valuation models based on them. A detailed accounting treatment of free cash flows and more-complicated valuation models follow in subsequent sections.

Defining Free Cash Flow

Free cash flow to the firm is the cash flow available to the company's suppliers of capital after all operating expenses (including taxes) have been paid and necessary investments in working capital (e.g., inventory) and fixed capital (e.g., equipment) have been made. FCFF is the cash flow from operations minus capital expenditures. A company's suppliers of capital include common stockholders, bondholders, and, sometimes, preferred stockholders. The equations analysts use to calculate FCFF depend on the accounting information available.

Free cash flow to equity is the cash flow available to the company's holders of common equity after all operating expenses, interest, and principal payments have been paid and necessary investments in working and fixed capital have been made. FCFE is the cash flow from operations minus capital expenditures minus payments to (plus receipts from) debtholders.

The way in which free cash flow is related to a company's net income, cash flow from operations, and measures such as EBITDA (earnings before interest, taxes, depreciation, and amortization) is important: The analyst must understand the relationship between a company's reported accounting data and free cash flow in order to forecast free cash flow and its expected growth. Although a company reports cash flow from operations (CFO) on the statement of cash flows, CFO is *not* free cash flow. Net income and CFO data can be used, however, in determining a company's free cash flow.

The advantage of FCFF and FCFE over other cash-flow concepts is that they can be used directly in a DCF framework to value the firm or to value equity. Other cash flow— or earnings-related measures, such as CFO, net income, EBIT, and EBITDA, do not have this property because they either double-count or omit cash flows in some way. For example, EBIT and EBITDA are before-tax measures, and the cash flows available to investors (in the firm or in the equity of the firm) must be after tax. From the stockholders' perspective, EBITDA and similar measures do not account for differing capital structures (the after-tax interest expenses or preferred dividends) or for the funds that bondholders supply to finance investments in operating assets. Moreover, these measures do not account for the reinvestment of cash flows that the company makes in capital assets and working capital to maintain or maximize the long-run value of the firm.

Using free cash flow in valuation is more challenging than using dividends because in forecasting free cash flow, the analyst must integrate the cash flows from the company's operations with those from its investing and financing activities. Because FCFF is the after-tax cash flow going to all suppliers of capital to the firm, the value of the firm is estimated by discounting FCFF at the weighted average cost of capital

(WACC). An estimate of the value of equity is then found by subtracting the value of debt from the estimated value of the firm. The value of equity can also be estimated directly by discounting FCFE at the required rate of return for equity (because FCFE is the cash flow going to common stockholders, the required rate of return on equity is the appropriate risk-adjusted rate for discounting FCFE).

The two free cash flow approaches for valuing equity, FCFF and FCFE, theoretically should yield the same estimates if all inputs reflect identical assumptions. An analyst may prefer to use one approach rather than the other, however, because of the characteristics of the company being valued. For example, if the company's capital structure is relatively stable, using FCFE to value equity is more direct and simpler than using FCFF. The FCFF model is often chosen, however, in two other cases:

- *A levered company with negative FCFE.* In this case, working with FCFF to value the company's equity might be easiest. The analyst would discount FCFF to find the present value of operating assets, adding the value of excess cash ("excess" in relation to operating needs) and marketable securities and of any other significant non-operating assets to get total firm value. He or she would then subtract the market value of debt to obtain an estimate of the intrinsic value of equity.

- *A levered company with a changing capital structure.* First, if historical data are used to forecast free cash flow growth rates, FCFF growth might reflect fundamentals more clearly than does FCFE growth, which reflects fluctuating amounts of net borrowing. Second, in a forward-looking context, the required return on equity might be expected to be more sensitive to changes in financial leverage than changes in the WACC, making the use of a constant discount rate difficult to justify.

Specialized DCF approaches are also available to facilitate the equity valuation when the capital structure is expected to change. The **adjusted present value** (APV) approach is one example of such models. In the APV approach, firm value is calculated as the sum of (1) the value of the company under the assumption that debt is not used (i.e., unlevered firm value) and (2) the net present value of any effects of debt on firm value (such as any tax benefits of using debt and any costs of financial distress). In this approach, the analyst estimates unlevered company value by discounting FCFF (under the assumption of no debt) at the unlevered cost of equity (the cost of equity given that the firm does not use debt). For more info, see Luehrman (1997), who explained APV in a capital budgeting context.

In the following section, we present the general form of the FCFF valuation model and the FCFE valuation model.

Present Value of Free Cash Flow

The two distinct approaches to using free cash flow for valuation are the FCFF valuation approach and the FCFE valuation approach. The general expressions for these valuation models are similar to the expression for the general dividend discount model. In the DDM, the value of a share of stock equals the present value of forecasted dividends from Time 1 through infinity discounted at the required rate of return for equity.

Present Value of FCFF

The FCFF valuation approach estimates the value of the firm as the present value of future FCFF discounted at the weighted average cost of capital:

$$\text{Firm value} = \sum_{t=1}^{\infty} \frac{FCFF_t}{(1 + WACC)^t} \qquad (1)$$

Because FCFF is the cash flow available to all suppliers of capital, using WACC to discount FCFF gives the total value of all of the firm's capital. The value of equity is the value of the firm minus the market value of its debt:

$$\text{Equity value} = \text{Firm value} - \text{Market value of debt.} \tag{2}$$

Dividing the total value of equity by the number of outstanding shares gives the value per share.

The cost of capital is the required rate of return that investors should demand for a cash flow stream like that generated by the company being analyzed. WACC depends on the riskiness of these cash flows. The calculation and interpretation of WACC were discussed earlier under the topic of return concepts; that is, WACC is the weighted average of the after (corporate) tax required rates of return for debt and equity, where the weights are the proportions of the firm's total market value from each source, debt and equity. As an alternative, analysts may use the weights of debt and equity in the firm's target capital structure when those weights are known and differ from market value weights. The formula for WACC is

$$\text{WACC} = \frac{\text{MV(Debt)}}{\text{MV(Debt)} + \text{MV(Equity)}} r_d (1 - \text{Tax rate})$$
$$+ \frac{\text{MV(Equity)}}{\text{MV(Debt)} + \text{MV(Equity)}} r. \tag{3}$$

MV(Debt) and MV(Equity) are the current market values of debt and equity, not their book or accounting values, and the ratios of MV(Debt) and MV(Equity) to the total market value of debt plus equity define the weights in the WACC formula. The quantities $r_d(1 - \text{Tax rate})$ and r are, respectively, the after-tax cost of debt and the after-tax cost of equity (in the case of equity, one could just write "cost of equity" because net income, the income belonging to equity, is after tax). In Equation 3, the tax rate is in principle the marginal corporate income tax rate.

Present Value of FCFE

The value of equity can also be found by discounting FCFE at the required rate of return on equity, r:

$$\text{Equity value} = \sum_{t=1}^{\infty} \frac{\text{FCFE}_t}{(1+r)^t}. \tag{4}$$

Because FCFE is the cash flow remaining for equity holders after all other claims have been satisfied, discounting FCFE by r (the required rate of return on equity) gives the value of the firm's equity. Dividing the total value of equity by the number of outstanding shares gives the value per share.

Single-Stage (Constant-Growth) FCFF and FCFE Models

In the DDM approach, the Gordon (constant- or stable-growth) model makes the assumption that dividends grow at a constant rate. The assumption that free cash flows grow at a constant rate leads to a single-stage (stable-growth) FCFF or FCFE model.

Constant-Growth FCFF Valuation Model

Assume that FCFF grows at a constant rate, g, such that FCFF in any period is equal to FCFF in the previous period multiplied by $(1 + g)$:

$$\text{FCFF}_t = \text{FCFF}_{t-1}(1 + g).$$

If FCFF grows at a constant rate,

g: constant growth rate of FCFF

$$\text{Firm value} = \frac{\text{FCFF}_1}{\text{WACC} - g} = \frac{\text{FCFF}_0(1 + g)}{\text{WACC} - g}. \tag{5}$$

Subtracting the market value of debt from the firm value gives the value of equity.

EXAMPLE 1

Using the Constant-Growth FCFF Valuation Model

Cagiati Enterprises has FCFF of 700 million Swiss francs (CHF) and FCFE of CHF620 million. Cagiati's before-tax cost of debt is 5.7%, and its required rate of return for equity is 11.8%. The company expects a target capital structure consisting of 20% debt financing and 80% equity financing. The tax rate is 33.33%, and FCFF is expected to grow forever at 5.0%. Cagiati Enterprises has debt outstanding with a market value of CHF2.2 billion and has 200 million outstanding common shares.

---

1. What is Cagiati's weighted average cost of capital?

Solution:

From Equation 3, WACC is calculated as follows:

$$\text{WACC} = 0.20(5.7\%)(1 - 0.3333) + 0.80(11.8\%) = 10.2\%.$$

---

2. What is the value of Cagiati's equity using the FCFF valuation approach?

Solution:

The firm value of Cagiati Enterprises is the present value of FCFF discounted by using WACC. For FCFF growing at a constant 5% rate, the result is

$$\text{Firm value} = \frac{\text{FCFF}_1}{\text{WACC} - g} = \frac{\text{FCFF}_0(1 + g)}{\text{WACC} - g} = \frac{700(1.05)}{0.102 - 0.05}$$

$$= \frac{735}{0.052} = \text{CHF}14,134.6 \text{ million.}$$

The value of equity is the value of the firm minus the value of debt:

$$\text{Equity value} = 14,134.6 - 2,200 = \text{CHF}11,934.6 \text{ million.}$$

---

3. What is the value per share using this FCFF approach?

Solution:

Dividing CHF11,934.6 million by the number of outstanding shares gives the estimated value per share, V_0:

$$V_0 = \text{CHF}11,934.6 \text{ million}/200 \text{ million shares}$$

$$= \text{CHF}59.67 \text{ per share.}$$

Constant-Growth FCFE Valuation Model

The constant-growth FCFE valuation model assumes that FCFE grows at constant rate g. FCFE in any period is equal to FCFE in the preceding period multiplied by $(1 + g)$:

$$\text{FCFE}_t = \text{FCFE}_{t-1}(1 + g).$$

The value of equity if FCFE is growing at a constant rate is

$$\text{Equity value} = \frac{\text{FCFE}_1}{r - g} = \frac{\text{FCFE}_0(1 + g)}{r - g}. \qquad g: \text{constant growth rate of FCFE} \tag{6}$$

The discount rate is r, the required rate of return on equity. Note that the growth rate of FCFF and the growth rate of FCFE need not be and frequently are not the same.

In this section, we presented the basic ideas underlying free cash flow valuation and the simplest implementation, single-stage free cash flow models. The next section examines the precise definition of free cash flow and introduces the issues involved in forecasting free cash flow.

FORECASTING FREE CASH FLOW AND COMPUTING FCFF FROM NET INCOME

2

☐ | explain the appropriate adjustments to net income, earnings before interest and taxes (EBIT), earnings before interest, taxes, depreciation, and amortization (EBITDA), and cash flow from operations (CFO) to calculate FCFF and FCFE

☐ | calculate FCFF and FCFE

☐ | describe approaches for forecasting FCFF and FCFE

Estimating FCFF or FCFE requires a complete understanding of the company and its financial statements. To provide a context for the estimation of FCFF and FCFE, we first discuss the calculation of free cash flows, including the relationship between free cash flow and accounting measures of income. We then describe approaches to forecasting free cash flow. For most of this section, we assume that the company has two sources of capital: debt and common stock. We then incorporate preferred stock as a third source of capital.

Computing FCFF from Net Income

FCFF is the cash flow available to the company's suppliers of capital after all operating expenses (including taxes) have been paid and operating investments have been made. The company's suppliers of capital include bondholders and common shareholders (plus, occasionally, holders of preferred stock, which we ignore until later). Keeping in mind that a noncash charge is a charge or expense that does not involve the outlay of cash, we can write the expression for FCFF as follows:

FCFF = Net income available to common shareholders (NI)
Plus: Net noncash charges (NCC)
Plus: Interest expense × (1 − Tax rate)
Less: Investment in fixed capital (FCInv)
Less: Investment in working capital (WCInv).

This equation can be written more compactly as

$$FCFF = NI + NCC + Int(1 − Tax rate) − FCInv − WCInv. \tag{7}$$

Consider each component of FCFF. The starting point in Equation 7 is net income available to common shareholders—usually, but not always, the bottom line in an income statement. It represents income after depreciation, amortization, interest expense, income taxes, and the payment of dividends to preferred shareholders (but not payment of dividends to common shareholders).

To derive cash flow from net income, it is necessary to make adjustments for any items that involved decreases and increases in net income but did not involve cash inflows or outflows. These items are referred to as noncash charges (NCC). If noncash decreases in net income exceed the increases, as is usually the case, the total adjustment is positive. If noncash increases exceed noncash decreases, the total adjustment is negative. The most common noncash charge is depreciation expense. The depreciation expense reduces net income but is not a cash outflow. Depreciation expense is thus one (the most common) noncash charge that must be added back in computing FCFF. In the case of intangible assets, there is a similar noncash charge, amortization expense, which must be added back. Other noncash charges vary from company to company and are discussed later.

After-tax interest expense must be added back to net income to arrive at FCFF. This step is required because interest expense net of the related tax savings was deducted in arriving at net income, but interest is a cash flow available to one of the company's capital providers (i.e., the company's creditors). In many countries, interest is tax deductible (reduces taxes) for the company (borrower) and taxable for the recipient (lender). As we explain later, when we discount FCFF, we use an after-tax cost of capital. For consistency, we thus compute FCFF by using the after-tax interest paid. Note that we could compute WACC on a pretax basis and compute FCFF by adding back interest paid with no tax adjustment. Whichever approach is adopted, the analyst must use mutually consistent definitions of FCFF and WACC.

Similar to the treatment of after-tax interest expense, dividends on preferred stock that are deducted in arriving at net income available to common shareholders must be added back to derive FCFF. The reason for the add-back is that preferred stock dividends are also a cash flow available to one of the company's capital providers and thus constitute part of overall FCFF.

Investments in fixed capital represent the outflows of cash to purchase the fixed capital necessary to support the company's current and future operations. These investments are capital expenditures for long-term assets, such as the property, plant, and equipment (PP&E) necessary to support the company's operations. Necessary capital expenditures may also include intangible assets, such as trademarks. In the case of a cash acquisition of another company instead of a direct acquisition of PP&E, the cash purchase amount can also be treated as a capital expenditure that reduces the company's free cash flow (note that this treatment is conservative because it reduces FCFF). In the case of large acquisitions (and all noncash acquisitions), analysts must take care in evaluating the impact on future free cash flow. If a company receives cash in disposing of any of its fixed capital, the analyst must deduct this cash in calculating investment in fixed capital. For example, suppose a company sells equipment for $100,000. This cash inflow would reduce the company's cash outflows for investments in fixed capital.

The company's statement of cash flows is an excellent source of information on capital expenditures as well as on sales of fixed capital. Analysts should be aware that some companies acquire fixed capital without using cash—for example, through an exchange for stock or debt. Such acquisitions do not appear in a company's statement of cash flows but, if material, must be disclosed in the footnotes. Although noncash exchanges do not affect historical FCFF, if the capital expenditures are necessary and may be made in cash in the future, the analyst should use this information in forecasting future FCFF.

Finally, the adjustment for net increases in working capital represents the net investment in current assets (such as accounts receivable) less current liabilities (such as accounts payable). Analysts can find this information by examining either the company's balance sheet or its statement of cash flows.

Although working capital is often defined as current assets minus current liabilities, working capital for cash flow and valuation purposes is defined to exclude cash and short-term debt (which includes notes payable and the current portion of long-term debt). When finding the net increase in working capital for the purpose of calculating free cash flow, we define working capital to exclude cash and cash equivalents as well as notes payable and the current portion of long-term debt. Cash and cash equivalents are excluded because a change in cash is what we are trying to explain. Notes payable and the current portion of long-term debt are excluded because they are liabilities with explicit interest costs that make them financing items rather than operating items.

Example 2 shows the adjustments to net income required to find FCFF.

EXAMPLE 2

Calculating FCFF from Net Income

1. Cane Distribution, Inc., incorporated on 31 December 2017 with initial capital infusions of $224,000 of debt and $336,000 of common stock, acts as a distributor of industrial goods. The company managers immediately invested the initial capital in fixed capital of $500,000 and working capital of $60,000. Working capital initially consisted solely of inventory. The fixed capital consisted of nondepreciable property of $50,000 and depreciable property of $450,000. The depreciable property has a 10-year useful life with no salvage value. Exhibit 1, Exhibit 2, and Exhibit 3 provide Cane's financial statements for the three years following incorporation. Starting with net income, calculate Cane's FCFF for each year.

Exhibit 1: Cane Distribution, Inc., Income Statement (in Thousands)

	Years Ending 31 December		
	2018	2019	2020
Earnings before interest, taxes, depreciation, and amortization (EBITDA)	$200.00	$220.00	$242.00
Depreciation expense	45.00	49.50	54.45
Operating income	155.00	170.50	187.55
Interest expense (at 7%)	15.68	17.25	18.97
Income before taxes	139.32	153.25	168.58
Income taxes (at 30%)	41.80	45.97	50.58
Net income	$97.52	$107.28	$118.00

Exhibit 2: Cane Distribution, Inc., Balance Sheet (in Thousands)

	Years Ending 31 December			
	2017	2018	2019	2020
Cash	$0.00	$108.92	$228.74	$360.54
Accounts receivable	0.00	100.00	110.00	121.00
Inventory	60.00	66.00	72.60	79.86
Current assets	60.00	274.92	411.34	561.40
Fixed assets	500.00	500.00	550.00	605.00
Less: Accumulated depreciation	0.00	45.00	94.50	148.95
Total assets	$560.00	$729.92	$866.84	$1,017.45
Accounts payable	$0.00	$50.00	$55.00	$60.50
Current portion of long-term debt	0.00	0.00	0.00	0.00

	Years Ending 31 December			
	2017	**2018**	**2019**	**2020**
Current liabilities	0.00	50.00	55.00	60.50
Long-term debt	224.00	246.40	271.04	298.14
Common stock	336.00	336.00	336.00	336.00
Retained earnings	0.00	97.52	204.80	322.80
Total liabilities and equity	$560.00	$729.92	$866.84	$1,017.45

Exhibit 3: Cane Distribution, Inc., Working Capital (in Thousands)

	Years Ending 31 December			
	2017	**2018**	**2019**	**2020**
Current assets excluding cash				
Accounts receivable	$0.00	$100.00	$110.00	$121.00
Inventory	60.00	66.00	72.60	79.86
Total current assets excluding cash	60.00	166.00	182.60	200.86
Current liabilities excluding short-term debt				
Accounts payable	0.00	50.00	55.00	60.50
Working capital	$60.00	$116.00	$127.60	$140.36
Increase in working capital		$56.00	$11.60	$12.76

Solution:

Following the logic in Equation 7, we calculate FCFF from net income as follows: We add noncash charges (here, depreciation) and after-tax interest expense to net income and then subtract the investment in fixed capital and the investment in working capital. The format for presenting the solution follows the convention that parentheses around a number indicate subtraction. The calculation follows (in thousands):

	Years Ending 31 December		
	2018	**2019**	**2020**
Net income	$97.52	$107.28	$118.00
Noncash charges – Depreciation	45.00	49.50	54.45
Interest expense × (1 – Tax rate)	10.98	12.08	13.28
Investment in fixed capital	(0.00)	(50.00)	(55.00)
Investment in working capital	(56.00)	(11.60)	(12.76)
Free cash flow to the firm	$97.50	$107.26	$117.97

COMPUTING FCFF FROM THE CASH FLOW STATEMENT

3

☐ explain the appropriate adjustments to net income, earnings before interest and taxes (EBIT), earnings before interest, taxes, depreciation, and amortization (EBITDA), and cash flow from operations (CFO) to calculate FCFF and FCFE

☐ calculate FCFF and FCFE

☐ describe approaches for forecasting FCFF and FCFE

FCFF is the cash flow that is available to all providers of capital (debt and equity). Analysts frequently use cash flow from operations, taken from the statement of cash flows, as a starting point to compute free cash flow because CFO incorporates adjustments for noncash expenses (such as depreciation and amortization) as well as for net investments in working capital.

In most cases, companies include interest paid as part of operating cash flow. Under US generally accepted accounting principles (GAAP), companies must include interest paid in operating cash flow. Under International Financial Reporting Standards (IFRS), companies may include interest paid in either financing or operating. According to Gordon, Henry, Jorgensen, and Linthicum (2017), most IFRS-reporting European firms choose to classify interest paid within the operating cash flow section of the statement of cash flows. This will be discussed later. Assuming that interest paid is included in operating cash flow, FCFF can be estimated as follows:

Free cash flow to the firm = Cash flow from operations
Plus: Interest expense × (1 − Tax rate)
Less: Investment in fixed capital,

or

$$FCFF = CFO + Int(1 - \text{Tax rate}) - FCInv. \tag{8}$$

To reiterate, as with the calculation shown as Equation 7, the after-tax interest expense is added back because it was previously taken out of net income but must be included in FCFF because it is a component of the total cash flows available to all suppliers of the firm's capital. In comparison with Equation 7, neither depreciation nor the investment in working capital appears in Equation 8 because both are already included in CFO. Example 3 illustrates the use of CFO to calculate FCFF. In this example, the operating section of the statement of cash flows begins with net income and presents each adjustment required to derive operating cash flow. This presentation, known as the "indirect" method because it derives operating cash flows indirectly from net income via adjustments, is the most common presentation of the statement of cash flows.

EXAMPLE 3

Calculating FCFF from CFO

1. Use the information from the statement of cash flows given in Exhibit 4 to calculate FCFF for the three years 2018–2020. The tax rate (as given in Exhibit 1) is 30%.

> **Exhibit 4: Cane Distribution, Inc., Statement of Cash Flows: Indirect Method (in Thousands)**
>
> | | Years Ending 31 December | | |
> | --- | --- | --- | --- |
> | | **2018** | **2019** | **2020** |
> | **Cash flow from operations** | | | |
> | Net income | $97.52 | $107.28 | $118.00 |
> | Plus: Depreciation | 45.00 | 49.50 | 54.45 |
> | Increase in accounts receivable | (100.00) | (10.00) | (11.00) |
> | Increase in inventory | (6.00) | (6.60) | (7.26) |
> | Increase in accounts payable | 50.00 | 5.00 | 5.50 |
> | Cash flow from operations | 86.52 | 145.18 | 159.69 |
> | **Cash flow from investing activities** | | | |
> | Purchases of PP&E | 0.00 | (50.00) | (55.00) |
> | **Cash flow from financing activities** | | | |
> | Borrowing (repayment) | 22.40 | 24.64 | 27.10 |
> | Total cash flow | 108.92 | 119.82 | 131.80 |
> | Beginning cash | 0.00 | 108.92 | 228.74 |
> | Ending cash | $108.92 | $228.74 | $360.54 |
> | *Notes:* | | | |
> | Cash paid for interest | ($15.68) | ($17.25) | ($18.97) |
> | Cash paid for taxes | ($41.80) | ($45.98) | ($50.57) |

Solution:

As shown in Equation 8, FCFF equals CFO plus after-tax interest expense minus the investment in fixed capital:

	Years Ending 31 December		
	2018	**2019**	**2020**
Cash flow from operations	$86.52	$145.18	$159.69
Interest expense × (1 − Tax rate)	10.98	12.08	13.28
Investment in fixed capital	(0.00)	(50.00)	(55.00)
Free cash flow to the firm	$97.50	$107.26	$117.97

4   ADDITIONAL CONSIDERATIONS IN COMPUTING FCFF

☐ calculate FCFF and FCFE
☐ describe approaches for forecasting FCFF and FCFE

Whether an analyst selects net income or cash flow from operations as a starting point in calculating free cash flows, some situations warrant a closer examination. In this section, we first describe classification of certain items on the statement of cash flows that merit attention when deriving free cash flow using cash flow from operations as a starting point. We then review the common adjustments for noncash charges made in deriving cash flow from net income and highlight several areas that merit additional attention from an analyst.

Classification of Certain Items on the Statement of Cash Flow

As noted above, IFRSallow the company to classify interest paid as either an operating or financing activity. Furthermore, IFRS allow dividends paid to be classified as either an operating or financing activity. In contrast, under US GAAP, interest paid to providers of debt capital must be classified as part of cash flow from operations (as are interest income and dividend income), but payment of dividends to providers of equity capital is classified as a financing activity.

Exhibit 5 summarizes IFRS and US GAAP treatment of interest and dividends.

Exhibit 5: IFRS vs. US GAAP Treatment of Interest and Dividends		
	IFRS	**US GAAP**
Interest received	Operating or investing	Operating
Interest paid	Operating or financing	Operating
Dividends received	Operating or investing	Operating
Dividends paid	Operating or financing	Financing

To estimate FCFF by starting with CFO, it is necessary to examine the classification of these items. For example, if the after-tax interest expense was taken out of net income and out of CFO, which is required under US GAAP and allowed under IFRS, then after-tax interest must be added back to get FCFF. However, if interest paid was not classified as an operating cash outflow (i.e., it was classified as a financing cash outflow as allowed under IFRS), then it is not necessary to add interest when operating cash flow is the starting point for calculating FCFF.

Adjustments to Derive Operating Cash Flow from Net Income

The operating cash flow section of the statement of cash flows provides detail on the adjustments made in deriving operating cash flow from net income. Exhibit 6 summarizes the common adjustments (other than changes in working capital) to derive operating cash flow from net income and indicates whether each item is added to or subtracted from net income in arriving at FCFF.

Exhibit 6: Noncash Items and FCFF	
Noncash Item	**Adjustment to NI to Arrive at FCFF**
Depreciation expense	Added back
Amortization expense and impairment of intangibles	Added back
Restructuring charges (expense)	Added back

Noncash Item	Adjustment to NI to Arrive at FCFF
Restructuring charges (income resulting from reversal)	Subtracted
Amortization of long-term bond discounts	Added back
Amortization of long-term bond premiums	Subtracted
Losses on non-operating activity	Added back
Gains on non-operating activity	Subtracted
Deferred taxes	Added back but calls for special attention

An adjustment to reported net income is required for any item that was treated as an expense in calculating net income on the income statement but did not result in an equivalent cash outflow in the reporting period. For example, both depreciation and amortization expenses reduce net income, but neither involves a cash outflow in the period. Therefore, to derive operating cash flow or FCFF from net income, it is necessary to add back these amounts to net income.

Adjustments to eliminate the amount of gains and losses are made for two reasons in general. First, such transactions are typically not operating activities (e.g., a sale of fixed assets, which is an investing activity), and thus the effects must be removed from the operating section of the statement of cash flows. Second, the amount of gain or loss reported in the income statement is not necessarily equivalent to the amount of cash involved in the transaction. For example, if a company sells a piece of equipment with a book value of €60,000 for €100,000, it reports the €40,000 gain as part of net income. The €40,000 gain, however, is not equivalent to the transaction's cash flow and, therefore, must be subtracted to derive operating cash flow from net income. Further, the €100,000 *is* a cash flow, and that amount will appear as a component of the company's cash flow for investing activity. Alternatively, if the company had sold the equipment with a book value of €60,000 for €40,000 and thus reported a loss of €20,000 as part of net income, that amount would be added back in deriving operating cash flow and FCFF.

Adjustments to Derive Operating Cash Flow from Net Income That May Merit Additional Attention from an Analyst

The item "deferred taxes" in Exhibit 6 requires special attention because deferred taxes result from differences in the timing of reporting income and expenses in the company's financial statements and the company's tax return. The income tax expense deducted in arriving at net income for financial reporting purposes is not the same as the amount of cash taxes paid. Over time, these differences between book income and taxable income should offset each other and have no impact on aggregate cash flows. Generally, if the analyst's purpose is forecasting and, therefore, identifying the persistent components of FCFF, then the analyst should not add back deferred tax changes that are expected to reverse in the near future. In some circumstances, however, a company may be able to consistently defer taxes until a much later date. If a company is growing and has the ability to indefinitely defer its tax liability, adding back deferred taxes to net income is warranted. Nevertheless, an acquirer must be aware that these taxes may be payable at some time in the future.

Similarly, companies often record expenses (e.g., restructuring charges) for financial reporting purposes that are not deductible for tax purposes or record revenues that are taxable in the current period but not yet recognized for financial reporting purposes. In these cases, taxable income exceeds financial statement income, so cash outflows for current tax payments are greater than the taxes reported in the income statement. This situation results in a deferred tax *asset* and a necessary adjustment to subtract that amount in deriving operating cash flow from net income. If, however, the deferred tax asset is expected to reverse in the near future, to avoid underestimating future cash flows, the analyst should not subtract the deferred tax asset in a cash flow forecast. If the company is expected to have these charges on a continual basis, however, a subtraction that will lower the forecast of future cash flows is warranted.

A second area that may warrant an analyst's attention to the adjustments made in derivation of operating cash flow from net income pertains to employee share-based compensation (stock options). Under both IFRS and US GAAP, companies must record in the income statement an expense for options provided to employees. The granting and expensing of options themselves do not result in a cash outflow and are thus a noncash charge; however, the granting of options has long-term cash flow implications. When the employee exercises the option, the company receives some cash related to the exercise price of the option at the strike price. This cash flow is considered a financing cash flow. Also, in some cases, a company receives a tax benefit from issuing options, which could increase operating cash flow but not net income. Both IFRS and US GAAP require that a portion of the tax effect be recorded as a financing cash flow rather than an operating cash flow in the statement of cash flows. Analysts should review the statement of cash flows and footnotes to determine the impact of options on operating cash flows. If these cash flows are not expected to persist in the future, analysts should not include them in their forecasts of cash flows. Analysts should also consider the impact of stock options on the number of shares outstanding. When computing equity value, analysts may want to use the number of shares *expected* to be outstanding (based on the exercise of employee stock options) rather than the number currently outstanding.

Finally, an analyst may benefit from a careful examination of adjustments in developing expectations about the sustainability of free cash flow. When any financial forecast is developed by using historical amounts as a baseline, it is necessary to ensure that the baseline amounts are not distorted by non-recurring items. Similarly, when a forecast of free cash flows is developed using historical amounts of FCFF or FCFE as a baseline, it is necessary to ensure that the baseline amounts are not distorted by non-recurring items. Example 4 is a historical case that is adapted to illustrate issues that an analyst may face when forecasting free cash flows. Specifically, the example illustrates that when forecasting cash flows for valuation purposes, analysts should consider the sustainability of historical working capital effects on free cash flow.

EXAMPLE 4

Sustainability of Working Capital Effects on Free Cash Flow

Duplico Holdings PLC has operations in Ireland, the United Kingdom, Continental Europe, and Morocco. The operating activities section of its statement of cash flows and a portion of the investing activities section are presented in Exhibit 7. The statement of cash flows was prepared in accordance with IFRS.

Exhibit 7: Duplico Holdings PLC Excerpt from Statement of Cash Flows (Euros in Millions)			
	Year Ended 31 March		
	2022	**2021**	**2020**
Operating activities			
Profit before tax	633.0	420.9	341.0

	Year Ended 31 March		
	2022	2021	2020
Adjustments to reconcile profits before tax to net cash provided by operating activities			
Depreciation	309.2	277.7	235.4
Increase in inventories	(0.1)	(0.2)	(0.4)
Increase in trade receivables	(0.9)	(6.3)	(2.5)
Decrease (increase) in other current assets	34.5	(20.9)	11.6
Increase (decrease) in trade payables	30.4	(3.2)	21.3
Increase in accrued expenses	11.6	135.0	189.7
Increase (decrease) in other creditors	19.7	(10.0)	30.1
Increase (decrease) in maintenance provisions	6.6	(7.9)	30.7
Gain on disposal of property, plant, and equipment	(10.4)	—	(2.0)
Loss on impairment of available-for-sale financial asset	—	—	13.5
Decrease (increase) in interest receivable	—	1.6	(1.2)
Increase (decrease) in interest payable	1.1	2.3	(0.5)
Retirement costs	(0.1)	(0.1)	(0.1)
Share-based payments	(0.7)	3.3	4.9
Income tax paid	(13.6)	(5.9)	—
Net cash provided by operating activities	1,020.3	786.3	871.5
Investing activities			
Capital expenditure (purchase of property, plant, and equipment)	(317.6)	(897.2)	(997.8)

Analysts predict that as Duplico grows in the coming years, depreciation expense will increase substantially. Based on the information given, address the following:

1. Contrast reported depreciation expense to reported capital expenditures, and describe the implications of future growth in depreciation expense (all else being equal) for future net income and future cash from operating activities.

Solution:

In the 2020–22 period, the amount of depreciation expense relative to the amount of capital expenditures changed significantly. For example, in 2022, capital expenditures of €317.6 million were just slightly more than the €309.2 million depreciation expense. In 2020, capital expenditures of €997.8 million were over 4 times more than depreciation charges of €235.4 million. The rate of growth in depreciation expense will be highly dependent on future capital expenditures.

In calculating net income, depreciation is a deduction. Therefore, as depreciation expense increases in the coming years, net income will decrease. Specifically, net income will be reduced by (Depreciation expense) × (1 − Tax rate). In calculating CFO, however, depreciation is added back in full to net income. The difference between depreciation expense—the amount added back to net income to calculate CFO—and the amount by which net income is reduced by depreciation expense is (Tax rate) × (Depreciation expense), which represents a positive increment to CFO. Thus, the projected increase in depreciation expense is a negative for future net income but a positive for future CFO. (At worst, if the company operates at a loss, depreciation is neutral for CFO.)

2. Explain the effects on free cash flow to equity of changes in 2022 in working capital accounts, such as inventory, accounts receivable, and accounts payable, and comment on the long-term sustainability of such changes.

Solution:

In 2022, the increases in inventory and accounts receivable ("trade receivables") resulted in negative adjustments to net income (i.e., the changes reduced cash flow relative to net income). The adjustments are negative because increases in these accounts are a use of cash. On the current liabilities side, the increase in trade payables, accrued expenses, and "other creditors" are added back to net income and are sources of cash because such increases represent increased amounts for which cash payments have yet to be made. Because CFO is a component of FCFE, the items that had a positive (negative) effect on CFO also have a positive (negative) effect on FCFE.

Although not the case here, declining balances for assets, such as inventory, or for liabilities, such as accounts payable, are not sustainable indefinitely. In the extreme case, the balance declines to zero and no further reduction is possible. Given the growth in its net income and the expansion of PP&E evidenced by capital expenditures, Duplico appears to be growing and investors should expect its working capital requirements to grow accordingly.

COMPUTING FCFE FROM FCFF

5

- [ ] explain the ownership perspective implicit in the FCFE approach
- [ ] calculate FCFF and FCFE
- [ ] describe approaches for forecasting FCFF and FCFE

FCFE is cash flow available to equity holders only. To find FCFE, therefore, we must reduce FCFF by the after-tax value of interest paid to debtholders and add net borrowing (which is debt issued less debt repaid over the period for which one is calculating free cash flow):

Free cash flow to equity = Free cash flow to the firm
Less: Interest expense × (1 − Tax rate)
Plus: Net borrowing,

or

$$\text{FCFE} = \text{FCFF} - \text{Int}(1 - \text{Tax rate}) + \text{Net borrowing.} \tag{9}$$

As Equation 9 shows, FCFE is found by starting from FCFF, subtracting after-tax interest expenses, and adding net new borrowing. The analyst can also find FCFF from FCFE by making the opposite adjustments—by adding after-tax interest expenses and subtracting net borrowing: $\text{FCFF} = \text{FCFE} + \text{Int}(1 - \text{Tax rate}) - \text{Net borrowing}$.

Exhibit 8 uses the values for FCFF for Cane Distribution calculated in Example 3 to show the calculation of FCFE when starting with FCFF. To calculate FCFE in this manner, we subtract after-tax interest expense from FCFF and then add net borrowing (equal to new debt borrowing minus debt repayment).

Exhibit 8: Calculating FCFE from FCFF

	Years Ending 31 December		
	2018	2019	2020
Free cash flow to the firm	97.50	107.26	117.97
Interest paid × (1 − Tax rate)	(10.98)	(12.08)	(13.28)
New debt borrowing	22.40	24.64	27.10
Debt repayment	(0)	(0)	(0)
Free cash flow to equity	108.92	119.82	131.79

To reiterate, FCFE is the cash flow available to common stockholders—the cash flow remaining after all operating expenses (including taxes) have been paid, capital investments have been made, and other transactions with other suppliers of capital have been carried out. The company's other capital suppliers include creditors, such as bondholders, and preferred stockholders. The cash flows (net of taxes) that arise from transactions with creditors and preferred stockholders are deducted from FCFF to arrive at FCFE.

FCFE is the amount that the company can afford to pay out as dividends. In actuality, for various reasons companies often pay out substantially more or substantially less than FCFE, so FCFE often differs from dividends paid. One reason for this difference is that the dividend decision is a discretionary decision of the board of directors. Most corporations "manage" their dividends; they prefer to raise them gradually over time, partly because they do not want to cut dividends. Many companies raise dividends slowly even when their earnings are increasing rapidly, and companies often maintain their current dividends even when their profitability has declined. Consequently, earnings are much more volatile than dividends.

In Equations 7 and 8, we showed the calculation of FCFF starting with, respectively, net income and cash flow from operations. As Equation 9 showed, FCFE = FCFF − Int(1 − Tax rate) + Net borrowing. By subtracting after-tax interest expense and adding net borrowing to Equations 7 and 8, we have equations to calculate FCFE starting with, respectively, net income and CFO:

$$\text{FCFE} = \text{NI} + \text{NCC} - \text{FCInv} - \text{WCInv} + \text{Net borrowing}. \tag{10}$$

$$\text{FCFE} = \text{CFO} - \text{FCInv} + \text{Net borrowing}. \tag{11}$$

Example 5 illustrates how to adjust net income or CFO to find FCFF and FCFE.

EXAMPLE 5

Adjusting Net Income or CFO to Find FCFF and FCFE

The balance sheet, income statement, and statement of cash flows for the Pitts Corporation are shown in Exhibit 9. Note that the statement of cash flows follows a convention according to which the positive numbers of $400 million and $85 million for "cash *used for* investing activities" and "cash *used for* financing activities," respectively, indicate outflows and thus amounts to be *subtracted*. Analysts will also encounter a convention in which the value "(400)" for "cash provided by (used for) investing activities" would be used to indicate a subtraction of $400.

Exhibit 9: Financial Statements for Pitts Corporation (in Millions, Except for Per-Share Data)

	Year Ended 31 December	
Balance Sheet	**2019**	**2020**
Assets		
Current assets		
Cash and equivalents	$190	$200
Accounts receivable	560	600
Inventory	410	440
Total current assets	1,160	1,240
Gross fixed assets	2,200	2,600
Accumulated depreciation	(900)	(1,200)
Net fixed assets	1,300	1,400
Total assets	$2,460	$2,640
Liabilities and shareholders' equity		
Current liabilities		
Accounts payable	$285	$300
Notes payable	200	250
Accrued taxes and expenses	140	150
Total current liabilities	625	700
Long-term debt	865	890
Common stock	100	100
Additional paid-in capital	200	200
Retained earnings	670	750
Total shareholders' equity	970	1,050
Total liabilities and shareholders' equity	$2,460	$2,640

Statement of Income Year Ended 31 December	**2020**
Total revenues	$3,000
Operating costs and expenses	2,200
EBITDA	800
Depreciation	300
Operating income (EBIT)	500
Interest expense	100
Income before tax	400
Taxes (at 40%)	160
Net income	$ 240

Statement of Income Year Ended 31 December	2020
Dividends	$ 160
Change in retained earnings (calculated as net income minus dividends)	$ 80
Earnings per share (EPS)	$0.48
Dividends per share	$0.32

Statement of Cash Flows Year Ended 31 December	2020
Operating activities	
Net income	$240
Adjustments	
Depreciation	300
Changes in working capital	
Accounts receivable	(40)
Inventories	(30)
Accounts payable	15
Accrued taxes and expenses	10
Cash provided by operating activities	$495
Investing activities	
Purchases of fixed assets	400
Cash used for investing activities	$400
Financing activities	
Notes payable	(50)
Long-term financing issuances	(25)
Common stock dividends	160
Cash used for financing activities	$85
Cash and equivalents increase (decrease)	10
Cash and equivalents at beginning of year	190
Cash and equivalents at end of year	$200
Supplemental cash flow disclosures	
Interest paid	$100
Income taxes paid	$160

Note that the Pitts Corporation had net income of $240 million in 2020. Show the calculations required to do each of the following:

1. Calculate FCFF starting with the net income figure.

Solution:

The analyst can use Equation 7 to find FCFF from net income (amounts are in millions):

Net income available to common shareholders	$240
Plus: Net noncash charges	300

Plus: Interest expense × (1 – Tax rate)	60
Less: Investment in fixed capital	400
Less: Investment in working capital	45
Free cash flow to the firm	$155

In the format shown and throughout the solutions, "Less: . . . *x*" is interpreted as "subtract *x*."

This equation can also be written as

$$FCFF = NI + NCC + Int(1 - Tax\ rate) - FCInv - WCInv$$

$$= 240 + 300 + 60 - 400 - 45 = \$155\ million.$$

Some of these items need explanation. Capital spending is $400 million, which is the increase in gross fixed assets shown on the balance sheet and in capital expenditures shown as an investing activity in the statement of cash flows. The increase in working capital is $45 million, which is the increase in accounts receivable of $40 million ($600 million – $560 million) plus the increase in inventories of $30 million ($440 million – $410 million) minus the increase in accounts payable of $15 million ($300 million – $285 million) minus the increase in accrued taxes and expenses of $10 million ($150 million – $140 million). When finding the increase in working capital, we ignore cash because the change in cash is what we are calculating. We also ignore short-term debt, such as notes payable, because such debt is part of the capital provided to the company and is not considered an operating item. The after-tax interest cost is the interest expense times (1 – Tax rate): $100 million × (1 – 0.40) = $60 million. The values of the remaining items in Equation 7 can be taken directly from the financial statements.

---

2. Calculate FCFE starting from the FCFF calculated in Part 1.

Solution:

Finding FCFE from FCFF can be done with Equation 9:

Free cash flow to the firm	$155
Less: Interest expense × (1 – Tax rate)	60
Plus: Net borrowing	75
Free cash flow to equity	$170

Or it can be done by using the equation

$$FCFE = FCFF - Int(1 - Tax\ rate) + Net\ borrowing$$

$$= 155 - 60 + 75 = \$170\ million.$$

---

3. Calculate FCFE starting with the net income figure.

Solution:

The analyst can use Equation 10 to find FCFE from NI.

Net income available to common shareholders	$240
Plus: Net noncash charges	300
Less: Investment in fixed capital	400

Less: Investment in working capital	45
Plus: Net borrowing	75
Free cash flow to equity	$170

Or the analyst can use the equation

$$FCFE = NI + NCC - FCInv - WCInv + Net\ borrowing$$

$$= 240 + 300 - 400 - 45 + 75 = \$170\ million.$$

Because notes payable increased by $50 million ($250 million – $200 million) and long-term debt increased by $25 million ($890 million – $865 million), net borrowing is $75 million.

4. Calculate FCFF starting with CFO.

Solution:

Equation 8 can be used to find FCFF from CFO:

Cash flow from operations	$495
Plus: Interest expense × (1 – Tax rate)	60
Less: Investment in fixed capital	400
Free cash flow to the firm	$155

Or

$$FCFF = CFO + Int(1 - Tax\ rate) - FCInv$$

$$= 495 + 60 - 400 = \$155\ million.$$

5. Calculate FCFE starting with CFO.

Solution:

Equation 11 can be used to find FCFE from CFO:

Cash flow from operations	$495
Less: Investment in fixed capital	400
Plus: Net borrowing	75
Free cash flow to equity	$170

Or

$$FCFE = CFO - FCInv + Net\ borrowing$$

$$= 495 - 400 + 75 = \$170\ million.$$

FCFE is usually less than FCFF. In this example, however, FCFE ($170 million) exceeds FCFF ($155 million) because external borrowing was large during this year.

FINDING FCFF AND FCFE FROM EBITA OR EBITDA

6

☐   explain the appropriate adjustments to net income, earnings before interest and taxes (EBIT), earnings before interest, taxes, depreciation, and amortization (EBITDA), and cash flow from operations (CFO) to calculate FCFF and FCFE

☐   calculate FCFF and FCFE

FCFF and FCFE are most frequently calculated from a starting basis of net income or CFO (as shown earlier). Two other starting points are EBIT and EBITDA from the income statement.

To show the relationship between EBIT and FCFF, we start with Equation 7 and assume that the only noncash charge (NCC) is depreciation (Dep):

$$FCFF = NI + Dep + Int(1 - Tax\ rate) - FCInv - WCInv.$$

Net income (NI) can be expressed as

$$NI = (EBIT - Int)(1 - Tax\ rate) = EBIT(1 - Tax\ rate) - Int(1 - Tax\ rate).$$

Substituting this equation for NI in Equation 7, we have

$$FCFF = EBIT(1 - Tax\ rate) + Dep - FCInv - WCInv. \tag{12}$$

To get FCFF from EBIT, we multiply EBIT by (1 − Tax rate), add back depreciation, and then subtract the investments in fixed capital and working capital.

The relationship between FCFF and EBITDA can also be easily shown. Net income can be expressed as

$$NI = (EBITDA - Dep - Int)(1 - Tax\ rate)$$

$$= EBITDA(1 - Tax\ rate) - Dep(1 - Tax\ rate) - Int(1 - Tax\ rate).$$

Substituting this equation for NI in Equation 7 results in

$$FCFF = EBITDA(1 - Tax\ rate) + Dep(Tax\ rate) - FCInv - WCInv. \tag{13}$$

FCFF equals EBITDA times (1 − Tax rate) plus depreciation times the tax rate minus investments in fixed capital and working capital. In comparing Equation 12 and Equation 13, note the difference in how depreciation is handled.

Many adjustments for noncash charges that are required to calculate FCFF when starting from net income are not required when starting from EBIT or EBITDA. In the calculation of net income, many noncash charges are made after computing EBIT or EBITDA, so they do not need to be added back when calculating FCFF based on EBIT or EBITDA. Another important consideration is that some noncash charges, such as depreciation, are tax deductible. A noncash charge that affects taxes must be accounted for.

In summary, in calculating FCFF from EBIT or EBITDA, whether an adjustment for a noncash charge is needed depends on where in the income statement the charge has been deducted; furthermore, the form of any needed adjustment depends on whether the noncash charge is a tax-deductible expense.

We can also calculate FCFE (instead of FCFF) from EBIT or EBITDA. An easy way to obtain FCFE based on EBIT or EBITDA is to use Equation 12 (the expression for FCFF in terms of EBIT) or Equation 13 (the expression for FCFF in terms of EBITDA), respectively, and then subtract Int(1 − Tax rate) and add net borrowing because FCFE is related to FCFF as follows (see Equation 9):

$$FCFE = FCFF - Int(1 - Tax\ rate) + Net\ borrowing.$$

Example 6 uses the Pitts Corporation financial statements to find FCFF and FCFE from EBIT and EBITDA.

EXAMPLE 6

Adjusting EBIT and EBITDA to Find FCFF and FCFE

The Pitts Corporation (financial statements provided in Example 5) had EBIT of $500 million and EBITDA of $800 million in 2020. Show the adjustments that would be required to find FCFF and FCFE:

1. Starting from EBIT.

Solution:

To get FCFF from EBIT using Equation 12, we carry out the following (in millions):

EBIT(1 − Tax rate) = 500(1 − 0.40)	$300
Plus: Net noncash charges	300
Less: Net investment in fixed capital	400
Less: Net increase in working capital	45
Free cash flow to the firm	$155

Or

$$FCFF = EBIT(1 - \text{Tax rate}) + Dep - FCInv - WCInv$$
$$= 500(1 - 0.40) + 300 - 400 - 45 = \$155 \text{ million.}$$

To obtain FCFE, make the appropriate adjustments to FCFF:

$$FCFE = FCFF - Int(1 - \text{Tax rate}) + \text{Net borrowing}$$
$$= 155 - 100(1 - 0.40) + 75 = \$170 \text{ million.}$$

2. Starting from EBITDA.

Solution:

To obtain FCFF from EBITDA using Equation 13, we do the following (in millions):

EBITDA(1 − Tax rate) = $800(1 − 0.40)	$480
Plus: Dep(Tax rate) = $300(0.40)	120
Less: Net investment in fixed capital	400
Less: Net increase in working capital	45
Free cash flow to the firm	$155

Or

$$FCFF = EBITDA(1 - \text{Tax rate}) + Dep(\text{Tax rate}) - FCInv - WCInv$$
$$= 800(1 - 0.40) + 300(0.40) - 400 - 45 = \$155 \text{ million.}$$

Again, to obtain FCFE, make the appropriate adjustments to FCFF:

$$FCFE = FCFF - Int(1 - \text{Tax rate}) + \text{Net borrowing}$$
$$= 155 - 100(1 - 0.40) + 75 = \$170 \text{ million.}$$

FCFF AND FCFE ON A USES-OF-FREE-CASH-FLOW BASIS

7

☐ | calculate FCFF and FCFE

☐ | explain how dividends, share repurchases, share issues, and changes in leverage may affect future FCFF and FCFE

Prior sections illustrated the calculation of FCFF and FCFE from various income or cash flow starting points (e.g., net income or cash flow from operations). Those approaches to calculating free cash flow can be characterized as showing the *sources* of free cash flow. An alternative perspective examines the *uses* of free cash flow. In the context of calculating FCFF and FCFE, analyzing free cash flow on a uses basis serves as a consistency check on the sources calculation and may reveal information relevant to understanding a company's capital structure policy or cash position.

In general, a firm has the following alternative uses of positive FCFF: (1) retain the cash and thus increase the firm's balances of cash and marketable securities; (2) use the cash for payments to providers of debt capital (i.e., interest payments and principal payments in excess of new borrowings); and (3) use the cash for payments to providers of equity capital (i.e., dividend payments and/or share repurchases in excess of new share issuances). Similarly, a firm has the following general alternatives for covering negative free cash flows: draw down cash balances, borrow additional cash, or issue equity.

The effects on the company's capital structure of its transactions with capital providers should be noted. For a simple example, assume that free cash flows are zero and that the company makes no change to its cash balances. Obtaining cash via net new borrowings and using the cash for dividends or net share repurchases will increase the company's leverage, whereas obtaining cash from net new share issuances and using that cash to make principal payments in excess of new borrowings will reduce leverage.

We calculate uses of FCFF as follows:

Uses of FCFF =

Increases (or minus decreases) in cash balances

Plus: Net payments to providers of debt capital, which are calculated as:

- Plus: Interest expense $\times$ (1 − Tax rate).
- Plus: Repayment of principal in excess of new borrowing (or minus new borrowing in excess of debt repayment if new borrowing is greater).

Plus: Payments to providers of equity capital, which are calculated as:

- Plus: Cash dividends.
- Plus: Share repurchases in excess of share issuance (or minus new share issuance in excess of share repurchases if share issuance is greater).

Uses of FCFF must equal sources of FCFF as previously calculated.

Free cash flows to equity reflect free cash flows to the firm net of the cash used for payments to providers of debt capital. Accordingly, we can calculate FCFE as follows:

Uses of FCFE =

Increases (or decreases) in cash balances

Plus: Payments to providers of equity capital, which are calculated as:

- Plus: Cash dividends.
- Plus: Share repurchases in excess of share issuance (or minus new share issuance in excess of share repurchases if share issuance is greater).

Again, the uses of FCFE must equal the sources of FCFE (calculated previously).

To illustrate the equivalence of sources and uses of FCFF and FCFE for the Pitts Corporation, whose financial statements are given in Exhibit 9 in Example 5, note the following for 2020:

- The increase in the balance of cash and equivalents was $10, calculated as $200 − $190.
- After-tax interest expense was $60, calculated as Interest expense × (1 − Tax rate) = $100 × (1 − 0.40).
- Net borrowing was $75, calculated as increase in borrowing minus repayment of debt = $50 (increase in notes payable) + $25 (increase in long-term debt).
- Cash dividends totaled $160.
- Share repurchases and issuance both equaled $0.

FCFF, previously calculated, was $155. Pitts Corporation used the FCFF as follows (note that payments of principal to providers of debt capital in excess of new borrowings are a use of free cash flow. Here, the corporation did not use its free cash flow to repay debt; rather, it borrowed new debt, which increased the cash flows available to be used for providers of equity capital):

Increase in balance of cash and cash equivalents		$10
Plus:	After-tax interest payments to providers of debt capital	$60
Minus:	New borrowing	($75)
Plus:	Payments of dividends to providers of equity capital	$160
Plus:	Share repurchases in excess of share issuances (or minus new share issuance in excess of share repurchases)	$0
Total uses of FCFF		$155

FCFE, previously calculated, was $170. Pitts Corporation used the FCFE as follows:

Increase in balance of cash and cash equivalents		$10
Plus:	Payments of dividends to providers of equity capital	$160
Plus:	Share repurchases in excess of share issuances (or minus new share issuance in excess of share repurchases)	$0
Total uses of FCFE		$170

In summary, an analysis of the uses of free cash flows shows that Pitts Corporation was using free cash flows to manage its capital structure by increasing debt. The additional debt was not needed to cover capital expenditures; the statement of cash flows showed that the company's operating cash flows of $495 were more than adequate to cover its capital expenditures of $400. Instead, the additional debt was used, in part, to make dividend payments to the company's shareholders.

FORECASTING FCFF AND FCFE

8

☐ | describe approaches for forecasting FCFF and FCFE

Computing FCFF and FCFE from historical accounting data is relatively straightforward. In some cases, these data are used directly to extrapolate free cash flow growth in a single-stage free cash flow valuation model. On other occasions, however, the analyst may expect that the future free cash flows will not bear a simple relationship to the past. The analyst who wishes to forecast future FCFF or FCFE directly for such a company must forecast the individual components of free cash flow. This section extends our previous presentation on *computing* FCFF and FCFE to the more complex task of *forecasting* FCFF and FCFE.

One method for forecasting free cash flow involves applying some constant growth rate to a current level of free cash flow (possibly adjusted, if necessary, to eliminate non-recurring components). The simplest basis for specifying the future growth rate is to assume that a historical growth rate will also apply to the future. This approach is appropriate if a company's free cash flow has tended to grow at a constant rate and if historical relationships between free cash flow and fundamental factors are expected to continue. Example 7 asks that the reader apply this approach to the Pitts Corporation based on 2020 FCFF of $155 million as calculated in Examples 5 and 6.

EXAMPLE 7

Constant Growth in FCFF

Use Pitts Corporation data to compute its FCFF for the next three years. Assume that growth in FCFF remains at the historical levels of 15% a year. The answer is as follows (in millions):

	2020 Actual	2021 Estimate	2022 Estimate	2023 Estimate
FCFF	155.00	178.25	204.99	235.74

A more complex approach is to forecast the components of free cash flow. This approach is able to capture the complex relationships among the components. One popular method is to forecast the individual components of free cash flow—EBIT(1 – Tax rate), net noncash charges, investment in fixed capital, and investment in working capital. EBIT can be forecasted directly or by forecasting sales and the company's EBIT margin based on an analysis of historical data and the current and expected economic environment. Similarly, analysts can base forecasts of capital needs on historical relationships between increases in sales and investments in fixed and working capital.

In this discussion, we illustrate a simple sales-based forecasting method for FCFF and FCFE based on the following major assumption:

> Investment in fixed capital in excess of depreciation (FCInv – Dep) and investment in working capital (WCInv) both bear a constant relationship to forecast increases in the size of the company as measured by increases in sales.

In addition, for FCFE forecasting, we assume that the capital structure represented by the debt ratio (DR)—debt as a percentage of debt plus equity—is constant. Under that assumption, DR indicates the percentage of the investment in fixed capital in excess of depreciation (also called "net new investment in fixed capital") and in working capital that will be financed by debt. This method involves a simplification because it considers depreciation as the only noncash charge, so the method does not work well when that approximation is not a good assumption.

If depreciation reflects the annual cost for maintaining the existing capital stock, the difference between fixed capital investment and depreciation—incremental FCInv—should be related to the capital expenditures required for growth. In this case, the following inputs are needed:

- forecasts of sales growth rates;
- forecasts of the after-tax operating margin (for FCFF forecasting) or profit margin (for FCFE forecasting);
- an estimate of the relationship of incremental FCInv to sales increases;
- an estimate of the relationship of WCInv to sales increases; and
- an estimate of DR.

In the case of FCFF forecasting, FCFF is calculated by forecasting EBIT(1 − Tax rate) and subtracting incremental fixed capital expenditures and incremental working capital expenditures. To estimate FCInv and WCInv, we multiply their past proportion to sales increases by the forecasted sales increases. Incremental fixed capital expenditures as a proportion of sales increases are computed as follows:

$$\frac{\text{Capital expenditures} - \text{Depreciation expense}}{\text{Increase in sales}}.$$

Similarly, incremental working capital expenditures as a proportion of sales increases are

$$\frac{\text{Increase in working capital}}{\text{Increase in sales}}.$$

When depreciation is the only significant net noncash charge, this method yields the same results as the previous equations for estimating FCFF or FCFE. Rather than adding back all depreciation and subtracting all capital expenditures when starting with EBIT(1 − Tax rate), this approach simply subtracts the net capital expenditures in excess of depreciation.

Although the recognition may not be obvious, this approach recognizes that capital expenditures have two components: those expenditures necessary to maintain existing capacity (fixed capital replacement) and those incremental expenditures necessary for growth. In forecasting, the expenditures to maintain capacity are likely to be related to the current level of sales and the expenditures for growth are likely to be related to the forecast of sales growth.

When forecasting FCFE, analysts often make an assumption that the financing of the company involves a "target" debt ratio. In this case, they assume that a specified percentage of the sum of (1) net new investment in fixed capital (new fixed capital minus depreciation expense) and (2) the increase in working capital is financed based on a target DR. This assumption leads to a simplification of FCFE calculations. If we assume that depreciation is the only noncash charge, Equation 10, which is FCFE = NI + NCC − FCInv − WCInv + Net borrowing, becomes

$$\text{FCFE} = \text{NI} - (\text{FCInv} - \text{Dep}) - \text{WCInv} + \text{Net borrowing.} \qquad (14)$$

Note that FCInv − Dep represents the incremental fixed capital expenditure net of depreciation. By assuming a target DR, we eliminated the need to forecast net borrowing and can use the expression

$$\text{Net borrowing} = \text{DR}(\text{FCInv} - \text{Dep}) + \text{DR}(\text{WCInv}).$$

By using this expression, we do not need to forecast debt issuance and repayment on an annual basis to estimate net borrowing. Equation 14 then becomes

$$FCFE = NI - (FCInv - Dep) - WCInv + (DR)(FCInv - Dep) + (DR)(WCInv)$$

or

$$FCFE = NI - (1 - DR)(FCInv - Dep) - (1 - DR)(WCInv). \qquad (15)$$

Equation 15 says that FCFE equals NI minus the amount of fixed capital expenditure (net of depreciation) and working capital investment that is financed by equity. Again, for Equation 15, we have assumed that the only noncash charge is depreciation.

Example 8 and Example 9 illustrate this sales-based method for forecasting free cash flow to the firm.

EXAMPLE 8

Free Cash Flow Tied to Sales

Carla Espinosa is an analyst following Pitts Corporation at the end of 2020. From the data in Example 5, she can see that the company's sales for 2020 were $3,000 million, and she assumes that sales grew by $300 million from 2019 to 2020. Espinosa expects Pitts Corporation's sales to increase by 10% a year thereafter. Pitts Corporation is a fairly stable company, so Espinosa expects it to maintain its historical EBIT margin and proportions of incremental investments in fixed and working capital. Pitts Corporation's EBIT for 2020 is $500 million, its EBIT margin is 16.67% (500/3,000), and its tax rate is 40%.

Note from Pitts Corporation's 2020 statement of cash flows (Exhibit 9) the amount for "purchases of fixed assets" (i.e., capital expenditures) of $400 million and depreciation of $300 million. Thus, incremental fixed capital investment in 2020 was

$$\frac{\text{Capital expenditures} - \text{Depreciation expense}}{\text{Increase in sales}}$$

$$= \frac{400 - 300}{300} = 33.33\%.$$

Incremental working capital investment in the past year was

$$\frac{\text{Increase in working capital}}{\text{Increase in sales}} = \frac{45}{300} = 15\%.$$

So, for every $100 increase in sales, Pitts Corporation invests $33.33 in new equipment in addition to replacement of depreciated equipment and $15 in working capital. Espinosa forecasts FCFF for 2013 as follows (dollars in millions):

Sales	$3,300	Up 10%
EBIT	550	16.67% of sales
EBIT(1 − Tax rate)	330	Adjusted for 40% tax rate
Incremental FC	(100)	33.33% of sales increase
Incremental WC	(45)	15% of sales increase
FCFF	$185	

This model can be used to forecast multiple periods and is flexible enough to allow varying sales growth rates, EBIT margins, tax rates, and rates of incremental capital increases.

[Handwritten margin note:] - This assumes the only noncash charge is depreciation. When the company has significant non-cash charges other than depreciation this method will result in a less accurate estimate of FCFE than one obtained by forecasting all the individual components of FCFE.

EXAMPLE 9

Free Cash Flow Growth Tied to Sales Growth

Continuing her work, Espinosa decides to forecast FCFF for the next five years. She is concerned that Pitts Corporation will not be able to maintain its historical EBIT margin and that the EBIT margin will decline from the current 16.67% to 14.5% in the next five years. Exhibit 10 summarizes her forecasts.

Exhibit 10: Free Cash Flow Growth for Pitts Corporation (Dollars in Millions)

	Year 1	Year 2	Year 3	Year 4	Year 5
Sales growth	10.00%	10.00%	10.00%	10.00%	10.00%
EBIT margin	16.67%	16.00%	15.50%	15.00%	14.50%
Tax rate	40.00%	40.00%	40.00%	40.00%	40.00%
Incremental FC investment	33.33%	33.33%	33.33%	33.33%	33.33%
Incremental WC investment	15.00%	15.00%	15.00%	15.00%	15.00%
Prior-year sales	$3,000.00				
Sales forecast	$3,300.00	$3,630.00	$3,993.00	$4,392.30	$4,831.53
EBIT forecast	550.00	580.80	618.92	658.85	700.57
EBIT(1 − Tax rate)	330.00	348.48	371.35	395.31	420.34
Incremental FC	(100.00)	(110.00)	(121.00)	(133.10)	(146.41)
Incremental WC	(45.00)	(49.50)	(54.45)	(59.90)	(65.88)
FCFF	$185.00	$188.98	$195.90	$202.31	$208.05

The model need not begin with sales; it could start with net income, cash flow from operations, or EBITDA.

A similar model can be designed for FCFE, as shown in Example 10. In the case of FCFE, the analyst should begin with net income and must also forecast any net new borrowing or net preferred stock issue.

EXAMPLE 10

Finding FCFE from Sales Forecasts

Espinosa decides to forecast FCFE for the year 2021. She uses the same expectations derived in Example 8. Additionally, she expects the following:

- the net profit margin will remain at 8% (= 240/3,000), and
- the company will finance incremental fixed and working capital investments with 50% debt—the target DR.

Espinosa's forecast for 2021 is as follows (dollars in millions):

Sales	$3,300	Up 10%
NI	264	8.0% of sales
Incremental FC	(100)	33.33% of sales increase
Incremental WC	(45)	15% of sales increase
Net borrowing	72.50	(100 FCInv + 45 WCInv) × 50%
FCFE	$191.50	

When the company being analyzed has significant noncash charges other than depreciation expense, the approach we have just illustrated will result in a less accurate estimate of FCFE than one obtained by forecasting all the individual components of FCFE. In some cases, the analyst will have specific forecasts of planned components, such as capital expenditures. In other cases, the analyst will study historical relationships, such as previous capital expenditures and sales levels, to develop a forecast.

OTHER ISSUES IN FREE CASH FLOW ANALYSIS

9

☐ | compare the FCFE model and dividend discount models

☐ | explain how dividends, share repurchases, share issues, and changes in leverage may affect future FCFF and FCFE

☐ | evaluate the use of net income and EBITDA as proxies for cash flow in valuation

We have already presented a number of practical issues that arise in using free cash flow valuation models. Other issues relate to analyst adjustments to CFO, the relationship between free cash flow and dividends, and valuation with complicated financial structures.

Analyst Adjustments to CFO

Although many corporate financial statements are straightforward, some are not transparent (i.e., the quality of the reported numbers and of disclosures is not high). Sometimes, difficulties in analysis arise either because of lack of transparency or because the companies and their transactions are more complicated than the Pitts Corporation example we just provided.

For instance, in many corporate financial statements, the changes in balance sheet items (the increase in an asset or the decrease in a liability) differ from the changes reported in the statement of cash flows. Financial statements in which the changes in the balance sheet working capital accounts do not equal the working capital amounts reported on the statement of cash flows are described as lacking "articulation." Research on financial statement non-articulation (which is not an uncommon occurrence) identifies several reasons for these differences (Casey, Gao, Kirschenheiter, Li, and Pandit 2016; Huefner, Ketz, and Largay 1989; Bahnson, Miller, and Budge 1996; Wilkins and Loudder 2000; Hribar and Collins 2002; and Shi and Zhang 2011). Two of the factors that can cause discrepancies between changes in balance sheet accounts and the changes reported in the statement of cash flows include (1) acquisitions or divestitures (and related discontinued operations) and (2) the presence of nondomestic subsidiaries. For example, an increase in an inventory account may result from purchases from suppliers (which is an operating activity) or from an acquisition or merger with another company that has inventory on its balance sheet (which is an investing activity). Discrepancies may also occur from currency translations of the earnings of nondomestic subsidiaries.

Particularly for companies with major acquisition or divestiture activity where the CFO figure from the statement of cash flows may be distorted by cash flows related to financing and/or investing activities, an analyst may need to use greater detail in forecasting. For example, the analyst may need to adjust the amount of CFO that is used as the starting point for free cash flow calculations. Alternatively, instead of (or in addition to) developing a cash flow forecast by extrapolating from reported OCF, an analyst might forecast individual components and pay careful attention to the relation between sales forecast and forecast of specific working capital items.

Free Cash Flow versus Dividends and Other Earnings Components

Many analysts have a strong preference for free cash flow valuation models over dividend discount models. Although one type of model may have no theoretical advantage over another type, legitimate reasons to prefer one model can arise in the process of applying free cash flow models versus DDMs. First, many corporations pay no, or very low, cash dividends. Using a DDM to value these companies is difficult because they require forecasts about when dividends will be initiated, the level of dividends at initiation, and the growth rate or rates from that point forward. Second, dividend payments are at the discretion of the corporation's board of directors. Therefore, they may imperfectly signal the company's long-run profitability. Some corporations clearly pay dividends that are substantially less than their free cash flow, and others pay dividends that are substantially more. Finally, as mentioned earlier, dividends are the cash flow actually going to shareholders whereas free cash flow to equity is the cash flow available to be distributed to shareholders without impairing the company's value. If a company is being analyzed because it is a target for takeover, free cash flow is the appropriate cash flow measure; once the company is taken over, the new owners will have discretion over how free cash flow is used (including its distribution in the form of dividends).

We have defined FCFF and FCFE and presented alternative (equivalent) ways to calculate both. So, the reader should have a good idea of what is included in FCFF or FCFE but may wonder why some cash flows are not included. Specifically, what role do dividends, share repurchases, share issuance, or changes in leverage have on FCFF and FCFE? The simple answer is not much. Recall the formulas for FCFF and FCFE:

$$FCFF = NI + NCC + Int(1 - Tax\ rate) - FCInv - WCInv,$$

and

$$FCFE = NI + NCC - FCInv - WCInv + Net\ borrowing.$$

Notice that dividends and share repurchases and issuance are absent from the formulas. The reason is that FCFF and FCFE are the cash flows *available* to investors or to stockholders; dividends and share repurchases are *uses* of these cash flows. So, the simple answer is that transactions between the company and its shareholders (through cash dividends, share repurchases, and share issuances) do not affect free cash flow. Leverage changes, such as the use of more debt financing, have some impact because they increase the interest tax shield (reduce corporate taxes because of the tax deductibility of interest) and reduce the cash flow available to equity. In the long run, the investing and financing decisions made today will affect future cash flows.

If all the inputs were known and mutually consistent, a DDM and an FCFE model would result in identical valuations for a stock. One possibility would be that FCFE equals cash dividends each year. Then, both cash flow streams would be discounted at the required return for equity and would have the same present value.

Generally, however, FCFE and dividends will differ, but the same economic forces that lead to low (high) dividends lead to low (high) FCFE. For example, a rapidly growing company with superior investment opportunities will retain a high proportion of earnings and pay low dividends. This same company will have high investments in fixed capital and working capital and have a low FCFE (which is clear from the expression FCFE = NI + NCC − FCInv − WCInv + Net borrowing). Conversely, a mature company that is investing relatively little might have high dividends and high FCFE. Despite this tendency, however, FCFE and dividends will usually differ.

FCFF and FCFE, as defined here, are measures of cash flow designed for valuation of the firm or its equity. Other definitions of free cash flow frequently appear in textbooks, articles, and vendor-supplied databases of financial information on public companies. In many cases, these other definitions of free cash flow are not designed for valuation purposes and thus should not be used for valuation. Using numbers supplied by others without knowing exactly how they are defined increases the likelihood of making errors in valuation. As consumers and producers of research, analysts should understand (if consumers) or make clear (if producers) the definition of free cash flow being used.

Because using free cash flow analysis requires considerable care and understanding, some practitioners erroneously use earnings components such as NI, EBIT, EBITDA, or CFO in a discounted cash flow valuation. Such mistakes may lead the practitioner to systematically overstate or understate the value of a stock. Shortcuts can be costly.

A common shortcut is to use EBITDA as a proxy for the cash flow to the firm. Equation 13 clearly shows the differences between EBITDA and FCFF:

$$FCFF = EBITDA(1 − Tax\ rate) + Dep(Tax\ rate) − FCInv − WCInv.$$

Depreciation charges as a percentage of EBITDA differ substantially for different companies and industries, as does the depreciation tax shield (the depreciation charge times the tax rate). Although FCFF captures this difference, EBITDA does not. EBITDA also does not account for the investments a company makes in fixed capital or working capital. Hence, EBITDA is a poor measure of the cash flow available to the company's investors. Using EBITDA (instead of free cash flow) in a DCF model has another important aspect as well: EBITDA is a before-tax measure, so the discount rate applied to EBITDA would be a before-tax rate. The WACC used to discount FCFF is an after-tax cost of capital.

EBITDA is a poor proxy for free cash flow to the firm because it does not account for the depreciation tax shield and the investment in fixed capital and working capital, but it is an even poorer proxy for free cash flow to equity. From a stockholder's perspective, additional defects of EBITDA include its failure to account for the after-tax interest costs or cash flows from new borrowing or debt repayments. Example 11 shows the mistakes sometimes made in discussions of cash flows.

EXAMPLE 11

The Mistakes of Using Net Income for FCFE and EBITDA for FCFF

1. A recent job applicant made some interesting comments about FCFE and FCFF: "I don't like the definitions for FCFE and FCFF because they are unnecessarily complicated and confusing. The best measure of FCFE, the funds available to pay dividends, is simply net income. You take the net income number straight from the income statement and don't need to make any further adjustments. Similarly, the best measure of FCFF, the funds available to the company's suppliers of capital, is EBITDA. You can take EBITDA straight from the income statement, and you don't need to consider using anything else."

How would you respond to the job applicant's definition of (1) FCFE and (2) FCFF?

Solution:

The FCFE is the cash generated by the business's operations less the amount it must reinvest in additional assets plus the amounts it is borrowing. Equation 10, which starts with net income to find FCFE, shows these items:

Free cash flow to equity   =   Net income available to common shareholders

Plus: Net noncash charges

Less: Investment in fixed capital

Less: Investment in working capital

Plus: Net borrowing

Net income does not include several cash flows. So, net income tells only part of the overall story. Investments in fixed or working capital reduce the cash available to stockholders, as do loan repayments. New borrowing increases the cash available. FCFE, however, includes the cash generated from operating the business and also accounts for the investing and financing activities of the company. Of course, a special case exists in which net income and FCFE are the same. This case occurs when new investments exactly equal depreciation and the company is not investing in working capital or engaging in any net borrowing.

Solution:

Assuming that EBITDA equals FCFF introduces several possible mistakes. Equation 13 highlights these mistakes:

Free cash flow to the firm   =   EBITDA(1 − Tax rate)

Plus: Depreciation(Tax rate)

Less: Investment in fixed capital

Less: Investment in working capital

The applicant is ignoring taxes, which obviously reduce the cash available to the company's suppliers of capital, and is also ignoring depreciation and the investments in fixed capital and working capital.

Free Cash Flow and Complicated Capital Structures

For the most part, the discussion of FCFF and FCFE so far has assumed the company has a simple capital structure with two sources of capital—namely, debt and equity. Including preferred stock as a third source of capital requires the analyst to add terms to the equations for FCFF and FCFE to account for the dividends paid on preferred stock and for the issuance or repurchase of preferred shares. Instead of including those terms in all of the equations, we chose to leave preferred stock out because only a few corporations use preferred stock. For companies that do have preferred stock, however, the effects of the preferred stock can be incorporated in the valuation models. For example, in Equation 7, which calculates FCFF starting with net income available to common shareholders, preferred dividends paid would be added to the cash flows to obtain FCFF. In Equation 10, which calculates FCFE starting with net income available to common shareholders, if preferred dividends were already subtracted when arriving at net income, no further adjustment for preferred dividends would be required. Issuing (redeeming) preferred stock increases (decreases) the cash flow available to common stockholders, however, so this term would have to be added in.

The existence of preferred stock in the capital structure has many of the same effects as the existence of debt, except that unlike interest payments on debt, preferred stock dividends paid are not tax deductible.

Example 12 shows how to calculate WACC, FCFF, and FCFE when the company has preferred stock.

EXAMPLE 12

FCFF Valuation with Preferred Stock in the Capital Structure

Welch Corporation uses bond, preferred stock, and common stock financing. The market value of each of these sources of financing and the before-tax required rates of return for each are given in Exhibit 11:

Exhibit 11: Welch Corporation Capital Structure (Dollars in Millions)		
	Market Value ($)	**Required Return (%)**
Bonds	400	8.0
Preferred stock	100	8.0
Common stock	500	12.0
Total	1,000	

Other financial information (dollars in millions):

- Net income available to common shareholders = $110.
- Interest expenses = $32.
- Preferred dividends = $8.
- Depreciation = $40.
- Investment in fixed capital = $70.
- Investment in working capital = $20.
- Net borrowing = $25.
- Tax rate = 30%.
- Stable growth rate of FCFF = 4.0%.
- Stable growth rate of FCFE = 5.4%.

---

1. Calculate Welch Corporation's WACC.

Solution:

Based on the weights and after-tax costs of each source of capital, the WACC is

$$\text{WACC} = \frac{400}{1,000}8\%\,(1-0.30) + \frac{100}{1,000}8\% + \frac{500}{1,000}12\% = 9.04\%.$$

---

2. Calculate the current value of FCFF.

Solution:

If the company did not issue preferred stock, FCFF would be

$$FCFF = NI + NCC + Int(1 - \text{Tax rate}) - FCInv - WCInv.$$

If preferred stock dividends have been paid (and net income is income available to common shareholders), the preferred dividends must be added back just as after-tax interest expenses are. The modified equation (including preferred dividends) for FCFF is

$$FCFF = NI + NCC + Int(1 - \text{Tax rate}) + \text{Preferred dividends} - FCInv - WCInv.$$

For Welch Corporation, FCFF is

$$FCFF = 110 + 40 + 32(1 - 0.30) + 8 - 70 - 20 = \$90.4 \text{ million}.$$

3. Based on forecasted Year 1 FCFF, what is the total value of Welch Corporation and the value of its equity?

Solution:

The total value of the firm is

$$\text{Firm value} = \frac{FCFF1}{WACC - g} = \frac{90.4(1.04)}{0.0904 - 0.04}$$

$$= \frac{94.016}{0.0504} = \$1,865.40 \text{ million}.$$

The value of (common) equity is the total value of the company minus the value of debt and preferred stock:

$$\text{Equity} = 1,865.40 - 400 - 100 = \$1,365.40 \text{ million}.$$

4. Calculate the current value of FCFE.

Solution:

With no preferred stock, FCFE is

$$FCFE = NI + NCC - FCInv - WCInv + \text{Net borrowing}.$$

If the company has preferred stock, the FCFE equation is essentially the same. Net borrowing in this case is the total of new debt borrowing and net issuances of new preferred stock. For Welch Corporation, FCFE is

$$FCFE = 110 + 40 - 70 - 20 + 25 = \$85 \text{ million}.$$

5. Based on forecasted Year 1 FCFE, what is the value of equity?

Solution:

Valuing FCFE, which is growing at 5.4%, produces a value of equity of

$$\text{Equity} = \frac{FCFE_1}{r - g} = \frac{85(1.054)}{0.12 - 0.054} = \frac{89.59}{0.066} = \$1,357.42 \text{ million}.$$

Paying cash dividends on common stock does not affect FCFF or FCFE, which are the amounts of cash *available* to all investors or to common stockholders. It is simply a use of the available cash. Share repurchases of common stock also do not affect FCFF or FCFE. Share repurchases are, in many respects, a substitute for cash dividends. Similarly, issuing shares of common stock does not affect FCFF or FCFE.

Changing leverage (changing the amount of debt financing in the company's capital structure), however, does have some effects on FCFE particularly. An increase in leverage will not affect FCFF (although it might affect the calculations used to arrive at FCFF). An increase in leverage affects FCFE in two ways. In the year the debt is issued, it increases the FCFE by the amount of debt issued. After the debt is issued, FCFE is then reduced by the after-tax interest expense.

In this section, we have discussed the concepts of FCFF and FCFE and their estimation. The next section presents additional valuation models that use forecasts of FCFF or FCFE to value the firm or its equity. These free cash flow models are similar in structure to dividend discount models, although the analyst must face the reality that estimating free cash flows is more time-consuming than estimating dividends.

FREE CASH FLOW MODEL VARIATIONS

10

☐ | explain the use of sensitivity analysis in FCFF and FCFE valuations

This section presents several extensions of the free cash flow models presented earlier. In many cases, especially when inflation rates are volatile, analysts will value real cash flows instead of nominal values. As with dividend discount models, free cash flow models are sensitive to the data inputs, so analysts routinely perform sensitivity analyses of their valuations.

Earlier, we presented the single-stage free cash flow model, which has a constant growth rate. In the following, we use the single-stage model to address selected valuation issues; we then present multistage free cash flow models.

An International Application of the Single-Stage Model

Valuation by using real (inflation-adjusted) values instead of nominal values has much appeal when inflation rates are high and volatile. Many analysts use this adaptation for both domestic and nondomestic stocks, but the use of real values is especially helpful for valuing international stocks. Special challenges to valuing equities from multiple countries include (1) incorporating economic factors—such as interest rates, inflation rates, and growth rates—that differ among countries and (2) dealing with varied accounting standards. Furthermore, performing analyses in multiple countries challenges the analyst—particularly a team of analysts—to use *consistent* assumptions for all countries.

Several securities firms have adapted the single-stage FCFE model to address some of the challenges of international valuation. They choose to analyze companies by using real cash flows and real discount rates instead of nominal values. To estimate real discount rates, they use a modification of the build-up method mentioned earlier under the topic of return concepts. Starting with a "country return," which is a real required rate of return for stocks from a particular country, they then make adjustments to the country return for the stock's industry, size, and leverage:

Country return (real)	x.xx%
+/− Industry adjustment	x.xx%
+/− Size adjustment	x.xx%
+/− Leverage adjustment	x.xx%
Required rate of return (real)	x.xx%

The adjustments in the model should have sound economic justification. They should reflect factors expected to affect the relative risk and return associated with an investment.

The securities firms making these adjustments predict the growth rate of FCFE also in real terms. The firms supply their analysts with estimates of the real economic growth rate for each country, and each analyst chooses a real growth rate for the stock being analyzed that is benchmarked against the real country growth rate. This approach is particularly useful for countries with high or variable inflation rates.

The value of the stock is found with an equation essentially like Equation 6 except that all variables in the equation are stated in real terms:

$$V_0 = \frac{FCFE_0\left(1 + g_{real}\right)}{r_{real} - g_{real}}.$$

Whenever real discount rates and real growth rates can be estimated more reliably than nominal discount rates and nominal growth rates, this method is worth using. Example 13 shows how this procedure can be applied.

EXAMPLE 13

Using Real Cash Flows and Discount Rates for International Stocks

Mukamba Ventures is a consumer staples company headquartered in Kinshasa, Democratic Republic of the Congo. Although the company's cash flows have been volatile, an analyst has estimated a per-share normalized FCFE of 1,400 Congolese francs (CDF) for the year just ended. The real country return for the Democratic Republic of the Congo is 7.30%; adjustments to the country return for Mukamba Ventures are an industry adjustment of +0.80%, a size adjustment of −0.33%, and a leverage adjustment of −0.12%. The long-term real growth rate for the Democratic Republic of the Congo is estimated to be 3.0%, and the real growth rate of Mukamba Ventures is expected to be about 0.5% below the country rate. The real required rate of return for Mukamba Ventures is calculated as follows:

Country return (real)	7.30%
Industry adjustment	+ 0.80%
Size adjustment	− 0.33%
Leverage adjustment	− 0.12%
Required rate of return	7.65%

The real growth rate of FCFE is expected to be 2.5% (3.0% − 0.5%), so the value of one share is

$$V_0 = \frac{FCFE_0\left(1 + g_{real}\right)}{r_{real} - g_{real}} = \frac{1,400\,(1.025)}{0.0765 - 0.025} = \frac{1,435}{0.0515} = CDF27,864.$$

Sensitivity Analysis of FCFF and FCFE Valuations

In large measure, growth in FCFF and in FCFE depends on a company's future profitability. Sales growth and changes in net profit margins dictate future net profits. Sales growth and profit margins depend on the growth phase of the company and the profitability of the industry. A highly profitable company in a growing industry can enjoy years of profit growth. Eventually, however, its profit margins are likely to be eroded by increased competition; sales growth is also likely to abate because of fewer opportunities for expansion of market size and market share. Growth rates and the duration of growth are difficult to forecast.

The base-year values for the FCFF and FCFE growth models are also critical. Given the same required rates of return and growth rates, the value of the firm or the value of equity will increase or decrease proportionately with the initial value of FCFF or FCFE used.

To examine how sensitive the final valuation is to changes in each of a valuation model's input variables, analysts can perform a sensitivity analysis. Some input variables have a much larger impact on stock valuation than others. Example 14 shows the sensitivity of the valuation of Petroleo Brasileiro to four input variables.

EXAMPLE 14

Sensitivity Analysis of an FCFE Valuation

1. Antonio Sousa is valuing the equity of Petroleo Brasileiro, commonly known as Petrobras, by using the single-stage (constant-growth) FCFE model. Estimated FCFE per share for the year just ended is 2.59 Brazilian reals (BRL). Sousa's best estimates of input values for the analysis are as follows:

   - The FCFE growth rate is 7.0%.
   - The risk-free rate is 8.9%.
   - The equity risk premium is 5.3%.
   - Beta is 1.4.

   Using the capital asset pricing model (CAPM), Sousa estimates that the required rate of return for Petrobras is

   $$r = E(R_i) = R_F + \beta_i \left[E(R_M) - R_F \right] = 8.9\% + 1.4(5.3\%) = 16.32\%.$$

   The estimated value per share is

   $$V_0 = \frac{FCFE_0(1+g)}{r-g} = \frac{2.59(1.07)}{0.1632 - 0.07} = BRL29.73.$$

   Exhibit 12 shows Sousa's base case and the highest and lowest reasonable alternative estimates. The column "Valuation with Low Estimate" gives the estimated value of Petrobras based on the low estimate for the variable on the same row of the first column and the base-case estimates for the remaining three variables. "Valuation with High Estimate" gives a similar estimated value based on the high estimate for the variable at issue.

   Exhibit 12: Sensitivity Analysis for Petrobras Valuation

Variable	Base-Case Estimate	Low Estimate	High Estimate	Valuation with Low Estimate	Valuation with High Estimate
Beta	1.4	1.2	1.6	BRL33.55	BRL26.70
Risk-free rate	8.9%	7.9%	9.9%	BRL33.31	BRL26.85
Equity risk premium	5.3%	4.3%	6.3%	BRL34.99	BRL25.85
FCFE growth rate	7.0%	5.0%	9.0%	BRL24.02	BRL38.57

As Exhibit 12 shows, the value of Petrobras is very sensitive to the inputs. The value is negatively related to changes in the beta, the risk-free rate, and the equity risk premium and positively related to changes in the FCFE growth rate. Of the four variables considered, the stock valuation is most sensitive to the range of estimates for the FCFE growth rate (a range from BRL24.02 to BRL38.57. The ranges of the estimates for the other three variables, while still large, are less than the range for changes in the FCFE growth rate. Of course, the variables to which a stock price is most sensitive vary from case to case. A sensitivity analysis gives the analyst a guide as to which variables are most critical to the final valuation.

11 TWO-STAGE FREE CASH FLOW MODELS

☐ explain the single-stage (stable-growth), two-stage, and three-stage FCFF and FCFE models and justify the selection of the appropriate model given a company's characteristics

☐ estimate a company's value using the appropriate free cash flow model(s)

☐ describe approaches for calculating the terminal value in a multistage valuation model; and

Several two-stage and multistage models exist for valuing free cash flow streams, just as several such models are available for valuing dividend streams. The free cash flow models are much more complex than the dividend discount models because to find FCFF or FCFE, the analyst usually incorporates sales, profitability, investments, financing costs, and new financing.

In two-stage free cash flow models, the growth rate in the second stage is a long-run sustainable growth rate. For a declining industry, the second-stage growth rate could be slightly below the GDP growth rate. For an industry that is expected to grow in the future faster than the overall economy, the second-stage growth rate could be slightly greater than the GDP growth rate.

The two most popular versions of the two-stage FCFF and FCFE models are distinguished by the pattern of the growth rates in Stage 1. In one version, the growth rate is constant in Stage 1 before dropping to the long-run sustainable rate in Stage 2. In the other version, the growth rate declines in Stage 1 to reach the sustainable rate at the beginning of Stage 2. This second type of model is like the H-model for discounted dividend valuation, in which dividend growth rates decline in Stage 1 and are constant in Stage 2.

Unlike multistage DDMs, in which the growth rates are consistently dividend growth rates, in free cash flow models, the "growth rate" may refer to different variables (which variables should be stated or should be clear from the context). The growth rate could be the growth rate for FCFF or FCFE, the growth rate for income (either net income or operating income), or the growth rate for sales. If the growth rate is for net income, the changes in FCFF or FCFE also depend on investments in operating assets and the financing of these investments. When the growth rate in income declines, such as between Stage 1 and Stage 2, investments in operating assets probably decline at the same time. If the growth rate is for sales, changes in net profit margins as well as investments in operating assets and financing policies will determine FCFF and FCFE.

A general expression for the two-stage FCFF valuation model is

$$\text{Firm value} = \sum_{t=1}^{n} \frac{\text{FCFF}_t}{(1 + \text{WACC})^t} + \frac{\text{FCFF}_{n+1}}{(\text{WACC} - g)} \frac{1}{(1 + \text{WACC})^n}. \tag{16}$$

The summation gives the present value of the first n years of FCFF. The terminal value of the FCFF from Year $n + 1$ forward is $\text{FCFF}_{n+1}/(\text{WACC} - g)$, which is discounted at the WACC for n periods to obtain its present value. Subtracting the value of outstanding debt gives the value of equity. The value per share is then found by dividing the total value of equity by the number of outstanding shares.

The general expression for the two-stage FCFE valuation model is

$$\text{Equity value} = \sum_{t=1}^{n} \frac{\text{FCFE}_t}{(1 + r)^t} + \left(\frac{\text{FCFE}_{n+1}}{r - g} \right) \left[\frac{1}{(1 + r)^n} \right]. \tag{17}$$

In this case, the summation is the present value of the first n years of FCFE and the terminal value of $\text{FCFE}_{n+1}/(r - g)$ is discounted at the required rate of return on equity for n years. The value per share is found by dividing the total value of equity by the number of outstanding shares.

In Equation 17, the terminal value of the stock at $t = n$, TV_n, is found by using the constant-growth FCFE model. In this case, $\text{TV}_n = \text{FCFE}_{n+1}/(r - g)$. (Of course, the analyst might choose to estimate terminal value another way, such as by using a P/E multiplied by the company's forecasted EPS.) The terminal value estimation is critical for a simple reason: The present value of the terminal value is often a substantial portion of the total value of the stock. For example, in Equation 17, when the analyst is calculating the total present value of the first n cash flows (FCFE) and the present value of the terminal value, the present value of the terminal value is often substantial. In the examples that follow, the terminal value usually represents a substantial part of total estimated value. The same is true in practice.

Fixed Growth Rates in Stage 1 and Stage 2

The simplest two-stage FCFF or FCFE growth model has a constant growth rate in each stage. Example 15 finds the value of a firm that has a 20% sales growth rate in Stage 1 and a 6% sales growth rate in Stage 2.

EXAMPLE 15

A Two-Stage FCFE Valuation Model with a Constant Growth Rate in Each Stage

1. Uwe Henschel is doing a valuation of TechnoSchaft on the basis of the following information:

   - Year 0 sales per share = €25.
   - Sales growth rate = 20% annually for three years and 6% annually thereafter.
   - Net profit margin = 10% forever.
   - Net investment in fixed capital (net of depreciation) = 50% of the sales increase.
   - Annual increase in working capital = 20% of the sales increase.
   - Debt financing = 40% of the net investments in capital equipment and working capital.

- TechnoSchaft beta = 1.20; the risk-free rate of return = 7%; the equity risk premium = 4.5%.

The required rate of return for equity is

$$r = E(R_i) = R_F + \beta_i[E(R_M) - R_F] = 7\% + 1.2(4.5\%) = 12.4\%.$$

Exhibit 13 shows the calculations for FCFE.

Exhibit 13: FCFE Estimates for TechnoSchaft (in Euros)

	Year					
	1	2	3	4	5	6
Sales growth rate	20%	20%	20%	6%	6%	6%
Sales per share	30.000	36.000	43.200	45.792	48.540	51.452
Net profit margin	10%	10%	10%	10%	10%	10%
EPS	3.000	3.600	4.320	4.579	4.854	5.145
Net FCInv per share	2.500	3.000	3.600	1.296	1.374	1.456
WCInv per share	1.000	1.200	1.440	0.518	0.550	0.582
Debt financing per share	1.400	1.680	2.016	0.726	0.769	0.815
FCFE per share	0.900	1.080	1.296	3.491	3.700	3.922
Growth rate of FCFE		20%	20%	169%	6%	6%

In Exhibit 13, sales are shown to grow at 20% annually for the first three years and then at 6% thereafter. Profits, which are 10% of sales, grow at the same rates. The net investments in fixed capital and working capital are, respectively, 50% of the increase in sales and 20% of the increase in sales. New debt financing equals 40% of the total increase in net fixed capital and working capital. FCFE is EPS minus the net investment in fixed capital per share minus the investment in working capital per share plus the debt financing per share.

Notice that FCFE grows by 20% annually for the first three years (i.e., between $t = 0$ and $t = 3$). Then, between Year 3 and Year 4, when the sales growth rate drops from 20% to 6%, FCFE increases substantially. In fact, FCFE increases by 169% from Year 3 to Year 4. This large increase in FCFE occurs because profits grow at 6% but the investments in capital equipment and working capital (and the increase in debt financing) drop substantially from the previous year. In Years 5 and 6 in Exhibit 13, sales, profit, investments, financing, and FCFE are all shown to grow at 6%.

The stock value is the present value of the first three years' FCFE plus the present value of the terminal value of the FCFE from Years 4 and later. The terminal value is

$$TV_3 = \frac{FCFE_4}{r-g} = \frac{3.491}{0.124 - 0.06} = €54.55.$$

The present values are

$$V_0 = \frac{0.900}{1.124} + \frac{1.080}{(1.124)^2} + \frac{1.296}{(1.124)^3} + \frac{54.55}{(1.124)^3}$$
$$= 0.801 + 0.855 + 0.913 + 38.415 = €40.98.$$

The estimated value of this stock is €40.98 per share.

As mentioned previously, the terminal value may account for a large portion of the value of a stock. In the case of TechnoSchaft, the present value of the terminal value is €38.415 out of a total value of €40.98. The present value (PV) of the terminal value is almost 94% of the total value of TechnoSchaft stock.

Declining Growth Rate in Stage 1 and Constant Growth in Stage 2

Growth rates usually do not drop precipitously as they do between the stages in the two-stage model just described, but growth rates can decline over time for many reasons. Sometimes, a small company has a high growth rate that is not sustainable as its market share increases. A highly profitable company may attract competition that makes it harder for the company to sustain its high profit margins.

In this section, we present two examples of the two-stage model with declining growth rates in Stage 1. In the first example, the growth rate of EPS declines during Stage 1. As a company's profitability declines and the company is no longer generating high returns, the company will usually reduce its net new investment in operating assets. The debt financing accompanying the new investments will also decline. Many highly profitable, growing companies have negative or low free cash flows. Later, when growth in profits slows, investments will tend to slow and the company will experience positive cash flows. Of course, the negative cash flows incurred in the high-growth stage help determine the cash flows that occur in future years.

Example 16 models FCFE per share as a function of EPS that declines constantly during Stage 1. Because of declining earnings growth rates, the company in the example also reduces its new investments over time. The value of the company depends on these free cash flows, which are substantial after the high-growth (and high-profitability) period has largely elapsed.

EXAMPLE 16

A Two-Stage FCFE Valuation Model with Declining Net Income Growth in Stage 1

1. Vishal Noronha needs to prepare a valuation of Sindhuh Enterprises. Noronha has assembled the following information for his analysis. It is now the first day of 2020.

   - EPS for 2019 is $2.40.
   - For the next five years, the growth rate in EPS is given in the following table. After 2024, the growth rate will be 7%.

	2020	2021	2022	2023	2024
Growth rate for EPS	30%	18%	12%	9%	7%

- Net investments in fixed capital (net of depreciation) for the next five years are given in the following table. After 2024, capital expenditures are expected to grow at 7% annually.

	2020	2021	2022	2023	2024
Net capital expenditure per share	$3.00	$2.50	$2.00	$1.50	$1.00

- The investment in working capital each year will equal 50% of the net investment in capital items.
- 30% of the net investment in fixed capital and investment in working capital will be financed with new debt financing.
- Current market conditions dictate a risk-free rate of 6.0%, an equity risk premium of 4.0%, and a beta of 1.10 for Sindhuh Enterprises.
- What is the per-share value of Sindhuh Enterprises on the first day of 2020?
- What should be the trailing P/E on the first day of 2020 and the first day of 2024?

Solution:

The required return for Sindhuh should be

$$r = E(R_i) = R_F + \beta_i [E(R_M) - R_F] = 6\% + 1.1(4\%) = 10.4\%.$$

The FCFEs for the company for years 2020 through 2024 are given in Exhibit 14.

Exhibit 14: FCFE Estimates for Sindhuh Enterprises (Per-Share Data in US Dollars)

	Year				
	2020	2021	2022	2023	2024
Growth rate for EPS	30%	18%	12%	9%	7%
EPS	3.120	3.682	4.123	4.494	4.809
Net FCInv per share	3.000	2.500	2.000	1.500	1.000
WCInv per share	1.500	1.250	1.000	0.750	0.500
Debt financing per share[a]	1.350	1.125	0.900	0.675	0.450
FCFE per share[b]	−0.030	1.057	2.023	2.919	3.759
PV of FCFE discounted at 10.4%	−0.027	0.867	1.504	1.965	

[a]30% of (Net FCInv + WCInv).
[b]EPS – Net FCInv per share – WCInv per share + Debt financing per share.

Earnings are $2.40 in 2019. Earnings increase each year by the growth rate given in the table. Net capital expenditures (capital expenditures minus depreciation) are the amounts that Noronha assumed. The increase in working capital each year is 50% of the increase in net capital expenditures. Debt financing is 30% of the total outlays for net capital expenditures and working capital each year. The FCFE each year is net income minus net capital expenditures minus increase in working capital plus new debt financing. Finally, for years 2020 through 2023, the present value of FCFE is found by discounting FCFE by the 10.4% required rate of return for equity.

After 2024, FCFE will grow by a constant 7% annually, so the constant-growth FCFE valuation model can be used to value this cash flow stream. At the end of 2023, the value of the future FCFE is

$$V_{2016} = \frac{FCFE_{2017}}{r-g} = \frac{3.759}{0.104-0.07} = \$110.56 \text{ per share.}$$

[handwritten: 2023 under 2016]

To find the present value of V_{2016} as of the end of 2019, V_{2019}, we discount V_{2016} at 10.4% for four years: [handwritten: 2023]

$$PV = 110.56/(1.104)^4 = \$74.425 \text{ per share.}$$

The total present value of the company is the present value of the first four years' FCFE plus the present value of the terminal value, or

$$V_{2012} = -0.027 + 0.867 + 1.504 + 1.965 + 74.42 = \$78.73 \text{ per share.}$$

[handwritten: 2019 under 2012]

Solution:

Using the estimated $78.73 stock value, we find that the trailing P/E at the beginning of 2020 is

$$P/E = 78.73/2.40 = 32.8.$$

At the beginning of 2024, the expected stock value is $110.56, and the previous year's EPS is $4.494, so the trailing P/E at this time would be

$$P/E = 110.56/4.494 = 24.6.$$

After its high-growth phase has ended, the P/E for the company declines substantially.

The FCFE in Example 16 was based on forecasts of future EPS. Analysts often model a company by forecasting future sales and then estimating the profits, investments, and financing associated with those sales levels. For large companies, analysts may estimate the sales, profitability, investments, and financing for each division or large subsidiary. Then, they aggregate the free cash flows for all of the divisions or subsidiaries to get the free cash flow for the company as a whole.

Example 17 is a two-stage FCFE model with declining sales growth rates in Stage 1, with profits, investments, and financing keyed to sales. In Stage 1, the growth rate of sales and the profit margin on sales both decline as the company matures and faces more competition and slower growth.

EXAMPLE 17

A Two-Stage FCFE Valuation Model with Declining Sales Growth Rates

Medina Werks, a manufacturing company headquartered in Canada, has a competitive advantage that will probably deteriorate over time. Analyst Flavio Torino expects this deterioration to be reflected in declining sales growth rates as well as declining profit margins. To value the company, Torino has accumulated the following information:

- Current sales are C$600 million. Over the next six years, the annual sales growth rate and the net profit margin are projected to be as follows:

	Year 1 (%)	Year 2 (%)	Year 3 (%)	Year 4 (%)	Year 5 (%)	Year 6 (%)
Sales growth rate	20	16	12	10	8	7
Net profit margin	14	13	12	11	10.5	10

Beginning in Year 6, the 7% sales growth rate and 10% net profit margin should persist indefinitely.

- Capital expenditures (net of depreciation) in the amount of 60% of the sales increase will be required each year.
- Investments in working capital equal to 25% of the sales increase will also be required each year.
- Debt financing will be used to fund 40% of the investments in net capital items and working capital.
- The beta for Medina Werks is 1.10; the risk-free rate of return is 6.0%; the equity risk premium is 4.5%.
- The company has 70 million outstanding shares.

1. What is the estimated total market value of equity?

Solution:

The required return for Medina is

$$r = E(R_i) = R_F + \beta_i[E(R_M) - R_F] = 6\% + 1.10(4.5\%) = 10.95\%.$$

The annual sales and net profit can be readily found as shown in Exhibit 15.

Exhibit 15: FCFE Estimates for Medina Werks (C$ in Millions)

	Year					
	1	2	3	4	5	6
Sales growth rate	20%	16%	12%	10%	8%	7%
Net profit margin	14%	13%	12%	11%	10.50%	10%
Sales	720.000	835.200	935.424	1,028.966	1,111.284	1,189.074
Net profit	100.800	108.576	112.251	113.186	116.685	118.907
Net FCInv	72.000	69.120	60.134	56.125	49.390	46.674
WCInv	30.000	28.800	25.056	23.386	20.579	19.447
Debt financing	40.800	39.168	34.076	31.804	27.988	26.449
FCFE	39.600	49.824	61.137	65.480	74.703	79.235
PV of FCFE at 10.95%	35.692	40.475	44.763	43.211	44.433	

As can be seen, sales are expected to increase each year by a declining sales growth rate. Net profit each year is the year's net profit margin times the year's sales. Capital investment (net of depreciation) equals 60% of the sales increase from the previous year. The investment in working capital is 25% of the sales increase from the previous year. The debt financing each year is equal to 40% of the total net investment in capital items and working capital for that year. FCFE is net income minus the net capital investment minus the working capital investment plus the debt financing. The present value of each year's FCFE is found by discounting FCFE at the required rate of return for equity, 10.95%.

In Year 6 and beyond, Torino predicts sales to increase at 7% annually. Net income will be 10% of sales, so net profit will also grow at a 7% annual rate. Because they are pegged to the 7% sales increase, the investments in capital items and working capital and debt financing will also grow at the same 7% rate. The amounts in Year 6 for net income, investment in capital items, investment in working capital, debt financing, and FCFE will grow at 7%. The terminal value of FCFE in Year 6 and beyond is

$$TV_5 = \frac{FCFE_6}{r-g} = \frac{79.235}{0.1095-0.07} = C\$2,005.95 \text{ million.}$$

The present value of this amount is

$$PV \text{ of } TV_5 = \frac{2,005.95}{(1.1095)^5} = C\$1,193.12 \text{ million.}$$

The estimated total market value of the firm is the present value of FCFE for Years 1 through 5 plus the present value of the terminal value:

$$MV = 35.692 + 40.475 + 44.763 + 43.211 + 44.433 + 1,193.12$$

$$= C\$1,401.69 \text{ million.}$$

2. What is the estimated value per share?

Solution:

Dividing C\$1,401.69 million by the 70 million outstanding shares gives the estimated value per share of C\$20.02.

THREE-STAGE FREE CASH FLOW MODELS

12

☐ explain the single-stage (stable-growth), two-stage, and three-stage FCFF and FCFE models and justify the selection of the appropriate model given a company's characteristics

☐ estimate a company's value using the appropriate free cash flow model(s)

☐ describe approaches for calculating the terminal value in a multistage valuation model; and

Three-stage models are a straightforward extension of the two-stage models. One common version of a three-stage model is to assume a constant growth rate in each of the three stages. The growth rates could be for sales, profits, and investments in fixed and working capital; external financing could be a function of the level of sales or changes in sales. A simpler model would apply the growth rate to FCFF or FCFE.

A second common model is a three-stage model with constant growth rates in Stages 1 and 3 and a declining growth rate in Stage 2. Again, the growth rates could be applied to sales or to FCFF or FCFE. Although future FCFF and FCFE are unlikely to follow the assumptions of either of these three-stage growth models, analysts often find such models to be useful approximations.

Example 18 is a three-stage FCFF valuation model with declining growth rates in Stage 2. The model directly forecasts FCFF instead of deriving FCFF from a more complicated model that estimates cash flow from operations and investments in fixed and working capital.

EXAMPLE 18

A Three-Stage FCFF Valuation Model with Declining Growth in Stage 2

Charles Jones is evaluating Reliant Home Furnishings by using a three-stage growth model. He has accumulated the following information:

- Current FCFF = $745 million.
- Outstanding shares = 309.39 million.
- Equity beta = 0.90; risk-free rate = 5.04%; equity risk premium = 5.5%.
- Cost of debt = 7.1%.
- Marginal tax rate = 34%.
- Capital structure = 20% debt, 80% equity.
- Long-term debt = $1.518 billion.
- Growth rate of FCFF =
  - 8.8% annually in Stage 1, Years 1–4.
  - 7.4% in Year 5, 6.0% in Year 6, 4.6% in Year 7.
  - 3.2% in Year 8 and thereafter.

From the information that Jones has accumulated, estimate the following:

1. WACC.

Solution:

The required return for equity is

$$r = E(R_i) = R_F + \beta_i [E(R_M) - R_F] = 5.04\% + 0.9(5.5\%) = 9.99\%.$$

WACC is

$$\text{WACC} = 0.20(7.1\%)(1 - 0.34) + 0.80(9.99\%) = 8.93\%.$$

2. Total value of the firm.

Solution:

Exhibit 16 displays the projected FCFF for the next eight years and the present value of each FCFF discounted at 8.93%:

Exhibit 16: Forecasted FCFF for Reliant Home Furnishings

	Year							
	1	2	3	4	5	6	7	8
Growth rate	8.80%	8.80%	8.80%	8.80%	7.40%	6.00%	4.60%	3.20%
FCFF	811	882	959	1,044	1,121	1,188	1,243	1,283
PV at 8.93%	744	743	742	741	731	711	683	

The terminal value at the end of Year 7 is

$$TV_7 = \frac{FCFF_8}{WACC - g} = \frac{1,283}{0.0893 - 0.032} = \$22,391 \text{ million.}$$

The present value of this amount discounted at 8.93% for seven years is

$$PV \text{ of } TV_7 = \frac{22,391}{(1.0893)^7} = \$12,304 \text{ million.}$$

The total present value of the first seven years of FCFF is \$5,097 million. The total value of the firm is 12,304 + 5,097 = \$17,401 million.

3. Total value of equity.

Solution:

The value of equity is the value of the firm minus the market value of debt:

17,401 − 1,518 = \$15,883 million.

4. Value per share.

Solution:

Dividing the equity value by the number of shares yields the value per share:

\$15,883 million/309.39 million = \$51.34.

INTEGRATING ESG IN FREE CASH FLOW MODELS

13

- [ ] explain the single-stage (stable-growth), two-stage, and three-stage FCFF and FCFE models and justify the selection of the appropriate model given a company's characteristics
- [ ] estimate a company's value using the appropriate free cash flow model(s)
- [ ] describe approaches for calculating the terminal value in a multistage valuation model; and
- [ ] evaluate whether a stock is overvalued, fairly valued, or undervalued based on a free cash flow valuation model

Integrating environmental, social, and governance (ESG) considerations in valuation models can have a material impact on valuation. ESG factors may be either quantitative or qualitative. Quantitative ESG-related information, such as the effect of a projected environmental fine on cash flows, is more straightforward to integrate in valuation models. By contrast, qualitative ESG-related information is more challenging to integrate. One approach to address this challenge is to adjust the cost of equity by adding a risk premium in a valuation model. This approach can estimate the effect of ESG-related issues that are deemed material by an analyst but are difficult to quantify. When making an adjustment to the cost of equity by adding a risk premium, the analyst relies on his or her judgment to determine what value constitutes a reasonable adjustment. Example 19 provides a case study of how an analyst may develop a multistage (three-stage, in this case) FCFF valuation model that integrates ESG considerations.

EXAMPLE 19

Integrating ESG in a Three-Stage FCFF Model

American Copper Mining Company (ACMC) is a large US-based company. Copper has many uses in manufacturing, building, and other industries. The mining of copper is resource-intensive and is highly regulated.

ACMC recently announced that it is acquiring a new copper mine in a very dry region of Latin America. After the announcement, the market welcomed the news, and ACMC's share price rose to its current level of US$110 per share. The company expects the new mine to have a useful life of approximately 15 years.

Jane Dodd is a research analyst who follows ACMC and has a "hold" rating on its shares. She is preparing a new report to determine whether ACMC's acquisition of the new copper mine changes her fundamental assessment of the company. Overall, Dodd believes that the evaluation of ESG considerations can provide critical insights into the feasibility, economics, and valuation of mining companies and mining projects.

Dodd begins her analysis by evaluating the current political, labor, and environmental situation for ACMC's new mine. She has identified three primary ESG considerations that, in her opinion, may have the greatest effects on the value of the new mine and the company:

1. Local government issues
2. Labor issues
3. Water-related issues

Dodd then assesses how each of these ESG considerations may affect ACMC's operations and cash flow.

1. *Local government issues*: To operate the new mine, ACMC must obtain a mining license from the local government in the region where the mine is located. Before obtaining the mining license, ACMC is required to submit a comprehensive rehabilitation plan indicating how the new mine's natural habitat will be restored. Dodd notices that in its other mining sites, ACMC has struggled to produce comprehensive rehabilitation plans that have been approved by government authorities in a timely manner. She concludes that ACMC is overly optimistic about the time required to get approval for the mining license. She expects that rather than three years, as management anticipates, it will likely take five years before the mine can begin operating.

2. *Labor issues*: ACMC's compensation of its employees is slightly lower than its competitors in the region of the new mine. In addition, unlike many of its competitors, ACMC does not tie executive compensation to worker safety. Some competitors in the region have experienced labor strikes (and thus production interruptions) because their employees' wages are not adjusted for inflation. Because of ACMC's compensation policies, Dodd is concerned about the potential for labor unrest and subsequent reputational risk for the company.

3. *Water-related issues*: Because a large volume of water is used for mining operations, water-related costs are typically among the largest expenditures for mining companies. Given that the development of

the new mine is located in a very dry region of Latin America, Dodd believes that ACMC has significantly underestimated the required capital expenditures necessary to build water wells.

Valuation Analysis

After identifying and assessing these ESG considerations, Dodd proceeds to value ACMC's share price using a three-stage FCFF model. The three stages are as follows:

- Stage 1: the period prior to expected operation of the new mine (2020–2024)
- Stage 2: the period during expected operation of the new mine (2025–2039)
- Stage 3: the period subsequent to the expected closing of the mine (2040 and onward)

Dodd makes the following assumptions in her model.

Revenues

ACMC's total revenues during 2020 were $1 billion. Dodd expects total revenues (i.e., excluding those of the new mine) to increase 2% annually through 2024 and then remain constant during 2025–2039, when the new mine operates. When the new mine begins operations under Dodd's assumption (in 2025), Dodd expects the mine to add US$400 million to ACMC's revenues in its first year. Dodd also expects that these additional revenues from the new mine will increase by 10% annually for the next six years (2026 through 2031) and then remain constant for the remaining life of the mine (2032 through 2039). Dodd assumes that once the new mine closes in 2039, the company's total revenues will grow by 1% in perpetuity. The following is a summary of revenues for the three stages:

Stage 1 (prior to expected operation of mine):

Years 2020–2024: annual total revenue growth of 2%

Stage 2 (during expected operation of new mine):

2025: constant growth of revenues excluding the new mine; additional revenue of US$400 million from new mine

2026–2039: constant growth of revenues excluding new mine during years 2026–2039); 10% annual growth of revenue from new mine during years 2026–2031; constant growth of revenues from new mine during years 2032–2039

Stage 3 (after expected closing of new mine):

2040 and beyond: annual total revenue growth of 1%

Dodd also makes the following financial assumptions for ACMC:

EBITDA:	30% of total revenues for all three stages
Taxes:	25%
Investment in fixed capital (not including water-related investments):	50% of EBITDA for all three stages
Depreciation:	40% of capital expenditures for all three stages
Investment in working capital:	10% of total revenue for all three stages

Required return (pretax) on ACMC debt:	5%
Risk-free rate:	3%
ACMC equity beta:	1.2
Equity risk premium:	5%
Debt ratio:	50%

In addition to these "traditional" financial assumptions, Dodd also reflects ESG considerations in her analysis.

Water-related investment in fixed capital

10% of non-water-related capital expenditures, which are added to the capital expenditures noted previously.

ESG equity risk premium adjustment

Dodd concludes that the potential for labor issues discussed earlier exposes ACMC to higher financial and reputational risk compared to its peers. Dodd further believes that the ESG considerations she has identified are not recognized fully in the market price of ACMC shares. As a result, Dodd estimates that a 75 basis point premium should be added to ACMC's cost of equity.

Dodd calculates the WACC as follows:

Cost of debt = (5%)(1 − 25%) = 3.75%.

Cost of equity = 3% + (1.2)(5%) + 0.75% ESG equity risk premium adjustment = 9.75%.

WACC = (0.5)(3.75%) + (0.5)(9.75%) = 6.75%.

Exhibit 17 presents the results of Dodd's model for valuing ACMC's equity. Dodd's analysis suggests that the fair value for ACMC's equity is $97 per share. By integrating ESG considerations in a traditional valuation framework, Dodd's estimate of the fair value of ACMC's shares decreased. Given that the stock is trading at US$110, she issues a "sell" recommendation for ACMC's shares.

The next section discusses an important technical issue, the treatment of non-operating assets in valuation.

14 NON-OPERATING ASSETS AND FIRM VALUE

☐ | estimate a company's value using the appropriate free cash flow model(s)

Free cash flow valuation focuses on the value of assets that generate or are needed to generate operating cash flows. If a company has significant non-operating assets, such as excess cash (excess in relation to what is needed for generating operating cash flows), excess marketable securities, or land held for investment, then analysts often calculate the value of the firm as the value of its operating assets (e.g., as estimated by FCFF valuation) plus the value of its non-operating assets:

Exhibit 17: Estimating Fair Value of ACMC Shares (in Millions of US Dollars, Except for Per-Share Items)

			Expected Operation of New Mine											Expected Closing of Mine	
	2020	2021	2022	2023	2024	2025	2026	2027	...	2030	2031	...	2034	2035	2036
Total revenues	1,000	1,020	1,040	1,061	1,082	1,482	1,522	1,566	...	1,727	1,791	...	1,791	1,791	1,809
Revenues from new mine only						400.0	440.0	484.0		644.2	708.6		708.6	708.6	
EBITDA	300.0	306.0	312.1	318.4	324.7	444.7	456.7	469.9	...	518.0	537.3	...	537.3	537.3	542.7
EBITDA(1 − Tax rate)	225.0	229.5	234.1	238.8	243.5	333.5	342.5	352.4		388.5	403.0		403.0	403.0	407.0
Depreciation(Tax rate)	15.0	15.3	15.6	15.9	16.2	22.2	22.8	23.5	...	25.9	26.9	...	26.9	26.9	27.1
Investment in fixed capital, or FCInv	(150.0)	(153.0)	(156.1)	(159.2)	(162.4)	(222.4)	(228.4)	(235.0)	...	(259.0)	(268.7)	...	(268.7)	(268.7)	(271.3)
Investment in working capital, or WCInv*	(2.0)	(2.0)	(2.0)	(2.1)	(2.1)	(40.0)	(4.0)	(4.4)		(5.9)	(6.4)		0.0	0.0	(1.8)
Additional FCInv (water-related)	—	—	—	—	—	(22.2)	(22.8)	(23.5)	...	(25.9)	(26.9)	...	(26.9)	(26.9)	
FCFF	**88.0**	**89.8**	**91.6**	**93.4**	**95.3**	**71.2**	**110.2**	**113.1**	...	**123.6**	**127.9**	...	**134.3**	**134.3**	**161.0**
PV of FCFF up to 2039 (@ WACC of 6.75%)	82.5	78.8	75.3	71.9	68.7	48.1	69.7	67.1	...	60.3	58.4	...	38.8	36.4	
PV of FCFF Years 2016–2035	1,178														
PV of perpetual FCFF 2036 onward	758														
Total PV of future FCFF	**1,936**														
Market value of debt (50% debt ratio)	968														
Fair value of equity	968														
Fair value per share (10 million shares outstanding)	97														

					Expected Operation of New Mine							Expected Closing of Mine		
Supplemental items:														
Depreciation	60.0	61.2	62.4	63.7	65.0	89.0	91.4	94.0	103.6	107.5	...	107.5	107.5	63.7
Working capital	100.0	102.0	104.0	106.1	108.2	148.2	152.2	156.6	172.7	179.1	...	179.1	179.1	180.9

Note: The 2020 investment in working capital (WCInv) reflects the change in working capital from 2019 to 2020. For simplicity, Dodd uses the same change in WCInv for 2020 as in 2021.

$$\text{Value of firm} = \text{Value of operating assets} + \text{Value of nonoperating assets.} \tag{18}$$

In general, if any company asset is excluded from the set of assets being considered in projecting a company's future cash flows, the analyst should add that omitted asset's estimated value to the cash flow–based value estimate. Some companies have substantial noncurrent investments in stocks and bonds that are not operating subsidiaries but, rather, financial investments. These investments should be reflected at their current market value. Those securities reported at book values on the basis of accounting conventions should be revalued to market values.

SUMMARY

Discounted cash flow models are widely used by analysts to value companies.

- Free cash flow to the firm (FCFF) and free cash flow to equity (FCFE) are the cash flows available to, respectively, all of the investors in the company and to common stockholders.

- Analysts like to use free cash flow (either FCFF or FCFE) as the return

  - if the company is not paying dividends;
  - if the company pays dividends but the dividends paid differ significantly from the company's capacity to pay dividends;
  - if free cash flows align with profitability within a reasonable forecast period with which the analyst is comfortable; or
  - if the investor takes a control perspective.

- The FCFF valuation approach estimates the value of the firm as the present value of future FCFF discounted at the weighted average cost of capital:

$$\text{Firm value} = \sum_{t=1}^{\infty} \frac{\text{FCFF}_t}{(1 + \text{WACC})^t}.$$

  The value of equity is the value of the firm minus the value of the firm's debt:

$$\text{Equity value} = \text{Firm value} - \text{Market value of debt}.$$

  Dividing the total value of equity by the number of outstanding shares gives the value per share.

  The WACC formula is

$$\text{WACC} = \frac{\text{MV(Debt)}}{\text{MV(Debt)} + \text{MV(Equity)}} r_d (1 - \text{Tax rate})$$
$$+ \frac{\text{MV(Equity)}}{\text{MV(Debt)} + \text{MV(Equity)}} r.$$

- The value of the firm if FCFF is growing at a constant rate is

$$\text{Firm value} = \frac{\text{FCFF}_1}{\text{WACC} - g} = \frac{\text{FCFF}_0 (1 + g)}{\text{WACC} - g}.$$

- With the FCFE valuation approach, the value of equity can be found by discounting FCFE at the required rate of return on equity, r:

$$\text{Equity value} = \sum_{t=1}^{\infty} \frac{\text{FCFE}_t}{(1+r)^t}.$$

Dividing the total value of equity by the number of outstanding shares gives the value per share.

- The value of equity if FCFE is growing at a constant rate is

$$\text{Equity value} = \frac{\text{FCFE}_1}{r-g} = \frac{\text{FCFE}_0(1+g)}{r-g}.$$

- FCFF and FCFE are frequently calculated by starting with net income:

$$\text{FCFF} = \text{NI} + \text{NCC} + \text{Int}(1 - \text{Tax rate}) - \text{FCInv} - \text{WCInv}.$$

$$\text{FCFE} = \text{NI} + \text{NCC} - \text{FCInv} - \text{WCInv} + \text{Net borrowing}.$$

- FCFF and FCFE are related to each other as follows:

$$\text{FCFE} = \text{FCFF} - \text{Int}(1 - \text{Tax rate}) + \text{Net borrowing}.$$

- FCFF and FCFE can be calculated by starting from cash flow from operations:

$$\text{FCFF} = \text{CFO} + \text{Int}(1 - \text{Tax rate}) - \text{FCInv}.$$

$$\text{FCFE} = \text{CFO} - \text{FCInv} + \text{Net borrowing}.$$

- FCFF can also be calculated from EBIT or EBITDA:

$$\text{FCFF} = \text{EBIT}(1 - \text{Tax rate}) + \text{Dep} - \text{FCInv} - \text{WCInv}.$$

$$\text{FCFF} = \text{EBITDA}(1 - \text{Tax rate}) + \text{Dep}(\text{Tax rate}) - \text{FCInv} - \text{WCInv}.$$

FCFE can then be found by using FCFE = FCFF − Int(1 − Tax rate) + Net borrowing.

- Finding CFO, FCFF, and FCFE may require careful interpretation of corporate financial statements. In some cases, the necessary information may not be transparent.
- Earnings components such as net income, EBIT, EBITDA, and CFO should not be used as cash flow measures to value a firm. These earnings components either double-count or ignore parts of the cash flow stream.
- FCFF or FCFE valuation expressions can be easily adapted to accommodate complicated capital structures, such as those that include preferred stock.
- A general expression for the two-stage FCFF valuation model is

$$\text{Firm value} = \sum_{t=1}^{n} \frac{\text{FCFF}_t}{(1 + \text{WACC})^t} + \frac{\text{FCFF}_{n+1}}{(\text{WACC} - g)} \frac{1}{(1 + \text{WACC})^n}.$$

- A general expression for the two-stage FCFE valuation model is

$$\text{Equity value} = \sum_{t=1}^{n} \frac{\text{FCFE}_t}{(1+r)^t} + \left(\frac{\text{FCFE}_{n+1}}{r - g} \right) \left[\frac{1}{(1+r)^n} \right].$$

- One common two-stage model assumes a constant growth rate in each stage, and a second common model assumes declining growth in Stage 1 followed by a long-run sustainable growth rate in Stage 2.

- To forecast FCFF and FCFE, analysts build a variety of models of varying complexity. A common approach is to forecast sales, with profitability, investments, and financing derived from changes in sales.

- Three-stage models are often considered to be good approximations for cash flow streams that, in reality, fluctuate from year to year.

- Non-operating assets, such as excess cash and marketable securities, noncurrent investment securities, and nonperforming assets, are usually segregated from the company's operating assets. They are valued separately and then added to the value of the company's operating assets to find total firm value.

REFERENCES

Bahnson, P., P. B. Miller, B. P. Budge. 1996. "Nonarticulation in Cash Flow Statements and Implications for Education, Research and Practice." Accounting Horizons10 (4): 1–15.

Casey, Ryan J., Feng Gao, Michael T. Kirschenheiter, Siyi Li, Shailendra Pandit. 2016. "Do Compustat Financial Statement Data Articulate?" Journal of Financial Reporting1 (1): 37–59. 10.2308/jfir-51329

Gordon, Elizabeth A., Elaine Henry, Bjorn N. Jorgensen, Cheryl L. Linthicum. 2017. "Flexibility in Cash-Flow Classification under IFRS: Determinants and Consequences." Review of Accounting Studies22 (2): 839–72. 10.1007/s11142-017-9387-1

Hribar, P., D. W. Collins. 2002. "Errors in Estimating Accruals: Implications for Empirical Research." Journal of Accounting Research40 (1): 105–34. 10.1111/1475-679X.00041

Huefner, R. J., J. E. Ketz, J. A. Largay. 1989. "Foreign Currency Translation and the Cash Flow Statement." Accounting Horizons3 (2): 66–75.

Luehrman, T. A. 1997. "Using APV (Adjusted Present Value): A Better Tool for Valuing Operations." Harvard Business Review75 (3): 145–46, 148, 150–54.

Pinto, Jerald E., Thomas R. Robinson, John D. Stowe. 2019. "Equity Valuation: A Survey of Professional Practice." Review of Financial Economics37 (2): 219–33. 10.1002/rfe.1040

Shi, Linna, Huai Zhang. 2011. "On Alternative Measures of Accruals." Accounting Horizons25 (4): 811–36. 10.2308/acch-50050

Wilkins, M. S., M. L. Loudder. 2000. "Articulation in Cash Flow Statements: A Resource for Financial Accounting Courses." Journal of Accounting Education18:115–26. 10.1016/S0748-5751(00)00007-5

PRACTICE PROBLEMS

The following information relates to questions 1-2

Shimotsuke Co. LTD. has FCFF of 1.7 billion Japanese yen (JPY) and FCFE of JPY1.3 billion. Shimotsuke Co.'s WACC is 11%, and its required rate of return for equity is 13%. FCFF is expected to grow forever at 7%, and FCFE is expected to grow forever at 7.5%. Shimotsuke Co. has debt outstanding of JPY15 billion.

1. What is the total value of Shimotsuke Co.'s equity using the FCFF valuation approach?

2. What is the total value of Shimotsuke Co.'s equity using the FCFE valuation approach?

The following information relates to questions 3-6

Elina Kuznetsova is planning to value BCC Corporation, a provider of a variety of industrial metals and minerals. Kuznetsova uses a single-stage FCFF approach. The financial information Kuznetsova has assembled for her valuation is as follows:

- The company has 1,852 million shares outstanding.
- The market value of its debt is $3.192 billion.
- The FCFF is currently $1.1559 billion.
- The equity beta is 0.90; the equity risk premium is 5.5%; the risk-free rate is 5.5%.
- The before-tax cost of debt is 7.0%.
- The tax rate is 40%.
- To calculate WACC, he will assume the company is financed 25% with debt.
- The FCFF growth rate is 4%.

Using Kuznetsova's information, calculate the following:

3. WACC.

4. Value of the firm.

5. Total market value of equity.

6. Value per share.

The following information relates to questions 7-13

Yandie Izzo manages a dividend growth strategy for a large asset management firm. Izzo meets with her investment team to discuss potential investments in three companies: Company A, Company B, and Company C. Statements of cash flow for the three companies are presented in Exhibit 1.

Exhibit 1: Statements of Cash Flow, Most Recent Fiscal Year End (Amounts in Millions of Dollars)

	Company A	Company B	Company C
Cash Flow from Operating Activities			
Net Income	4,844	1,212	15,409
Adjustments			
Depreciation	500	288	3,746
Other noncash expenses	1,000	—	—
Changes in working capital			
(Increase) Decrease accounts receivable	(452)	(150)	(536)
(Increase) Decrease inventories	—	(200)	(803)
Increase (Decrease) accounts payable	(210)	100	(3)
Increase (Decrease) other current liabilities	540	14	350
Net cash from operating activities	6,222	1,264	18,163
Cash Flow from Investing Activities			
(Purchase) Sale of fixed assets	2,379	(1,000)	(3,463)
Net cash from investing activities	2,379	(1,000)	(3,463)
Cash Flow from Financing Activities			
Increase (Decrease) notes payable	25	3000	1,238
Increase (Decrease) long-term debt	(1,500)	(1,000)	(1,379)
Payment of common stock dividends	(1,000)	(237)	(15,000)
Net cash from financing activities	(2,475)	1,763	(15,141)
Net change in cash and cash equivalents	6,126	2,027	(441)
Cash and equivalents at beginning of year	50	100	3,000
Cash and equivalents at end of year	6,176	2,127	2,559
Supplemental Cash Flow Disclosures			
Interest	(353)	(50)	(552)

	Company A	Company B	Company C
Income taxes	(1,605)	(648)	(3,787)

Izzo's team first discusses key characteristics of Company A. The company has a history of paying modest dividends relative to FCFE, has a stable capital structure, and is owned by a controlling investor.

The team also considers the impact of Company A's three noncash transactions in the most recent year on its FCFE, including the following:

Transaction 1: A $900 million loss on a sale of equipment

Transaction 2: An impairment of intangibles of $400 million

Transaction 3: A $300 million reversal of a previously recorded restructuring charge

In addition, Company A's annual report indicates that the firm expects to incur additional noncash charges related to restructuring over the next few years.

To value the three companies' shares, one team member suggests valuing the companies' shares using net income as a proxy for FCFE. Another team member proposes forecasting FCFE using a sales-based methodology based on the following equation:

$$FCFE = NI - (1 - DR)(FCInv - Dep) - (1 - DR)(WCInv).$$

Izzo's team ultimately decides to use actual free cash flow to value the three companies' shares. Selected data and assumptions are provided in Exhibit 2.

Exhibit 2: Supplemental Data and Valuation Assumptions

	Company A	Company B	Company C
Tax rate	35%	35%	30%
Beta	1.00	0.90	1.10
Before-tax cost of debt	6%	7%	6%
Target debt ratio	50%	30%	40%
Market data:			
Risk-free rate: 3%			
Market risk premium: 7%			

The team calculates the intrinsic value of Company B using a two-stage FCFE model. FCFE growth rates for the first four years are estimated at 10%, 9%, 8%, and 7%, respectively, before declining to a constant 6% starting in the fifth year.

To calculate the intrinsic value of Company C's equity, the team uses the FCFF approach assuming a single-stage model where FCFF is expected to grow at 5% indefinitely.

7. Based on Company A's key characteristics, which discounted cash flow model would *most likely* be used by the investment team to value Company A's shares?

   A. DDM

   B. FCFE

   C. FCFF

8. Which noncash transaction should be subtracted from net income in arriving at Company A's FCFE?

   A. Transaction 1

   B. Transaction 2

   C. Transaction 3

9. Based on Exhibit 1, Company A's FCFE for the most recent year is *closest* to:

   A. $5,318 million.

   B. $6,126 million.

   C. $7,126 million.

10. Based on Exhibit 1, using net income as a proxy for Company B's FCFE would result in an intrinsic value that is:

    A. lower than the intrinsic value if actual FCFE were used.

    B. equal to the intrinsic value if actual FCFE were used.

    C. higher than the intrinsic value if actual FCFE were used.

11. Based on Exhibit 1, using the proposed sales-based methodology to forecast FCFE would produce an inaccurate FCFE projection for which company?

    A. Company A

    B. Company B

    C. Company C

12. Based on Exhibits 1 and 2 and the proposed two-stage FCFE model, the intrinsic value of Company B's equity is *closest* to:

    A. $70,602 million.

    B. $73,588 million.

    C. $79,596 million.

13. Based on Exhibits 1 and 2 and the proposed single-stage FCFF model, the intrinsic value of Company C's equity is *closest* to:

    A. $277,907 million.

    B. $295,876 million.

    C. $306,595 million.

The following information relates to questions 14-15

The term "free cash flow" is frequently applied to cash flows that differ from the definition for FCFF that should be used to value a firm. Two such definitions of free cash flow are given below. Compare these two definitions for free cash flow with the technically correct definition of FCFF used in our coverage of the topic.

14. FCF = Net income + Depreciation and amortization – Cash dividends – Capital expenditures.

15. FCF = Cash flow from operations (from the statement of cash flows) – Capital expenditures.

The following information relates to questions 16-18

LaForge Systems, Inc., has net income of $285 million for the year 2020. Using information from the company's financial statements given here, show the adjustments to net income that would be required to find:

16. FCFF.

17. FCFE.

18. In addition, show the adjustments to FCFF that would result in FCFE.

The following information relates to questions 19-20

Do Pham is evaluating Phaneuf Accelerateur by using the FCFF and FCFE valuation approaches. Pham has collected the following information (currency in euros):

- Phaneuf has net income of €250 million, depreciation of €90 million, capital expenditures of €170 million, and an increase in working capital of €40 million.
- Phaneuf will finance 40% of the increase in net fixed assets (capital expenditures less depreciation) and 40% of the increase in working capital with debt financing.
- Interest expenses are €150 million. The current market value of Phaneuf's outstanding debt is €1,800 million.
- FCFF is expected to grow at 6.0% indefinitely, and FCFE is expected to grow at 7.0%.
- The tax rate is 30%.
- Phaneuf is financed with 40% debt and 60% equity. The before-tax cost of debt is 9%, and the before-tax cost of equity is 13%.
- Phaneuf has 10 million outstanding shares.

19. Using the FCFF valuation approach, estimate the total value of the firm, the total market value of equity, and the per-share value of equity.

20. Using the FCFE valuation approach, estimate the total market value of equity and the per-share value of equity.

The following information relates to questions 21-22

LaForge Systems, Inc., Balance Sheet (in Millions)		
Years Ended 31 December	**2019**	**2020**
Assets		
Current assets		
Cash and equivalents	$210	$248
Accounts receivable	474	513
Inventory	520	564
Total current assets	1,204	1,325
Gross fixed assets	2,501	2,850
Accumulated depreciation	(604)	(784)
Net fixed assets	1,897	2,066
Total assets	$3,101	$3,391
Liabilities and shareholders' equity		
Current liabilities		
Accounts payable	$295	$317
Notes payable	300	310
Accrued taxes and expenses	76	99
Total current liabilities	671	726
Long-term debt	1,010	1,050
Common stock	50	50
Additional paid-in capital	300	300
Retained earnings	1,070	1,265
Total shareholders' equity	1,420	1,615
Total liabilities and shareholders' equity	$3,101	$3,391

Statement of Income In Millions, except Per-Share Data	31 December 2020
Total revenues	$2,215
Operating costs and expenses	1,430
EBITDA	785
Depreciation	180
EBIT	605

Statement of Income In Millions, except Per-Share Data	31 December 2020
Interest expense	130
Income before tax	475
Taxes (at 40%)	190
Net income	285
Dividends	90
Addition to retained earnings	195

Statement of Cash Flows In Millions	31 December 2020
Operating activities	
Net income	$285
Adjustments	
Depreciation	180
Changes in working capital	
Accounts receivable	(39)
Inventories	(44)
Accounts payable	22
Accrued taxes and expenses	23
Cash provided by operating activities	$427
Investing activities	
Purchases of fixed assets	349
Cash used for investing activities	$349
Financing activities	
Notes payable	$(10)
Long-term financing issuances	(40)
Common stock dividends	90
Cash used for financing activities	$40
Cash and equivalents increase (decrease)	38
Cash and equivalents at beginning of year	210
Cash and equivalents at end of year	$248
Supplemental cash flow disclosures	
Interest paid	$130
Income taxes paid	$190

Note: The statement of cash flows shows the use of a convention by which the positive numbers of $349 and $40 for cash used for investing activities and cash used for financing activities, respectively, are understood to be subtractions, because "cash used" is an outflow.

For LaForge Systems, whose financial statements are given in Problem 2, show the adjustments from the current levels of CFO (which is $427 million), EBIT ($605 million), and EBITDA ($785 million) to find:

21. FCFF.

22. FCFE.

The following information relates to questions 23-28

Ryan Leigh is preparing a presentation that analyzes the valuation of the common stock of two companies under consideration as additions to his firm's recommended list, Emerald Corporation and Holt Corporation. Leigh has prepared preliminary valuations of both companies using an FCFE model and is also preparing a value estimate for Emerald using a dividend discount model. Holt's 2019 and 2020 financial statements, contained in Exhibits 1 and 2, are prepared in accordance with US GAAP.

Exhibit 1: Holt Corporation Consolidated Balance Sheets (US$ Millions)

		As of 31 December		
		2020		2019
Assets				
Current assets				
Cash and cash equivalents		$ 372		$ 315
Accounts receivable		770		711
Inventories		846		780
Total current assets		1,988		1,806
Gross fixed assets	4,275		3,752	
Less: Accumulated depreciation	1,176	3,099	906	2,846
Total assets		$5,087		$4,652
Liabilities and shareholders' equity				
Current liabilities				
Accounts payable		$ 476		$ 443
Accrued taxes and expenses		149		114
Notes payable		465		450
Total current liabilities		1,090		1,007
Long-term debt		1,575		1,515
Common stock		525		525
Retained earnings		1,897		1,605
Total liabilities and shareholders' equity		$5,087		$4,652

Exhibit 2: Holt Corporation Consolidated Income Statement for the Year Ended 31 December 2020 (US$ Millions)

Total revenues	$3,323
Cost of goods sold	1,287
Selling, general, and administrative expenses	858

Earnings before interest, taxes, depreciation, and amortization (EBITDA)	1,178
Depreciation expense	270
Operating income	908
Interest expense	195
Pretax income	713
Income tax (at 32%)	228
Net income	$ 485

Leigh presents his valuations of the common stock of Emerald and Holt to his supervisor, Alice Smith. Smith has the following questions and comments:

1. "I estimate that Emerald's long-term expected dividend payout rate is 20% and its return on equity is 10% over the long term."

2. "Why did you use an FCFE model to value Holt's common stock? Can you use a DDM instead?"

3. "How did Holt's FCFE for 2008 compare with its FCFF for the same year? I recommend you use an FCFF model to value Holt's common stock instead of using an FCFE model because Holt has had a history of leverage changes in the past."

4. "In the last three years, about 5% of Holt's growth in FCFE has come from decreases in inventory."

Leigh responds to each of Smith's points as follows:

1. "I will use your estimates and calculate Emerald's long-term, sustainable dividend growth rate."

2. "There are two reasons why I used the FCFE model to value Holt's common stock instead of using a DDM. The first reason is that Holt's dividends have differed significantly from its capacity to pay dividends. The second reason is that Holt is a takeover target and once the company is taken over, the new owners will have discretion over the uses of free cash flow."

3. "I will calculate Holt's FCFF for 2020 and estimate the value of Holt's common stock using an FCFF model."

4. "Holt is a growing company. In forecasting either Holt's FCFE or FCFF growth rates, I will not consider decreases in inventory to be a long-term source of growth."

23. Which of the following long-term FCFE growth rates is *most* consistent with the facts and stated policies of Emerald?

    A. 5% or lower

    B. 2% or higher

    C. 8% or higher

24. Do the reasons provided by Leigh support his use of the FCFE model to value Holt's common stock instead of using a DDM?

    A. Yes

    B. No, because Holt's dividend situation argues in favor of using the DDM

    C. No, because FCFE is not appropriate for investors taking a control perspective

25. Holt's FCFF (in millions) for 2020 is *closest* to:

    A. $308.

    B. $370.

    C. $422.

26. Holt's FCFE (in millions) for 2020 is *closest* to:

    A. $175.

    B. $250.

    C. $364.

27. Leigh's comment about not considering decreases in inventory to be a source of long-term growth in free cash flow for Holt is:

    A. inconsistent with a forecasting perspective.

    B. mistaken because decreases in inventory are a use rather than a source of cash.

    C. consistent with a forecasting perspective because inventory reduction has a limit, particularly for a growing firm.

28. Smith's recommendation to use an FCFF model to value Holt is:

    A. logical, given the prospect of Holt changing capital structure.

    B. not logical because an FCFF model is used only to value the total firm.

    C. not logical because FCFE represents a more direct approach to free cash flow valuation.

29. Indicate the effect on this period's FCFF and FCFE of a change in each of the items listed here. Assume a $100 increase in each case and a 40% tax rate.

    A. Net income.

    B. Cash operating expenses.

    C. Depreciation.

    D. Interest expense.

    E. EBIT.

    F. Accounts receivable.

    G. Accounts payable.

    H. Property, plant, and equipment.

    I. Notes payable.

    J. Cash dividends paid.

   K. Proceeds from issuing new common shares.

   L. Common shares repurchased.

The following information relates to questions 30-32

The management of Telluride, an international diversified conglomerate, believes that the recent strong performance of its wholly owned medical supply subsidiary, Sundanci, has gone unnoticed. To realize Sundanci's full value, Telluride has announced that it will divest Sundanci in a tax-free spin-off.

Sue Carroll is director of research at Kesson and Associates. In developing an investment recommendation for Sundanci, Carroll has gathered the information shown in Exhibit 1 and Exhibit 2.

Exhibit 1: Sundanci Actual 2019 and 2020 Financial Statements for Fiscal Years Ending 31 May (Dollars in Millions except Per-Share Data)

Income Statement	2019	2020
Revenue	$474	$598
Depreciation	20	23
Other operating costs	368	460
Income before taxes	86	115
Taxes	26	35
Net income	60	80
Dividends	18	24
EPS	$0.714	$0.952
Dividends per share	$0.214	$0.286
Common shares outstanding	84.0	84.0

Balance Sheet	2019	2020
Current assets (includes $5 cash in 2007 and 2008)	$201	$326
Net property, plant, and equipment	474	489
Total assets	675	815
Current liabilities (all non-interest-bearing)	57	141
Long-term debt	0	0
Total liabilities	57	141
Shareholders' equity	618	674
Total liabilities and equity	675	815

Balance Sheet	2019	2020
Capital expenditures	34	38

Exhibit 2: Selected Financial Information

Required rate of return on equity	14%
Industry growth rate	13%
Industry P/E	26

Abbey Naylor has been directed by Carroll to determine the value of Sundanci's stock by using the FCFE model. Naylor believes that Sundanci's FCFE will grow at 27% for two years and at 13% thereafter. Capital expenditures, depreciation, and working capital are all expected to increase proportionately with FCFE.

30. Calculate the amount of FCFE per share for 2020 by using the data from Exhibit 22.

31. Calculate the current value of a share of Sundanci stock based on the two-stage FCFE model.

32. Describe limitations that the two-stage DDM and FCFE models have in common.

The following information relates to questions 33-38

Gurmeet Singh, an equity portfolio manager at a wealth management company, meets with junior research analyst Cindy Ho to discuss potential investments in three companies: Sienna Limited, Colanari Manufacturing, and Bern Pharmaceutical.

Singh and Ho review key financial data from Sienna's most recent annual report, which are presented in Exhibits 1 and 2, to assess the company's ability to generate free cash flow.

Exhibit 1: Selected Data from Sienna Limited's Statement of Income for the Year Ended 31 December 2019 (Amounts in Millions of Euros)

EBITDA	4,000
Depreciation expense	800
Operating income (EBIT)	3,200
Interest expense	440
Tax rate	35%

Exhibit 2: Sienna Limited's Statement of Cash Flows for the Year Ended 31 December 2019 (Amounts in Millions of Euros)	
Cash flow from operations	
Net income	1,794
Plus: Depreciation	800
Increase in accounts receivable	(2,000)
Increase in inventory	(200)
Increase in accounts payable	1,000
Cash flow from operations	1,394
Cash flow from investing activities	
Purchases of PP&E	(1,000)
Cash flow from financing activities	
Borrowing (repayment)	500
Total cash flow	894

Singh and Ho also discuss the impact of dividends, share repurchases, and leverage on Sienna's free cash flow. Ho tells Singh the following:

Statement 1   Changes in leverage do not impact free cash flow to equity.

Statement 2   Transactions between the company and its shareholders, such as the payment of dividends or share repurchases, do affect free cash flow.

Singh and Ho next analyze Colanari. Last year, Colanari had FCFF of €140 million. Singh instructs Ho to perform an FCFF sensitivity analysis of Colanari's firm value using the three sets of estimates presented in Exhibit 3. In her analysis, Ho assumes a tax rate of 35% and a stable capital structure of 30% debt and 70% equity.

Exhibit 3: Sensitivity Analysis for Colanari Valuation

Variable	Base-Case Estimate	Low Estimate	High Estimate
FCFF growth rate	4.6%	4.2%	5.0%
Before-tax cost of debt	4.9%	3.9%	5.9%
Cost of equity	11.0%	10.0%	12.0%

Finally, Singh and Ho analyze Bern. Selected financial information on Bern is presented in Exhibit 4.

Exhibit 4: Selected Financial Data on Bern Pharmaceutical

	Market Value	Required Return
Debt	€15,400 million	6.0%
Preferred stock	€4,000 million	5.5%
Common stock	€18,100 million	11.0%

	Market Value	Required Return
FCFF, most recent year	€3,226 million	
Corporate tax rate	26.9%	

Singh notes that Bern has two new drugs that are currently in clinical trials awaiting regulatory approval. In addition to its operating assets, Bern owns a parcel of land from a decommissioned manufacturing facility with a current market value of €50 million that is being held for investment. Singh and Ho elect to value Bern under two scenarios:

Scenario 1   Value Bern assuming the two new drugs receive regulatory approval. In this scenario, FCFF is forecast to grow at 4.5% into perpetuity.

Scenario 2   Value Bern assuming the two new drugs do not receive regulatory approval. In this scenario, FCFF is forecast using a stable growth in FCFF of 1.5% for the next three years and then 0.75% thereafter into perpetuity.

33. Based on Exhibits 1 and 2, Sienna's FCFF in 2019 is:

   A. €680 million.

   B. €1,200 million.

   C. €3,080 million.

34. Based on Exhibits 1 and 2, Sienna's FCFE in 2019 is:

   A. €894 million.

   B. €1,466 million.

   C. €2,894 million.

35. Which of Ho's statements regarding free cash flow is (are) correct?

   A. Statement 1 only

   B. Statement 2 only

   C. Neither Statement 1 nor Statement 2

36. Based on Exhibit 3, Ho's FCFF sensitivity analysis should conclude that Colanari's value is *most* sensitive to the:

   A. FCFF growth rate.

   B. before-tax cost of debt.

   C. required rate of return for equity.

37. Based on Exhibit 4, Bern's firm value under Scenario 1 is *closest* to:

   A. €100,951.3 million.

B. €105,349.1 million.

C. €105,399.1 million.

38. Based on Exhibit 4, Singh and Ho should conclude that under Scenario 2, shares of Bern are:

   A. undervalued.

   B. fairly valued.

   C. overvalued.

39. PHB Company currently sells for £32.50 per share. In an attempt to determine whether PHB is fairly priced, an analyst has assembled the following information:

   ▪ The before-tax required rates of return on PHB debt, preferred stock, and common stock are, respectively, 7.0%, 6.8%, and 11.0%.

   ▪ The company's target capital structure is 30% debt, 15% preferred stock, and 55% common stock.

   ▪ The market value of the company's debt is £145 million, and its preferred stock is valued at £65 million.

   ▪ PHB's FCFF for the year just ended is £28 million. FCFF is expected to grow at a constant rate of 4% for the foreseeable future.

   ▪ The tax rate is 35%.

   ▪ PHB has 8 million outstanding common shares.

   What is PHB's estimated value per share? Is PHB's stock underpriced?

The following information relates to questions 40-41

An aggressive financial planner who claims to have a superior method for picking undervalued stocks is trying to steal one of your clients. The planner claims that the best way to find the value of a stock is to divide EBITDA by the risk-free bond rate. The planner is urging your client to invest in NewMarket, Inc. The planner says that NewMarket's EBITDA of $1,580 million divided by the long-term government bond rate of 7% gives a total value of $22,571.4 million. With 318 million outstanding shares, NewMarket's value per share found by using this method is $70.98. Shares of NewMarket currently trade for $36.50.

40. Provide your client with an alternative estimate of NewMarket's value per share based on a two-stage FCFE valuation approach. Use the following assumptions:

   ▪ Net income is currently $600 million. Net income will grow by 20% annually for the next three years.

   ▪ The net investment in operating assets (capital expenditures less depreciation plus investment in working capital) will be $1,150 million next year and grow at 15% for the following two years.

   ▪ 40% of the net investment in operating assets will be financed with net new debt financing.

   ▪ NewMarket's beta is 1.3; the risk-free bond rate is 7%; the equity risk premium is 4%.

- After three years, the growth rate of net income will be 8% and the net investment in operating assets (capital expenditures minus depreciation plus increase in working capital) each year will drop to 30% of net income.
- Debt is, and will continue to be, 40% of total assets.
- NewMarket has 318 million shares outstanding.

41. Criticize the valuation approach that the aggressive financial planner used.

The following information relates to questions 42–44

John Jones is head of the research department of Peninsular Research and is estimating the value of Mackinac Inc. The company has released its June 2019 financial statements, shown in Exhibit 1, Exhibit 2, and Exhibit 3.

Exhibit 1: Mackinac Inc. Annual Income Statement 30 June 2019 (in Thousands, except Per-Share Data)

Sales	$250,000
Cost of goods sold	125,000
Gross operating profit	125,000
Selling, general, and administrative expenses	50,000
EBITDA	75,000
Depreciation and amortization	10,500
EBIT	64,500
Interest expense	11,000
Pretax income	53,500
Income taxes	16,050
Net income	$37,450
Shares outstanding	13,000
EPS	$2.88

Exhibit 2: Mackinac Inc. Balance Sheet 30 June 2019 (in Thousands)

Current Assets		
Cash and equivalents	$20,000	
Receivables	40,000	
Inventories	29,000	
Other current assets	23,000	
Total current assets		$112,000
Noncurrent Assets		
Property, plant, and equipment	$145,000	
Less: Accumulated depreciation	43,000	
Net property, plant, and equipment		102,000

Investments	70,000	
Other noncurrent assets	36,000	
Total noncurrent assets		208,000
Total assets		$320,000
Current Liabilities		
Accounts payable	$41,000	
Short-term debt	12,000	
Other current liabilities	17,000	
Total current liabilities		$ 70,000
Noncurrent Liabilities		
Long-term debt	100,000	
Total noncurrent liabilities		100,000
Total liabilities		170,000
Shareholders' Equity		
Common equity	40,000	
Retained earnings	110,000	
Total equity		150,000
Total liabilities and equity		$320,000

**Exhibit 3: Mackinac Inc. Statement of Cash Flows
30 June 2019 (in Thousands)**

Cash Flow from Operating Activities		
Net income		$37,450
Depreciation and amortization		10,500
Change in Working Capital		
(Increase) decrease in receivables	($5,000)	
(Increase) decrease in inventories	(8,000)	
Increase (decrease) in payables	6,000	
Increase (decrease) in other current liabilities	1,500	
Net change in working capital		(5,500)
Net cash from operating activities		$42,450
Cash Flow from Investing Activities		
Purchase of property, plant, and equipment	($15,000)	
Net cash from investing activities		($15,000)
Cash Flow from Financing Activities		
Change in debt outstanding	$4,000	
Payment of cash dividends	(22,470)	
Net cash from financing activities		(18,470)
Net change in cash and cash equivalents		$8,980
Cash at beginning of period		11,020
Cash at end of period		$20,000

Mackinac has announced that it has finalized an agreement to handle North American production of a successful product currently marketed by a company headquartered outside North America. Jones decides to value Mackinac by using the DDM and FCFE models. After reviewing Mackinac's financial statements and forecasts related to the new production agreement, Jones concludes the following:

- Mackinac's earnings and FCFE are expected to grow 17% a year over the next three years before stabilizing at an annual growth rate of 9%.
- Mackinac will maintain the current payout ratio.
- Mackinac's beta is 1.25.
- The government bond yield is 6%, and the market equity risk premium is 5%.

42. Calculate the value of a share of Mackinac's common stock by using the two-stage DDM.

43. Calculate the value of a share of Mackinac's common stock by using the two-stage FCFE model.

44. Jones is discussing with a corporate client the possibility of that client acquiring a 70% interest in Mackinac. Discuss whether the DDM or FCFE model is more appropriate for this client's valuation purposes.

The following information relates to questions 45-46

James Smith is valuing McInish Corporation and performing a sensitivity analysis on his valuation. He uses a single-stage FCFE growth model. The base-case values for each of the parameters in the model are given, together with possible low and high estimates for each variable, in the following table.

Variable	Base-Case Value	Low Estimate	High Estimate
Normalized $FCFE_0$	£0.88	£0.70	£1.14
Risk-free rate	5.08%	5.00%	5.20%
Equity risk premium	5.50%	4.50%	6.50%
Beta	0.70	0.60	0.80
FCFE growth rate	6.40%	4.00%	7.00%

45. Use the base-case values to estimate the current value of McInish Corporation.

46. Calculate the range of stock prices that would occur if the base-case value for $FCFE_0$ were replaced by the low estimate and the high estimate for $FCFE_0$. Similarly, using the base-case values for all other variables, calculate the range of stock prices caused by using the low and high values for beta, the risk-free rate, the equity risk premium, and the growth rate. Based on these ranges, rank the sensitivity of the stock price to each of the five variables.

The following information relates to questions 47-48

KMobile Telecom is an Asian mobile network operator headquartered in Seoul, South Korea. Sol Kim has estimated the normalized FCFE per share for KMobile to be 1,300 Korean won (KRW) for the year just ended. The real country return for South Korea is 6.50%. To estimate the required return for KMobile, Kim makes the following adjustments to the real country return: an industry adjustment of +0.60%, a size adjustment of –0.10%, and a leverage adjustment of +0.25%. The long-term real growth rate for South Korea is estimated to be 3.5%, and Kim expects the real growth rate of KMobile to track the country rate.

47. What is the real required rate of return for KMobile Telecom?

48. Using the single-stage FCFE valuation model and real values for the discount rate and FCFE growth rate, estimate the value of one share of KMobile.

49. Hugo Dubois is evaluating NYL Manufacturing Company, Ltd. In 2020, when Dubois is performing his analysis, the company is unprofitable. Furthermore, NYL pays no dividends on its common shares. Dubois decides to value NYL Manufacturing by using his forecasts of FCFE. Dubois gathers the following facts and assumptions:

- The company has 17.0 billion shares outstanding.
- Sales will be €5.5 billion in 2021, increasing at 28% annually for the next four years (through 2025).
- Net income will be 32% of sales.
- Investment in fixed assets will be 35% of sales; investment in working capital will be 6% of sales; depreciation will be 9% of sales.
- 20% of the net investment in assets will be financed with debt.
- Interest expenses will be only 2% of sales.
- The tax rate will be 10%. NYL Manufacturing's beta is 2.1; the risk-free government bond rate is 6.4%; the equity risk premium is 5.0%.
- At the end of 2025, Dubois projects NYL terminal stock value at 18 times earnings.

What is the value of one ordinary share of NYL Manufacturing Company?

50. Bron has EPS of $3.00 in 2019 and expects EPS to increase by 21% in 2020. EPS are expected to grow at a decreasing rate for the following five years, as shown in the following table.

	2020	2021	2022	2023	2024	2025
Growth rate for EPS	21%	18%	15%	12%	9%	6%
Net capital expenditures per share	$5.00	$5.00	$4.50	$4.00	$3.50	$1.50

In 2025, the growth rate will be 6%, and it is expected to stay at that rate thereafter. Net capital expenditures (capital expenditures minus depreciation) will be $5.00 per share in 2019 and then follow the pattern predicted in the table. In 2025, net capital expenditures are expected to be $1.50, and they will then grow at 6% annually. The investment in working capital parallels the increase in net capital expenditures and is predicted to equal 25% of net capital expenditures each year. In 2025, investment in working capital will be $0.375, and it is predicted to grow at 6% thereafter. Bron will use debt financing to fund 40% of net capital expenditures and 40% of the investment in working capital. The required rate of return for Bron is 12%.

Estimate the value of a Bron share using a two-stage FCFE valuation approach.

51. Minsuh Park is preparing a valuation of QuickChange Auto Centers, Inc. Park has decided to use a three-stage FCFE valuation model and the following estimates. The FCFE per share for the current year is $0.75. The FCFE is expected to grow at 10% for next year, then at 26% annually for the following three years, and then at 6% in Year 5 and thereafter. QuickChange's estimated beta is 2.00, and Park believes that current market conditions dictate a 4.5% risk-free rate of return and a 5.0% equity risk premium. Given Park's assumptions and approach, estimate the value of a share of QuickChange.

52. Astrid Nilsson has valued the operating assets of Gothenburg Extrusion AB at 720 million Swedish kronor (SEK). The company also has short-term cash and securities with a market value of SEK60 million that are not needed for Gothenburg's operations. The noncurrent investments have a book value of SEK30 million and a market value of SEK45 million. The company also has an overfunded pension plan, with plan assets of SEK210 million and plan liabilities of SEK170 million. Gothenburg Extrusion has SEK215 million of notes and bonds outstanding and 100 million outstanding shares. What is the value per share of Gothenburg Extrusion stock?

SOLUTIONS

1. The firm value is the present value of FCFF discounted at the WACC, or

$$\text{Firm value} = \frac{\text{FCFF}_1}{\text{WACC} - g} = \frac{\text{FCFF}_0(1+g)}{\text{WACC} - g} = \frac{1.7(1.07)}{0.11 - 0.07}$$

$$= \frac{1.819}{0.04} = \text{JPY45.475 billion.}$$

The market value of equity is the value of the firm minus the value of debt:

Equity = 45.475 − 15 = JPY30.475 billion.

2. Using the FCFE valuation approach, we find the present value of FCFE discounted at the required rate of return on equity to be

$$\text{PV} = \frac{\text{FCFE}_1}{r - g} = \frac{\text{FCFE}_0(1+g)}{r - g} = \frac{1.3(1.07)}{0.13 - 0.075} = \frac{1.3975}{0.055}$$

= JPY25.409 billion.

The value of equity using this approach is JPY25.409 billion.

3. The required return on equity is

$$r = E(R_i) = R_F + \beta_i \left[E(R_M) - R_F \right] = 5.5\% + 0.90(5.5\%) = 10.45\%.$$

The weighted-average cost of capital is

WACC = 0.25(7.0%)(1 − 0.40) + 0.75(10.45%) = 8.89%.

4.

$$\text{Firm value} = \frac{\text{FCFF}_0(1+g)}{\text{WACC} - g}.$$

$$\text{Firm value} = \frac{1.1559(1.04)}{0.0889 - 0.04} = \$24.583.$$

5. Equity value = Firm value − Market value of debt.
   Equity value = 24.583 − 3.192 = $21.391 billion.

6. Value per share = Equity value/Number of shares.
   Value per share = $21.391 billion/1.852 billion = $11.55.

7. B is correct. Company A has a history of paying modest dividends relative to FCFE. An FCFF or FCFE model provides a better estimate of value over a DDM model when dividends paid differ significantly from the company's capacity to pay dividends. Also, Company A has a controlling investor; with control comes discretion over the uses of free cash flow. Therefore, there is the possibility that the controlling shareholder could change the dividend policy. Finally, Company A has a stable capital structure; using FCFE is a more direct and simpler method to value a company's equity than using FCFF when a company's capital structure is stable.

8. C is correct. The applicable noncash adjustments to net income in arriving at FCFE are as follows:

Noncash Item	Adjustment to Net Income	Amount (millions)
Transaction 1: Loss on sale of equipment	Added back	+900

Noncash Item	Adjustment to Net Income	Amount (millions)
Transaction 2: Impairment of intangibles	Added back	+400
Transaction 3: Reversal of restructuring charge	Subtracted	−300

In the case of Transaction 1, a loss reduces net income and thus must be added back in arriving at FCFE. Similarly, an impairment of intangibles (Transaction 2) reduces net income and thus must be added back in arriving at FCFE. Transaction 3 (reversal of a restructuring charge) would increase net income and thus must be subtracted in arriving at FCFE.

9. C is correct. FCFE for Company A for the most recent year is calculated as follows:

Net income	$4,844
Plus: Net noncash charges	1,500
Less: Investment in working capital	122
Plus: Proceeds from sale of fixed capital	2,379
Less: Net borrowing repayment	1,475
FCFE (millions)	$7,126

Net noncash charges are found by adding depreciation to other noncash expenses:

$500 million + $1,000 million = $1,500 million.

Investment in working capital is calculated by netting the increase in accounts receivable, the decrease in accounts payable, and the increase in other current liabilities:

−$452 million − $210 million + $540 million = −$122 million (outflow).

Net borrowing repayment is calculated by netting the increase in notes payable and the decrease in long-term debt:

$25 million − $1,500 million = −$1,475 million (outflow).

10. A is correct. FCFE is significantly higher than net income for Company B:

Net income = $1,212 million.

FCFE for Company B is calculated as follows:

Net income	$1,212
Plus: Net noncash charges	288
Less: Investment in WC	236
Less: Investment in fixed assets	1,000
Plus: Net borrowing	2,000
FCFE (millions)	$2,264

Investment in working capital is calculated by adding the increase in accounts receivable, the increase in inventories, the increase in accounts payable, and the increase in other current liabilities: −$150 million − $200 million + $100 million + $14 million = −$236 million. Net borrowing is calculated by adding the increase in notes payable to the decrease in long-term debt: $3,000 million − $1,000 million = $2,000 million.

Therefore, using net income of $1,212 million as a proxy for FCFE ($2,264 million) for Company B would result in a much lower valuation estimate than if actual FCFE were used.

11. A is correct. In addition to significant noncash charges other than depreciation in the most recent year, the annual report indicates that Company A expects to recognize additional noncash charges related to restructuring over the next few years. The given equation for forecasting assumes that the only noncash charge is depreciation. When the company being analyzed has significant noncash charges other than depreciation expense, this sales-based methodology will result in a less accurate estimate of FCFE than one obtained by forecasting all the individual components of FCFE.

12. C is correct.

FCFE for the most recent year for Company B is calculated as follows:

Net income	$1,212
Plus: Net noncash charges	288
Less: Investment in WC	236
Less: Investment in fixed assets	1,000
Plus: Net borrowing	2,000
FCFE (millions)	$2,264

The required rate of return on equity for Company B is

$r = E(R_i) = R_F + \beta_i[E(R_M) - R_F] = 3\% + 0.90(7\%) = 9.3\%.$

The most recent FCFE grows for the next four years at annual growth rates of 10%, 9%, 8%, and 7%, respectively, and then 6% thereafter:

t	g	Calculation	FCFE (millions)
1	10%	$2,264.00 × 1.10	$2,490.40
2	9%	$2,490.40 × 1.09	$2,714.54
3	8%	$2,714.54 × 1.08	$2,931.70
4	7%	$2,931.70 × 1.07	$3,136.92
5	6%	$3,136.92 × 1.06	$3,325.13

The present value of FCFE for the first four years is calculated as follows:

$$PV = \frac{2,490.40}{1.093^1} + \frac{2,714.54}{1.093^2} + \frac{2,931.70}{1.093^3} + \frac{3,136.92}{1.093^4}.$$

$PV = 2,278.50 + 2,272.25 + 2,245.22 + 2.197.97 = 8,993.94.$

The present value of the terminal value is calculated as follows:

$$PV \text{ of } TV_4 = \frac{3,325.13}{(0.093 - 0.06)(1.093)^4} = 70,601.58.$$

So, the estimated total market value of the equity is 8,993.94 + 70,601.58 = 79,595.52 ≈ $79,596 million.

13. C is correct. Company C's firm value is calculated as follows:

The required rate of return on equity for Company C is

$r = E(R_i) = R_F + \beta_i[E(R_M) - R_F] = 3\% + 1.1(7\%) = 10.7\%.$

$$WACC = \frac{MV\,(Debt)}{MV\,(Debt) + MV\,(Equity)} r_d(1 - Tax\ rate) + \frac{MV\,(Equity)}{MV\,(Debt) + MV\,(Equity)} r_e.$$

WACC = 0.40(6%)(1 − 0.30) + 0.60(10.7%) = 1.68% + 6.42% = 8.10%.

FCFF for the most recent year for Company C is calculated as follows:

Net income	$15,409.00
Plus: Net noncash charges	3,746.00
Less: Investment in working capital	992.00
Less: Investment in fixed capital	3,463.00
Plus: Interest expense × (1 − Tax rate)	386.40
FCFF (in millions)	$15,086.40

Investment in working capital is found by adding the increase in accounts receivable, the increase in inventories, the decrease in accounts payable, and the increase in other current liabilities: −$536 million − $803 million − $3 million + $350 million = −$992 million.

FCFF is expected to grow at 5.0% indefinitely. Thus,

$$\text{Firm value} = \frac{\text{FCFF}_1}{\text{WACC} - g} = \frac{\text{FCFF}_0(1 + g)}{\text{WACC} - g} = \frac{15,086.4(1.05)}{0.081 - 0.05} = \$510,990.97 \text{ million.}$$

The value of equity is the value of the firm minus the value of debt. The value of debt is found by multiplying the target debt ratio by the total firm value:

Debt value = 0.40($510,990.97) = $204,396.39.

Therefore, equity value = $510,990.97 − $204,396.39 = $306,594.58 million.

14. FCF = Net income + Depreciation and amortization − Cash dividends − Capital expenditures. This definition of free cash flow is sometimes used to determine how much "discretionary" cash flow the management has at its disposal. Management discretion concerning dividends is limited by investor expectations that dividends will be maintained. Comparing this definition with Equation 7, FCFF = NI + NCC + Int(1 − Tax rate) − FCInv − WCInv, we find that FCFF includes a reduction for investments in working capital and the addition of after-tax interest expense. Common stock dividends are not subtracted from FCFF because dividends represent a distribution of the cash available to investors. (If a company pays preferred dividends and they were previously taken out when net income available to common shareholders was calculated, they are added back in Equation 7 to include them in FCFF.)

15. FCF = Cash flow from operations (from the statement of cash flows) − Capital expenditures. Comparing this definition of free cash flow with Equation 8, FCFF = CFO + Int(1 − Tax rate) − FCInv, highlights the relationship of CFO to FCFF: The primary point is that when Equation 8 is used, after-tax interest is added back to CFO to arrive at the cash flow to all investors. Then FCInv is subtracted to arrive at the amount of that cash flow that is "free" in the sense of available for distribution to those investors after taking care of capital investment needs. If preferred dividends were subtracted to obtain net income (in CFO), they would also have to be added back in. This definition is commonly used to approximate FCFF, but it generally understates the actual FCFF by the amount of after-tax interest expense.

16. Free cash flow to the firm, found with Equation 7, is

FCFF = NI + NCC + Int(1 − Tax rate) − FCInv − WCInv.
FCFF = 285 + 180 + 130(1 − 0.40) − 349 − (39 + 44 − 22 − 23).
FCFF = 285 + 180 + 78 − 349 − 38 = $156 million.

17. Free cash flow to equity, found with Equation 10, is

$$FCFE = NI + NCC - FCInv - WFCInv + \text{Net borrowing}.$$
$$FCFE = 285 + 180 - 349 - (39 + 44 - 22 - 23) + (10 + 40).$$
$$FCFE = 285 + 180 - 349 - 38 + 50 = \$128 \text{ million}.$$

18. To find FCFE from FCFF, one uses the relationship in Equation 9:

$$FCFE = FCFF - Int(1 - \text{Tax rate}) + \text{Net borrowing}.$$
$$FCFE = 156 - 130(1 - 0.40) + (10 + 40).$$
$$FCFE = 156 - 78 + 50 = \$128 \text{ million}.$$

19. The FCFF is (in euros)

$$FCFF = NI + NCC + Int(1 - \text{Tax rate}) - FCInv - WCInv.$$
$$FCFF = 250 + 90 + 150(1 - 0.30) - 170 - 40.$$
$$FCFF = 250 + 90 + 105 - 170 - 40 = 235 \text{ million}.$$

The weighted-average cost of capital is

$$WACC = 9\%(1 - 0.30)(0.40) + 13\%(0.60) = 10.32\%.$$

The value of the firm (in euros) is

$$\text{Firm value} = \frac{FCFF_1}{WACC - g} = \frac{FCFF_0(1 + g)}{WACC - g} = \frac{235(1.06)}{0.1032 - 0.06}$$
$$= \frac{249.1}{0.0432} = 5,766.20 \text{ million}.$$

The total value of equity is the total firm value minus the value of debt: Equity = €5,766.20 million – €1,800 million = €3,966.20 million. Dividing by the number of shares gives the per-share estimate of V_0 = €3,966.20 million/10 million = €396.62 per share.

20. The free cash flow to equity is

$$FCFE = NI + NCC - FCInv - WCInv + \text{Net borrowing}.$$
$$FCFE = 250 + 90 - 170 - 40 + 0.40(170 - 90 + 40).$$
$$FCFE = 250 + 90 - 170 - 40 + 48 = €178 \text{ million}.$$

Because the company is borrowing 40% of the increase in net capital expenditures (170 – 90) and working capital (40), net borrowing is €48 million.

The total value of equity is the FCFE discounted at the required rate of return of equity:

$$\text{Equity value} = \frac{FCFE_1}{r - g} = \frac{FCFE_0(1 + g)}{r - g} = \frac{178(1.07)}{0.13 - 0.07}$$
$$= \frac{190.46}{0.06} = €3,174.33 \text{ million}.$$

The value per share is V_0 = €3,174.33 million/10 million = €317.43 per share.

21. To find FCFF from CFO, EBIT, or EBITDA, the analyst can use Equations 8, 12, and 13.

To find FCFF from CFO:

$$FCFF = CFO + Int(1 - \text{Tax rate}) - FCInv.$$
$$FCFF = 427 + 130(1 - 0.40) - 349 = 427 + 78 - 349 = \$156 \text{ million}.$$

To find FCFF from EBIT:

$$\text{FCFF} = \text{EBIT}(1 - \text{Tax rate}) + \text{Dep} - \text{FCInv} - \text{WCInv}.$$
$$\text{FCFF} = 605(1 - 0.40) + 180 - 349 - 38.$$
$$\text{FCFF} = 363 + 180 - 349 - 38 = \$156 \text{ million.}$$

Finally, to obtain FCFF from EBITDA:

$$\text{FCFF} = \text{EBITDA}(1 - \text{Tax rate}) + \text{Dep}(\text{Tax rate}) - \text{FCInv} - \text{WCInv}.$$
$$\text{FCFF} = 785(1 - 0.40) + 180(0.40) - 349 - 38.$$
$$\text{FCFF} = 471 + 72 - 349 - 38 = \$156 \text{ million.}$$

22. The simplest approach is to calculate FCFF from CFO, EBIT, or EBITDA as was done in Part A and then to find FCFE by making the appropriate adjustments to FCFF:

$$\text{FCFE} = \text{FCFF} - \text{Int}(1 - \text{Tax rate}) + \text{Net borrowing.}$$
$$\text{FCFE} = 156 - 130(1 - 0.40) + 50 = 156 - 78 + 50 = \$128 \text{ million.}$$

The analyst can also find FCFE by using CFO, EBIT, or EBITDA directly. Starting with CFO and using Equation 11, FCFE is found to be

$$\text{FCFE} = \text{CFO} - \text{FCInv} + \text{Net borrowing.}$$
$$\text{FCFE} = 427 - 349 + 50 = \$128 \text{ million.}$$

Starting with EBIT, on the basis of Equations 9 and 12, FCFE is

$$\text{FCFE} = \text{EBIT}(1 - \text{Tax rate}) + \text{Dep} - \text{Int}(1 - \text{Tax rate}) - \text{FCInv}$$
$$- \text{WCInv} + \text{Net borrowing.}$$
$$\text{FCFE} = 605(1 - 0.40) + 180 - 130(1 - 0.40) - 349 - 38 + 50.$$
$$\text{FCFE} = 363 + 180 - 78 - 349 - 38 + 50 = \$128 \text{ million.}$$

Finally, starting with EBITDA, on the basis of Equations 9 and 13, FCFE is

$$\text{FCFE} = \text{EBITDA}(1 - \text{Tax rate}) + \text{Dep}(\text{Tax rate})$$
$$- \text{Int}(1 - \text{Tax rate}) - \text{FCInv} - \text{WCInv} + \text{Net borrowing.}$$
$$\text{FCFE} = 785(1 - 0.40) + 180(0.40) - 130(1 - 0.40) - 349 - 38 + 50.$$
$$\text{FCFE} = 471 + 72 - 78 - 349 - 38 + 50 = \$128 \text{ million.}$$

23. C is correct. The sustainable growth rate is return on equity (ROE) multiplied by the retention ratio. ROE is 10%, and the retention ratio is 1 − Payout ratio, or 1.0 − 0.2 = 0.8. The sustainable growth rate is 0.8 × 10% = 8%. FCFE growth should be at least 8% per year in the long term.

24. A is correct. Justifications for choosing the FCFE model over the DDM include the following:

   - The company pays dividends, but its dividends differ significantly from the company's capacity to pay dividends (the first reason given by Leigh).
   - The investor takes a control perspective (the second reason given by Leigh).

25. A is correct. FCFF = NI + NCC + Interest expense(1 − Tax rate) − FCInv − WCInv. In this case:

NI	=	$485 million
NCC	=	Depreciation expense = $270 million
Interest expense(1 − Tax rate) = 195(1 − 0.32) = $132.6 million		
FCInv	=	Net purchase of fixed assets = Increase in gross fixed assets
	=	4,275 − 3,752 = $523 million
WCInv	=	Increase in accounts receivable + Increase in inventory − Increase in accounts payable − Increase in accrued liabilities

$$= (770 - 711) + (846 - 780) - (476 - 443) - (149 - 114)$$
$$= \$57 \text{ million}$$

FCFF $= 485 + 270 + 132.6 - 523 - 57 = 307.6$, or $308 million

26. B is correct. FCFE = NI + NCC – FCInv – WCInv + Net borrowing. In this case:

NI = $485 million.

NCC = Depreciation expense = $270 million.

FCInv = Net purchase of fixed assets = Increase in gross fixed
assets
= 4,275 – 3,752 = $523 million.

WCInv = Increase in accounts receivable + Increase in
inventory – Increase in accounts payable – Increase
in accrued liabilities
= (770 – 711) + (846 – 780) – (476 – 443) – (149 – 114)
= $57 million.

Net borrowing = Increase in notes payable + Increase in long-term debt

= (465 – 450) + (1,575 – 1,515) = $75 million.

FCFE = 485 + 270 – 523 – 57 + 75 = $250 million.

An alternative calculation is

FCFE = FCFF – Int(1 – Tax rate) + Net borrowing.

FCFE = 307.6 – 195(1 – 0.32) + (15 +60) = $250 million.

27. C is correct. Inventory cannot be reduced below zero. Furthermore, sales growth
tends to increase inventory.

28. A is correct. The FCFF model is often selected when the capital structure is expected to change because FCFF estimation may be easier than FCFE estimation
in the presence of changing financial leverage.

29.

For a $100 increase in:	Change in FCFF (in US Dollars)	Change in FCFE (in US Dollars)
A. Net income	+100	+100
B. Cash operating expenses	−60	−60
C. Depreciation	+40	+40
D. Interest expense	0	−60
E. EBIT	+60	+60
F. Accounts receivable	−100	−100
G. Accounts payable	+100	+100
H. Property, plant, and equipment	−100	−100
I. Notes payable	0	+100
J. Cash dividends paid	0	0
K. Proceeds from issuing new common shares	0	0
L. Common shares repurchased	0	0

30. FCFE is defined as the cash flow remaining after the company meets all financial obligations, including debt payment, and covers all capital expenditure and working capital needs. Sundanci's FCFE for the year 2020 is calculated as follows:

Net income	= $80 million
Plus: Depreciation expense	= 23
Less: Capital expenditures	= 38
Less: Investment in WC	= 41
Equals: FCFE	= $24 million

Thus, FCFE per share equals ($24 million)/(84 million shares) = $0.286.

31. The FCFE model requires forecasts of FCFE for the high-growth years (2021 and 2022) plus a forecast for the first year of stable growth (2023) to allow for an estimate of the terminal value in 2022 based on constant perpetual growth. Because all of the components of FCFE are expected to grow at the same rate, the values can be obtained by projecting the FCFE at the common rate. (Alternatively, the components of FCFE can be projected and aggregated for each year.)

The following table provides the process for estimating Sundanci's current value on a per-share basis.

Free Cash Flow to Equity

Base assumptions:					
Shares outstanding (millions)	84				
Required return on equity, r	14%				

			Projected 2021	Projected 2022	Projected 2023
			$g = 27\%$	$g = 27\%$	$g = 13\%$
	Total	Per share			
Earnings after tax	$80	$0.952	$1.2090	$1.5355	$1.7351
Plus: Depreciation expense	$23	$0.274	$0.3480	$0.4419	$0.4994
Less: Capital expenditures	$38	$0.452	$0.5740	$0.7290	$0.8238
Less: Increase in net working capital	$41	$0.488	$0.6198	$0.7871	$0.8894
Equals: FCFE	$24	$0.286	$0.3632	$0.4613	$0.5213
Terminal value[a]				$52.1300	
Total cash flows to equity[b]			$0.3632	$52.5913	
Discounted value[c]			$0.3186	$40.4673	
Current value per share[d]		$40.7859			

[a]*Projected 2022 terminal value = Projected 2023 FCFE/(r − g).*
[b]*Projected 2022 total cash flows to equity = Projected 2022 FCFE + Projected 2022 terminal value.*
[c]*Discounted values obtained by using r = 14%.*
[d]*Current value per share = Discounted value 2021 + Discounted value 2022.*

32. The following limitations of the DDM *are* addressed by the FCFE model: The DDM uses a strict definition of cash flow to equity; that is, cash flows to equity are the dividends on the common stock. The FCFE model expands the definition of cash flow to include the balance of residual cash flows after all financial obligations and investment needs have been met. Thus, the FCFE model explicitly recognizes the company's investment and financing policies as well as its dividend policy. In instances of a change of corporate control, and thus the possibility

of changing dividend policy, the FCFE model provides a better estimate of value.

Both two-stage valuation models allow for two distinct phases of growth—an initial finite period when the growth is abnormal followed by a stable growth period that is expected to last forever. These two-stage models share the same limitations with respect to the growth assumptions:

First, the analyst must confront the difficulty of defining the duration of the extraordinary growth period. A long period of high growth will produce a higher valuation, and the analyst may be tempted to assume an unrealistically long period of extraordinary growth.

Second, the analyst must realize that assuming a sudden shift from high growth to lower, stable growth is unrealistic. The transformation is more likely to occur gradually over time.

Third, because value is quite sensitive to the steady-state growth assumption, overestimating or underestimating this rate can lead to large errors in value.

The two models also share other limitations—notably, difficulties in accurately estimating required rates of return.

33. A is correct. Sienna's FCFF in 2019 is calculated as

    FCFF = EBIT(1 − Tax rate) + Dep − FCInv − WCInv.

    FCInv = Purchases of PP&E = 1,000 (outflow).

    WCInv = Increase in accounts receivable (outflow) + Increase in inventory (outflow) + Increase in accounts payable (inflow).

    WCInv = −2,000 (outflow) + −200 (outflow) + 1,000 (inflow) = −1,200 (outflow).

    FCFF = 3,200(1 − 0.35) + 800 − 1,000 −1,200.

    FCFF = €680 million.

    FCFF can also be computed from CFO:

    FCFF = CFO + Int(1 − Tax rate) − FCInv.

    FCFF = 1,394 + 440(1 − 0.35) − 1,000.

    FCFF = €680 million.

34. A is correct. Sienna's FCFE in 2019 is calculated as

    FCFE = CFO − FCInv + Net borrowing

    = 1,394 − 1,000 + 500

    = €894 million.

    Alternatively, FCFE may be calculated as

    FCFE = FCFF − Int(1 − Tax rate) + Net borrowing.

    = 680 − 440(1 − 0.35) + 500

    = €894 million.

35. C is correct. Transactions between the company and its shareholders (through cash dividends, share repurchases, and share issuances) do not affect free cash flow. However, leverage changes, such as the use of more debt financing, have some impact on free cash flow because they increase the interest tax shield (re-

duce corporate taxes because of the tax deductibility of interest) and reduce the cash flow available to equity.

36. C is correct. Colanari's valuation is most sensitive to the cost of equity (r_e) because the range of estimated values is larger than the valuation ranges estimated from the sensitivity analysis of both the FCFF growth rate (GFCFF) and the before-tax cost of debt (r_d).

Variable	Base Case	Low Estimate	High Estimate	Valuation with Low Estimate (€ millions)	Valuation with High Estimate (€ millions)	Range (€ millions)
GFCFF	4.6%	4.2%	5.0%	3,274.16	4,021.34	747.18
r_d	4.9%	3.9%	5.9%	3,793.29	3,445.24	348.05
r_e	11.0%	10.0%	12.0%	4,364.18	3,079.38	1,284.80

$$\text{WACC} = [w_d \times r_d(1 - \text{Tax rate})] + (w_e \times r_e).$$

$$\text{Firm value} = \text{FCFF}_0(1 + g)/(\text{WACC} - g).$$

Cost of equity sensitivity

Using the base case estimates for the FCFF growth rate and the before-tax cost of debt and using the low estimate for the cost of equity (r_e) of 10.0%, the valuation estimate is

$$\text{WACC} = [(0.30)(0.049)(1 - 0.35)] + (0.70)(0.10) = 7.96\%.$$

Firm value = 140 million(1 + 0.046)/(0.0796 − 0.046) = €4,364.18 million.

Using the base case estimates for the FCFF growth rate and the before-tax cost of debt and using the high estimate for the cost of equity (r_e) of 12.0%, the valuation estimate is

$$\text{WACC} = [(0.30)(0.049)(1 - 0.35)] + (0.70)(0.120) = 9.36\%.$$

Firm value = 140 million(1 + 0.046)/(0.0936 − 0.046) = €3,079.38 million.

Therefore, the range in valuation estimates from using the highest and lowest estimates of the cost of equity is €1,284.80 million.

FCFF growth rate sensitivity

Using the base case estimates for the cost of equity and the before-tax cost of debt and using the low estimate for the FCFF growth rate (GFCFF) of 4.2%, the valuation estimate is

$$\text{WACC} = [(0.30)(0.049)(1 - 0.35)] + (0.70)(0.11) = 8.66\%.$$

Firm value = 140 million(1 + 0.042)/(0.0866 − 0.042) = €3,274.16 million.

Using the base case estimates for the cost of equity and the before-tax cost of debt and using the high estimate for the FCFF growth rate (GFCFF) of 5.0%, the valuation estimate is

$$\text{WACC} = [(0.30)(0.049)(1 - 0.35)] + (0.70)(0.11) = 8.66\%.$$

Firm value = 140 million(1 + 0.05)/(0.0866 − 0.05) = €4,021.34 million.

Therefore, the range in valuation estimates from using the highest and lowest estimates of the FCFF growth rate is €747.18 million.

Before-tax cost of debt sensitivity

Using the base case estimates for the FCFF growth rate and the cost of equity and using the low estimate for the before-tax cost of debt (r_d) of 3.9%, the valuation estimate is

WACC = [(0.30)(0.039)(1 − 0.35)] + (0.70)(0.11) = 8.46%.

Firm value = 140 million(1 + 0.046)/(0.0846 − 0.046) = €3,793.29 million.

Using the base case estimates for the FCFF growth rate and the cost of equity and using the high estimate for the before-tax cost of debt (r_d) of 5.9%, the valuation estimate is

WACC = [(0.30)(0.059)(1 − 0.35)] + (0.70)(0.11) = 8.85%.

Firm value = 140 million(1 + 0.046)/(0.0885 − 0.046) = €3,445.24 million.

Therefore, the range in valuation estimates from using the highest and lowest estimates of the before-tax cost of debt is €348.05 million.

37. C is correct. Based on Scenario 1, where Bern receives regulatory approval for its new drugs, the growth rate in FCFF for Bern will be constant at 4.5%. Therefore, a constant-growth valuation model can be used to calculate firm value.

Bern's weighted average cost of capital is calculated as

WACC = $[w_d \times r_d(1 − \text{Tax rate})] + (w_p \times r_p) + (w_e \times r_e)$.

The total market value of the firm is the sum of the debt, preferred stock, and common stock market values: 15,400 + 4,000 + 18,100 = 37,500.

WACC = [(15,400/37,500)(0.060)(1 − 0.269] + (4,000/37,500)(0.055) + (18,100/37,500)(0.11)

= 7.70%.

Value of operating assets = $\text{FCFF}_0(1 + g)/(\text{WACC} − g)$.

Value of operating assets = 3,226 million(1 + 0.045)/(0.0770 − 0.045)

= €105,349.06 million.

Total value of the company

= Value of operating assets + Value of non-operating assets.

Total value of the company = 105,349.06 million + 50 million

= €105,399.06 million.

38. A is correct.

The total market value of the firm is the sum of the debt, preferred stock, and common stock market values: 15,400 + 4,000 + 18,100 = 37,500 million.

WACC = $[w_d \times r_d(1 − \text{Tax rate})] + (w_p \times r_p) + (w_e \times r_e)$

= [(15,400/37,500)(0.060)(1 − 0.269] + (4,000/37,500)(0.055) + (18,100/37,500)(0.11)

= 7.70%.

Under the assumption that Bern has a low growth rate because it did not receive regulatory approval for its new drugs, the value of Bern can be analyzed using a two-stage valuation model.

Company value = $\sum_{t=1}^{n} \dfrac{\text{FCFF}_t}{(1 + \text{WACC})^t} + \dfrac{\text{FCFF}_{n+1}}{(\text{WACC} − g)} \dfrac{1}{(1 + \text{WACC})^n}$.

Year	0	1	2	3	4
g		1.50%	1.50%	1.50%	0.75%
$FCFF_n$ (€ millions)	3,226	3,274.39	3,323.51	3,373.36	3,398.66
Present Value Factor		0.928529	0.862167	0.800547	
Present Value (€ millions)		3,040.37	2,865.42	2,700.53	

The terminal value at the end of Year 3 is $TV_3 = FCFF_4/(WACC - g_4)$.

$TV_3 = 3,398.66/(0.0770 - 0.0075) = €48,901.58$ million.

The total value of operating assets

$= (3,040.37 + 2,865.42 + 2,700.53) + 48,901.58/(1 + 0.0770)^3$

$= 8,606.32 + 39,144.95$

$= €47,751.27$ million.

Value of Bern's common stock

$=$ Value of operating assets $+$ Value of non-operating assets $-$ Market value of debt $-$ Preferred stock

$= 47,751.27 + 50.00 - 15,400 - 4,000$

$= €28,401.27$ million.

Since the current market value of Bern's common stock (€18,100 million) is less than the estimated value (€28,401.27 million), the shares are undervalued.

39. The WACC for PHB Company is

$WACC = 0.30(7.0\%)(1 - 0.35) + 0.15(6.8\%) + 0.55(11.0\%) = 8.435\%$.

The firm value is

$$\text{Firm value} = \frac{FCFF_0(1 + g)}{WACC - g}.$$

$$\text{Firm value} = \frac{28(1.04)}{0.08435 - 0.04}$$

$$= \frac{29.12}{0.04435}$$

$$= £656.60 \text{ million.}$$

The value of equity is the firm value minus the value of debt minus the value of preferred stock: Equity = 656.60 − 145 − 65 = £446.60 million. Dividing this amount by the number of shares gives the estimated value per share of £446.60 million/8 million shares = £55.82.

The estimated value for the stock is greater than the market price of £32.50, so the stock appears to be undervalued.

40. Using the CAPM, the required rate of return for NewMarket is

$$r = E(R_i) = R_F + \beta_i[E(R_M) - R_F] = 7\% + 1.3(4\%) = 12.2\%.$$

To estimate FCFE, we use Equation 15:

$$FCFE = \text{Net income} - (1 - DR)(FCInv - Depreciation)$$
$$- (1 - DR)(WCInv),$$

which can be written

$$FCFE = \text{Net income} - (1 - DR)(FCInv - Depreciation + WCInv)$$
$$= \text{Net income} - (1 - DR)(\text{Net investment in operating assets}).$$

The following table shows that net income grows at 20% annually for Years 1, 2, and 3 and then grows at 8% for Year 4. The net investment in operating assets is $1,150 million in Year 1 and grows at 15% annually for Years 2 and 3. Debt financing is 40% of this investment. FCFE is NI – Net investment in operating assets + New debt financing. Finally, the present value of FCFE for Years 1, 2, and 3 is found by discounting at 12.2%.

(in $ Millions)	Year			
	1	2	3	4
Net income	720.00	864.00	1,036.80	1,119.74
Net investment in operating assets	1,150.00	1,322.50	1,520.88	335.92
New debt financing	460.00	529.00	608.35	134.37
FCFE	30.00	70.50	124.27	918.19
PV of FCFE discounted at 12.2%	26.74	56.00	87.98	

In Year 4, net income is 8% larger than in Year 3. In Year 4, the investment in operating assets is 30% of net income and debt financing is 40% of this investment. The FCFE in Year 4 is $918.19 million. The value of FCFE after Year 3 is found by using the constant-growth model:

$$V_3 = \frac{FCFE_4}{r - g} = \frac{918.19}{0.122 - 0.08} = \$21,861.67 \text{ million.}$$

The present value of V_3 discounted at 12.2% is $15,477.64 million. The total value of equity, the present value of the first three years' FCFE plus the present value of V_3, is $15,648.36 million. Dividing this amount by the number of outstanding shares (318 million) gives a value per share of $49.21. For the first three years, NewMarket has a small FCFE because of the large investments it is making during the high-growth phase. In the normal-growth phase, FCFE is much larger because the investments required are much smaller.

41. The planner's estimate of the share value of $70.98 is much higher than the FCFE model estimate of $49.21 for several reasons. First, taxes and interest expenses have a prior claim to the company's cash flow and should be taken out of the cash flows used in estimating the value of equity because these amounts are not available to equity holders. The planner did not do this.

Second, EBITDA does not account for the company's reinvestments in operating assets. So, EBITDA overstates the funds available to stockholders if reinvestment needs exceed depreciation charges, which is the case for growing companies such as NewMarket.

Third, EBITDA does not account for the company's capital structure. Using EBITDA to represent a benefit to stockholders (as opposed to stockholders and bondholders combined) is a mistake.

Finally, dividing EBITDA by the bond rate is a major error. The risk-free bond rate is an inappropriate discount rate for risky equity cash flows; the proper measure is the required rate of return on the company's equity. Dividing by a fixed rate also assumes, erroneously, that the cash flow stream is a fixed perpetuity. EBITDA cannot be a perpetual stream because if it were distributed, the stream would eventually decline to zero (lacking capital investments). NewMarket is actually a growing company, so assuming it to be a nongrowing perpetuity is a mistake.

42. When a two-stage DDM is used, the value of a share of Mackinac, dividends per share (DPS), is calculated as follows:

DPS_0 = Cash dividends/Shares outstanding = $22,470/13,000

      = $1.7285.

DPS_1 = $DPS_0 \times 1.17$ = $2.0223.

DPS_2 = $DPS_0 \times 1.17^2$ = $2.3661.

DPS_3 = $DPS_0 \times 1.17^3$ = $2.7683.

DPS_4 = $DPS_0 \times 1.17^3 \times 1.09$ = $3.0175.

When the CAPM is used, the required return on equity, r, is

$$r = \text{Government bond rate} + (\text{Beta} \times \text{Equity risk premium})$$

$$= 0.06 + (1.25 \times 0.05) = 0.1225, \text{ or } 12.25\%.$$

Value per share = $DPS_1/(1+r) + DPS_2/(1+r)^2 + DPS_3/(1+r)^3$

      $+ \left[DPS_4/(r - g_{stable}) \right] /(1+r)^3.$

Value per share = $2.0223/1.1225 + $2.3661/1.1225^2

    $+ $2.7683/1.1225^3$

    $+ [$3.0175/(0.1225 - 0.09)]/1.1225^3$

= $1.8016 + $1.8778 + $1.9573 + $65.6450

= $71.28.

43. When the two-stage FCFE model is used, the value of a share of Mackinac is calculated as follows (in $ thousands except per-share data):

Net income = $37,450.

Depreciation = $10,500.

Capital expenditures = $15,000.

Change in working capital = $5,500.

New debt issuance − Principal repayments = Change in debt outstanding = $4,000

$FCFE_0$ = Net income + Depreciation − Capital expenditures−

                Change in working capital − Principal repayments +

                New debt issues.

$FCFE_0$ = $37,450 + $10,500 − $15,000 − $5,500 + $4,000

        = $31,450.

$FCFE_0 per share$ = $31,450/13,000 = $2.4192.

$FCFE_1$ = $FCFE_0 \times 1.17$ = $2.8305.

$FCFE_2$ = $FCFE_0 \times 1.17^2$ = $3.3117.

$FCFE_3$ = $FCFE_0 \times 1.17^3$ = $3.8747.

$FCFE_4$ = $FCFE_0 \times 1.17^3 \times 1.09$ = $4.2234.

From the answer to A, r = 12.25%.

Value per share = $FCFE_1/(1+r) + FCFE_2/(1+r)^2 + FCFE_3/(1+r)^3$

    $+ \left[FCFE_4/(r - g_{stable}) \right] /(1+r)^3.$

Value per share $= \$2.8305/1.1225 + \$3.3117/1.1225^2$

$\quad + \$3.8747/1.1225^3$

$\quad + [\$4.2234/(0.1225 - 0.09)]/1.1225^3$

$= \$2.5216 + \$2.6283 + \$2.7395 + \$91.8798$

$= \$99.77.$

44. The FCFE model is best for valuing companies for takeovers or in situations that have a reasonable chance of a change in corporate control. Because controlling stockholders can change the dividend policy, they are interested in estimating the maximum residual cash flow after meeting all financial obligations and investment needs. The DDM is based on the premise that the only cash flows received by stockholders are dividends. FCFE uses a more expansive definition to measure what a company can afford to pay out as dividends.

45. The required rate of return for McInish found with the CAPM is

$$r = E(R_i) = R_F + \beta_i [E(R_M) - R_F] = 5.08\% + 0.70(5.50\%) = 8.93\%.$$

The value per share is

$$V_0 = \frac{FCFE_0(1+g)}{r-g} = \frac{0.88(1.064)}{0.0893 - 0.064} = \$37.01.$$

46. The following table shows the calculated price for McInish based on the base-case values for all values except the variable being changed from the base-case value.

Variable	Estimated Price with Low Value (£)	Estimated Price with High Value (£)	Range (Rank) (£)
Normalized $FCFE_0$	29.44	47.94	18.50 (3)
Risk-free rate	38.22	35.33	2.89 (5)
Equity risk premium	51.17	28.99	22.18 (2)
Beta	47.29	30.40	16.89 (4)
FCFE growth rate	18.56	48.79	30.23 (1)

As the table shows, the value of McInish is most sensitive to the changes in the FCFE growth rate, with the price moving over a wide range. McInish's stock price is least sensitive to alternative values of the risk-free rate. Alternative values of beta, the equity risk premium, or the initial FCFE value also have a large impact on the value of the stock, although the effects of these variables are smaller than the effect of the growth rate.

47. The real required rate of return for KMobile is

Country return (real)	6.50%
Industry adjustment	+0.60%
Size adjustment	−0.10%
Leverage adjustment	+0.25%
Required rate of return	7.25%

48. The real growth rate of FCFE is expected to be the same as the country rate of 3.5%. The value of one share is

$$V_0 = \frac{\text{FCFE}_0\,(1 + g_{real})}{r_{real} - g_{real}} = \frac{1,300\,(1.035)}{0.0725 - 0.035} = \text{KRW35},880.$$

49. The required rate of return found with the CAPM is

$$r = E(R_i) = R_F + \beta_i\left[E(R_M) - R_F\right] = 6.4\% + 2.1\,(5.0\%) = 16.9\%.$$

The following table shows the values of sales, net income, capital expenditures less depreciation, and investments in working capital. FCFE equals net income less the investments financed with equity:

$$\text{FCFE} = \text{Net income} - (1 - \text{DR})\,(\text{Capital expenditures} - \text{Depreciation})$$
$$- (1 - \text{DR})\,(\text{Investment in working capital}),$$

where DR is the debt ratio (debt financing as a percentage of debt and equity). Because 20% of net new investments are financed with debt, 80% of the investments are financed with equity, which reduces FCFE by 80% of (Capital expenditures − Depreciation) and 80% of the investment in working capital.

(All Data in Billions of Euros)	2021	2022	2023	2024	2025
Sales (growing at 28%)	5.500	7.040	9.011	11.534	14.764
Net income = 32% of sales	1.760	2.253	2.884	3.691	4.724
FCInv − Dep = (35% − 9%) × Sales	1.430	1.830	2.343	2.999	3.839
WCInv = (6% of Sales)	0.330	0.422	0.541	0.692	0.886
0.80 × (FCInv − Dep + WCInv)	1.408	1.802	2.307	2.953	3.780
FCFE = NI − 0.80 × (FCInv − Dep + WCInv)	0.352	0.451	0.577	0.738	0.945
PV of FCFE discounted at 16.9%	0.301	0.330	0.361	0.395	0.433
Terminal stock value		85.032			
PV of terminal value discounted at 16.9%		38.950			
PV of FCFE (first five years)		1.820			
Total value of equity		40.770			

The terminal stock value is 18.0 times the earnings in 2025, or 18 × 4.724 = €85.03 billion. The present value of the terminal value (€38.95 billion) plus the present value of the first five years' FCFE (€1.82 billion) is €40.77 billion. Because NYL Manufacturing has 17 billion outstanding shares, the value per ordinary share is €2.398.

50. The following table develops the information to calculate FCFE per share (amounts are in US dollars).

	2020	2021	2022	2023	2024	2025
Growth rate for EPS	21%	18%	15%	12%	9%	6%
EPS	3.630	4.283	4.926	5.517	6.014	6.374
Net capital expenditure per share	5.000	5.000	4.500	4.000	3.500	1.500
Investment in WC per share	1.250	1.250	1.125	1.000	0.875	0.375
New debt financing = 40% of (Capital expenditure + WCInv)	2.500	2.500	2.250	2.000	1.750	0.750
FCFE = NI − Net capital expenditure − WCInv + New debt financing	−0.120	0.533	1.551	2.517	3.389	5.249
PV of FCFE discounted at 12%	−0.107	0.425	1.104	1.600	1.923	

Earnings per share for 2019 are $3.00, and the EPS estimates for 2020 through 2025 in the table are found by increasing the previous year's EPS by that year's growth rate. The net capital expenditures each year were specified by the analyst. The increase in working capital per share is equal to 25% of net capital expenditures. Finally, debt financing is 40% of that year's total net capital expenditures and investment in working capital. For example, in 2020, the per-share amount for net capital expenditures plus investment in working capital is $5.00 + $1.25 = $6.25. Debt financing is 40% of $6.25, or $2.50. Debt financing for 2021 through 2025 is found in the same way.

FCFE equals net income minus net capital expenditures minus investment in working capital plus new debt financing. Notice that FCFE is negative in 2020 because of large capital investments and investments in working capital. As these investments decline relative to net income, FCFE becomes positive and substantial.

The present values of FCFE from 2020 through 2024 are given in the bottom row of the table. These five present values sum to $4.944 per share. Because FCFE from 2025 onward will grow at a constant 6%, the constant-growth model can be used to value these cash flows.

$$V_{2024} = \frac{FCFE_{2025}}{r - g} = \frac{5.249}{0.12 - 0.06} = \$87.483.$$

The present value of this stream is $87.483/(1.12)^5 = $49.640. The value per share is the present value of the first five FCFEs (2020–2024) plus the present value of the FCFE after 2024, or $4.944 + $49.640 = $54.58.

51. The required return for QuickChange, found by using the CAPM, is $r = E(R_i) = R_F + \beta_i[E(R_M) - R_F] = 4.5\% + 2.0(5.0\%) = 14.5\%$. The estimated future values of FCFE per share are given in the following exhibit (amounts in US dollars):

Year t	Variable	Calculation	Value in Year t	Present Value at 14.5%
1	$FCFE_1$	0.75(1.10)	0.825	0.721
2	$FCFE_2$	0.75(1.10)(1.26)	1.040	0.793
3	$FCFE_3$	$0.75(1.10)(1.26)^2$	1.310	0.873
4	$FCFE_4$	$0.75(1.10)(1.26)^3$	1.650	0.960
4	TV_4	$FCFE_5/(r - g)$ $= 0.75(1.10)(1.26)^3(1.06)/(0.145 - 0.06)$ $= 1.749/0.085.$	20.580	11.974
0	Total value $=$	PV of FCFE for Years 1–4 + PV of terminal value		15.32

The FCFE grows at 10% for Year 1 and then at 26% for Years 2–4. These calculated values for FCFE are shown in the exhibit. The present values of the FCFE for the first four years discounted at the required rate of return are given in the last column of the table. After Year 4, FCFE will grow at 6% forever, so the constant-growth FCFE model is used to find the terminal value at Time 4, which is $TV_4 = FCFE_5/(r - g)$. TV_4 is discounted at the required return for four periods to find its present value, as shown in the table. Finally, the total value of the stock, $15.32, is the sum of the present values of the first four years' FCFE per share plus the present value of the terminal value per share.

52. The total value of non-operating assets is

SEK60	million short-term securities
SEK45	million market value of noncurrent assets

| SEK40 | million pension fund surplus |
| SEK145 | million non-operating assets |

The total value of the firm is the value of the operating assets plus the value of the non-operating assets, or SEK720 million plus SEK145 million = SEK865 million. The equity value is the value of the firm minus the value of debt, or SEK865 million − SEK215 million = SEK650 million. The value per share is SEK650 million/100 million shares = SEK6.50 per share.

2

Market-Based Valuation: Price and Enterprise Value Multiples

by Jerald E. Pinto, PhD, CFA, Elaine Henry, PhD, CFA, Thomas R. Robinson, PhD, CFA, CAIA, and John D. Stowe, PhD, CFA.

Jerald E. Pinto, PhD, CFA, is at CFA Institute (USA). Elaine Henry, PhD, CFA, is at Stevens Institute of Technology (USA). Thomas R. Robinson, PhD, CFA, CAIA, Robinson Global Investment Management LLC, (USA). John D. Stowe, PhD, CFA, is at Ohio University (USA).

LEARNING OUTCOMES

Mastery	The candidate should be able to:
☐	contrast the method of comparables and the method based on forecasted fundamentals as approaches to using price multiples in valuation and explain economic rationales for each approach
☐	calculate and interpret a justified price multiple
☐	describe rationales for and possible drawbacks to using alternative price multiples and dividend yield in valuation
☐	calculate and interpret alternative price multiples and dividend yield
☐	calculate and interpret underlying earnings, explain methods of normalizing earnings per share (EPS), and calculate normalized EPS
☐	explain and justify the use of earnings yield (E/P)
☐	describe fundamental factors that influence alternative price multiples and dividend yield
☐	calculate and interpret a predicted P/E, given a cross-sectional regression on fundamentals, and explain limitations to the cross-sectional regression methodology
☐	calculate and interpret the justified price-to-earnings ratio (P/E), price-to-book ratio (P/B), and price-to-sales ratio (P/S) for a stock, based on forecasted fundamentals
☐	calculate and interpret the P/E-to-growth (PEG) ratio and explain its use in relative valuation
☐	calculate and explain the use of price multiples in determining terminal value in a multistage discounted cash flow (DCF) model
☐	evaluate whether a stock is overvalued, fairly valued, or undervalued based on comparisons of multiples

LEARNING OUTCOMES

Mastery	The candidate should be able to:
☐	evaluate a stock by the method of comparables and explain the importance of fundamentals in using the method of comparables
☐	explain alternative definitions of cash flow used in price and enterprise value (EV) multiples and describe limitations of each definition
☐	calculate and interpret EV multiples and evaluate the use of EV/ EBITDA
☐	explain sources of differences in cross-border valuation comparisons
☐	describe momentum indicators and their use in valuation
☐	explain the use of the arithmetic mean, the harmonic mean, the weighted harmonic mean, and the median to describe the central tendency of a group of multiples

1   INTRODUCTION

☐	contrast the method of comparables and the method based on forecasted fundamentals as approaches to using price multiples in valuation and explain economic rationales for each approach

Among the most familiar and widely used valuation tools are price and enterprise value multiples. **Price multiples** are ratios of a stock's market price to some measure of fundamental value per share. **Enterprise value multiples**, by contrast, relate the total market value of all sources of a company's capital to a measure of fundamental value for the entire company.

The intuition behind price multiples is that investors evaluate the price of a share of stock—judge whether it is fairly valued, overvalued, or undervalued—by considering what a share buys in terms of per share earnings, net assets, cash flow, or some other measure of value (stated on a per share basis). The intuition behind enterprise value multiples is similar; investors evaluate the market value of an entire enterprise relative to the amount of earnings before interest, taxes, depreciation, and amortization (EBITDA), sales, or operating cash flow it generates. As valuation indicators (measures or indicators of value), multiples have the appealing qualities of simplicity in use and ease in communication. A multiple summarizes in a single number the relationship between the market value of a company's stock (or of its total capital) and some fundamental quantity, such as earnings, sales, or **book value** (owners' equity based on accounting values).

Among the questions we will study for answers that will help in making correct use of multiples as valuation tools are the following:

- What accounting issues affect particular price and enterprise value multiples, and how can analysts address them?
- How do price multiples relate to fundamentals, such as earnings growth rates, and how can analysts use this information when making valuation comparisons among stocks?

- For which types of valuation problems is a particular price or enterprise value multiple appropriate or inappropriate?
- What challenges arise in applying price and enterprise value multiples internationally?

Multiples may be viewed as valuation indicators relating to individual securities. Another type of valuation indicator used in security selection is **momentum indicators**. They typically relate either price or a fundamental (such as earnings) to the time series of its own past values or, in some cases, to its expected value. The logic behind the use of momentum indicators is that such indicators may provide information on future patterns of returns over some time horizon. Because the purpose of momentum indicators is to identify potentially rewarding investment opportunities, they can be viewed as a class of valuation indicators with a focus that is different from and complementary to the focus of price and enterprise value multiples.

We first put the use of price and enterprise value multiples in an economic context and present certain themes common to the use of any price or enterprise value multiple. We then present price multiples. The treatment of each multiple follows a common format: usage considerations, the relationship of the multiple to investors' expectations about fundamentals, and using the multiple in valuation based on comparables. The subsequent sections present enterprise value multiples, international considerations in using multiples, and treatment of momentum indicators. We then discuss several practical issues that arise in using valuation indicators.

Price and Enterprise Value Multiples in Valuation

In practice, two methods underpin analysts' use of price and enterprise value multiples: the method of comparables and the method based on forecasted fundamentals. Each of these methods relates to a definite economic rationale. In this section, we introduce the two methods and their associated economic rationales.

The Method of Comparables

The **method of comparables** refers to the valuation of an asset based on multiples of comparable (similar) assets—that is, valuation based on multiples benchmarked to the multiples of similar assets. The similar assets may be referred to as the **comparables**, the **comps**, or the **guideline assets** (or in the case of equity valuation, **guideline companies**). For example, multiplying a benchmark value of the price-to-earnings (P/E) multiple by an estimate of a company's earnings per share (EPS) provides a quick estimate of the value of the company's stock that can be compared with the stock's market price. Equivalently, comparing a stock's actual price multiple with a relevant benchmark multiple should lead the analyst to the same conclusion on whether the stock is relatively fairly valued, relatively undervalued, or relatively overvalued.

The idea behind price multiples is that a stock's price cannot be evaluated in isolation. Rather, it needs to be evaluated in relation to what it buys in terms of earnings, net assets, or some other measure of value. Obtained by dividing price by a measure of value per share, a price multiple gives the price to purchase one unit of value in whatever way value is measured. For example, a P/E of 20 means that it takes 20 units of currency (for example, €20) to buy one unit of earnings (for example, €1 of earnings). This scaling of price per share by value per share also makes possible comparisons among various stocks. For example, an investor pays more for a unit of earnings for a stock with a P/E of 25 than for another stock with a P/E of 20. Applying the method of comparables, the analyst would reason that if the securities are otherwise closely similar (if they have similar risk, profit margins, and growth prospects, for example), the security with the P/E of 20 is undervalued relative to the one with the P/E of 25.

The word *relative* is necessary. An asset may be undervalued relative to a comparison asset or group of assets, and an analyst may thus expect the asset to outperform the comparison asset or assets on a relative basis. If the comparison asset or assets themselves are not efficiently priced, however, the stock may not be undervalued: It could be fairly valued or even overvalued (on an absolute basis, i.e., in relation to its intrinsic value). Example 1 presents the method of comparables in its simplest application.

EXAMPLE 1

The Method of Comparables at Its Simplest

Company A's EPS is $1.50. Its closest competitor, Company B, is trading at a P/E of 22. Assume the companies have a similar operating and financial profile.

---

1. If Company A's stock is trading at $37.50, what does that indicate about its value relative to Company B?

Solution:

If Company A's stock is trading at $37.50, its P/E will be 25 ($37.50 divided by $1.50). If the companies are similar, this P/E would indicate that Company A is overvalued relative to Company B.

---

2. If we assume that Company A's stock should trade at about the same P/E as Company B's stock, what will we estimate as an appropriate price for Company A's stock?

Solution:

If we assume that Company A's stock should trade at about the same P/E as Company B's stock, we will estimate that an appropriate price for Company A's stock is $33 ($1.50 times 22).

The method of comparables applies also to enterprise value multiples. In this application, we would evaluate the market value of an entire company in relation to some measure of value relevant to all providers of capital, not only providers of equity capital. For example, multiplying a benchmark multiple of enterprise value (EV) to earnings before interest, taxes, depreciation, and amortization (EBITDA) times an estimate of a company's EBITDA provides a quick estimate of the value of the entire company. Similarly, comparing a company's actual enterprise value multiple with a relevant benchmark multiple allows an assessment of whether the company is relatively fairly valued, relatively undervalued, or relatively overvalued.

Many choices for the benchmark value of a multiple have appeared in valuation methodologies, including the multiple of a closely matched individual stock and the average or median value of the multiple for the stock's industry peer group. The economic rationale underlying the method of comparables is the **law of one price**—the economic principle that two identical assets should sell at the same price. The method of comparables is perhaps the most widely used approach for analysts *reporting* valuation judgments on the basis of price multiples. For this reason, the use of multiples in valuation is sometimes viewed solely as a type of relative-valuation approach; however, multiples can also be derived from, and expressed in terms of, fundamentals, as discussed in the next section.

The Method Based on Forecasted Fundamentals

The **method based on forecasted fundamentals** refers to the use of multiples that are derived from forecasted fundamentals—characteristics of a business related to profitability, growth, or financial strength. For brevity, we sometimes use the phrase "based on fundamentals" in describing multiples derived using this approach. Fundamentals drive cash flows, and we can relate multiples to company fundamentals through a discounted cash flow (DCF) model. Algebraic expressions of price multiples in terms of fundamentals facilitate an examination of how valuation differences among stocks relate to different expectations for those fundamentals.

One process for relating multiples to forecasted fundamentals begins with a valuation based on a DCF model. Recall that DCF models estimate the intrinsic value of a firm or its equity as the present value of expected cash flows and that fundamentals drive cash flows. Multiples are stated with respect to a single value of a fundamental, but any price or enterprise value multiple relates to the entire future stream of expected cash flows through its DCF value.

We can illustrate this concept by first taking the present value of the stream of expected future cash flows and then expressing the result relative to a forecasted fundamental. For example, if the DCF value of a UK stock is £10.20 and its forecasted EPS is £1.2, the forward P/E multiple consistent with the DCF value is £10.20/£1.2 = 8.5. (The term **forward P/E** refers to a P/E calculated on the basis of a forecast of EPS and is discussed in further detail later in this reading.) This exercise of relating a valuation to a price multiple applies to any definition of price multiple and any DCF model or residual income model.

In summary, we can approach valuation by using multiples from two perspectives. First, we can use the method of comparables, which involves comparing an asset's multiple to a standard of comparison. Similar assets should sell at similar prices. Second, we can use the method based on forecasted fundamentals, which involves forecasting the company's fundamentals rather than making comparisons with other companies. The price multiple of an asset should be related to its expected future cash flows. We can also incorporate the insights from the method based on forecasted fundamentals in explaining valuation differences based on comparables, because we seldom (if ever) find exact comparables. In the sections covering each multiple, we will present the method based on forecasted fundamentals first so we can refer to it when using the method of comparables.

Using either method, how can an analyst communicate a view about the value of a stock? Of course, the analyst simply can offer a qualitative judgment about whether the stock appears to be fairly valued, overvalued, or undervalued (and offer specific reasons for the view). The analyst may also be more precise by communicating a **justified price multiple** for the stock. The justified price multiple is the estimated **fair value** of that multiple, which can be justified on the basis of the method of comparables or the method of forecasted fundamentals.

For an example of a justified multiple based on the method of comparables, suppose we use the price-to-book (P/B) multiple in a valuation and find that the median P/B for the company's peer group, which would be the standard of comparison, is 2.2. Note that we are using the median rather than the mean value of the peer group's multiple to avoid distortions from outliers—an important issue when dealing with peer groups that often consist of a small number of companies. The stock's justified P/B based on the method of comparables is 2.2 (without making any adjustments for differences in fundamentals). We can compare the justified P/B with the actual P/B based on market price to form an opinion about value. If the justified P/B is larger (smaller) than the actual P/B, the stock may be undervalued (overvalued). We can also, on the assumption that the comparison assets are fairly priced, translate the justified

P/B based on comparables into an estimate of absolute fair value of the stock. If the current book value per share is $23, then the fair value of the stock is 2.2 × $23 = $50.60, which can be compared with its market price.

For an example of a justified multiple based on fundamentals, suppose that we are using a residual income model and estimate that the value of the stock is $46. Then, the justified P/B based on forecasted fundamentals is $46/$23 = 2.0, which we can again compare with the actual value of the stock's P/B. We can also state our estimate of the stock's absolute fair value as 2 × $23 = $46. (Note that the analyst could report valuation judgments related to a DCF model in terms of the DCF value directly; price multiples are a familiar form, however, in which to state valuations.) Furthermore, we can incorporate the insights from the method based on fundamentals to explain differences from results based on comparables.

In the next section, we begin a discussion of specific price and enterprise value multiples used in valuation.

2   PRICE/EARNINGS: THE BASICS

- [ ] calculate and interpret a justified price multiple
- [ ] describe rationales for and possible drawbacks to using alternative price multiples and dividend yield in valuation
- [ ] calculate and interpret alternative price multiples and dividend yield
- [ ] calculate and interpret underlying earnings, explain methods of normalizing earnings per share (EPS), and calculate normalized EPS
- [ ] explain and justify the use of earnings yield (E/P)

In this section, we first discuss the most familiar price multiple, the price-to-earnings ratio. In the context of that discussion, we introduce a variety of practical issues that have counterparts for most other multiples. These issues include analyst adjustments to the denominator of the ratio for accuracy and comparability and the use of inverse price multiples. Then, we discuss four other major price multiples from the same practical perspective.

Price/Earnings

In the first edition of *Security Analysis* (Graham and Dodd 1934, p. 351), Benjamin Graham and David L. Dodd described common stock valuation based on P/Es as the standard method of that era, and the P/E is still the most familiar valuation measure today.

We begin our discussion with rationales offered by analysts for the use of P/E and with the possible drawbacks of its use. We then define the two chief variations of the P/E: the trailing P/E and the forward P/E (also called the "leading P/E"). The multiple's numerator, market price, is (as in other multiples) definitely determinable; it presents no special problems of interpretation. But the denominator, EPS, is based on the complex rules of accrual accounting and presents significant interpretation issues. We discuss those issues and the adjustments analysts can make to obtain more-meaningful P/Es. Finally, we conclude the section by examining how analysts use P/Es to value a stock using the method of forecasted fundamentals and the method of comparables. As mentioned earlier, we discuss fundamentals first so that we can draw insights from that discussion when using comparables.

Several rationales support the use of P/E multiples in valuation:

- Earning power is a chief driver of investment value, and EPS, the denominator in the P/E ratio, is perhaps the chief focus of security analysts' attention. Surveys show that P/E ranks first among price multiples used in market-based valuation (2007 survey of CFA Institute members; for more details, see Pinto, Robinson, and Stowe 2018) and that it is the most popular valuation metric when making investment decisions (2012 BofA Merrill Lynch Institutional Factor Survey).

- The P/E ratio is widely recognized and used by investors.

- Differences in stocks' P/Es may be related to differences in long-run average returns on investments in those stocks, according to empirical research (Chan and Lakonishok 2004).

Potential drawbacks to using P/Es derive from the characteristics of EPS:

- EPS can be zero, negative, or insignificantly small relative to price, and P/E does not make economic sense with a zero, negative, or insignificantly small denominator.

- The ongoing or recurring components of earnings that are most important in determining intrinsic value can be practically difficult to distinguish from transient components.

- The application of accounting standards requires corporate managers to choose among acceptable alternatives and to use estimates in reporting. In making such choices and estimates, managers may distort EPS as an accurate reflection of economic performance. Such distortions may affect the comparability of P/Es among companies.

Methods to address these potential drawbacks will be discussed later in the reading. In the next section, we discuss alternative definitions of P/E based on alternative specifications of earnings.

Alternative Definitions of P/E

In calculating a P/E, the numerator most commonly used is the current price of the common stock, which is generally easily obtained and unambiguous for publicly traded companies. Selecting the appropriate EPS figure to be used in the denominator is not as straightforward. The following two issues must be considered:

- the time horizon over which earnings are measured, which results in alternative definitions of P/E, and

- adjustments to accounting earnings that the analyst may make so that P/Es for various companies can be compared.

Common alternative definitions of P/E are trailing P/E and forward P/E.

- A stock's **trailing P/E** (sometimes referred to as a current P/E) is its current market price divided by the most recent four quarters' EPS. In such calculations, EPS is sometimes referred to as "trailing 12-month (TTM) EPS." Note, however, that the Value Line Investment Survey uses "current P/E" to mean a P/E based on EPS for the most recent six months plus the projected EPS for the coming six months. That calculation blends historical and forward-looking elements.

- The **forward P/E** (also called the **leading P/E** or **prospective P/E**) is a stock's current price divided by next year's expected earnings. Trailing P/E is the P/E usually presented first in stock profiles that appear in financial databases, but most databases also provide the forward P/E. In practice, the forward P/E has a number of important variations that depend on how "next year" is defined, as we discuss later.

Other names and time-horizon definitions for P/E exist. For example, Thomson First Call (part of Refinitiv) provides various P/Es, including ratios that have as the denominator a stock's trailing 12-month EPS, last reported annual EPS, and EPS forecasted for one year to three years ahead. Another example is Value Line's company reports which display a median P/E, which is a rounded average of the four middle values of the range of annual average P/Es over the past 10 years.

In using the P/E, an analyst should apply the same definition to all companies and time periods under examination. Otherwise, the P/Es are not comparable, for a given company over time or for various companies at a specific point in time. One reason is that the differences in P/Es calculated by different methods may be systematic (as opposed to random). For example, for companies with rising earnings, the forward P/E will be smaller than the trailing P/E because the denominator in the forward P/E calculation will be larger.

Valuation is a forward-looking process, so analysts usually focus on the forward P/E when earnings forecasts are available. For large public companies, an analyst can develop earnings forecasts and/or obtain consensus earnings forecasts from a commercial database. When earnings are not readily predictable, however, a trailing P/E (or another valuation metric) may be more appropriate than a forward P/E. Furthermore, logic sometimes indicates that a particular definition of the P/E is not relevant. For example, a major acquisition or divestiture or a significant change in financial leverage may change a company's operating or financial risk so much that the trailing P/E based on past EPS is not informative about the future and thus not relevant to a valuation. In such a case, the forward P/E is the appropriate measure. In the following sections, we address issues that arise in calculating trailing and forward P/Es.

Trailing P/Es and forward P/Es are based on a single year's EPS. If that number is negative or viewed as unrepresentative of a company's earning power, however, an analyst may base the P/E calculation on a longer-run expected average EPS value. P/Es based on such normalized EPS data may be called **normalized P/Es**. Because the denominators in normalized P/Es are typically based on historical information, they are covered in the next section on calculating the trailing P/E.

Calculating the Trailing P/E

When using trailing earnings to calculate a P/E, the analyst must take care in determining the EPS to be used in the denominator. The analyst must consider the following:

- potential **dilution** of EPS (a reduction in proportional ownership interest as a result of the issuance of new shares.);
- transitory, nonrecurring components of earnings that are company specific;
- transitory components of earnings ascribable to cyclicality (business or industry cyclicality); and
- differences in accounting methods (when different companies' stocks are being compared).

Among the considerations mentioned, potential dilution of EPS generally makes the least demands on analysts' accounting expertise because companies are themselves required to present both basic EPS and diluted EPS. **Basic earnings per share** data reflect total earnings divided by the weighted average number of shares actually outstanding during the period. **Diluted earnings per share** reflects division by the number of shares that would be outstanding if holders of securities such as executive stock options, equity warrants, and convertible bonds exercised their options to obtain common stock. The diluted EPS measure also reflects the effect of such conversion on the numerator, earnings. For example, conversion of a convertible bond affects both the numerator (earnings) and the denominator (number of shares) in the EPS calculation. Because companies present both EPS numbers, the analyst does not need to make the computation. Companies also typically report details of the EPS computation in a footnote to the financial statements. Example 2, illustrating the first bullet point, shows the typical case in which the P/E based on diluted EPS is higher than the P/E based on basic EPS.

EXAMPLE 2

Basic versus Diluted EPS

For the fiscal year ended 30 September 2018, Siemens AG (SIE-DE) reported basic EPS of €7.12 and diluted EPS of €7.01. Based on a closing stock price of €95.94 on 29 March 2019, the trailing P/E for Siemens is 13.47 if basic EPS is used and 13.69 if diluted EPS is used.

When comparing companies, analysts generally prefer to use diluted EPS so that the EPS of companies with differing amounts of dilutive securities are on a comparable basis. The other bulleted considerations frequently lead to analyst adjustments to reported earnings numbers and are discussed in order below.

Analyst Adjustments for Nonrecurring Items

Items in earnings that are not expected to recur in the future are generally removed by analysts because valuation concentrates on future cash flows. The analyst's focus is on estimating **underlying earnings** (other names for this concept include **persistent earnings**, **continuing earnings**, and **core earnings**)—that is, earnings that exclude nonrecurring items. An increase in underlying earnings reflects an increase in earnings that the analyst expects to persist into the future. Companies may disclose adjusted earnings, which may be called non-IFRS earnings (because they differ, as a result of adjustments, from earnings as reportable under International Financial Reporting Standards), non-GAAP earnings (because they differ, as a result of adjustments, from earnings as reportable under US generally accepted accounting principles), pro forma earnings, adjusted earnings, or, as in Example 3, core earnings. All of these terms indicate that the earnings number differs in some way from that presented in conformity with accounting standards. Example 3 shows the calculation of EPS and P/E before and after analyst adjustments for nonrecurring items.

EXAMPLE 3

Calculating Trailing 12-Month EPS and Adjusting EPS for Nonrecurring Items

You are calculating a trailing P/E for Evergreen PLC as of 31 May 20X9, when the share price closed at £50.11 in London. In its first quarter of 20X9, ended 31 March, Evergreen reported basic and diluted EPS according to IFRS of £0.81, which included £0.34 of restructuring costs and £0.26 of amortization of intangibles arising from acquisitions. Adjusting for all of these items, Evergreen reported "core EPS" of £1.41 for the first quarter of 20X9, compared with core EPS of £1.81 for the first quarter of 20X8. Because the core EPS differed from the EPS calculated under IFRS, the company provided a reconciliation of the two EPS figures.

[Handwritten margin note: – When comparing companies, if any of the companies have a complex capital structure, the P/Es must be compared on the basis of diluted EPS]

Other data for Evergreen as of 31 March 20X9 are given below. The trailing 12-month diluted EPS for 31 March 20X9 includes one quarter in 20X9 and three quarters in 20X8.

Measure	Full Year 20X8 (a)	Less 1st Quarter 20X8 (b)	Three Quarters of 20X8 (c = a − b)	Plus 1st Quarter 20X9 (d)	Trailing 12-Month EPS (e = c + d)
Reported diluted EPS	£4.98	£1.27	£3.71	£0.81	£4.52
Core EPS	£6.41	£1.81	£4.60	£1.41	£6.01
EPS excluding 20X8 legal provisions	£5.07	£1.28	£3.79	£0.81	£4.60

Based on the table and information about Evergreen, address the following:

Suppose you expect the amortization charges to continue for some years and note that, although Evergreen excluded restructuring charges from its core earnings calculation, Evergreen has reported restructuring charges in previous years. After reviewing all relevant data, you conclude that, in this instance, only the legal provision related to a previously disclosed legal matter should be viewed as clearly nonrecurring.

1. Based on the company's reported EPS, determine the trailing P/E of Evergreen as of 31 March 20X9.

Solution:

Based on reported EPS and without any adjustments for nonrecurring items, the trailing P/E is £50.11/£4.52 = 11.1.

2. Determine the trailing P/E of Evergreen as of 31 March 20X9 using core earnings as determined by Evergreen.

Solution:

Using the company's reported core earnings, you find that the trailing EPS would be £6.01 and the trailing P/E would be £50.11/£6.01 = 8.3.

3. Determine the trailing P/E based on your adjustment to EPS.

Solution:

The trailing EPS excluding only what you consider to be nonrecurring items is £4.60, and the trailing P/E on that basis is £50.11/£4.60 = 10.9.

Example 3 makes several important points:

- By any of its various names, underlying earnings, or core earnings, is a non-IFRS concept without prescribed rules for its calculation.

- An analyst's calculation of underlying earnings may well differ from that of the company supplying the earnings numbers. Company-reported core earnings may not be comparable among companies because of differing bases of calculation. Analysts should thus always carefully examine the calculation and, generally, should not rely on such company-reported core earnings numbers.

- In general, the P/E that an analyst uses in valuation should reflect the analyst's judgment about the company's underlying earnings and should be calculated on a consistent basis among all stocks under review.

The identification of nonrecurring items often requires detailed work—in particular, examination of the income statement, the footnotes to the income statement, and the management discussion and analysis section. The analyst cannot rely on income statement classifications alone to identify nonrecurring components of earnings. Nonrecurring items (for example, gains and losses from the sale of assets, asset **write-downs**, goodwill impairment, provisions for future losses, and changes in **accounting estimates**) often appear in the income from continuing operations portion of a business's income statement. An analyst may decide not to exclude income/loss from discontinued operations when assets released from discontinued operations are redirected back into the company's earnings base. An analyst who takes income statement classifications at face value may draw incorrect conclusions in a valuation.

This discussion does not exhaust the analysis that may be necessary to distinguish earnings components that are expected to persist into the future from those that are not. For example, earnings may be decomposed into cash flow and accrual components (where the accrual component of earnings is the difference between a cash measure of earnings and a measure of earnings under the relevant set of accounting standards). Some research indicates that the cash flow component of earnings should receive a greater weight than the accrual component of earnings in valuation, and analysts may attempt to reflect that conclusion in the earnings used in calculating P/Es.

Analyst Adjustments for Business-Cycle Influences

In addition to company-specific effects, such as restructuring costs, transitory effects on earnings can come from business-cycle or industry-cycle influences. These effects are somewhat different from company-specific effects. Because business cycles repeat, business-cycle effects, although transitory, can be expected to recur in subsequent cycles.

Because of cyclical effects, the most recent four quarters of earnings may not accurately reflect the average or long-term earning power of the business, particularly for **cyclical businesses**—those with high sensitivity to business- or industry-cycle influences, such as automobile and steel manufacturers. Trailing EPS for such stocks is often depressed or negative at the bottom of a cycle and unusually high at the top of a cycle. Empirically, P/Es for cyclical companies are often highly volatile over a cycle even without any change in business prospects: High P/Es on depressed EPS at the bottom of the cycle and low P/Es on unusually high EPS at the top of the cycle reflect the countercyclical property of P/Es known as the **Molodovsky effect**, named after Nicholas Molodovsky, who wrote on this subject in the 1950s and referred to using average earnings as a simple starting point for understanding a company's underlying earnings power. Analysts address this problem by normalizing EPS—that is, estimating the level of EPS that the business could be expected to achieve under mid-cyclical conditions (**normalized EPS** or **normal EPS**). Please note that we are using the term "normalized earnings" to refer to earnings adjusted for the effects of a business cycle. Some sources use the term "normalized earnings" also to refer to earnings adjusted for nonrecurring items.

Two of several available methods to calculate normalized EPS are as follows:

- The method of *historical average EPS*, in which normalized EPS is calculated as average EPS over the most recent full cycle

- The method of *average return on equity*, in which normalized EPS is calculated as the average return on equity (ROE) from the most recent full cycle, multiplied by current book value per share

The first method is one of several possible statistical approaches to the problem of cyclical earnings; however, this method does not account for changes in a business's size. The second alternative, by using recent book value per share, reflects more accurately the effect on EPS of growth or shrinkage in the company's size. For that reason, the

Book value per share here is the value of shareholders' equity less any value attributable to preferred stock (i.e., market value of preferred stock)

method of average ROE is sometimes preferred. When reported current book value does not adequately reflect company size in relation to past values (because of items such as large write-downs), the analyst can make appropriate accounting adjustments. The analyst can also estimate normalized earnings by multiplying total assets by an estimate of the long-run return on total assets or by multiplying shareholders' equity by an estimate of the long-run return on total shareholders' equity. These methods are particularly useful for a period in which a cyclical company has reported a loss.

Example 4 illustrates this concept. The example uses data for an **American Depositary Receipt** (ADR) but is applicable to any equity security. An ADR is intended to facilitate US investment in non-US companies. It is a negotiable certificate issued by a depositary bank that represents ownership in a non-US company's deposited equity (i.e., equity held in custody by the depositary bank in the company's home market). One ADR may represent one, more than one, or less than one deposited share. The number of or fraction of deposited securities represented by one ADR is referred to as the "ADR ratio."

EXAMPLE 4

Normalizing EPS for Business-Cycle Effects

You are researching the valuation of Zenlandia Chemical Company, a large (fictitious) manufacturer of specialty chemicals. Your research is for a US investor who is interested in the company's ADRs rather than the company's shares listed on the Zenlandia Stock Exchange. On 5 July 2021, the closing price of the US-listed ADR was $18.21. The chemical industry is notably cyclical, so you decide to normalize earnings as part of your analysis. You believe that data from 2014 reasonably capture the beginning of the most recent business cycle, and you want to evaluate a normalized P/E. Exhibit 1 supplies data on EPS (based on Zenlandia GAAP) for one ADR, book value per share (BVPS) for one ADR, and the company's ROE.

Exhibit 1: Zenlandia Chemical Company (Currency in US Dollars)							
Measure	2014	2015	2016	2017	2018	2019	2020
EPS (ADR)	$0.74	$0.63	$0.61	$0.54	$1.07	$0.88	$1.08
BVPS (ADR)	$3.00	$2.93	$2.85	$2.99	$3.80	$4.03	$4.82
ROE	24.7%	21.5%	21.4%	18.1%	28.2%	21.8%	22.4%

Note: This example involves a single company. When the analyst compares multiple companies on the basis of P/Es based on normalized EPS and uses this normalization approach, the analyst should be sure that the ROEs are being calculated consistently by the subject companies. In this example, ROE for each year is being calculated by using ending BVPS and, essentially, trailing earnings are being normalized.

Using the data in Exhibit 1:

1. Calculate a normalized EPS by the method of historical average EPS and then calculate the P/E based on that estimate of normalized EPS.

Solution:

Averaging EPS over the 2014–20 period, you would find it to be ($0.74 + $0.63 + $0.61 + $0.54 + $1.07 + $0.88 + $1.08)/7 = $0.79. Thus, according to the method of historical average EPS, normalized EPS is $0.79. The P/E based on this estimate is $18.21/$0.79 = 23.1.

2. Calculate a normalized EPS by the method of average ROE and the P/E based on that estimate of normalized EPS.

Solution:

Average ROE over the 2014–20 period is (24.7% + 21.5% + 21.4% + 18.1% + 28.2% + 21.8% + 22.4%)/7 = 22.6%. Based on the current BVPS of $4.82, the method of average ROE gives 0.226 × $4.82 = $1.09 as normalized EPS. The P/E based on this estimate is $18.21/$1.09 = 16.7.

3. Explain the source of the differences in the normalized EPS calculated by the two methods, and contrast the impact on the estimate of a normalized P/E.

Solution:

From 2014 to 2020, BVPS increased from $3.00 to $4.82, an increase of about 61%. The estimate of normalized EPS of $1.09 from the average ROE method reflects the use of information on the current size of the company better than does the $0.79 calculated from the historical average EPS method. Because of that difference, the company appears more conservatively valued (as indicated by a lower P/E) when the method based on average ROE is used.

Analyst Adjustments for Comparability with Other Companies

Analysts adjust EPS for differences in accounting methods between the company and companies it is being compared with so that the P/Es will be comparable. For example, if an analyst is comparing a company that uses the last-in, first-out (LIFO) method of inventory accounting as permitted by US GAAP (but not by IFRS) with another company that uses the first-in, first-out (FIFO) method, the analyst should adjust earnings to provide comparability in all ratio and valuation analyses. In general, any adjustment made to a company's reported financials for purposes of financial statement analysis should be incorporated into an analysis of P/E and other multiples.

Dealing with Extremely Low, Zero, or Negative Earnings

Having addressed the challenges that arise in calculating P/E because of nonrecurring items and business-cycle influences and for comparability among companies, we present in this section the methods analysts have developed for dealing with extremely low, zero, or negative earnings.

Stock selection disciplines that use P/Es or other price multiples often involve ranking stocks from highest value of the multiple to lowest value of the multiple. The security with the lowest positive P/E has the lowest purchase cost per currency unit of earnings among the securities ranked. Zero earnings and negative earnings pose a problem if the analyst wishes to use P/E as the valuation metric. Because division by zero is undefined, P/Es cannot be calculated for zero earnings.

A P/E can technically be calculated in the case of negative earnings. Negative earnings, however, result in a negative P/E. A negative-P/E security will rank below the lowest positive-P/E security, but because earnings are negative, the negative-P/E security is actually the most costly in terms of earnings purchased. Thus, negative P/Es are not meaningful.

In some cases, an analyst might handle negative EPS by using normalized EPS instead. Also, when trailing EPS is negative, the year-ahead EPS and thus the forward P/E may be positive. An argument in favor of either of these approaches based on positive earnings is that if a company is appropriately treated as a going concern, losses cannot be the usual operating result.

If the analyst is interested in a ranking, however, one solution (applicable to any ratio involving a quantity that can be negative or zero) is the use of an **inverse price ratio**—that is, the reciprocal of the original ratio, which places price in the denominator. The use of inverse price multiples addresses the issue of consistent ranking because price is never negative. In the case of the P/E, the inverse price ratio is earnings to price (E/P), known as the **earnings yield**. Ranked by earnings yield from highest to lowest, the securities are correctly ranked from cheapest to most costly in terms of the amount of earnings one unit of currency buys. Earnings yield can be based on normalized EPS, expected next-year EPS, or trailing EPS. In these cases also, earnings yield provides a consistent ranking.

Exhibit 2 illustrates these points for a group of automobile companies, one of which has a negative EPS. When reporting a P/E based on negative earnings, analysts should report such P/Es as "NM" (not meaningful).

Exhibit 2: P/E and E/P for Five Automobile Companies (as of 28 June 2019; in US Dollars)

Company	Current Price	Diluted EPS (TTM)	P/E (TTM)	E/P (%)
Ford Motor Co. (F)	10.28	0.78	13.2	7.59
Honda Motor Co.	25.85	3.12	8.3	12.06
Fiat Chrysler	13.88	2.32	6.0	16.71
General Motors	38.57	6.29	11.72	8.53
Tesla Inc.	224.45	−7.72	NM	−2.51

Source: Yahoo! Finance.

In addition to zero and negative earnings, extremely low earnings can pose problems when using P/Es—particularly for evaluating the distribution of P/Es of a group of stocks under review. In this case, again, inverse price ratios can be useful. The P/E of a stock with extremely low earnings may, nevertheless, be extremely high because an earnings rebound is anticipated. An extremely high P/E—an outlier P/E—can overwhelm the effect of the other P/Es in the calculation of the mean P/E. Although the use of median P/Es and other techniques can mitigate the problem of skewness caused by outliers, the distribution of inverse price ratios is inherently less susceptible to outlier-induced skewness.

As mentioned, earnings yield is but one example of an inverse price ratio—that is, the reciprocal of a price ratio. Exhibit 3 summarizes inverse price ratios for all the price ratios we discuss in this reading.

Exhibit 3: Summary of Price and Inverse Price Ratios

Price Ratio	Inverse Price Ratio	Comments
Price to earnings (P/E)	Earnings yield (E/P)	Both forms commonly used.
Price to book (P/B)	Book to market (B/P)*	Book value is less commonly negative than EPS. Book to market is favored in research but not common in practitioner usage.
Price to sales (P/S)	Sales to price (S/P)	S/P is rarely used except when all other ratios are being stated in the form of inverse price ratios; sales is not zero or negative in practice for going concerns.

Price Ratio	Inverse Price Ratio	Comments
Price to cash flow (P/CF)	Cash flow yield (CF/P)	Both forms are commonly used.
Price to dividends (P/D)	Dividend yield (D/P)	Dividend yield is much more commonly used because P/D is not calculable for non-dividend-paying stocks, but both D/P and P/D are used in discussing index valuation.

"Book to market" is probably more common usage than "book to price." Book to market is variously abbreviated B/M, BV/MV (for "book value" and "market value"), or B/P.
Note: B, S, CF, and D are in per-share terms.

Forward P/E

The forward P/E is a major and logical alternative to the trailing P/E because valuation is naturally forward looking. In the definition of forward P/E, analysts have interpreted "next year's expected earnings" as expected EPS for

- the next four quarters,
- the next 12 months, or
- the next fiscal year.

In this section, unless otherwise stated, we use the first definition of forward P/E (i.e., the next four quarters), which is closest to how cash flows are dated in our discussion of DCF valuation. To illustrate the calculation, suppose the current market price of a stock is $15 as of 1 March 2020 and the most recently reported quarterly EPS (for the quarter ended 31 December 2019) is $0.22. Our forecasts of EPS are as follows:

- $0.15 for the quarter ending 31 March 2020,
- $0.18 for the quarter ending 30 June 2020,
- $0.18 for the quarter ending 30 September 2020, and
- $0.24 for the quarter ending 31 December 2020.

The sum of the forecasts for the next four quarters is $0.15 + $0.18 + $0.18 + $0.24 = $0.75, and the forward P/E for this stock is $15/$0.75 = 20.0.

Another important concept related to the forward P/E is the next 12-month (NTM) P/E, which corresponds in a forward-looking sense to the TTM P/E concept of trailing P/E. A stock's **NTM P/E** is its current market price divided by an estimated next 12-month EPS, which typically combines the annual EPS estimates from two fiscal years, weighted to reflect the relative proximity of the fiscal year. For example, assume that in late August 2020, an analyst is looking at Microsoft Corporation. Microsoft has a June 30 fiscal year end, so at the time of the analyst's scrutiny, there were 10 months remaining until the end of the company's 2021 fiscal year (i.e., September 2020 through June 2021, inclusive). The estimated next 12-month EPS for Microsoft would be calculated as $[(10/12) \times \text{FY21E EPS}] + [(2/12) \times \text{FY22E EPS}]$. NTM P/E is useful because it facilitates comparison of companies with different fiscal year ends without the need to use quarterly estimates, which for many companies are not available.

Applying the fiscal year concept, Thomson First Call reports a stock's "forward P/E" in two ways: first, based on the mean of analysts' *current fiscal year* (FY1 = Fiscal Year 1) forecasts, for which analysts may have actual EPS in hand for some quarters, and second, based on analysts' *following fiscal year* (FY2 = Fiscal Year 2) forecasts, which must be based entirely on forecasts. For Thomson First Call, "forward P/E" contrasts with "current P/E," which is based on the last reported annual EPS.

Clearly, analysts must be consistent in the definition of forward P/E when comparing stocks. Example 5 and Example 6 illustrate two ways of calculating forward P/E.

EXAMPLE 5

Calculating a Forward P/E (1)

A market price for the common stock of IBM in late June 2019 was $137.90. IBM's fiscal year coincides with the calendar year. At that time, the consensus EPS forecast of the 22 analysts covering IBM was $13.91 for 2019 (FY1), and the consensus EPS forecast of 20 analysts covering IBM was $14.17 for 2020 (FY2).

1. Calculate IBM's forward P/E based on the fiscal year consensus forecasted EPS for FY1.

Solution:

IBM's forward P/E is $137.90/$13.91 = 9.9 based on FY1 forecasted EPS. Note that this EPS number includes the reported first quarter earnings and a forecast of the three remaining quarters as of late June 2019.

2. Calculate IBM's forward P/E based on a fiscal year definition and the FY2 consensus forecasted EPS.

Solution:

IBM's forward P/E is $137.90/$14.17 = 9.7 based on FY2 forecasted EPS.

In Example 5, the company's EPS was expected to increase by slightly less than 2%, so the forward P/Es based on the two different EPS specifications differed from one another somewhat but not significantly. Example 6 presents the calculation of forward P/Es for a company with volatile earnings.

EXAMPLE 6

Calculating a Forward P/E (2)

In this example, we use alternative definitions of "forward" to compute forward P/Es. Exhibit 4 presents actual and forecasted EPS for Selene Gaming Corp. (Selene), which owns and operates gaming entertainment properties.

Exhibit 4: Quarterly EPS for Selene (in US Dollars; Excluding Nonrecurring Items and Discontinued Operations)					
Year	31 March	30 June	30 September	31 December	Annual Estimate
2020	0.10	0.00	E(0.10)	E(0.50)	(0.50)
2021	E0.70	E0.80	E0.30	E(0.30)	1.50

Source: The Value Line Investment Survey.

On 9 August 2020, Selene closed at $12.20. Selene's fiscal year ends on 31 December. As of 9 August 2020, solve the following problems by using the information in Exhibit 4:

1. Calculate Selene's forward P/E based on the next four quarters of forecasted EPS.

Solution:

We sum forecasted EPS as follows:

3Q:2020 EPS (estimate)	($0.10)
4Q:2020 EPS (estimate)	($0.50)
1Q:2021 EPS (estimate)	$0.70
2Q:2021 EPS (estimate)	$0.80
Sum	$0.90

The forward P/E by this definition is $12.20/$0.90 = 13.6.

2. Calculate Selene's NTM P/E.

Solution:

As of 9 August 2020, approximately five months remained in FY2020. Therefore, the estimated next 12-month EPS for Selene would be based on annual estimates in the last column of Exhibit 4: $[(5/12) \times$ FY20E EPS$] + [(7/12) \times$ FY21E EPS$] = (5/12)(-0.50) + (7/12)(1.50) = 0.67$. The NTM P/E would be $12.20/$0.67 = 18.2.

3. Calculate Selene's forward P/E based on a fiscal year definition and current fiscal year (2020) forecasted EPS.

Solution:

We sum EPS as follows:

1Q:2020 EPS (actual)	$0.10
2Q:2020 EPS (actual)	$0.00
3Q:2020 EPS (estimate)	($0.10)
4Q:2020 EPS (estimate)	($0.50)
Sum	($0.50)

The forward P/E is $12.20/($0.50) = -24.4, which is not meaningful.

4. Calculate Selene's forward P/E based on a fiscal year definition and next fiscal year (2021) forecasted EPS.

Solution:

We sum EPS as follows:

1Q:2021 EPS (estimate)	$0.70
2Q:2021 EPS (estimate)	$0.80
3Q:2021 EPS (estimate)	$0.30
4Q:2021 EPS (estimate)	($0.30)
Sum	$1.50

The forward P/E by this definition is $12.20/$1.50 = 8.1.

As illustrated in Example 6, for companies with volatile earnings, forward P/Es and thus valuations based on forward P/Es can vary dramatically depending on the definition of earnings. The analyst would probably be justified in normalizing EPS for Selene. The gaming industry is highly sensitive to discretionary spending; thus, Selene's earnings are strongly procyclical.

Having explored the issues involved in calculating P/Es, we turn to using them in valuation.

3   PRICE/EARNINGS: VALUATION BASED ON FORECASTED FUNDAMENTALS

☐ | describe fundamental factors that influence alternative price multiples and dividend yield

☐ | calculate and interpret a predicted P/E, given a cross-sectional regression on fundamentals, and explain limitations to the cross-sectional regression methodology

The analyst who understands DCF valuation models can use them not only in developing an estimate of the justified P/E for a stock but also to gain insight into possible sources of valuation differences when the method of comparables is used. Linking P/Es to a DCF model helps us address what value the market should place on a dollar of EPS when we are given a particular set of expectations about the company's profitability, growth, and cost of capital.

Justified P/E

The simplest of all DCF models is the Gordon (constant) growth form of the dividend discount model (DDM). Presentations of discounted dividend valuation commonly show that the P/E of a share can be related to the value of a stock as calculated in the Gordon growth model through the expressions

$$\frac{P_0}{E_1} = \frac{D_1/E_1}{r-g} = \frac{1-b}{r-g} \tag{1}$$

for the forward P/E and

$$\frac{P_0}{E_0} = \frac{D_0(1+g)/E_0}{r-g} = \frac{(1-b)(1+g)}{r-g} \tag{2}$$

for the trailing P/E, where

P = price

E = earnings

D = dividends

r = required rate of return

g = dividend growth rate

b = retention rate

Under the assumption of constant dividend growth, the first expression gives the justified forward P/E and the second gives the justified trailing P/E. Note that both expressions state P/E as a function of two fundamentals: the stock's required rate of return, r, which reflects its risk, and the expected (stable) dividend growth rate, g. The dividend payout ratio, $1 - b$, also enters into the expressions.

A particular value of the P/E is associated with a set of forecasts of the fundamentals and the dividend payout ratio. This value is the stock's **justified (fundamental) P/E** based on forecasted fundamentals (that is, the P/E justified by fundamentals). All else being equal, the higher the expected dividend growth rate or the lower the stock's required rate of return, the higher the stock's intrinsic value and the higher its justified P/E.

This intuition carries over to more-complex DCF models. Using any DCF model, all else being equal, justified P/E is

- inversely related to the stock's required rate of return and
- positively related to the growth rate(s) of future expected cash flows, however defined.

We illustrate the calculation of a justified forward P/E in Example 7.

EXAMPLE 7

Forward P/E Based on Fundamental Forecasts (1)

BP p.l.c. (London: BP) is one of the world's largest integrated oil producers. The company has continued to deal with litigation concerns surrounding its role in a 2010 drilling rig accident. Jan Unger, an energy analyst, forecasts a long-term earnings retention rate, b, for BP of 40% and a long-term growth rate of 3.5%. Given the significant legal uncertainties still facing BP shareholders, Unger estimates a required rate of return of 7.6%. Based on Unger's forecasts of fundamentals and Equation 1, BP's justified forward P/E is

$$\frac{P_0}{E_1} = \frac{1-b}{r-g} = \frac{1-0.40}{0.076-0.035} = 14.6.$$

When using a complex DCF model to value the stock (e.g., a model with varying growth rates and varying assumptions about dividends), the analyst may not be able to express the P/E as a function of fundamental, constant variables. In such cases, the analyst can still calculate a justified P/E by dividing the value per share (that results from a DCF model) by estimated EPS, as illustrated in Example 8. Approaches similar to this one can be used to develop other justified multiples.

EXAMPLE 8

Forward P/E Based on Fundamental Forecasts (2)

Toyota Motor Corporation is one of the world's largest vehicle manufacturers. The company's most recent fiscal year ended on 31 March 2019. In late June 2019, you are valuing Toyota stock, which closed at ¥6,688 on the previous day. You have used a free cash flow to equity (FCFE) model to value the company stock and have obtained a value of ¥6,980 for the stock. For ease of communication, you want to express your valuation in terms of a forward P/E based on your forecasted fiscal year 2020 EPS of ¥720. Toyota's fiscal year 2020 is from 1 April 2019 through 31 March 2020.

1. What is Toyota's justified P/E based on forecasted fundamentals?

Solution:

Value of the stock derived from FCFE = ¥6,980.

Forecasted 2014 EPS = ¥720.
¥6,980/¥720 = 9.7 is the justified forward P/E.

2. Based on a comparison of the current price of ¥6,688 with your estimated intrinsic value of ¥6,980, the stock appears to be undervalued by approximately 4%. Use your answer to Part 1 to state this evaluation in terms of P/Es.

Solution:

The justified P/E of 9.7 is about 4% higher than the forward P/E based on current market price, ¥6,688/¥720 = 9.3.

The next section illustrates another, but less commonly used, approach to relating price multiples to fundamentals.

Predicted P/E Based on Cross-Sectional Regression

A predicted P/E, which is conceptually similar to a justified P/E, can be estimated from cross-sectional regressions of P/E on the fundamentals believed to drive security valuation. Kisor and Whitbeck (1963) and Malkiel and Cragg (1970) pioneered this approach. Their studies measured P/Es for a group of stocks and the characteristics thought to determine P/E: growth rate in earnings, payout ratio, and a measure of volatility, such as standard deviation of earnings changes or beta. An analyst can conduct such cross-sectional regressions by using any set of explanatory variables considered to determine investment value; the analyst must bear in mind, however, potential distortions that can be introduced by multicollinearity among independent variables. Example 9 illustrates the prediction of P/E using cross-sectional regression.

EXAMPLE 9

Predicted P/E Based on a Cross-Sectional Regression

You are valuing a food company with a beta of 0.9, a dividend payout ratio of 0.45, and an earnings growth rate of 0.08. The estimated regression for a group of other stocks in the same industry is

Predicted P/E = 12.12 + (2.25 × DPR) − (0.20 × Beta) + (14.43 × EGR),

where DPR is the dividend payout ratio and EGR is the five-year earnings growth rate.

1. Based on this cross-sectional regression, what is the predicted P/E for the food company?

Solution:

Predicted P/E = 12.12 + (2.25 × 0.45) − (0.20 × 0.9) + (14.43 × 0.08) = 14.1. The predicted P/E is 14.1.

2. If the stock's actual trailing P/E is 18, is the stock fairly valued, overvalued, or undervalued?

Solution:

Because the predicted P/E of 14.1 is less than the actual P/E of 18, the stock appears to be overvalued. That is, it is selling at a higher multiple than is justified by its fundamentals.

A cross-sectional regression summarizes a large amount of data in a single equation and can provide a useful additional perspective on a valuation. It is not frequently used as a main tool, however, because it is subject to at least three limitations:

- The method captures valuation relationships only for the specific stock (or sample of stocks) over a particular time period. The predictive power of the regression for a different stock and different time period is not known.

- The regression coefficients and explanatory power of the regressions tend to change substantially over a number of years. The relationships between P/E and fundamentals may thus change over time. Empirical evidence suggests that the relationships between P/Es and such characteristics as earnings growth, dividend payout, and beta are not stable over time (Damodaran 2012). Furthermore, because distributions of multiples change over time, the predictive power of results from a regression at any point in time can be expected to diminish with the passage of time (Damodaran 2012).

- Because regressions based on this method are prone to the problem of multicollinearity (correlation within linear combinations of the independent variables), interpreting individual regression coefficients is difficult.

Overall, rather than examining the relationship between a stock's P/E multiple and economic variables, the bulk of capital market research examines the relationship between companies' stock prices (and returns on the stock) and explanatory variables, one of which is often earnings (or unexpected earnings). A classic example of such research is the Fama and French (1992) study showing that, used alone, a number of factors explained cross-sectional stock returns in the 1963–90 period; the factors were E/P, size, leverage, and the book-to-market multiples. When these variables were used in combination, however, size and book to market had explanatory power that absorbed the roles of the other variables in explaining cross-sectional stock returns. Research building on that study eventually resulted in the Fama–French three-factor model (with the factors of size, book to market, and beta). Another classic academic study providing evidence that accounting variables appear to have predictive power for stock returns is Lakonishok, Shleifer, and Vishny (1994), which also provided evidence that value strategies—buying stocks with low prices relative to earnings, book value, cash flow, and sales growth—produced superior five-year buy-and-hold returns in the 1968–90 period without involving greater fundamental risk than a strategy of buying growth stocks.

PRICE/EARNINGS: USING THE P/E IN VALUATION

4

- [ ] calculate and interpret the justified price-to-earnings ratio (P/E), price-to-book ratio (P/B), and price-to-sales ratio (P/S) for a stock, based on forecasted fundamentals
- [ ] calculate and interpret the P/E-to-growth (PEG) ratio and explain its use in relative valuation
- [ ] calculate and explain the use of price multiples in determining terminal value in a multistage discounted cash flow (DCF) model
- [ ] evaluate whether a stock is overvalued, fairly valued, or undervalued based on comparisons of multiples

The most common application of the P/E approach to valuation is to estimate the value of a company's stock by applying a benchmark multiple to the company's actual or forecasted earnings. An essentially equivalent approach is to compare a stock's actual price multiple with a benchmark value of the multiple. This section explores these comparisons for P/Es. Using any multiple in the method of comparables involves the following steps:

- Select and calculate the price multiple that will be used in the comparison.
- Select the comparison asset or assets and calculate the value of the multiple for the comparison asset(s). For a group of comparison assets, calculate a median or mean value of the multiple for the assets. The result in either case is the **benchmark value of the multiple**.
- Use the benchmark value of the multiple, possibly subjectively adjusted for differences in fundamentals, to estimate the value of a company's stock. (Equivalently, compare the subject stock's actual multiple with the benchmark value.)
- When feasible, assess whether differences between the estimated value of the company's stock and the current price of the company's stock are explained by differences in the fundamental determinants of the price multiple and modify conclusions about relative valuation accordingly. (An essentially equivalent approach is to assess whether differences between a company's actual multiple and the benchmark value of the multiple can be explained by differences in fundamentals.)

These bullet points provide the structure for this reading's presentation of the method of comparables. The first price multiple that will be used in the comparison is the P/E. Practitioners' choices for the comparison assets and the benchmark value of the P/E derived from these assets include the following:

- the average or median value of the P/E for the company's peer group of companies within an industry, including an average past value of the P/E for the stock relative to this peer group;
- the average or median value of the P/E for the company's industry or sector, including an average past value of the P/E for the stock relative to the industry or sector;
- the P/E for a representative equity index, including an average past value of the P/E for the stock relative to the equity index; and
- an average past value of the P/E for the stock.

To illustrate the first bullet point, the company's P/E (say, 15) may be compared to the median P/E for the peer companies currently (say, 10), or the ratio 15/10 = 1.5 may be compared to its average past value. The P/E of the most closely matched individual stock can also be used as a benchmark; because of averaging, however, using a group of stocks or an equity index is typically expected to generate less valuation error than using a single stock. We later illustrate a comparison with a single closely matched individual stock.

Economists and investment analysts have long attempted to group companies by similarities and differences in their business operations. A country's economy overall is typically grouped most broadly into **economic sectors** or large industry groupings. These groupings differ depending on the source of the financial information, and an analyst should be aware of differences among data sources. Classifications often attempt to group companies by what they supply (e.g., energy, consumer goods), by demand characteristics (e.g., consumer discretionary), or by financial market or economic "theme" (e.g., consumer cyclical, consumer noncyclical).

Two classification systems that are widely used in equity analysis are the Global Industry Classification System (GICS) sponsored by Standard & Poor's and MSCI and the Industrial Classification Benchmark (ICB). Many other classification schemes developed by commercial and governmental organizations and by academics are also in use.

The GICS structure assigns each company to one of 158 subindustries, an industry (69 in total), an industry group (24 in total), and an economic sector (11 in total: consumer discretionary, consumer staples, energy, financials, health care, industrials, information technology, materials, real estate, telecommunication services, and utilities). The assignment is made by a judgment as to the company's principal business activity, which is based primarily on sales. Because a company is classified on the basis of one business activity, a given company appears in just one group at each level of the classification. A classification ("industrial conglomerates") is available under the capital goods sector of industrials for companies that cannot be assigned to a principal business activity.

The ICB, like GICS, has four levels, but the terminology of ICB uses "sector" and "industry" in nearly opposite senses. The ICB is managed by FTSE Russell. At the bottom of the four levels are 173 subsectors, each of which belongs to one of 45 sectors; each sector belongs to one of 20 supersectors; and each supersector belongs to one of 11 industries at the highest level of classification. (The numbers in the groups were changed effective 1 July 2019; changes are made to the classification from time to time. See www.ftserussell.com/data/industry-classification-benchmark-icbwww.icbenchmark.com for updates.) The industries are technology, telecommunications, health care, financials, real estate, consumer discretionary, consumer staples, industrials, basic materials, energy, and utilities.

For these classification systems, analysts often choose the narrowest grouping (i.e., subindustry for GICS and subsector for ICB) as an appropriate starting point for comparison asset identification. To narrow the list of comparables in the subsector, an analyst might use information on company size (as measured by revenue or market value of equity) and information on the specific markets served.

Analysts should be aware that, although different organizations often group companies in a broadly similar fashion, sometimes they differ sharply. The lists of peer companies or competitors given by each of these organizations can be, as a result, quite distinct.

The comparable companies—selected by using any of the choices described previously—provide the basis for calculating a benchmark value of the multiple. In analyzing differences between the subject company's multiple and the benchmark value of the multiple, financial ratio analysis serves as a useful tool. Financial ratios can point out

- a company's ability to meet short-term financial obligations (liquidity ratios);
- the efficiency with which assets are being used to generate sales (asset turnover ratios);
- the use of debt in financing the business (leverage ratios);
- the degree to which fixed charges, such as interest on debt, are being met by earnings or cash flow (coverage ratios); and
- profitability (profitability ratios).

With this understanding of terms in hand, we turn to using the method of comparables. We begin with cross-sectional P/Es derived from industry peer groups and move to P/Es derived from comparison assets that are progressively less closely matched to the stock. We then turn to using historical P/Es—that is, P/Es derived from the company's own history. Finally, we sketch how both fundamentals- and comparables-driven models for P/Es can be used to calculate the terminal value in a multistage DCF valuation.

Peer-Company Multiples

Companies operating in the same industry as the subject company (i.e., its peer group) are frequently used as comparison assets. The advantage of using a peer group is that the constituent companies are typically similar in their business mix to the company being analyzed. This approach is consistent with the idea underlying the method of comparables—that similar assets should sell at similar prices. The subject stock's P/E is compared with the median or mean P/E for the peer group to arrive at a relative valuation. Equivalently, multiplying the benchmark P/E by the company's EPS provides an estimate of the stock's value that can be compared with the stock's market price. The value estimated in this way represents an estimate of intrinsic value if the comparison assets are efficiently (fairly) priced.

In practice, analysts often find that the stock being valued has some significant differences from the median or mean fundamental characteristics of the comparison assets. In applying the method of comparables, analysts usually attempt to judge whether differences from the benchmark value of the multiple can be explained by differences in the fundamental factors believed to influence the multiple. The following relationships for P/E hold, all else being equal:

- If the subject stock has higher-than-average (or higher-than-median) expected earnings growth, a higher P/E than the benchmark P/E is justified.
- If the subject stock has higher-than-average (or higher-than-median) risk (operating or financial), a lower P/E than the benchmark P/E is justified.

Another perspective on these two points is that for a group of stocks with comparable relative valuations, the stock with the greatest expected growth rate (or the lowest risk) is, all else equal, the most attractively valued. Example 10 illustrates a simple comparison of a company with its peer group.

EXAMPLE 10

A Simple Peer-Group Comparison

As a telecommunication industry analyst at a brokerage firm, you are valuing Verizon Communications, Inc., a telecommunication company. The valuation metric that you have selected is the trailing P/E. You are evaluating the P/E using the median trailing P/E of peer-group companies as the benchmark value. According to GICS, Verizon is in the telecommunication services sector and, within it, the integrated telecommunication services subindustry. Exhibit 5 presents the relevant data.

Exhibit 5: Trailing P/Es of Telecommunication Services Companies

Company	Trailing P/E
AT&T	13.20
Comcast Corporation	16.23
CenturyLink	NMF
China Telecom	13.14
Charter Communications Corp.	70.67

Company	Trailing P/E
Verizon Communications	15.03
Windstream Holdings	19.01
Mean*	24.55
Median	15.03

Mean, six firms excluding CenturyLink.

NMF = not meaningful.

Based on the data in Exhibit 5, address the following:

1. Given the definition of the benchmark stated above, determine the most appropriate benchmark value of the P/E for Verizon.

Solution:

As stated earlier, the use of median values mitigates the effect of outliers on the valuation conclusion. In this instance, the P/Es for CenturyLink and Charter Communications are clearly outliers. Therefore, the median trailing P/E for the group, 15.03, is more appropriate than the mean trailing P/E of 24.55 for use as the benchmark value of the P/E. Note that when a group includes an odd number of companies, as here, the median value will be the middle value when the values are ranked (in either ascending or descending order). When the group includes an even number of companies, the median value will be the average of the two middle values.

2. State whether Verizon is relatively fairly valued, relatively overvalued, or relatively undervalued, assuming no differences in fundamentals among the peer group companies. Justify your answer.

Solution:

If you assume no differences in fundamentals among the peer group companies, Verizon appears to be fairly valued because its P/E is identical to the median P/E of 15.03.

3. Identify the stocks in this group of telecommunication companies that appear to be relatively undervalued when the median trailing P/E is used as a benchmark. Explain what further analysis might be appropriate to confirm your answer.

Solution:

AT&T, China Telecom, and CenturyLink appear to be undervalued relative to their peers because their trailing P/Es are lower than the median P/E. Verizon appears to be relatively fairly valued because its P/E equals the median P/E. Charter Communications, Comcast Corporation, and Windstream appear to be overvalued.

To confirm this valuation conclusion, you should look at other metrics. One issue for this particular industry is that earnings may differ significantly from cash flow. These companies invest considerable amounts of money to build out their networks—whether it be landlines or increasing bandwidth capacity for mobile users. Because telecommunication service providers are frequently required to take large noncash charges on their infrastructure, reported earnings are typically very volatile and frequently much lower than cash flow.

A metric that appears to address the impact of earnings growth on P/E is the P/E-to-growth (PEG) ratio. The **PEG ratio** is calculated as the stock's P/E divided by the expected earnings growth rate (in percentage terms). The ratio, in effect, is a calculation of a stock's P/E per percentage point of expected growth. Stocks with lower PEG ratios are more attractive than stocks with higher PEG ratios, all else being equal. Some consider that a PEG ratio less than 1 is an indicator of an attractive value level. The PEG ratio is useful but must be used with care for several reasons:

- The PEG ratio assumes a linear relationship between P/E and growth. The model for P/E in terms of the DDM shows that, in theory, the relationship is not linear.

- The PEG ratio does not factor in differences in risk, an important determinant of P/E.

- The PEG ratio does not account for differences in the duration of growth. For example, dividing P/Es by short-term (five-year) growth forecasts may not capture differences in long-term growth prospects.

The way in which fundamentals can add insight to comparables is illustrated in Example 11.

EXAMPLE 11

A Peer-Group Comparison Modified by Fundamentals

Continuing with the valuation of telecommunication service providers, you gather information on selected fundamentals related to risk (beta), profitability (five-year earnings growth forecast), and valuation (trailing and forward P/Es). Analysts may also use other measures of risk in comparables work. These data are reported in Exhibit 6, which lists companies in order of descending earnings growth forecast. The use of forward P/Es recognizes that differences in trailing P/Es could be the result of transitory effects on earnings.

Exhibit 6: Valuation Data for Telecommunication Services Companies (as of 11 September 2013)

Company	Trailing P/E	Forward P/E	Five-Year EPS Growth Forecast	Forward PEG Ratio	Beta
AT&T	13.20	9.36	1.83%	7.20	0.56
Comcast Corporation	16.23	12.92	11.20	1.45	1.09
CenturyLink	NMF	8.89	8.52	1.04	0.81
China Telecom	13.14	10.31	6.90	1.90	0.81
Charter Communications	70.67	30.32	45.30	1.56	1.24
Verizon	15.03	11.99	2.51	5.99	0.50
Windstream Holdings	19.01	16.29	3.19	5.96	0.45
Mean	24.55	14.30	11.30	3.59	0.78
Median	15.03	11.99	6.90	1.90	0.78

Notes: NMF = not meaningful. The trailing P/E for CenturyLink is a negative number, which would result in a P/E that is not meaningful.

Source: www.finviz.com.

Based on the data in Exhibit 6, answer the following questions:

1. In Example 10, Part 3, AT&T, China Telecom, and CenturyLink were identified as possibly relatively undervalued compared with the peer group as a whole, and Verizon was identified as relatively fairly valued. What does the additional information relating to profitability and risk suggest about the relative valuation of the stocks in Exhibit 6?

Solution:

Among the three companies identified as underpriced (based on their low trailing P/Es), CenturyLink has the highest five-year EPS growth forecast and the lowest PEG ratio. AT&T and China Telecom have lower growth rates and higher PEG ratios than CenturyLink. Among the other companies in Exhibit 6, Comcast and Charter Communications had the highest EPS growth forecasts and the second and third lowest PEG ratios. The three stocks with the lowest trailing P/Es (AT&T, CenturyLink, and China Telecom) also had the lowest forward P/Es.

The two stocks with the highest growth forecasts, Comcast and Charter Communications, also had the highest betas, which is consistent with studies that have shown that growth stocks tend to have higher beta values than those of value stocks. Based on the high trailing and forward P/Es, it appears that investors in Charter Communications have high expectations concerning the company's future earnings potential. However, the high beta value is likely reflective of the uncertainty surrounding the earnings forecast and the possibility that actual future earnings may be less than expected.

Some analysts consider a PEG ratio below 1 to be a signal of undervaluation. However, one limitation of the PEG ratio is that it does not account for the overall growth rate of an industry or the economy as a whole. Hence, it is typically a good idea for an investor to compare a stock's PEG ratio to an average or median PEG ratio for the industry, as well as the entire market, to get an accurate sense of how fairly valued a stock is. The PEG ratio of CenturyLink is not below 1, but it is significantly lower than the PEG ratios for the other telecommunication companies—further indicating that this company is relatively undervalued.

2. AT&T has a consensus year-ahead EPS forecast of $3.63. Suppose the median P/E of 11.99 for the peer group is subjectively adjusted upward to 13.00 to reflect AT&T's superior profitability and below-average risk. Estimate AT&T's intrinsic value.

Solution:

$3.63 × 13.0 = $47.19 is an estimate of intrinsic value.

3. AT&T's current market price is $33.98. State whether AT&T appears to be fairly valued, overvalued, or undervalued when compared with the intrinsic value estimated in the answer to Part 2.

Solution:

Because the estimated intrinsic value of $47.19 is greater than the current market price of $33.98, AT&T appears to be undervalued by the market on an absolute basis.

In Problem 2 of the Example 11, a peer median P/E of 11.99 was subjectively adjusted upward to 13.00. Depending on the context, the justification for using the specific value of 13.00 as the relevant benchmark rather than some other value could be raised. To avoid that issue, one way to express the analysis and results would be as follows: Given its modest growth and lower risk, AT&T should trade at a premium to the median P/E (11.99) of its peer group. Of course, this is a bullish outlook for AT&T because its forward P/E is only 9.36.

Analysts frequently compare a stock's multiple with the median or mean value of the multiple for larger sets of assets than a company's peer group. The next sections examine comparisons with these larger groups.

Industry and Sector Multiples

Median or mean P/Es for industries and for economic sectors are frequently used in relative valuations. Although median P/Es have the advantage that they are insensitive to outliers, some databases report only mean values of multiples for industries.

The mechanics of using industry multiples are identical to those used for peer-group comparisons. Taking account of relevant fundamental information, we compare a stock's multiple with the median or mean multiple for the company's industry.

Using industry and sector data can help an analyst explore whether the peer-group comparison assets are themselves appropriately priced. Comparisons with broader segments of the economy can potentially provide insight about whether the relative valuation based on comparables accurately reflects intrinsic value. For example, Value Line reports a relative P/E that is calculated as the stock's current P/E divided by the median P/E of all issues under Value Line review. The less closely matched the stock is to the comparison assets, the more dissimilarities are likely to be present to complicate the analyst's interpretation of the data. Arguably, however, the larger the number of comparison assets, the more likely that mispricings of individual assets cancel out. In some cases, we may be able to draw inferences about an industry or sector overall. For example, during the 1998–2000 internet bubble, comparisons of an individual internet stock's value with the overall market would have been more likely to point to overvaluation than comparisons of relative valuation only among internet stocks.

Overall Market Multiple

Although the logic of the comparables approach suggests the use of industry and peer companies as comparison assets, equity market indexes also have been used as comparison assets. The mechanics of using the method of comparables do not change in such an approach, although the user should be cognizant of any size differences between the subject stock and the stocks in the selected index.

The question of whether the overall market is fairly priced has captured analyst interest throughout the entire history of investing. We mentioned one approach to market valuation (using a DDM) in an earlier reading.

Example 12 shows a valuation comparison to the broad equity market on the basis of P/E.

EXAMPLE 12

Valuation Relative to the Market

You are analyzing three large-cap US stock issues with approximately equal earnings growth prospects and risk. As one step in your analysis, you have decided to check valuations relative to the S&P 500 Index. Exhibit 7 provides the data.

Exhibit 7: Comparison with an Index Multiple (Prices and EPS in US Dollars; as of 28 June 2019)				
Measure	Stock A	Stock B	Stock C	S&P 500
Current price	23	50	80	2,941.76
P/E	15.2	30.0	15.2	21.8
Five-year average P/E (as a % of S&P 500 P/E)	80	120	105	

Source: www.us.spindices.com for S&P 500 data.

Based only on the data in Exhibit 7, address the following:

1. Explain which stock appears relatively undervalued when compared with the S&P 500.

Solution:

Stock C appears to be undervalued when compared to the S&P 500. Stock A and Stock C are both trading at a P/E of 15.2 relative to trailing earnings, versus a P/E of 21.8 for the S&P 500. But the last row of Exhibit 7 indicates that Stock A has historically traded at a P/E reflecting a 20% discount to the S&P 500 (which, based on the current level of the S&P 500, would imply a P/E of $0.8 \times 21.8 = 17.4$). In contrast, Stock C has usually traded at a premium to the S&P 500 P/E but now trades at a discount to it. Stock B is trading at a high P/E, even higher than its historical relationship to the S&P 500's P/E ($1.2 \times 21.8 = 16.1$).

2. State the assumption underlying the use of five-year average P/E comparisons.

Solution:

Using historical relative-value information in investment decisions relies on an assumption of stable underlying economic relationships (that is, that the past is relevant for the future).

Because many equity indexes are market-capitalization weighted, financial databases often report the average market P/E with the individual P/Es weighted by the company's market capitalization. As a consequence, the largest constituent stocks heavily influence the calculated P/E. If P/Es differ systematically by market capitalization, however, differences in a company's P/E multiple from the index's multiple may be explained by that effect. Therefore, particularly for stocks in the middle-cap range, the analyst should favor using the median P/E for the index as the benchmark value of the multiple.

As with other comparison assets, the analyst may be interested in whether the equity index itself is efficiently priced. A common comparison is the index's P/E in relation to historical values. Siegel (2014) noted that recent P/Es were more than twice as high as the average P/E for US stocks over a long time period. Potential justifications for a higher-than-average P/E include lower-than-average interest rates and/or higher-than-average expected growth rates. An alternative hypothesis in a situation (historical high P/Es) is that the market as a whole is overvalued or, alternatively, that earnings are abnormally low.

The time frame for comparing average multiples is important. For example, at the end of the fourth quarter of 2008, the P/E for the S&P 500 was 60.70. That value is much higher than the 15.8 historical average since 1935. From 2006 through 2018, the highest quarterly P/E was 122.4 (30 June 2009) and the lowest was 13.0 (30 September 2011), and the quarterly P/E ranged between 18.9 and 24.1 over the five years ending in 2018. The use of past data relies on the key assumption that the past (sometimes the distant past) is relevant for the future.

We end this section with an introduction to valuation of the equity market itself on the basis of P/E. A well-known comparison is the earnings yield (the E/P) on a group of stocks and the interest yield on a bond. The so-called Fed model, based on a paper written by three analysts at the US Federal Reserve, predicts the return on the S&P 500 on the basis of the relationship between forecasted earnings yields and yields on bonds (Lander, Orphanides, and Douvogiannis 1997). Example 13 illustrates the Fed model.

EXAMPLE 13

The Fed Model

One of the main drivers of P/E for the market as a whole is the level of interest rates. The inverse relationship between value and interest rates can be seen from the expression of P/E in terms of fundamentals, because the risk-free rate is one component of the required rate of return that is inversely related to value. The Fed model relates the earnings yield on the S&P 500 to the yield to maturity on 10-year US Treasury bonds. As we have defined it, the earnings yield (E/P) is the inverse of the P/E; the Fed model uses expected earnings for the next 12 months in calculating the ratio.

Based on the premise that the two yields should be closely linked, on average, the trading rule based on the Fed model considers the stock market to be overvalued when the market's current earnings yield is less than the 10-year Treasury bond (T-bond) yield. The intuition is that when risk-free T-bonds offer a yield that is higher than that of stocks—which are a riskier investment—stocks are an unattractive investment.

According to the model, the justified or fair value P/E for the S&P 500 is the reciprocal of the 10-year T-bond yield. As of 28 December 2018, according to the model, with a 10-year T-bond yielding 2.72%, the justified P/E on the S&P 500 was 1/0.0272 = 36.8. The trailing P/E based for 31 December 2018 was 18.9.

We previously presented an expression for the justified P/E in terms of the Gordon growth model. That expression indicates that the expected growth rate in dividends or earnings is a variable that enters into the intrinsic value of a stock (or an index of stocks). A concern in considering the Fed model is that this variable is lacking in the model. Please note that the earnings yield is, in fact, the expected rate of return on a no-growth stock (under the assumption that price equals value). With the PVGO (present value of growth opportunities) and setting price equal to value, we obtain

$P_0 = E_1/r + \text{PVGO}$. Setting the present value of growth opportunities equal to zero and rearranging, we obtain $r = E_1/P_0$. Example 14 presents a valuation model for the equity market that incorporates the expected growth rate in earnings.

EXAMPLE 14

The Yardeni Model

Yardeni (2000) developed a model that incorporates the expected growth rate in earnings—a variable that is missing in the Fed model. This model is presented as one example of more-complex models than the Fed model. Yardeni's model is

$$CEY = CBY - b \times LTEG + \text{Residual},$$

where CEY is the current earnings yield on the market index, CBY is the current Moody's Investors Service A rated corporate bond yield, and LTEG is the consensus five-year earnings growth rate forecast for the market index. The coefficient b measures the weight the market gives to five-year earnings projections. (Recall that the expression for P/E in terms of the Gordon growth model is based on the long-term sustainable growth rate and that five-year forecasts of growth may not be sustainable.) Although CBY incorporates a default risk premium relative to T-bonds, it does not incorporate an equity risk premium per se. For example, in the bond yield plus risk premium model for the cost of equity, an analyst typically adds 300–400 basis points to a corporate bond yield.

Yardeni found that, prior to publication of the model in 2000, the coefficient b had averaged 0.10. In recent years, he has reported valuations based on growth weights of 0.10, 0.20, and 0.25. Noting that CEY is E/P and taking the inverse of both sides of this equation, Yardeni obtained the following expression for the justified P/E on the market:

$$\frac{P}{E} = \frac{1}{CBY - b \times LTEG}.$$

Consistent with valuation theory, in Yardeni's model, higher current corporate bond yields imply a lower justified P/E and higher expected long-term growth results in a higher justified P/E.

Critics of the Fed model point out that it ignores the equity risk premium (Stimes and Wilcox 2011). The model also inadequately reflects the effects of inflation and incorrectly incorporates the differential effects of inflation on earnings and interest payments (e.g., Siegel 2014). Some empirical evidence has shown that prediction of future returns based on simple P/E outperforms prediction based on the Fed model's differential with bond yields (for the US market, see Arnott and Asness 2003; for nine other markets, see Aubert and Giot 2007).

Another drawback to the Fed model is that the relationship between interest rates and earnings yields is not a linear one. This drawback is most noticeable at low interest rates; Example 13 provided an example of this limitation of the model. Furthermore, small changes in interest rates and/or corporate profits can significantly alter the justified P/E predicted by the model. Overall, an analyst should look to the Fed model only as one tool for calibrating the overall value of the stock market and should avoid overreliance on the model as a predictive method, particularly in periods of low inflation and low interest rates.

Own Historical P/E

As an alternative to comparing a stock's valuation with that of other stocks, one traditional approach uses past values of the stock's own P/E as a basis for comparison. Underlying this approach is the idea that a stock's P/E may regress to historical average levels.

An analyst can obtain a benchmark value in a variety of ways with this approach. Value Line reports as a "P/E median" a rounded average of four middle values of a stock's average annual P/E for the previous 10 years. The five-year average trailing P/E is another reasonable metric. In general, trailing P/Es are more commonly used than forward P/Es in such computations. In addition to "higher" and "lower" comparisons with this benchmark, justified price based on this approach may be calculated as follows:

$$\text{Justified price} = (\text{Benchmark value of own historical P/Es}) \times (\text{Most recent EPS}). \tag{3}$$

Normalized EPS replaces most recent EPS in this equation when EPS is negative and whenever otherwise appropriate.

Example 15 illustrates the use of past values of the stock's own P/E as a basis for reaching a valuation conclusion.

EXAMPLE 15

Valuation Relative to Own Historical P/Es

As of June 2019, you are valuing Honda Motor Company, among the market leaders in Japan's auto manufacturing industry. You are applying the method of comparables using Honda's five-year average P/E as the benchmark value of the multiple. Exhibit 8 presents the data.

Exhibit 8: Historical P/Es for Honda Motor Company						
2018	**2017**	**2016**	**2015**	**2014**	**Mean**	**Median**
6.9	10.0	10.9	10.8	9.7	9.7	10.0

Sources: The Value Line Investment Survey for average annual P/Es; calculations for mean and median P/Es.

1. State a benchmark value for Honda's P/E.

Solution:

From Exhibit 8, the benchmark value based on the median P/E value is 10.0 and based on the mean P/E value is 9.7.

2. Given forecasted EPS for fiscal year 2019 (ended 31 December) of ¥381.93, calculate and interpret a justified price for Honda.

Solution:

The calculation is 10.0 × ¥381.93 = ¥3,819 when the median-based benchmark P/E is used and 9.7 × ¥381.93 = ¥3,704 when the mean-based benchmark P/E is used.

3. Compare the justified price with the stock's recent price of ¥2,837.

Solution:

The stock's recent price is 26.2% (calculated as 2,817/3,819 − 1) less than the justified price of the stock based on median historical P/E but 23.9% (calculated as 2,817/3,704 − 1) less than the justified price of the stock based on mean historical P/E. The stock may be undervalued, and misvaluation, if present, appears significant.

In using historical P/Es for comparisons, analysts should be alert to the impact on P/E levels of changes in a company's business mix and leverage over time. If the company's business has changed substantially within the time period being examined, the method based on a company's own past P/Es is prone to error. Shifts in the use of financial leverage may also impair comparability based on average own past P/E.

Changes in the interest rate environment and economic fundamentals over different time periods can be another limitation to using an average past value of P/E for a stock as a benchmark. A specific caution is that inflation can distort the economic meaning of reported earnings. Consequently, if the inflationary environments reflected in current P/E and average own past P/E are different, a comparison between the two P/Es may be misleading. Changes in a company's ability to pass through cost inflation to higher prices over time may also affect the reliability of such comparisons, as illustrated in Example 16 in the next section.

P/Es in Cross-Country Comparisons

When comparing the P/Es of companies in different countries, the analyst should be aware of the following effects that may influence the comparison:

- The effect on EPS of differences in accounting standards: Comparisons (without analyst adjustments) among companies preparing financial statements based on different accounting standards may be distorted. Such distortions may occur when, for example, the accounting standards differ as to permissible recognition of revenues, expenses, or gains.

- The effect on market-wide benchmarks of differences in their macroeconomic contexts: Differences in macroeconomic contexts may distort comparisons of benchmark P/E levels among companies operating in different markets.

A specific case of the second bullet point is differences in inflation rates and in the ability of companies to pass through inflation in their costs in the form of higher prices to their customers. For two companies with the same pass-through ability, the company operating in the environment with higher inflation will have a lower justified P/E; if the inflation rates are equal but pass-through rates differ, the justified P/E should be lower for the company with the lower pass-through rate. Example 16 provides analysis in support of these conclusions.

EXAMPLE 16

An Analysis of P/Es and Inflation

Assume a company with no real earnings growth, such that its earnings growth can result only from inflation, will pay out all its earnings as dividends. Based on the Gordon (constant growth) DDM, the value of a share is

$$P_0 = \frac{E_0(1+I)}{r-I},$$

where

P_0 = current price, which is substituted for the intrinsic value, V_0, for purposes of analyzing a justified P/E

E_0 = current EPS, which is substituted for current dividends per share, D_0, because the assumption in this example is that all earnings are paid out as dividends

I = rate of inflation, which is substituted for expected growth, g, because of the assumption in this example that the company's only growth is from inflation

r = required return

Suppose the company has the ability to pass on some or all inflation to its customers, and let λ represent the percentage of inflation in costs that the company can pass through to earnings. The company's earnings growth may then be expressed as λI, and the equation becomes

$$P_0 = \frac{E_0(1 + \lambda I)}{r - \lambda I} = \frac{E_1}{r - \lambda I}.$$

Now, introduce a real rate of return, defined here as r minus I and represented as ρ. The value of a share and the justified forward P/E can now be expressed, respectively, as follows:

$$P_0 = \frac{E_1}{\rho + (1 - \lambda)I},$$

and

$$\frac{P_0}{E_1} = \frac{1}{\rho + (1 - \lambda)I}.$$

(Note that the denominator of this equation is derived from the previous equation as follows: $r - \lambda I = r - I + I - I\lambda = (r - I) + (1 - \lambda)I = \rho + (1 - \lambda)I$.

If a company can pass through all inflation, such that $\lambda = 1$ (100%), then the P/E is equal to $1/\rho$. But if the company can pass through no inflation, such that $\lambda = 0$, then the P/E is equal to $1/(\rho + I)$—that is, $1/r$.

You are analyzing two companies, Company M and Company P. The real rate of return required on the shares of Company M and Company P is 3% per year. Using the analytic framework provided, address the following:

1. Suppose both Company M and Company P can pass through 75% of cost increases. Cost inflation is 6% for Company M but only 2% for Company P.

   A. Estimate the justified P/E for each company.

   B. Interpret your answer to Part A.

Solution:

   A. For Company M, $\dfrac{1}{0.03 + (1 - 0.75)0.06} = 22.2$.

   For Company P, $\dfrac{1}{0.03 + (1 - 0.75)0.02} = 28.6$.

   B. With less than 100% cost pass-through, the justified P/E is inversely related to the inflation rate.

2. Suppose both Company M and Company P face 6% a year inflation. Company M can pass through 90% of cost increases, but Company P can pass through only 70%.

   A. Estimate the justified P/E for each company.

   B. Interpret your answer to Part A.

Solution:

A. For Company M, $\dfrac{1}{0.03 + (1 - 0.90)\,0.06} = 27.8$.

For Company P, $\dfrac{1}{0.03 + (1 - 0.70)\,0.06} = 20.8$.

B. For equal inflation rates, the company with the higher pass-through rate has a higher justified P/E.

Note that this example follows the analysis of Solnik and McLeavey (2004, pp. 289–290).

Example 16 illustrates that with less than 100% cost pass-through, the justified P/E is inversely related to the inflation rate (with complete cost pass-through, the justified P/E should not be affected by inflation). The higher the inflation rate, the greater the impact of incomplete cost pass-through on P/E. From Example 16, one can also infer that the higher the inflation rate, the more serious the effect on justified P/E of a pass-through rate that is less than 100%.

Using P/Es to Obtain Terminal Value in Multistage Dividend Discount Models

In using a DDM to value a stock, whether applying a multistage model or modeling within a spreadsheet (forecasting specific cash flows individually up to some horizon), estimation of the terminal value of the stock is important. The key condition that must be satisfied is that terminal value reflects earnings growth that the company can sustain in the long run. Analysts frequently use price multiples—in particular, P/Es and P/Bs—to estimate terminal value. We can call such multiples **terminal price multiples**. Choices for the terminal multiple, with a terminal P/E multiple used as the example, include the following two types:

Terminal price multiple based on fundamentals: As illustrated earlier, analysts can restate the Gordon growth model as a multiple by, for example, dividing both sides of the model by EPS. For terminal P/E multiples, dividing both sides of the Gordon growth model by EPS at time n, where n is the point in time at which the final stage begins (i.e., E_n), gives a trailing terminal price multiple; dividing both sides by EPS at time $n + 1$ (i.e., E_{n+1}) gives a leading terminal price multiple. Of course, an analyst can use the Gordon growth model to estimate terminal value and need not go through the process of deriving a terminal price multiple and then multiplying by the same value of the fundamental to estimate terminal value. Because of their familiarity, however, multiples may be useful in communicating an estimate of terminal value.

Terminal price multiple based on comparables: Analysts have used various choices for the benchmark value, including:

- median industry P/E,
- average industry P/E, and
- average of own past P/Es.

Having selected a terminal multiple, the expression for terminal value when using a terminal P/E multiple is

V_n = Benchmark value of trailing terminal P/E × E_n

or

V_n = Benchmark value of forward terminal P/E × E_{n+1}, where V_n = Terminal value at time n.

The use of a comparables approach has the strength that it is entirely grounded in market data. In contrast, the Gordon growth model calls for specific estimates (the required rate of return, the dividend payout ratio, and the expected mature growth rate), and the model's output is very sensitive to changes in those estimates. A possible disadvantage to the comparables approach is that when the benchmark value reflects mispricing (over- or undervaluation), so will the estimate of terminal value. Example 17 illustrates the use of P/Es and the Gordon growth model to estimate terminal value.

EXAMPLE 17

Using P/Es and the Gordon Growth Model to Value the Mature Growth Phase

As an energy analyst, you are valuing the stock of an oil exploration company. You have projected earnings and dividends three years out (to $t = 3$), and you have gathered the following data and estimates:

- Required rate of return = 0.10.
- Average dividend payout rate for mature companies in the market = 0.45.
- Industry average ROE = 0.13.
- E_3 = $3.00.
- Industry average P/E = 14.3.

On the basis of this information, carry out the following:

1. Calculate terminal value based on comparables, using your estimated industry average P/E as the benchmark.

Solution:

V_n = Benchmark value of P/E × E_n = 14.3 × $3.00 = $42.90.

2. Contrast your answer in Part 1 to an estimate of terminal value using the Gordon growth model.

Solution:

Recall that the Gordon growth model expresses intrinsic value, V, as the present value of dividends divided by the required rate of return, r, minus the growth rate, g: $V_0 = D_0(1 + g)/(r - g)$. Here we are estimating terminal value, so the relevant expression is $V_n = D_n(1 + g)/(r - g)$. You would estimate that the dividend at $t = 3$ will equal earnings in Year 3 of $3.00 times the average payout ratio of 0.45, or D_n = $3.00 × 0.45 = $1.35. Recall also the sustainable growth rate expression—that is, $g = b ×$ ROE, where b is the retention rate and equivalent to 1 minus the dividend payout ratio. In this example, $b = (1 - 0.45) = 0.55$, and you can use ROE = 0.13 (the industry average). Therefore, $g = b ×$ ROE = 0.55 × 0.13 = 0.0715. Given the required rate of return of 0.10, you obtain the estimate V_n = ($1.35)(1 + 0.0715)/(0.10 − 0.0715) = $50.76. In this example, therefore, the Gordon growth model estimate of terminal value is 18.3% higher than the estimate based on comparables calculated in Part 1 (i.e., 0.1832 = $50.76/$42.90 − 1).

PRICE/BOOK VALUE

5

☐ | calculate and interpret a justified price multiple

☐ | describe rationales for and possible drawbacks to using alternative price multiples and dividend yield in valuation

☐ | calculate and interpret alternative price multiples and dividend yield

☐ | describe fundamental factors that influence alternative price multiples and dividend yield

☐ | calculate and interpret the justified price-to-earnings ratio (P/E), price-to-book ratio (P/B), and price-to-sales ratio (P/S) for a stock, based on forecasted fundamentals

☐ | evaluate a stock by the method of comparables and explain the importance of fundamentals in using the method of comparables

☐ | evaluate whether a stock is overvalued, fairly valued, or undervalued based on comparisons of multiples

The ratio of market price per share to book value per share (P/B), like P/E, has a long history of use in valuation practice. According to the 2012 BofA Merrill Lynch Institutional Factor Survey, 53% of respondents considered P/B when making investment decisions.

In the P/E multiple, the measure of value (EPS) in the denominator is a flow variable relating to the income statement. In contrast, the measure of value in the P/B's denominator (book value per share) is a stock or level variable coming from the balance sheet. (*Book* refers to the fact that the measurement of value comes from accounting records or books, in contrast to market value.) Intuitively, therefore, we note that book value per share attempts to represent, on a per-share basis, the investment that common shareholders have made in the company. To define book value per share more precisely, we first find **shareholders' equity** (total assets minus total liabilities). Because our purpose is to value common stock (as opposed to valuing the company as a whole), we subtract from shareholders' equity any value attributable to preferred stock to obtain common shareholders' equity, or the **book value of equity** (often called simply book value). Dividing book value by the number of common stock shares outstanding, we obtain **book value per share**, the denominator in P/B.

In the remainder of this section, we present the reasons analysts have offered for using P/B and possible drawbacks to its use. We then illustrate the calculation of P/B and discuss the fundamental factors that drive P/B. We end the section by showing the use of P/B based on the method of comparables.

Analysts have offered several rationales for the use of P/B; some specifically compare P/B with P/E:

- Because book value is a cumulative balance sheet amount, book value is generally positive even when EPS is zero or negative. An analyst can generally use P/B when EPS is zero or negative, whereas P/E based on a zero or negative EPS is not meaningful.

- Because book value per share is more stable than EPS, P/B may be more meaningful than P/E when EPS is abnormally high or low or is highly variable.

- As a measure of net asset value per share, book value per share has been viewed as appropriate for valuing companies composed chiefly of liquid assets, such as finance, investment, insurance, and banking institutions

(Wild, Bernstein, and Subramanyam 2001, p. 233). For such companies, book values of assets may approximate market values. When information on individual corporate assets is available, analysts may adjust reported book values to market values where they differ.

- Book value has also been used in the valuation of companies that are not expected to continue as a going concern (Martin 1998, p. 22).

- Differences in P/Bs may be related to differences in long-run average returns, according to empirical research (Bodie, Kane, and Marcus 2008).

Possible drawbacks of P/Bs in practice include the following:

- Assets in addition to those recognized in financial statements may be critical operating factors. For example, in many service companies, **human capital**—the value of skills and knowledge possessed by the workforce—is more important than physical capital as an operating factor, but it is not reflected as an asset on the balance sheet. Similarly, the good reputation that a company develops by consistently providing high-quality goods and services is not reflected as an asset on the balance sheet.

- P/B may be misleading as a valuation indicator when the levels of assets used by the companies under examination differ significantly. Such differences may reflect differences in business models.

- Accounting effects on book value may compromise how useful book value is as a measure of the shareholders' investment in the company. In general, intangible assets that are generated internally (as opposed to being acquired) are not shown as assets on a company's balance sheet. For example, companies account for advertising and marketing as expenses, so the value of internally generated brands, which are created and maintained by advertising and marketing activities, do not appear as assets on a company's balance sheet under IFRS or US GAAP. Similarly, when accounting standards require that research and development (R&D) expenditures be treated as expenses, the value of internally developed patents does not appear as assets. Certain R&D expenditures can be capitalized, although rules vary among accounting standards. Accounting effects such as these may impair the comparability of P/B among companies and countries unless appropriate analyst adjustments are made.

- Book value reflects the reported value of assets and liabilities. Some assets and liabilities, such as some financial instruments, may be reported at fair value as of the balance sheet date; other assets, such as property, plant, and equipment, are generally reported at historical cost, net of accumulated depreciation, amortization, depletion, and/or impairment. It is important to examine the notes to the financial statements to identify how assets and liabilities are measured and reported. For assets measured at net historical cost, inflation and technological change can eventually result in significant divergence between the book value and the market value of assets. As a result, book value per share often does not accurately reflect the value of shareholders' investments. When comparing companies, significant differences in the average age of assets may lessen the comparability of P/Bs.

- Share repurchases or issuances may distort historical comparisons.

As an example of the effects of share repurchases, consider Colgate-Palmolive Company. As of 13 September 2013, Colgate-Palmolive's trailing P/E and P/B were, respectively, 24.84 and 36.01. Five years earlier, Colgate-Palmolive's trailing P/E and P/B were 23.55 and 15.94. In other words, the company's P/E widened by 5.5% (= 24.84/23.55 − 1) while its P/B widened by 125.9% (= 36.01/15.94 − 1). The majority of the difference in changes in these two multiples can be attributed to the substantial amount of shares that Colgate-Palmolive repurchased over those five years, as reflected by book value (i.e., total common equity) declining from $2.48 billion as of 30 June 2008 to $1.53 billion as of 30 June 2013. Because of those share repurchases, Colgate-Palmolive's book value declined at an annual rate of 9.2%. In summary, when a company repurchases shares at a price higher than the current book value per share, it lowers the overall book value per share for the company. All else being equal, the effect is to make the stock appear more expensive if the current P/B is compared to its historical values.

Example 18 illustrates another potential limitation to using P/B in valuation.

EXAMPLE 18

Differences in Business Models Reflected in Differences in P/Bs

The US banking industry has a wide range of P/Bs. Much of these differences in P/Bs can be attributed to differences in company-specific business models. Exhibit 9 presents P/Bs for three major US banks as of 31 December 2018.

Exhibit 9: P/Bs for Selected US Banks

Entity	P/B
Citigroup, Inc.	0.69
Wells Fargo & Company	1.21
US Bancorp	1.63

Source: S&P Capital IQ

Citigroup's low P/B versus its peers is a reflection of the "one-stop shopping" business model it and some other mega-banks pursued in the 1990s. Citigroup suffered huge losses during the global financial crisis and had to be rescued in November 2008 by the US government.

Wells Fargo derives most of its revenue from loans and service fees. Its business model focuses on cross-selling multiple products, and in 2012 it was responsible for originating close to a third of all US home loans. Wells Fargo is also predominantly a domestic business, whereas other large banks are much more exposed to overseas markets.

US Bancorp's relatively risk-averse business model is focused on consumer and business banking as well as trusts and payment processing. Compared with other mega-banks, US Bancorp has a much smaller presence in investment banking and capital markets. Another reason for the bank's relatively high P/B was its acquisition activity, which has helped it grow its business considerably.

Determining Book Value

In this section, we illustrate how to calculate book value and how to adjust book value to improve the comparability of P/Bs among companies. To compute book value per share, we need to refer to the business's balance sheet, which has a shareholders' (or stockholders') equity section. The computation of book value is as follows:

- (Shareholders' equity) − (Total value of equity claims that are senior to common stock) = Common shareholders' equity.

- (Common shareholders' equity)/(Number of common stock shares outstanding) = Book value per share.

Possible claims senior to the claims of common stock, which would be subtracted from shareholders' equity, include the value of preferred stock and the dividends in arrears on preferred stock. Example 19 illustrates the calculation.

EXAMPLE 19

Computing Book Value per Share

Headquartered in Toronto, Canada, the Toronto-Dominion Bank and its subsidiaries are collectively known as TD Bank Group (TD). With operations organized into four segments (Canadian Personal and Commercial Banking, US Personal and Commercial Banking, Wholesale Banking, and Wealth and Insurance), in 2018 TD provided financial products and services to approximately 26 million customers. Exhibit 10 presents data from the equity section of TD's consolidated balance sheets for the years 2016–2018. TD's fiscal years end on 31 October.

Exhibit 10: Equity Data for TD Bank Group (Millions of Canadian Dollars)

	31 October 2018	31 October 2017	31 October 2016
Equity			
Common shares	CAD21,221	CAD20,931	CAD20,711
Millions of shares issued and outstanding:			
2018: 1,830.4			
2017: 1,842.5			
2016: 1,857.6			
Preferred shares	5,000	4,750	4,400
Millions of shares issued and outstanding:			
2018: 200.0			
2017: 190.0			
2016: 176.0			
Treasury shares—common	(151)	(183)	(36)
Millions of shares held:			
2018: 2.1			
2017: 2.9			
2016: 0.4			
Treasury shares—preferred	(1)	—	(1)
2018: nil			
2017: nil			
2016: nil			
Contributed surplus	193	214	203
Retained earnings	46,145	40,489	35,452
Accumulated and other comprehensive income	6,639	8,006	11,834
	79,047	74,207	72,564
Non-controlling interests in subsidiaries	993	983	1,650
Total equity	**CAD80,040**	**CAD75,190**	**CAD74,214**

Source: TD Bank Group 2018 annual report.

1. Using the data in Exhibit 10, calculate book value per share for 2016, 2017, and 2018.

Solution:

Because preferred shareholders have a claim on income and assets that is senior to that of the common shareholders, total equity must be adjusted by the value of outstanding and repurchased preferred shares. The divisor is the number of common shares outstanding.

2018: Book value per share = (80,040 – 5,000)/1,830.4 = CAD41.00.

2017: Book value per share = (75,190 – 4,750)/1,842.5 = CAD38.23.

2016: Book value per share = (74,214 – 4,400)/1,857.6 = CAD37.58.

2. Given a closing price of CAD73.03 on 31 October 2018, calculate TD's 2018 P/B.

Solution:

P/B = CAD73.03/CAD41.00 = 1.78.

Example 19 illustrated the calculation of book value per share without any adjustments. Adjusting P/B has two purposes: (1) to make the book value per share more accurately reflect the value of shareholders' investment and (2) to make P/B more useful for making comparisons among different stocks. Some adjustments are as follows:

- Some services and analysts report a **tangible book value per share**. Computing tangible book value per share involves subtracting reported intangible assets on the balance sheet from common shareholders' equity. The analyst should be familiar with the calculation. From the viewpoint of financial theory, however, the general exclusion of all intangibles may not be warranted. In the case of individual intangible assets, such as patents, which can be separated from the entity and sold, exclusion may not be justified. Exclusion may be appropriate, however, for goodwill from acquisitions, particularly for comparative purposes. **Goodwill** represents the excess of the purchase price of an acquisition beyond the fair value of acquired tangible assets and specifically identifiable intangible assets. Many analysts believe that goodwill does not represent an asset because it is not separable and may reflect overpayment for an acquisition.

- Certain adjustments may be appropriate for enhancing comparability. For example, one company may use FIFO whereas a peer company uses LIFO, which in an inflationary environment will generally understate inventory values. To accurately assess the relative valuation of the two companies, the analyst should restate the book value of the company using LIFO to what it would be based on FIFO. For a more complete discussion of adjustments to balance sheet amounts, refer to readings on financial statement analysis.

- For book value per share to most accurately reflect current values, the balance sheet should be adjusted for significant off-balance-sheet assets and liabilities. An example of an off-balance-sheet liability is a guarantee to pay a debt of another company in the event of that company's default. US accounting standards require companies to disclose off-balance-sheet liabilities.

Example 20 illustrates adjustments an analyst might make to a financial firm's P/B to obtain an accurate firm value.

EXAMPLE 20

Adjusting Book Value (Historical Example)

Edward Stavos is a junior analyst at a major US pension fund. Stavos is researching Barclays PLC for his fund's Credit Services Portfolio and is preparing background information prior to an upcoming meeting with the company. Headquartered in London, United Kingdom, Barclays is a major global financial services provider engaged in personal banking, credit cards, corporate and investment banking, and wealth and investment management with an extensive international presence in Europe, the Americas, Africa, and Asia.

Stavos is particularly interested in Barclays' P/B and how adjusting asset and liability accounts to their current fair value impacts the ratio. He gathers the condensed 2012 balance sheet (as of 31 December) and footnote data from Barclay's website as shown in Exhibit 11.

Exhibit 11: Barclays PLC 2012 Condensed Consolidated Balance Sheet and Footnote Data (£ in Millions)

	2012
Assets	
Cash and balances at central banks	£86,175
Items in the course of collection from other banks	1,456
Trading portfolio assets	145,030
Financial assets designated at fair value	46,061
Derivative financial instruments	469,146
Available for sale investments	75,109
Loans and advances to banks	40,489
Loans and advances to customers	425,729
Reverse repurchase agreements and other similar secured lending	176,956
Prepayments, accrued income, and other assets	4,360
Investments in associates and joint ventures	570
Property, plant, and equipment	5,754
Goodwill and intangible assets	7,915
Current tax assets	252
Deferred tax assets	3,016
Retirement benefit assets	2,303
Total assets	£1,490,321
Liabilities	
Deposits from banks	77,010
Items in the course of collection due to other banks	1,573

	2012
Customer accounts	385,707
Repurchase agreements and other similar secured borrowing	217,342
Trading portfolio liabilities	44,794
Financial liabilities designated at fair value	78,280
Derivative financial instruments	462,468
Debt securities in issue	119,581
Subordinated liabilities	24,018
Accruals, deferred income, and other liabilities	12,232
Provisions	2,766
Current tax liabilities	621
Deferred tax liabilities	719
Retirement benefit liabilities	253
Total liabilities	1,427,364
Shareholders' equity	
Shareholders' equity excluding non-controlling interests	53,586
Non-controlling interests	9,371
Total shareholders' equity	62,957
Total liabilities and shareholders' equity	£1,490,321

Excerpt from Footnotes to the Barclays Financial Statements: Financial Assets and Liabilities at Carrying Amount and Fair Value

	2012	
	Carrying amount	Fair value
Financial assets		
Loans and advances to banks	£40,489	£40,489
Loans and advances to customers:		
—Home loans	174,988	164,608
—Credit cards, unsecured and other retail lending	66,414	65,357
—Corporate loans	184,327	178,492
Reverse repurchase agreements and other similar secured lending	176,956	176,895
	£643,174	£625,841
Financial liabilities		
Deposits from banks	77,010	77,023
Customer accounts:		
—Current and demand accounts	127,819	127,819
—Savings accounts	99,875	99,875
—Other time deposits	158,013	158,008
Debt securities in issue	119,581	119,725

	2012	
	Carrying amount	**Fair value**
Repurchase agreements and other similar secured borrowing	217,342	217,342
Subordinated liabilities	24,018	23,467
	£823,658	£823,259

Source: Barclays' 2012 annual report.

The 31 December 2012 share price for Barclays was £2.4239, and the diluted weighted average number of shares was 12,614 million. Stavos computes book value per share initially by dividing total shareholders' equity by the share count and arrives at a book value per share of £4.9910 (£62,957/12,614) and a P/B of 0.49 (£2.4239/£4.9910).

Stavos then computes tangible book value per share as £4.3636 (calculated as £62,957 minus £7,915 of goodwill and intangible assets, which is then divided by 12,614 shares). The P/B based on tangible book value per share is 0.56 (£2.4239/£4.3636).

Stavos then turns to the footnotes to examine the fair value data. He notes the fair value of financial assets is £17,333 million less than their carrying amount (£643,174 − £625,841) and the fair value of financial liabilities is £399 million less than their carrying amount (£823,658 − £823,259). Including these adjustments to tangible book value results in an adjusted book value per share of £3.0211 [(£62,957 − £7,915 − £17,333 + £399)/12,614]. Stavos' adjusted P/B is 0.80 (£2.4239/£3.0211).

Stavos is concerned about the wide range in his computed P/Bs. He knows that if quoted prices are not available for financial assets and liabilities, IAS 39 allows for the use of valuation models to estimate fair value. He decides to question management regarding the use of models to value assets, liabilities, and derivatives and the sensitivity of these accounts to changes in interest rates and currency values.

An analyst should also be aware of differences in accounting standards related to how assets and liabilities are valued in financial statements. Accounting standards currently require companies to report some assets and liabilities at fair value and others at historical cost (with some adjustments).

Financial assets, such as investments in marketable securities, are usually reported at fair value. Investments classified as "held to maturity" and reported on a historical cost basis are an exception. (Instead of the term "held-to-maturity," IFRS refer to this category of investments as financial assets measured at amortized cost.) Some financial liabilities also are reported at fair value.

Nonfinancial assets, such as land and equipment, are generally reported at their historical acquisition costs, and in the case of equipment, the assets are depreciated over their useful lives. The value of these assets may have increased over time, however, or the value may have decreased more than is reflected in the accumulated depreciation. When the reported amount of an asset—that is, its carrying value—exceeds its recoverable amount, both international accounting standards (IFRS) and US accounting standards (GAAP) require companies to reduce the reported amount of the asset and show the reduction as an impairment loss (the two sets of standards differ in the measurement of impairment losses). US GAAP, however, prohibit subsequent reversal of impairment losses, whereas IFRS permit subsequent reversals. In addition, as mentioned above, IFRS allow companies to measure fixed assets using either the historical cost model or a revaluation model, under which the assets are reported at their current value. When assets are reported at fair value, P/Bs become more comparable among companies; for this reason, P/Bs are considered to be more comparable for companies with significant amounts of financial assets.

Valuation Based on Forecasted Fundamentals

We can use forecasts of a company's fundamentals to estimate a stock's justified P/B. For example, assuming the Gordon growth model and using the expression $g = b \times$ ROE for the sustainable growth rate, the expression for the justified P/B based on the most recent book value (B_0) is

$$\frac{P_0}{B_0} = \frac{\text{ROE} - g}{r - g}. \tag{4}$$

For example, if a business's ROE is 12%, its required rate of return is 10%, and its expected growth rate is 7%, then its justified P/B based on fundamentals is (0.12 – 0.07)/(0.10 – 0.07) = 1.67.

> **DERIVING THE JUSTIFIED P/B EXPRESSION**
>
> According to the Gordon growth model, $V_0 = E_1 \times (1 - b)/(r - g)$. Defining ROE as E_1/B_0 so that $E_1 = B_0 \times$ ROE and substituting for E_1 into the prior expression, we have $V_0 = B_0 \times$ ROE $\times (1 - b)/(r - g)$, giving $V_0/B_0 =$ ROE $\times (1 - b)/(r - g)$. The sustainable growth rate expression is $g = b \times$ ROE. Substituting $b = g/$ROE into the expression just given for V_0/B_0, we have $V_0/B_0 = ($ROE $- g)/(r - g)$. Because justified price is intrinsic value, V_0, we obtain Equation 4.

E_1 = earnings

B_0: book value

Equation 4 states that the justified P/B is an increasing function of ROE, all else equal. Because the numerator and denominator are differences of, respectively, ROE and r from the same quantity, g, what determines the justified P/B in Equation 4 is ROE in relation to the required rate of return, r. The larger ROE is in relation to r, the higher is the justified P/B based on fundamentals. This relationship can be seen clearly if we set g equal to 0 (the no-growth case): $P_0/B_0 =$ ROE$/r$.

A practical insight from Equation 4 is that we cannot conclude whether a particular value of the P/B reflects undervaluation without taking into account the business's profitability. Equation 4 also suggests that if we are evaluating two stocks with the same P/B, the one with the higher ROE is relatively undervalued, all else equal. These relationships have been confirmed through cross-sectional regression analyses (Harris and Marston 1994; Fairfield, 1994).

Further insight into P/B comes from the residual income model, which is discussed in detail in another reading. The expression for the justified P/B based on the residual income valuation is

$$\frac{P_0}{B_0} = 1 + \frac{\text{Present value of expected future residual earnings}}{B_0}. \tag{5}$$

Equation 5, which makes no special assumptions about growth, states the following:

- If the present value of expected future residual earnings is zero—for example, if the business just earns its required return on investment in every period—the justified P/B is 1.

- If the present value of expected future residual earnings is positive (negative), the justified P/B is greater than (less than) 1.

JUSTIFIED P/B EXPRESSION BASED ON RESIDUAL INCOME

Noting that $(ROE - r) \times B_0$ would define a level residual income stream, we can show that Equation 4 is consistent with Equation 5 (a general expression) as follows. In $P_0/B_0 = (ROE - g)/(r - g)$, we can successively rewrite the numerator $(ROE - g) + r - r = (r - g) + (ROE - r)$, so $P_0/B_0 = [(r - g) + (ROE - r)]/(r - g) = 1 + (ROE - r)/(r - g)$, which can be written $P_0/B_0 = 1 + [(ROE - r)/(r - g)] \times B_0/B_0 = 1 + [(ROE - r) \times B_0/(r - g)]/B_0$; the second term in the final expression is the present value of residual income divided by B_0 as in Equation 5.

Valuation Based on Comparables

To use the method of comparables for valuing stocks using a P/B, we follow the steps given earlier. In contrast to EPS, however, analysts' forecasts of book value are not aggregated and widely disseminated by financial data vendors; in practice, most analysts use trailing book value in calculating P/Bs. Evaluation of relative P/Bs should consider differences in ROE, risk, and expected earnings growth. The use of P/Bs in the method of comparables is illustrated in Example 21.

EXAMPLE 21

P/B Comparables Approach (Historical Example)

1. You are working on a project to value an independent securities brokerage firm. You know the industry had a significant decline in valuations during the 2007–09 financial crisis. You decide to perform a time series analysis on three firms: E*TRADE Financial Corp. (ETFC), the Charles Schwab Corporation (SCHW), and TD Ameritrade Holding Corp. (AMTD). Exhibit 12 presents information on these firms.

Exhibit 12: Price-to-Book Comparables

	Price-to-Book Value Ratio								
Entity	2006	2007	2008	2009	2010	2011	2012	As of 19 July 2013	Mean
ETFC	2.37	2.38	0.68	0.88	0.84	0.74	0.54	0.65	1.14
Forecasted growth in book value: 1.5%									
Forecasted growth in revenues: −1.0%									
Beta: 1.65									
SCHW	4.23	6.69	6.14	3.54	3.15	2.50	1.96	2.31	3.81
Forecasted growth in book value: 10.5%									
Forecasted growth in revenues: 5.0%									
Beta: 1.20									
AMTD	6.96	4.85	3.33	2.60	2.68	2.44	2.20	2.53	3.45
Forecasted growth in book value: 9.0%									
Forecasted growth in revenues: 3.5%									
Beta: 1.10									

Source: The Value Line Investment Survey. The price-to-book value ratio is based on the average of the annual high and low prices and end-of-year book value.

Based only on the information in Exhibit 12, discuss the relative valuation of ETFC relative to the other two companies.

Solution:

ETFC is currently selling at a P/B that is less than 30% of the P/B for either SCHW or AMTD. It is also selling at a P/B that is less than 60% of its average P/B for the time period noted in the exhibit. The likely explanation for ETFC's low P/B is that its growth forecasts for book value and revenues are lower and its beta is higher than those for SCHW and AMTD. In deciding whether ETFC is overvalued or undervalued, an analyst would likely decide how his or her growth forecast and the uncertainty surrounding that forecast compare to the market consensus.

PRICE/SALES

6

☐   calculate and interpret a justified price multiple

☐   describe rationales for and possible drawbacks to using alternative price multiples and dividend yield in valuation

☐   calculate and interpret alternative price multiples and dividend yield

☐   describe fundamental factors that influence alternative price multiples and dividend yield

☐   calculate and interpret the justified price-to-earnings ratio (P/E), price-to-book ratio (P/B), and price-to-sales ratio (P/S) for a stock, based on forecasted fundamentals

☐   evaluate a stock by the method of comparables and explain the importance of fundamentals in using the method of comparables

☐   evaluate whether a stock is overvalued, fairly valued, or undervalued based on comparisons of multiples

Certain types of privately held companies, including investment management companies and many types of companies in partnership form, have long been valued by a multiple of annual revenues. In recent decades, the ratio of price to sales has become well known as a valuation indicator for the equity of publicly traded companies as well. Based on US data, O'Shaughnessy (2005) characterized P/S as the best ratio for selecting undervalued stocks.

According to the 2012 BofA *Merrill Lynch Institutional Factor Survey*, about 30% of respondents consistently used P/S in their investment process. Analysts have offered the following rationales for using P/S:

- Sales are generally less subject to distortion or manipulation than are other fundamentals, such as EPS or book value. For example, through discretionary accounting decisions about expenses, company managers can distort EPS as a reflection of economic performance. In contrast, total sales, as the top line in the income statement, is prior to any expenses.

- Sales are positive even when EPS is negative. Therefore, analysts can use P/S when EPS is negative, whereas the P/E based on a zero or negative EPS is not meaningful.

- Because sales are generally more stable than EPS, which reflects operating and financial leverage, P/S is generally more stable than P/E. P/S may be more meaningful than P/E when EPS is abnormally high or low.

- P/S has been viewed as appropriate for valuing the stocks of mature, cyclical, and zero-income companies (Martin 1998).

- Differences in P/S multiples may be related to differences in long-run average returns, according to empirical research (Nathan, Sivakumar and Vijayakumar, 2001; O'Shaughnessy, 2005).

Possible drawbacks of using P/S in practice include the following:

- A business may show high growth in sales even when it is not operating profitably as judged by earnings and cash flow from operations. To have value as a going concern, a business must ultimately generate earnings and cash.

- Share price reflects the effect of debt financing on profitability and risk. In the P/S multiple, however, price is compared with sales, which is a prefinancing income measure—a logical mismatch. For this reason, some experts use a ratio of enterprise value to sales because enterprise value incorporates the value of debt.

- P/S does not reflect differences in cost structures among different companies.

- Although P/S is relatively robust with respect to manipulation, revenue recognition practices have the potential to distort P/S.

Despite the contrasts between P/S to P/E, the ratios have a relationship with which analysts should be familiar. The fact that (Sales) × (Net profit margin) = Net income means that (P/E) × (Net profit margin) = P/S. For two stocks with the same positive P/E, the stock with the higher P/S has a higher (actual or forecasted) net profit margin, calculated as the ratio of P/S to P/E.

Determining Sales

P/S is calculated as price per share divided by annual net sales per share (net sales is total sales minus returns and customer discounts). Analysts usually use annual sales from the company's most recent fiscal year in the calculation, as illustrated in Example 22. Because valuation is forward looking in principle, the analyst may also develop and use P/S multiples based on forecasts of next year's sales.

EXAMPLE 22

Calculating P/S

1. Stora Enso Oyj (Helsinki Stock Exchange: STERV) is an integrated paper, packaging, and forest products company headquartered in Finland. In its fiscal year ended 31 December 2018, Stora Enso reported net sales of €10,486

million and had 788.4 million shares outstanding. Calculate the P/S for Stora Enso based on a closing price of €10.34 on 28 June 2019.

Solution:

Sales per share = €10,486 million/788.6 million shares = €13.30. So, P/S = €10.34/€13.30 = 0.778.

Although the determination of sales is more straightforward than the determination of earnings, the analyst should evaluate a company's revenue recognition practices—in particular those tending to speed up the recognition of revenues—before relying on the P/S multiple. An analyst using a P/S approach who does not also assess the quality of accounting for sales may place too high a value on the company's shares. Example 23 illustrates the problem.

Valuation Based on Forecasted Fundamentals

Like other multiples, P/S can be linked to DCF models. In terms of the Gordon growth model, we can state P/S as

$$\frac{P_0}{S_1} = \frac{\left(\frac{E_1}{S_1}\right)(1-b)}{r-g}.$$

[handwritten annotations:]
$E_1 = \frac{D_1}{1-b} \Rightarrow D_1 = E_1(1-b)$

D_1: dividend
$(1-b)$: dividend payout ratio
(6)
E_1: earnings
b: retention rate

where E_1/S_1 is the business's forward-looking profit margin (the equation can be obtained from the Gordon Growth model $P_0 = D_1/(r-g)$, by substituting $D_1 = E_1(1-b)$ into the numerator and then dividing both sides by S_1). Equation 6 states that the justified P/S is an increasing function of the profit margin and earnings growth rate, and the intuition behind Equation 6 generalizes to more-complex DCF models.

EXAMPLE 23

Revenue Recognition Practices (1)

Analysts label stock markets "bubbles" when market prices appear to lose contact with intrinsic values. To many analysts, the run-up in the prices of internet stocks in the US market in the 1998–2000 period represented a bubble. During that period, many analysts adopted P/S as a metric for valuing the many internet stocks that had negative earnings and cash flow. Perhaps at least partly as a result of this practice, some internet companies engaged in questionable revenue recognition practices to justify their high valuations. To increase sales, some companies engaged in bartering website advertising with other internet companies. For example, InternetRevenue.com might barter $1,000,000 worth of banner advertising with RevenueIsUs.com. Each could then show $1,000,000 of revenue and $1,000,000 of expenses. Although neither had any net income or cash flow, each company's revenue growth and market valuation was enhanced (at least temporarily). In addition, the value placed on the advertising was frequently questionable.

As a result of these and other questionable activities, the US SEC issued a stern warning to companies and formalized revenue recognition practices for barter in Staff Accounting Bulletin No. 101. Similarly, international accounting standard setters issued Standing Interpretations Committee Interpretation 31 to define revenue recognition principles for barter transactions involving advertising services. The analyst should review footnote disclosures to assess whether a company may be recognizing revenue prematurely or otherwise aggressively.

Example 24 illustrates another classic instance in which an analyst should look behind the accounting numbers.

EXAMPLE 24

Revenue Recognition Practices (2)

Sales on a **bill-and-hold basis** involve selling products but not delivering those products until a later date. Sales on this basis have the effect of accelerating the recognition of those sales into an earlier reporting period. In its form 10-K filed 30 September 2008, Diebold, a provider of bank security systems and ATMs, provided the following note:

Revenues

Bill and Hold—The largest of the revenue recognition adjustments relates to the Company's previous long-standing method of accounting for bill and hold transactions under Staff Accounting Bulletin 104, Revenue Recognition in Financial Statements (SAB 104), in its North America and International businesses. On January 15, 2008, the Company announced that it had concluded its discussions with the OCA in regard to its practice of recognizing certain revenue on a bill and hold basis in its North America business segment. As a result of those discussions, the Company determined that its previous, long-standing method of accounting for bill and hold transactions was in error, representing a misapplication of GAAP. To correct for this error, the Company announced it would discontinue the use of bill and hold as a method of revenue recognition in its North America and International businesses and restate its financial statements for this change.

The Company completed an analysis of transactions and recorded adjusting journal entries related to revenue and costs recognized previously under a bill and hold basis that is now recognized upon customer acceptance of products at a customer location. Within the North America business segment, when the Company is contractually responsible for installation, customer acceptance will be upon completion of the installation of all of the items at a job site and the Company's demonstration that the items are in operable condition. Where items are contractually only delivered to a customer, revenue recognition of these items will continue upon shipment or delivery to a customer location depending on the terms in the contract. Within the International business segment, customer acceptance is upon either delivery or completion of the installation depending on the terms in the contract with the customer. The Company restated for transactions affecting both product revenue for hardware sales and service revenue for installation and other services that had been previously recognized on a bill and hold basis.

Other Revenue Adjustments—The Company also adjusted for other specific revenue transactions in both its North America and International businesses related to transactions largely where the Company recognized revenue in incorrect periods. The majority of these adjustments were related to misapplication of GAAP related to revenue recognition requirements as defined within SAB 104. Generally, the Company recorded adjustments for transactions when the Company previously recognized revenue prior to title and/or risk of loss transferring to the customer.

In 2010, Diebold agreed to pay $25 million to settle Securities and Exchange Commission charges that it manipulated its earnings from at least 2002 through 2007. During that period, the company misstated the company's reported pre-tax earnings by at least $127 million.

According to the SEC, Diebold's financial management received reports, sometimes on a daily basis, comparing the company's actual earnings to analyst earnings forecasts. Diebold's management would prepare "opportunity lists" of ways to close the gap between the company's actual financial results and analyst forecasts. Many of the methods were fraudulent accounting transactions designed to improperly recognize revenue or otherwise inflate Diebold's financial performance. Among the fraudulent practices identified by the SEC were the following: improper use of bill and hold accounting, recognition of revenue on a lease agreement subject to a side buy-back agreement, manipulating reserves and accruals, improperly delaying and capitalizing expenses, and writing up the value of used inventory.

Example 25 briefly summarizes another example of aggressive revenue recognition practices.

EXAMPLE 25

Revenue Recognition Practices (3)

Groupon is a deal-of-the-day website that features discounted gift certificates usable at local or national companies. Before going public in November 2011, Groupon amended its registration statement eight times. One SEC-mandated restatement forced it to change an auditor-sanctioned method of reporting revenue, reducing sales by more than 50%. Essentially, Groupon had initially counted the gross amount its members paid for coupons or certificates as revenue, without deducting the share (typically half or more) that it sends to local merchants. The SEC also demanded Groupon remove from its offering document a non-GAAP metric it had invented called "adjusted consolidated segment operating income." This measure was considered misleading because it ignored marketing expenses, which are one of the major risks of Groupon's business model.

Even when a company discloses its revenue recognition practices, the analyst cannot always determine precisely by how much sales may be overstated. If a company is engaging in questionable revenue recognition practices and the amount being manipulated is unknown, the analyst might do well to suggest avoiding investment in that company's securities. At the very least, the analyst should be skeptical and assign the company a higher risk premium than otherwise, which would result in a lower justified P/S.

Valuation Based on Forecasted Fundamentals

Like other multiples, P/S can be linked to DCF models. In terms of the Gordon growth model, we can state P/S as

$$\frac{P_0}{S_0} = \frac{(E_0/S_0)\ (1-b)\ (1+g)}{r-g},$$

(7)

where E_0/S_0 is the business's profit margin (the equation can be obtained from the Gordon growth model, $P_0 = D_0(1+g)/(r-g)$, by substituting $D_0 = E_0(1-b)$ into the numerator and then dividing both sides by S_0). Although the profit margin is stated in terms of trailing sales and earnings, the analyst may use a long-term forecasted profit margin in Equation 7. Equation 7 states that the justified P/S is an increasing function of the profit margin and earnings growth rate, and the intuition behind Equation 7 generalizes to more-complex DCF models.

Profit margin is a determinant of the justified P/S not only directly but also through its effect on g. We can illustrate this concept by restating the equation for the sustainable growth rate [g = (Retention rate, b) × ROE], as follows:

$$g = b \times PM_0 \times \frac{Sales}{Total\ assets} \times \frac{Total\ assets}{Shareholders'\ equity},$$

where PM_0 is profit margin and the last three terms come from the DuPont analysis of ROE. An increase (decrease) in the profit margin produces a higher (lower) sustainable growth rate as long as sales do not decrease (increase) proportionately. Example 26 illustrates the use of justified P/S and how to apply it in valuation.

EXAMPLE 26

Justified P/S Based on Forecasted Fundamentals

As a health care analyst, you are valuing the stocks of three medical equipment manufacturers, including the Swedish company Getinge AB (GETI) in March 2019. Based on an average of estimates obtained from capital asset pricing model (CAPM) and bond yield plus risk premium approaches, you estimate that GETI's required rate of return is 9%. You have gathered the following data from GETI's annual reports (amounts in millions of Swedish krona, or SEK):

	2009	2010	2011	2012	2013	2014	2015	2016	2017	2018
Net sales	22,816	22,712	21,854	24,248	25,287	26,669	30,235	29,756	22,496	24,172
Growth rates (geometric)										
2009–2018	0.6%									
2014–2018	−2.4%									
Year / Year		−0.5%	−3.8%	11.0%	4.3%	5.5%	13.4%	−1.6%	−24.4%	7.5%
Net profit	1,914	2,280	2,537	2,531	2,285	1,433	1,390	1,188	1,376	−967
Growth rates (geometric)										
2009–2018	NMF									
2014–2018	NMF									
Year / Year		19.1%	11.3%	−0.2%	−9.7%	−37.3%	−3.0%	−14.5%	15.8%	−170.3%
Net profit margin	8.4%	10.0%	11.6%	10.4%	9.0%	5.4%	4.6%	4.0%	6.1%	−4.0%
Averages										
2009–2018	6.6%									
2014–2018	3.2%									
Dividend payout ratio	0.3%	34.0%	35.3%	39.2%	43.3%	69.3%	49.7%	57.7%	36.0%	−43.8%
Averages										
2009–2018	32.1%									
2014–2018	33.8%									

Sales growth and profitability have been quite variable in recent years, particularly in 2017 and 2018, making it difficult to extrapolate future trends. Based on further research on the company and its industry, , you make the following long-term forecasts:

Profit margin = 9.0%

Dividend payout ratio = 35.0%

Earnings growth rate = 7.0%

1. Based on these data, calculate GETI's justified P/S.

Solution: 6

From Equation 7, GETI's justified P/S is calculated as follows:

$$\frac{P_0}{S_1} = \frac{(E_1/S_1)\,(1-b)}{r-g} = \frac{0.09 \times 0.35}{0.09 - 0.07} = 1.575$$

2. Given a forecast of GETI's sales per share (in Swedish krona) for 2019 of SEK94.3, estimate the intrinsic value of GETI stock.

Solution:

An estimate of the intrinsic value of GETI stock is 1.575 × SEK94.3 = SEK148.52.

3. Given a market price for GETI of SEK133.70 on 26 August 2019 and your answer to Part 2, determine whether GETI stock appears to be fairly valued, overvalued, or undervalued.

Solution:

GETI stock appears to be undervalued because its current market value of SEK133.70 is less than its estimated intrinsic value of SEK148.52.

Valuation Based on Comparables

Using P/S in the method of comparables to value stocks follows the steps given in Section 3. As mentioned earlier, P/Ss are usually reported on the basis of trailing sales. Analysts may also base relative valuations on P/S multiples calculated on forecasted sales. In doing so, analysts may make their own sales forecasts or may use forecasts supplied by data vendors. In valuing stocks using the method of comparables, analysts should also gather information on profit margins, expected earnings growth, and risk. As always, the quality of accounting also merits investigation. Example 27 illustrates the use of P/S in the comparables approach.

EXAMPLE 27

P/S Comparables Approach

Continuing with the project to value Getinge AB, you have compiled the information on GETI and peer companies Cantel Medical Corporation (CMD) and New Genomics (NEO) given in Exhibit 13.

Exhibit 13: P/S Comparables (as of 26 October 2019)			
Measure	GETI	CMD	NEO
Price/Sales (TTM)	1.54	3.96	8.79

Measure	GETI	CMD	NEO
Profit Margin (TTM)	−2.49%	6.95%	14.53%
Quarterly Revenue Growth (YoYy)	9.50%	5.20%	1.50%
Total Debt/Equity (mrq)	58.43	35.58	28.50
Enterprise Value/Revenue (TTM)	1.88	4.14	8.23

Source: Yahoo! Finance.

Use the data in Exhibit 13 to address the following:

1. Based on the P/S but referring to no other information, assess GETI's relative valuation.

Solution:

Because the P/S for GETI, 1.54, is the lowest of the three P/S multiples, if no other information is referenced, GETI appears to be relatively undervalued.

2. State whether GETI is more closely comparable to CMD or to NEO. Justify your answer.

Solution:

On the basis of the information given, GETI appears to be more closely matched to CMD than to NEO. NEO's P/S is significantly higher than the P/S for GETI and CMD. The profit margin and revenue growth are key fundamentals in the P/S approach, and NEO's higher P/S reflects its high profit margin. GETI's funding (Total debt/Equity) is higher than that of CMD and NEO, and its Enterprise value/Revenue is low and much closer to CMD's ratio than to that of NEO. Overall, GETI's valuation seems to be more like that of CMD than that of NEO. GETI's low P/S is consistent with its other relative-valuation metrics in Exhibit 13.

7   PRICE/CASH FLOW

- [ ] calculate and interpret a justified price multiple
- [ ] describe rationales for and possible drawbacks to using alternative price multiples and dividend yield in valuation
- [ ] calculate and interpret alternative price multiples and dividend yield
- [ ] describe fundamental factors that influence alternative price multiples and dividend yield
- [ ] calculate and interpret the justified price-to-earnings ratio (P/E), price-to-book ratio (P/B), and price-to-sales ratio (P/S) for a stock, based on forecasted fundamentals
- [ ] evaluate a stock by the method of comparables and explain the importance of fundamentals in using the method of comparables
- [ ] evaluate whether a stock is overvalued, fairly valued, or undervalued based on comparisons of multiples

Price to cash flow is a widely reported valuation indicator. According to the 2012 BofA Merrill Lynch Institutional Factor Survey, price to free cash flow trailed only P/E, beta, enterprise value/EBITDA, ROE, size, and P/B in popularity as a valuation factor and was used as a valuation metric by approximately half of the institutions surveyed.

In this section, we present price to cash flow based on alternative major cash flow concepts. Note that "price to cash flow" is used to refer to the ratio of share price to any one of these definitions of cash flow whereas "P/CF" is reserved for the ratio of price to the earnings-plus-noncash-charges definition of cash flow, explained later. Because of the wide variety of cash flow concepts in use, the analyst should be especially careful to understand (and communicate) the exact definition of "cash flow" that is the basis for the analysis.

Analysts have offered the following rationales for the use of price to cash flow:

- Cash flow is less subject to manipulation by management than earnings.
- Because cash flow is generally more stable than earnings, price to cash flow is generally more stable than P/E.
- Using price to cash flow rather than P/E addresses the issue of differences in accounting conservatism between companies (differences in the quality of earnings).
- Differences in price to cash flow may be related to differences in long-run average returns, according to empirical research (O'Shaughnessy 2005).

Possible drawbacks to the use of price to cash flow include the following:

- When cash flow from operations is defined as EPS plus noncash charges, items affecting actual cash flow from operations, such as noncash revenue and net changes in working capital, are ignored. So, for example, aggressive recognition of revenue (front-end loading) would not be accurately captured in the earnings-plus-noncash-charges definition because the measure would not reflect the divergence between revenues as reported and actual cash collections related to that revenue.
- Theory views free cash flow to equity (FCFE) rather than cash flow as the appropriate variable for price-based valuation multiples. We can use P/FCFE, but FCFE does have the possible drawback of being more volatile than cash flow for many businesses. FCFE is also more frequently negative than cash flow.
- As analysts' use of cash flow has increased over time, some companies have increased their use of accounting methods that enhance cash flow measures. Operating cash flow, for example, can be enhanced by securitizing accounts receivable to speed up a company's operating cash inflow or by outsourcing the payment of accounts payable to slow down the company's operating cash outflow (while the outsource company continues to make timely payments and provides financing to cover any timing differences). Mulford and Comiskey (2005) described a number of opportunistic accounting choices that companies can make to increase their reported operating cash flow.
- Operating cash flow from the statement of cash flows under IFRS may not be comparable to operating cash flow under US GAAP because IFRS allow more flexibility in classification of interest paid, interest received, and dividends received. Under US GAAP, all three of these items are classified in operating cash flow, but under IFRS, companies have the option to classify them as operating or investing (for interest and dividends received) and as operating or financing (for interest paid).

One approximation of cash flow in practical use is EPS plus per-share depreciation, amortization, and depletion. This simple approximation is used in Example 28 to highlight issues of interest to the analyst in valuation.

EXAMPLE 28

Accounting Methods and Cash Flow

1. Consider two hypothetical companies, Company A and Company B, that have constant cash revenues and cash expenses (as well as a constant number of shares outstanding) in 2018, 2019, and 2020. In addition, both companies incur total depreciation of $15.00 per share during the three-year period, and both use the same depreciation method for tax purposes. The two companies use different depreciation methods, however, for financial reporting. Company A spreads the depreciation expense evenly over the three years (straight-line depreciation, or SLD). Because its revenues, expenses, and depreciation are constant over the period, Company A's EPS is also constant. In this example, Company A's EPS is assumed to be $10 each year, as shown in Column 1 in Exhibit 14.

   Company B is identical to Company A except that it uses accelerated depreciation. Company B's depreciation is 150% of SLD in 2018 and declines to 50% of SLD in 2020, as shown in Column 5.

Exhibit 14: Earnings Growth Rates and Cash Flow (All Amounts per Share)

	Company A			Company B		
Year	Earnings (1)	Depreciation (2)	Cash Flow (3)	Earnings (4)	Depreciation (5)	Cash Flow (6)
2018	$10.00	$5.00	$15.00	$7.50	$7.50	$15.00
2019	10.00	5.00	15.00	10.00	5.00	15.00
2020	10.00	5.00	15.00	12.50	2.50	15.00
Total		$15.00			$15.00	

Because of the different depreciation methods used by Company A and Company B for financial reporting purposes, Company A's EPS (Column 1) is flat at $10.00 whereas Company B's EPS (Column 4) shows 29% compound growth: $(\$12.50/\$7.50)^{1/2} - 1.00 = 0.29$. Thus, Company B appears to have positive earnings momentum. Analysts comparing Companies A and B might be misled by using the EPS numbers as reported instead of putting EPS on a comparable basis. For both companies, however, cash flow per share is level at $15.

Depreciation may be the simplest noncash charge to understand; write-offs and other noncash charges may offer more latitude for the management of earnings.

Determining Cash Flow

In practice, analysts and data vendors often use simple *approximations* of cash flow from operations in calculating cash flow for price-to-cash-flow analysis. For many companies, depreciation and amortization are the major noncash charges regularly added to net income in the process of calculating cash flow from operations by the add-back method, so the approximation focuses on them. A representative approximation specifies cash flow per share as EPS plus per-share depreciation, amortization, and depletion. We call this estimation the "earnings-plus-noncash-charges" definition and in this section use the acronym CF for it. Keep in mind, however, that this definition is only one commonly used in calculating price to cash flow, not a technically accurate definition from an accounting perspective. We will also describe more technically accurate cash flow concepts: cash flow from operations, free cash flow to equity, and EBITDA (an estimate of pre-interest, pretax operating cash flow).

Most frequently, trailing price to cash flow is reported. A trailing price to cash flow is calculated as the current market price divided by the sum of the most recent four quarters' cash flow per share. A fiscal year definition is also possible, as in the case of EPS.

Example 29 illustrates the calculation of P/CF with cash flow defined as earnings plus noncash charges.

EXAMPLE 29

Calculating Price to Cash Flow with Cash Flow Defined as Earnings plus Noncash Charges

1. In 2018, Koninklijke Philips Electronics N.V. (PHIA) reported net income from continuing operations of €1,310 million, equal to EPS of €1.41. The company's depreciation and amortization was €1,089 million, or €1.17 per share. An AEX price for PHIA as of 29 March 2019 was €36.31. Calculate the P/CF for PHIA.

Solution:

CF (defined as EPS plus per-share depreciation, amortization, and depletion) is €1.41 + €1.17 = €2.58 per share. Thus, P/CF = €36.31/€2.58 = 14.1.

Rather than use an approximate EPS-plus-noncash-charges concept of cash flow, analysts can use cash flow from operations (CFO) in a price multiple. CFO is found in the statement of cash flows. Similar to the adjustments to normalize earnings, adjustments to CFO for components not expected to persist into future time periods may also be appropriate. In addition, adjustments to CFO may be required when comparing companies that use different accounting standards. For example, as noted above, under IFRS, companies have flexibility in classifying interest payments, interest receipts, and dividend receipts across operating, investing, and financing. US GAAP require companies to classify interest payments, interest receipts, and dividend receipts as operating cash flows.

As an alternative to CF and CFO, the analyst can relate price to FCFE, the cash flow concept with the strongest link to valuation theory. Because the amounts of capital expenditures in proportion to CFO generally differ among companies being compared, the analyst may find that rankings by price to cash flow from operations (P/CFO) and by P/CF will differ from rankings by P/FCFE. Period-by-period FCFE may be more volatile than CFO (or CF), however, so a trailing P/FCFE is not necessarily more informative in a valuation. For example, consider two similar businesses with

[handwritten margin note] FCFE: cash flow available to shareholders after deducting all operating expenses, interest and debt payments, and investments in working capital

the same CFO and capital expenditures over a two-year period. If the first company times its capital expenditures to fall toward the beginning of the period and the second times its capital expenditures to fall toward the end of the period, the P/FCFEs for the two stocks may differ sharply without representing a meaningful economic difference. The analyst could, however, appropriately use the FCFE discounted cash flow model value, which incorporates all expected future free cash flows to equity. This concern can be addressed, at least in part, by using price to average free cash flow, as in Hackel, Livnat, and Rai (1994).

Another cash flow concept used in multiples is EBITDA (earnings before interest, taxes, depreciation, and amortization). To forecast EBITDA, analysts usually start with their projections of EBIT and simply add depreciation and amortization to arrive at an estimate for EBITDA. In calculating EBITDA from historical numbers, one can start with earnings from continuing operations, excluding nonrecurring items. To that earnings number, interest, taxes, depreciation, and amortization are added.

In practice, both EV/EBITDA and P/EBITDA have been used by analysts as valuation metrics. EV/EBITDA has been the preferred metric, however, because its numerator includes the value of debt; therefore, it is the more appropriate method because EBITDA is pre-interest and is thus a flow to both debt and equity. EV/EBITDA is discussed in detail in a later section.

Valuation Based on Forecasted Fundamentals

The relationship between the justified price to cash flow and fundamentals follows from the familiar mathematics of the present value model. The justified price to cash flow, all else being equal, is inversely related to the stock's required rate of return and positively related to the growth rate(s) of expected future cash flows (however defined). We can find a justified price to cash flow based on fundamentals by finding the value of a stock using the most suitable DCF model and dividing that number by cash flow (based on our chosen definition of cash flow). Example 30 illustrates the process.

EXAMPLE 30

Justified Price to Cash Flow Based on Forecasted Fundamentals

As a consumer staples analyst, you are working on the valuation of Colgate-Palmolive (CL), a global consumer products supplier. As a first estimate of value, you are applying an FCFE model under the assumption of a stable long-term growth rate in FCFE:

$$V_0 = \frac{(1 + g)\, FCFE_0}{r - g},$$

where g is the expected growth rate of FCFE. You estimate trailing FCFE at $2.66 per share and trailing CF (based on the earnings-plus-noncash-charges definition) at $3.26. Your other estimates are a 7.4% required rate of return and a 3.2% expected growth rate of FCFE.

1. What is the intrinsic value of CL according to a constant growth FCFE model?

Solution:

Calculate intrinsic value as (1.032 × $2.66)/(0.074 − 0.032) = $58.41.

2. What is the justified P/CF based on forecasted fundamentals?

Solution:

Calculate a justified P/CF based on forecasted fundamentals as $58.41/$3.26 = 24.6.

3. What is the justified P/FCFE based on forecasted fundamentals?

Solution:

The justified P/FCFE is $58.41/$2.66 = 22.0.

Valuation Based on Comparables

The method of comparables for valuing stocks based on price to cash flow follows the steps given previously and illustrated for P/E, P/B, and P/S. Example 31 is a simple exercise in the comparables method based on price-to-cash-flow measures.

EXAMPLE 31

Price to Cash Flow and Comparables

1. Exhibit 15 provides information on P/CF, P/FCFE, and selected fundamentals as of 16 April 2020 for two hypothetical companies. Using the information in Exhibit 15, compare the valuations of the two companies.

Exhibit 15: Comparison of Two Companies (All Amounts per Share)

Company	Current Price (£)	Trailing CF per Share (£)	P/CF	Trailing FCFE per Share (£)	P/FCFE	Consensus Five-Year CF Growth Forecast (%)	Beta
Company A	17.98	1.84	9.8	0.29	62	13.4	1.50
Company B	15.65	1.37	11.4	−0.99	NMF	10.6	1.50

Company A is selling at a P/CF (9.8) approximately 14% smaller than the P/CF of Company B (11.4). Based on that comparison, we expect that, all else equal, investors would anticipate a higher growth rate for Company B. Contrary to that expectation, however, the consensus five-year earnings growth forecast for Company A is 280 basis points higher than it is for Company B. As of the date of the comparison, Company A appears to be relatively undervalued compared with Company B, as judged by P/CF and expected growth. The information in Exhibit 15 on FCFE supports the proposition that Company A may be relatively undervalued. The positive FCFE for Company A indicates that operating cash flows and new debt borrowing are more than sufficient to cover capital expenditures. Negative FCFE for Company B suggests the need for external funding of growth.

8   PRICE/DIVIDENDS AND DIVIDEND YIELD

☐   calculate and interpret a justified price multiple

☐   describe rationales for and possible drawbacks to using alternative price multiples and dividend yield in valuation

☐   calculate and interpret alternative price multiples and dividend yield

☐   describe fundamental factors that influence alternative price multiples and dividend yield

☐   calculate and interpret the justified price-to-earnings ratio (P/E), price-to-book ratio (P/B), and price-to-sales ratio (P/S) for a stock, based on forecasted fundamentals

☐   evaluate a stock by the method of comparables and explain the importance of fundamentals in using the method of comparables

☐   evaluate whether a stock is overvalued, fairly valued, or undervalued based on comparisons of multiples

The total return on an equity investment has a capital appreciation component and a dividend yield component. Dividend yield data are frequently reported to provide investors with an estimate of the dividend yield component in total return. Dividend yield is also used as a valuation indicator. Although the 2012 BofA Merrill Lynch Institutional Factor Survey did not survey this metric, in its surveys from 1989 to 2006 slightly more than one-quarter of respondents on average reported using dividend yield as a factor in the investment process.

Analysts have offered the following rationales for using dividend yields in valuation:

- Dividend yield is a component of total return.
- Dividends are a less risky component of total return than capital appreciation.

Possible drawbacks of using dividend yields include the following:

- Dividend yield is only one component of total return; not using all information related to expected return is suboptimal.

- Investors may trade off future earnings growth to receive higher current dividends. That is, holding return on equity constant, dividends paid now displace earnings in all future periods (a concept known as the **dividend displacement of earnings**). Arnott and Asness (2003) and Zhou and Ruland (2006), however, showed that caution must be exercised in assuming that dividends displace future earnings in practice, because dividend payout may be correlated with future profitability.

- The argument about the relative safety of dividends presupposes that market prices reflect in a biased way differences in the relative risk of the components of return.

Calculation of Dividend Yield

This reading so far has presented multiples with market price (or market capitalization) in the numerator. P/Ds have sometimes appeared in valuation, particularly with respect to indexes. Many stocks, however, do not pay dividends, and P/D is undefined with zero in the denominator. For such non-dividend-paying stocks, dividend yield (D/P) *is* defined: It is equal to zero. For practical purposes, then, dividend yield is the preferred way to present this multiple.

Trailing dividend yield is generally calculated by using the dividend rate divided by the current market price per share. The annualized amount of the most recent dividend is known as the **dividend rate**. For companies paying quarterly dividends, the dividend rate is calculated as four times the most recent quarterly per-share dividend. (Some data sources use the dividends in the last four quarters as the dividend rate for purposes of a trailing dividend yield.) For companies that pay semiannual dividends comprising an interim dividend that typically differs in magnitude from the final dividend, the dividend rate is usually calculated as the most recent annual per-share dividend.

The dividend rate indicates the annual amount of dividends per share under the assumption of no increase or decrease over the year. The analyst's forecast of leading dividends could be higher or lower and is the basis of the leading dividend yield. The **leading dividend yield** is calculated as forecasted dividends per share over the next year divided by the current market price per share. Example 32 illustrates the calculation of dividend yield.

EXAMPLE 32

Calculating Dividend Yield

Exhibit 16 gives quarterly dividend data for Canadian telecommunications company BCE Inc. (BCE) and semiannual dividend data for the ADRs of BT Group (BT), formerly British Telecom.

Exhibit 16: Dividends Paid per Share for BCE Inc. and for BT Group ADRs

Period	BCE ($)	BT ADR ($)
4Q:2016	0.51	
1Q:2017	0.54	0.685
2Q:2017	0.53	
3Q:2017	0.57	0.339
Total	2.15	1.024
4Q:2017	0.56	
1Q:2018	0.60	0.675
2Q:2018	0.58	
3Q:2018	0.58	0.301
Total	2.32	0.976

Source: Value Line.

1. Given a price per share for BCE of $39.53 during 4Q:2018, calculate this company's trailing dividend yield.

Solution:

The dividend rate for BCE is $0.58 × 4 = $2.32. The dividend yield is $2.32/$39.53 = 0.0587, or 5.87%. ↳ annualized amount of the most recent dividend of $.58

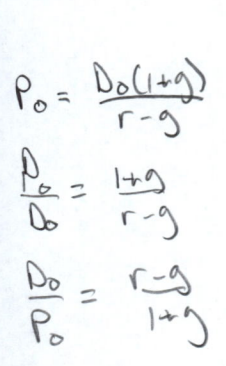

$$P_0 = \frac{D_0(1+g)}{r-g}$$

$$\frac{P_0}{D_0} = \frac{1+g}{r-g}$$

$$\frac{D_0}{P_0} = \frac{r-g}{1+g}$$

2. Given a price per ADR for BT of $15.20 during 4Q:2018, calculate the trailing dividend yield for the ADRs.

Solution:

Because BT pays semiannual dividends that differ in magnitude between the interim and final dividends, the dividend rate for BT's ADR is the total dividend in the most recent year, $0.976. The dividend yield is $0.976/$15.20 = 0.0642, or 6.52%.

Valuation Based on Forecasted Fundamentals

The relationship of dividend yield to fundamentals can be illustrated in the context of the Gordon growth model. From that model, we obtain the expression

$$\frac{D_0}{P_0} = \frac{r-g}{1+g}. \tag{8}$$

Equation 8 shows that dividend yield is negatively related to the expected rate of growth in dividends and positively related to the stock's required rate of return. The first point implies that the selection of stocks with relatively high dividend yields is consistent with an orientation to a value rather than growth investment style.

Valuation Based on Comparables

Using dividend yield with comparables is similar to the process that has been illustrated for other multiples. An analyst compares a company with its peers to determine whether it is attractively priced, considering its dividend yield and risk. The analyst should examine whether differences in expected growth explain the differences in dividend yield. Another consideration used by some investors is the security of the dividend (the probability that it will be reduced or eliminated). A useful metric in assessing the safety of the dividend is the payout ratio: A high payout relative to other companies operating in the same industry may indicate a less secure dividend because the dividend is less well covered by earnings. Balance sheet metrics are equally important in assessing the safety of the dividend, and relevant ratios to consider include the interest coverage ratio and the ratio of net debt to EBITDA. Example 33 illustrates use of the dividend yield in the method of comparables.

EXAMPLE 33

Dividend Yield Comparables

1. William Leiderman is a portfolio manager for a US pension fund's domestic equity portfolio. The portfolio is exempt from taxes, so any differences in the taxation of dividends and capital gains are not relevant. Leiderman's client requires high current income. Leiderman is considering the purchase of utility stocks for the fund in August 2019. In the course of his review, he considers the four large-cap US electric utilities shown in Exhibit 17.

Exhibit 17: Using Dividend Yield to Compare Stocks

Company	Consensus Earnings Growth Forecast (%)	Beta	Dividend Yield (%)	Payout Ratio (%)
Duke Energy	7.20	0.18	4.24	89
NiSource Inc.	4.63	0.22	2.70	NMF
Portland General Electric Co.	5.20	0.24	2.76	59
PPL Corp.	0.60	0.55	5.37	63

Sources: www.finviz.com and Yahoo! Finance.

All of the securities exhibit similar low market risk; they each have a beta substantially less than 1.00. The dividend payout ratio for NiSource is not meaningful due to a negative EPS. Duke Energy's dividend payout ratio of 89%, the highest of the group, also suggests that its dividend may be subject to greater risk. Leiderman notes that PPL Corp.'s relatively low payout ratio means that the dividend is well supported; however, the expected low earnings growth rate is a negative factor. Summing Portland General Electric's dividend yield and expected earnings growth rate, Leiderman estimates Portland General Electric's expected total return is about 7.96%; because the total return estimate is relatively attractive and because Portland General Electric does not appear to have any strong negatives, Leiderman decides to focus his further analysis on Portland General Electric.

ENTERPRISE VALUE/EBITDA

9

- [ ] explain alternative definitions of cash flow used in price and enterprise value (EV) multiples and describe limitations of each definition
- [ ] calculate and interpret EV multiples and evaluate the use of EV/EBITDA
- [ ] evaluate whether a stock is overvalued, fairly valued, or undervalued based on comparisons of multiples

Enterprise value multiples are multiples that relate the enterprise value of a company to some measure of value (typically, a pre-interest income measure). Perhaps the most frequently advanced argument for using enterprise value multiples rather than price multiples in valuation is that enterprise value multiples are relatively less sensitive to the effects of financial leverage than price multiples when one is comparing companies that use differing amounts of leverage. Enterprise value multiples, in defining the numerator as they do, take a control perspective (discussed in more detail later). Thus, even where leverage differences are not an issue, enterprise value multiples may complement the perspective of price multiples. Indeed, although some analysts strictly favor one type of multiple, other analysts report both price and enterprise value multiples.

Enterprise Value/EBITDA

Enterprise value to EBITDA is by far the most widely used enterprise value multiple. Earlier, EBITDA was introduced as an estimate of pre-interest, pretax operating cash flow. Because EBITDA is a flow to both debt and equity, as noted, defining an EBITDA multiple by using a measure of total company value in the numerator, such as EV, is appropriate. Recall that **enterprise value** is total company value (the market value of debt, common equity, and preferred equity) minus the value of cash and short-term investments. Thus, EV/EBITDA is a valuation indicator for the overall company rather than solely its common stock. If, however, the analyst can assume that the business's debt and preferred stock (if any) are efficiently priced, the analyst can use EV/EBITDA to draw an inference about the valuation of common equity. Such an inference is often reasonable.

Analysts have offered the following rationales for using EV/EBITDA:

- EV/EBITDA is usually more appropriate than P/E alone for comparing companies with different financial leverage (debt), because EBITDA is a pre-interest earnings figure, in contrast to EPS, which is postinterest.

- By adding back depreciation and amortization, EBITDA controls for differences in depreciation and amortization among businesses, in contrast to net income, which is postdepreciation and postamortization. For this reason, EV/EBITDA is frequently used in the valuation of capital-intensive businesses (for example, cable companies and steel companies). Such businesses typically have substantial depreciation and amortization expenses.

- EBITDA is frequently positive when EPS is negative.

Possible drawbacks to using EV/EBITDA include the following (Moody's 2000; Grant and Parker 2001):

- EBITDA will overestimate cash flow from operations if working capital is growing. EBITDA also ignores the effects of differences in revenue recognition policy on cash flow from operations.

- Free cash flow to the firm (FCFF), which directly reflects the amount of the company's required capital expenditures, has a stronger link to valuation theory than does EBITDA. Only if depreciation expenses match capital expenditures do we expect EBITDA to reflect differences in businesses' capital programs. This qualification to EBITDA comparisons may be particularly meaningful for the capital-intensive businesses to which EV/EBITDA is often applied.

Determining Enterprise Value

We illustrated the calculation of EBITDA previously. As discussed, analysts commonly define enterprise value as follows:

Market value of common equity (Number of shares outstanding × Price per share)

Plus: Market value of preferred stock (if any) and any minority interest (unless included elsewhere)

Plus: Market value of debt

Less: Cash and investments (specifically, cash, cash equivalents, and short-term investments)

Equals: Enterprise value.

P/EBITDA does not take into account differences in the use of financial leverage.

Cash and investments (sometimes termed **nonearning assets**) are subtracted because EV is designed to measure the net price an acquirer would pay for the company as a whole. The acquirer must buy out current equity and debt providers but then receives access to the cash and investments, which lower the net cost of the acquisition. (For example, cash and investments can be used to pay off debt or loans used to finance the purchase.) The same logic explains the use of market values: In repurchasing debt, an acquirer has to pay market prices. Some debt, however, may be private and does not trade; some debt may be publicly traded but may trade infrequently. When analysts do not have market values, they often use book values obtained from the balance sheet. Alternatively, they may use so-called matrix price estimates of debt market values in such cases; where they are available, they may be more accurate. Matrix price estimates are based on characteristics of the debt issue and information on how the marketplace prices those characteristics. Example 34 illustrates the calculation of EV/EBITDA.

EXAMPLE 34

Calculating EV/EBITDA

1. Colgate-Palmolive (CL) provides a variety of household products. Exhibit 18 presents the company's consolidated balance sheet as of 31 December 2018.

Exhibit 18: Colgate-Palmolive Condensed Consolidated Balance Sheet (in Millions except Par Values; Unaudited)

Assets	
Current assets:	
Cash and cash equivalents	$726
Accounts receivable, net	1,400
Inventories	1,250
Other current assets	417
Total current assets	3,793
Property and equipment, net	3,881
Goodwill and other intangible assets, net	4,167
Other non-current assets	320
Total assets	$12,161

Liabilities and Shareholders' Equity	
Current liabilities:	
Accounts payable	$1,222
Accrued income taxes	411
Other accruals	1,696
Current portion of long-term debt	0
Notes and loans payable	12
Total current liabilities	3,341
Long-term debt	6,354
Other non-current liabilities	2,269

Liabilities and Shareholders' Equity	
Total liabilities	$11,964
Shareholders' equity:	
Preference stock	—
Common stock outstanding—863 million shares	1,466
Additional paid-in capital	2,204
Accumulated comprehensive income (loss)	(4,191)
Retained earnings	21,615
Treasury stock—common shares at cost	(21,196)
Noncontrolling interests	299
Total shareholders' equity	197
Total liabilities and shareholders' equity	$12,161

Source: Company financial report.

This financial statement is audited because US companies are required to have audits only for their annual financial statements. Quarterly statements are labeled as unaudited.

From CL's financial statements, the income statement and statement of cash flows for the year ended 31 December 2018 provided the following items (in millions):

Item	Source	Year Ended 31 December 2018
Net income	Income statement	$2,400
Interest expense (net of interest income)	Income statement	143
Income tax provision	Income statement	906
Depreciation and amortization	Statement of cash flows	511

The company's share price as of 15 February 2019 was $66.48. Based on the above information, calculate EV/EBITDA.

Solution:

- For EV, we first calculate the total value of CL's equity: 863 million shares outstanding times $66.48 price per share equals $57,372 million market capitalization.

  CL has only one class of common stock, no preferred shares, and no **minority interest**. For companies that have multiple classes of common stock, market capitalization includes the total value of all classes of common stock. Similarly, for companies that have preferred stock and/or minority interest, the market value of preferred stock and the amount of minority interest are added to market capitalization.

  EV also includes the value of long-term debt obligations. Per CL's balance sheet, this is the sum of long-term debt ($6,354 million), the current portion of long-term debt ($0 million), and other non-current liabilities ($2,034 million), or $8,388 million. Typically, the book value of long-term debt is used in EV. If, however, the market value of the debt is readily available and materially different from the book value, the market value should be used.

EV excludes cash, cash equivalents, and short-term investments. Per CL's balance sheet, the total of cash and cash equivalents is $726 million.

So, CL's EV is $57,372 million + $8,388 million − $720 million = $65,040 million.

- For EBITDA, we use the trailing 12-month (TTM) data, which are shown in the table above for the year ending 31 December 2018. The EBITDA calculation is

EBITDA = Net income + Interest + Income taxes + Depreciation and amortization.

EBITDA = $2,400 + $143 + $906 + $511 = $3,960 million.

CL does not have preferred equity. Companies that do have preferred equity typically present in their financial statement net income available to common shareholders. In those cases, the EBITDA calculation uses net income available to *both* preferred and common equity holders.

For CL, we conclude that EV/EBITDA = ($65,040 million)/($3,960 million) = 16.4.

Valuation Based on Forecasted Fundamentals

As with other multiples, intuition about the fundamental drivers of enterprise value to EBITDA can help when applying the method of comparables. All else being equal, the justified EV/EBITDA based on fundamentals should be positively related to the expected growth rate in free cash flow to the firm, positively related to expected profitability as measured by return on invested capital, and negatively related to the business's weighted average cost of capital. **Return on invested capital** (ROIC) is calculated as operating profit after tax divided by invested capital. In analyzing ratios such as EV/EBITDA, ROIC is the relevant measure of profitability because EBITDA flows to all providers of capital.

Valuation Based on Comparables

All else equal, a lower EV/EBITDA value relative to peers indicates that a company is relatively undervalued. An analyst's recommendations, however, are usually not completely determined by relative EV/EBITDA; from an analyst's perspective, EV/EBITDA is simply one piece of information to consider.

Example 35 presents a comparison of enterprise value multiples for four peer companies. The example includes a measure of total firm value—**total invested capital** (TIC), sometimes also known as the **market value of invested capital**—that is an alternative to enterprise value. Similar to EV, TIC includes the market value of equity and debt but does not deduct cash and investments.

EXAMPLE 35

Comparable Enterprise Value Multiples

Exhibit 19 presents EV multiples on 27 August 2019 for four companies in the household products industry: Colgate-Palmolive (CL), Kimberly Clark Corp. (KMB), Clorox Co. (CLX), and Church & Dwight Co. (CHD).

Exhibit 19: Enterprise Value Multiples for Industry Peers (Amounts in $ Millions, Except Where Indicated Otherwise)

Measure	CL	KMB	CLX	CHD
Price	$72.60	$140.25	$156.96	$79.15
Times: Shares outstanding (millions)	860	344	127	247
Equals: Equity market cap	62.44	48.25	19.93	19.55
Plus: Debt (most recent quarter)	7.33	8.46	2.69	2.38
Plus: Preferred stock	—	—	—	—
Equals: Market value of TIC	69.77	56.71	22.62	21.93
Less: Cash	0.93	0.53	0.11	0.10
Equals: Enterprise value (EV)	$68.84	$56.18	$22.51	$21.83
EBITDA (TTM)	$4.07	$3.81	$1.28	$0.97
TIC/EBITDA	17.1	14.9	17.7	22.6
EV/EBITDA	16.9	14.7	17.6	22.5
Profit margin (TTM)	14.8%	9.8%	13.2%	5.0%
Quarterly revenue growth (year over year)	−0.5%	−0.2%	−3.8%	13.8%

Sources: Yahoo! Finance; authors' calculations.

1. Exhibit 19 provides two alternative enterprise value multiples, TIC/EBITDA and EV/EBITDA. The ranking of the companies' multiples is identical by both multiples. In general, what could cause the rankings to vary?

Solution:

The difference between TIC and EV is that EV excludes cash, cash equivalents, and marketable securities. So, a material variation among companies in cash, cash equivalents, or marketable securities relative to EBITDA could cause the rankings to vary.

2. Each EBITDA multiple incorporates a comparison with enterprise value. How do these multiples differ from price-to-cash-flow multiples?

Solution:

These multiples differ from price-to-cash-flow multiples in that the numerator is a measure of firm value rather than share price, to match the denominator, which is a pre-interest measure of earnings. These multiples thus provide a more appropriate comparison than price to cash flow when companies have significantly different capital structures.

3. Based solely on the information in Exhibit 19, how does the valuation of CL compare with that of the other three companies?

Solution:

Based on its lower TIC/EBITDA and EV/EBITDA multiples of 17.1 and 16.9, respectively, CL appears undervalued relative to CLX and CHD and overvalued relative to KMB. These valuation ratios may be warranted given differences in profitability and growth rates. Compared with CHD, CL has a similar profit margin and lower revenue growth, which may explain CL's lower valuation multiples. Compared with KMB, the enterprise value mul-

> tiples of CL are higher, which is consistent with CL being more profitable than KMB (profit margin of 14.8% versus 9.8%).

OTHER ENTERPRISE VALUE MULTIPLES

10

☐ explain alternative definitions of cash flow used in price and enterprise value (EV) multiples and describe limitations of each definition

☐ calculate and interpret EV multiples and evaluate the use of EV/EBITDA

☐ evaluate whether a stock is overvalued, fairly valued, or undervalued based on comparisons of multiples

Although EV/EBITDA is the most widely known and used enterprise value multiple, other enterprise value multiples are used together with or in place of EV/EBITDA—either in a broad range of applications or for valuations in a specific industry. EV/FCFF is an example of a broadly used multiple; an example of a special-purpose multiple is EV/EBITDAR (where R stands for rent expense), which is favored by airline industry analysts. Here we review the most common such multiples (except EV/sales, which is covered in the next section). In each case, a valuation metric could be formulated in terms of TIC rather than EV.

Major alternatives to using EBITDA in the denominator of enterprise value multiples include FCFF (free cash flow to the firm), EBITA (earnings before interest, taxes, and amortization), and EBIT (earnings before interest and taxes). Exhibit 20 summarizes the components of each of these measurements and how they relate to net income. Note that, in practice, analysts typically forecast EBITDA by forecasting EBIT and adding depreciation and amortization.

Exhibit 20: Alternative Denominators in Enterprise Value Multiples

Free Cash Flow to the Firm =	Net Income	plus Interest Expense	minus Tax Savings on Interest	plus Depreciation	plus Amortization	less Investment in Working Capital	less Investment in Fixed Capital
EBITDA =	Net Income	plus Interest Expense	plus Taxes	plus Depreciation	plus Amortization		
EBITA =	Net Income	plus Interest Expense	plus Taxes		plus Amortization		
EBIT =	Net Income	plus Interest Expense	plus Taxes				

Note that the calculation of all the measures given in Exhibit 20 add interest back to net income, which reflects that these measures are flows relevant to all providers of both debt and equity capital. As one moves down the rows of Exhibit 20, the measures incorporate increasingly less precise information about a company's tax position and its capital investments, although each measure has a rationale. For example, EBITA may be chosen in cases in which amortization (associated with intangibles) but not depreciation (associated with tangibles) is a major expense for companies being compared. EBIT may be chosen where neither depreciation nor amortization is a major item.

In addition to enterprise value multiples based on financial measures, in some industries or sectors, the analyst may find it appropriate to examine enterprise value multiples based on a nonfinancial measurement that is specific to that industry or sector. For example, for satellite and cable TV broadcasters, an analyst might usefully examine EV to subscribers. For a resource-based company, a multiple based on reserves of the resource may be appropriate.

Regardless of the specific denominator used in an enterprise value multiple, the concept remains the same—namely, to relate the market value of the total company to some fundamental financial or nonfinancial measure of the company's value.

Enterprise Value to Sales

Enterprise value to sales is a major alternative to the price-to-sales ratio. The P/S multiple has the conceptual weakness that it fails to recognize that for a debt-financed company, not all sales belong to a company's equity investors. Some of the proceeds from the company's sales will be used to pay interest and principal to the providers of the company's debt capital. For example, a P/S for a company with little or no debt would not be comparable to a P/S for a company that is largely financed with debt. EV/S would be the basis for a valid comparison in such a case. In summary, EV/S is an alternative sales-based ratio that is particularly useful when comparing companies with diverse capital structures. Example 36 illustrates the calculation of EV/S multiples.

EXAMPLE 36

Calculating Enterprise Value to Sales

1. As described in Example 22, Stora Enso Oyj (Helsinki Stock Exchange: STERV) reported net sales of €10,486 million for 2018. Based on 788.6 million shares outstanding and a stock price of €10.34 on 28 June 2019, the total market value of the company's equity was €8,154 million. The company reported non-current debt of €2,970 million and cash of €1,130 million. Assume that the market value of the company's debt is equal to the amount reported. Calculate the company's EV/S.

Solution:

Enterprise value = €8,145 million + €2,970 million − €1,130 million = €9,994 million. So, EV/S = €9,994 million/€10,486 million = 0.953.

Price and Enterprise Value Multiples in a Comparable Analysis: Some Illustrative Data

In previous sections, we explained the major price and enterprise value multiples. Analysts using multiples and a benchmark based on closely similar companies should be aware of the range of values for multiples for peer companies and should track the fundamentals that may explain differences. For the sake of illustration, Exhibit 21 shows the median value of various multiples by GICS economic sector, the median dividend payout ratio, and median values of selected fundamentals:

- ROE and its determinants (net profit margin, asset turnover, and financial leverage)
- The compound average growth rate in operating margin for the three years ending with FY2007 (shown in the last column under "3-Year CAGR Operating Margin")

Because EV includes the market values of both debt and equity, logically the ranking based on EV/Sales should be compared with a pre-interest measure of profitability, namely, operating margin

Exhibit 21 is based on the S&P 1500 Composite Index for US equities, consisting of the S&P 500, the S&P MidCap 400 Index, and the S&P SmallCap 600 Index. GICS was described earlier.

At the level of aggregation shown in Exhibit 21, the data are, arguably, most relevant to relative sector valuation. For the purposes of valuing individual companies, analysts would most likely use more narrowly defined industry or sector classification.

INTERNATIONAL CONSIDERATIONS WHEN USING MULTIPLES

11

☐ | explain sources of differences in cross-border valuation comparisons

Clearly, to perform a relative-value analysis, an analyst must use comparable companies and underlying financial data prepared by applying comparable methods. Therefore, using relative-valuation methods in an international setting is difficult. Comparing companies across borders frequently involves differences in accounting methods, cultural differences, economic differences, and resulting differences in risk and growth opportunities. P/Es for individual companies in the same industry but in different countries have been found to vary widely. Furthermore, P/Es of different national markets often vary substantially at any single point in time.

Although international accounting standards are converging, significant differences still exist across borders, sometimes making comparisons difficult. Even when harmonization of accounting principles is achieved, the need to adjust accounting data for comparability will remain. As we showed earlier, even within a single country's accounting standards, differences between companies result from accounting choices (e.g., FIFO versus average cost for inventory valuation). Prior to 2008, the US SEC required non-US companies whose securities trade in US markets to provide a reconciliation between their earnings from home-country accounting principles to US GAAP. This requirement not only assisted the analyst in making necessary adjustments but also provided some insight into appropriate adjustments for other companies not required to provide this data. In December 2007, however, the SEC eliminated the reconciliation requirement for non-US companies that use IFRS. Research analyzing reconciliations by EU companies with US listings shows that most of those companies reported net income under IFRS that was higher than they would have reported under US GAAP and lower shareholders' equity than they would have under US GAAP, with a result that more of the sample companies reported higher ROE under IFRS than under US GAAP.

In a study of companies filing such reconciliations to US GAAP, Harris and Muller (1999) classified common differences into seven categories, as shown in Exhibit 22.

Exhibit 21: Fundamental and Valuation Statistics by GICS Economic Sector: Median Values from S&P 1500, FY2007

GICS Sector (count)	Valuation Statistics							Fundamental Statistics					
	Trailing P/E	P/B	P/S	P/CF	Dividend Yield (%)	EV/ EBITDA	EV/S	Net Profit Margin (%)	Asset Turnover	Financial Leverage	ROE (%)	Dividend Payout Ratio (%)	3-Year CAGR Operating Margin (%)
Energy (85)	14.406	2.531	2.186	8.622	0.4	7.733	2.64	13.942	0.573	2.103	19.688	4.024	12.035
Materials (85)	15.343	2.254	0.888	9.588	1.4	7.686	1.095	5.568	0.995	2.465	15.728	17.874	4.157
Industrials (207)	17.275	2.578	1.045	11.642	1.0	8.979	1.209	6.089	1.139	2.143	15.262	16.066	5.337
Consumer Discretionary (279)	15.417	2.254	0.789	9.986	0.7	7.634	0.928	4.777	1.383	2.12	13.289	0	-2.682
Consumer Staples (80)	19.522	3.048	1.122	13.379	1.4	10.66	1.237	5.306	1.351	2.208	17.264	23.133	-0.88
Health Care (167)	23.027	3.088	2.061	15.762	0	11.623	2.274	6.637	0.83	1.854	12.399	0	-1.708
Financials (257)	14.648	1.559	1.888	11.186	3.1	9.482	4.017	13.113	0.113	5.848	10.348	41.691	-4.124
Information Technology (252)	20.205	2.444	2.162	45.073	0	11.594	1.811	7.929	0.743	1.587	10.444	0	1.524
Telecommunication Services (13)	19.585	2.485	1.527	5.266	0.8	6.681	2.345	7.109	0.471	2.367	5.43	6.862	-2.421
Utilities (75)	16.682	1.784	1.151	8.405	3.1	9.056	1.903	7.21	0.439	3.52	11.853	52.738	0.361
Overall (1,500)	17.148	2.246	1.398	11.328	0.8	9.108	1.626	7.318	0.839	2.227	12.701	8.051	0.181

Source: Standard & Poor's Research Insight.

Exhibit 22: Reconciliation of IFRS to US GAAP: Average Adjustment		
Category	**Earnings**	**Equity**
Differences in the treatment of goodwill	Minus	Plus
Deferred income taxes	Plus	Plus
Foreign exchange adjustments	Plus	Minus
Research and development costs	Minus	Minus
Pension expense	Minus	Plus
Tangible asset revaluations	Plus	Minus
Other	Minus	Minus

In a more recent study of reconciliation data, Henry, Lin, and Yang (2009) found that among 20 categories of reconciliations, the most frequently occurring adjustments are in the pension category (including post-retirement benefits) and the largest value of adjustments are in the goodwill category.

Although the SEC's decision to eliminate the requirement for reconciliation has eliminated an important resource for analysts, accounting research can provide some insight into areas where differences between IFRS and US GAAP have commonly arisen. Going forward, analysts must be aware of differences between standards and make adjustments when disclosures provide sufficient data to do so.

International accounting differences affect the comparability of all price multiples. Of the price multiples we examined, P/CFO and P/FCFE will generally be least affected by accounting differences. P/B, P/E, and multiples based on such concepts as EBITDA, which start from accounting earnings, will generally be the most affected.

MOMENTUM VALUATION INDICATORS   12

☐ | describe momentum indicators and their use in valuation

The valuation indicators we call momentum indicators relate either price or a fundamental, such as earnings, to the time series of their own past values or, in some cases, to the fundamental's expected value. One style of growth investing uses positive momentum in various senses as a selection criterion, and practitioners sometimes refer to such strategies as "growth/momentum investment strategies." Momentum indicators based on price, such as the relative-strength indicator we will discuss here, have also been referred to as **technical indicators**. According to the BofA Merrill Lynch Institutional Factor Survey, various momentum indicators were used by many institutional investors. In this section, we review three representative momentum indicators: earnings surprise, standardized unexpected earnings, and relative strength.

To define standardized unexpected earnings, we define **unexpected earnings** (also called **earnings surprise**) as the difference between reported earnings and expected earnings:

$$UE_t = \text{EPS}_t - E(\text{EPS}_t),$$

where UE_t is the unexpected earnings for quarter t, EPS_t is the reported EPS for quarter t, and $E(\text{EPS}_t)$ is the expected EPS for the quarter.

For example, a stock with reported quarterly earnings of $1.05 and expected earnings of $1.00 would have a positive earnings surprise of $0.05. Often, the percentage earnings surprise (i.e., earnings surprise divided by expected EPS) is reported by data providers; in this example, the percentage earning surprise would be $0.05/$1.00 = 0.05, or 5%. When used directly as a valuation indicator, earnings surprise is generally scaled by a measure reflecting the variability or range in analysts' EPS estimates. The principle is that the less disagreement among analysts' forecasts, the more meaningful the EPS forecast error of a given size in relation to the mean. A way to accomplish such scaling is to divide unexpected earnings by the standard deviation of analysts' earnings forecasts, which we refer to as the **scaled earnings surprise**. Example 37 illustrates the calculation of such a scaled earnings surprise.

EXAMPLE 37

Calculating Scaled Earnings Surprise by Using Analysts' Forecasts

1. During the third quarter of 2019, the mean consensus earnings forecast for BP plc for the fiscal year ending December 2019 was $3.26. Of the 11 estimates, the low forecast was $2.76, the high forecast was $3.74, and the standard deviation was $0.29. If actual reported earnings for 2019 come in equal to the high forecast, what would be the measure of the earnings surprise for BP scaled to reflect the dispersion in analysts' forecasts?

Solution:

In this case, scaled earnings surprise would be ($3.74 − $3.26)/$0.29 = $0.48/$0.29 = 1.66.

The rationale behind using earnings surprise is the thesis that positive surprises may be associated with persistent positive abnormal returns, or alpha. The same rationale lies behind a momentum indicator that is closely related to earnings surprise but more highly researched—namely, **standardized unexpected earnings** (SUE). The SUE measure is defined as

$$SUE_t = \frac{EPS_t - E(EPS_t)}{\sigma[EPS_t - E(EPS_t)]},$$

where

EPS_t = Actual EPS for time t

$E(EPS_t)$ = Expected EPS for time t

$\sigma[EPS_t - E(EPS_t)]$ = Standard deviation of $[EPS_t - E(EPS_t)]$ over some historical time period

In words, the numerator is the unexpected earnings at time t and the denominator is the standard deviation of past unexpected earnings over some period prior to time t—for example, the 20 quarters prior to t, as in Latané and Jones (1979), the article that introduced the SUE concept (for a summary of the research on SUE, see Brown 1997). In SUE, the magnitude of unexpected earnings is scaled by a measure of the size of historical forecast errors or surprises. The principle is that the smaller (larger) the historical size of forecast errors, the more (less) meaningful a given size of EPS forecast error.

Suppose that for a stock with a $0.05 earnings surprise, the standard deviation of past surprises is $0.20. The $0.05 surprise is relatively small compared with past forecast errors, which would be reflected in a SUE score of $0.05/$0.20 = 0.25. If the standard error of past surprises were smaller—say, $0.07—the SUE score would be $0.05/$0.07 = 0.71. Example 38 applies analysis of SUE to two companies.

EXAMPLE 38

Unexpected Earnings (Historical Example)

Exhibit 23 and Exhibit 24 provide information about the earnings surprise history for two companies: Exxon Mobil Corporation and Volkswagen AG (VW).

Exhibit 23: Earnings Surprise History for Exxon Mobil Corporation (in US$)

Quarter Ending	EPS Release Date	Mean Consensus EPS Forecast	Actual EPS	% Surprise	Std. Dev.	SUE Score
Sep 2013	31 Oct 2013	1.77	1.79	0.88	0.1250	0.16
Jun 2013	1 Aug 2013	1.90	1.55	−18.39	0.0997	−3.51
Mar 2013	25 Apr 2013	2.05	2.12	3.59	0.0745	0.94
Dec 2012	1 Feb 2013	2.00	2.20	10.20	0.0463	4.32

Exhibit 24: Earnings Surprise History for Volkswagen AG (in Euros)

Quarter Ending	EPS Release Date	Mean Consensus EPS Forecast	Actual EPS	% Surprise	Std. Dev.	SUE Score
Sep 2013	30 Oct 2013	4.53	3.79	−16.37	0.2846	−2.60
Jun 2013	30 Jul 2013	5.10	5.86	14.99	0.3858	1.97
Mar 2013	24 Apr 2013	4.15	4.24	2.17	1.1250	0.08
Dec 2012	22 Feb 2013	5.56	3.54	−36.33	0.5658	−3.57

Source: Thomson Surprise Report.

1. Explain how Exxon's SUE score of 0.16 for the quarter ending September 2013 is calculated.

Solution:

The amount of Exxon's unexpected earnings (i.e., its earnings surprise) for the quarter ending September 2013 was $1.79 – $1.77 = $0.02. Dividing by the standard deviation of $0.1250 gives a SUE score of 0.16.

2. Based on these exhibits, for which company were the consensus forecasts less accurate over the past four quarters?

Solution:

The answer depends on whether accuracy is measured by the percentage surprise or by the SUE score. If accuracy is measured by the percentage surprise, then VW's consensus forecasts were less accurate: Percentage surprise varied from −36.33% to +14.99% for VW versus −18.39% to +10.20% for Exxon. Using SUE, Exxon's consensus forecasts were less accurate: SUE varied from −3.51 to +4.32 for Exxon versus −3.57 to +1.13 for VW. The reason for these differing results is that the standard deviation of the earnings estimates is relatively smaller for Exxon than it is for VW.

3. Was the consensus forecast more accurate for Exxon or VW for the quarter ending March 2013?

Solution:

For the quarter ending March 2013, the consensus forecast was more accurate for VW than Exxon. Both the percentage surprise and SUE were lower for VW in this quarter.

Another set of indicators, **relative-strength indicators**, compares a stock's performance during a particular period either with its own past performance or with the performance of some group of stocks. The simplest relative-strength indicator that compares a stock's performance during a period with its past performance is the stock's compound rate of return over some specified time horizon, such as six months or one year. This indicator has also been referred to as **price momentum** in the academic literature. Despite its simplicity, this measure has been used in numerous studies. The rationale behind its use is the thesis that patterns of persistence or reversal exist in stock returns that may be shown empirically to depend on the investor's time horizon (Lee and Swaminathan 2000).

Other definitions of relative strength relate a stock's return over a recent period to its return over a longer period that includes the more recent period. For example, a classic study of technical momentum indicators (Brock, Lakonishok, and LeBaron 1992) examined trading strategies based on two technical rules—namely, a moving-average oscillator and a trading-range break (i.e., resistance and support levels)—in which buy and sell signals are determined by the relationship between a short period's moving average and a longer period's moving average (and bands around those averages). The reader should keep in mind that research on patterns of historical stock returns is notoriously vulnerable to data snooping and hindsight biases. Furthermore, investing strategies based purely on technical momentum indicators are viewed as inherently self-destructing, in that "once a useful technical rule (or price pattern) is discovered, it ought to be invalidated when the mass of traders attempts to exploit it" (Bodie, Kane, and Marcus 2008, p. 377). Yet, the possibility of discovering a profitable trading rule and exploiting it prior to mass use continues to motivate research.

A simple relative-strength indicator of the second type (i.e., the stock's performance relative to the performance of some group of stocks) is the stock's performance divided by the performance of an equity index. If the value of this ratio increases, the stock price increases relative to the index and displays positive relative strength. Often, the relative-strength indicator is scaled to 1.0 at the beginning of the study period. If the stock goes up at a higher (lower) rate than the index, then relative strength will be above (below) 1.0. Relative strength in this sense is often calculated for industries and individual stocks. Example 39 explores this indicator.

EXAMPLE 39

Relative Strength in Relation to an Equity Index

Exhibit 25 shows the values of the S&P 500 and three exchange-traded funds (ETFs) for the end of each of 18 months from March 2018 through August 2019. The ETFs are for long-term US Treasury securities, for the STOXX Europe 50 Index, and for emerging markets. SPDRs and iShares are families of exchange-traded funds managed by State Street Global Advisors and by Blackrock, Inc.

[handwritten note in left margin:] - High relative strength would be relevant for a portfolio managed with a growth/momentum investment style.

Exhibit 25: A Relative-Strength Comparison

First Day of	S&P 500 Index	iShares 20+ Year Treasury Bond ETF (TLT)	SPDR STOXX Europe 50 ETF (FEU)	iShares Emerging Markets ETF (EEM)
Mar-18	2,640.87	121.90	34.64	48.28
Apr-18	2,648.05	119.10	35.36	46.92
May-18	2,705.27	121.22	34.29	45.69
Jun-18	2,718.37	121.72	33.43	43.33
Jul-18	2,816.29	119.70	34.94	44.86
Aug-18	2,901.52	121.00	33.53	43.17
Sep-18	2,913.98	117.27	33.60	42.92
Oct-18	2,711.74	113.58	31.51	39.16
Nov-18	2,760.17	115.33	31.61	41.08
Dec-18	2,506.85	121.51	29.89	39.06
Jan-19	2,704.10	121.97	31.38	43.10
Feb-19	2,784.49	120.02	32.61	42.44
Mar-19	2,834.40	126.44	33.09	42.92
Apr-19	2,945.83	123.65	34.14	43.93
May-19	2,752.06	131.83	32.71	40.71
Jun-19	2,941.76	132.81	34.17	42.91
Jul-19	2,980.38	132.89	33.22	41.77
Aug-19	2,923.65	144.04	32.47	39.70

To produce the information for Exhibit 26, we divided each ETF value by the S&P 500 value for the same month and then scaled those results so that the value of the relative-strength indicator (RSTR) for March 2018 would equal 1.0. To illustrate, on 1 March 2018, the value of TLT divided by the S&P 500 was 121.90/2,640.87 = 0.04616. The RSTR for TLT on that date, by design, is then 0.04616/0.04616 = 1.0. In April, the value of TLT divided by the S&P 500 was 119.10/2,648.05 = 0.04498, which we scaled by the April number. The RSTR for 1 April 2018 for TLT is 0.04498/0.04616 = 0.9744, shown in Exhibit 26 as 0.974.

Exhibit 26: Relative-Strength Indicators

First Day of	RSTR iShares 20+ Year Treasury Bond ETF (TLT)	RSTR SPDR STOXX Europe 50 ETF (FEU)	RSTR iShares Emerging Markets ETF (EEM)
Mar-18	1.000	1.000	1.000
Apr-18	0.974	1.018	0.969
May-18	0.971	0.966	0.924
Jun-18	0.970	0.938	0.872
Jul-18	0.921	0.946	0.871
Aug-18	0.903	0.881	0.814
Sep-18	0.872	0.879	0.806
Oct-18	0.907	0.886	0.790
Nov-18	0.905	0.873	0.814

First Day of	RSTR iShares 20+ Year Treasury Bond ETF (TLT)	RSTR SPDR STOXX Europe 50 ETF (FEU)	RSTR iShares Emerging Markets ETF (EEM)
Dec-18	1.050	0.909	0.852
Jan-19	0.977	0.885	0.872
Feb-19	0.934	0.893	0.834
Mar-19	0.966	0.890	0.828
Apr-19	0.909	0.884	0.816
May-19	1.038	0.906	0.809
Jun-19	0.978	0.886	0.798
Jul-19	0.966	0.850	0.767
Aug-19	1.067	0.847	0.743

On the basis of Exhibit 25 and Exhibit 26, address the following:

1. State the relative strength of long-term US Treasury securities, the STOXX Europe 50 Index, and emerging market stocks over the entire time period March 2018 through August 2019. Interpret the relative strength for each sector over that period.

Solution:

The relative-strength indicator for long-term US Treasuries is 1.067. This number represents 1.067 − 1.000 = 0.067, or 6.7% overperformance relative to the S&P 500 over the time period. The relative-strength indicator for the STOXX Europe 50 Index is 0.995. This number represents 0.847 − 1.000 = −0.153, or 15.3% underperformance relative to the S&P 500 over the time period. The relative-strength indicator for the emerging market ETF is 0.743, indicating that it underperformed the S&P 500 by 25.7% over the time frame.

2. Discuss the relative performance of the STOXX Europe 50 Index ETF and the emerging market ETF in the month of December 2018.

Solution:

The December 2018 performance is found by comparing the RSTR at 1 December 2018 and 1 January 2019. The December 2019 RSTR for the STOXX Europe 50 Index ends at 0.885, which is 2.7% lower than its value for the prior month (0.909). The emerging market RSTR, at 0.872, is higher than the prior month value of 0.852 by 2.3%. In December 2018, the emerging market ETF outperformed the STOXX Europe 50 Index ETF. The relative performance for that one month differs from the relative performance over the entire period, during which the STOXX Europe 50 Index significantly outperformed the emerging market ETF.

Overall, momentum indicators have a substantial following among professional investors. Some view momentum indicators as signals that should prompt an analyst to consider whether a stock price is moving successively *farther from* or successively *closer to* the fundamental valuations derived from models and multiples. In other words, an analyst might be correct about the intrinsic value of a firm, and the momentum indicators might provide a clue about when the market price will converge with that intrinsic value. The use of such indicators continues to be a subject of active research in industry and in business schools.

VALUATION INDICATORS: ISSUES IN PRACTICE

13

☐ explain the use of the arithmetic mean, the harmonic mean, the weighted harmonic mean, and the median to describe the central tendency of a group of multiples

All the valuation indicators discussed are quantitative aids but not necessarily solutions to the problem of security selection. In this section, we discuss some issues that arise in practice when averages are used to establish benchmark multiples and then illustrate the use of multiple valuation indicators.

Averaging Multiples: The Harmonic Mean

The harmonic mean and the weighted harmonic mean are often applied to average a group of price multiples.

Consider a hypothetical portfolio that contains two stocks. For simplicity, assume the portfolio owns 100% of the shares of each stock. One stock has a market capitalization of €715 million and earnings of €71.5 million, giving it a P/E of 10. The other stock has a market capitalization of €585 million and earnings of €29.25 million, for a P/E of 20. Note that the P/E for the portfolio is calculated directly by aggregating the companies' market capitalizations and earnings: (€715 + €585)/(€71.50 + €29.25) = €1,300/€100.75 = 12.90. The question that will be addressed is, What calculation of portfolio P/E, based on the individual stock P/Es, best reflects the value of 12.90?

If the ratio of an individual holding is represented by X_i, the expression for the simple **harmonic mean of the ratio** is

$$X_H = \frac{n}{\sum_{i=1}^{n}(1/X_i)},$$ (9)

which is the reciprocal of the arithmetic mean of the reciprocals.

The expression for the **weighted harmonic mean** is

$$X_{WH} = \frac{1}{\sum_{i=1}^{n}(w_i/X_i)},$$ (10)

where the w_i are portfolio value weights (summing to 1) and $X_i > 0$ for $i = 1, 2, \ldots, n$.

Exhibit 27 displays the calculation of the hypothetical portfolio's simple arithmetic mean P/E, weighted mean P/E, (simple) harmonic mean P/E, and weighted harmonic mean P/E.

Exhibit 27: Alternative Mean P/Es

	Market Cap		Earnings	Stock				
Security	(€ Millions)	Percent	(€ Millions)	P/E	(1)	(2)	(3)	(4)
Stock 1	715	55	71.50	10	0.5 × 10	0.55 × 10	0.5 × 0.1	0.55 × 0.1

Security	Market Cap (€ Millions)	Percent	Earnings (€ Millions)	Stock P/E	(1)	(2)	(3)	(4)
Stock 2	585	45	29.25	20	0.5 × 20	0.45 × 20	0.5 × 0.05	0.45 × 0.05
					15	14.5	0.075	0.0775
Arithmetic mean P/E (1)					15			
Weighted mean P/E (2)						14.5		
Harmonic mean P/E (3)							1/0.075 = 13.33	
Weighted harmonic mean P/E (4)								1/0.0775 = 12.90

The weighted harmonic mean P/E precisely corresponds to the portfolio P/E value of 12.90. This example explains why index fund vendors frequently use the weighted harmonic mean to calculate the "average" P/E or average value of other price multiples for indexes. In some applications, an analyst might not want or be able to incorporate the market value weight information needed to calculate the weighted harmonic mean. In such cases, the simple harmonic mean can still be calculated.

Note that the simple harmonic mean P/E is smaller than the arithmetic mean and closer to the directly calculated value of 12.90 in this example. The harmonic mean inherently gives less weight to higher P/Es and more weight to lower P/Es. In general, unless all the observations in a data set have the same value, the harmonic mean is less than the arithmetic mean.

As explained and illustrated earlier, using the median rather than the arithmetic mean to derive an average multiple mitigates the effect of outliers. The harmonic mean is sometimes also used to reduce the impact of large outliers—which are typically the major concern in using the arithmetic mean multiple—but not the impact of small outliers (i.e., those close to zero). The harmonic mean tends to mitigate the impact of large outliers. The harmonic mean may aggravate the impact of small outliers, but such outliers are bounded by zero on the downside.

We can use the group of telecommunications companies examined earlier (see Exhibit 5) to illustrate differences between the arithmetic mean and the harmonic mean. This group includes two large outliers for P/E: CenturyLink, with a P/E that is not meaningful, and Charter Communications, with a P/E of 70.67. Exhibit 28 shows mean values excluding CenturyLink and excluding both CenturyLink and Charter Communications (two outliers).

Exhibit 28: Arithmetic versus Harmonic Mean

Company	Trailing P/E (without CenturyLink)	Trailing P/E (No Outliers)
AT&T	13.20	13.20
Comcast Corporation	16.23	16.23
CenturyLink	NMF	
China Telecom	13.14	13.14
Charter Communications Corp.	70.67	
Verizon Communications	15.03	15.03
Windstream Holdings	24.55	24.55

Company	Trailing P/E (without CenturyLink)	Trailing P/E (No Outliers)
Arithmetic mean	25.30	16.43
Median	15.23	15.03
Harmonic mean	17.70	15.39

Note that for the entire group, the arithmetic mean (25.30) is far higher than the median (15.23) because of the high P/E of Charter Communications (CenturyLink was not included). The harmonic mean (17.70) is much closer to the median and more plausible as representing central tendency. Once the outliers are eliminated, the values for the arithmetic mean (16.43), median (15.03), and harmonic mean (15.39) are more tightly grouped. The lower value for the harmonic mean reflects the fact that this approach mitigates the effect of the relatively high P/E for Charter Communications.

This example illustrates the importance for the analyst of understanding how an average has been calculated, particularly when the analyst is reviewing information prepared by another analyst, and the usefulness of examining several summary statistics.

Using Multiple Valuation Indicators

Because each carefully selected and calculated price multiple, momentum indicator, or fundamental may supply some piece of the puzzle of stock valuation, many investors and analysts use more than one valuation indicator (in addition to other criteria) in stock valuation and selection. Example 40 illustrates the use of multiple indicators.

EXAMPLE 40

Multiple Indicators in Stock Valuation

Analysts may use more valuation indicators than they describe in their company reports. The two following excerpts, adapted from past equity analyst reports, illustrate the use of multiple ratios in communicating views about a stock's value. In the first excerpt, from a report on Aussie Beverage Ltd. (ABEV), the analyst has used a discounted cash flow valuation as the preferred methodology but notes that the stock is also attractive when a price-to-earnings ratio (PER in the report) is used. In the second excerpt, from a report on Südliche Logistik (SLOG), an analyst evaluates the stock price (then trading at 42.80) by using two multiples, price to earnings (P/E) and EV/EBITDA, in relation to revised forecasts.

Aussie Beverage

Our DCF for ABEV is A$0.82ps, which represents a 44% prem. to the current price. Whilst the DCF valuation is our preferred methodology, we recognise that ABEV also looks attractive on different metrics.

Applying a mid-cycle PER multiple of 10.5 × (30% disc to mkt) to FY08 EPS of 7.6cps, we derive a valuation of A$0.80. Importantly, were the stock to reach our target of A$0.75ps in 12mths, ABEV would be trading on a fwd PER of 9.1×, which we do not view as demanding. At current levels, the stock is also offering an attractive dividend yield of 5.7% (fully franked). [*Note*: "Fully franked" is a concept specific to the Australian market and refers to tax treatment of the dividend.]

Südliche Logistik

> Based on our slightly increased estimates, the shares are valued at a P/E and EV/EBITDA 2012 of 12.4x and 9x, slightly below the valuation of peer companies. Given its stronger profit growth, SLOG could command a premium. We raise our target price from EUR52 to EUR53, implying a 24% upside. Buy.

In selecting stocks, institutional investors surveyed in the BofA Merrill Lynch Institutional Factor Surveys from 1989 to 2012 used an average of 9.3 factors in selecting stocks (does not include 2008–2010 due to a lack of sufficient responses). The survey factors included not only price multiples, momentum indicators, and the DDM but also the fundamentals ROE, debt to equity, projected five-year EPS growth, EPS variability, EPS estimate dispersion, size, beta, foreign exposure, low price, and neglect. Exhibit 29 lists the factors classified by percentage of investors indicating that they use that factor in making investment decisions, out of 137 responders in 2012.

Exhibit 29: Frequency of Investor Usage of Factors in Making Investment Decisions

High (●) >50%; Med (♦) >30% <50%;
Low (○) <30%

Factor	Frequency
P/E	●
Beta	●
EV/EBITDA	●
ROE	●
Size	●
P/B	●
P/FCF	♦
Share Repurchase	♦
Earnings Estimate Revision	♦
Margins	♦
Relative Strength	♦
EPS Momentum	♦
D/E	♦
EPS Variability	♦
DDM/DCF	♦
PEG Ratio	♦
Long-Term Price Trend	♦
P/CF	♦
Analyst Neglect	♦
Dividend Growth	♦
Projected 5-Year EPS Growth	♦
Mean Reversion	♦
Normalized P/E	♦
P/S	♦
Net Debt/EBITDA	○
EPS Surprise	○

	High (●) >50%; Med (♦) >30% <50%; Low (○) <30%	
Factor		Frequency
ROC		○
ROA		○
EPS Estimate Dispersion		○
Analyst Rating Revisions		○
Foreign Exposure		○
Long-Term Price Trend w/ Short-Term Reversal		○
Trading Volume		○
Price Target		○
Ownership		○
Short-Term Price Trend		○
EV/Sales		○
Low Price		○
Altman Z-Score		○
Equity Duration		○

Source: 2012 BofA Merrill Lynch Institutional Factor Survey.

An issue concerning the use of ratios in an investing strategy is look-ahead bias. **Look-ahead bias** is the use of information that was not contemporaneously available in computing a quantity. Investment analysts often use historical data to back test an investment strategy that involves stock selection based on price multiples or other factors. When back testing, an analyst should be aware that time lags in the reporting of financial results create the potential for look-ahead bias in such research. For example, as of early January 2019, most companies had not reported EPS for the last quarter of 2018, so at that time, a company's trailing P/E would be based on EPS for the first, second, and third quarters of 2018 and the last quarter of 2017. Any investment strategy based on a trailing P/E that used actual EPS for the last quarter of 2018 could be implemented only after the data became available. Thus, if an analysis assumed that an investment was made in early January 2019 based on full-year 2018 data, the analysis would involve look-ahead bias. To avoid this bias, an analyst would calculate the trailing P/E based on the most recent four quarters of EPS then being reported. The same principle applies to other multiples calculated on a trailing basis.

The application of a set of criteria to reduce an investment universe to a smaller set of investments is called **screening**. Stock screens often include not only criteria based on the valuation measures that featured in our discussion but also on fundamental criteria that may explain differences in such measures. Computerized stock screening is an efficient way to narrow a search for investments and is a part of many stock selection disciplines. The limitations to many commercial databases and screening tools usually include lack of control by the user of the calculation of important inputs (such as EPS); the absence of qualitative factors in most databases is another important limitation. Example 41 illustrates the use of a screen in stock selection.

EXAMPLE 41

Using Screens to Find Stocks for a Portfolio

Janet Larsen manages an institutional portfolio and is currently looking for new stocks to add to the portfolio. Larsen has a commercial database with information on US stocks. She has designed several screens to select stocks with low

P/Es and low P/B multiples. Because Larsen is aware that screening for low P/E and low P/B multiples may identify stocks with low expected growth, she also wants stocks that have a PEG ratio less than 1.0. She decides to screen for stocks with a dividend yield of at least 3.0% and a total market capitalization over $10 billion. Exhibit 30 shows the number of stocks that successively met each of the five criteria as of 17 July 2019 (so, the number of stocks that met all five criteria is 10).

Exhibit 30: Stock Screen

Criterion	Stocks Meeting Each Criterion Successively
P/E < 20.0	2,096
P/B < 2.0	1,384
PEG ratio < 1.0	89
Dividend yield ≥ 3.0%	23
Market capitalization over $10 billion	10

Other information:

- The screening database indicates that the trailing P/E was 22.3, P/B was 3.5, and the dividend yield was 1.9% for the S&P 500 as of the date of the screen.

- The "S&P U.S. Style Indices Methodology" (June 2019) indicates that the style indexes measure growth and value by the following six factors, which S&P standardizes and uses to compute growth and value scores for each company:

  Three Growth Factors

  Three-year change in EPS over price per share

  Three-year sales per-share growth rate

  Momentum (12-month percentage price change)

  Three Value Factors

  Book value-to-price ratio

  Earnings-to-price ratio

  Sales-to-price ratio

- In February of 2019, the S&P Dow Jones US Index Committee raised the market cap guidelines used when selecting companies for the S&P 500, S&P MidCap 400 and S&P SmallCap 600. The new guidelines are as follows:

  S&P 500: Over $8.2 billion

  S&P MidCap 400: $2.4 billion to $8.2 billion

  S&P SmallCap 600: $600 million to $2.4 billion

Using the information supplied, answer the following questions:

1. What type of valuation indicators does Larsen *not* include in her stock screen?

Solution:

Larsen has not included momentum indicators in the screen.

2. Characterize the overall orientation of Larsen as to investment style.

Solution:

Larsen can be characterized as a large-cap value investor, based on the specified market capitalization. Although her screen does include a PEG ratio, it excludes explicit growth rate criteria, such as those used by S&P, and it excludes momentum indicators usually associated with a growth orientation, such as positive earnings surprise. Larsen also uses a cutoff for P/B that is less than the average P/B for the S&P 500. Note that her criteria for multiples are all "less than" criteria.

3. State two limitations of Larsen's stock screen.

Solution:

Larsen does not include any profitability criteria or risk measurements. These omissions are a limitation because a stock's expected low profitability or high risk may explain its low P/E. Another limitation of her screen is that the computations of the value indicators in a commercial database may not reflect the appropriate adjustments to inputs. The absence of qualitative criteria is also a possible limitation.

[handwritten note in right margin: — As a rule, a screen that includes a maximum P/E should include criteria requiring positive earnings; otherwise, the screen could select companies with negative P/Es]

Investors also apply all the metrics that we have illustrated in terms of individual stocks to industries and economic sectors. For example, average price multiples and momentum indicators can be used in sector rotation strategies to determine relatively under- or overvalued sectors. A sector rotation strategy is an investment strategy that overweights economic sectors that are anticipated to outperform or lead the overall market.

SUMMARY

We have defined and explained the most important valuation indicators in professional use and illustrated their application to a variety of valuation problems.

- Price multiples are ratios of a stock's price to some measure of value per share.

- Price multiples are most frequently applied to valuation in the method of comparables. This method involves using a price multiple to evaluate whether an asset is relatively undervalued, fairly valued, or overvalued in relation to a benchmark value of the multiple.

- The benchmark value of the multiple may be the multiple of a similar company or the median or average value of the multiple for a peer group of companies, an industry, an economic sector, an equity index, or the company's own median or average past values of the multiple.

- The economic rationale for the method of comparables is the law of one price.

- Price multiples may also be applied to valuation in the method based on forecasted fundamentals. Discounted cash flow (DCF) models provide the basis and rationale for this method. Fundamentals also interest analysts who use the method of comparables because differences between a price multiple and its benchmark value may be explained by differences in fundamentals.

- The key idea behind the use of price-to-earnings ratios (P/Es) is that earning power is a chief driver of investment value and earnings per share (EPS) is probably the primary focus of security analysts' attention. The EPS figure, however, is frequently subject to distortion, often volatile, and sometimes negative.

- The two alternative definitions of P/E are trailing P/E, based on the most recent four quarters of EPS, and forward P/E, based on next year's expected earnings.

- Analysts address the problem of cyclicality by normalizing EPS—that is, calculating the level of EPS that the business could achieve currently under mid-cyclical conditions (normalized EPS).

- Two methods to normalize EPS are the method of historical average EPS (calculated over the most recent full cycle) and the method of average return on equity (EPS = average ROE multiplied by current book value per share).

- Earnings yield (E/P) is the reciprocal of the P/E. When stocks have zero or negative EPS, a ranking by earnings yield is meaningful whereas a ranking by P/E is not.

- Historical trailing P/Es should be calculated with EPS lagged a sufficient amount of time to avoid look-ahead bias. The same principle applies to other multiples calculated on a trailing basis.

- The fundamental drivers of P/E are the expected earnings growth rate and the required rate of return. The justified P/E based on fundamentals bears a positive relationship to the first factor and an inverse relationship to the second factor.

- The PEG (P/E-to-growth) ratio is a tool to incorporate the impact of earnings growth on P/E. The PEG ratio is calculated as the ratio of the P/E to the consensus growth forecast. Stocks with low PEG ratios are, all else equal, more attractive than stocks with high PEG ratios.

- We can estimate terminal value in multistage DCF models by using price multiples based on comparables. The expression for terminal value, V_n, is (using P/E as the example)

$$V_n = \text{Benchmark value of trailing P/E} \times E_n$$

or

$$V_n = \text{Benchmark value of forward P/E} \times E_{n+1}.$$

- Book value per share is intended to represent, on a per-share basis, the investment that common shareholders have in the company. Inflation, technological change, and accounting distortions, however, may impair the use of book value for this purpose.

- Book value is calculated as common shareholders' equity divided by the number of shares outstanding. Analysts adjust book value to accurately reflect the value of the shareholders' investment and to make P/B (the price-to-book ratio) more useful for comparing different stocks.

- The fundamental drivers of P/B are ROE and the required rate of return. The justified P/B based on fundamentals bears a positive relationship to the first factor and an inverse relationship to the second factor.

- An important rationale for using the price-to-sales ratio (P/S) is that sales, as the top line in an income statement, are generally less subject to distortion or manipulation than other fundamentals, such as EPS or book value. Sales are also more stable than earnings and are never negative.

- P/S fails to take into account differences in cost structure between businesses, may not properly reflect the situation of companies losing money, and may be subject to manipulation through revenue recognition practices.

- The fundamental drivers of P/S are profit margin, growth rate, and the required rate of return. The justified P/S based on fundamentals bears a positive relationship to the first two factors and an inverse relationship to the third factor.

- Enterprise value (EV) is total company value (the market value of debt, common equity, and preferred equity) minus the value of cash and investments.

- The ratio of EV to total sales is conceptually preferable to P/S because EV/S facilitates comparisons among companies with varying capital structures.

- A key idea behind the use of price to cash flow is that cash flow is less subject to manipulation than are earnings. Price-to-cash-flow multiples are often more stable than P/Es. Some common approximations to cash flow from operations have limitations, however, because they ignore items that may be subject to manipulation.

- The major cash flow (and related) concepts used in multiples are earnings plus noncash charges (CF), cash flow from operations (CFO), free cash flow to equity (FCFE), and earnings before interest, taxes, depreciation, and amortization (EBITDA).

- In calculating price to cash flow, the earnings-plus-noncash-charges concept is traditionally used, although FCFE has the strongest link to financial theory.

- CF and EBITDA are not strictly cash flow numbers because they do not account for noncash revenue and net changes in working capital.

- The fundamental drivers of price to cash flow, however defined, are the expected growth rate of future cash flow and the required rate of return. The justified price to cash flow based on fundamentals bears a positive relationship to the first factor and an inverse relationship to the second.

- EV/EBITDA is preferred to P/EBITDA because EBITDA, as a pre-interest number, is a flow to all providers of capital.

- EV/EBITDA may be more appropriate than P/E for comparing companies with different amounts of financial leverage (debt).

- EV/EBITDA is frequently used in the valuation of capital-intensive businesses.

- The fundamental drivers of EV/EBITDA are the expected growth rate in free cash flow to the firm, profitability, and the weighted average cost of capital. The justified EV/EBITDA based on fundamentals bears a positive relationship to the first two factors and an inverse relationship to the third.

- Dividend yield has been used as a valuation indicator because it is a component of total return and is less risky than capital appreciation.

- Trailing dividend yield is calculated as four times the most recent quarterly per-share dividend divided by the current market price.

- The fundamental drivers of dividend yield are the expected growth rate in dividends and the required rate of return.

- Comparing companies across borders frequently involves dealing with differences in accounting standards, cultural differences, economic differences, and resulting differences in risk and growth opportunities.

- Momentum indicators relate either price or a fundamental to the time series of the price's or fundamental's own past values (in some cases, to their expected values).

- Momentum valuation indicators include earnings surprise, standardized unexpected earnings (SUE), and relative strength.

- Unexpected earnings (or earnings surprise) equals the difference between reported earnings and expected earnings.

- SUE is unexpected earnings divided by the standard deviation in past unexpected earnings.

- Relative-strength indicators allow comparison of a stock's performance during a period either with its own past performance (first type) or with the performance of some group of stocks (second type). The rationale for using relative strength is the thesis that patterns of persistence or reversal in returns exist.

- Screening is the application of a set of criteria to reduce an investment universe to a smaller set of investments and is a part of many stock selection disciplines. In general, limitations of such screens include the lack of control in vendor-provided data of the calculation of important inputs and the absence of qualitative factors.

REFERENCES

Arnott, Robert D., Clifford S. Asness. 2003. "Surprise! Higher Dividends = Higher Earnings Growth." Financial Analysts Journal59 (1): 70–87. 10.2469/faj.v59.n1.2504

Aubert, Samuel, Pierre Giot. 2007. "An International Test of the Fed Model." Journal of Asset Management8 (2): 86–100. 10.1057/palgrave.jam.2250063

Bodie, Zvi, Alex Kane, Alan J. Marcus. 2008. Investments. 7th ed.New York: McGraw-Hill.

Brock, William, Joseph Lakonishok, Blake LeBaron. 1992. "Simple Technical Trading Rules and the Stochastic Properties of Stock Returns." Journal of Finance47 (5): 1731–64. 10.1111/j.1540-6261.1992.tb04681.x

Brown, Lawrence D. 1997. "Earnings Surprise Research: Synthesis and Perspectives." Financial Analysts Journal53 (2): 13–20. 10.2469/faj.v53.n2.2067

Chan, L. K. C., J. Lakonishok. 2004. "Value and Growth Investing: Review and Update." Financial Analysts Journal60 (1): 71–86. 10.2469/faj.v60.n1.2593

Damodaran, Aswath. 2012. Investment Valuation: Tools and Techniques for Determining the Value of Any Asset. 3rd ed.Hoboken, NJ: John Wiley & Co.

Fairfield, Patricia M. 1994. "P/E, P/B and the Present Value of Future Dividends." Financial Analysts Journal50 (4): 23–31. 10.2469/faj.v50.n4.23

Fama, Eugene F., Kenneth R. French. 1992. "The Cross-Section of Expected Stock Returns." Journal of Finance47 (2): 427–65. 10.1111/j.1540-6261.1992.tb04398.x

Graham, Benjamin, David L. Dodd. 1934. Security Analysis. McGraw-Hill Professional Publishing.

Grant, Julia, Larry Parker. 2001. "EBITDA!" Research in Accounting Regulation15:205–11.

Hackel, Kenneth S., Joshua Livnat, Atul Rai. 1994. "The Free Cash Flow/Small-Cap Anomaly." Financial Analysts Journal50 (5): 33–42. 10.2469/faj.v50.n5.33

Harris, Robert S., Felicia C. Marston. 1994. "Value versus Growth Stocks: Book-to-Market, Growth, and Beta." Financial Analysts Journal50 (5): 18–24. 10.2469/faj.v50.n5.18

Harris, Mary, Karl A. Muller. 1999. "The Market Valuation of IAS versus U.S. GAAP Accounting Measures Using Form 20-F Reconciliations." Journal of Accounting and Economics26 (1–3): 285–312. 10.1016/S0165-4101(99)00003-8

Henry, E., S. Lin, Y. Yang. 2009. "The European–U.S. GAAP Gap: Amount, Type, Homogeneity, and Value Relevance of IFRS to U.S. GAAP Form 20-F Reconciliations." Accounting Horizons23 (2): 121–50. 10.2308/acch.2009.23.2.121

Kisor, Manown, Volkert S. Whitbeck. 1963. "A New Tool in Investment Decision-Making." Financial Analysts Journal19 (3): 55–62. 10.2469/faj.v19.n3.55

Lakonishok, J., A. Shleifer, R. W. Vishny. 1994. "Contrarian Investment, Extrapolation and Risk." Journal of Finance49 (5): 1541–78. 10.1111/j.1540-6261.1994.tb04772.x

Lander, Joel, Athanasios Orphanides, Martha Douvogiannis. 1997. "Earnings Forecasts and the Predictability of Stock Returns: Evidence from Trading the S&P." Journal of Portfolio Management23 (4): 24–35. 10.3905/jpm.1997.409620

Latané, Henry A., Charles P. Jones. 1979. "Standardized Unexpected Earnings—1971–77." Journal of Finance34 (3): 717–24.

Lee, Charles M.C., Bhaskaran Swaminathan. 2000. "Price Momentum and Trading Volume." Journal of Finance55 (5): 2017–69. 10.1111/0022-1082.00280

Malkiel, Burton, John Cragg. 1970. "Expectations and the Structure of Share Prices." American Economic Review60 (4): 601–17.

Martin, Thomas A. 1998. "Traditional Equity Valuation Methods." In Equity Research and Valuation Techniques. Charlottesville, VA: AIMR. 10.2469/cp.v1998.n2.5

Mulford, Charles W., Eugene E. Comiskey. 2005. Creative Cash Flow Reporting: Uncovering Sustainable Financial Performance. Hoboken, NJ: John Wiley & Sons.

Nathan, Siva, Kumar Sivakumar, Jayaraman Vijayakumar. 2001. "Returns to Trading Strategies Based on Price-to-Earnings and Price-to-Sales Ratios." Journal of Investing10 (2): 17–28. 10.3905/joi.2001.319458

O'Shaughnessy, James P. 2005. What Works on Wall Street: A Guide to the Best-Performing Investment Strategies of All Time. 3rd ed.New York: McGraw-Hill Professional Publishing.

Pinto, Jerald, Thomas Robinson, John Stowe. 2018. "Equity Valuation: A Survey of Professional Practice." Review of Financial Economics37:219–33. 10.1002/rfe.1040

Siegel, Jeremy. 2014. Stocks for the Long Run. 5th ed.New York: McGraw-Hill.

Solnik, Bruno, Dennis McLeavey. 2004. International Investments. 5th ed.Boston: Pearson Addison-Wesley.

Stimes, Peter C., Stephen E. Wilcox. 2011. "Equity Market Valuation." Chap. 11 in Investments: Principles of Portfolio and Equity Analysis. Hoboken, NJ: John Wiley & Sons.

Wild, John J., Leopold A. Bernstein, K. R. Subramanyam. 2001. Financial Statement Analysis. 7th ed.New York: McGraw-Hill Irwin.

Yardeni, Edward. 2000. "How to Value Earnings Growth." Topical Study #49. Deutsche Banc Alex Brown.

Zhou, Ping, William Ruland. 2006. "Dividend Payout and Future Earnings Growth." Financial Analysts Journal62 (3): 58–69. 10.2469/faj.v62.n3.4157

PRACTICE PROBLEMS

The following information relates to questions 1-3

As of February 2020, you are researching Jonash International, a hypothetical company subject to cyclical demand for its services. Jonash shares closed at $57.98 on 2 February 2019. You believe the 2015–18 period reasonably captures average profitability:

Measure	2019	2018	2017	2016	2015
EPS	E$3.03	$1.45	$0.23	$2.13	$2.55
BV per share	E$19.20	$16.21	$14.52	$13.17	$11.84
ROE	E16.0%	8.9%	1.6%	16.3%	21.8%

1. Define normalized EPS.

2. Calculate a normalized EPS for Jonash based on the method of historical average EPS, and then calculate the P/E based on normalized EPS.

3. Calculate a normalized EPS for Jonash based on the method of average ROE and the P/E based on normalized EPS.

The following information relates to questions 4-5

An analyst plans to use P/E and the method of comparables as a basis for recommending purchasing shares of one of two peer-group companies in the business of manufacturing personal digital assistants. Neither company has been profitable to date, and neither is expected to have positive EPS over the next year. Data on the companies' prices, trailing EPS, and expected growth rates in sales (five-year compounded rates) are given in the following table:

Company	Price	Trailing EPS	P/E	Expected Growth (Sales)
Hand	$22	−$2.20	NMF	45%
Somersault	$10	−$1.25	NMF	40%

Unfortunately, because the earnings for both companies have been negative, their P/Es are not meaningful. On the basis of this information, address the following:

4. Discuss how the analyst might make a relative valuation in this case.

5. State which stock the analyst should recommend.

The following information relates to questions 6-7

May Stewart, CFA, a retail analyst, is performing a P/E-based comparison of two hypothetical jewelry stores as of early 2020. She has the following data for Hallwhite Stores (HS) and Ruffany (RUF).

- HS is priced at $44. RUF is priced at $22.50.
- HS has a simple capital structure, earned $2.00 per share (basic and diluted) in 2019, and is expected to earn $2.20 (basic and diluted) in 2020.
- RUF has a complex capital structure as a result of its outstanding stock options. Moreover, it had several unusual items that reduced its basic EPS in 2019 to $0.50 (versus the $0.75 that it earned in 2018).
- For 2020, Stewart expects RUF to achieve net income of $30 million. RUF has 30 million shares outstanding and options outstanding for an additional 33,333,333 shares.

6. Which P/E (trailing or forward) should Stewart use to compare the two companies' valuation?

7. Which of the two stocks is relatively more attractive when valued on the basis of P/Es (assuming that all other factors are approximately the same for both stocks)?

The following information relates to questions 8-9

You are researching the valuation of the stock of a company in the food-processing industry. Suppose you intend to use the mean value of the forward P/Es for the food-processing industry stocks as the benchmark value of the multiple. This mean P/E is 18.0. The forward or expected EPS for the next year for the stock you are studying is $2.00. You calculate 18.0 × $2.00 = $36, which you take to be the intrinsic value of the stock based only on the information given here. Comparing $36 with the stock's current market price of $30, you conclude the stock is undervalued.

8. Give two reasons why your conclusion that the stock is undervalued may be in error.

9. What additional information about the stock and the peer group would support your original conclusion?

The following information relates to questions 10-16

Mark Cannan is updating research reports on two well-established consumer companies before first quarter 2021 earnings reports are released. His supervisor, Sharolyn Ritter, has asked Cannan to use market-based valuations when updating the reports.

Delite Beverage is a manufacturer and distributor of soft drinks and recently acquired a major water bottling company in order to offer a broader product line. The acquisition will have a significant impact on Delite's future results.

You Fix It is a US retail distributor of products for home improvement, primarily for those consumers who choose to do the work themselves. The home improvement industry is cyclical; the industry was adversely affected by the recent downturn in the economy, the level of foreclosures, and slow home sales. Although sales and earnings at You Fix It weakened, same store sales are beginning to improve as consumers undertake more home improvement projects. Poor performing stores were closed, resulting in significant restructuring charges in 2020.

Before approving Cannan's work, Ritter wants to discuss the calculations and choices of ratios used in the valuation of Delite and You Fix It. The data used by Cannan in his analysis are summarized in Exhibit 1.

Exhibit 1: Select Financial Data for Delite Beverage and You Fix It

	Delite Beverage	You Fix It
2020 earnings per share (EPS)	$3.44	$1.77
2021 estimated EPS	$3.50	$1.99
Book value per share end of year	$62.05	$11.64
Current share price	$65.50	$37.23
Sales (billions)	$32.13	$67.44
Free cash flow per share	$2.68	$0.21
Shares outstanding end of year	2,322,034,000	1,638,821,000

Cannan advises Ritter that he is considering three different approaches to value the shares of You Fix It:

Approach 1	Price-to-book ratio (P/B)
Approach 2	Price-to-earnings ratio (P/E) using trailing earnings
Approach 3	Price-to-earnings ratio using normalized earnings

Cannan tells Ritter that he calculated the price-to-sales ratio (P/S) for You Fix It but chose not to use it in the valuation of the shares. Cannan states to Ritter that it is more appropriate to use the P/E than the P/S because

Reason 1	Earnings are more stable than sales.
Reason 2	Earnings are less easily manipulated than sales.
Reason 3	The P/E reflects financial leverage, whereas the P/S does not.

Cannan also informs Ritter that he did not use a price-to-cash-flow multiple in valuing the shares of Delite or You Fix It. The reason is that he could not identify a cash flow measure that would both account for working capital and noncash revenues and be after interest expense and thus not be mismatched with share price. Ritter advises Cannan that such a cash flow measure does exist.

Ritter provides Cannan with financial data on three close competitors as well as the overall beverage sector, which includes other competitors, in Exhibit 2. She asks Cannan to determine, based on the P/E-to-growth (PEG) ratio, whether Delite shares are overvalued, fairly valued, or undervalued.

Exhibit 2: Beverage Sector Data

	Forward P/E	Earnings Growth
Delite	—	12.41%
Fresh Iced Tea Company	16.59	9.52%
Nonutter Soda	15.64	11.94%
Tasty Root Beer	44.10	20%
Beverage sector average	16.40	10.80%

After providing Ritter his answer, Cannan is concerned about the inclusion of Tasty Root Beer in the comparables analysis. Specifically, Cannan says to Ritter:

"I feel we should mitigate the effect of large outliers but not the impact of small outliers (i.e., those close to zero) when calculating the beverage sector P/E. What measure of central tendency would you suggest we use to address this concern?"

Ritter requests that Cannan incorporate their discussion points before submitting the reports for final approval.

10. Based on the information in Exhibit 1, the *mostappropriate* price-to-earnings ratio to use in the valuation of Delite is *closest* to:

   A. 18.71.

   B. 19.04.

   C. 24.44.

11. Based on the information in Exhibit 1, the price-to-sales ratio for You Fix It is *closest* to:

   A. 0.28.

   B. 0.55.

   C. 0.90.

12. Which valuation approach would be *most* appropriate in valuing shares of You Fix It?

   A. Approach 1

   B. Approach 2

   C. Approach 3

13. Cannan's preference to use the P/E over the P/S is *best* supported by:

   A. Reason 1.

   B. Reason 2.

   C. Reason 3.

14. The cash flow measure that Ritter would *most likely* recommend to address Cannan's concern is:

   A. free cash flow to equity.

   B. earnings plus noncash charges.

    C. earnings before interest, tax, depreciation, and amortization.

15. Based on the information in Exhibits 1 and 2, Cannan would most likely conclude that Delite's shares are:

    A. overvalued.

    B. undervalued.

    C. fairly valued.

16. The measure of central tendency that Ritter will *most likely* recommend is the:

    A. median.

    B. harmonic mean.

    C. arithmetic mean.

The following information relates to questions 17-22

Andrea Risso is a junior analyst with AquistareFianco, an independent equity research firm. Risso's supervisor asks her to update, as of 1 January 2020, a quarterly research report for Centralino S.p.A., a telecommunications company headquartered in Italy. On that date, Centralino's common share price is €50 and its preferred shares trade for €5.25 per share.

Risso gathers information on Centralino. Exhibit 1 presents earnings and dividend data, and Exhibit 2 presents balance sheet data. Net sales were €3.182 billion in 2019. Risso estimates a required return of 15% for Centralino and forecasts growth in dividends of 6% into perpetuity.

Exhibit 1: Earnings and Dividends for Centralino, 2016–2020

	2016	2017	2018	2019	2020(E)
Earnings per share (EPS, €)	4.93	5.25	4.46	5.64	6.00
Dividends per share (DPS, €)	2.45	2.60	2.60	2.75	2.91
Return on equity (ROE)	13.01%	13.71%	11.58%	14.21%	14.96%

Note: The data for 2016–2019 are actual and for 2020 are estimated.

Exhibit 2: Summary Balance Sheet for Centralino, Year Ended 31 December 2019

Assets (€ millions)		Liabilities and Shareholders' Equity (€ millions)	
Cash and cash equivalents	102	Current liabilities	259
Accounts receivable	305	Long-term debt	367
Inventory	333	**Total liabilities**	626
Total current assets	740	Preferred shares	80

Assets (€ millions)		Liabilities and Shareholders' Equity (€ millions)	
Property and equipment, net	913	Common shares	826
Total assets	1,653	Retained earnings	121
		Total shareholders' equity	1,027
		Total liabilities and shareholders' equity	1,653

Notes: The market value of long-term debt is equal to its book value. Shares outstanding are 41.94 million common shares and 16.00 million preferred shares.

Exhibit 3 presents forward price-to-earnings ratios (P/Es) for Centralino's peer group. Risso assumes no differences in fundamentals among the peer-group companies.

Exhibit 3: Peer Group Forward P/Es

Company	Forward P/E
Brinaregalo	5.9
Camporio	8.3
Esperto	3.0
Fornodissione	15.0
Radoresto	4.6

Risso also wants to calculate normalized EPS using the average return on equity method. She determines that the 2016–19 time period in Exhibit 1 represents a full business cycle for Centralino.

17. Based on Exhibit 1, the trailing P/E for Centralino as of 1 January 2020, ignoring any business-cycle influence, is *closest to*:

    A. 8.3.

    B. 8.9.

    C. 9.9.

18. Based on Exhibit 1 and Risso's estimates of return and dividend growth, Centralino's justified forward P/E based on the Gordon growth dividend discount model is *closest* to:

    A. 5.4.

    B. 5.7.

    C. 8.3.

19. Based on Exhibit 2, the price-to-book multiple for Centralino is *closest* to:

    A. 2.0.

    B. 2.2.

    C. 2.5.

20. Based on Exhibit 2, the multiple of enterprise value to sales for Centralino as of

31 December 2019 is *closest* to:

A. 0.67.

B. 0.74.

C. 0.77.

21. Based on Exhibit 1 and using the harmonic mean of the peer group forward P/Es shown in Exhibit 3 as a valuation indicator, the common shares of Centralino are:

A. undervalued.

B. fairly valued.

C. overvalued.

22. Based on Exhibits 1 and 2, the normalized earnings per share for Centralino as calculated by Risso should be *closest* to:

A. €2.94.

B. €3.21.

C. €5.07.

The following information relates to questions 23-29

Cátia Pinho is a supervisor in the equity research division of Suite Securities. Pinho asks Flávia Silveira, a junior analyst, to complete an analysis of Adesivo S.A., Enviado S.A., and Gesticular S.A.

Pinho directs Silveira to use a valuation metric that would allow for a meaningful ranking of relative value of the three companies' shares. Exhibit 1 provides selected financial information for the three companies.

Exhibit 1: Selected Financial Information for Adesivo, Enviado, and Gesticular (Brazilian Real, BRL)

	Adesivo	Enviado	Gesticular
Stock's current price	14.72	72.20	132.16
Diluted EPS (last four quarters)	0.81	2.92	−0.05
Diluted EPS (next four quarters)	0.91	3.10	2.85
Dividend rate (annualized most recent dividend)	0.44	1.24	0.00

Silveira reviews underlying trailing EPS for Adesivo. Adesivo has basic trailing EPS of BRL0.84. Silveira finds the following note in Adesivo's financial statements:

"On a per share basis, Adesivo incurred in the last four quarters

i. from a lawsuit, a nonrecurring gain of BRL0.04; and

ii. from factory integration, a nonrecurring cost of BRL0.03 and a recurring cost of BRL0.01 in increased depreciation."

Silveira notes that Adesivo is forecasted to pay semiannual dividends of BRL0.24 next year. Silveira estimates five-year earnings growth rates for the three companies, which are presented in Exhibit 2.

Exhibit 2: Earnings Growth Rate Estimates over Five Years

Company	Earnings Growth Rate Estimate (%)
Adesivo	16.67
Enviado	21.91
Gesticular	32.33

Pinho asks Silveira about the possible use of the price-to-sales ratio (P/S) in assessing the relative value of the three companies. Silveira tells Pinho:

Statement 1　　　The P/S is not affected by revenue recognition practices.

Statement 2　　　The P/S is less subject to distortion from expense accounting than is the P/E.

Pinho asks Silveira about using the Fed and Yardeni models to assess the value of the equity market. Silveira states:

Statement 1　　　The Fed model concludes that the market is undervalued when the market's current earnings yield is greater than the 10-year Treasury bond yield.

Statement 2　　　The Yardeni model includes the consensus five-year earnings growth rate forecast for the market index.

Silveira also analyzes the three companies using the enterprising value (EV)-to-EBITDA multiple. Silveira notes that the EBITDA for Gesticular for the most recent year is BRL560 million and gathers other selected information on Gesticular, which is presented in Exhibit 4.

Exhibit 3: Selected Information on Gesticular at Year End (BRL Millions)

Market Value of Debt	Market Value of Common Equity	Market Value of Preferred Equity	Cash	Short-Term Investments
1,733	6,766	275	581	495

Pinho asks Silveira about the use of momentum indicators in assessing the shares of the three companies. Silveira states:

Statement 1　　　Relative-strength indicators compare an equity's performance during a period with the performance of some group of equities or its own past performance.

Statement 2　　　In the calculation of standardized unexpected earnings (SUE), the magnitude of unexpected earnings is typically scaled by the standard deviation of analysts' earnings forecasts.

23. Based on Pinho's directive and the data from the last four quarters presented in Exhibit 1, the valuation metric that Silveira should use is the:

    A. price-to-earnings ratio (P/E).

    B. production-to-demand ratio (P/D).

    C. earnings-to-price ratio (E/P).

24. Based on Exhibit 1 and the note to Adesivo's financial statements, the trailing P/E for Adesivo using underlying EPS is *closest* to:

    A. 17.7.

    B. 18.2.

    C. 18.4.

25. Based on Exhibits 1 and 2, which company's shares are the most attractively priced based on the five-year forward P/E-to-growth (PEG) ratio?

    A. Adesivo

    B. Enviado

    C. Gesticular

26. Which of Silveira's statements concerning the use of the P/S is correct?

    A. Statement 1 only

    B. Statement 2 only

    C. Both Statement 1 and Statement 2

27. Which of Silveira's statements concerning the Fed and Yardeni models is correct?

    A. Statement 3 only

    B. Statement 4 only

    C. Both Statement 3 and Statement 4

28. Based on Exhibit 4, Gesticular's EV/EBITDA multiple is *closest* to:

    A. 11.4.

    B. 13.7.

    C. 14.6.

29. Which of Silveira's statements concerning momentum indicators is correct?

    A. Statement 5 only

    B. Statement 6 only

    C. Both Statement 5 and Statement 6

The following information relates to questions 30-31

Christie Johnson, CFA, has been assigned to analyze Sundanci. Johnson assumes that Sundanci's earnings and dividends will grow at a constant rate of 13%. Exhibits 1 and 2 provide financial statements for the most recent two years (2020 and 2021) and other information for Sundanci.

Exhibit 1: Sundanci Actual 2020 and 2021 Financial Statements for Fiscal Years Ending 31 May (in Millions except Per-Share Data)

Income Statement	2020	2021
Revenue	$474	$598
Depreciation	20	23
Other operating costs	368	460
Income before taxes	86	115
Taxes	26	35
Net income	60	80
Dividends	18	24
Earnings per share	$0.714	$0.952
Dividends per share	$0.214	$0.286
Common shares outstanding	84.0	84.0
Balance Sheet	**2020**	**2021**
Current assets	$201	$326
Net property, plant, and equipment	474	489
Total assets	675	815
Current liabilities	57	141
Long-term debt	0	0
Total liabilities	57	141
Shareholders' equity	618	674
Total liabilities and equity	675	815
Other Information		
Capital expenditures	34	38

Exhibit 2: Selected Financial Information	
Required rate of ROE	14%
Growth rate of industry	13%
Industry P/E	26

30. Based on information in Exhibits 1 and 2 and on Johnson's assumptions for Sundanci, calculate justified trailing and forward P/Es for this company.

31. Identify, within the context of the constant dividend growth model, how *each* of the following fundamental factors would affect the P/E:

  i.   The risk (beta) of Sundanci increases substantially.

  ii. The estimated growth rate of Sundanci's earnings and dividends increases.

  iii. The equity risk premium increases.

  Note: A change in a fundamental factor is assumed to happen in isolation; interactive effects between factors are ignored. That is, every other item of the company is unchanged.

32. Suppose an analyst uses an equity index as a comparison asset in valuing a stock. In making a decision to recommend purchase of an individual stock, which price multiple(s) would cause concern about the impact of potential overvaluation of the equity index?

The following information relates to questions 33-34

Tom Smithfield is valuing the stock of a food-processing business. He feels confident explicitly projecting earnings and dividends to three years (to $t = 3$). Other information and estimates are as follows:

- Required rate of return = 0.09.
- Average dividend payout rate for mature companies in the market = 0.45.
- Industry average ROE = 0.10.
- E_3 = $3.00.
- Industry average P/E = 12.

On the basis of this information, answer the following questions:

33. Compute terminal value (V_3) based on comparables.

34. Contrast your answer in Part A to an estimate of terminal value based on the Gordon growth model.

35. Discuss three types of stocks or investment situations for which an analyst could appropriately use P/B in valuation.

The following information relates to questions 36-37

Aratatech is a multinational distributor of semiconductor chips and related products to businesses. Its leading competitor around the world is Trymye Electronics. Aratatech has a current market price of $10.00, 20 million shares outstanding, annual sales of $1 billion, and a 5% profit margin. Trymye has a market price of $20.00, 30 million shares outstanding, annual sales of $1.6 billion, and a profit margin of 4.9%. Based on the information given, answer the following questions:

36. Which of the two companies has a more attractive valuation based on P/S?

37. Identify and explain one advantage of P/S over P/E as a valuation tool.

The following information relates to questions 38-41

GN Growing AG (GG) is currently selling for €240, with TTM EPS and dividends per share of €1.5 and €0.9, respectively. The company's trailing P/E is 16.0, P/B is 3.2. P/Sales based on forecast sales, is 1.5. ROE is 20%, and for the profit margin on sales is 10.0%. The Treasury bond rate is 4.9%, the equity risk premium is 5.5%, and GG's beta is 1.2.

38. What is GG's required rate of return, based on the capital asset pricing model (CAPM)?

39. Assume that the dividend and earnings growth rates are 8%. What trailing P/E and P/B multiples would be justified in light of the required rate of return in Part A and current values of the dividend payout ratio and ROE ?

40. Calculate the justified P/Sales ratio based on the forward-looking margin of 10% and current values of dividend payout.

41. Given that the assumptions and constant growth model are appropriate, state and justify whether GG, based on fundamentals, appears to be fairly valued, overvalued, or undervalued.

42. Define the major alternative cash flow concepts, and state one limitation of each.

43. Data for two hypothetical companies in the pharmaceutical industry, DriveMed and MAT Technology, are given in the following table. For both companies, expenditures on fixed capital and working capital during the previous year reflect anticipated average expenditures over the foreseeable horizon.

Measure	DriveMed	MAT Technology
Current price	$46.00	$78.00
Trailing CF per share	$3.60	$6.00
P/CF	12.8	13.0
Trailing FCFE per share	$1.00	$5.00
P/FCFE	46.0	15.6
Consensus five-year growth forecast	15%	20%

Measure	DriveMed	MAT Technology
Beta	1.25	1.25

On the basis of the information supplied, discuss the valuation of MAT Technology relative to DriveMed. Justify your conclusion.

The following information relates to questions 44-46

Jorge Zaldys, CFA, is researching the relative valuation of two companies in the aerospace/defense industry, NCI Heavy Industries (NCI) and Relay Group International (RGI). He has gathered relevant information on the companies in the following table.

EBITDA Comparisons (in € Millions except Per-Share and Share-Count Data)		
Company	RGI	NCI
Price per share	150	100
Shares outstanding	5 million	2 million
Market value of debt	50	100
Book value of debt	52	112
Cash and investments	5	2
Net income	49.5	12
Net income from continuing operations	49.5	8
Interest expense	3	5
Depreciation and amortization	8	4
Taxes	2	3

Using the information in the table, answer the following questions:

44. Calculate P/EBITDA for NCI and RGI.

45. Calculate EV/EBITDA for NCI and RGI.

46. Which company should Zaldys recommend as relatively undervalued? Justify the selection.

The following information relates to questions 47-48

Wilhelm Müller, CFA, has organized the selected data on four food companies that appear below (TTM stands for trailing 12-month):

Measure	Hoppelli Foods	Telli Foods	Drisket Co.	Whiteline Foods
Stock price	€25.70	€11.77	€23.65	€24.61

Measure	Hoppelli Foods	Telli Foods	Drisket Co.	Whiteline Foods
Shares outstanding (thousands)	138,923	220,662	108,170	103,803
Market cap (€ millions)	3,570	2,597	2,558	2,555
Enterprise value (€ millions)	3,779	4,056	3,846	4,258
Sales (€ millions)	4,124	10,751	17,388	6,354
Operating income (€ millions)	285	135	186	396
Operating profit margin	6.91%	1.26%	1.07%	6.23%
Net income (€ millions)	182	88	122	252
TTM EPS	€1.30	€0.40	€1.14	€2.43
Return on equity	19.20%	4.10%	6.40%	23.00%
Net profit margin	4.41%	0.82%	0.70%	3.97%

On the basis of the data given, answer the following questions:

47. Calculate the trailing P/E and EV/sales for each company.

48. Explain, on the basis of fundamentals, why these stocks have different EV/S multiples.

49. John Jones, CFA, is head of the research department at Peninsular Research. Peninsular has a client who has inquired about the valuation method best suited for comparing companies in an industry with the following characteristics:

   - Principal competitors within the industry are located in the United States, France, Japan, and Brazil.
   - The industry is currently operating at a cyclical low, with many companies reporting losses.

   Jones recommends that the client consider the following valuation ratios:

   1. P/E
   2. P/B
   3. EV/S

   Determine which *one* of the three valuation ratios is most appropriate for comparing companies in this industry. Support your answer with *one* reason that makes that ratio superior to either of the other two ratios in this case.

The following information relates to questions 50–51

Your value-oriented investment management firm recently hired a new analyst, Bob Westard, because of his expertise in the life sciences and biotechnology areas. At the firm's weekly meeting, during which each analyst proposes a stock idea for inclusion in the firm's approved list, Westard recommends Hitech Clothing International (HCI). He bases his recommendation on two considerations. First, HCI has pending patent applications but a P/E that he judges to be low in light of the potential earnings from the patented products. Second, HCI has had high relative strength versus the S&P 500 over the past month.

50. Explain the difference between Westard's two approaches—that is, the use of price multiples and the relative-strength approach.

51. State which, if any, of the bases for Westard's recommendation is consistent with the investment orientation of your firm.

The following information relates to questions 52-53

Kirstin Kruse, a portfolio manager, has an important client who wants to alter the composition of her equity portfolio, which is currently a diversified portfolio of 60 global common stocks. Because of concerns about the economy and based on the thesis that the consumer staples sector will be less hurt than others in a recession, the client wants to add stocks trading in the United States (including ADRs) from the consumer staples sector. In addition, the client wants the stocks to meet the following criteria:

- Stocks must be considered large cap (i.e., have a large market capitalization).
- Stocks must have a dividend yield of at least 4.0%.
- Stocks must have a forward P/E no greater than 15.

The following table shows how many stocks satisfied each screen, which was run in June 2019.

Screen	Number Satisfying
Consumer staples sector	424
Large cap	361
Dividend yield of at least 4.0%	887
P/E less than 15	5,409
All four screens	3

The stocks meeting all four screens were Altria Group, Inc.; British American Tobacco PLC (the company's ADR); and Kraft Heinz Co.

52. Critique the construction of the screen.

53. Do these criteria identify appropriate additions to this client's portfolio?

SOLUTIONS

1. Normalized EPS is the level of earnings per share that the company could currently achieve under mid-cyclical conditions.

2. Averaging EPS over the 2015–18 period, we find that ($2.55 + $2.13 + $0.23 + $1.45)/4 = $1.59. According to the method of historical average EPS, Jonash's normalized EPS is $1.59. The P/E based on this estimate is $57.98/$1.59 = 36.5.

3. Averaging ROE over the 2015–18 period, we find that (0.218 + 0.163 + 0.016 + 0.089)/4 = 0.1215. For current BV per share, you would use the estimated value of $19.20 for year end 2019. According to the method of average ROE, 0.1215 × $19.20 = $2.33 is the normalized EPS. The P/E based on this estimate is $57.98/$2.33 = 24.9.

4. The analyst can rank the two stocks by earnings yield (E/P). Whether EPS is positive or negative, a lower E/P reflects a richer (higher) valuation and a ranking from high to low E/P has a meaningful interpretation.

   In some cases, an analyst might handle negative EPS by using normalized EPS in its place. Neither business, however, has a history of profitability. When year-ahead EPS is expected to be positive, forward P/E is positive. Thus, the use of forward P/Es sometimes addresses the problem of trailing negative EPS. Forward P/E is not meaningful in this case, however, because next year's earnings are expected to be negative.

5. Hand has an E/P of –0.100, and Somersault has an E/P of –0.125. A higher earnings yield has an interpretation that is similar to that of a lower P/E, so Hand appears to be relatively undervalued. The difference in earnings yield cannot be explained by differences in sales growth forecasts. In fact, Hand has a higher expected sales growth rate than Somersault. Therefore, the analyst should recommend Hand.

6. Because investing looks to the future, analysts often favor forward P/E when earnings forecasts are available, as they are here. A specific reason to use forward P/Es is the fact given that RUF had some unusual items affecting EPS for 2008. The data to make appropriate adjustments to RUF's 2008 EPS are not given. In summary, Stewart should use forward P/Es.

7. Because RUF has a complex capital structure, the P/Es of the two companies must be compared on the basis of diluted EPS.

   For HS, forward P/E = $44/2.20 = 20.

   For RUF, forward P/E per diluted share

   = $22.50/($30,000,000/33,333,333) = $22.50/$0.90 = 25.

   Therefore, HS has the more attractive valuation at present.

   The problem illustrates some of the considerations that should be taken into account in using P/Es and the method of comparables.

8. Your conclusion may be in error because of the following:

   - The peer-group stocks themselves may be overvalued; that is, the mean P/E of 18.0 may be too high in terms of intrinsic value. If so, using 18.0 as a multiplier of the stock's expected EPS will lead to an estimate of stock value in excess of intrinsic value.

- The stock's fundamentals may differ from those of the mean food-processing industry stock. For example, if the stock's expected growth rate is lower than the mean industry growth rate and its risk is higher than the mean, the stock may deserve a lower P/E than the industry mean.

In addition, mean P/E may be influenced by outliers.

9. The following additional evidence would support the original conclusion:

- Evidence that stocks in the industry are, at least on average, fairly valued (that stock prices reflect fundamentals)
- Evidence that no significant differences exist in the fundamental drivers of P/E for the stock being compared and the average industry stock

10. A is correct. The forward P/E should be used given the recent significant acquisition of the water bottling company. Since a major change such as an acquisition or divestiture can affect results, the forward P/E, also known as the leading P/E or prospective P/E, is the most appropriate P/E to use for Delite. Earnings estimates for 2021 should incorporate the performance of the water bottling company. The forward P/E is calculated as the current price divided by the projected earnings per share, or $65.50/$3.50 = 18.71.

11. C is correct. The price-to-sales ratio is calculated as price per share divided by annual net sales per share.

Price per share = $37.23.

Annual net sales per share = $67.44 billion/1.638821 billion shares = $41.15.

Price-to-sales ratio (P/S) = $37.23/$41.15 = 0.90.

12. C is correct. You Fix It is in the cyclical home improvement industry. The use of normalized earnings should address the problem of cyclicality in You Fix It earnings by estimating the level of earnings per share that the company could achieve currently under mid-cyclical conditions.

13. C is correct. The price to sales ratio (P/S) fails to consider differences in cost structures. Also, while share price reflects the effect of debt financing on profitability and risk, sales is a pre-financing income measure and does not incorporate the impact of debt in the firm's capital structure. Earnings reflect operating and financial leverage, and thus the price-to-earnings ratio (P/E) incorporates the impact of debt in the firm's capital structure.

14. A is correct. Free cash flow to equity (FCFE) is defined as cash flow available to shareholders after deducting all operating expenses, interest and debt payments, and investments in working and fixed capital. Cannan's requirement that the cash flows include interest expense, working capital, and noncash revenue is satisfied by FCFE.

15. C is correct. The P/E-to-growth (PEG) ratio is calculated by dividing a stock's P/E by the expected earnings growth rate, expressed as a percentage. To calculate Delite's PEG ratio, first calculate the P/E: $65.50/$3.50 = 18.71. In this case, the forward earnings should be used given the recent acquisition of the water bottling company. Next, calculate Delite's PEG ratio: 18.71/12.41 = 1.51.

Comparing Delite's PEG ratio of 1.51 with the PEG ratios of 1.74 (16.59/9.52) for Fresh Iced Tea and 1.31 (15.64/11.94) for Nonutter Soda and with the beverage sector average of 1.52 (16.40/10.80), it appears that Delite's shares are fairly valued. This is determined by the fact that Delite's PEG ratio is in the middle of the range of PEG ratios and very close to the sector average. Therefore, the shares appear to be fairly valued.

16. B is correct. The harmonic mean is sometimes used to reduce the impact of large outliers—which are typically the major concern in using the arithmetic mean multiple—but not the impact of small outliers (i.e., those close to zero). The harmonic mean may aggravate the impact of small outliers, but such outliers are bounded by zero on the downside.

17. B is correct. The trailing P/E is calculated as follows:

    Stock's current price/Most recent four quarters' EPS =

    €50/€5.64 = 8.9.

18. A is correct. The justified forward P/E is calculated as follows:

$$\frac{P_0}{E_1} = \frac{D_1/E_1}{r - g}$$

$$= \frac{(2.91/6.00)}{(0.15 - 0.06)} = 5.4.$$

19. B is correct. Price to book is calculated as the current market price per share divided by book value per share. Book value per share is common shareholders' equity divided by the number of common shares outstanding. Common shareholders' equity is calculated as total shareholders' equity minus the value of preferred stock.

    Thus,

    Common shareholders' equity = €1,027 − €80 = €947 million.

    Book value per share = €947 million/41.94 million = €22.58.

    Price-to-book ratio (P/B) for Centralino = €50/€22.58 = 2.2.

20. C is correct. Enterprise value (EV) is calculated as follows:

    EV = Market value of common equity + Market value of preferred stock + Market value of debt − Cash, cash equivalents, and short-term investments

    = (€50 × 41.94 million) + (€5.25 × 16.00 million) + €367 million − €102 million

    = €2,446 million (or €2.446 billion).

    So, EV/sales = €2.446 billion/€3.182 billion = 0.77.

21. C is correct. The harmonic mean is calculated as follows:

$$x_H = \frac{n}{\sum\limits_{i=1}^{n}\left(\frac{1}{x_i}\right)} = \frac{5}{\left(\frac{1}{5.9}\right) + \left(\frac{1}{8.3}\right) + \left(\frac{1}{3.0}\right) + \left(\frac{1}{15.0}\right) + \left(\frac{1}{4.6}\right)} = 5.5.$$

    The forward P/E for Centralino is €50/€6.00 = 8.3. Because Centralino's forward P/E is higher than the harmonic mean of the peer group, the shares of Centralino appear relatively overvalued.

22. A is correct. Based on the method of average ROE, normalized EPS are calculated as the average ROE from the most recent full business cycle multiplied by current book value per share. The most recent business cycle was 2011–2014, and the average ROE over that period was

$$\frac{0.1301 + 0.1371 + 0.1158 + 0.1421}{4} = 0.131.$$

The book value of (common) equity, or simply book value, is the value of shareholders' equity less any value attributable to the preferred stock: €1,027 million − €84 million = €943 million.

Current book value per share (BVPS) is calculated as €943 million/41.94 million = €22.48.

So, normalized EPS is calculated as

Average ROE × BVPS = 0.131 × €22.48 = €2.94.

23. C is correct. The E/P based on trailing earnings would offer the most meaningful ranking of the shares. Using E/P places Gesticular's negative EPS in the numerator rather than the denominator, leading to a more meaningful ranking.

24. C is correct. The EPS figure that Silveira should use is diluted trailing EPS of BRL0.81, adjusted as follows:

    1. Subtract the BRL0.04 nonrecurring legal gain.

    2. Add BRL0.03 for the nonrecurring factory integration charge.

    No adjustment needs to be made for the BRL0.01 charge related to depreciation because it is a recurring charge.

    Therefore, underlying trailing EPS = BRL0.81 − BRL0.04 + BRL0.03 = BRL0.80 and trailing P/E using underlying trailing EPS = BRL14.72/BRL0.80 = 18.4.

25. A is correct. The forward PEG ratios for the three companies are calculated as follows:

    Forward P/E = Stock's current price/Forecasted EPS.

    Forward PEG ratio

    = Forward P/E ÷ Expected earnings growth rate (in percentage terms).

    Adesivo forward P/E = BRL14.72/BRL0.91 = 16.18.

    Adesivo forward PEG ratio = 16.18/16.67 = 0.97.

    Enviado forward P/E = BRL72.20/BRL3.10 = 23.29.

    Enviado forward PEG ratio = 23.29/21.91 = 1.06.

    Gesticular forward P/E = BRL132.16/BRL2.85 = 46.37.

    Gesticular forward PEG ratio = 46.37/32.33 = 1.43.

    Adesivo has the lowest forward PEG ratio, 0.97, indicating that it is the most undervalued of the three equities based on the forward PEG ratio.

26. B is correct. Statement 2 is correct because sales, as the top line of the income statement, are less subject to accounting distortion or manipulation than are other fundamentals, such as earnings. Statement 1 is incorrect because sales figures can be distorted by revenue recognition practices, in particular those tending to speed up the recognition of revenues.

27. C is correct. The Fed model considers the equity market to be undervalued when the market's current earnings yield is greater than the 10-year Treasury bond yield. The Yardeni model incorporates the consensus five-year earnings growth rate forecast for the market index, a variable missing in the Fed model.

28. B is correct. The EV for Gesticular is calculated as follows:

EV = Market value of debt + Market value of common equity +
Market value of preferred equity − Cash and short-term investments.

EV = BRL1,733 million + BRL6,766 million + BRL275 million − BRL581 million − BRL495 million

  = BRL7,698 million.

EV/EBITDA = BRL7,698 million/BRL560 million = 13.7.

29. A is correct. Relative-strength indicators compare an equity's performance with the performance of a group of equities or with its own past performance. SUE is unexpected earnings scaled by the standard deviation in past unexpected earnings (not the standard deviation of analysts' earnings forecasts, which is used in the calculation of the scaled earnings surprise).

30. The formula for calculating the justified forward P/E for a stable-growth company is the payout ratio divided by the difference between the required rate of return and the growth rate of dividends. If the P/E is being calculated on trailing earnings (Year 0), the payout ratio is increased by 1 plus the growth rate. According to the 2020 income statement, the payout ratio is 18/60 = 0.30; the 2021 income statement gives the same number (24/80 = 0.30). Thus, we can find the following:

P/E based on trailing earnings:

$$P/E = [Payout\ ratio \times (1 + g)] / (r - g)$$
$$= (0.30 \times 1.13) / (0.14 - 0.13) = 33.9.$$

P/E based on next year's earnings:

$$P/E = Payout\ ratio / (r - g)$$
$$= 0.30 / (0.14 - 0.13) = 30.$$

31.

Fundamental Factor	Effect on P/E	Explanation (Not Required in Question)
The risk (beta) of Sundanci increases substantially.	Decrease	P/E is a decreasing function of risk; that is, as risk increases, P/E decreases. Increases in the risk of Sundanci stock would be expected to lower its P/E.
The estimated growth rate of Sundanci's earnings and dividends increases.	Increase	P/E is an increasing function of the growth rate of the company; that is, the higher the expected growth, the higher the P/E. Sundanci would command a higher P/E if the market price were to incorporate expectations of a higher growth rate.
The equity risk premium increases.	Decrease	P/E is a decreasing function of the equity risk premium. An increased equity risk premium increases the required rate of return, which lowers the price of a stock relative to its earnings. A higher equity risk premium would be expected to lower Sundanci's P/E.

32. In principle, the use of any price multiple for valuation is subject to the concern stated. If the stock market is overvalued, an asset that appears to be fairly or even

undervalued in relation to an equity index may also be overvalued.

33. V_n = Benchmark value of P/E $\times$ E_n = 12 $\times$ \$3.00 = \$36.0.

34. In the expression for the sustainable growth rate, $g = b \times$ ROE, you can use $(1 - 0.45) = 0.55 = b$ and ROE = 0.10 (the industry average), obtaining 0.55 $\times$ 0.10 = 0.055. Given the required rate of return of 0.09, you obtain the estimate \$3.00(0.45)(1.055)/(0.09 - 0.055) = \$40.69. In this case, the estimate of terminal value obtained from the Gordon growth model is higher than the estimate based on multiples. The two estimates may differ for a number of reasons, including the sensitivity of the Gordon growth model to the values of the inputs.

35. Although the measurement of book value has a number of widely recognized shortcomings, P/B may still be applied fruitfully in several circumstances:

   - The company is not expected to continue as a going concern. When a company is likely to be liquidated (so ongoing earnings and cash flow are not relevant), the value of its assets less its liabilities is of utmost importance. Naturally, the analyst must establish the fair value of these assets.

   - The company is composed mainly of liquid assets, which is the case for finance, investment, insurance, and banking institutions.

   - The company's EPS is highly variable or negative.

36. Aratatech: P/S = (\$10 price per share)/[(\$1 billion sales)/(20 million shares)] = \$10/(\$1,000,000,000/20,000,000) = 0.2.

   Trymye: P/S = (\$20 price per share)/[(\$1.6 billion sales)/(30 million shares)] = \$20/(\$1,600,000,000/30,000,000) = 0.375.

   Aratatech has a more attractive valuation than Trymye based on its lower P/S but a comparable profit margin.

37. One advantage of P/S over P/E is that companies' accounting decisions typically have a much greater impact on reported earnings than they are likely to have on reported sales. Although companies are able to make a number of legitimate business and accounting decisions that affect earnings, their discretion over reported sales (revenue recognition) is limited. Another advantage is that sales are almost always positive, so using P/S eliminates issues that arise when EPS is zero or negative.

38. Based on the CAPM, the required rate of return is 4.9% + 1.2 $\times$ 5.5% = 11.5%.

39. The dividend payout ratio is €0.9/€1.50 = 0.6. The justified values for the trailing P/E and P/BV ratios should be

$$\frac{P_0}{E_0} = \frac{(1 - b) \times (1 + g)}{r - g} = \frac{0.6 \times (1 + 0.08)}{0.115 - 0.08} = 18.5$$

$$\frac{P_0}{E_0} = \frac{ROE - g}{r - g} = \frac{0.20 - 0.08}{0.115 - 0.08} = 3.4$$

40. The justified P/S ratio based on assumed profit margin of 10% should be

$$\frac{P_0}{S_1} = \frac{\left(\frac{E_1}{S_1}\right)(1 - b)}{r - g} = \frac{0.10 \times 0.6}{0.115 - 0.08} = 1.7$$

41. The justified trailing P/E is higher than the trailing P/E (18.5 versus 16), the justified trailing P/B is higher than the actual trailing P/B (3.4 versus 3.2). The justified P/S based on forward looking margin assumptions is higher than the actual P/S

based of forecast sales (1.7 versus 1.5). Therefore, based on these three measures, GG appears to be slightly undervalued.

42. The major concepts are as follows:

   - EPS plus per-share depreciation, amortization, and depletion (CF)

     Limitation: Ignores changes in working capital and noncash revenue; not a free cash flow concept.

   - Cash flow from operations (CFO)

     Limitation: Not a free cash flow concept, so not directly linked to theory.

   - Free cash flow to equity (FCFE)

     Limitation: Often more variable and more frequently negative than other cash flow concepts.

   - Earnings before interest, taxes, depreciation, and amortization (EBITDA)

     Limitation: Ignores changes in working capital and noncash revenue; not a free cash flow concept. Relative to its use in P/EBITDA, EBITDA is mismatched with the numerator because it is a pre-interest concept.

43. MAT Technology is relatively undervalued compared with DriveMed on the basis of P/FCFE. MAT Technology's P/FCFE multiple is 34% the size of DriveMed's FCFE multiple (15.6/46 = 0.34, or 34%). The only comparison slightly in DriveMed's favor, or approximately equal for both companies, is the comparison based on P/CF (i.e., 12.8 for DriveMed versus 13.0 for MAT Technology). However, FCFE is more strongly grounded in valuation theory than P/CF. Because DriveMed's and MAT Technology's expenditures for fixed capital and working capital during the previous year reflected anticipated average expenditures over the foreseeable horizon, you would have additional confidence in the P/FCFE comparison.

44. EBITDA = Net income (from continuing operations) + Interest expense + Taxes + Depreciation + Amortization.

    EBITDA for RGI = €49.5 million + €3 million + €2 million + €8 million = €62.5 million.

    Per-share EBITDA = (€62.5 million)/(5 million shares) = €12.5.

    P/EBITDA for RGI = €150/€12.5 = 12.

    EBITDA for NCI = €8 million + €5 million + €3 million + €4 million = €20 million.

    Per-share EBITDA = (€20 million)/(2 million shares) = €10.

    P/EBITDA for NCI = €100/€10 = 10.

45. For RGI:

    Market value of equity = €150 × 5 million = €750 million.

    Market value of debt = €50 million.

    Total market value = €750 million + €50 million = €800 million.

    EV = €800 million − €5 million (cash and investments) = €795 million.

    Now, Zaldys would divide EV by total (as opposed to per-share) EBITDA:

    EV/EBITDA for RGI = (€795 million)/(€62.5 million) = 12.72.

    For NCI:

Market value of equity = €100 × 2 million = €200 million.

Market value of debt = €100 million.

Total market value = €200 million + €100 million = €300 million.

EV = €300 million − €2 million (cash and investments) = €298 million.

Now, Zaldys would divide EV by total (as opposed to per-share) EBITDA:

EV/EBITDA for NCI = (€298 million)/(€20 million) = 14.9.

46. Zaldys should select RGI as relatively undervalued.

First, it is correct that NCI *appears* to be relatively undervalued based on P/EBITDA, because NCI has a lower P/EBITDA multiple:

- P/EBITDA = €150/€12.5 = 12 for RGI.
- P/EBITDA = €100/€10 = 10 for NCI.

RGI is relatively undervalued on the basis of EV/EBITDA; however, because RGI has the lower EV/EBITDA multiple,

- EV/EBITDA = (€795 million)/(€62.5 million) = 12.72 for RGI.
- EV/EBITDA = (€298 million)/(€20 million) = 14.9 for NCI.

EBITDA is a pre-interest flow; therefore, it is a flow to both debt and equity and the EV/EBITDA multiple is more appropriate than the P/EBITDA multiple. Zaldys would rely on EV/EBITDA to reach his decision if the two ratios conflicted. Note that P/EBITDA does not take into account differences in the use of financial leverage. Substantial differences in leverage exist in this case (NCI uses much more debt), so the preference for using EV/EBITDA rather than P/EBITDA is supported.

47. The P/Es are as follows:

Hoppelli	25.70/1.30 = 19.8.
Telli	11.77/0.40 = 29.4.
Drisket	23.65/1.14 = 20.7.
Whiteline	24.61/2.43 = 10.1.

The EV/S multiples for each company are as follows:

Hoppelli	3,779/4,124 = 0.916.
Telli	4,056/10,751 = 0.377.
Drisket	3,846/17,388 = 0.221.
Whiteline	4,258/6,354 = 0.670.

48. The data for the problem include measures of profitability, such as operating profit margin, ROE, and net profit margin. Because EV includes the market values of both debt and equity, logically the ranking based on EV/S should be compared with a pre-interest measure of profitability—namely, operating profit margin. The ranking of the stocks by EV/S from highest to lowest and the companies' operating margins are shown below:

Company	EV/S	Operating Profit Margin (%)
Hoppelli	0.916	6.91

Company	EV/S	Operating Profit Margin (%)
Whiteline	0.670	6.23
Telli	0.377	1.26
Drisket	0.221	1.07

The differences in EV/S appear to be explained, at least in part, by differences in cost structure as measured by operating profit margin.

49. For companies in the industry described, EV/S would be superior to either of the other two ratios. Among other considerations, EV/S is:

   ▪ more useful than P/E in valuing companies with negative earnings;

   ▪ better than either P/E or P/B for comparing companies in different countries that are likely to use different accounting standards (a consequence of the multinational nature of the industry);

   ▪ less subject to manipulation than earnings (i.e., through aggressive accounting decisions by management, who may be more motivated to manage earnings when a company is in a cyclical low, rather than in a high, and thus likely to report losses).

50. Relative strength is based strictly on price movement (a technical indicator). As used by Westard, the comparison is between the returns on HCI and the returns on the S&P 500. In contrast, the price multiple approaches are based on the relationship of current price not to past prices but to some measure of value, such as EPS, book value, sales, or cash flow.

51. Only the reference to the P/E in relationship to the pending patent applications in Westard's recommendation is consistent with the company's value orientation. High relative strength would be relevant for a portfolio managed with a growth/momentum investment style.

52. As a rule, a screen that includes a maximum P/E should include criteria requiring positive earnings; otherwise, the screen could select companies with negative P/Es. The screen may be too narrowly focused on value measures. It did not include criteria related to expected growth, required rate of return, risk, or financial strength.

53. The screen results in a very concentrated portfolio. The screen selected only three companies, including two tobacco companies, which typically pay high dividends. Owning these three stocks would provide little diversification.

3

Residual Income Valuation

by Jerald E. Pinto, PhD, CFA, Elaine Henry, PhD, CFA, Thomas R. Robinson, PhD, CFA, CAIA, and John D. Stowe, PhD, CFA.

Jerald E. Pinto, PhD, CFA, is at CFA Institute (USA). Elaine Henry, PhD, CFA, is at Stevens Institute of Technology (USA). Thomas R. Robinson, PhD, CFA, CAIA, Robinson Global Investment Management LLC, (USA). John D. Stowe, PhD, CFA, is at Ohio University (USA).

LEARNING OUTCOMES

Mastery	The candidate should be able to:
☐	calculate and interpret residual income, economic value added, and market value added
☐	describe the uses of residual income models
☐	calculate the intrinsic value of a common stock using the residual income model and compare value recognition in residual income and other present value models
☐	explain fundamental determinants of residual income
☐	explain the relation between residual income valuation and the justified price-to-book ratio based on forecasted fundamentals
☐	calculate and interpret the intrinsic value of a common stock using single-stage (constant-growth) and multistage residual income models
☐	calculate the implied growth rate in residual income, given the market price-to-book ratio and an estimate of the required rate of return on equity
☐	explain continuing residual income and justify an estimate of continuing residual income at the forecast horizon, given company and industry prospects
☐	compare residual income models to dividend discount and free cash flow models
☐	explain strengths and weaknesses of residual income models and justify the selection of a residual income model to value a company's common stock
☐	describe accounting issues in applying residual income models

1 INTRODUCTION

☐ | calculate and interpret residual income, economic value added, and market value added

☐ | describe the uses of residual income models

Residual income models of equity value have become widely recognized tools in both investment practice and research. Conceptually, residual income is net income less a charge (deduction) for common shareholders' opportunity cost in generating net income. It is the residual or remaining income after considering the costs of all of a company's capital. The appeal of residual income models stems from a shortcoming of traditional accounting. Specifically, although a company's income statement includes a charge for the cost of debt capital in the form of interest expense, it does not include a charge for the cost of equity capital. A company can have positive net income but may still not be adding value for shareholders if it does not earn more than its cost of equity capital. Residual income models explicitly recognize the costs of all the capital used in generating income.

As an economic concept, residual income has a long history, dating back to Alfred Marshall in the late 1800s (Alfred Marshall, 1890). As far back as the 1920s, General Motors used the concept in evaluating business segments. More recently, residual income has received renewed attention and interest, sometimes under names such as economic profit, abnormal earnings, or economic value added. Although residual income concepts have been used in a variety of contexts, including the measurement of internal corporate performance, we will focus on the residual income model for estimating the intrinsic value of common stock. Among the questions we will study to help us apply residual income models are the following:

- How is residual income measured, and how can an analyst use residual income in valuation?
- How does residual income relate to fundamentals, such as return on equity and earnings growth rates?
- How is residual income linked to other valuation methods, such as a price-multiple approach?
- What accounting-based challenges arise in applying residual income valuation?

The following section develops the concept of residual income, introduces the use of residual income in valuation, and briefly presents alternative measures used in practice. The subsequent sections present the residual income model and illustrate its use in valuing common stock, show practical applications, and describe the relative strengths and weaknesses of residual income valuation compared with other valuation methods. The last section addresses accounting issues in the use of residual income valuation. We then conclude with a summary.

Residual Income

Traditional financial statements, particularly the income statement, are prepared to reflect earnings available to owners. As a result, the income statement shows net income after deducting an expense for the cost of debt capital (i.e., interest expense). The income statement does not, however, deduct dividends or other charges for equity capital. Thus, traditional financial statements essentially let the owners decide whether earnings cover their opportunity costs. Conversely, the economic concept of residual income explicitly deducts the estimated cost of equity capital, the finance concept that measures shareholders' opportunity costs. The cost of equity is the marginal cost of equity, also referred to as the required rate of return on equity. The cost of equity is a marginal cost because it represents the cost of additional equity, whether generated internally or by selling more equity interests. Example 1 illustrates, in a stylized setting, the calculation and interpretation of residual income. To simplify this introduction, we assume that net income accurately reflects clean surplus accounting, a condition that income (earnings) reflects all changes in the book value of equity other than ownership transactions. This concept will be explained later. Our discussions also assume that companies' financing consists only of common equity and debt. In the case of a company that also has preferred stock financing, the residual income calculation would reflect the deduction of preferred stock dividends from net income.

EXAMPLE 1

Calculation of Residual Income

Axis Manufacturing Company, Inc. (AXCI), a very small company in terms of market capitalization, has total assets of €2 million financed 50% with debt and 50% with equity capital. The cost of debt is 7% before taxes; this example assumes that interest is tax deductible, so the after-tax cost of debt is 4.9%. Note that in countries where corporate interest is not tax deductible, the after-tax cost of debt equals the pretax cost of debt. The cost of equity capital is 12%. The company has earnings before interest and taxes (EBIT) of €200,000 and a tax rate of 30%. Net income for AXCI can be determined as follows:

EBIT	€200,000
Less: Interest Expense	€70,000
Pretax Income	€130,000
Less: Income Tax Expense	€39,000
Net Income	€91,000

With earnings of €91,000, AXCI is clearly profitable in an accounting sense. But was the company's profitability adequate return for its owners? Unfortunately, it was not. To incorporate the cost of equity capital, compute residual income. One approach to calculating residual income is to deduct an **equity charge** (the estimated cost of equity capital in money terms) from net income. Compute the equity charge as follows:

Equity charge = Equity capital × Cost of equity capital

$$= €1,000,000 × 12\%$$

$$= €120,000.$$

As stated, residual income is equal to net income minus the equity charge:

Net Income	€91,000
Less: Equity Charge	€120,000
Residual Income	(€29,000)

AXCI did not earn enough to cover the cost of equity capital. As a result, it has negative residual income. Although AXCI is profitable in an accounting sense, it is not profitable in an economic sense.

In Example 1, residual income is calculated based on net income and a charge for the cost of equity capital. Analysts will also encounter another approach to calculating residual income that yields the same results under certain assumptions. In this second approach, which takes the perspective of all providers of capital (both debt and equity), a **capital charge** (the company's total cost of capital in money terms) is subtracted from the company's after-tax operating profit. In the case of AXCI in Example 1, the capital charge is €169,000:

Equity charge	$0.12 \times €1,000,000 =$	€120,000
Debt charge	$0.07(1 - 0.30) \times €1,000,000 =$	€49,000
Total capital charge		€169,000

The company's net operating profit after taxes (NOPAT) is €140,000 (€200,000 – 30% taxes). The capital charge of €169,000 is higher than the after-tax operating profit of €140,000 by €29,000, the same figure obtained in Example 1.

As the following table illustrates, both approaches yield the same results in this case because of two assumptions. First, this example assumes that the marginal cost of debt equals the current cost of debt—that is, the cost used to determine net income. Specifically, in this instance, the after-tax interest expense incorporated in net income [€49,000 = €70,000 × (1 – 30%)] is equal to the after-tax cost of debt incorporated into the capital charge. Second, this example assumes that the weights used to calculate the capital charge are derived from the book value of debt and equity. Specifically, it uses the weights of 50% debt and 50% equity.

Approach 1		Reconciliation	Approach 2	
Net income	€91,000	Plus the after-tax interest expense of €49,000	Net operating profit after tax	€140,000
Less: Equity charge	€120,000	Plus the after-tax capital charge for debt of €49,000	Less: Capital charge	€169,000
Residual income	(€29,000)		Residual income	(€29,000)

Handwritten annotation near Approach 2: $EBIT(1-0.3)$; $200,000 \times (1-0.3)$

That the company is not profitable in an economic sense can also be seen by comparing the company's cost of capital with its return on capital. Specifically, the company's capital charge is greater than its after-tax return on total assets or capital. The after-tax net operating return on total assets or capital is calculated as profits divided by total assets (or total capital). In this example, the after-tax net operating return on total assets is 7% (€140,000/€2,000,000), which is 1.45 percentage points less than the company's effective capital charge of 8.45% (€169,000/€2,000,000). The amount of after-tax net operating profits as a percentage of total assets or capital has been called **return on invested capital** (ROIC). Residual income can also be calculated as (ROIC – Effective capital charge) × Beginning capital.

Handwritten annotation in left margin:
$ROIC: \dfrac{EBIT \times (1-\tau)}{Total\ Assets}$

↓

I think this is the same

as $\dfrac{NOPAT}{Total\ Assets}$

Yes,

$EBIT(1-t) = NOPAT$

The Use of Residual Income in Equity Valuation

A company that is generating more income than its cost of obtaining capital—that is, one with positive residual income—is creating value. Conversely, a company that is not generating enough income to cover its cost of capital—that is, a company with negative residual income—is destroying value. Thus, all else equal, higher (lower) residual income should be associated with higher (lower) valuations.

To illustrate the effect of residual income on equity valuation using the case of AXCI presented in Example 1, assume the following:

- Initially, AXCI equity is selling for book value or €1 million with 100,000 shares outstanding. Thus, AXCI's book value per share and initial share price are both €10.

- Earnings per share (EPS) is €0.91 (€91,000/100,000 shares).
- Earnings will continue at the current level indefinitely.
- All net income is distributed as dividends.

Because AXCI is not earning its cost of equity, as shown in Example 1, the company's share price should fall. Given the information, AXCI is destroying €29,000 of value per year, which equals €0.29 per share (€29,000/100,000 shares). Discounted at 12% cost of equity, the present value of the perpetuity is €2.42 (€0.29/12%). The current share price minus the present value of the value being destroyed equals €7.58 (€10 – €2.42).

Another way to look at these data is to note that the earnings yield (E/P) for a no-growth company is an estimate of the expected rate of return. Therefore, when price reaches the point at which E/P equals the required rate of return on equity, an investment in the stock is expected to just cover the stock's required rate of return. With EPS of €0.91, the earnings yield is exactly 12% (AXCI's cost of equity) when its share price is €7.58333 (i.e., €0.91/€7.58333 = 12%). At a share price of €7.58333, the total market value of AXCI's equity is €758,333. When a company has negative residual income, shares are expected to sell at a discount to book value. In this example, AXCI's price-to-book ratio (P/B) at this level of discount from book value would be 0.7583. In contrast, if AXCI were earning positive residual income, then its shares should sell at a premium to book value. In summary, higher residual income is expected to be associated with higher market prices (and higher P/Bs), all else being equal.

Residual income (RI) models have been used to value both individual stocks and stock indexes such as the Dow Jones Industrial Average (see Fleck, Craig, Bodenstab, Harris, and Huh 2001; and Lee, Myers, and Swaminathan 1999). Recall that **impairment** in an accounting context means downward adjustment, and **goodwill** is an intangible asset that may appear on a company's balance sheet as a result of its purchase of another company.

Residual income and residual income models have been referred to by a variety of names. Residual income has sometimes been called **economic profit** because it estimates the company's profit after deducting the cost of all capital: debt and equity. In forecasting future residual income, the term **abnormal earnings** is also used. Under the assumption that in the long term the company is expected to earn its cost of capital (from all sources), any earnings in excess of the cost of capital can be termed abnormal earnings. The residual income model has also been called the **discounted abnormal earnings model** and the **Edwards–Bell–Ohlson model** after the names of researchers in the field. Our focus is on a general residual income model that analysts can apply using publicly available data and nonproprietary accounting adjustments. A number of commercial implementations of the approach, however, are also very well known. Before returning to the general residual income model we briefly discuss one such commercial implementation and the related concept of market value added.

Commercial Implementations

One example of several competing commercial implementations of the residual income concept is **economic value added** (EVA, an acronym trademarked by Stern Stewart & Co. and generally associated with a specific set of adjustments proposed by Stern Stewart & Co.). EVA aims to produce a value that is a good approximation of economic profit (see Stewart 1991 and Peterson and Peterson 1996). The previous section illustrated a calculation of residual income starting from net operating profit after taxes, and EVA takes the same broad approach. Specifically, economic value added is computed as

$$\text{EVA} = \text{NOPAT} - (\text{C\%} \times \text{TC}), \quad (1)$$

NOPAT: net operating profit after tax

C = WACC TC: Total capital

where NOPAT is the company's net operating profit after taxes, C% is the cost of capital, and TC is total capital. In this model, both NOPAT and TC are determined under generally accepted accounting principles and adjusted for a number of items. Some of the more common adjustments include the following:

- Research and development (R&D) expenses are capitalized and amortized rather than expensed (i.e., R&D expense, net of estimated amortization, is added back to earnings to compute NOPAT).

- In the case of strategic investments that are not expected to generate an immediate return, a charge for capital is suspended until a later date.

- Deferred taxes are eliminated such that only cash taxes are treated as an expense.

- Any inventory LIFO (last in, first out) reserve is added back to capital, and any increase in the LIFO reserve is added in when calculating NOPAT.

- Operating leases are treated as capital leases, and non-recurring items are adjusted.

Because of the adjustments made in calculating EVA, a different numerical result will be obtained, in general, than that resulting from the use of the simple computation presented in Example 1. In practice, general (nonbranded) residual income valuation also considers the effect of accounting methods on reported results. Analysts' adjustments to reported accounting results in estimating residual income, however, will generally reflect some differences from the set specified for EVA. A later section will explore accounting considerations in more detail.

Over time, a company must generate economic profit for its market value to increase. A concept related to economic profit (and EVA) is market value added (MVA):

$$\text{MVA} = \text{Market value of the company} - \text{Accounting book value of total capital} \tag{2}$$

A company that generates positive economic profit should have a market value in excess of the accounting book value of its capital.

Research on the ability of value-added concepts to explain equity value and stock returns has reached mixed conclusions. Peterson and Peterson (1996) found that value-added measures are slightly more highly correlated with stock returns than traditional measures, such as return on assets and return on equity. Bernstein and Pigler (1997) and Bernstein, Bayer, and Pigler (1998) found that value-added measures are no better at predicting stock performance than are such measures as earnings growth.

A variety of commercial models related to the residual income concept have been marketed by other major accounting and consulting firms. Interestingly, the application focus of these models is not, in general, equity valuation. Rather, these implementations of the residual income concept are marketed primarily for measuring internal corporate performance and determining executive compensation.

[handwritten margin note: Market value of company = Market value of equity + Market value of debt]

THE RESIDUAL INCOME MODEL

☐ | calculate the intrinsic value of a common stock using the residual income model and compare value recognition in residual income and other present value models

☐ | explain fundamental determinants of residual income

☐ | explain the relation between residual income valuation and the justified price-to-book ratio based on forecasted fundamentals

In the previous section, we discussed the concept of residual income and briefly introduced the relationship of residual income to equity value. In the long term, companies that earn more than the cost of capital should sell for more than book value, and companies that earn less than the cost of capital should sell for less than book value. The **residual income model** of valuation analyzes the intrinsic value of equity as the sum of two components:

- the current book value of equity, and
- the present value of expected future residual income.

Note that when the change is made from valuing total shareholders' equity to directly valuing an individual common share, earnings per share rather than net income is used. According to the residual income model, the intrinsic value of common stock can be expressed as follows:

$$V_0 = B_0 + \sum_{t=1}^{\infty} \frac{RI_t}{(1+r)^t} = B_0 + \sum_{t=1}^{\infty} \frac{E_t - rB_{t-1}}{(1+r)^t} \qquad (3)$$

note the time subscripts here

where

V_0 = value of a share of stock today ($t = 0$)

B_0 = current per-share book value of equity

B_t = expected per-share book value of equity at any time t

r = required rate of return on equity investment (cost of equity)

E_t = expected EPS for period t

RI_t = expected per-share residual income, equal to $E_t - rB_{t-1}$

— If intrinsic value is
< BVPS → future residual earnings will be negative
> BVPS → future residual earnings will be positive

The per-share residual income in period t, RI_t, is the EPS for the period, E_t, minus the per-share equity charge for the period, which is the required rate of return on equity multiplied by the book value per share at the beginning of the period, or rB_{t-1}. Whenever earnings per share exceed the per-share cost of equity, per-share residual income is positive; and whenever earnings are less, per-share residual income is negative. Example 2 illustrates the calculation of per-share residual income.

EXAMPLE 2

Per-Share Residual Income Forecasts

1. David Smith is evaluating the expected residual income as of the end of January 2019 of the Canadian Railway Company (CNR). Using an adjusted beta of 1.02 relative to the TSX 300 Index, a 10-year government bond yield of

1.75%, and an estimated equity risk premium of 7.5%, Smith uses the capital asset pricing model (CAPM) to estimate CNR's required rate of return, r, at 9.40% [1.75% + (1.02 × 7.5%)]. Smith obtains the following (in Canadian dollars, CAD) as of the close on 1 February 2019:

Current market price	109.12
Book value per share as of 31 December 2018	24.32
Consensus annual earnings estimates	
FY 2019 (ending December)	6.23
FY 2020	6.96
Annualized dividend per share forecast	
FY 2019	2.15
FY 2020	2.32 2.31

What is the forecast residual income for fiscal years ended December 2019 and December 2020?

Solution:

Forecasted residual income and calculations are shown in Exhibit 1.

Exhibit 1: Canadian National Railway Company (all data in CAD)

Year	2019	2020
Forecasting book value per share		
Beginning book value (B_{t-1})	24.32	28.40
Earnings per share forecast (E_t)	6.23	6.96
Less dividend forecast (D_t)	2.15	2.31
Add Change in retained earnings ($E_t - D_t$)	4.08	4.65
Forecast ending book value per share ($B_{t-1} + E_t - D_t$)	28.40	33.05
Calculating the equity charge		
Beginning book value per share	24.32	28.40
Multiply cost of equity	× 0.094	× 0.094
Per-share equity charge ($r \times B_{t-1}$)	2.29	2.67
Estimating per share residual income		
EPS forecast	6.23	6.96
Less equity charge	2.29	2.67
Per-share residual income	3.94	4.29

The use of Equation 3, the expression for the estimated intrinsic value of common stock, is illustrated in Example 3.

EXAMPLE 3

Using the Residual Income Model (1)

Bugg Properties' expected EPS is $2.00, $2.50, and $4.00 for the next three years. Analysts expect that Bugg will pay dividends of $1.00, $1.25, and $12.25 for the three years. The last dividend is anticipated to be a liquidating dividend; analysts expect Bugg will cease operations after Year 3. Bugg's current book value is $6.00 per share, and its required rate of return on equity is 10%.

1. Calculate per-share book value and residual income for the next three years.

Solution:

The book value and residual income for the next three years are shown in Exhibit 2.

Exhibit 2			
Year	1	2	3
Beginning book value per share (B_{t-1})	$6.00	$7.00	$8.25
Net income per share (EPS)	2.00	2.50	4.00
Less dividends per share (D)	1.00	1.25	12.25
Change in retained earnings ($EPS - D$)	1.00	1.25	−8.25
Ending book value per share ($B_{t-1} + EPS - D$)	$7.00	$8.25	$0.00
Net income per share (EPS)	2.00	2.50	4.000
Less per-share equity charge (rB_{t-1})	0.60	0.70	0.825
Residual income (EPS − Equity charge)	$1.40	$1.80	$3.175

(handwritten annotations: .1 × 6.00 = 0.60; .1 × 7 0.70; .1 × 8.25 → 0.825)

2. Estimate the stock's value using the residual income model given in Equation 3

$$V_0 = B_0 + \sum_{t=1}^{\infty} \frac{E_t - r B_{t-1}}{(1+r)^t}$$

Solution:

The value using the residual income model is

$$V_0 = 6.00 + \frac{1.40}{(1.10)} + \frac{1.80}{(1.10)^2} + \frac{3.175}{(1.10)^3}$$
$$= 6.00 + 1.2727 + 1.4876 + 2.3854$$
$$= \$11.15$$

3. Confirm your valuation estimate in Part 2 using the discounted dividend approach (i.e., estimating the value of a share as the present value of expected future dividends).

Solution:

The value using a discounted dividend approach is

$$V_0 = \frac{1.00}{(1.10)} + \frac{1.25}{(1.10)^2} + \frac{12.25}{(1.10)^3}$$
$$= 0.9091 + 1.0331 + 9.2036$$
$$= \$11.15$$

Example 3 illustrates two important points about residual income models. First, the RI model is fundamentally similar to other valuation models, such as the dividend discount model (DDM), and given consistent assumptions will yield equivalent results. Second, recognition of value typically occurs earlier in RI models than in the DDM. In Example 3, the RI model attributes \$6.00 of the \$11.15 total value to the beginning of the *first* period. In contrast, the DDM attributes \$9.2036 of the \$11.15 total value to the present value of the *final* period. The rest of this section develops the most familiar general expression for the RI model and illustrates the model's application.

The General Residual Income Model

The residual income model has a clear relationship to other valuation models, such as the DDM. In fact, the residual income model given in Equation 3 can be derived from the DDM. The general expression for the DDM is

$$V_0 = \frac{D_1}{(1+r)^1} + \frac{D_2}{(1+r)^2} + \frac{D_3}{(1+r)^3} + \ldots$$

The **clean surplus relation** states the relationship among earnings, dividends, and book value as follows:

$$B_t = B_{t-1} + E_t - D_t$$

In other words, the ending book value of equity equals the beginning book value plus earnings minus dividends, apart from ownership transactions. The condition that income (earnings) reflects all changes in the book value of equity other than ownership transactions is known as clean surplus accounting. By rearranging the clean surplus relation, the dividend for each period can be viewed as the net income minus the earnings retained for the period, or net income minus the increase in book value:

$$D_t = E_t - (B_t - B_{t-1}) = E_t + B_{t-1} - B_t$$

Substituting $E_t + B_{t-1} - B_t$ for D_t in the expression for V_0 results in:

$$V_0 = \frac{E_1 + B_0 - B_1}{(1+r)^1} + \frac{E_2 + B_1 - B_2}{(1+r)^2} + \frac{E_3 + B_2 - B_3}{(1+r)^3} + \ldots$$

This equation can be rewritten as follows:

$$V_0 = B_0 + \frac{E_1 - rB_0}{(1+r)^1} + \frac{E_2 - rB_1}{(1+r)^2} + \frac{E_3 - rB_2}{(1+r)^3} + \ldots$$

Expressed with summation notation, the following equation restates the residual income model given in Equation 3:

$$V_0 = B_0 + \sum_{t=1}^{\infty} \frac{RI_t}{(1+r)^t} = B_0 + \sum_{t=1}^{\infty} \frac{E_t - rB_{t-1}}{(1+r)^t}$$

According to the expression, the value of a stock equals its book value per share plus the present value of expected future per-share residual income. Note that when the present value of expected future per-share residual income is positive (negative), intrinsic value, V_0, is greater (smaller) than book value per share, B_0.

The residual income model used in practice today has its origins largely in the academic work of Ohlson (1995) and Feltham and Ohlson (1995) along with the earlier work of Edwards and Bell (1961), although in the United States this method has been used to value small businesses in tax cases since the 1920s. In tax valuation, the approach is known as the **excess earnings method** (Hitchner 2017 and US IRS Revenue Ruling 68-609). The general expression for the residual income model based on this work (Hirst and Hopkins 2000) can also be stated as:

$$V_0 = B_0 + \sum_{t=1}^{\infty} \frac{(\text{ROE}_t - r)\, B_{t-1}}{(1 + r)^t} \tag{4}$$

Equation 4 is equivalent to the expressions for V_0 given earlier because in any year, t, $\text{RI}_t = (\text{ROE}_t - r)B_{t-1}$. Other than the required rate of return on common stock, the inputs to the residual income model come from accounting data. Note that return on equity (ROE) in this context uses beginning book value of equity in the denominator, whereas in financial statement analysis ROE is frequently calculated using the average book value of equity in the denominator. Example 4 illustrates the estimation of value using Equation 4.

EXAMPLE 4

Using the Residual Income Model (2)

1. To recap the data from Example 3, Bugg Properties has expected earnings per share of $2.00, $2.50, and $4.00 and expected dividends per share of $1.00, $1.25, and $12.25 for the next three years. Analysts expect that the last dividend will be a liquidating dividend and that Bugg will cease operating after Year 3. Bugg's current book value per share is $6.00, and its estimated required rate of return on equity is 10%.

   Using this data, estimate the value of Bugg Properties' stock using a residual income model of the form:

   $$V_0 = B_0 + \sum_{t=1}^{\infty} \frac{(\text{ROE}_t - r)\, B_{t-1}}{(1 + r)^t}$$

Solution:

To value the stock, forecast residual income. Exhibit 3 illustrates the calculation of residual income. (Note that Exhibit 3 arrives at the same estimates of residual income as Exhibit 2 in Example 3.)

Exhibit 3			
Year	**1**	**2**	**3**
Earnings per share	$2.00	$2.50	$4.00
Divided by beginning book value per share	÷ 6.00	÷ 7.00	÷ 8.25
ROE	0.3333	0.3571	0.4848
Less required rate of return on equity	− 0.1000	− 0.1000	− 0.1000
Abnormal rate of return (ROE − r)	0.2333	0.2571	0.3848
Multiply by beginning book value per share	× 6.00	× 7.00	× 8.25
Residual income (ROE − r) × Beginning BV	$1.400	$1.800	$3.175

Estimate the stock value as follows:

$$V_0 = 6.00 + \frac{1.40}{(1.10)} + \frac{1.80}{(1.10)^2} + \frac{3.175}{(1.10)^3}$$
$$= 6.00 + 1.2727 + 1.4876 + 2.3854$$
$$= \$11.15$$

Note that the value is identical to the estimate obtained using Equation 3, as illustrated in Example 3, because the assumptions are the same and Equation 3 and Equation 4 are equivalent expressions:

$$V_0 = \frac{B_0 + \sum_{t=1}^{\infty} \frac{E_t - rB_{t-1}}{(1+r)^t}}{\text{Equation 3}} = \frac{B_0 + \sum_{t=1}^{\infty} \frac{(ROE_t - r)B_{t-1}}{(1+r)^t}}{\text{Equation 4}}$$

Example 4 showed that residual income value can be estimated using current book value, forecasts of earnings, forecasts of book value, and an estimate of the required rate of return on equity. The forecasts of earnings and book value translate into ROE forecasts.

EXAMPLE 5

Valuing a Company Using the General Residual Income Model

1. Robert Sumargo, an equity analyst, is considering the valuation of Alphabet Inc. Class C shares (GOOG), in mid 2019 when a recent closing price is $1,037.39. (Alphabet Inc. is the parent company of Google.) Sumargo notes that in general, Alphabet had a fairly high ROE during the past 10 years and that consensus analyst forecasts for EPS for the next two fiscal years reflect a fairly high expected ROE percentage. He expects that a high ROE may not be sustainable in the future. Sumargo usually takes a present value approach to valuation. As of the date of the valuation, Alphabet does not pay dividends; although a discounted dividend valuation is possible, Sumargo does not feel confident about predicting the date of a dividend initiation. He decides to apply the residual income model to value Alphabet and uses the following data and assumptions:

   - According to the CAPM, Alphabet has a required rate of return of approximately 8.2%.
   - Alphabet's book value per share on 31 December 2018 was $255.40.
   - ROE is expected to be 20.2% for 2019. Because of competitive pressures, Sumargo expects Google's ROE to decline in the following years and incorporates an assumed decline of 0.5% each year until it reaches the CAPM required rate of return. In 2043, the ROE will be 8.2%, and residual income that year and after will be zero.
   - Google does not currently pay a dividend. Sumargo does not expect the company to pay a dividend in the foreseeable future, so all earnings will be reinvested. In addition, Sumargo expects that share repurchases will approximately offset new share issuances.

   Compute the value of Google using the residual income model (Equation 4).

Solution:

Book value per share is initially $255.40. Based on a ROE forecast of 20.2% in the first year, the forecast EPS would be $51.59. Because no dividends are paid and the clean surplus relation is assumed to hold, book value at the end of the period is forecast to be $306.99 ($255.40 + $51.59). For 2019, residual income is measured as projected EPS of $51.59 minus an equity charge of $20.94, or $30.65. This amount is equivalent to the beginning book value per share of $255.40 multiplied by the difference between ROE of 20.2% and r of 8.2% [i.e., $255.40 × (0.20.2 − 0.082) = $30.65]. The present value of $30.65 at 8.2% for one year is $28.33. This process is continued year by year as presented in Exhibit 4. The value of Alphabet using this residual income model would be the present value of each year's residual income plus the current book value per share. Because residual income is zero starting in 2043, no forecast is required beyond that period. The estimated value under this model is $972.25, as shown in Exhibit 4.

Handwritten margin notes:

EPS of $51.59 = ROE × BVPS
= .202 × $255.40

Equity charge of $20.94 =
Cost of equity × $BVPS_{t-1}$
.082 × 255.40

Exhibit 4: Valuation of Alphabet Using the Residual Income Model

Year	Projected Income EPS	Projected Dividend per Share	Book Value per Share	Forecast ROE (Based on Beginning Book Value)	Cost of Equity	Equity Charge	Residual Income (RI)	PV of BV and RI
	[Plus]	[Minus]	255.40					255.40
2019	$51.59	$0.00	$306.99	20.20%	8.20%	$20.94	$30.65	28.33
2020	60.48	0.00	367.47	19.70%	8.20%	25.17	35.30	30.16
2021	70.55	0.00	438.02	19.20%	8.20%	30.13	40.42	31.91
2022	81.91	0.00	519.93	18.70%	8.20%	35.92	45.99	33.56
2023	94.63	0.00	614.56	18.20%	8.20%	42.63	51.99	35.06
2024	108.78	0.00	723.34	17.70%	8.20%	50.39	58.38	36.39
2025	124.41	0.00	847.75	17.20%	8.20%	59.31	65.10	37.50
2026	141.57	0.00	989.32	16.70%	8.20%	69.52	72.06	38.36
2027	160.27	0.00	1,149.60	16.20%	8.20%	81.12	79.15	38.94
2028	180.49	0.00	1,330.08	15.70%	8.20%	94.27	86.22	39.20
2029	202.17	0.00	1,532.25	15.20%	8.20%	109.07	93.11	39.13
2030	225.24	0.00	1,757.50	14.70%	8.20%	125.64	99.60	38.68
2031	249.56	0.00	2,007.06	14.20%	8.20%	144.11	105.45	37.85
2032	274.97	0.00	2,282.03	13.70%	8.20%	164.58	110.39	36.62
2033	301.23	0.00	2,583.25	13.20%	8.20%	187.13	114.10	34.99
2034	328.07	0.00	2,911.33	12.70%	8.20%	211.83	116.25	32.94
2035	355.18	0.00	3,266.51	12.20%	8.20%	238.73	116.45	30.50
2036	382.18	0.00	3,648.69	11.70%	8.20%	267.85	114.33	27.67
2037	408.65	0.00	4,057.35	11.20%	8.20%	299.19	109.46	24.49
2038	434.14	0.00	4,491.48	10.70%	8.20%	332.70	101.43	20.97
2039	458.13	0.00	4,949.61	10.20%	8.20%	368.30	89.83	17.17
2040	480.11	0.00	5,429.73	9.70%	8.20%	405.87	74.24	13.11
2041	499.53	0.00	5,929.26	9.20%	8.20%	445.24	54.30	8.86
2042	515.85	0.00	6,445.11	8.70%	8.20%	486.20	29.65	4.47
Total								972.25

Handwritten annotations in Equity Charge column: 255.40 × .082 (for 2019 row, $20.94); 306.99 × .082 (for 2020 row, 25.17)

> *Note:* PV is present value and BV is book value. This table was created in Excel, so numbers may differ from what will be obtained using a calculator, because of rounding.

Example 5 refers to the assumption of clean surplus accounting. The residual income model, as stated earlier, assumes clean surplus accounting. The clean surplus accounting assumption is illustrated in Exhibit 4, for example, in which ending book value per share is computed as beginning book value plus net income minus dividends. Under International Financial Reporting Standards (IFRS) and US generally accepted accounting principles (US GAAP), several items of income and expense occurring during a period, such as changes in the market value of certain securities, bypass the income statement and affect a company's book value of equity directly. Items that bypass the income statement (dirty surplus items) are referred to as **other comprehensive income** (the relationship is Comprehensive income = Net income + Other comprehensive income). Strictly speaking, residual income models involve all items of income and expense (income under clean surplus accounting). If an analyst can reliably estimate material differences from clean surplus accounting expected in the future, an adjustment to net income may be appropriate. We explore violations of the clean surplus accounting assumption in more detail later.

Fundamental Determinants of Residual Income

In general, the residual income model makes no assumptions about future earnings and dividend growth. If constant earnings and dividend growth are assumed, a version of the residual income model that usefully illustrates the fundamental drivers of residual income can be derived. The following expression is used for justified P/B based on forecasted fundamentals, assuming the Gordon (constant growth) DDM and the sustainable growth rate equation, $g = b \times$ ROE:

Justified P/B $\longrightarrow$

$$\frac{P_0}{B_0} = \frac{\text{ROE} - g}{r - g},$$

which is mathematically equivalent to

$$\frac{P_0}{B_0} = 1 + \frac{\text{ROE} - r}{r - g}.$$

The justified price is the stock's intrinsic value ($P_0 = V_0$). Therefore, using the previous equation and remembering that residual income is earnings less the cost of equity, or (ROE $\times B_0$) − ($r \times B_0$), a stock's intrinsic value under the residual income model, assuming constant growth, can be expressed as:

$$V_0 = B_0 + \frac{\text{ROE} - r}{r - g} B_0 \tag{5}$$

Under this model, the estimated value of a share is the book value per share (B_0) plus the present value [(ROE − r)B_0/($r − g$)] of the expected stream of residual income. In the case of a company for which ROE exactly equals the cost of equity, the intrinsic value is equal to the book value per share. Equation 5 is considered a single-stage (or constant-growth) residual income model.

In an idealized world, where the book value of equity represents the fair value of net assets and clean surplus accounting prevails, the term B_0 reflects the value of assets owned by the company less its liabilities. The second term, (ROE − r)B_0/($r − g$), represents additional value expected because of the company's ability to generate returns in excess of its cost of equity; the second term is the present value of the company's expected economic profits. However, both IFRS and US GAAP allow companies to exclude some liabilities from their balance sheets, and neither set of rules reflects the fair value of many corporate assets. Internationally, however, a move toward fair value accounting is occurring, particularly for financial assets. Further, controversies, such as the failure of Enron Corporation in the United States, have highlighted the importance of identifying off-balance-sheet financing techniques.

The residual income model is most closely related to the P/B. A stock's justified P/B is directly related to expected future residual income. Another closely related concept is **Tobin's q**, the ratio of the market value of debt and equity to the replacement cost of total assets:

$$\text{Tobin's } q = \frac{\text{Market value of debt and equity}}{\text{Replacement cost of total assets}}$$

Although similar to P/B, Tobin's q also has some obvious differences. The numerator includes the market value of total capital (debt as well as equity). The denominator uses total assets rather than equity. Further, assets are valued at replacement cost rather than at historical accounting cost; replacement costs take into account the effects of inflation. All else equal, Tobin's q is expected to be higher the greater the productivity of a company's assets (note that Tobin theorized that q would average to 1 for all companies because the economic rents or profits earned by assets would average to zero). One difficulty in computing Tobin's q is the lack of information on the replacement cost of assets. If available, market values of assets or replacement costs can be more useful in a valuation than historical costs.

SINGLE-STAGE AND MULTISTAGE RESIDUAL INCOME VALUATION

3

☐ | calculate and interpret the intrinsic value of a common stock using single-stage (constant-growth) and multistage residual income models

☐ | calculate the implied growth rate in residual income, given the market price-to-book ratio and an estimate of the required rate of return on equity

☐ | explain continuing residual income and justify an estimate of continuing residual income at the forecast horizon, given company and industry prospects

☐ | compare residual income models to dividend discount and free cash flow models

☐ | explain strengths and weaknesses of residual income models and justify the selection of a residual income model to value a company's common stock

The single-stage (constant-growth) residual income model assumes that a company has a constant return on equity and constant earnings growth rate through time. This model was given in Equation 5:

$$V_0 = B_0 + \frac{\text{ROE} - r}{r - g} B_0$$

EXAMPLE 6

Single-Stage Residual Income Model (1)

1. Joseph Yoh is evaluating a purchase of Koninklijke Philips N.V. Current book value per share is €13.22, and the current price per share is €35.40. Yoh expects the long-term ROE to be 12% and long-term growth to be 6.75%. Assuming a cost of equity of 8.5%, what is the intrinsic value of Canon stock calculated using a single-stage residual income model?

Solution:

Using Equation 5:

$$V_0 = 13.22 + \frac{0.12 - 0.085}{0.085 - 0.675} \times 13.22$$
$$V_0 = €39.66$$

Similar to the Gordon growth DDM, the single-stage RI model can be used to assess the market expectations of residual income growth—that is, an implied growth rate—by inputting the current price into the model and solving for g.

EXAMPLE 7

Single-Stage Residual Income Model (2)

Joseph Yoh is curious about the market-perceived growth rate, given that he is comfortable with his other inputs. By using the current price per share of €35.40 for Philips, Yoh solves the following equation for g:

$$35.40 = 13.22 + \frac{0.12 - 0.085}{0.085 - g} \times 13.22$$

He finds an implied growth rate of 6.41%.

In Example 6 and Example 7, the company was valued at almost 2.7× its book value because its ROE exceeded its cost of equity. If ROE was equal to the cost of equity, the company would be valued at book value. If ROE was lower than the cost of equity, the company would have negative residual income and be valued at less than book value. (When a company has no prospect of being able to cover its cost of capital, a liquidation of the company and redeployment of assets may be appropriate.) In many applications, a drawback to the single-stage model is that it assumes the excess ROE above the cost of equity will persist indefinitely. More likely, a company's ROE will revert to a mean value of ROE over time, and at some point, the company's residual income will be zero. If a company or industry has an abnormally high ROE, other companies will enter the marketplace, thus increasing competition and lowering returns for all companies. Similarly, if an industry has a low ROE, companies will exit the industry (through bankruptcy or otherwise) and ROE will tend to rise over time. As with the single-stage DDM, the single-stage residual income model also assumes a constant growth rate through time. In light of these considerations, the residual income model has been adapted in practice to handle declining residual income. For example, Lee and Swaminathan (1999) and Lee, Myers, and Swaminathan (1999) used a residual income model to value the Dow 30 by assuming that ROE fades (reverts) to the industry mean over time. Lee and Swaminathan found that the residual income model had more ability than traditional price multiples to predict future returns.

Fortunately, other models are available that enable analysts to relax the assumption of indefinite persistence of excess returns. The following section describes a multistage residual income model.

Multistage Residual Income Valuation

As with other valuation approaches, such as DDM and free cash flow, a multistage residual income approach can be used to forecast residual income for a certain time horizon and then estimate a terminal value based on continuing residual income at the end of that time horizon. **Continuing residual income** is residual income after the forecast horizon. As with other valuation models, the forecast horizon for the initial stage should be based on the ability to explicitly forecast inputs in the model. Because ROE has been found to revert to mean levels over time and may decline to the cost of equity in a competitive environment, residual income approaches often model ROE fading toward the cost of equity. As ROE approaches the cost of equity, residual income approaches zero. An ROE equal to the cost of equity would result in residual income of zero.

In residual income valuation, the current book value often captures a large portion of total value and the terminal value may not be a large component of total value because book value is larger than the periodic residual income and because ROE may fade over time toward the cost of equity. This contrasts with other multistage approaches (DDM and DCF), in which the present value of the terminal value is frequently a significant portion of total value.

Analysts make a variety of assumptions concerning continuing residual income. Frequently, one of the following assumptions is made:

- residual income continues indefinitely at a positive level;
- residual income is zero from the terminal year forward;
- residual income declines to zero as ROE reverts to the cost of equity through time; or
- residual income reflects the reversion of ROE to some mean level.

The following examples illustrate several of these assumptions.

One finite-horizon model of residual income valuation assumes that at the end of time horizon T, a certain premium over book value $(P_T - B_T)$ exists for the company, in which case, current value equals the following (Bauman, 1999):

$$V_0 = B_0 + \sum_{t=1}^{T} \left[\frac{(E_t - r B_{t-1})}{(1 + r)^t} \right] + \frac{P_T - B_T}{(1 + r)^T} \tag{6}$$

Alternatively,

$$V_0 = B_0 + \sum_{t=1}^{T} \left[\frac{(ROE_t - r) B_{t-1}}{(1 + r)^t} \right] + \frac{P_T - B_T}{(1 + r)^T} \tag{7}$$

The last component in both specifications represents the premium over book value at the end of the forecast horizon. The longer the forecast period, the greater the chance that the company's residual income will converge to zero. For long forecast periods, this last term may be treated as zero. For shorter forecast periods, a forecast of the premium should be calculated.

EXAMPLE 8

Multistage Residual Income Model (1)

Diana Rosato, CFA, is considering an investment in Zenlandia Chemical Company, a fictitious manufacturer of specialty chemicals. Rosato obtained the following facts and estimates as of August 2020:

- Current price equals ZL$95.6.
- Cost of equity equals 12%.
- Zenlandia Chemical's ROE has ranged from 18% to 22.9% during the period 2015–2019. The only time ROE was below 20% during that period was in 2016.
- In 2019, the company paid a cash dividend of ZL$2.9995.
- Book value per share was ZL$28.8517 at the end of 2019.
- Rosato's forecasts of EPS are ZL$7.162 for 2020 and ZL$8.356 for 2021. She expects dividends of ZL$2.9995 for 2020 and ZL$3.2995 for 2021.
- Rosato expects Zenlandia Chemical's ROE to be 25% from 2022 through 2026 and then decline to 20% through 2039.
- For the period after 2021, Rosato assumes an earnings retention ratio of 60%.
- Rosato assumes that after 2039, ROE will be 12% and residual income will be zero; therefore, the terminal value would be zero. Rosato's residual income model is shown in Exhibit 5.

Exhibit 5: Zenlandia Chemical

Year	Book Value (ZL$)	Projected Income (ZL$)	Dividend per Share (ZL$)	Forecasted ROE (Beg. Equity, %)	COE (%)	COE (ZL$)	Residual Income (ZL$)	Present Value of Residual Income (ZL$)
2019	28.8517							28.85
2020	33.0142	7.1620	2.9995	24.82	12.00	3.4622	3.6998	3.30
2021	38.0707	8.3560	3.2995	25.31	12.00	3.9617	4.3943	3.50
2022	43.7813	9.5177	3.8071	25.00	12.00	4.5685	4.9492	3.52
2023	50.3485	10.9453	4.3781	25.00	12.00	5.2538	5.6916	3.62
2024	57.9008	12.5871	5.0349	25.00	12.00	6.0418	6.5453	3.71
2025	66.5859	14.4752	5.7901	25.00	12.00	6.9481	7.5271	3.81
2026	76.5738	16.6465	6.6586	25.00	12.00	7.9903	8.6562	3.92
2027	85.7626	15.3148	6.1259	20.00	12.00	9.1889	6.1259	2.47
2028	96.0541	17.1525	6.8610	20.00	12.00	10.2915	6.8610	2.47
2029	107.5806	19.2108	7.6843	20.00	12.00	11.5265	7.6843	2.47
2030	120.4903	21.5161	8.6065	20.00	12.00	12.9097	8.6065	2.47
2031	134.9492	24.0981	9.6392	20.00	12.00	14.4588	9.6392	2.47
2032	151.1431	26.9898	10.7959	20.00	12.00	16.1939	10.7959	2.47
2033	169.2802	30.2286	12.0914	20.00	12.00	18.1372	12.0914	2.47
2034	189.5938	33.8560	13.5424	20.00	12.00	20.3136	13.5424	2.47
2035	212.3451	37.9188	15.1675	20.00	12.00	22.7513	15.1675	2.47
2036	237.8265	42.4690	16.9876	20.00	12.00	25.4814	16.9876	2.47

Handwritten annotations: Row 2019 — "28.8517 + 7.1620 − 2.9995"; "7.1620 / 28.8517"; "28.8517 × .12"; "7.1620 − 3.4622". Row 2020 — arrow near 33.0142.

Year	Book Value (ZL$)	Projected Income (ZL$)	Dividend per Share (ZL$)	Forecasted ROE (Beg. Equity, %)	COE (%)	COE (ZL$)	Residual Income (ZL$)	Present Value of Residual Income (ZL$)
2037	266.3657	47.5653	19.0261	20.00	12.00	28.5392	19.0261	2.47
2038	298.3296	53.2731	21.3093	20.00	12.00	31.9639	21.3093	2.47
2039	334.1291	59.6659	23.8664	20.00	12.00	35.7996	23.8664	2.47
							Present value ZL$	86.41

Terminal Premium = 0.00

The market price of ZL$95.6 exceeds the estimated value of ZL$86.41. The market price reflects higher forecasts of residual income during the period to 2039, a higher terminal premium than Rosato forecasts, and/or a lower cost of equity. If Rosato is confident in her forecasts she may conclude that the company is overvalued in the current marketplace.

Lee and Swaminathan (1999) and Lee, Myers, and Swaminathan (1999) have presented a residual income model based on explicit forecasts of residual income for three years. Thereafter, ROE is forecast to fade to the industry mean value of ROE. The terminal value at the end of the forecast horizon (T) is estimated as the terminal-year residual income discounted in perpetuity. Lee and Swaminathan stated that this assumes any growth in earnings after T is value neutral. Exhibit 6 presents sector ROE data from CSIMarket. In forecasting a fading ROE, the analyst should also consider any trends in industry ROE.

Exhibit 6: US Sector ROEs

Sectors	ROE (%)
Basic Materials	11.14
Consumer Goods	19.96
Consumer Non-cyclicals	26.59
Energy	8.81
Financial	12.76
Healthcare	19.95
Industrial Goods	23.16
Retail	23.37
Technology	28.97
Transportation	21.49
Utilities	8.18

Source: Based on data from CSIMarket on 5 August 2019.

EXAMPLE 9

Multistage Residual Income Model (2)

Rosato's supervisor questions her assumption that Zenlandia Chemical will have no premium at the end of her forecast period. Rosato assesses the effect of a terminal value based on a perpetuity of Year 2039 residual income. She computes the following terminal value:

TV = ZL\$23.8664/0.12 = ZL\$198.8867

The present value of this terminal value is as follows:

PV = ZL\$198.8867/$(1.12)^{20}$ = ZL\$20.6179

Adding ZL\$20.6179 to the previous value of ZL\$86.41 (for which the terminal value was zero) yields a total value of ZL\$107.03. Because the current market price of ZL\$95.6 is less than ZL\$107.03, market participants expect a continuing residual income that is lower than her new assumptions and/or are forecasting a lower interim ROE. If Rosato agrees with her supervisor and is confident in her new forecasts, she may now conclude that the company is undervalued.

Another multistage model assumes that ROE fades over time to the cost of equity. In this approach, ROE can be explicitly forecast each period until reaching the cost of equity. The forecast would then end and the terminal value would be zero. Dechow, Hutton, and Sloan (1999) presented an analysis of a residual income model in which residual income fades over time:

$$V_0 = B_0 + \sum_{t=1}^{T-1} \frac{(E_t - rB_{t-1})}{(1+r)^t} + \frac{E_T - rB_{T-1}}{(1+r-\omega)(1+r)^{T-1}} \tag{8}$$

This model adds a persistence factor, ω, which is between zero and one. A persistence factor of one implies that residual income will not fade at all; rather it will continue at the same level indefinitely (i.e., in perpetuity). A persistence factor of zero implies that residual income will not continue after the initial forecast horizon. The higher the value of the persistence factor, the higher the stream of residual income in the final stage, and the higher the valuation, all else being equal. Dechow et al. found that in a large sample of company data from 1976 to 1995, the persistence factor equaled 0.62, which was interpreted by Bauman (1999) as equivalent to residual income decaying at an average rate of 38% a year. The persistence factor considers the long-run mean-reverting nature of ROE, assuming that in time ROE regresses toward r and that resulting residual income fades toward zero. Clearly, the persistence factor varies from company to company. For example, a company with a strong market leadership position would have a lower expected rate of decay (Bauman 1999). Dechow et al. provided insight into some characteristics, listed in Exhibit 7, that can indicate a lower or higher level of persistence.

Exhibit 7: Final-Stage Residual Income Persistence

Lower Residual Income Persistence	Higher Residual Income Persistence
Extreme accounting rates of return (ROE)	Low dividend payout
Extreme levels of special items (e.g., non-recurring items)	High historical persistence in the industry
Extreme levels of accounting accruals	

Example 10 illustrates the assumption that continuing residual income will decline to zero as ROE approaches the required rate of return on equity.

EXAMPLE 10

Multistage Residual Income Model (3)

Rosato extends her analysis to consider the possibility that ROE will slowly decay toward r in 2040 and beyond, rather than using a perpetuity of Year 2037 residual income. Rosato estimates a persistence parameter of 0.60. The present value of the terminal value is determined as

$$\frac{E_T - rB_{T-1}}{(1 + r - \omega)(1 + r)^{T-1}},$$

with T equal to 20 and 2037 residual income equal to 23.8664, in which the 1.12 growth factor reflects a 12% growth rate calculated as the retention ratio multiplied by ROE, or (0.60)(20%) = 0.12.

$$\frac{23.8664}{(1 + 0.12 - 0.60)(1.12)^{19}} = 5.33$$

Total value is ZL\$86.26, calculated by adding the present value of the terminal value, ZL\$5.33, to ZL\$83.93 (the sum of the PV of residual income in the first 19 years). Rosato concludes that if Zenlandia Chemical's residual income does not persist at a stable level past 2039 and deteriorates through time, the shares are modestly overvalued at a price of ZL\$95.6.

In the previous example, the company's terminal residual value was estimated based on the residual income in the final year of stage 1 and on future growth or decay functions. As shown in Equations 6 and 7, the terminal residual value of the firm is $P_T - B_T$, the terminal price minus the terminal book value. The terminal price could be based on any valuation model, such as a DDM, a price–earnings multiple, or a price–book multiple. Example 11 uses a two-stage residual income model in which the terminal price per share is based on a P/B.

EXAMPLE 11

Two-Stage Residual Income Model

Andreea Popescu is using the two-stage residual income model to value the shares of URS Holdings. For her analysis, she assumes the following:

- Beginning book value per share is €15.00.
- EPS will be 25% of beginning book value for the next six years.
- Cash dividends will be 30% of EPS each year.
- At the end of six years, market price per share will be 1.80× book value per share.
- Cost of equity = 7.95% *(handwritten)*

1. Calculate per-share book value and residual income for the next three years.

Solution:

Exhibit 8 shows the book values, net income, dividends, and residual income.

Exhibit 8: Residual Income for URS Holdings

Year	Beginning Book Value	Net Income	Dividends	Ending Book Value	Residual Income	Present Value of Residual Income
1	15.000	3.750	1.125	17.625	2.558	2.369
2	17.625	4.406	1.322	20.709	3.005	2.579
3	20.709	5.177	1.553	24.334	3.531	2.807
4	24.334	6.083	1.825	28.592	4.149	3.055
5	28.592	7.148	2.144	33.595	4.875	3.325
6	33.595	8.399	2.520	39.475	5.728	3.620
				Sum of PV of Residual Income		17.755

Each year, net income is 25% of beginning book value, dividends are 30% of net income, ending book value is beginning book value plus net income minus dividends, and residual income is net income minus 7.95% of beginning book value.

2. Estimate the stock's value using the residual income model given in Equation 6:

$$V_0 = B_0 + \sum_{t=1}^{T} \frac{(E_t - rB_{t-1})}{(1+r)^t} + \frac{P_T - B_T}{(1+r)^T}$$

Solution:

In Exhibit 8, the present values of residual income are found by discounting at the 7.95% cost of equity. Using the logic in Equation 6, the value per share is:

Current book value per share		15.000
Present value of 6 years' residual income	$(1.8 \times 39.475) - 39.475$	17.755
Terminal value $[P_T - B_T = (1.8 \times B_T) - B_T]$	↓ 31.580	
Present value of terminal value (at 7.95%)		18,856
Value per share		€52.711

3. Confirm your valuation estimate in Part 2 using the discounted dividend approach (i.e., estimating the value of a share as the present value of expected future dividends and terminal price).

Solution:

The value using a discounted dividend approach is

$$V_0 = \sum_{t=1}^{T} \frac{D_t}{(1+r)^t} + \frac{P_T}{(1+r)^T}$$

Exhibit 9: DDM Valuation of URS Holdings		
Year	**Dividends**	**PV of Dividends**
1	1.125	1.042
2	1.322	1.134
3	1.553	1.235
4	1.825	1.344
5	2.144	1.463
6	2.520	1.592
Sum of PVs of six years' dividends		7.810
Terminal price = $1.8 \times B_T$	71.054	
PV of terminal price (@7.95%)		44.901
Value per share using DDM		€52.711

RELATIONSHIP TO OTHER APPROACHES

4

☐ compare residual income models to dividend discount and free cash flow models

☐ explain strengths and weaknesses of residual income models and justify the selection of a residual income model to value a company's common stock

Before addressing accounting issues in using the residual income model, we briefly summarize the relationship of the residual income model to other valuation models.

Valuation models based on discounting dividends or on discounting free cash flows are as theoretically sound as the residual income model. Unlike the residual income model, however, the discounted dividend and free cash flow models forecast future cash flows and find the value of stock by discounting them back to the present using the required return. Recall that the required return is the cost of equity for both the DDM and the free cash flows to equity (FCFE) model. For the free cash flow to the firm (FCFF) model, the required return is the overall weighted average cost of capital. The RI model approaches this process differently. It starts with a value based on the balance sheet, the book value of equity, and adjusts this value by adding the present values of expected future residual income. Thus, in theory, the recognition of value is different, but the total present value, whether using expected dividends, expected free cash flow, or book value plus expected residual income, should be consistent (Shrieves and Wachowicz, 2001).

Example 12 again illustrates the important point that the recognition of value in residual income models typically occurs earlier than in dividend discount models. In other words, residual income models tend to assign a relatively small portion of a security's total present value to the earnings that occur in later years. Note also that this example makes use of the fact that the present value of a perpetuity in the amount of X can be calculated as X/r.

EXAMPLE 12

Valuing a Perpetuity with the Residual Income Model

Assume the following data:

- A company will earn $1.00 per share forever.
- The company pays out all earnings as dividends.
- Book value per share is $6.00.
- The required rate of return on equity (or the percent cost of equity) is 10%.

1. Calculate the value of this stock using the DDM.

Solution:

Because the dividend, D, is a perpetuity, the present value of D can be calculated as D/r.

$$V_0 = D/r = \$1.00/0.10 = \$10.00 \text{ per share}$$

2. Calculate the level amount of per-share residual income that will be earned each year.

Solution:

Because each year all net income is paid out as dividends, book value per share will be constant at $6.00. Therefore, with a required rate of return on equity of 10%, for all future years, per-share residual income will be as follows:

$$RI_t = E_t - rB_{t-1} = \$1.00 - 0.10(\$6.00) = \$1.00 - \$0.60 = \$0.40$$

3. Calculate the value of the stock using a RI model.

Solution:

Using a residual income model, the estimated value equals the current book value per share plus the present value of future expected residual income (which in this example can be valued as a perpetuity):

V_0 = Book value + PV of expected future per-share residual income

= $6.00 + $0.40/0.10

= $6.00 + $4.00

= $10.00

4. Create a table summarizing the year-by-year valuation using the DDM and the RI model.

Solution:

Exhibit 10 summarizes the year-by-year valuation using the DDM and the RI models.

Exhibit 10: Value Recognition in the DDM and the RI Model				
Dividend Discount Model			**Residual Income Model**	
Year	D_t	PV of D_t	B_0 or RI_t	PV of B_0 or RI_t
0			$6.00	$6.000
1	$1.00	$0.909	0.40	0.364
2	1.00	0.826	0.40	0.331
3	1.00	0.751	0.40	0.301
4	1.00	0.683	0.40	0.273
5	1.00	0.621	0.40	0.248
6	1.00	0.564	0.40	0.226
7	1.00	0.513	0.40	0.205
8	1.00	0.467	0.40	0.187
⋮	⋮	⋮	⋮	⋮
Total		$10.00		$10.00

In the RI model, most of the stock's total value is attributed to the earlier periods. Specifically, the current book value of $6.00 represents 60% of the stock's total present value of $10.

In contrast, in the DDM, value is derived from the receipt of dividends, and typically, a smaller proportion of value is attributed to the earlier periods. Less than $1.00 of the total $10 derives from the first year's dividend, and collectively, the first five years' dividends ($0.909 + $0.826 + $0.751 + $0.683 + $0.621 = $3.79) contribute only about 38% of the total present value of $10.

As shown earlier and illustrated again in Example 11, the dividend discount and residual income models are in theory mutually consistent. Because of the real-world uncertainty in forecasting distant cash flows, however, the earlier recognition of value in a residual income approach relative to other present value approaches is a practical advantage. In the dividend discount and free cash flow models, a stock's value is often modeled as the sum of the present value of individually forecasted dividends or free cash flows up to some terminal point plus the present value of the expected terminal value of the stock. In practice, a large fraction of a stock's total present value, in either the discounted dividend or free cash flow models, is represented by the present value of the expected terminal value. Substantial uncertainty, however, often surrounds the terminal value. In contrast, residual income valuations typically are less sensitive to terminal value estimates. (In some residual income valuation contexts, the terminal value may actually be set equal to zero.) The derivation of value from the earlier portion of a forecast horizon is one reason residual income valuation can be a useful analytical tool.

Strengths and Weaknesses of the Residual Income Model

Now that the implementation of the residual income model has been illustrated with several examples, a summary of the strengths and weaknesses of the residual income approach follows:

The strengths of residual income models include the following:

- Terminal values do not make up a large portion of the total present value, relative to other models.

- RI models use readily available accounting data.
- The models can be readily applied to companies that do not pay dividends or to companies that do not have positive expected near-term free cash flows.
- The models can be used when cash flows are unpredictable.
- The models have an appealing focus on economic profitability.

The potential weaknesses of residual income models include the following:

- The models are based on accounting data that can be subject to manipulation by management.
- Accounting data used as inputs may require significant adjustments.
- The models require either that the clean surplus relation (explained later) holds or that the analyst makes appropriate adjustments when the clean surplus relation does not hold.
- The residual income model's use of accounting income assumes that the cost of debt capital is reflected appropriately by interest expense.

Broad Guidelines for Using a Residual Income Model

The above list of potential weaknesses helps explain the following section's focus on accounting considerations. In light of its strengths and weaknesses, the following are broad guidelines for using a residual income model in common stock valuation.

A residual income model is most appropriate when:

- a company does not pay dividends, or its dividends are not predictable;
- a company's expected free cash flows are negative within the analyst's comfortable forecast horizon; or
- great uncertainty exists in forecasting terminal values using an alternative present value approach.

Residual income models are least appropriate when:

- significant departures from clean surplus accounting exist, or
- significant determinants of residual income, such as book value and ROE, are not predictable.

Because various valuation models can be derived from the same underlying theoretical model, when fully consistent assumptions are used to forecast earnings, cash flow, dividends, book value, and residual income through a full set of pro forma (projected) financial statements, and the same required rate of return on equity is used as the discount rate, the same estimate of value should result when using each model. Practically speaking, however, it may not be possible to forecast each of these items with the same degree of certainty. For example, if a company has near-term negative free cash flow and forecasts for the terminal value are uncertain, a residual income model may be more appropriate. But a company with positive, predictable cash flow that does not pay a dividend would be well suited for a discounted free cash flow valuation (Penman and Sougiannis 1998; Penman 2001; Lundholm and O'Keefe 2001a; and Lundholm and O'Keefe 2001b).

Residual income models, just like the discounted dividend and free cash flow models, can also be used to establish justified market multiples, such as P/E or P/B. For example, the value can be determined by using a residual income model and dividing by earnings to arrive at a justified P/E.

A residual income model can also be used in conjunction with other models to assess the consistency of results. If a wide variation of estimated value is found and each model appears appropriate, the inconsistency may lie with the assumptions used in the models. The analyst would need to perform additional work to determine whether the assumptions are mutually consistent and which model is most appropriate for the subject company.

ACCOUNTING AND INTERNATIONAL CONSIDERATIONS

5

☐ | describe accounting issues in applying residual income models

To most accurately apply the residual income model in practice, the analyst may need to adjust book value of common equity for off-balance-sheet items and adjust reported net income to obtain **comprehensive income** (all changes in equity other than contributions by, and distributions to, owners). In this section, we will discuss issues relating to these tasks.

Bauman (1999) has noted that the strength of the residual income model is that the two components (book value and future earnings) of the model have a balancing effect on each other, provided that the clean surplus relationship is followed:

> All other things held constant, companies making aggressive (conservative) accounting choices will report higher (lower) book values and lower (higher) future earnings. In the model, the present value of differences in future income is exactly offset by the initial differences in book value. (Bauman 1999, page 31)

Unfortunately, this argument has several problems in practice because the clean surplus relationship does not prevail, and analysts often use past earnings to predict future earnings. IFRS and US GAAP permit a variety of items to bypass the income statement and be reported directly in stockholders' equity. Further, off-balance-sheet liabilities or nonoperating and non-recurring items of income may obscure a company's financial performance. The analyst must thus be aware of such items when evaluating the book value of equity and return on equity to be used as inputs into a residual income model.

With regard to the possibility that aggressive accounting choices will lead to lower reported future earnings, consider an example in which a company chooses to capitalize an expenditure in the current year rather than expense it. Doing so overstates current-year earnings as well as current book value. If an analyst uses current earnings (or ROE) naively in predicting future residual earnings, the RI model will overestimate the company's value. Take, for example, a company with $1,000,000 of book value and $200,000 of earnings before taxes, after expensing an expenditure of $50,000. Ignoring taxes, this company has a ROE of 20%. If the company capitalized the expenditure rather than expensing it immediately, it would have a ROE of 23.81% ($250,000/$1,050,000). Although at some time in the future this capitalized item will likely be amortized or written off, thus reducing realized future earnings, analysts' expectations often rely on historical data. If capitalization of expenditures persists over time for a company whose size is stable, ROE can decline because net income will normalize over the long term, but book value will be overstated. For a growing company, for which the expenditure in question is increasing, ROE can continue at high levels over time. In practice, because the RI model uses primarily accounting data as inputs, the model can be sensitive to accounting choices, and aggressive accounting methods (e.g., accelerating revenues or deferring expenses) can result in valuation errors. The analyst must, therefore, be particularly careful in analyzing a company's reported data for use in a residual income model.

Two principal drivers of residual earnings are ROE and book value. Analysts must understand how to use historical reported accounting data for these items to the extent they use historical data in forecasting future ROE and book value. Elsewhere we have explained the DuPont analysis of ROE, which can be used as a tool in forecasting, and discussed the calculation of book value. We extend these discussions below with specific application to residual income valuation, particularly in addressing the following accounting considerations:

- violations of the clean surplus relationship;
- balance sheet adjustments for fair value;
- intangible assets;
- non-recurring items;
- aggressive accounting practices; and
- international considerations.

In any valuation, close attention must be paid to the accounting practices of the company being valued. The following sections address the aforementioned issues with respect to how they specifically affect residual income valuation.

Violations of the Clean Surplus Relationship

One potential accounting issue in applying a residual income model is a violation of the clean surplus accounting assumption. Violations of this assumption occur when accounting standards permit charges directly to stockholders' equity, bypassing the income statement. An example is the case of changes in the market value of "available-for-sale" investments under US GAAP and "equity instruments measured at fair value through other comprehensive income" under IFRS. Under both IFRS (IFRS 9 Financial Instruments, paragraph 5.7.5) and US GAAP (ASC 320-10-35-1), these categories of investments are shown on the balance sheet at market value. Any unrealized change in their market value, however, is reflected in other comprehensive income rather than as income on the income statement.

As stated earlier, comprehensive income is defined as all changes in equity during a period other than contributions by, and distributions to, owners. Comprehensive income includes net income reported on the income statement and *other comprehensive income*, which is the result of other events and transactions that result in a change to equity but are not reported on the income statement. Items that commonly bypass the income statement include

- unrealized changes in the fair value of some financial instruments, as already discussed;
- foreign currency translation adjustments;
- certain pension adjustments;
- a portion of gains and losses on certain hedging instruments;
- changes in revaluation surplus related to property, plant, and equipment or intangible assets (applicable under IFRS but not under US GAAP); and
- for certain categories of liabilities, a change in fair value attributable to changes in the liability's credit risk (applicable under IFRS but not under US GAAP).

Under both international and US standards, such items as fair value changes for some financial instruments and foreign currency translation adjustments bypass the income statement. In addition, under IFRS, which unlike US GAAP permits revaluation of fixed assets (IAS 16, paragraph 39–42), some changes in the fair value of fixed assets also bypass the income statement and directly affect equity.

In all of these cases in which items bypass the income statement, the book value of equity is stated accurately because it includes "accumulated other comprehensive income," but net income is not stated properly from the perspective of residual income valuation. The analyst should be most concerned with the effect of these items on forecasts of net income and ROE, which has net income in the numerator, and hence residual income. Note that for best results, historical ROE should be calculated at the aggregate level (e.g., as net income divided by shareholders' equity, rather than as earnings per share divided by book value per share), because such actions as share issuance and share repurchases can distort ROE calculated on a per-share basis. Because some items (including those listed earlier) bypass the income statement, they are excluded from historical ROE data. As noted by Frankel and Lee (1999), bias will be introduced into the valuation only if the present expected value of the clean surplus violations does not net to zero. In other words, reductions in income from some periods may be offset by increases from other periods. The analyst must examine the equity section of the balance sheet and the related statements of shareholders' equity and comprehensive income carefully for items that have bypassed the income statement. The analyst can then assess whether amounts are likely to be offsetting and can assess the effect on future ROE.

EXAMPLE 13

Evaluating Clean Surplus Violations

1. Excerpts from two companies' statements of changes in stockholders' equity are shown in Exhibit 11 and Exhibit 12. The first statement, prepared under IFRS as of 31 December 2018, is for Nokia Corporation, a provider of network equipment, software, and services to telecom network companies. The second statement, prepared under US GAAP as of 31 December 2018, is for SAP AG, which is headquartered in Germany and is a worldwide provider of enterprise application software, including enterprise resource planning, customer relationship management, and supply chain management software.

Exhibit 12: SAP AG and Subsidiaries Statement of Changes in Shareholders' Equity (€ millions)

	Issued Capital	Share Premium	Retained Earnings	Other Components of Equity	Treasury Shares	Total	Non-controlling interests	Total Equity
						Equity Attributable to Owners of Parent		
1 January 2018	1,229	570	24,987	347	−1,591	25,542	31	25,573
Profit after tax			4,083			4,083	6	4,088
Other comprehensive income			11	887		898		898
Comprehensive income			**4,093**	**887**	**0**	**4,980**	**6**	**4,986**
Share-based payments		−40				−40		−40
Dividends			−1,671			−1,671	−13	−1,684

Exhibit 11: Nokia Corporation Statement of Changes in Shareholders' Equity (€ millions except number of shares)

	Number of Shares Outstanding	Share Capital	Share Issue Premium	Treasury Shares	Translation Differences	Fair Value and Other Reserves	Reserve for Invested Unrestricted Equity	(Accumulated Deficit)/ Retained Earnings	Attributable to Equity Holders of the Parent	Non-controlling Interests	Total Equity
As of 1 January 2018	5,579,517	246	447	−1,480	−932	842	15,616	1,345	16,084	80	16,164
Re-measurements and defined benefit pension plans, net of tax						293			293		293
Translation differences					402				402		402
Net investment hedges, net of tax					−61	3			−58		−58
Cash flow hedges, net of tax						−43			−43		−43
Financial assets at fair value through other comprehensive income, net of tax						−38			−38		−38
Other increase, net						6			5	1	6
Loss for the year									−340	5	−335
Total comprehensive income for the year					**341**	**221**			**221**	**6**	**227**
Share-based payment			68						68		68

Exhibit 11: Continued

	Number of Shares Outstanding	Share Capital	Share Issue Premium	Treasury Shares	Translation Differences	Fair Value and Other Reserves	Reserve for Invested Unrestricted Equity	(Accumulated Deficit)/ Retained Earnings	Attributable to Equity Holders of the Parent	Non-controlling Interests	Total Equity
Excess tax benefit on share-based payment	13,221		6						6		6
Settlement of performance and restricted shares			−85	72			−11		−24		−24
Cancellation of treasury shares	424			1,000				−1,000			
Stock options exercised							1		1		1
Dividends								−1,063	−1,063	−5	−1,068
Acquisitions of non-controlling interests								−1	−1	1	0
Other movements					−1			−2	−3		−3
Total other equity movements		0	−11	1,072	−1	0	−10	−2,066	−1,016	-4	-1020
As of December 31, 2018	5,593,162	246	436	−408	−592	1,063	15,606	−1,062	15,289	82	15371

	Issued Capital	Share Premium	Retained Earnings	Other Components of Equity	Treasury Shares	Equity Attributable to Owners of Parent		Total Equity
						Total	Non-controlling interests	
Reissuance of treasury shares under share-based payments	13				11	24		24
Shares to be issued			7			7		7
Hyperinflation			−8			−8		−8
Changes in non-controlling interests						0	19	19
Other changes			−2			−2	3	1
12/31/2018	1,229	543	27,407	1,234	−1,580	28,832	45	28,877

Source: www.sap.com.

For Nokia, items that have bypassed the income statement in 2018 are those in the columns labeled "Share issue premium," "Translation differences," "Fair value and other reserves," and "Reserve for invested unrestricted equity." For SAP, the amounts that bypassed the income statement in 2018 are "Share premium" and "Other components of equity."

To illustrate the issues in interpreting these items, consider the columns "Translation differences" (Nokia) and "Other components of equity" (SAP). The amounts in these columns reflect currency translation adjustments to equity that have bypassed the income statement. For Nokia, the adjustment for the year 2018 was €341 million. Because this is a positive adjustment to stockholders' equity, this item would have increased income if it had been reported on the income statement. For SAP, the "Other components of equity" adjustment (which includes translation adjustment for the year 2018) was €887 million. Again, because this is a positive adjustment to stockholders' equity, this item would have increased income if it had been reported on the income statement. If the analyst expects this trend of positive translation adjustments to continue and has used historical data as the basis for initial estimates of ROE to be used in residual income valuation, an upward adjustment in that estimated future ROE might be warranted. It is possible, however, that future exchange rate movements will reverse this trend.

The examples we have explored used the actual beginning equity and a forecasted level of ROE (return on beginning equity) to compute the forecasted net income. Because equity includes accumulated other comprehensive income (AOCI), the assumptions about future other comprehensive income (OCI) will affect forecasted net income and thus residual income. To illustrate, Exhibit 13 shows a hypothetical company's financials for a single previous year, labeled year $t - 1$, followed by three different forecasts for the following two years. In year $t - 1$, the company reports net income of $120, which is a 12% return on beginning equity of $1,000. The company paid no dividends, so ending retained earnings equal $120. In year $t - 1$, the company also reports OCI of −$100, a loss, so the ending amount shown in AOCI is −$100. (Companies typically label this line item "accumulated other comprehensive income (loss)," indicating that the amount is an accumulated loss when given in parentheses.) All three forecasts in Exhibit 13 assume that ROE will be 12% and use this assumption to forecast net income for year t and $t + 1$ by using the expression 0.12 × Beginning book value. Each forecast, however, incorporates different assumptions about future

Exhibit 13: Hypothetical Company Alternative Forecasts with Different Assumptions about Comprehensive Income

	Actual	Forecast A		Forecast B		Forecast C	
Year	$t-1$	t	$t+1$	t	$t+1$	t	$t+1$
Beginning Balance Sheet							
Assets	$1,000.00	$1,020.00	$1,142.40	$1,020.00	$1,042.40	$1,020.00	$1,242.40
Liabilities	—	—	—	—	—	—	—
Common stock	1,000.00	1,000.00	1,000.00	1,000.00	1,000.00	1,000.00	1,000.00
Retained earnings	—	120.00	242.40	120.00	242.40	120.00	242.40
AOCI	—	(100.00)	(100.00)	(100.00)	(200.00)	(100.00)	—
Total equity	1,000.00	1,020.00	1,142.40	1,020.00	1,042.40	1,020.00	1,242.40
Total liabilities and total equity	$1,000.00	$1,020.00	$1,142.40	$1,020.00	$1,042.40	$1,020.00	$1,242.40
Net income	120.00	122.40	137.09	122.40	125.09	122.40	149.09
Dividends	—	—	—	—	—	—	—
Other comprehensive income	(100.00)	—	—	(100.00)	(100.00)	100.00	—
Ending Balance Sheet							
Assets	$1,020.00	$1,142.40	$1,279.49	$1,042.40	$1,067.49	$1,242.40	$1,391.49
Liabilities	—	—	—	—	—	—	—
Common stock	1,000.00	1,000.00	1,000.00	1,000.00	1,000.00	1,000.00	1,000.00
Retained earnings	120.00	242.40	379.49	242.40	367.49	242.40	391.49
AOCI	(100.00)	(100.00)	(100.00)	(200.00)	(300.00)	—	—
Total equity	$1,020.00	$1,142.40	$1,279.49	$1,042.40	$1,067.49	$1,242.40	$1,391.49
Total liabilities and total equity	$1,020.00	$1,142.40	$1,279.49	$1,042.40	$1,067.49	$1,242.40	$1,391.49
Residual income calculation based on beginning total equity							
Net income	120.00	122.40	137.09	122.40	125.09	122.40	149.09
Equity charge at 10%	100.00	102.00	114.24	102.00	104.24	102.00	124.24
Residual income	$20.00	$20.40	$22.85	$20.40	$20.85	$20.40	$24.85

OCI. Forecast A assumes that the company will have no OCI in year t or year $t + 1$, so the amount of AOCI does not change. Forecast B assumes that the company will continue to have the same amount of OCI in year t and year $t + 1$ as it had in the prior year, so the amount of AOCI becomes more negative each year. Forecast C assumes that the company's OCI will reverse in year t, so at the end of year t, AOCI will be zero. As shown, because the forecasts use the assumed ROE to compute forecasted net income, the forecasts for net income and residual income in year $t + 1$ vary significantly.

Because this example assumes all earnings are retained, a forecast of 12% ROE also implies that net income and residual income will grow at 12%. Only the year t to year $t + 1$ under Forecast A, which assumes no future OCI, correctly reflects that relationship. Specifically, in Forecast A, both net income and residual income increase by 12% from year t to year $t + 1$. Net income grows from $122.40 to $137.09, an increase of 12% [($137.09/$122.40) − 1]; and residual income grows from $20.40 to $22.85, an increase of 12% [($22.85/$20.40) − 1]. In contrast to Forecast A, neither Forecast B nor Forecast C correctly reflects the relationship between ROE and growth in income (net and residual). Growth in residual income from year t to year $t + 1$ was 2.2% under Forecast B and 21.8% under Forecast C.

If, alternatively, the forecasts of future ROE and the residual income computation had incorporated total comprehensive income (net income plus OCI), the results of the residual income computation would have differed significantly. For example, suppose that in Forecast B, which assumes the company will continue to have the same amount of OCI, the estimated future ROE was 2.0%, using total comprehensive income [($120 − $100)/$1,000 = $20/$1,000]. If the residual income computation had then also used forecasted total comprehensive income at time t, the amount of residual income would be negative. Specifically, for time t, forecast comprehensive income would be $22.40 (net income plus other comprehensive income), the equity charge would be $102 (required return of 10% multiplied by beginning equity of $1,020), and residual income would be −$79.60 (comprehensive income of $22.40 minus equity charge of $102). Clearly, residual income on this basis significantly falls short of the positive $20.40 when the violation of clean surplus is ignored. As this example demonstrates, using an ROE forecast or a net income forecast that ignores violations of clean surplus accounting will distort estimates of residual income. Unless the present value of such distortions net to zero, using those forecasts will also distort valuations.

What are the implications for implementing a residual-income-based valuation? If future OCI is expected to be significant relative to net income and if the year-to-year amounts of OCI are not expected to net to zero, the analyst should attempt to incorporate these items so that residual income forecasts are closer to what they would be if the clean surplus relation held. Specifically, when possible, the analyst should incorporate explicit assumptions about future amounts of OCI.

Example 14 illustrates, by reference to the DDM value, the error that results when OCI is omitted from residual income calculations (assuming an analyst has a basis for forecasting future amounts of OCI). The example also shows that the growth rate in residual income generally does not equal the growth rate of net income or dividends.

EXAMPLE 14

Incorporating Adjustments in the Residual Income Model

Exhibit 14 gives per-share forecasts for Mannistore, Inc., a hypothetical company operating a chain of retail stores. The company's cost of equity capital is 10%.

Exhibit 14: Forecasts for Mannistore, Inc.

	Year				
Variable	1	2	3	4	5
Shareholders' equity$_{t-1}$	$8.58	$10.32	$11.51	$14.68	$17.86
Plus net income	2.00	2.48	3.46	3.47	4.56
Less dividends	0.26	0.29	0.29	0.29	0.38
Less other comprehensive income	0.00	1.00	0.00	0.00	0.00
Equals shareholders' equity$_t$	$10.32	$11.51	$14.68	$17.86	$22.04

(handwritten annotation near Year 2 dividends: "-% of CI")

1. Assuming the forecasted terminal price of Mannistore's shares at the end of Year 5 (time $t = 5$) is $68.40, estimate the value per share of Mannistore using the DDM.

Solution:

The estimated value using the DDM is

$$V_0 = \frac{\$0.26}{(1.10)^1} + \frac{\$0.29}{(1.10)^2} + \frac{\$0.29}{(1.10)^3} + \frac{\$0.29}{(1.10)^4} + \frac{\$0.38}{(1.10)^5}$$

$$+ \frac{\$68.40}{(1.10)^5} = \$43.59$$

2. Given that the forecast terminal price of Mannistore's shares at the end of Year 5 (time $t = 5$) is $68.40, estimate the value of a share of Mannistore using the RI model and calculate residual income based on:

   A. net income without adjustment, and

   B. net income plus other comprehensive income.

Solution:

A. Calculating residual income as net income (NI) minus the equity charge, which is beginning shareholders' equity (SE) multiplied by the cost of equity capital (r), gives the following for years 1 through 5:

	Year				
	1	2	3	4	5
RI = NI − (SE$_{t-1}$ × r)	1.14	1.45	2.30	2.00	2.77

So, the estimated value using the RI model (using Equation 6), with residual income calculated based on net income, is

$$V_0 = \$8.58 + \frac{\$1.14}{(1.10)^1} + \frac{\$1.45}{(1.10)^2} + \frac{\$2.30}{(1.10)^3} + \frac{\$2.00}{(1.10)^4} + \frac{\$2.77}{(1.10)^5}$$

$$+ \frac{\$68.40 - \$22.04}{(1.10)^5}$$

$$V_0 = \$8.58 + 35.84 = \$44.42$$

B. Calculating residual income as net income adjusted for OCI (NI + OCI) minus the equity charge, which equals beginning shareholders' equity (SE) multiplied by the cost of equity capital (r), gives the following for years 1 through 5:

	Year				
	1	2	3	4	5
RI = (NI + OCI) − (SE$_{t-1}$ × r)	$1.14	$0.45	$2.30	$2.00	$2.77

So, the estimated value using the RI model, with residual income based on net income adjusted for OCI, is

$$V_0 = \$8.58 + \frac{\$1.14}{(1.10)^1} + \frac{\$.45}{(1.10)^2} + \frac{\$2.30}{(1.10)^3} + \frac{\$2.00}{(1.10)^4} + \frac{\$2.77}{(1.10)^5}$$
$$+ \frac{\$68.40 - \$22.04}{(1.10)^5}$$
$$V_0 = \$8.58 + 35.01 = \$43.59$$

3. Interpret your answers to Parts 2A and 2B.

Solution:

The first calculation (2A) incorrectly omits an adjustment for a violation of the clean surplus relation. The second calculation (2B) includes an adjustment and yields the correct value estimate, which is consistent with the DDM estimate.

4. Assume that a forecast of the terminal price of Mannistore's shares at the end of Year 5 (time $t = 5$) is not available. Instead, an estimate of terminal price based on the Gordon growth model is appropriate. You estimate that the growth in net income and dividends from $t = 5$ to $t = 6$ will be 8%. Predict residual income for Year 6, and based on that 8% growth estimate, determine the growth rate in forecasted residual income from $t = 5$ to $t = 6$.

Solution:

Given the estimated 8% growth in net income and dividends in Year 6, the estimated Year 6 net income is $4.92 ($4.56 × 1.08), and the estimated amount of Year 6 dividends is $0.42 ($0.38 × 1.08).

Residual income will then equal $2.72 (which is net income of $4.92 minus the equity charge of beginning book value of $22.04 multiplied by the cost of capital of 10%). So, the growth rate in residual income is negative at approximately −2% ($2.72/$2.77 − 1).

Lacking a basis for explicit assumptions about future amounts of OCI, the analyst should nonetheless be aware of the potential effect of OCI on residual income and adjust ROE accordingly. Finally, as noted earlier, the analyst may decide that an alternative valuation model is more appropriate.

ACCOUNTING CONSIDERATIONS: OTHER

6

☐ | describe accounting issues in applying residual income models

To have a reliable measure of book value of equity, an analyst should identify and scrutinize significant off-balance-sheet assets and liabilities. Additionally, reported assets and liabilities should be adjusted to fair value when possible. Off-balance-sheet assets and liabilities may become apparent through an examination of the financial statement footnotes. Probably the most common example is the use of operating leases. Operating leases do not affect the amount of equity (because leases involve off-balance-sheet assets that offset the off-balance-sheet liabilities) but can affect an assessment of future earnings for the residual income component of value. Other assets and liabilities may be stated at values other than fair value. For example, inventory may be stated at LIFO and require adjustment to restate to current value. (LIFO is not permitted under IFRS.) The following are some common items to review for balance sheet adjustments. Note, however, that this list is not comprehensive:

- inventory;
- deferred tax assets and liabilities;
- operating leases;
- reserves and allowances (for example, bad debts); and
- intangible assets.

Additionally, the analyst should examine the financial statements and footnotes for items unique to the subject company.

Intangible Assets

Intangible assets can have a significant effect on book value. In the case of specifically identifiable intangibles that can be separated from the entity (e.g., sold), it is generally appropriate to include these in determining book value of equity. If these assets have a finite useful life, they will be amortized over time as an expense. Intangible assets, however, require special consideration because they are often not recognized as an asset unless they are obtained in an acquisition. For example, advertising expenditures can create a highly valuable brand, which is clearly an intangible asset. Advertising expenditures, however, are shown as an expense, and the value of a brand would not appear as an asset on the financial statements unless the company owning the brand was acquired.

To demonstrate this, consider a simplified example involving two companies, Alpha and Beta, with the following summary financial information (all amounts in thousands, except per-share data):

	Alpha (€)	Beta (€)
Cash	1,600	100
Property, plant, and equipment	3,400	900
Total assets	5,000	1,000
Equity	5,000	1,000
Net income	600	150

Each company pays out all net income as dividends (no growth), and the clean surplus relation holds. Alpha has a 12% ROE and Beta has a 15% ROE, both expected to continue indefinitely. Each has a 10% required rate of return. The fair market value of each company's property, plant, and equipment is the same as its book value. What is the value of each company in a residual income framework?

Using total book value rather than per-share data, the value of Alpha would be €6,000, determined as follows (note that result would be the same if calculated on a per-share basis):

$$V_0 = B_0 + \frac{\text{ROE} - r}{r - g} B_0 = 5,000 + \frac{0.12 - 0.10}{0.10 - 0.00} 5,000 = 6,000$$

Similarly, the value of Beta would be €1,500:

$$V_0 = B_0 + \frac{\text{ROE} - r}{r - g} B_0 = 1,000 + \frac{0.15 - 0.10}{0.10 - 0.00} 1,000 = 1,500$$

The value of the companies on a combined basis would be €7,500. Note that both companies are valued more highly than the book value of equity because they have ROE in excess of the required rate of return. Absent an acquisition transaction, the financial statements of Alpha and Beta do not reflect this value. If either is acquired, however, an acquirer would allocate the purchase price to the acquired assets, with any excess of the purchase price above the acquired assets shown as goodwill.

Suppose Alpha acquires Beta by paying Beta's former shareholders €1,500 in cash. Alpha has just paid €500 in excess of the value of Beta's total reported assets of €1,000. Assume that Beta's property, plant and equipment is already shown at its fair market value of €1,000, and that the €500 is considered to be the fair value of a license owned by Beta, say an exclusive right to provide a service. Assume further that the original cost of obtaining the license was an immaterial application fee, which does not appear on Beta's balance sheet, and that the license covers a period of 10 years. Because the entire purchase price of €1,500 is allocated to identifiable assets, no goodwill is recognized. Alpha's balance sheet immediately after the acquisition would be as follows:

	Alpha (€)
Cash	200
Property, plant, and equipment	4,300
License	500
Total assets	5,000
Equity	5,000

Note that the total book value of Alpha's equity did not change, because the acquisition was made for cash and thus did not require Alpha to issue any new shares. Also note that, for example, cash of €200 is calculated as €1,600 (cash of Alpha) + €100 (cash of Beta) − €1,500 (purchase price of Beta).

Under the assumption that the license is amortized over a 10-year period, the combined company's expected net income would be €700 (€600 + €150 − €50 amortization). If this net income number is used to derive expected ROE, the expected ROE would be 14%. Under a residual income model, with no adjustment for amortization, the value of the combined company would be

[handwritten note: ↓ This means that amortization expense is not added back befor computing ROE]

$$V_0 = B_0 + \frac{\text{ROE} - r}{r - g} B_0 = 5,000 + \frac{0.14 - 0.10}{0.10 - 0.00} 5,000 = 7,000$$

Why would the combined company be worth less than the two separate companies? If the assumption is made that a fair price was paid to Beta's former shareholders, the combined value should not be lower. The lower value using the residual income model results from a reduction in ROE as a result of the amortization of the intangible license asset. If this asset were not amortized (or if the amortization expense were added back before computing ROE), net income would be €750 and ROE would be 15%. The value of the combined entity would be

$$V_0 = B_0 + \frac{\text{ROE} - r}{r - g}B_0 = 5,000 + \frac{0.15 - 0.10}{0.10 - 0.00}5,000 = 7,500$$

This amount, €7,500, is the same as the sum of the values of the companies on a separate basis.

Would the answer be different if the acquiring company used newly issued stock rather than cash in the acquisition? The form of currency used to pay for the transaction should not affect the total value. If Alpha used €1,500 of newly issued stock to acquire Beta, its balance sheet would be as follows:

	Alpha (€)
Cash	1,700
Property, plant, and equipment	4,300
License	500
Total assets	6,500
Equity	6,500

Projected earnings, excluding the amortization of the license, would be €750, and projected ROE would be 11.538%. Value under the residual income model would be

$$V_0 = B_0 + \frac{\text{ROE} - r}{r - g}B_0 = 6,500 + \frac{0.11538 - 0.10}{0.10 - 0.00}6,500 = 7,500$$

The overall value remains unchanged. The book value of equity is higher but offset by the effect on ROE. Once again, this example assumes that the buyer paid a fair value for the acquisition. If an acquirer overpays for an acquisition, the overpayment should become evident in a reduction in future residual income.

Research and development (R&D) costs provide another example of an intangible asset that must be given careful consideration. Under US GAAP, R&D is generally expensed to the income statement directly (except in certain cases such as ASC 985-20-25, which permits the capitalization of R&D expenses related to software development after product feasibility has been established). Also, under IFRS, some R&D costs can be capitalized and amortized over time. R&D expenditures are reflected in a company's ROE, and hence residual income, over the long term. If a company engages in unproductive R&D expenditures, these will lower residual income through the expenditures made. If a company engages in productive R&D expenditures, these should result in higher revenues to offset the expenditures over time. In summary, on a continuing basis for a mature company, ROE should reflect the productivity of R&D expenditures without requiring an adjustment.

As explained in Lundholm and Sloan (2007), including and subsequently amortizing an asset that was omitted from a company's reported assets has no effect on valuation under a residual income model. Such an adjustment would increase the estimated equity value by adding the asset to book value at time zero but decrease the estimated value by an equivalent amount, which would include a) the present value of the asset when amortized in the future and b) the present value of a periodic capital charge based on the amount of the asset multiplied by the cost of equity. Expensing R&D, however, results in an immediately lower ROE vis-à-vis capitalizing R&D. But expensing R&D will result in a slightly higher ROE relative to capitalizing R&D in future years because this capitalized R&D is amortized. Because ROE is used in a number of expressions derived from the residual income model and may also be used in forecasting net income, the analyst should carefully consider a company's R&D expenditures and their effect on long-term ROE.

Non-recurring Items

In applying a residual income model, it is important to develop a forecast of future residual income based on recurring items. Companies often report non-recurring charges as part of earnings, which can lead to overestimates and underestimates of future residual earnings if no adjustments are made. No adjustments to book value are necessary for these items, however, because non-recurring gains and losses are reflected in the value of assets in place. Hirst and Hopkins (2000) noted that non-recurring items sometimes result from accounting rules and at other times result from "strategic" management decisions. Regardless, they highlighted the importance of examining the financial statement notes and other sources for items that may warrant adjustment in determining recurring earnings, such as

- unusual items;
- extraordinary items (applicable under US GAAP but not under IFRS);
- restructuring charges;
- discontinued operations; and
- accounting changes.

In some cases, management may record restructuring or unusual charges in every period. In these cases, the item may be considered an ordinary operating expense and may not require adjustment.

Companies sometimes inappropriately classify non-operating gains as a reduction in operating expenses (such as selling, general, and administrative expenses). If material, this inappropriate classification can usually be uncovered by a careful reading of financial statement footnotes and press releases. Analysts should consider whether these items are likely to continue and contribute to residual income in time. More likely, they should be removed from operating earnings when forecasting residual income.

Other Aggressive Accounting Practices

Companies may engage in accounting practices that result in the overstatement of assets (book value) and/or overstatement of earnings. We discussed some of these practices in the preceding sections. Other activities that a company may engage in include accelerating revenues to the current period or deferring expenses to a later period (Schilit and Perler 2010). Both activities simultaneously increase earnings and book value. For example, a company might ship unordered goods to customers at year-end, recording revenues and a receivable. As another example, a company could capitalize rather than expense a cash payment, resulting in lower expenses and an increase in assets.

Conversely, companies have also been criticized for the use of "cookie jar" reserves (reserves saved for future use), in which excess losses or expenses are recorded in an *earlier* period (for example, in conjunction with an acquisition or restructuring) and then used to reduce expenses and increase income in future periods. The analyst should carefully examine the use of reserves when assessing residual earnings. Overall, the analyst must evaluate a company's accounting policies carefully and consider the integrity of management when assessing the inputs in a residual income model.

International Considerations

Accounting standards differ internationally. These differences result in different measures of book value and earnings internationally and suggest that valuation models based on accrual accounting data might not perform as well as other present value models in international contexts. It is interesting to note, however, that Frankel and Lee (1999) found that the residual income model works well in valuing companies on an international basis. Using a simple residual income model without any of the adjustments discussed here, they found that their residual income valuation model accounted for 70% of the cross-sectional variation of stock prices among 20 countries. Frankel and Lee concluded that there are three primary considerations in applying a residual income model internationally:

- the availability of reliable earnings forecasts;
- systematic violations of the clean surplus assumption; and
- "poor quality" accounting rules that result in delayed recognition of value changes.

Analysts should expect the model to work best in situations in which earnings forecasts are available, clean surplus violations are limited, and accounting rules do not result in delayed recognition. Because Frankel and Lee found good explanatory power for a residual income model using unadjusted accounting data, one expects that if adjustments are made to the reported data to correct for clean surplus and other violations, international comparisons should result in comparable valuations. For circumstances in which clean surplus violations exist, accounting choices result in delayed recognition, or accounting disclosures do not permit adjustment, the residual income model would not be appropriate and the analyst should consider a model less dependent on accounting data, such as a FCFE model.

It should be noted, however, that IFRS is increasingly becoming widely used. As of 2019, according to AICPA (an accociation representing the accounting profession), approximately 120 nations and reporting jurisdictions permit or require IFRS for domestic listed companies, although approximately 90 countries have fully conformed with IFRS as promulgated by the IASB and include a statement acknowledging such conformity in audit reports. Furthermore, standard setters in numerous countries continue to work toward convergence between IFRS and home-country GAAP. In time, concerns about the use of different accounting standards should become less severe. Nonetheless, even within a single set of accounting standards, companies make choices and estimates that can affect valuation.

SUMMARY

We have discussed the use of residual income models in valuation. Residual income is an appealing economic concept because it attempts to measure economic profit, which are profits after accounting for all opportunity costs of capital.

- Residual income is calculated as net income minus a deduction for the cost of equity capital. The deduction, called the equity charge, is equal to equity capital multiplied by the required rate of return on equity (the cost of equity capital in percent).

- Economic value added (EVA) is a commercial implementation of the residual income concept. EVA = NOPAT − (C% × TC), where NOPAT is net operating profit after taxes, C% is the percent cost of capital, and TC is total capital.

- Residual income models (including commercial implementations) are used not only for equity valuation but also to measure internal corporate performance and for determining executive compensation.

- We can forecast per-share residual income as forecasted earnings per share minus the required rate of return on equity multiplied by beginning book value per share. Alternatively, per-share residual income can be forecasted as beginning book value per share multiplied by the difference between forecasted ROE and the required rate of return on equity.

■ In the residual income model, the intrinsic value of a share of common stock is the sum of book value per share and the present value of expected future per-share residual income. In the residual income model, the equivalent mathematical expressions for intrinsic value of a common stock are

$$V_0 = B_0 + \sum_{t=1}^{\infty} \frac{RI_t}{(1+r)^t} = B_0 + \sum_{t=1}^{\infty} \frac{E_t - rB_{t-1}}{(1+r)^t}$$

$$= B_0 + \sum_{t=1}^{\infty} \frac{(ROE_t - r)B_{t-1}}{(1+r)^t}$$

where

V_0 = value of a share of stock today ($t = 0$)

B_0 = current per-share book value of equity

B_t = expected per-share book value of equity at any time t

r = required rate of return on equity (cost of equity)

E_t = expected earnings per share for period t

RI_t = expected per-share residual income, equal to $E_t - rB_{t-1}$ or to $(ROE - r) \times B_{t-1}$

ROE_T = return on equity

• In the two-stage model with continuing residual income in stage two, the intrinsic value of a share of stock is

$$V_0 = B_0 + \sum_{t=1}^{T} \frac{RI_t}{(1+r)^t} + \frac{P_T - B_T}{(1+r)^T} = B_0 + \sum_{t=1}^{T} \frac{(E_t - rB_{t-1})}{(1+r)^t} + \frac{P_T - B_T}{(1+r)^T}$$

$$V_0 = B_0 + \sum_{t=1}^{T} \frac{(ROE_t - r)B_{t-1}}{(1+r)^t} + \frac{P_T - B_T}{(1+r)^T}$$

where

P_T = expected per share price at terminal time T

B_T = expected per share book value at terminal time T

■ In most cases, value is recognized earlier in the residual income model compared with other present value models of stock value, such as the dividend discount model.

■ Strengths of the residual income model include the following:

- Terminal values do not make up a large portion of the value relative to other models.

- The models use readily available accounting data.

- The models can be used in the absence of dividends and near-term positive free cash flows.

- The models can be used when cash flows are unpredictable.

■ Weaknesses of the residual income model include the following:

- The models are based on accounting data that can be subject to manipulation by management.

- Accounting data used as inputs may require significant adjustments.
- The models require that the clean surplus relation holds, or that the analyst makes appropriate adjustments when the clean surplus relation does not hold.

■ The residual income model is most appropriate in the following cases:

- A company is not paying dividends or if it exhibits an unpredictable dividend pattern.
- A company has negative free cash flow many years out but is expected to generate positive cash flow at some point in the future.
- A great deal of uncertainty exists in forecasting terminal values.

■ The fundamental determinants or drivers of residual income are book value of equity and return on equity.

■ Residual income valuation is most closely related to P/B. When the present value of expected future residual income is positive (negative), the justified P/B based on fundamentals is greater than (less than) one.

■ When fully consistent assumptions are used to forecast earnings, cash flow, dividends, book value, and residual income through a full set of pro forma (projected) financial statements, and the same required rate of return on equity is used as the discount rate, the same estimate of value should result from a residual income, dividend discount, or free cash flow valuation. In practice, however, analysts may find one model easier to apply and possibly arrive at different valuations using the different models.

■ Continuing residual income is residual income after the forecast horizon. Frequently, one of the following assumptions concerning continuing residual income is made:

- Residual income continues indefinitely at a positive level. (One variation of this assumption is that residual income continues indefinitely at the rate of inflation, meaning it is constant in real terms.)
- Residual income is zero from the terminal year forward.
- Residual income declines to zero as ROE reverts to the cost of equity over time.
- Residual income declines to some mean level.

■ The residual income model assumes the clean surplus relation of $B_t = B_{t-1} + E_t - D_t$. In other terms, the ending book value of equity equals the beginning book value plus earnings minus dividends, apart from ownership transactions.

■ In practice, to apply the residual income model most accurately, the analyst may need to do the following:

- adjust book value of common equity for:

  ▪ off-balance-sheet items;

  ▪ discrepancies from fair value; or

  ▪ the amortization of certain intangible assets.

- adjust reported net income to reflect clean surplus accounting.
- adjust reported net income for non-recurring items misclassified as recurring items.

REFERENCES

Bauman, Mark P. 1999. "Importance of Reported Book Value in Equity Valuation." Journal of Financial Statement Analysis, vol. 4, no. 2:31–40.

Bernstein, Richard, Carmen Pigler. 1997. "An Analysis of EVA*." Quantitative Viewpoint. Merrill Lynch. 19 December.

Bernstein, Richard, Kari Bayer, Carmen Pigler. 1998. "An Analysis of EVA* Part II." Quantitative Viewpoint. Merrill Lynch. 3 February.

Dechow, Patricia M., Amy P. Hutton, Richard G. Sloan. 1999. "An Empirical Assessment of the Residual Income Valuation Model." Journal of Accounting and Economics, vol. 26, no. 1-3:1–34. 10.1016/S0165-4101(98)00049-4

Feltham, Gerald A., James A. Ohlson. 1995. "Valuation and Clean Surplus Accounting for Operating and Financial Activities." Contemporary Accounting Research, vol. 11, no. 4:689–731. 10.1111/j.1911-3846.1995.tb00462.x

Fleck, Shelby A., Scott D. Craig, Michael Bodenstab, Trevor Harris, Elmer Huh. 2001. Technology: Electronics Manufacturing Services. Industry Overview; Morgan Stanley Dean Witter. 28 March.

Frankel, Richard M., Charles M.C. Lee. 1999. "Accounting Diversity and International Valuation." Working Paper, May.

Hirst, D. Eric, Patrick E. Hopkins. 2000. Earnings: Measurement, Disclosure, and the Impact on Equity Valuation. Charlottesville, VA: Research Foundation of AIMR and Blackwell Series in Finance.

Hitchner, James R. 2017. Financial Valuation: Applications and Models, 4th edition. Hoboken, NJ: John Wiley & Sons.

Lee, Charles M.C., Bhaskaran Swaminathan. 1999. "Valuing the Dow: A Bottom-Up Approach." Financial Analysts Journal, vol. 55, no. 5:4–23. 10.2469/faj.v55.n5.2295

Lee, Charles M.C., James Myers, Bhaskaran Swaminathan. 1999. "What is the Intrinsic Value of the Dow?" Journal of Finance, vol. 54, no. 5:1693–1741. 10.1111/0022-1082.00164

Lundholm, Russell J., Terrence B. O'Keefe. 2001a. "Reconciling Value Estimates from the Discounted Cash Flow Model and the Residual Income Model." Contemporary Accounting Research, vol. 18, no. 2:311–335. 10.1506/W13B-K4BT-455N-TTR2

Lundholm, Russell J., Terrence B. O'Keefe. 2001b. "On Comparing Residual Income and Discounted Cash Flow Models of Equity Valuation: A Response to Penman 2001." Contemporary Accounting Research, vol. 18, no. 4:693–696. 10.1506/Y51R-C3YF-MT0T-BWE2

Lundholm, Russell J., Richard G. Sloan. 2007. Equity Valuation and Analysis with eVal, 2nd edition. McGraw-Hill Irwin. New York.

Ohlson, James A. 1995. "Earnings, Book Values, and Dividends in Equity Valuation." Contemporary Accounting Research, vol. 11, no. 4:661–687. 10.1111/j.1911-3846.1995.tb00461.x

Penman, Stephen H. 2001. "On Comparing Cash Flow and Accrual Accounting Models for Use in Equity Valuation: A Response to Lundholm and O'Keefe." Contemporary Accounting Research, vol. 18, no. 4:681–692. 10.1506/DT0R-JNEG-QL60-7CBP

Penman, Stephen H., Theodore Sougiannis. 1998. "A Comparison of Dividend, Cash Flow and Earnings Approaches to Equity Valuation." Contemporary Accounting Research, vol. 15, no. 3:343–383. 10.1111/j.1911-3846.1998.tb00564.x

Peterson, Pamela P., David R. Peterson. 1996. Company Performance and Measures of Value Added. Charlottesville, VA: The Research Foundation of the ICFA.

Schilit and Perler2010. Financial Shenanigans. 3rd ed., McGraw-Hill.

Shrieves, Ronald E., John M. Wachowicz. 2001. "Free Cash Flow (FCF), Economic Value Added (EVA™), and Net Present Value (NPV): A Reconciliation of Variations of Discounted-Cash-Flow (DCF) Valuation." Engineering Economist, vol. 46, no. 1:33–52. 10.1080/00137910108967561

Stewart, G. Bennett. 1991. The Quest for Value. New York: HarperCollins.

PRACTICE PROBLEMS

1. Based on the following information, determine whether Vertically Integrated Manufacturing (VIM) earned any residual income for its shareholders:

    - VIM had total assets of $3,000,000, financed with twice as much debt capital as equity capital.
    - VIM's pretax cost of debt is 6% and cost of equity capital is 10%.
    - VIM had EBIT of $300,000 and was taxed at a rate of 40%.

    Calculate residual income by using the method based on deducting an equity charge.

2. Because New Market Products (NMP) markets consumer staples, it is able to make use of considerable debt in its capital structure; specifically, 90% of the company's total assets of $450,000,000 are financed with debt capital. Its cost of debt is 8% before taxes, and its cost of equity capital is 12%. NMP achieved a pretax income of $5.1 million in 2006 and had a tax rate of 40%. What was NMP's residual income?

3. In 2020, Smithson–Williams Industries (SWI) achieved an operating profit after taxes of €10 million on total assets of €100 million. Half of its assets were financed with debt with a pretax cost of 9%. Its cost of equity capital is 12%, and its tax rate is 40%. Did SWI achieve a positive residual income?

The following information relates to questions 4-6

Calculate the economic value added or residual income, as requested, for each of the following:

4. NOPAT = $100
    Beginning book value of debt = $200
    Beginning book value of equity = $300
    Weighted average cost of capital (WACC) = 11%
    Calculate EVA.

5. Net income = €5.00
    Dividends = €1.00
    Beginning book value of equity = €30.00
    Required rate of return on equity = 11%
    Calculate residual income.

6. Return on equity = 18%
    Required rate of return on equity = 12%
    Beginning book value of equity = €30.00
    Calculate residual income.

The following information relates to questions 7-8

Jim Martin is using economic value added and market value added to measure the performance of Sundanci. Martin uses the fiscal year 2020 information below for his analysis.

- Adjusted net operating profit after taxes is $100 million.
- Total capital is $700 million (no debt).
- Closing stock price is $26.
- Total shares outstanding is 84 million.
- The cost of equity is 14%.

Calculate the following for Sundanci. Show your work.

7. EVA for fiscal year 2020.

8. MVA as of fiscal year-end 2020.

The following information relates to questions 9-16

Mangoba Nkomo, CFA, a senior equity analyst with Robertson-Butler Investments, South Africa, has been assigned a recent graduate, Manga Mahlangu, to assist in valuations. Mahlangu is interested in pursuing a career in equity analysis. In their first meeting, Nkomo and Mahlangu discuss the concept of residual income and its commercial applications. Nkomo asks Mahlangu to determine the market value added for a hypothetical South African firm using the data provided in Exhibit 1.

Exhibit 1: Hypothetical Firm Data (amounts in South African rand)	
Current share price	R25.43
Book value per share	R20.00
Total shares outstanding	30 million
Cost of equity	13%
Market value of debt	R55 million
Accounting book value of total capital	R650 million
Intrinsic share value of equity derived from residual income model	R22.00

Nkomo also shares his valuation report of the hypothetical firm with Mahlangu. Nkomo's report concludes that the intrinsic value of the hypothetical firm, based on the residual income model, is R22.00 per share. To assess Mahlangu's knowledge of residual income valuation, Nkomo asks Mahlangu two questions about the hypothetical firm:

| Question 1 | What conclusion can we make about future residual earnings given the current book value per share and my estimate of intrinsic value per share? |

Question 2   Suppose you estimated the intrinsic value of a firm's shares using a constant growth residual income model, and you found that your estimate of intrinsic value equaled the book value per share. What would that finding imply about that firm's return on equity?

Satisfied with Mahlangu's response, Nkomo requests that Mahlangu use the single-stage residual income model to determine the intrinsic value of the equity of Jackson Breweries, a brewery and bottling company, using data provided in Exhibit 2.

Exhibit 2: Jackson Breweries Data (amounts in South African rand)

Constant long-term growth rate	9.5%
Constant long-term ROE	13%
Current market price per share	R150.70
Book value per share	R55.81
Cost of equity	11%

Nkomo also wants to update an earlier valuation of Amersheen, a food retailer. The valuation report, completed at the end of 2020, concluded an intrinsic value per share of R11.00 for Amersheen. The share price at that time was R8.25. Nkomo points out to Mahlangu that in late 2020, Amersheen announced a significant restructuring charge, estimated at R2 million, that would be reported as part of operating earnings in Amersheen's 2020 annual income statement. Nkomo asks Mahlangu the following question about the restructuring charge:

Question 1   What was the correct way to treat the estimated R2 million restructuring charge in my 2020 valuation report?

Satisfied with Mahlangu's response, Nkomo mentions to Mahlangu that Amersheen recently (near the end of 2021) completed the acquisition of a chain of convenience stores. Nkomo requests that Mahlangu complete, as of the beginning of 2022, an updated valuation of Amersheen under two scenarios:

Scenario 1   Estimate the value of Amersheen shares using a multistage residual income model with the data provided in Exhibit 3. Under Scenario 1, expected ROE in 2025 is 26%, but it is assumed that the firm's ROE will slowly decline towards the cost of equity thereafter.

Scenario 2   Estimate the value of Amersheen shares using a multistage residual income model with the data provided in Exhibit 3, but assume that at the end of 2024, share price is expected to equal book value per share.

Scenario 3

Exhibit 3: Amersheen Data (amounts in South African rand)

Long-term growth rate starting in 2025	9.0%
Expected ROE in 2025	26%

Current market price per share	R16.55
Book value per share, beginning of 2022	R7.60
Cost of equity	10%
Persistence factor	0.70

	2022	2023	2024
Expected earnings per share	R3.28	R3.15	R2.90
Expected dividend per share	R2.46	R2.36	R2.06

9. Based on the information in Exhibit 1, the market value added of the hypothetical firm is *closest* to:

   A. R65 million.

   B. R113 million.

   C. R168 million.

10. The *most* appropriate response to Nkomo's Question 1 would be that the present value of future residual earnings is expected to be:

   A. zero.

   B. positive.

   C. negative.

11. The *most* appropriate response to Nkomo's Question 2 would be that the firm's return on equity is:

   A. equal to the firm's cost of equity.

   B. lower than the firm's cost of equity.

   C. higher than the firm's cost of equity.

12. Based on the information in Exhibit 2, the intrinsic value per share of the equity of Jackson Breweries is *closest* to:

   A. R97.67.

   B. R130.22.

   C. R186.03.

13. If Nkomo's 2020 year-end estimate of Amersheen shares' intrinsic value was accurate, then Amersheen's shares were *most likely*:

   A. overvalued.

   B. undervalued.

   C. fairly valued.

14. The *most* appropriate treatment of the estimated restructuring charge, in re-

sponse to Nkomo's Question 3, would be:

A. an upward adjustment to book value.

B. an upward adjustment to the cost of equity.

C. to exclude it from the estimate of net income.

15. Under Scenario 1, the intrinsic value per share of the equity of Amersheen is *closest* to:

A. R13.29.

B. R15.57.

C. R16.31.

16. Under Scenario 2, the intrinsic value per share of the equity of Amersheen is *closest* to:

A. R13.29.

B. R15.57.

C. R16.31.

The following information relates to questions 17-26

Elena Castovan is a junior analyst with Contralith Capital, a long-only equity investment manager. She has been asked to value three stocks on Contralith's watch list: Portous, Inc. (PTU), SSX Financial (SSX), and Tantechi Ltd. (TTCI).

During their weekly meeting, Castovan and her supervisor, Ariana Beckworth, discuss characteristics of residual income models. Castovan tells Beckworth the following.

Statement 1   The present value of the terminal value in RI models is often a larger portion of the total intrinsic value than it is in other DCF valuation models.

Statement 2   The RI model's use of accounting income assumes that the cost of debt capital is appropriately reflected by interest expense.

Statement 3   RI models cannot be readily applied to companies that do not have positive expected near-term free cash flows.

Beckworth asks Castovan why an RI model may be more appropriate for valuing PTU than the dividend discount model or a free cash flow model. Castovan tells Beckworth that, over her five-year forecast horizon, she expects PTU to perform the following actions.

Reason 1   Pay dividends that are unpredictable

Reason 2   Generatepositiveand fairly predictable free cash flows

Reason 3   Report significant amounts of other comprehensive income

At the conclusion of their meeting, Beckworth asks Castovan to value SSX using RI models. Selected financial information on SSX is presented in Exhibit 1.

Exhibit 1: SSX Financial (SSX) Selected Financial Data

Total assets (millions)	€4,000.00
Capital structure	60% debt/40% equity
EBIT (millions)	€700.00
Tax rate	35.00%
Return on equity (ROE)	23.37%
Pretax cost of debt[a]	5.20%
Cost of equity	15.00%
Market price per share	€48.80
Price-to-book ratio	2.10

[a] *Interest expense is tax-deductible.*

Castovan's final assignment is to determine the intrinsic value of TTCI using both a single-stage and a multistage RI model. Selected data and assumptions for TTCI are presented in Exhibit 2.

Exhibit 2: Tantechi Ltd. (TTCI) Selected Financial Data and Assumptions

Book value per share	€45.25
Market price per share	€126.05
Constant long-term ROE	12.00%
Constant long-term earnings growth rate	4.50%
Cost of equity	8.70%

For the multistage model, Castovan forecasts TTCI's ROE to be higher than its long-term ROE for the first three years. Forecasted earnings per share and dividends per share for TTCI are presented in Exhibit 3. Starting in Year 4, Castovan forecasts TTCI's ROE to revert to the constant long-term ROE of 12% annually. The terminal value is based on an assumption that residual income per share will be constant from Year 3 into perpetuity.

Exhibit 3: Tantechi Ltd. (TTCI) Forecasts of Earnings and Dividends

	Year 1	Year 2	Year 3
Earnings per share (€)	7.82	8.17	8.54
Dividends per share (€)	1.46	1.53	1.59

Beckworth questions Castovan's assumption regarding the implied persistence factor used in the multistage RI valuation. She tells Castovan that she believes that a persistence factor of 0.10 is appropriate for TTCI.

17. Which of Castovan's statements regarding residual income models is correct?

    A. Statement 1

    B. Statement 2

    C. Statement 3

18. Which of Castovan's reasons *best* justifies the use of a residual income model to value PTU?

    A. Reason 1

    B. Reason 2

    C. Reason 3

19. The forecasted item described in Reason 3 will *most likely* affect:

    A. earnings per share.

    B. dividends per share.

    C. book value per share.

20. Based on Exhibit 1, residual income for SSX is *closest* to:

    A. €40.9 million.

    B. €90.2 million.

    C. €133.9 million.

21. Based on Exhibit 1 and the single-stage residual income model, the implied growth rate of earnings for SSX is *closest* to:

    A. 5.8%.

    B. 7.4%.

    C. 11.0%.

22. Based on the single-stage RI model and Exhibit 2, Castovan should conclude that TTCI is:

    A. undervalued.

    B. fairly valued.

    C. overvalued.

23. Based on Exhibit 2, the justified price-to-book ratio for TTCI is *closest* to:

    A. 1.79.

    B. 2.27.

    C. 2.79.

24. Based on Exhibits 2 and 3 and the multistage RI model, Castovan should estimate

the intrinsic value of TTCI to be *closest* to:

A. €54.88.

B. €83.01.

C. €85.71.

25. The persistence factor suggested by Beckworth will lead to a multistage value estimate of TTCI's shares that is:

A. less than Castovan's multistage value estimate.

B. equal to Castovan's multistage value estimate.

C. greater than Castovan's multistage value estimate.

26. The *best* justification for Castovan to use Beckworth's suggested persistence factor is that TTCI has:

A. a low dividend payout.

B. extreme accounting rates of return.

C. a strong market leadership position.

27. Use the following information to estimate the intrinsic value of VIM's common stock using the residual income model:

- VIM had total assets of $3,000,000, financed with twice as much debt capital as equity capital.
- VIM's pretax cost of debt is 6% and cost of equity capital is 10%.
- VIM had EBIT of $300,000 and was taxed at a rate of 40%. EBIT is expected to continue at $300,000 indefinitely.
- VIM's book value per share is $20.
- VIM has 50,000 shares of common stock outstanding.

28. Palmetto Steel, Inc. (PSI) maintains a dividend payout ratio of 80% because of its limited opportunities for expansion. Its return on equity is 15%. The required rate of return on PSI equity is 12%, and its long-term growth rate is 3%. Compute the justified P/B based on forecasted fundamentals, consistent with the residual income model and a constant growth rate assumption.

The following information relates to questions 29-30

Protected Steel Corporation (PSC) has a book value of $6 per share. PSC is expected to earn $0.60 per share forever and pays out all of its earnings as dividends. The required rate of return on PSC's equity is 12%. Calculate the value of the stock using the following:

29. Dividend discount model.

30. Residual income model.

The following information relates to questions 31-32

Notable Books (NB) is a family controlled company that dominates the retail book market. NB has book value of $10 per share, is expected to earn $2.00 per share forever, and pays out all of its earnings as dividends. Its required return on equity is 12.5%. Value the stock of NB using the following:

31. Dividend discount model.

32. Residual income model.

The following information relates to questions 33-35

Simonson Investment Trust International (SITI) is expected to earn $4.00, $5.00, and $8.00 per share for the next three years. SITI will pay annual dividends of $2.00, $2.50, and $20.50 in each of these years. The last dividend includes a liquidating payment to shareholders at the end of Year 3 when the trust terminates. SITI's book value is $8 per share and its required return on equity is 10%.

33. What is the current value per share of SITI according to the dividend discount model?

34. Calculate per-share book value and residual income for SITI for each of the next three years and use those results to find the stock's value using the residual income model.

35. Calculate return on equity and use it as an input to the residual income model to calculate SITI's value.

36. Foodsco Incorporated (FI), a leading distributor of food products and materials to restaurants and other institutions, has a remarkably steady track record in terms of both return on equity and growth. At year-end 2017, FI had a book value of $30 per share. For the foreseeable future, the company is expected to achieve a ROE of 15% (on trailing book value) and to pay out one-third of its earnings in dividends. The required return is 12%. Forecast FI's residual income for the year ending 31 December 2022.

The following information relates to questions 37-39

Thales S.A. (Paris: HO.PA) has a current stock price of €98.73. It also has book value per share of €26.83. and a P/B of 3.68. Assume that the single-stage growth model is appropriate for valuing the company. Thales S.A.'s adjusted beta is 0.68, the risk-free rate is 4.46%, and the equity risk premium is 5.50%.

37. If the growth rate is 5.50% and the ROE is 20%, what is the justified P/B for Thales?

38. If the growth rate is 5.50%, what ROE is required to yield Thales S.A.'s current P/B?

39. If the ROE is 20%, what growth rate is required for Thales to have its current P/B?

40. Retail fund manager Seymour Simms is considering the purchase of shares in upstart retailer Hottest Topic Stores (HTR). The current book value of HTS is $20 per share, and its market price is $35. Simms expects long-term ROE to be 18%, long-term growth to be 10%, and cost of equity to be 14%. What conclusion would you expect Simms to arrive at if he uses a single-stage residual income model to value these shares?

41. Dayton Manufactured Homes (DMH) builds prefabricated homes and mobile homes. Favorable demographics and the likelihood of slow, steady increases in market share should enable DMH to maintain its ROE of 15% and growth rate of 10% through time. DMH has a book value of $30 per share and the required rate of return on its equity is 12%. Compute the value of its equity using the single-stage residual income model.

42. Use the following inputs and the finite horizon form of the residual income model to compute the value of Southern Trust Bank (STB) shares as of 31 December 2020:

   - ROE will continue at 15% for the next five years (and 10% thereafter) with all earnings reinvested (no dividends paid).
   - Cost of equity equals 10%.
   - B_0 = $10 per share (at year-end 2020).
   - Premium over book value at the end of five years will be 20%.

The following information relates to questions 43-46

Shunichi Kobayashi is valuing Procter & Gamble Company (NYSE: PG). Kobayashi has made the following assumptions:

   - Book value per share is estimated at $21.30 on 31 March 2019.
   - EPS will be 18% of the beginning book value per share for the next eight years.
   - Cash dividends paid will be 70% of EPS.
   - At the end of the eight-year period, the market price per share will be four times the book value per share.
   - The beta for PG is 0.50, the risk-free rate is 2.0%, and the equity risk premium is 6.2%.

The current market price of PG is $107.50, which indicates a current P/B of 5.05.

43. Prepare a table that shows the beginning and ending book values, net income, and cash dividends annually for the eight-year period.

44. Estimate the residual income and the present value of residual income for the

eight years.

45. Estimate the value per share of PG stock using the residual income model.

46. Estimate the value per share of PG stock using the dividend discount model. How does this value compare with the estimate from the residual income model?

47. Consider the following information about Industrias Gómez.

- Current book value per share is €20.00.
- Expected earnings per share for the next five years are €1.50, €2.50, €3.50, €4.50, and €5.50.
- Dividends per share are projected to be €1.00 for the first three years and €2.00 for the last two years.
- The terminal share price (at the end of Year 5) is expected to be 14× trailing earnings.
- The required rate of return on equity is 9%.
- Estimate the residual income each year, the terminal residual value, and the value per share of Industrias Gómez shares using the residual income model.
- Estimate the value per share of Industrias Gómez shares using the dividend discount model.

48. Lendex Electronics (LE) had a great deal of turnover of top management for several years and was not followed by analysts during this period of turmoil. Because the company's performance has been improving steadily for the past three years, technology analyst Stephanie Kent recently reinitiated coverage of LE. A meeting with management confirms Kent's positive impression of LE's operations and strategic plan. Kent decides LE merits further analysis.

Careful examination of LE's financial statements revealed that the company had negative other comprehensive income from changes in the value of available-for-sale securities in each of the past five years. How, if at all, should this observation about LE's other comprehensive income affect the figures that Kent uses for the company's ROE and book value for those years?

SOLUTIONS

1. Yes, VIM earned a positive residual income of $8,000.

EBIT	$300,000
Interest	120,000 ($2,000,000 × 6%)
Pretax income	$180,000
Tax expense	72,000
Net income	$108,000

Equity charge = Equity capital × Required return on equity

= (1/3)($3,000,000) × 0.10

= $1,000,000 × 0.10 = $100,000

Residual income = Net income − Equity charge

= $108,000 − $100,000 = $8,000

2. In this problem (unlike Problems 1 and 2), interest expense has already been deducted in arriving at NMP's pretax income of $5.1 million. Therefore,

Net income	= Pretax income × (1 − Tax rate)
	= $5.1 million × (1 − 0.4)
	= $5.1 × 0.6 = $3.06 million
Equity charge	= Total equity × Cost of equity capital
	= (0.1 × $450 million) × 12%
	= $45 million × 0.12 = $5,400,000
Residual income	= Net income − Equity charge
	= $3,0600,000 - $5,400,000 = −$2,340,000

NMP had negative residual income of −$2,340,000.

3. To achieve a positive residual income, a company's net operating profit after taxes as a percentage of its total assets can be compared with its weighted average cost of capital. For SWI,

NOPAT/Assets = €10 million/€100 million = 10%

WACC = Percent of debt × After-tax cost of debt + Percent of equity × Cost of equity

= (0.5)(0.09)(0.6) + (0.5)(0.12)

= (0.5)(0.054) + (0.5)(0.12) = 0.027 + 0.06 = 0.087

= 8.7%

Therefore, SWI's residual income was positive. Specifically, residual income equals €1.3 million [(0.10 − 0.087) × €100 million].

4. EVA = NOPAT − WACC × Beginning book value of assets

= $100 − (11%) × ($200 + $300) = $100 − (11%) ($500) = $45

5. $RI_t = E_t - rB_{t-1}$
  $= €5.00 - (11\%)(€30.00) = €5.00 - €3.30 = €1.70$

6. $RI_t = (ROE_t - r) \times B_{t-1}$
  $= (18\% - 12\%) \times (€30) = €1.80$

7. Economic value added = Net operating profit after taxes – (Cost of capital × Total capital) = \$100 million – (14% × \$700 million) = \$2 million. In the absence of information that would be required to calculate the weighted average cost of debt and equity, and given that Sundanci has no long-term debt, the only capital cost used is the required rate of return on equity of 14%.

8. Market value added = Market value of capital – Total capital = \$26 stock price × 84 million shares – \$700 million = \$1,484,000,000.

  Market value added per share = \$1,484,000,000 / 84 million shares= \$17.67 per share.

9. C is correct. Market value added equals the market value of firm minus total accounting book value of total capital.

  Market value added = Market value of company – Accounting book value of total capital

  Market value of firm = Market value of debt + Market value of equity

  Market value of firm = R55 million + (30,000,000 × R25.43)

  Market value of firm = R55 million + R762.9 million = R817.9 million

  Market value added = R817.9 million – R650 million = R167.9 million, or approximately R168 million.

10. B is correct. The intrinsic value of R22.00 is greater than the current book value of R20.00. The residual income model states that the intrinsic value of a stock is its book value per share plus the present value of expected (future) per share residual income. The higher intrinsic value per share, relative to book value per share, indicates that the present value of expected per share residual income is positive.

11. A is correct because the intrinsic value is the book value per share, B_0, plus the expected residual income stream, or $B_0 + [(ROE - r)B_0/(r - g)]$. If ROE equals the cost of equity (r), then $V_0 = B_0$. This implies that ROE is equal to the cost of the equity, and therefore there is no residual income contribution to the intrinsic value. As a result, intrinsic value would be equal to book value.

12. B is correct. With a single-stage residual income (RI) model, the intrinsic value, V_0, is calculated assuming a constant return on equity (ROE) and a constant earnings growth (g).

  $$V_0 = B_0 + B_0 \frac{(ROE - r)}{(r - g)}$$
  $$V_0 = R55.81 + R55.81 \frac{(0.13 - 0.11)}{(0.11 - 0.095)}$$
  $$V_0 = R130.22$$

13. B is correct. The share price of R8.25 was lower than the intrinsic value of R11.00. Shares are considered undervalued when the current share price is less than intrinsic value per share.

14. C is correct. The restructuring charge is a non-recurring item and not indicative of future earnings. In applying a residual income model, it is important to develop a forecast of future residual income based on recurring items. Using the net income reported in Amersheen's 2020 net income statement to model subsequent future earnings, without adjustment for the restructuring charge, would understate the firm's future earnings. By upward adjusting the firm's net income, by adding back the R2 million restructuring charge to reflect the fact that the charge is non-recurring, future earnings will be more accurately forecasted.

15. C is correct. The multistage residual income model results in an intrinsic value of R16.31.

    This variation of the multistage residual income model, in which residual income fades over time, is:

$$V_0 = B_0 + \sum_{t=1}^{T-1} \frac{(E_t - rB_{t-1})}{(1+r)^t} + \frac{(E_T - rB_{T-1})}{(1 + r - \omega)(1+r)^{T-1}}$$

where ω is the persistence factor.

The first step is to calculate residual income per share for years 2022–2025:

	2022	2023	2024	2025
Beginning book value per share	R7.60 (given)	R7.60 + R3.28 − R2.46 = R8.42	R8.42 + R3.15 − R2.36 = R9.21	R9.21 + 2.90 − R2.06 = R10.05
ROE	R3.28/R7.60 = 0.4316	R3.15/R8.42 = 0.3741	R2.90/R9.21 = 0.3149	26% (given)
Retention rate	1 − (R2.46/R3.28) = 0.25	1 − (R2.36/R3.15) = 0.2508	1 − (R2.06/R2.90) = 0.2897	N/A
Growth rate	0.4316 × 0.25 =0.1079	0.3741 × 0.2508 = 0.0938	0.3149 × 0.2897 = 0.0912	9% (given)
Equity charge per share	R7.60 × 0.10 = R0.76	R8.42 × 0.10 = R0.842	R9.21 × 0.10 = R0.921	R10.05 × 0.10 = R1.005
Residual income per share	R3.28 − R0.76 = R2.52	R3.15 − R0.842 = R2.31	R2.90 − 0.921 = R1.98	[0.26 × R10.05] − R1.005 = R1.608

ROE = Earnings/Book value

Growth rate = ROE × Retention rate

Retention rate = 1 − (Dividends/Earnings)

Book value$_t$ = Book value$_{t-1}$ + Earnings$_{t-1}$ − Dividends$_{t-1}$

Residual income per share = EPS − Equity charge per share

Equity charge per share = Book value per share$_t$ × Cost of equity

Using the residual income per share for 2015 of R1.608, the second step is to calculate the present value of the terminal value:

$$\text{PV of Terminal Value} = \frac{R1.608}{(1 + 0.10 - 0.70)(1.10)^3} = R3.0203$$

Then, intrinsic value per share is:

$$V_0 = R7.60 + \frac{R2.52}{(1.10)} + \frac{R2.31}{(1.10)^2} + \frac{R1.98}{(1.10)^3} + R3.0203 = R16.31$$

16. A is correct. The multistage residual income model results in an intrinsic value of R13.29. The multistage residual income model, is:

$$V_0 = B_0 + \sum_{t=1}^{T} \frac{(E_t - rB_{t-1})}{(1+r)^t} + \frac{(P_T - B_T)}{(1+r)^T}$$

The first step is to calculate residual income per share for years 2022–2024:

	2022	**2023**	**2024**
Beginning book value per share	R7.60 (given)	R7.60 + R3.28 − R2.46 = R8.42	R8.42 + R3.15 − R2.36 = R9.21
ROE	R3.28/R7.60 = 0.4316	R3.15/R8.42 = 0.3741	R2.90/R9.21 = 0.3149
Retention rate	1 − (R2.46/R3.28) = 0.25	1 − (R2.36/R3.15) = 0.2508	1 − (R2.06/R2.90) = 0.2897
Growth rate	0.4316 × 0.25=0.1079	0.3741 × 0.2508 = 0.0938	0.3149 × 0.2897= 0.0912
Equity charge per share	R7.60 × 0.10 = R0.76	R8.42 × 0.10 = R0.842	R9.21 × 0.10 = R0.921
Residual income per share	R3.28 − R0.76 = R2.52	R3.15 − R0.842 = R2.31	R2.90 − 0.921= R1.98

ROE = Earnings/Book value

Growth rate = ROE × Retention rate

Retention rate = 1 − (Dividends/Earnings)

Book value$_t$ = Book value$_{t-1}$ + Earnings$_{t-1}$ − Dividends$_{t-1}$

Residual income per share = EPS − Equity charge per share

Equity charge per share = Book value per share$_t$ × Cost of equity

Under Scenario 2, at the end of 2024, it is assumed that share price will be equal to book value per share. This results in the second term in the equation above, the present value of the terminal value, being equal to zero.

Then, intrinsic value per share is:

$$V_0 = R7.60 + \frac{R2.52}{(1.10)} + \frac{R2.31}{(1.10)^2} + \frac{R1.98}{(1.10)^3} = R13.29$$

17. B is correct. The residual income model's use of accounting income assumes that the cost of debt capital is reflected appropriately by interest expense.

18. A is correct. Dividend payments are forecasted to be unpredictable over Castovan's five-year forecast horizon. A residual income model is appropriate when a company does not pay dividends or when its dividends are not predictable, which is the case for PTU.

19. C is correct. Other comprehensive income bypasses the income statement and goes directly to the statement of stockholders' equity (which is a violation of the clean surplus relationship). Therefore, book value per share for PTU will be affected by forecasted OCI.

20. C is correct. The residual income can be calculated using net income and the equity charge or using net operating profit after taxes and the total capital charge.

Residual income = Net income − Equity charge

Calculation of Net Income (values in millions):

EBIT	€700.0	
Less Interest expense	€124.8	(= €4,000 × 0.60 × 0.052)
Pretax income	€575.2	
Less Income tax expense	€201.3	(= €575.20 × 0.35)
Net income	€373.9	

Equity charge = Total assets × Equity weighting × Cost of equity

Equity charge = €4,000 million × 0.40 × 0.15 = €240 million

Therefore, residual income = €373.9 million − €240 million = €133.9 million. Alternatively, residual income can be calculated from NOPAT as follows.

Residual income = NOPAT − Total capital charge

NOPAT = EBIT × (1 − Tax rate)

NOPAT = €700 million × (1 − 0.35) = €455 million

The total capital charge is as follows.

Equity charge = Total assets × Equity weighting × Cost of equity

= €4,000 million × 0.40 × 0.15

= €240 million

Debt charge = Total assets × Debt weighting × Pretax cost of debt × (1 − Tax rate)

= €4,000 million × 0.60 × 0.052(1 − 0.35)

= €81.1 million

Total capital charge = €240 million + €81.1 million

= €321.1 million

Therefore, residual income = €455 million − €321.1 million = €133.9 million.

21. B is correct. The implied growth rate of earnings from the single-stage RI model is calculated by solving for g in the following equation:

$$V_0 = B_0 + \left(\frac{\text{ROE} - r}{r - g}\right) B_0$$

Book value per share can be calculated using the given price-to-book ratio and market price per share as follows.

Book value per share (B_0) = Market price per share/Price-to-book ratio

= €48.80/2.10 = €23.24

Then, solve for the implied growth rate.

$$€48.80 = €23.24 + \left(\frac{0.2337 - 0.15}{0.15 - g}\right) €23.24$$

$$g = 7.4\%$$

22. C is correct. Using the single-stage RI model, the intrinsic value of TTCI is calculated as

$$V_0 = B_0 + \left(\frac{\text{ROE} - r}{r - g}\right) B_0$$

$$= €45.25 + \left(\frac{0.12 - 0.087}{0.087 - 0.045}\right) €45.25$$

$$= €80.80$$

The intrinsic value of €80.80 is less than the market price of €126.05, so Castovan should conclude that the stock is overvalued.

23. A is correct. The justified price-to-book ratio is calculated as

$$\frac{P}{B} = 1 + \left(\frac{ROE - r}{r - g}\right)$$

$$= 1 + \left(\frac{0.12 - 0.087}{0.087 - 0.045}\right) = 1.79$$

24. C is correct. Residual income per share for the next three years is calculated as follows.

	Year 1	Year 2	Year 3
Beginning book value per share	45.25	51.61	58.25
Earnings per share	7.82	8.17	8.54
Less dividends per share	1.46	1.53	1.59
Change in retained earnings	6.36	6.64	6.95
Ending book value per share	51.61	58.25	65.20
Earnings per share	7.82	8.17	8.54
Less per share equity charge*	3.94	4.49	5.07
Residual income	3.88	3.68	3.47

*Per share equity charge = Beginning book value per share × Cost of equity
Year 1 per share equity charge = 45.25 × 0.087 = 3.94
Year 2 per share equity charge = 51.61 × 0.087 = 4.49
Year 3 per share equity charge = 58.25 × 0.087 = 5.07

Because Castovan forecasts that residual income per share will be constant into perpetuity, equal to Year 3 residual income per share, the present value of the terminal value is calculated using a persistence factor of 1.

$$\text{Present value of terminal value} = \frac{8.54 - (0.087 \times 58.25)}{(1 + 0.087 - 1)(1 + 0.087)^2}$$

$$= \frac{3.47}{(0.087)(1.087)^2}$$

$$= 33.78$$

So, the intrinsic value of TTCI is then calculated as follows.

$$V_0 = €45.25 + \frac{3.88}{1.087} + \frac{3.68}{1.087^2} + 33.78 = €85.71$$

25. A is correct. In Castovan's multistage valuation, she assumes that TTCI's residual income will remain constant in perpetuity after Year 3. This perpetuity assumption implies a persistence factor of 1 in the calculation of the terminal value. A persistence factor of 0.10 indicates that TTCI's residual income is forecasted to decline at an average rate of 90% per year. This assumption would lead to a lower valuation than Castovan's multistage value estimate, which assumes that residual income will remain constant in perpetuity after Year 3.

26. B is correct. Beckworth's suggested persistence factor for TTCI is 0.10, which is quite low. Companies with extreme accounting rates of return typically have low persistence factors. Companies with strong market leadership positions and low dividend payouts are likely to have high persistence factors.

27. According to the residual income model, the intrinsic value of a share of common stock equals book value per share plus the present value of expected future per-share residual income. Book value per share was given as $20. If we note that debt is $2,000,000 [(2/3)($3,000,000)] so that interest is $120,000 ($2,000,000 × 6%), VIM's residual income is $8,000, which is calculated (as in Problem 1) as

follows:

Residual income = Net income − Equity charge

= [(EBIT − Interest)(1 − Tax rate)] − [(Equity capital)(Required return on equity)]

= [($300,000 − $120,000)(1 − 0.40)] − [($1,000,000)(0.10)]

= $108,000 − $100,000

= $8,000

Therefore, residual income per share is $0.16 per share ($8,000/50,000 shares). Because EBIT is expected to continue at the current level indefinitely, the expected per-share residual income of $0.16 is treated as a perpetuity. The present value of $0.16 is discounted at the required return on equity of 10%, so the present value of the residual income is $1.60 ($0.16/0.10).

Intrinsic value = Book value per share +
PV of expected future income per-share residual income

= $20 + $1.60 = $21.60

28. With $g = b \times \text{ROE} = (1 − 0.80)(0.15) = (0.20)(0.15) = 0.03$,

P/B = (ROE − g)/(r − g)

= (0.15 − 0.03)/(0.12 − 0.03)

= 0.12/0.09 = 1.33

or

P/B = 1 + (ROE − r)/(r − g)

= 1 + (0.15 − 0.12)/(0.12 − 0.03)

= 1.33

29. Because the dividend is a perpetuity, the no-growth form of the DDM is applied as follows:

$V_0 = D/r$

= $0.60/0.12 = $5 per share

30. According to the residual income model, V_0 = Book value per share + Present value of expected future per-share residual income.
Residual income is calculated as:

$\text{RI}_t = E − rB_{t-1}$

= $0.60 − (0.12)($6) = −$0.12

Present value of perpetual stream of residual income is calculated as:

$\text{RI}_t/r = −$0.12/0.12 = −1.00

The value is calculated as:

$V_0 = $6.00 − $1.00 = $5.00 per share

31. According to the DDM, $V_0 = D/r$ for a no-growth company.

$V_0 = \$2.00/0.125 = \$16$ per share

32. Under the residual income model, $V_0 = B_0 +$ Present value of expected future per-share residual income.

   Residual income is calculated as:

   $RI_t = E - rB_{t-1}$

   $= \$2 - (0.125)(\$10) = \$0.75$

   Present value of stream of residual income is calculated as:

   $RI_t/r = 0.75/0.125 = \$6$

   The value is calculated as:

   $V_0 = \$10 + \$6 = \$16$ per share

33. $V_0 =$ Present value of the future dividends

   $= \$2/1.10 + \$2.50/(1.1)^2 + \$20.50/(1.1)^3$

   $= \$1.818 + \$2.066 + \$15.402 = \$19.286$

34. The book values and residual incomes for the next three years are as follows:

Year	1	2	3
Beginning book value	$ 8.00	$10.00	$12.50
Retained earnings (Net income – Dividends)	2.00	2.50	(12.50)
Ending book value	$10.00	$12.50	$ 0.00
Net income	$ 4.00	$ 5.00	$ 8.00
Less equity charge ($r \times$ Book value)	0.80	1.00	1.25
Residual income	$ 3.20	$ 4.00	$ 6.75

   Under the residual income model,

   $V_0 = B_0 +$ Present value of expected future per-share residual income

   $V_0 = \$8.00 + \$3.20/1.1 + \$4.00/(1.1)^2 + \$6.75/(1.1)^3$

   $V_0 = 8.00 + \$2.909 + \$3.306 + \$5.071 = \$19.286$

35.

Year	1	2	3
Net income (NI)	$4.00	$5.00	$8.00
Beginning book value (BV)	8.00	10.00	12.50
Return on equity (ROE) = NI/BV	50%	50%	64%
ROE – r	40%	40%	54%

Year	1	2	3
Residual income (ROE − r) × BV	$3.20	$4.00	$6.75

Under the residual income model,

$V_0 = B_0$ + Present value of expected future per-share residual income

$V_0 = \$8.00 + \$3.20/1.1 + \$4.00/(1.1)^2 + \$6.75/(1.1)^3$

$V_0 = 8.00 + \$2.909 + \$3.306 + \$5.071 = \$19.286$

36.

Year	2018	2019	2022
Beginning book value	$30.00	$33.00	$43.92
Net income = ROE × Book value	4.50	4.95	6.59
Dividends = payout × Net income	1.50	1.65	2.20
Equity charge (r × Book value)	3.60	3.96	5.27
Residual income = Net income − Equity charge	0.90	0.99	1.32
Ending book value	$33.00	$36.30	$48.32

The table shows that residual income in Year 2018 is $0.90, which equals Beginning book value × (ROE − r) = $30 × (0.15 − 0.12). The Year 2019 column shows that residual income grew by 10% to $0.99, which follows from the fact that growth in residual income relates directly to the growth in net income as this example is configured. When both net income and dividends are a function of book value and return on equity is constant, then growth, g, can be predicted from (ROE)(1 − Dividend payout ratio). In this case, g = 0.15 × (1 − 0.333) = 0.10 or 10%. Net income and residual income will grow by 10% annually.

Therefore, residual income in Year 2022 = (Residual income in Year 2018) × (1.1)^4 = 0.90 × 1.4641 = $1.32.

37. The justified P/B can be found with the following formula:

$$\frac{P_0}{B_0} = 1 + \frac{ROE - r}{r - g}$$

ROE is 20%, g is 5.5%, and r is 8.2% $[R_F + \beta_i[E(R_M) - RF] = 4.46\% + (0.68)(5.5\%)]$. Substituting in the values gives a justified P/B of

$$\frac{P_0}{B_0} = 1 + \frac{0.20 - 0.082}{0.082 - 0.055} = 4.37$$

The assumed parameters give a justified P/B of 4.37, slightly above the current P/B of 3.68.

38. To find the ROE that would result in a P/B of 3.68, we substitute 3.68, r, and g into the following equation:

$$\frac{P_0}{B_0} = 1 + \frac{ROE - r}{r - g}$$

This yields

$$3.68 = 1 + \frac{ROE - 0.082}{0.082 - 0.055}$$

Solving for ROE requires several steps to finally derive a ROE of 0.15435 or 15.4%. This value of ROE is consistent with a P/B of 3.68.

39. To find the growth rate that would result with a P/B of 3.68, use the expression given in Part B, but solve for g instead of ROE:

$$\frac{P_0}{B_0} = 1 + \frac{ROE - r}{r - g}$$

Substituting in the values gives:

$$3.68 = 1 + \frac{0.20 - 0.082}{0.082 - g}$$

The growth rate g is 0.03797, or 3.8%. If we assume that the single-stage growth model is applicable to Thales, the current P/B and current market price can be justified with values for ROE or g that are quite a bit lower than the starting values of 20% and 5.5%, respectively.

40. $V_0 = B_0 + (ROE - r)B_0/(r - g)$

= \$20 + (0.18 − 0.14) (\$20) / (0.14 − 0.10)

= \$20 + \$20 = \$40

Given that the current market price is \$35 and the estimated value is \$40, Simms will probably conclude that the shares are somewhat undervalued.

41. $V_0 = B_0 + (ROE - r)B_0/(r - g)$

= \$30 + (0.15 − 0.12) (\$30) / (0.12 − 0.10)

= \$30 + \$45 = \$75 per share

42.

Year	Net Income (Projected)	Ending Book Value	ROE (%)	Equity Charge (in Currency)	Residual Income	PV of RI
2020		\$10.00				
2021	\$1.50	11.50	15	\$1.00	\$0.50	\$0.45
2022	1.73	13.23	15	1.15	0.58	0.48
2023	1.99	15.22	15	1.32	0.67	0.50
2024	2.29	17.51	15	1.52	0.77	0.53
2025	2.63	20.14	15	1.75	0.88	0.55
						\$2.51

Using the finite horizon form of residual income valuation,

$V_0 = B_0 +$ Sum of discounted RIs + Premium (also discounted to present)

= \$10 + \$2.51 + (0.20)(20.14)/(1.10)^5

= \$10 + \$2.51 + \$2.50 = \$15.01

43. Columns (a) through (d) in the table show calculations for beginning book value, net income, dividends, and ending book value.

	(a)	(b)	(c)	(d)	(e)	(f)
Year	Beginning Book Value	Net Income	Dividends	Ending Book Value	Residual Income	PV of RI
1	\$21.300	\$3.834	\$2.684	\$22.450	\$2.748	\$2.614
2	22.450	4.041	2.829	23.663	2.896	2.622
3	23.663	4.259	2.981	24.940	3.052	2.629

Year	(a) Beginning Book Value	(b) Net Income	(c) Dividends	(d) Ending Book Value	(e) Residual Income	(f) PV of RI
4	24.940	4.489	3.142	26.287	3.217	2.637
5	26.287	4.732	3.312	27.707	3.391	2.644
6	27.707	4.987	3.491	29.203	3.574	2.652
7	29.203	5.256	3.680	30.780	3.767	2.659
8	30.780	5.540	3.878	32.442	3.971	2.667
Total						$21.125

For each year, net income is 18% of beginning book value. Dividends are 70% of net income. The ending book value equals the beginning book value plus net income minus dividends.

44. Column (e) of the table in Part A shows Residual income, which equals Net income − Cost of equity (%) × Beginning book value.

To find the cost of equity, use the CAPM:

$$r = R_F + \beta_i[E(R_M) - R_F] = 2\% + (0.50)(6.2\%) = 5.1\%$$

For Year 1 in the table,

$$\text{Residual income} = \text{RI}_t = E - rB_{t-1}$$

$$= 3.834 - (5.1\%)(21.30)$$

$$= 3.834 - 1.086 = \$2.748$$

This same calculation is repeated for Years 2 through 8.

Column (f) of the table gives the present value of the calculated residual income, discounted at 5.1%.

45. To find the stock value with the residual income method, use this equation:

$$V_0 = B_0 + \sum_{t=1}^{T} \frac{(E_t - rB_{t-1})}{(1 + r)^t} + \frac{P_T - B_T}{(1 + r)^T}$$

- In this equation, B_0 is the current book value per share of $21.30.
- The second term, the sum of the present values of the eight years' residual income is shown in the table, $21.125.
- To estimate the final term, the present value of the excess of the terminal stock price over the terminal book value, use the assumption that the terminal stock price is assumed to be 4.0× the terminal book value. So, by assumption, the terminal stock price is $129.767 [$P_T = 4.0(32.442)$]. $P_T - B_T$ is $97.325 (129.767 − 32.442), and the present value of this amount discounted at 5.1% for eight years is $65.374.
- Summing the relevant terms gives a stock price of $107.799 ($V_0 = 21.30 + 21.125 + 65.374$).

46. The appropriate DDM expression expresses the value of the stock as the sum of the present value of the dividends plus the present value of the terminal value:

$$V_0 = \sum_{t=1}^{T}\frac{D_t}{(1+r)^t}+\frac{P_T}{(1+r)^T}$$

Discounting the dividends from the table shown in the solution to Part A above at 8.30% gives:

Year	Dividend	PV of Dividend
1	$2.684	2.554
2	2.829	2.561
3	2.981	2.568
4	3.142	2.575
5	3.312	2.583
6	3.491	2.590
7	3.680	2.598
8	3.878	2.605
All		$20.634

- The present value of the eight dividends is $20.634. The estimated terminal stock price, calculated in the solution to Part C above is $125.767, which equals $87.165 discounted at 5.1% for eight years.

- The value for the stock, the present value of the dividends plus the present value of the terminal stock price, is $V_0 = 20.634 + 87.165 = \$107.799$.

- The stock values estimated with the residual income model and the dividend discount model are identical. Because they are based on similar financial assumptions, this equivalency is expected. Even though the two models differ in their timing of the recognition of value, their final results are the same.

47.

A. The value found with the residual income model is:

Year	Beginning BV	Net Income	Dividends	Ending BV	Residual Income	PV of Residual Income
1	20.00	1.50	1.00	20.50	−0.300	−0.275
2	20.50	2.50	1.00	22.00	0.655	0.551
3	22.00	3.50	1.00	24.50	1.520	1.174
4	24.50	4.50	2.00	27.00	2.295	1.626
5	27.00	5.50	2.00	30.50	3.070	1.995
			Sum PVRI			5.071
			Terminal $P_T - B_T$		46.500	
			PV of $P_T - B_T$			30.222
			B_0			20.000
			Total value:			€55.293

Residual income each year is Net income − 0.09 × (Beginning BV). The PV of residual income is found by discounting at 9%. The terminal price is 14 × EPS in Year 5, or 14 × 5.50 = €77.00. The terminal residual value is $P_T - B_T$

= 77.00 − 30.50 = €46.50. Discounted at 9%, the PV of €46.50 is €30.222. The value per share is B_0 + PV of residual income + PV of terminal residual value, which is €55.293.

B. The value found with the dividend discount model is as follows:

Year	Dividend or Price	PV of Dividend or Price
1	1.00	0.917
2	1.00	0.842
3	1.00	0.772
4	2.00	1.417
5	2.00	1.300
5	77.00	50.045
Total PV		€55.293

The values per share found with the DDM and the residual income model are an identical €55.293.

48. When such items as changes in the value of available-for-sale securities bypass the income statement, they are generally assumed to be nonoperating items that will fluctuate from year to year, although averaging to zero in a period of years. The evidence suggests, however, that changes in the value of available-for-sale securities are not averaging to zero but are persistently negative. Furthermore, these losses are bypassing the income statement. It appears that the company is either making an inaccurate assumption or misleading investors in one way or another. Accordingly, Kent might adjust LE's income downward by the amount of loss for other comprehensive income for each of those years. ROE would then decline commensurately. LE's book value would *not* be misstated because the decline in the value of these securities was already recognized and appears in the shareholders' equity account "Accumulated Other Comprehensive Income."

4

Private Company Valuation

by Raymond D. Rath, ASA, CEIV, CFA.

Raymond D. Rath, ASA, CEIV, CFA, is at Globalview Advisors LLC (USA).

LEARNING OUTCOMES

Mastery	The candidate should be able to:
☐	compare public and private company valuation
☐	describe uses of private business valuation and explain applications of greatest concern to financial analysts
☐	explain cash flow estimation issues related to private companies and adjustments required to estimate normalized earnings
☐	explain the income, market, and asset-based approaches to private company valuation and factors relevant to the selection of each approach
☐	explain factors that require adjustment when estimating the discount rate for private companies
☐	compare models used to estimate the required rate of return to private company equity (for example, the CAPM, the expanded CAPM, and the build-up approach)
☐	calculate the value of a private company using free cash flow, capitalized cash flow, and/or excess earnings methods
☐	calculate the value of a private company based on market approach methods and describe advantages and disadvantages of each method
☐	describe the asset-based approach to private company valuation
☐	explain and evaluate the effects on private company valuations of discounts and premiums based on control and marketability

1   INTRODUCTION

☐   compare public and private company valuation

☐   describe uses of private business valuation and explain applications of greatest concern to financial analysts

The valuation of the equity of private companies is a major field of application for equity valuation. Private companies are those whose shares are not listed on public markets. Generalist investment practitioners need to be familiar with issues associated with valuations of such companies. We use the terms "valuation" and "appraisal" interchangeably in this chapter.

Many public companies have start-up or other operations that can best be valued as if they were private companies. Companies may grow through the acquisition of competitors, including private companies, and analysts must be prepared to evaluate the price paid in such transactions. Furthermore, acquisitions often result in significant balances of intangible assets, including goodwill, that are reported on the balance sheets of acquiring companies. Goodwill balances require impairment assessment or formal testing on an annual basis under International Financial Reporting Standards (IFRS) and US GAAP. Impairment testing and other financial reporting initiatives increasingly result in the use of fair value estimates in financial statements. The concepts and methods we will discuss play important roles in this aspect of financial reporting. In addition, issues relating to private company valuation arise in the types of investment held by venture capital and other types of private equity funds.

The following sections illustrate key elements associated with the valuation of private companies and provide background for understanding private company valuation, including typical contrasts between public and private companies and the major purposes for which private valuations are performed. Later sections discuss earnings normalization and cash flow estimation; introduce the three major approaches recognized in private company valuation, valuation discounts, and premiums; and explain business valuation standards and practices.

The Scope of Private Company Valuation

Private companies range from single-employee, unincorporated businesses to formerly public companies that have been taken private in management buyouts or other transactions. Numerous large, successful companies also exist that have remained private since inception, such as IKEA and Bosch in Europe, Cargill and Bechtel in the United States, Alibaba in China, and Toyota in Japan. The diverse characteristics of private companies and the absence of a universally recognized body providing guidance on valuation methods and assumptions have contributed to the development of diverse valuation practices.

Private and Public Company Valuation: Similarities and Contrasts

We can gain some insight into the challenges of private company valuation by examining company- and stock-specific factors that mark key differences between private and public companies.

Company-Specific Factors

Company-specific factors characterize the company itself, including its life-cycle stage, size, markets, and the goals and characteristics of management.

- *Stage in life cycle.* Private companies include companies at the earliest stages of development, whereas public companies are typically further advanced in their life cycle. Private companies may have minimal capital, assets, or employees. Private companies, however, also include large, stable, going concerns and failed companies in the process of liquidation. The stage of life cycle influences the valuation process for a company.

- *Size.* Relative size—whether based on income statement, balance sheet, or other measures—frequently distinguishes public and private companies; private companies in a given line of business tend to be smaller than public ones. Size has implications for the level of risk and, hence, relative valuation. Small size typically increases risk levels, and risk premiums for small size have often been applied in estimating required rates of return for private companies. For some private companies, small size may reduce growth prospects by reducing access to capital to fund growth of operations. The public equity markets are generally the best source for such funding. Conversely, for small companies, the costs of operating as a public company including compliance costs may outweigh any financing benefits.

- *Overlap of shareholders and management.* For many private companies, and in contrast to most public companies, top management has a controlling ownership interest. Therefore, they may not face the same pressure from external investors as public companies. **Agency issues**, such as monitoring costs arising from potentially conflicting interests of owners (principals) and managers (agents), may also be mitigated in private companies. For that reason, private company management may be able to take a longer-term perspective in decisions than public company management.

- *Quality/depth of management.* A small private company, especially if it has limited growth potential, would be expected to be less attractive to management candidates and have less management depth than a typical public company. The smaller scale of operation might also lead to less management depth compared with a public company. To the extent these considerations apply, they may increase risk and reduce growth prospects for the private company.

- *Quality of financial and other information.* Compared with the levels of disclosure by public companies, the more limited availability of financial and other information for private companies results in an increased burden for the prospective investor considering an equity investment or loan. This type of information difference presumably leads to greater uncertainty and, hence, risk. All else equal, the higher risk should lead to a relatively lower valuation. Note, however, that in certain private company valuations, such as fairness opinions prepared in the context of an acquisition, the analyst usually has unlimited access to books, records, contracts, and other information that would be unavailable to the public stock analyst.

- *Pressure from short-term investors.* Earnings consistency and growth rates are often perceived as critical to the stock price performance of public companies. Continued management employment and levels of incentive compensation are often linked to stock price performance, but many investors' interests may be of a trading or short-term nature. As a result, management may be motivated to try to support share price in the short term.

According to some observers, private companies typically do not experience similar stock price performance pressure and such companies can take a longer-term investment focus.

- *Tax concerns.* Reduction of reported taxable income and corporate tax payments may be a more important goal for private companies than for public companies because of greater benefit to the owners.

Stock-Specific Factors

In addition to company-specific factors, the characteristics of the stock of private companies frequently differ markedly from that of public companies.

- *Liquidity of equity interests in business.* Stock in private companies is generally much less liquid than otherwise similar interests in public companies. Private companies typically have fewer shareholders. Shares of a private company have not been registered for sale in the public stock markets. The limited number of existing and potential buyers reduces the value of the shares in private companies.

- *Concentration of control.* Control of private companies is often concentrated in one or in very few investors. This concentration of control may lead to actions by a corporation that benefit some shareholders at the expense of other shareholders. Transactions with entities related to a controlling group at above-market prices would transfer value away from the corporation's non-controlling shareholders. Above-market compensation to a controlling shareholder is a typical perquisite. Please note that the "concentration of control" factor can also be viewed as a "company-specific" factor.

- *Potential agreements restricting liquidity.* Private companies may have shareholder agreements in place that restrict the ability to sell shares. These agreements may reduce the marketability of equity interests.

Generally, stock-specific factors are a negative for private company valuation, whereas company-specific factors are potentially positive or negative. The range of differences observed in private companies is such that the spectrum of risk and, therefore, the spectrum of return requirements are typically wider than for public companies. Another consequence is that the range of valuation methods and assumptions applied to private companies is typically more varied.

Reasons for Performing Valuations

Valuations of private businesses or equity interests therein fall into three groups: transaction related, compliance related, and litigation related.

Transactions encompass events affecting the ownership or financing of a business and represent a primary area of private company valuation. A variety of transaction types exist.

- *Private financing.* Raising capital is critical to development-stage companies. To reduce risk and maintain influence, **venture capital investors** (as equity investors in such companies are known) typically invest through multiple rounds of financing tied to the achievement of key developments ("milestones"). A high level of uncertainty concerning expected future cash flows results in valuations that are often informal and based on negotiations between the company and investors.

- *Initial public offering (IPO).* An IPO is one liquidity option for a private company. Investment banking firms prepare valuations as part of the IPO process. A key element of an IPO-related valuation is frequently the identification of any public companies that are similar to the one going public.

- *Acquisition.* Acquisition can be an attractive option for development-stage or mature companies. Acquisition related valuations may be performed (and negotiated) by management of the target and/or buyer. Smaller companies may be sold with the assistance of a business broker. The sale of many larger companies is handled by investment banking firms.

- *Bankruptcy.* For companies operating under bankruptcy protection, valuations of the business and its underlying assets may help assess whether a company is more valuable as a going concern or in liquidation. For viable going concerns operating in bankruptcy, insights from valuation may be critical to the restructuring of an overleveraged capital structure.

- *Share-based payment (compensation).* Share-based payments can be viewed as transactions between a company and its employees. These transactions often have accounting and tax implications to the issuer and the employee. Share-based payments can include stock option grants, restricted stock grants, and transactions involving an employee stock ownership plan (ESOP) in the United States and equivalent structures in other countries. Providing an incentive for improved employee performance is an important goal of such compensation mechanisms.

Compliance encompasses actions required by law or regulation. Compliance valuations are a second key area of valuation practice. Financial reporting and tax reporting are the two primary focuses of this type of valuation.

- *Financial reporting.* Financial reporting valuations are increasing in importance. Goodwill impairment is one of the most frequent financial reporting valuations that a securities analyst might observe. Goodwill impairment tests require a business valuation for a **cash-generating unit** (defined in IFRS as "the smallest identifiable group of assets that generates cash inflows that are largely independent of the cash inflows of other assets or groups of assets") of an entity or a **reporting unit** (defined in US GAAP as an operating segment or one level below an operating segment, called a component, that constitutes a business for which discrete financial information is available and for which segment management regularly reviews the operating results of that component). Essentially, components of public companies are valued using private company valuation techniques. For private companies, stock option grants will frequently require valuations.

- *Tax reporting.* Tax reporting is a longstanding area that requires valuations of private companies. Tax-related reasons for valuations include corporate and individual tax reporting. A variety of corporate activities, such as corporate restructurings, transfer pricing, and property tax matters, may require valuations. An individual's tax requirements, such as those arising from estate and gift taxation in some jurisdictions, may generate a need for private company valuations.

Litigation—legal proceedings including those related to damages, lost profits, shareholder disputes, and divorce—often requires valuations. Litigation may affect public or private companies or may be between shareholders with no effect at the corporate level.

As the foregoing descriptions make clear, each of the three major practice areas requires specialized knowledge and skills. This fact has led many valuation professionals to focus their efforts in one of these areas. Transactions, for example, often involve investment bankers. Compliance valuations are best performed by valuation professionals with knowledge of the relevant accounting or tax regulations. Litigation-related valuations require effective presentations in a legal setting.

Having provided an overview of the field of private company valuation, we can proceed to discussing how valuations are done. Logically, before developing an estimate of value, the valuator must understand the context of the valuation and its requirements. An important element in that process is knowing the definition(s) of value that the valuation must address, which we cover in the next section.

2   PRIVATE COMPANY VALUATION APPROACHES

☐ explain cash flow estimation issues related to private companies and adjustments required to estimate normalized earnings

Private company valuation experts distinguish three major approaches to valuation.

- The **income approach** values an asset as the present discounted value of the income expected from it. The income approach has several variations depending on the assumptions the valuator makes.
- The **market approach** values an asset based on pricing multiples from sales of assets viewed as similar to the subject asset. ("Pricing multiples" may refer to multiples based on share price or multiples based on a measure of total company value.)
- The **asset-based approach** values a private company based on the values of its underlying assets less the value of any related liabilities.

Valuation approaches for private companies are conceptually similar to those used for public companies, although the labels used for them by experts in each field and the details of application may differ. The income approach corresponds to what public equity analysts call discounted cash flow models or present value models. Along with asset-based models, discounted cash flow models are classified as absolute valuation models. By contrast, analysts use a relative valuation model when they apply a market-based approach in evaluating price and enterprise multiples relative to the value of a comparable.

Analysts select approach(es) depending on specific factors. The nature of operations and stage in life cycle are important considerations. For a development-stage company with the potential to operate as a successful large public company, the valuation methods may change over time. At the earliest stages of development, the company may best be valued using an asset-based approach because the going-concern **premise of value** may be uncertain and/or future cash flows may be extremely difficult to predict. With progress to a development-stage company in a high-growth mode, the company might be valued using a free cash flow method, which in private business appraisal is known as an income approach. A stable, mature company might be best valued on the basis of the market approach. Specific facts and circumstances may suggest different valuation methods.

Size is an important criterion in assessing valuation approaches and valuation methods. Multiples from public companies may be inappropriate for a small, relatively mature private company with very limited growth prospects. Comparisons to public companies are not a good basis of valuation for a private company if risk and growth prospects differ materially.

Public and private companies may consist of a variety of operating and non-operating assets. Non-operating assets are defined as assets not necessary to the ongoing operations of the business enterprise. Excess cash and investment balances are typical examples of non-operating assets. In principle, the value of a company is the sum of the value of operating assets and the value of non-operating assets. Thus, non-operating assets should be included in the valuation of an enterprise regardless of the valuation approach or method being used.

Before we illustrate the application of the three approaches to valuation, we need to address certain typical issues relating to valuation model inputs that arise when valuing private companies.

Earnings Normalization and Cash Flow Estimation Issues

The next two sections cover earnings normalization and cash flow estimation in the context of private company valuation. Potential acquirers of private companies may find that current earnings reflect inefficiencies or redundancies that detract from their relevance as a baseline for forecasting future earnings under new ownership. In such cases, the earnings should be adjusted or "normalized" to a basis that is relevant for forecasting future results, given that the company is acquired. Essentially, the valuator is seeking to understand accurately the earnings and cash flow capacity of the business enterprise if it is acquired and run efficiently.

Earnings Normalization Issues for Private Companies

Private company valuations may require significant adjustments to estimate the company's normalized earnings. As defined in the International Glossary of Business Valuation Terms (IGBVT, developed through joint efforts of several North American accountancy and appraisal bodies to explain frequently used terms), **normalized earnings** are "economic benefits adjusted for non-recurring, non-economic, or other unusual items to eliminate anomalies and/or facilitate comparisons." (Note that the term "normalized earnings" can also refer to earnings adjusted for the effects of a business cycle.) As a result of the concentration of control in many private businesses, reported earnings may reflect discretionary expenses or expenses that are not at arm's-length amounts. Tax and other motivations may also result in reporting earnings that may differ from the normalized earnings of a private company. The smaller size of many private companies potentially increases the relative impact of discretionary expenses on company value.

When comparing the reported earnings of private companies with those of public companies, a key area of difference is the possible effect of transactions between the company and owners working in the business or with entities controlled by controlling shareholders. Many adjustments required to normalize earnings involve items that reduce the reported earnings of a profitable, private company. The controlling or sole shareholder is often active in the business and controls the board of directors as well as all policy and operating decisions. Above-market compensation or other expenses will reduce taxable income and income tax expense at the corporate level and subsequent taxes upon the payment of dividends to the controlling shareholder and other shareholders. Above-market expenses can also result in the controlling shareholder receiving a disproportionately high return in relation to other shareholders.

Compensation expense is a key area requiring possible adjustment. Profitable, private companies may report compensation expense to owner/employees above amounts that would be paid to a non-owner employee. Family members may also be included as employees and paid amounts above the market value of their services. For private companies with limited profits or reported losses, expenses may actually be understated with the reported income of the entity overstated. Owners active in the business may not take compensation commensurate with market levels required by an employee for similar activities.

A number of other areas exist for consideration for possible adjustments. Personal expenses may be included as expenses of the private company. Personal-use assets and excess entertainment expenses are areas for consideration. Personal residences, aircraft, and luxury or excessive use of corporate vehicles for personal use may require an adjustment. Life insurance and loans to shareholders merit review.

Real estate used by the private company is also an area for consideration. When a private company owns real estate, some analysts separate the real estate from the operating company. This separation consists of removing any revenues and expenses associated with the real estate from the income statement. If the company is using owned property in its business operations, adding a market rental charge for the use of the real estate to the expenses of the company would produce a more accurate estimate of the earnings of the business operations. Adjusting reported earnings to include a provision for third-party real estate costs would produce a value of the business operations excluding the owned real estate. Because the real estate is still owned by the entity, its value would represent a non-operating asset of the entity. These adjustments for the financial impact of owned real estate can be appropriate because the business operations and real estate have different risk levels and growth expectations.

Without these adjustments to eliminate the effect of owned real estate on reported financial performance, the private company may be incorrectly valued. Rent charges for the use of real estate include return "of" and "on" investment components. Depreciation reflects return "of" investment. If real property is owned, depreciation expense would reflect the historical acquisition cost rather than current replacement cost. For owned real estate, the return "on" component of the rental charge would not be included at a market level charge. Applying a capitalization rate for the business operations to an earnings figure that includes some of the benefit from the owned real estate may misvalue the private company. The business operations and real estate may have different levels of risk and expected future growth that require separate valuation. If real estate is leased to the private company by a related entity, the level of expense may require an adjustment to a market rental rate. If real estate is leased from an unrelated party but the rental charge is not at a market level, an adjustment to normalize this expense may also be appropriate.

Example 1 illustrates a case in which a prospective buyer of a private business would need to make adjustments to reported financial results for a more accurate picture of the company's normalized earnings and value under new ownership.

EXAMPLE 1

Able Manufacturing: Normalized Earnings Adjustments

John Smith is the sole shareholder and CEO of Able Manufacturing, Inc. Smith has put Able up for sale in advance of his retirement. James Duvall, a manager in the corporate venturing unit of a public company, is evaluating the purchase of Able. Duvall notes the following facts affecting the most recent fiscal year's reported results:

- Smith's compensation for the year was $1.5 million. Duvall's executive compensation consultant believes a normalized compensation expense of $500,000 for a CEO of a company like Able is appropriate. Compensation is included in selling, general, and administrative expenses (SG&A).

- Certain corporate assets including ranch property and a condominium are in Duvall's judgment not required for the company's core operations. Fiscal year expenses associated with the ranch and condominium were $400,000, including $300,000 of such operating expenses as property upkeep, property taxes, and insurance reflected in SG&A expenses, and depreciation expense of $100,000. All other asset balances (including cash) are believed to be at normal levels required to support current operations.

- Able's debt balance of $2,000,000 (interest rate of 7.5%) was lower than the optimal level of debt expected for the company. As reported interest expense did not reflect an optimal charge, Duvall believes the use of an earnings figure that excludes interest expense altogether, specifically operating income after taxes, will facilitate the assessment of Able.

Duvall uses the reported income statement to show the derivation of reported operating income after taxes, as given in the following table.

Able Manufacturing, Inc. Operating Income after Taxes	
As of 31 December 2020	**As Reported**
Revenues	$50,000,000
Cost of goods sold	30,000,000
Gross profit	20,000,000
Selling, general, and admin. expenses	5,000,000
EBITDA	15,000,000
Depreciation and amortization	1,000,000
Earnings before interest and taxes	14,000,000
Pro forma taxes (at 30.0%)	4,200,000
Operating income after taxes	$9,800,000

Based only on the information given, address the following:

1. Identify the adjustments that Duvall would make to reported financials to estimate normalized operating income after taxes—that is, what the operating income after taxes would have been under ownership by Duvall's unit.

Solution:

First, SG&A should be reduced by $1,500,000 – $500,000 = $1,000,000 to reflect the expected level of salary expense under professional management at a market rate of compensation. Second, the ranch and condominium are non-operating assets—they are not needed to generate revenues—so expense items should be adjusted to reflect their removal (e.g., through a sale). Two income statement lines are affected: SG&A expenses should be reduced by $300,000, and depreciation and amortization reduced by $100,000.

2. Based on your answer to Part 1, construct a pro forma statement of normalized operating income after taxes for Able.

Solution:

The pro forma statement of normalized operating income after taxes would be as follows:

Able Manufacturing, Inc. Pro Forma Normalized Operating Income after Taxes

As of 31 December 2020	Pro Forma
Revenues	$50,000,000
Cost of goods sold	30,000,000
Gross profit	20,000,000
Selling, general, and admin. expenses	3,700,000
EBITDA	16,300,000
Depreciation and amortization	900,000
Earnings before interest and taxes	15,400,000
Pro forma taxes (at 30.0%)	4,620,000
Operating income after taxes	$10,780,000

In addition to the various adjustments noted, a variety of other areas exist for possible adjustment that are similar for valuing both public and private companies (e.g., adjustments related to inventory accounting methods, depreciation assumptions, and capitalization versus expensing of various costs). Private companies may have their financial statements reviewed rather than audited. **Reviewed financial statements** provide an opinion letter with representations and assurances by the reviewing accountant that are less than those in audited financial statements. The preparation of reviewed rather than audited financial statements as well as other factors suggest a potentially greater need for analyst adjustments to the reported financials of some private companies. **Compiled financial statements** (that are not accompanied by an auditor's opinion letter) suggest an even greater need for analytical adjustments.

Cash Flow Estimation Issues for Private Companies

In addition to earnings normalization, cash flow estimation is an important element of the valuation process. Free cash flow (FCF) is the relevant concept of cash flow in this context. Free cash flow to the firm (FCFF) represents free cash flow at the business enterprise level and is used to value the firm or, indirectly, the firm's equity. Alternatively, free cash flow to equity (FCFE) can be used to value equity directly.

Cash flow estimation for private companies raises some important challenges, including those related to the nature of the interest being valued, potentially acute uncertainties regarding future operations, and managerial involvement in forecasting.

The nature of assumptions in cash flow estimates depends on a variety of factors. The equity interest appraised and the intended use of the appraisal are key in determining the appropriate definition of value for a specific valuation. The assumptions included in cash flow estimates may differ if a small minority equity interest is appraised rather than the total equity of a business. For example, an investment value standard may lead to different cash flow estimates than a fair value standard related to a financial reporting valuation assignment.

In assessing future cash flow estimates, uncertainty regarding a potentially wide range of future cash flow possibilities also creates challenges for valuation using FCF. Many development-stage companies and some mature companies are subject to significant uncertainties regarding future operations and cash flows. One possible solution involves projecting the different possible future scenarios. For a privately held development-stage company, the possible scenarios could include initial public offering, acquisition, continued operation as a private company, or bankruptcy. For a larger, mature company, the scenarios might be chosen to cover the range of possible levels of growth and profitability.

In valuing an individual scenario, the discount rate chosen should reflect the risk of achieving the projected cash flows in that scenario. The analyst must also estimate the probability of each scenario occurring. The overall value estimate for a company is then a probability-weighted average of the company's estimated scenario values. Alternatively, the expected future cash flows based on the scenarios could be discounted using a conventional, single discount rate to obtain an overall value estimate. Although the trend is generally to more robust models, in current practice private company valuation more frequently reflects an average or most likely scenario than an explicit multiple scenario analysis.

Managers of private companies generally command much more information about their business than outside analysts. Management may develop cash flow forecasts to be used in a valuation with appraiser input, or appraisers may develop their own forecasts consulting management as needed. The appraiser should be aware of potential managerial biases, such as to possibly overstate values in the case of goodwill impairment testing or understate values in the case of incentive stock option grants. Appraisers should also pay attention to whether projections adequately capture capital needs.

The actual process for estimating FCFF and FCFE is similar for private and public companies.

EXAMPLE 2

Able Manufacturing: Pro Forma Free Cash Flow to the Firm

Duvall, the manager of the corporate venturing unit introduced in Example 1, has decided to make a bid for Able Manufacturing. Duvall has decided to use an income approach to value Able. As stated in Example 1, Able's debt is $2,000,000. Considering the nature of Able's business, its size, and the financial leverage used by competitors, Duvall has concluded that Able has a low level of debt relative to its capacity and that it will be optimal to increase its debt if Duvall's unit succeeds in purchasing Able. Because of that anticipated change in leverage, Duvall has decided to use a FCFF approach rather than FCFE to value Able.

Based on available information, Duvall makes the following assumptions:

- Long-term growth of revenues is 3% annually.
- The gross profit margin will remain at 40%.
- Depreciation will remain at 1.8% of sales.
- SG&A expenses can be maintained at the prior year's level of $3,700,000 at least for two years.
- Working capital equal to 10% of revenues is required (e.g., if the increase in revenues is $X from the prior year, additional working capital of 0.10 × $X would be needed).
- Capital expenditures are expected to equal projected depreciation expense (to support current operations) plus 3% of incremental revenues (to support future growth).

1. Should Duvall use reported earnings or normalized earnings in estimating FCFF for Able? Explain.

Solution:

For the valuation of Able in a purchase transaction, the normalized earnings of Able should be used to estimate FCFF. Normalized earnings would more accurately reflect the income expected by a willing buyer of Able than reported earnings.

2. Forecast FCFF for Able for the upcoming year (from the perspective of a knowledgeable buyer).

Solution:

Duvall assumed long-term growth of 3% into the foreseeable future. With the $50 million revenue base from the prior year and the 3% annual revenue growth, a $1.5 million increase in revenues is forecast when moving from the last historical year to the year ahead. Given depreciation of $927,000 (1.8% of $51.5 million) and incremental sales of $1,500,000, forecast capital expenditure sums to $927,000 + 0.03($1,500,000) = $927,000 + $45,000 = $972,000. A requirement for incremental working capital of 10% of the increase in revenues equates to a $150,000 deduction in calculating free cash flow. Based on these assumptions, free cash flow to the firm of $10,986,100 was calculated as follows.

Able Manufacturing, Inc. Calculation of Next Year's Projected Free Cash Flow to Firm	
Revenues ($50,000,000 × 1.03 =)	$51,500,000
Cost of goods sold (0.60 × Revenues =)	30,900,000
Gross profit (Revenue − Cost of goods sold =)	20,600,000
SG&A expenses (maintained at 2020 level)	3,700,000
Pro forma EBITDA	16,900,000
Deprec. and amort. (0.018 × $51,500,000 =)	927,000
Pro forma earnings before interest and taxes	15,973,000
Pro forma taxes on EBIT (at 30.0%)	4,791,900
Operating income after tax	11,181,100
Plus: Depreciation and amortization	927,000
Less: Capital expenditures ($927,000 + 0.035 × $1,500,000)	972,000
Less: Increase in working capital (0.10 × ($51,500,000 − $50,000,000).	150,000
Free cash flow to firm	$10,986,100

INCOME APPROACH METHODS AND REQUIRED RATE OF RETURN

> ☐   explain the income, market, and asset-based approaches to private company valuation and factors relevant to the selection of each approach
>
> ☐   explain factors that require adjustment when estimating the discount rate for private companies
>
> ☐   compare models used to estimate the required rate of return to private company equity (for example, the CAPM, the expanded CAPM, and the build-up approach)

The income approach obtains its conceptual support from the assumption that value is based on expectations of future income and cash flows. The income approach converts future economic benefits into a present value equivalent. For IFRS and US GAAP, assets are defined as probable future economic benefits. This definition provides strong support for the application of the income approach to valuation of an interest in a public or private company. The income approach takes three main forms.

- **Free cash flow method**. This method is often referred to as the **discounted cash flow method** in the appraisal community. It values an asset based on estimates of future cash flows that are discounted to present value by using a discount rate reflective of the risks associated with the cash flows. For a going concern, this method frequently includes a series of discrete cash flow projections followed by an estimate of the value of the business enterprise as a going concern at the end of the projection period.

- **Capitalized cash flow method**. Also referred to as the **capitalized income method** or **capitalization of earnings method**, this approach values a private company by using a single representative estimate of economic benefits and dividing that estimate by an appropriate capitalization rate to derive an indication of value.

- **Residual income method**. Frequently referred to as the **excess earnings method** in the valuation community, this method is sometimes categorized under the asset approach because it involves marking the tangible assets to market and estimating the value of intangible assets. For valuing a business enterprise, the excess earnings method consists of estimating the value of all of the company's intangible assets by capitalizing future earnings in excess of the estimated return requirements associated with working capital and fixed assets. The value of the intangible assets is added to the values of working capital and fixed assets to arrive at the value of the business enterprise.

[handwritten margin note: – The excess earnings method would rarely be applied to value a company's equity, particularly when it is not needed to value intangibles.]

Whichever income approach method is used, an appropriate required rate of return estimate is needed for discounting expected future cash flows.

Required Rate of Return: Models and Estimation Issues

A variety of factors make estimating a required rate of return for a private company challenging.

- *Application of size premiums.* In assessing private company valuations, size premiums are frequently used in developing equity return requirements by private company appraisers. This practice seems to be less prevalent in the valuation of public companies. Furthermore, size premium estimates based on public company data for the smallest market cap segments can capture premiums for financial and/or operating distress that may be irrelevant to the company being valued.

- *Use of the CAPM.* Some parties have questioned whether the CAPM is appropriate for developing discount rate estimates for small private company valuations. Small companies that have little prospect of going public or being acquired by a public company may be viewed as not comparable to the public companies for which market-data-based beta estimates are available.

- *Expanded CAPM.* The **expanded CAPM** is an adaptation of the CAPM that adds to the CAPM premiums for small size and company-specific risk (Pratt and Grabowski, 2014). Estimation of company-specific risk has been a very subjective element of the valuation process. Several valuation professionals have presented methodologies to develop quantitative estimates of company-specific risk. These tools are being vetted in the valuation community.

- *Elements of the build-up approach.* The build-up approach, introduced earlier as part of return concept topics, relies on building up the required rate of return as a set of premia added to the risk-free rate. The added premia are typically based on factors such as size and company risk. When **guideline public companies** (public-company comparables for the company being valued) are unavailable or of questionable comparability, appraisers may rely on a build-up method rather than the CAPM or other models. The build-up method, unlike the expanded CAPM, excludes the application of beta to the equity risk premium. In the build-up model, in which beta is implicitly assumed equal to 1, an argument exists to include an industry risk adjustment (premium or discount), although there are challenges in measuring industry risk adjustments. For the baseline implementation of the build-up model, we take the model with an industry risk adjustment.

- *Relative debt availability and cost of debt.* Another valuation challenge involves correctly estimating a private company's debt capacity. In calculating a weighted average cost of capital (WACC) for a valuation based on FCFF, analysts should note that a private company may have less access to debt financing than a similar public company. This lesser access means the private company may need to rely more on equity financing, which would tend to increase its WACC. Furthermore, a private company's typically smaller size could lead to greater operating risk and a higher cost of debt.

- *Discount rates in an acquisition context.* In evaluating an acquisition, finance theory indicates that the cost of capital used should be based on the target company's capital structure and the riskiness of the target company's cash flows—the buyer's cost of capital is irrelevant. In the context of acquisitions made by larger, more mature companies of smaller, riskier target companies, the buyer would be expected to have a lower cost of capital than the target.

Both of these practices in general incorrectly transfer value from the buyer to the seller because the buyer would be paying the seller for possible value it brings to a transaction (Damodaran, 2012).

- *Discount rate adjustment for projection risk.* Any lesser amount of information concerning a private company's operations or business model compared with a similar public company introduces greater uncertainty into projections that may lead to a higher required rate of return. As a second area of concern, management of a private company (on whom analysts may need to rely for forecasts) may have less experience forecasting future financial performance. Projections may reflect excessive optimism or pessimism. Any adjustments to a discount rate to account for projection risk or managerial inexperience in forecasting, however, would typically be highly judgmental.

EXAMPLE 3

Developing a Discount Rate for a Private Company

Duvall and his advisers have decided to use an income approach to value Able Manufacturing.

Because of its years of operating successfully and its owner's conservative nature, Able operated with little debt. Smith explored various sources of debt financing to operate Able with a lower overall cost of capital. Analysis of public companies in Able's industry indicated several guideline public companies for possible use in estimating a discount rate for Able. Duvall and his advisers agreed on the following estimates:

- Risk-free rate: Estimated at 3.8%.
- Equity risk premium: The parties agreed that a 5% equity risk premium was appropriate.
- Beta: A beta of 1.1 was estimated based on publicly traded companies in the same industry.
- Small stock premium: The smaller size and less diversified operations suggest greater risk for Able relative to public companies. A small stock premium of 3% was included in the equity return calculation for these expected risks.
- Company-specific risk premium: Assessment of Able indicated that beyond Smith's key role at the company, no other unusual elements created additional risk. A 1% company-specific risk adjustment was included.
- Industry risk premium (build-up method only): The industry risk premium was 0% because no industry-related factors were viewed as materially affecting the overall required return on equity estimate.
- Pre-tax cost of debt: Estimated at 7.5%.
- Ratio of debt to total capital for public companies in the same industry: Estimated at 20%.
- Optimal ratio of debt to total capital: The ratio was estimated at 10% based on discussions with various sources of financing. Able would be unable to achieve the industry capital structure based on its smaller size compared with public companies and the greater risk of its operations as a standalone company.
- Actual ratio of debt to total capital: For Able, the actual ratio was 2%.

- Combined corporate tax rate: Estimated at 30%.

Based only on the information given, address the following:

1. Calculate the required return on equity for Able using the CAPM.

Solution:

According to the CAPM, Required return on share i = Current expected risk-free return + β_i (Equity risk premium) = 3.8% + 1.1(5%) = 9.30%.

2. Calculate the required return on equity for Able using the expanded CAPM.

Solution:

The required rate of return is 13.3%, which is shown in the following tabular format.

Able Manufacturing, Inc. Expanded CAPM: Required Rate of Return on Equity	
Risk-free rate	3.8%
Plus: Equity risk premium adjusted for beta[a]	5.5
Plus: Small stock premium	3.0
Plus: Company-specific risk adjustment	1.0
Indicated required return on equity	13.3%

[a] *1.1 beta × 5% equity risk premium = 5.5%.*

3. Calculate the required return on equity for Able using the build-up method.

Solution:

The required rate of return is 12.8%. Note the absence of a beta adjustment. Note also that the fact that beta (1.1) is close to 1.0 possibly suggests any industry risk adjustment that could be made would be small in magnitude.

Able Manufacturing, Inc. Build-Up Method: Required Rate of Return on Equity	
Risk-free rate	3.8%
Plus: Equity risk premium	5.0
Plus: Small stock premium	3.0
Plus: Industry risk premium	0.0
Plus: Company-specific risk adjustment	1.0
Indicated return on equity	12.8%

4. Discuss the selection of the capital structure weights to use in determining the weighted average cost of capital for Able.

Solution:

For valuation concerning the possible sale of Able, it is appropriate to assume the weights in the optimal capital structure in calculating WACC because an acquirer would be able and motivated to establish the optimum.

Able's current capital structure involves less debt than the optimal one; thus the company's WACC is currently higher than it needs to be. Note, however, that the weight on debt of similar large public companies may be higher than what is optimal for Able. Large public companies would be expected to have better access to public debt markets. Also, Able's small size increases its risk relative to larger public companies. These two factors tend to increase Able's cost of debt relative to a large public comparable and lead to a lower optimal weight of debt compared with such a public company.

5. Calculate the WACC for Able using the current capital structure and a 13% cost of equity.

Solution:

The cost of capital for Able based on the existing capital structure was calculated as follows:

Able Manufacturing, Inc. Calculation of Weighted Average Cost of Capital Current Capital Structure		
Pre-tax cost of debt	7.5%	
Tax rate complement (1 − Tax rate)	0.70	
After-tax cost of debt	5.3%	
Weight	×0.02	
Weighted cost of debt		0.1%
Cost of equity	13.0%	
Weight	×0.98	
Weighted cost of equity		12.7%
Weighted average cost of capital		12.8%

6. Calculate the WACC for Able based on the optimal capital structure for Able and a 13% cost of equity.

Solution:

The overall cost of capital using the optimal capital structure for Able reflected a higher level of debt financing. The WACC was calculated as follows:

Able Manufacturing, Inc. Calculation of Weighted Average Cost of Capital Optimal Capital Structure		
Pre-tax cost of debt	7.5%	
Tax rate complement (1 − Tax rate)	0.70	
After-tax cost of debt	5.3%	
Weight	0.10	
Weighted cost of debt		0.5%
Cost of equity	13.0%	
Weight	0.90	
Weighted cost of equity		11.7%
Weighted average cost of capital		12.2%

Note: Rounded figures are used.

For early stage development companies, discount rate estimation concerns are magnified. Very high levels of company-specific risk, for example, may make using the CAPM problematic. Several life cycle stages exist with perceived broad ranges of absolute rate of return requirements for companies operating in each stage. Further, there can be uncertainty in classifying a company in a specific life cycle stage.

> **AICPA PRACTICE AIDS**
>
> The American Institute of Certified Public Accountants (AICPA) released practice aids ("Valuation of Privately-Held-Company Equity Securities Issued as Compensation" and "Assets Acquired in a Business Combination to Be Used in Research and Development Activities: A Focus on Software, Electronic Devices, and Pharmaceutical Industries") to provide technical guidance for stock valuation in the context of stock option grants and other share-based payments. Paragraph 119 of "Valuation of Privately-Held-Company Equity Securities Issued as Compensation" notes that "One of the objectives and benefits of becoming a public enterprise is the ability to access the public capital markets, with the associated benefits of a lower cost of both equity and debt capital." The practice aids also provide descriptive information on various stages in the early life cycle of development-stage companies and estimated return requirements.

4 FREE CASH FLOW, CAPITALIZED CASH FLOW, AND EXCESS EARNINGS METHODS

☐ explain the income, market, and asset-based approaches to private company valuation and factors relevant to the selection of each approach

☐ calculate the value of a private company using free cash flow, capitalized cash flow, and/or excess earnings methods

Free cash flow valuation for private and public companies is substantially similar. For example, in the case of Able Manufacturing, a FCF valuation might involve projecting individual free cash flows for a number of years, finding the present value of those projected free cash flows, followed by finding the present value of a terminal value estimate that captures the business enterprise value at the end of the initial projection period. In principle, discrete free cash flow forecasts should be made until cash flows are expected to stabilize at a constant growth rate.

To value the business enterprise at the end of the initial projection period, the capitalized cash flow method incorporating a sustainable long-term growth rate is a theoretically preferred method. Some appraisers, however, will calculate the terminal value using pricing multiples developed in the market approach. For a company in a high-growth industry, market multiples would be expected to capture rapid growth in the near future and "normal" growth into the indefinite future. If we use these multiples to estimate terminal value, the residual enterprise value may be inappropriate because rapid growth was incorporated twice: once in the cash flow projections over the projection period and also in the market multiple used in calculating the residual enterprise value.

Capitalized Cash Flow Method

The capitalized cash flow method (CCM) estimates value based on the expression for the value of a growing perpetuity and is essentially a stable growth (single-stage) free cash flow model. Although rarely used for the valuation of public companies, larger private companies, or in the context of acquisitions or financial reporting, the CCM may be appropriate in valuing a private company for which no projections are available and an expectation of stable future operations exists. If market pricing evidence from public companies or transactions is limited, a CCM valuation may also be a feasible alternative.

For companies that are not expected to grow at a constant rate, FCF valuation using a series of discrete cash flow projections is theoretically preferable to the CCM. The CCM could provide assistance in assessing the discount rate or growth assumptions embedded in value indications from the market approach.

At the firm level, the formula for the capitalized cash flow to the firm is

$$V_f = \text{FCFF}_1/(\text{WACC} - g_f) \tag{1}$$

— This is just like the DDM

where

V_f = value of the firm

FCFF_1 = free cash flow to the firm for next 12 months

WACC = weighted average cost of capital

g_f = sustainable growth rate of free cash flow to the firm

The value of equity is found as the value of the company less the market value of debt, or V_f − (Market value of debt). An implicit assumption in using WACC for discounting FCFF in Equation 1 is that a constant capital structure at market values in the future exists.

To value equity directly, the inputs for free cash flow would reflect FCFE and the equity return requirement would be substituted for the WACC:

$$V = \text{FCFE}_1/(r - g) \tag{2}$$

where r is the required return on equity and g is the sustainable growth rate of free cash flow to equity. In Equation 1 and Equation 2, the denominator is known as the **capitalization rate**. Thus, the estimate of value in each is calculated as the forecasted Year 1 FCF divided by the capitalization rate. Example 4 illustrates the application of the CCM.

EXAMPLE 4

Valuation Using the Capitalized Cash Flow Method

Duvall and his team are comfortable with the normalized earnings, growth, and discount rate estimated for Able. The company's management has not developed detailed projections for Able. Suppose that free cash flow to the firm is expected to grow at 3% annually from the level of $10,986,100 forecast earlier.

1. Explain the rationale for using the CCM in this case.

Solution:

The CCM is appropriate given the assumption that free cash flow to the firm grows at a constant rate (here 3%) is accurate. Otherwise, at best it provides a rough value estimate.

2. Calculate the value of the equity of Able using the CCM and a WACC of 12.2% based on Able's optimal capital structure.

Solution:

Using the estimated free cash flow to the firm, a capitalization rate of 9.2% (12.2% − 3%) was applied to derive a valuation indication for the business enterprise. Able's debt balance was subtracted to arrive at an equity value calculated as follows.

Able Manufacturing, Inc. Capitalized Cash Flow Method—Optimal Capital Structure		
Free cash flow to firm		$10,986,100
Weighted average cost of capital	12.2%	
Long-term growth rate	3.0%	
Capitalization rate		9.2%
Indicated value of invested capital		119,414,130
Less: Debt capital (actual, assumed to equal market value)		2,000,000
Indicated value of equity		$117,414,130

3. Calculate the value of Able's equity using the WACC of 12.8% based on the existing capital structure.

Solution:

This calculation is similar to the one in the Solution to 2 except for the use of a capitalization rate of 9.8% (12.8% − 3%).

Able Manufacturing, Inc. Capitalized Cash Flow Method—Existing Capital Structure		
Free cash flow to firm		$10,986,100
Weighted average cost of capital	12.8%	
Long-term growth rate	3.0%	
Capitalization rate		9.8%
Indicated value of invested capital		112,103,061
Less: Debt capital		2,000,000
Indicated value of equity		$110,103,0615

4. Discuss factors leading to the difference in the computed values.

Solution:

The low level of debt in the existing capital structure results in a higher WACC and a lower valuation conclusion for Able relative to the optimal capital structure.

Excess Earnings Method

In a business valuation context, the excess earnings method (EEM) involves estimating the earnings remaining after deducting amounts that reflect the required returns to working capital and fixed assets (i.e., the tangible assets). This residual amount of earnings (i.e., "excess earnings") is capitalized by using the growing perpetuity formula from the CCM to obtain an estimate of the value of intangible assets. Generally, the EEM has been used to value intangible assets and very small businesses when other such market approach methods are not feasible. For valuing the entire business, the values of working capital and fixed assets are added to the capitalized value of intangibles.

Applying the EEM to value a business enterprise involves the following steps:

1. Estimate values of working capital and fixed assets (typically, fair value estimates are used). Suppose these are €200,000 and €800,000, respectively.

2. Determine the normalized earnings of the business enterprise. Suppose normalized earnings are €120,000 for the year just ended.

3. Develop discount rates for working capital and fixed assets. Working capital is viewed as the lowest-risk and most liquid asset with the lowest required rate of return. Fixed assets require a somewhat greater rate of return. Intangible assets, given their limited liquidity and high risk, often require the highest return. Suppose the required returns on working capital and fixed assets are 5% and 11%, respectively.

4. Calculate required returns associated with working capital and fixed assets and subtract the required returns on working capital and fixed assets from the normalized earnings of the business enterprise to estimate the residual income. This residual income, if any, must reflect the value associated with intangible assets. In this case, residual income is €120,000 − 0.05(€200,000) − 0.11(€800,000) = €22,000. Assume that residual income grows at 3% annually.

5. Estimate discount rate and capitalization rate required for valuing the intangible assets. This estimate typically represents all intangible assets (including customer relationships, technology, trade names, and the assembled work force, among others). The details of such a calculation are outside the scope of our coverage. Significant judgement is associated with many of these estimates (for further discussion, see The Appraisal Foundation's best practice guide, "The Identification of Contributory Assets and Calculation of Economic Rents"). For the purpose of this illustration, assume the discount rate is 12%.

6. Value the enterprise's intangible assets using the formula for a growing perpetuity. The total value of intangible assets is (1.03)(€22,000)/(0.12 − 0.03) ≈ €251,778. (Because €22,000 is associated with normalized income for the most recent year, it is increased by its assumed 3% growth rate to obtain a forecast of the year-ahead residual income.)

7. Total of working capital, fixed assets, and intangibles equals the value of the business. The EEM estimate is €200,000 + €800,000 + €251,778 = €1,251,778.

As mentioned, the EEM is used only rarely in pricing entire private businesses, and then only for small ones. Some have viewed the specific return requirements for working capital, tangible assets, and the residual income associated with intangible assets as not readily measurable (again, for further detail, see The Appraisal Foundation's best practice guide, "The Identification of Contributory Assets and Calculation of Economic Rents").

For financial reporting, the concept of residual income is an important element of intangible asset valuations and has wide acceptance. Residual income is the subject of significant discussion among appraisers who perform purchase price allocation valuations of intangible assets pursuant to IFRS 3 or Accounting Standards Codification (ASC) 805. An analyst considering intangible asset amortization and goodwill impairment issues would benefit from an understanding of residual income concepts.

5   MARKET APPROACH METHODS AND THE GUIDELINE PUBLIC COMPANY METHOD

☐   explain the income, market, and asset-based approaches to private company valuation and factors relevant to the selection of each approach

☐   calculate the value of a private company based on market approach methods and describe advantages and disadvantages of each method

The market approach uses direct comparisons to public companies and acquired enterprises to estimate the fair value of an equity interest in a private company. Three major variations of the market approach exist:

- The **guideline public company method** (GPCM) establishes a value estimate based on the observed multiples from trading activity in the shares of public companies viewed as reasonably comparable to the subject private company. The multiples from the public companies are adjusted to reflect differences in the relative risk and growth prospects of the subject private company compared with the guideline public companies.

- The **guideline transactions method** (GTM) establishes a value estimate based on pricing multiples derived from the acquisition of control of entire public or private companies that were acquired. Whereas GPCM uses a multiple that could be associated with trades of any size, GTM uses a multiple that specifically relates to sales of entire companies.

- The **prior transaction method** (PTM) considers actual transactions in the stock of the subject private company. The actual price paid for shares or the pricing multiples implied by past transactions in the stock can be used for this method.

Because the market approach relies on data generated in actual market transactions, some consider it conceptually preferable to the income- and asset-based approaches for private company valuation. In the United States, tax courts assessing private company valuations have generally stated a preference for valuation based on market transactions, although they often accept valuations based on the income approach. IFRS 13 and ASC 820 also present a fair value hierarchy that gives the highest priority to market-based evidence. Specifically, IFRS 13 states that "fair value hierarchy gives the highest priority to quoted prices (unadjusted) in active markets for identical assets or liabilities (Level 1) and the lowest priority to unobservable inputs (Level 3)." The primary assumption of the market approach is that transactions providing pricing evidence are reasonably comparable to the subject company.

A primary challenge in using the market approach is finding comparable companies and accurately assessing their pricing. All of the company-specific factors noted previously may lead to different levels of expected risk and growth for a private company relative to a public one. Market multiples reflect both expected risk and growth. Risk and growth assumptions should be extracted and multiples adjusted to reflect any differences of the subject company vis-à-vis the chosen comparable(s). The stock-specific factors associated with private companies may create additional uncertainties regarding levels of risk and growth.

The pricing of shares in public companies reflects stock price volatility as a result of, in part, their ready marketability. Rapid movements in public companies' stock prices can lead to changes in pricing multiples that often serve as a basis for private company valuations. Interests in private companies have much more limited marketability and often require longer periods to completely sell. The extended period to sell such an interest in full and the likely movement of pricing multiples over the sale period create uncertainty in the determination of a pricing multiple and thus in the final value conclusion.

Factors for identifying guideline companies are similar for public and private companies. Key factors include industry membership, form of operations, trends, and current operating status, among others. As previously noted, life cycle and size differences may create significant challenges in applying the market approach.

Public and private company analysis may differ in the financial metrics used in the valuation process. Price-to-earnings methods are frequently cited in the valuation of public companies, with other multiples considered as well. For larger, mature private companies, pricing multiples are frequently based on EBITDA and/or EBIT. EBITDA is best compared with the **market value of invested capital** (MVIC), defined as the market value of debt and equity, in forming the valuation metric. In addition to MVIC, other similar terms include enterprise value (EV), business enterprise value (BEV), and firm value. Definitions for enterprise value vary but most frequently start with MVIC and subtract any cash and cash equivalents. BEV is typically synonymous with EV.

With a calculation of MVIC for a private company, the value of debt can be subtracted to produce an estimate of equity value. Because current transaction market values for debt are unavailable in many cases, some estimate of the market value of debt is needed. The use of the face value of debt as an estimate may be acceptable in many situations in which debt represents a small fraction of overall financing and operations are stable. For companies with highly leveraged financial conditions and/or significant volatility expected in future financial performance, the valuation of equity as the residual obtained by subtracting the face value of debt from the value of the business enterprise is frequently not appropriate. Consider highly leveraged companies or companies with significant volatility of financial performance whose debt may be valued at significant discounts from face value. In these cases, option pricing theory can be used to value each debt and equity instrument as a separate call option on the company's BEV. An alternative in such cases is to estimate market value based on debt characteristics, known as matrix prices. For many very small private companies with limited asset bases, net income–based multiples may be more commonly used than EBITDA multiples. For extremely small companies, multiples of revenue may even be commonly applied. This convention considers the likely absence of meaningful financial data and the greater impact and subjectivity associated with such items as owner compensation.

Non-financial metrics may be an appropriate means of valuation for certain industries. These metrics would probably best be used in addition to financial metrics. Significant reliance on these metrics would be appropriate only if the non-financial measure is generally accepted within the industry. Examples of non-financial metrics include price per subscriber in cable and price per bed for hospital and skilled nursing and other healthcare facilities.

[Handwritten margin notes:]

$$EV$$
$$\downarrow$$
$$MVIC = Enterprise\ Value$$
$$- Cash : cash\ equivalents$$

$$BEV = EV$$

$$MVIC = Working\ capital$$
$$+ fixed\ assets$$
$$+ intangible\ assets$$

Guideline Public Company Method

In private company valuation, as has been noted, valuation based on multiples of similar public companies is often referred to as the guideline public company method. The valuation process is essentially similar for a public or a private company. A group of public companies is identified, the relevant pricing multiples for the guideline companies are derived, and adjustments to the multiples are made that reflect the risk and growth prospects of the subject company relative to the publicly traded companies. For a private company, this method would lead to a conclusion of value. For a public company, applying this method helps assess over- or undervaluation of a company relative to similar companies at a specific point in time.

The primary advantage of this method is the potentially large pool of guideline companies and the significant descriptive, financial, and trading information available to the analyst/appraiser. Disadvantages include possible issues regarding comparability and subjectivity in the risk and growth adjustments to the pricing multiple.

Control premiums may be used in valuing a controlling interest in a company. Defined in the IGBVT, a **control premium** is an amount or percentage by which the pro rata value of a controlling interest exceeds the pro rata value of a non-controlling interest in a business enterprise, to reflect the power of control. For the valuation of a controlling interest, a control premium has often been added if the value is derived from the GPCM. The trading of interests in public companies typically reflects small blocks without control of the entity. Given this information, many but not all believe the resulting pricing multiples do not reflect control of the entity.

Control Premium Recommendation

The Appraisal Foundation's 2017 guide *The Measurement and Application of Market Participant Acquisition Premiums* proposes major changes to improve consistency among appraisers' practice in this area. In its draft form, the document recommends that any control premium be justified based on an analysis of projected cash flows after an acquisition and, when justified, that control premiums be calculated at the MVIC rather than the equity level.

A control premium adjustment may be appropriate depending on the specific facts. Historically, control premiums have been estimated based on transactions in which public companies were acquired. Several factors require careful consideration in estimating a control premium.

- *Type of transaction.* Some transaction databases classify acquisitions as either financial or strategic transactions. A **strategic transaction** involves a buyer that would benefit from certain synergies associated with owning the target firm. These synergies could include enhanced revenues, cost savings, or other possible benefits. A **financial transaction** involves a buyer having essentially no material synergies with the target. As an example, the purchase of a private company by a company in an unrelated industry would typically be a financial transaction. Compared with financial transactions, control premiums for an acquisition by a strategic buyer are typically larger because of the expected synergies.

- *Industry factors.* Industry sectors with acquisition activity are considered to be "in play" at a valuation date; that is, pricing of public companies in the sector may reflect some part of a possible control premium in the share prices. Control premiums measured at a date significantly before a valuation date might reflect a different industry environment from that of the valuation date.

- *Form of consideration.* Transactions involving the exchange of significant amounts of stock (as opposed to all-cash transactions) might be less relevant as a basis of measuring a control premium because of the possibility that acquiring companies time such transactions during periods when their management perceives that shares of their company are overvalued in the marketplace.

The multiple resulting from applying a control premium to pricing multiples from publicly traded companies should be assessed for reasonableness. Suppose that a public company, which is viewed as comparable to a private company being appraised, was acquired at an 8× pricing multiple. A control premium of 30% control is paid based on the stock's price prior to the acquisition. Pricing multiples for guideline public companies, however, are 10× at the valuation date. Applying a 30% control premium would suggest a 13× pricing multiple. The dramatically different value indications resulting from applying a 8× transaction multiple and a 13× multiple suggest the need for further investigation before accepting the 13× multiple. Comparability issues or dramatic pricing changes may be factors leading to this material difference.

EXAMPLE 5

Valuation Using Guideline Public Company Method

Duvall decides to use the GPCM to develop a value indication for Able that is independent of the FCF indication he is also pursuing. He believes that many acquirors apply a multiple of market value of invested capital to EBITDA to value companies in Able's industry. A search for comparable public companies indicated several companies that might serve as guidelines or benchmarks for valuing Able; however, all of these are much larger than Able. Duvall's research on guideline public companies indicates the following:

- The MVIC to EBITDA multiples of such public companies cluster near 7.0.

- A combined downward adjustment of 15% for relative risk and growth characteristics of Able compared with the guideline public companies suggests an adjusted MVIC to EBITDA multiple of 5.95, rounded to 6, for Able.

- A control premium of 20% was reported in a single strategic acquisition from several years ago. The transaction involved an exchange of stock with no cash consideration paid.

- Duvall is unaware of any strategic buyers that might incorporate synergies into their valuation of Able.

- Normalized EBITDA is $16,900,000.

- Market value of debt capital is $2,000,000.

---

1. Explain the elements included in the calculation of a pricing multiple for Able.

Solution:

Able's value in relation to a possible acquisition is desired. Pricing multiples from guideline public companies provide a starting point to develop a pricing multiple. The pricing multiples for the guideline public companies must be adjusted to reflect any differences in risk and growth expectations for Able compared with the guideline public companies. As a final element, the pricing multiple should consider the inclusion of a control premium given the possible sale of Able.

2. Calculate the pricing multiple appropriate for Able, including a control premium adjustment.

Solution:

Considering the absence of any strategic buyers, in the present instance a control premium of 0% is a reasonable baseline. There was a single strategic transaction for the acquisition of a public company several years prior to the acquisition. The age of the transaction, however, creates concern regarding the relevance of the indicated control premium.

Based on the information provided, the MVIC to EBITDA multiple for Able can be taken to approximately 6, reflecting no control premium adjustment.

Able Manufacturing, Inc. Development for Pricing Multiple for Guideline Public Company Method		
Initial MVIC to EBITDA from public companies		7.0
Relative risk and growth adjustment for Able	–15%	(1.05)
Multiple before control adjustment		5.95
Control Premium adjustment*	0%	0
Multiple after control adjustment		5.95
Rounded to		6.0

* Control premiums are measured based on the value of the equity or the MVIC of public companies before and after an acquisition. When an equity control premium has been estimated, a valuation on an MVIC basis (as is often the case in a transaction setting) would require an adjustment to the equity control premium. In the example, no control premium was concluded to be appropriate. Assuming an equity control premium of 30% was deemed appropriate based on different facts, a normalized capital structure of one-third debt and two-thirds equity would suggest a 20% control premium (two-thirds of 30%) if applied to an MVIC-multiple-based value from guideline public companies. Control premium data vary markedly, and divergence in practice exists in this area of valuation.

3. Calculate the value of Able using the guideline public company method.

Solution:

Able Manufacturing, Inc. Valuation Using Guideline Public Company Method	
Normalized EBITDA	$16,900,000
Pricing multiple	6.0
Indicated value of invested capital	101,400,000
Less: Debt capital	2,000,000
Indicated value of equity	$99,400,000

GUIDELINE TRANSACTIONS AND PRIOR TRANSACTION METHODS

6

☐ | calculate the value of a private company based on market approach methods and describe advantages and disadvantages of each method

The guideline transactions method is conceptually similar to the guideline public company method. Unlike the GPCM, the GTM uses pricing multiples derived from acquisitions of public or private companies. Transaction data available on publicly reported acquisitions are compiled from public filings made by parties to the transaction with the regulatory bodies, such as the Financial Conduct Authority in the United Kingdom or the Securities and Exchange Commission (SEC) in the United States. Data on transactions not subject to public disclosure may be available from certain transaction databases. Because information may be limited and is generally not readily confirmed, many appraisers challenge the reliability of this data. All other things equal, transaction multiples would be the most relevant evidence for valuation of a controlling interest in a private company.

— No control premium adjustment is necessary

A number of factors need to be considered in assessing transaction-based pricing multiples.

- *Synergies*. The pricing of strategic acquisitions may include payment for anticipated synergies. The relevance of payments for synergies to the case at hand merits consideration.

- *Contingent consideration*. **Contingent consideration** represents potential future payments to the seller that are contingent on the achievement of certain agreed-on occurrences. Obtaining some form of regulatory approval or achieving a targeted level of EBITDA are two types of contingencies. Contingent consideration may be included in the structure of acquisition. The inclusion of contingent consideration in the purchase price paid for an enterprise often reflects uncertainty regarding the entity's future financial performance. IFRS 3 and ASC 805 changed the requirements for measuring and reporting contingent consideration in the context of a business combination (further details in "Valuation of Contingent Consideration" by The Appraisal Foundation, February 2019).

- *Non-cash consideration*. Acquisitions may include stock in the consideration. The cash equivalent value of a large block of stock may create uncertainty regarding the transaction price. For example, the 2001 merger of America Online (AOL) and Time Warner Corporation was a stock swap that occurred at a time when AOL stock was trading based on expectations of significant future growth. In 2002, the combined company reported two charges for goodwill impairment expense totaling $99 billion. The level of this impairment expense raises questions regarding whether the initial transaction price reflected temporary overvaluation of AOL stock relative to its intrinsic value.

- *Availability of transactions*. Meaningful transactions for a specific private company may be limited. The relevance of pricing indications from a transaction that occurred a significant period prior to a valuation date can be challenged—especially if evidence indicates changes in the subject company, industry, or economy between the transaction date and the valuation date.

- *Changes between transaction date and valuation date.* Unlike the guideline public company method, which develops pricing multiples based on stock prices at or very near the valuation date, the guideline transactions method relies on pricing evidence from acquisitions of control of firms at different points in the past. In many industries, transactions are limited and transactions several months or more from a valuation date may be the only transaction evidence available. Changes in the marketplace could result in differing risk and growth expectations requiring an adjustment to the pricing multiple.

EXAMPLE 6

Valuation Using Guideline Transactions Method

In addition to the income approach and the guideline public company method, the guideline transactions method was considered and applied. Duvall and his advisers noted the following:

- Pricing multiples from several recent acquisitions of private companies in the industry indicated a MVIC to EBITDA multiple of 6.0.
- Several of the acquisitions studied were viewed as similar to Able because of similar revenue bases and limited diversification. The overall risk and growth characteristics of the acquired companies and Able were viewed as similar.

1. Discuss differences between pricing multiples from the guideline transactions and guideline public company methods.

Solution:

The guideline transactions method considers market transactions involving the acquisition of the total equity of companies. As such, the pricing multiple, compared to other methods, more accurately reflects the value of total companies. Pricing multiples from guideline public companies typically reflect public trading in small blocks of stock. The multiples may not reflect the value of the total equity of the public companies.

2. Explain the calculation of a pricing multiple using the guideline transactions method.

Solution:

The pricing multiples from acquisitions are the basis for the pricing multiple. The risk and growth prospects of the acquired companies and the subject private company are assessed and an adjustment factor is applied. Because the multiples reflect acquisitions of total equity, they reflect the value of total equity. No control premium adjustment is necessary.

3. Calculate the pricing multiple appropriate for Able.

Solution:

Calculation of the initial pricing multiple follows:

Able Manufacturing, Inc. Development of Pricing Multiple for Guideline Transactions Method		
Initial MVIC to EBITDA from transactions		6.0
Relative risk and growth adjustment for Able	0%	0.0
Indicated multiple		6.0
Rounded to		6.0

4. Calculate the value of Able using the guideline transactions method.

Solution:

Valuation using the guideline transactions method is similar to that from the guideline public company method, except any control premium is already incorporated in the transaction multiple.

Able Manufacturing, Inc. Guideline Transactions Method	
EBITDA	$16,900,000
Pricing multiple	6.0
Indicated value of invested capital	101,400,000
Less: Debt capital	2,000,000
Indicated value of equity	$99,400,000

Prior Transaction Method

The prior transaction method considers actual transactions in the stock of the subject company. Valuation can be based on either the actual price paid or the multiples implied from the transaction. The PTM is generally most relevant when considering the value of a minority equity interest in a company. For many private companies, there are no or very limited transactions in the stock.

If actual transactions in the stock of the subject company took place, were done at arm's length, and information is available, the PTM would be expected to provide the most meaningful evidence of value. The PTM provides less reliable valuation evidence if transactions are infrequent. Also, uncertainly regarding the parties' motivations, or special circumstances surrounding a prior transaction, can create uncertainty regarding PTM data reliability. Transactions at different points in time may require significant adjustment. As an example, an early stage venture capital–funded company experiences rapid value increases resulting from successful execution of its development plans. A transaction conducted prior to the company achieving a significant value event might not provide meaningful value insights at a subsequent date.

The PTM can provide insights on the value of development-stage entities when revenues and cash flows are highly speculative. Many development-stage companies fund development activities through several rounds of equity financing. As such, there may be a series of prior transactions providing valuation evidence. The equity financing often involves the sale of preferred stock with liquidation preferences and rights to convert to common stock. Because development-stage entities often have complex capital structures with

> different classes of equity securities that have differing rights, significant adjustments are required. This process is complex and requires significant judgment. The AICPA guide, "Valuation of Privately-Held-Company Equity Securities Issued as Compensation" (2013) provides further insights.

7   ASSET-BASED APPROACH

☐ explain the income, market, and asset-based approaches to private company valuation and factors relevant to the selection of each approach

☐ describe the asset-based approach to private company valuation

The principle underlying the asset-based approach is that the value of ownership of an enterprise is equivalent to the fair value of its assets less the fair value of its liabilities. Of the three approaches to valuation, the asset-based approach (also referred to as the **cost approach** by many in the valuation profession) is generally considered to be the weakest from a conceptual standpoint for valuing an ongoing business enterprise.

The asset-based approach is rarely used for the valuation of going concerns. Reasons include the limited market data available to directly value intangible assets, difficulties in valuing certain tangible assets (such as special use plant and equipment), and the more readily available information to value operating companies as an integrated whole rather than on an asset-by-asset basis.

An operating company with nominal profits relative to the values of assets used and without prospects for doing better in the future might best be valued using an asset-based approach assuming the winding up of operations. In this case, its value as a going concern might be less than its value in liquidation (the value that could be realized through the liquidation of its assets) because the assets might be redeployed by buyers to higher-valued uses. Resource and financial companies might also be valued based on an asset-based approach. Banks and finance companies largely consist of loan and securities portfolios that can be priced based on market variables. In such cases, a summation of individual asset value estimates may give a lower-bound-type estimate of the company's overall value. The asset-based approach may be appropriate for the valuation of holding (investment) companies, such as real estate investment trusts (REITs) and closed end investment companies (CEICs). For these entities, the underlying assets typically consist of real estate or securities that were valued using the market and/or income approaches. An asset-based approach may also be appropriate for very small businesses with limited intangible value or for early stage companies.

For the valuation of an interest in a pooled investment vehicle, certain factors may suggest a value different from the net asset value per share. Management and incentive fees may lead to an expectation of proceeds available to an investor and a value estimate that is less than the net asset value per share. The relative growth and profit as a result of management expertise may also merit an upward or downward adjustment to the net asset value. Other factors, such as the possible effect of tax attributes (tax basis in the assets held by the entity) and diversification, and professional management benefits may also affect value.

Exhibit 1 illustrates four definitions of values that a private business appraiser used to value the financial services subsidiary of a public company.

In a valuation of a financial services company, a business appraiser estimated four values for the company using four different approaches, which she characterized as follows:

1. *Discounted cash flow approach.* The appraiser estimated value as the present value of projected FCFE for the next 10 years plus the present value of the capitalized value of the 11th-year cash flow.

2. *Market approach.* The appraiser used the GPCM with price-to-cash flow, price-to-book (mainly in the case of financial services companies), and price-to-earnings multiples, and she made adjustments to reflect differences in risk and growth, applying the resulting multiples to the company's cash flow, book value, and earnings, respectively.

3. *Adjusted book value approach, going-concern basis.* The appraiser adjusted the book values of assets and liabilities to better reflect market values and obtained the adjusted book value of equity, which was the estimate of value based on this approach. The definition of market value used was: "Market value is...the most probable price that an asset should bring in a competitive and open market under all conditions requisite to a fair sale, the buyer and seller each acting prudently and knowledgeably, and assuming the price is not affected by undue stimulus." This approach is relevant mostly for financial services companies.

4. *Adjusted book value approach, orderly liquidation basis.* The appraiser adjusted the book values of assets and liabilities to better reflect orderly liquidation values and obtained the liquidation book value of equity, which was the estimate of value based on this approach. The definition of orderly liquidation value used was: "Orderly liquidation value [is] the price [the asset] would bring if exposed for sale on the open market, with a reasonable time allowed to find a purchaser, both buyer and seller having knowledge of the uses and purposes to which the asset is adapted and for which it is capable of being used, the seller being compelled to sell and the buyer being willing, but not compelled, to buy."

State and explain which of the foregoing methods would be expected to produce the lowest value estimate.

Methods 1, 2, and 3 recognize a going-concern value for the company; Method 4 does not, so the value estimates under 4 should be the lowest unless the entity is unable to generate sufficient income to justify continued operations. In general, using individual assets in a coordinated way in the operation of a business as implicitly assumed in 1 and 2 should increase value. Between Methods 3 and 4, the element of the seller being compelled to sell should result in 4 being the lowest estimate. Method 3 may also produce a low value because of difficulties in identifying and valuing intangible assets. Because goodwill includes a variety of items, including potential future customers and other intangibles that may be created, its direct valuation is extremely difficult.

VALUATION DISCOUNTS AND PREMIUMS

8

☐ explain and evaluate the effects on private company valuations of discounts and premiums based on control and marketability

Control and/or marketability adjustments are often included in valuations of interests in private companies. This area is one of the primary differences in the valuation of interests in private companies compared with public companies. The chart in Exhibit 2 is adapted from Hitchner (2017) and presents the relationship of these concepts and other concepts that we discuss. As the chart indicates, the inclusion of discounts depends, in part, on the starting point of a valuation.

Exhibit 2: Valuation of Private Companies

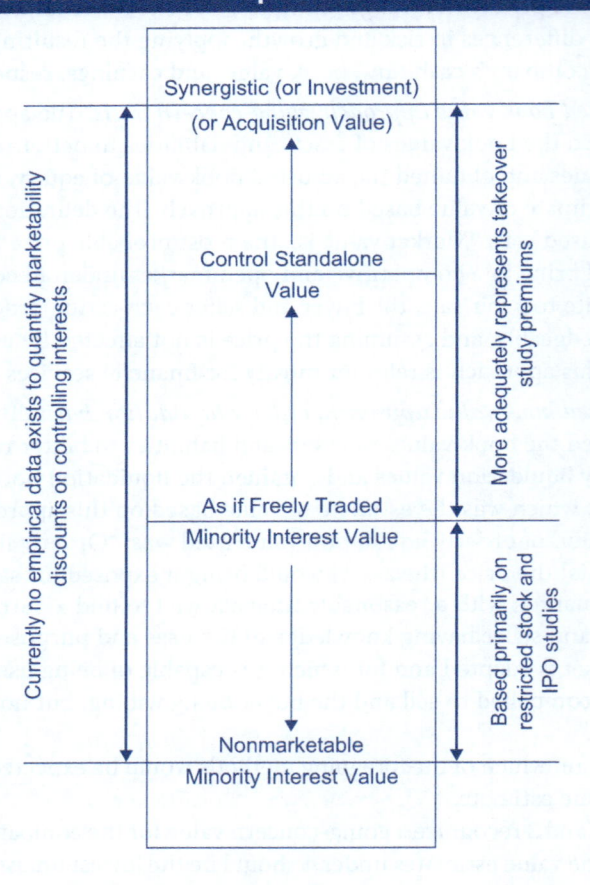

Starting at the top of the chart, the highest possible value indication for an entity would be its **investment value** to the optimal synergistic buyer. This value reflects a controlling interest assumption, which also increases value. Below the control value of the enterprise to a strategic buyer is the value of the enterprise to a standalone (financial) buyer. In this case, specific synergies to the buyer are unavailable. The "As If Freely Traded/Minority Interest Value" represents the value of a non-controlling equity interest that is readily marketable. This value would be equivalent to the price at which most publicly traded companies trade in the market. The lowest level of value is the "Nonmarketable/Minority Interest Value." This value reflects the reduction to value associated with the lack of control and ready marketability associated with small equity interests in private companies.

The application of both control premiums and lack of control and marketability discounts is fact-specific, and estimates may vary dramatically. Variations in estimated discounts and premiums may relate to the challenging comparability of the data used to quantify discounts. Discounts may also vary based on interpretation of the importance of the size of shareholding and distribution of shares, the relationship of parties, state law affecting minority shareholder rights, and other factors.

The timing of a potential liquidity event is one key consideration. An interest in a private company that is pursuing either an IPO or a strategic sale might be valued with relatively modest valuation discounts. An equity interest in a private company that has not paid dividends and has no prospect for a liquidity event would likely require much higher valuation discounts.

Lack of Control Discounts

A **discount for lack of control** (DLOC), as defined in the IGBVT, is an amount or percentage deducted from the pro rata share of 100% of the value of an equity interest in a business to reflect the absence of some or all of the powers of control.

Lack of control discounts may be necessary for valuing non-controlling equity interests in private companies if the value of total equity was developed on a controlling interests basis. The lack of control may be disadvantageous to an investor because of the inability to select directors, officers, and management that control an entity's operations. Without control, an investor is unable to distribute cash or other property, to buy and sell assets, to obtain financing, and to bring about other actions, all of which could affect the value of the investment, the timing of distributions, and the ultimate return to the investor.

Although an interest may lack control, the effect of this lack of control on value is uncertain. The US SEC suggests that evidence of "disproportionate returns" is important in supporting the application of lack of control discounts. Disproportionate returns would result when control shareholders increase their returns through above-market compensation and other actions that reduce the returns available to minority shareholders. For private companies seeking a liquidity event through an IPO or strategic sale of the entity, the likelihood decreases that a controlling group will take actions that reduce an entity's earnings.

Data available for estimating a lack of control discount are limited and interpretations can vary markedly. For interests in operating companies, control premium data from acquisitions of public companies have been used frequently in the past. The factors cited earlier on calculating a control premium should also be considered for estimating a lack of control discount. Noting the uncertainties in demonstrating the adverse financial impact of an interest's lack of control and finding appropriate data to measure that lack of control, the equation used frequently in the calculation of a lack of control discount is

— Lack of Control discount

DLOC = 1 − [1/(1 + Control premium)].

For example, if a 15% control premium is assumed, the associated DLOC is 1 − (1/1.15) = 0.130, or 13.0%.

The following sets forth the typical application of DLOC based on the different methods of valuation.

Method	Basis of Valuation	DLOC Expected?
GTM	Control	Yes
GPCM	Typically minority	No
CCM/FCF	Control or minority	Depends on cash flows

CEIC: closed-end investment company

Valuation indications from the CCM and FCF methods of the income approach are generally agreed to be a controlling interest value if cash flows and the discount rate are estimated on a controlling interest basis. If control cash flows are not used and/or the discount rate does not reflect an optimal capital structure, the resulting value is generally believed to reflect a lack of control basis.

Some analysts believe trading in REITs and CEICs may provide a basis for estimating lack of control discounts as well. Because individual REITs and CEICs may trade at premiums, discounts, or near their net asset value at different points in time, the use of this data to quantify the lack of control is challenging and outside the scope of our coverage.

Lack of Marketability Discounts

A **discount for lack of marketability** (DLOM), as defined in the IGBVT, is an amount or percentage deducted from the value of an ownership interest to reflect the relative absence (compared with publicly traded companies) of a ready market for a company's shares.

Lack of marketability discounts are frequently applied in the valuation of non-controlling equity interests in private companies. Although a DLOM is different from a DLOC, the two discounts are often linked; that is, if a valuation is on a non-controlling interest basis, a lack of marketability discount is typically appropriate. Key variables affecting a marketability discount include prospects for liquidity, contractual arrangements affecting marketability (such as lock-up agreements), restrictions on transferability, pool of potential buyers, risk or volatility, size and timing of distributions (duration of asset), uncertainty of value, and concentration of ownership (AICPA "Valuation of Privately-Held-Company Equity Securities", 2013). At a minimum, an interest that lacks marketability involves a potential opportunity cost associated with the inability to redeploy investment funds.

Restricted stock transactions and IPOs are two types of data used to quantify lack of marketability discounts. A variety of option pricing models are being used to develop marketability discount estimates as well. Although valuation professionals generally agree that these sources offer the best available data to support discounts, all of these approaches are subject to significant differences in their interpretation.

In the United States, SEC Rule 144 provides certain restrictions on the resale of unregistered stock in public companies. Shares acquired prior to an IPO are an example of shares that might be subject to Rule 144 restrictions. These restrictions prevent resale of shares subject to the requirements of Rule 144 in an attempt to maintain an orderly trading market for the publicly traded shares. Restricted stock is essentially identical to freely traded stock of a public company except for the trading restrictions. Unlike interests in private companies, restricted stock transactions typically involve shares that will enjoy ready marketability in the near future. Note that it is sometimes observed that the sale of blocks of restricted stock that significantly exceed public trading activity in the stock may be the most comparable data for quantifying a lack of marketability discount. If the block size significantly exceeds trading volumes, large blocks of restricted shares may still be illiquid when Rule 144 restrictions terminate. A private sale of such a block may reflect a valuation discount related to the price risk associated with the holding.

The relationship of stock sales prior to IPOs is another source of marketability discounts. In many companies (especially early stage or high-growth companies) approaching an IPO, value may be increasing as levels of risk and uncertainty decline because the company is progressing in its development. Reduction in risk associated with realization of the predicted cash flows or a narrowing of the ranges of possible future cash flows would lead to a reduction in the implied marketability discount. Some studies have attempted to adjust for this factor. According to AICPA ("Valuation of Privately-Held-Company Equity Securities", 2013, known as "Stock Practice Aid"), "The cost of equity capital for a private enterprise prior to its IPO generally ranges from 20% to 35%," (paragraph 117); and "By contrast, the cost of equity capital for a newly public enterprise generally ranges from 15% to 25%" (paragraph 119).

A variety of models involving put options have also been used to quantify lack of marketability discounts. As the first step of this process, an at-the-money put option is priced. The value of the put option as a percentage of the value of the stock before any DLOM provides an estimate of the DLOM as a percentage. DLOM based on put options are often used for equity interests in development stage companies. For these companies, liquidity in the short to intermediate term is frequently a key objective of investors.

The key assumptions are the expected term until a liquidity event and the level of volatility associated with the company. One advantage of the put option analysis is the ability to directly address perceived risk of the private company through the volatility estimate. The volatility estimate may better capture the risks of the stock compared with restricted stock or IPO transactions in which volatility may be one of many variables influencing the level of discount. An estimate of volatility can be developed at the valuation date based on either historical volatilities of public companies or the volatility estimates embedded in the prices of publicly traded options. Put options provide only price protection (the protection lasts for the life of the option). They do not, however, provide liquidity for the asset holding, raising a concern on the use of this form of estimate of the DLOM. Put options also allow the holder of the underlying security to benefit from potential price increases in the security's value and thus do not exactly model lack of marketability.

In addition to control and marketability discounts, a variety of other potential valuation discounts exist that may require consideration. These include key person discounts, portfolio discounts (discount for non-homogeneous assets), and possible discounts for non-voting shares.

If both lack of control and lack of marketability discounts are appropriate, these discounts are applied in sequence and are essentially multiplicative rather than additive. The discounts are multiplicative because the valuation process involves discrete steps—first moving from a controlling to a non-controlling basis and then moving from a marketable to a non-marketable basis. For an equity interest in which a 10% lack of control discount and a 20% lack of marketability discount are believed to be appropriate, the total discount is 28% [1 − (1 − 10%)(1 − 20%)] rather than 30% (10% + 20%).

Application of Valuation Discounts

Suppose that Jane Doe owns 10% of the stock of Able, and the remaining 90% is held by CEO John Smith. Smith is interested in selling Able to a third party. Smith advises Doe that if Able is not sold, he has no reason to purchase Doe's 10% interest. Assume the following:

- Valuation discounts assuming imminent transaction:
  - Lack of control discount = 0%.
  - Lack of marketability discount = 5%.
- Valuation discounts assuming continued operation as a private company:
  - Lack of control discount: incorporated through use of reported earnings rather than normalized earnings.

- Lack of marketability discount = 25%.
  - Indicated value of equity in operations:
    - $96,000,000 in sale scenario.
    - $80,000,000 in "stay private scenario."

1. Discuss the relevance of valuation discounts assuming an imminent sale of Able.

Solution:

The sale of Able can be completed only with Smith's concurrence, given his 90% equity interest. If a sale of Able seems imminent, valuation discounts associated with Doe's 10% equity interest would be modest. The controlling shareholder, Smith, would maximize the sales proceeds to himself and any other shareholder(s). Hence, the lack of control associated with a small minority equity interest would not be a factor. Note that when the controlling stockholder sells, he is not always obligated to offer the minority shareholders the same price. The analyst should investigate this fact and consider factors including 1) intent of the controlling stockholder, 2) articles of incorporation, and 3) legal statutes on corporate governance and shareholder rights. The pending transaction being driven by the controlling shareholder reduces the adverse impact of the limited marketability of an interest in a private company.

2. Explain which estimate of equity value should be used and calculate the value of Doe's equity interest in Able assuming a sale is likely.

Solution:

If a sale is viewed as highly likely, the $96,000,000 equity value would be appropriate. This equity value uses normalized earnings and a discount rate based on an optimal capital structure in calculating the capitalization rate applied to earnings.

Able Manufacturing, Inc. Valuation of Doe's 10% Equity Interest Sale of Company Viewed as Highly Likely	
Indicated value of equity in operations	$96,000,000
Interest appraised	10%
Pro rata value of 10% equity interest	9,600,000
Less: Lack of control discount of 0%	0
Value assuming ready marketability	9,600,000
Less: Lack of marketability discount of 5%	480,000
Indicated value of Doe's 10% equity interest	$9,120,000

3. Discuss the relevance of valuation discounts assuming Able continues as a private company.

Solution:

If Smith has no intent to sell the company, the above-market expenses may continue. With the above-market expenses, the reported earnings would be lower than the normalized earnings. Use of reported earnings rather than normalized earnings is one possible means of capturing the adverse impact associated with the lack of control of a small minority equity interest.

Given the absence of any potential liquidity event and the above-market expenses, little market for the stock exists. A higher lack of marketability discount would be appropriate for the interest in this situation.

4. Explain which estimate of equity value should be used and calculate the value of Doe's equity interest assuming Able continues as a private company.

Solution:

If continuing as a private company is viewed as highly likely, the $80,000,000 equity value would be appropriate. This equity value uses reported earnings and a discount rate based on the actual (not optimal) capital structure in calculating the capitalization rate applied to earnings.

Able Manufacturing, Inc. Valuation of Doe's 10% Equity Interest Continued Operation as a Private Company Likely	
Indicated value of equity in operations	$80,000,000
Interest appraised	10%
Pro rata value of 10% equity interest	8,000,000
Less: Lack of control discount*	0
Value assuming ready marketability	8,000,000
Less: Lack of marketability discount of 25%	2,000,000
Indicated value of Doe's 10% equity interest	$6,000,000

* As noted in the example, the impact on the value of the 10% equity interest was assumed to be captured in the use of reported rather than normalized earnings. Also, the actual capital structure was used rather than the optimal capital structure. A wide range of practice exists in the treatment of the lack of control for a minority equity interest in a private firm.

5. Contrast the valuation conclusions and discuss factors that contribute to the difference in the concluded values.

Solution:

The value of Doe's 10% minority equity interest differs markedly in the two scenarios. The imminent sale scenario results in a higher value indication for Doe's equity interest as a result of the company's higher value and the lower valuation discounts. The company's value would be higher because of the use of normalized earnings rather than reported earnings. A lower pricing multiple might also be warranted. The discount rate might be lower in the event an optimal capital structure is used rather than the existing structure. The lack of control becomes less important in the event of an imminent liquidity event such as a sale. The lack of marketability of a small equity interest also becomes less important in this instance.

Note that the treatment of non-operating assets varies when a minority interest in the stock is appraised. In the event of a sale, many buyers would not be interested in the non-operating assets—and those assets could be distributed to the shareholders prior to the sale of the stock to a buyer. Alternatively, Able could sell the operating assets and liabilities to a buyer, resulting in Able holding the real estate assets and cash from sale of the business

> operations. Specific circumstances would determine whether or not these assets and cash should be included in equity valuation.

We have seen that in private company valuation, as in most types of valuation beyond the simplest, a range of approaches and estimates can be argued even apart from differences resulting from different forecasts or business assumptions. The investment community also has the perception that valuation practices and estimates of value diverge from each other, as well as that valuation standards could benefit consumers of valuations.

SUMMARY

We have provided an overview of key elements of private company valuation and contrasted public and private company valuations.

- Company- and stock-specific factors may influence the selection of appropriate valuation methods and assumptions for private company valuations. Stock-specific factors may result in a lower value for an equity interest in a private company relative to a public company.

- Company-specific factors in which private companies differ from public companies include:

  - stage in life cycle;
  - size;
  - overlap of shareholders and management;
  - quality/depth of management;
  - quality of financial and other information;
  - pressure from short-term investors; and
  - tax concerns.

- Stock-specific factors that frequently affect the value of private companies include

  - liquidity of equity interests in business;
  - concentration of control; and
  - potential agreements restricting liquidity.

- Private company valuations are typically performed for three different reasons: transactions, compliance (financial or tax reporting), or litigation. Acquisition-related valuation issues and financial reporting valuation issues are of greatest importance in assessing public companies.

- Different definitions (standards) of value exist. The use of a valuation and key elements pertaining to the appraised company will help determine the appropriate definition. Key definitions of value include

  - fair market value;
  - market value;
  - fair value for financial reporting;
  - fair value in a litigation context;
  - investment value; and
  - intrinsic value.

- Private company valuations may require adjustments to the income statement to develop estimates of the company's normalized earnings. Adjustments may be required for non-recurring, non-economic, or other unusual items to eliminate anomalies and/or facilitate comparisons.

- Within the income approach, the FCF method is frequently used to value larger, mature private companies. For smaller companies or in special situations, the capitalized cash flow method and residual income method may also be used.

- Within the market approach, three methods are regularly used: the guideline public company method, guideline transactions method, and prior transactions method.

- An asset-based approach is infrequently used in valuing private companies. This approach may be appropriate for companies that are worth more in liquidation than as going concerns. This approach is also applied for asset holding companies, very small companies, or companies formed recently that have limited operating histories.

- Control and marketability issues are important and challenging elements in the valuation of private companies and equity interests therein.

- If publicly traded companies are used as the basis for pricing multiple(s), control premiums may be appropriate in measuring the total equity value of a private company. Control premiums have also been used to estimate lack of control discounts.

- Discounts for lack of control are used to convert a controlling interest value into a non-controlling equity interest value. Evidence of the adverse impact of the lack of control is an important consideration in assessing this discount.

- Discounts for lack of marketability are often used in valuing non-controlling equity interests in private companies. A DLOM may be inappropriate if the company has a high likelihood of a liquidity event in the immediate future.

- Quantification of DLOMs can be challenging because of limited data, differences in the interpretation of available data, and different interpretations of the lack of marketability's effect on a private company.

- DLOM can be estimated based on 1) private sales of restricted stock in public companies relative to their freely traded share price, 2) private sales of stock in companies prior to a subsequent IPO, and 3) the pricing of put options.

REFERENCES

AICPA"Valuation of Privately-Held-Company Equity Securities Issued as Compensation – Accounting and Valuation Guide" (2013)

Damodaran, Aswath. 2012. Investment Valuation Tools and Techniques for Determining the Value of Any Asset. Hoboken, NJ: John Wiley & Sons.

Hitchner, James R. 2017. Financial Valuation: Applications and Models. 4th ed.Hoboken, NJ: John Wiley & Sons. 10.1002/9781119362814

Pratt, Shannon P., Roger J. Grabowski. 2014. Cost of Capital: Applications and Examples. 5th ed.Hoboken, NJ: John Wiley & Sons. 10.1002/9781118846780

"Valuation of Contingent Consideration" by The Appraisal Foundation, February 2019.

PRACTICE PROBLEMS

The following information relates to questions 1-5

Alan Chin, CEO of Thunder Corporation, has asked his chief financial officer, Constance Ebinosa, to prepare a valuation of Thunder for the purpose of selling the company to a private investment partnership. Thunder is a profitable US-domiciled manufacturer of generic household products with $200 million in annual sales. Customers consist of several grocery store chains in the United States. Competitors include large companies such as Procter & Gamble, The Clorox Company, and Unilever. Thunder has been in business for 15 years and is privately owned by the original shareholders, none of whom are employed by the company. Thunder's senior management has been in charge of the company's operations for most of the past 15 years and expects to remain in that capacity after any sale.

The partnership has expectations about Thunder similar to the current shareholders and management of Thunder. These investors expect to hold Thunder for an intermediate period and then bring the company public when market conditions are more favorable than currently.

Chin is concerned about what definition of value to use in analyzing Thunder. He notes that the stock market has been very volatile recently. He also wonders whether fair market value can be realistically estimated when the most similar recent private market transactions may not have been at arm's length.

Chin asks Ebinosa whether there will be differences in the process of valuing a private company like Thunder compared with a public company. Ebinosa replies that differences do exist and mentions several factors an analyst must consider.

Ebinosa also explains that several approaches are available for valuing private companies. She mentions that one possibility is to use an asset-based approach because Thunder has a relatively large and efficient factory and warehouse for its products. A real estate appraiser can readily determine the value of these facilities. A second method would be the market approach and using an average of the price-to-earnings multiples for Procter & Gamble and Clorox. A third possibility is a discounted free cash flow approach. The latter would focus on a continuation of Thunder's trend of slow profitable growth during the past 10 years.

The private investment partnership has mentioned that it is likely to use an income approach as one of its valuation methods. Ebinosa decides to validate the estimates they make. She assumes that for the next 12 months, Thunder's revenues will increase by the long-term annual growth rate of 3%. She also makes the following assumptions to calculate the free cash flow to the firm for the next 12 months:

- Gross profit margin is 45%.
- Depreciation is 2% of revenues.
- Selling, general, and administrative expenses are 24% of revenues.
- Capital expenditures equal 125% of depreciation to support the current level of revenues.
- Additional capital expenditures of 15% of incremental revenues are needed to fund future growth.
- Working capital investment equals 8% of incremental revenues.

- Marginal tax rate on EBIT is 35%.

Chin knows that if an income approach is used, the choice of discount rate may have a large influence on the estimated value. He makes two statements regarding discount rate estimates:

1. If the CAPM method is used to estimate the discount rate with a beta estimate based on public companies with operations and revenues similar to Thunder, then a small stock premium should be added to the estimate.

2. The weighted average cost of capital of the private investment partnership should be used to value Thunder.

Ebinosa decides to calculate a value of Thunder's equity using the capitalized cash flow method and decides to use the build-up method to estimate Thunder's required return on equity. She makes the following assumptions:

- Growth of FCFE is at a constant annual rate of 3%.
- Free cash flow to equity for the year ahead is $2.5 million.
- Risk-free rate is 4.5%.
- Equity risk premium is 5.0%.
- Size premium is 2.0%.

1. The *least likely* factor that would be a source of differences in valuing Thunder compared with valuing a publicly traded company is:

    A. access to public debt markets.

    B. agency problems.

    C. the size of the company.

2. Ebinosa can *best* value Thunder using the:

    A. excess earnings approach.

    B. asset-based approach.

    C. discounted free cash flow approach.

3. The free cash flow to the firm is *closest* to:

    A. $23,031,000.

    B. $25,441,000.

    C. $36,091,000.

4. Regarding the two statements about discount rate estimates, Chin is:

    A. correct with respect to adding the small stock premium and correct with respect to the weighted average cost of capital.

    B. correct with respect to adding the small stock premium and incorrect with respect to the weighted average cost of capital.

    C. incorrect with respect to adding the small stock premium and incorrect with respect to the weighted average cost of capital.

5. The indicated value of Thunder's equity using the build-up method and the capitalized cash flow method (CCM) based on free cash flow to equity is *closest* to:

    A. $29.41 million.

    B. $38.46 million.

    C. $125.00 million.

6. Two companies are considering the acquisition of Target Company. Buyer A is a strategic buyer and Buyer B is a financial buyer. The following information pertains to Target Company:

    Sales = £28,000,000

    Reported EBITDA = £4,500,000

    Reported executive compensation = £1,000,000

    Normalized executive compensation = £500,000

    Reduced SG&A from eliminating duplicate general and administrative functions = £600,000

    Calculate the pro forma EBITDA estimates that the strategic and financial buyers would each develop in an acquisitions analysis of Target Company.

The following information relates to questions 7-12

The senior vice president of acquisitions for Northland Industries, Angela Lanton, and her head analyst, Michael Powell, are evaluating several potential investments. Northland is a diversified holding company for numerous businesses. One of Northland's divisions is a manufacturer of fine papers, and that division has alerted Lanton about Oakstar Timber, a supplier that may be available for purchase. Oakstar's sole owner, Felix Tanteromo, has expressed interest in exchanging his ownership of Oakstar for a combination of cash and Northland Industries securities.

Oakstar's main asset is 10,000 hectares of timberland in western Canada. The land is a combination of new and old growth Douglas fir trees. The value of this timberland has been steadily increasing since Oakstar acquired it. Oakstar manages the land on a sustained yield basis (i.e., so it continues to produce timber indefinitely) and contracts with outside forestry companies to evaluate, harvest, and sell the timber. Oakstar's income is in the form of royalties (fees paid to Oakstar based on the number of cubic meters harvested). Oakstar's balance sheet as of 31 December 20X0, in Canadian dollars, is as follows.

Oakstar Timber Balance Sheet
Year Ended 31 December 20X0

Assets	
Cash	C$500,000
Inventory	25,000
Accounts receivable	50,000
Plant and equipment (cost less depreciation)	750,000

Oakstar Timber Balance Sheet
Year Ended 31 December 20X0

Assets	
Land	10,000,000
Total assets	C$11,325,000

Liabilities and Equity	
Accounts payables	C$75,000
Long-term bank loan	1,500,000
Common stock	9,750,000
Total liabilities and equity	C$11,325,000

In addition to the balance sheet, Powell is gathering other data to assist in valuing Oakstar and has found information on recent sales of timberland in western Canada. Douglas fir properties have averaged C$6,178 per hectare for tracts that are not contiguous and do not have a developed road system for harvesting the timber. For tracts with these features, as possessed by Oakstar, the average price is C$8,750 per hectare. Properties near urban areas and having potential for residential and recreational second home development command up to C$20,000 per hectare. Oakstar's land lacks this potential. Lanton believes these values would form the basis of an asset-based valuation for Oakstar, with the additional assumption that other assets and liabilities on the balance sheet are assumed to be worth their stated values.

The second company under evaluation, FAMCO, Inc., is a family-owned electronic manufacturing company with annual sales of US$120 million. The family wants to monetize the value of its ownership in FAMCO with a view to later investing part of the proceeds in a diversified stock portfolio. Lanton has asked Powell to obtain data for both an income-based and market-based valuation. Powell has obtained the recent annual income statement and additional data needed to calculate normalized earnings as follows.

FAMCO, Inc.
Income Statement
Year Ending 31 December 20XO

Revenues		US$120,000,000
Gross profit		85,000,000
Selling, general, and administrative expenses		23,000,000
Pro forma EBITDA		US$62,000,000
Depreciation and amortization		3,500,000
Pro forma earnings before interest and taxes		US$58,500,000
Less: Interest		1,000,000
Earnings before taxes (EBT)		US$57,500,000
Pro forma taxes on EBT	40%	23,000,000
Operating income after tax		US$34,500,000

Additional data for FAMCO is provided in the following table. Included are estimates by Powell of the compensation paid to family members and the smaller amount of salary expense for replacement employees if Northland acquires the company (reflecting perceived above-market compensation of the family group executives). He believes the current debt of FAMCO can be replaced with a more optimal level of debt at a lower interest rate. The additional data will be reflected in a normalized income statement.

FAMCO, Inc.

Current debt level	US$10,000,000
Current interest rate	10%
Salaries of employed family members	US$7,000,000
Salaries of replacement employees	US$5,400,000
New debt level	US$25,000,000
New interest rate	8%

Powell also recognizes that a value needs to be assigned to FAMCO's intangibles consisting of patents and other intangible assets. Powell prepares an additional estimate of excess earnings and intangibles value using the capitalized cash flow method. He projects the following data for 20X1:

FAMCO, Inc.—Intangibles Valuation Data

Working capital balance	US$10,000,000
Fair value of fixed assets	US$45,000,000
Normalized income to the company	US$35,000,000
Required return on working capital	8%
Required return on fixed assets	12%
Required return on intangible assets	20%
Weighted average cost of capital	14.5%
Future growth rate	6%

Lanton asks Powell to also use the market approach to valuation with a focus on the guideline transactions method. Powell prepares a table showing relevant information regarding three recent guideline transactions and market conditions at the time of the transactions. Powell's assumptions about FAMCO include its expected fast growth and moderate level of risk.

Target Firm	Target's Risk	Target's Growth	Consideration	Market Conditions
Firm 1	High	Slow	Cash	Normal, rising trend
Firm 2	Moderate	Fast	Stock	Prices near peak
Firm 3	Moderate	Fast	Cash	Normal, rising trend

Although Northland is interested in acquiring all of the stock of FAMCO, the acquisition of a 15% equity interest in FAMCO is also an option. Lanton asks Powell about the valuation of small equity interests in private entities and notes that control and marketability are important factors that lead to adjustments in value estimates for small equity interests. Powell mentions that the control premium paid for the most similar guideline firm used in the analysis suggests a discount for lack of control of 20%. The discount for lack of marketability was estimated at 15%.

7. Which of the following statements concerning asset-based valuation as applied to Oakstar is *most* accurate? The approach is applicable:

A. only when a guideline public company is unavailable for the valuation.

    B. because natural resources with determinable market values constitute the majority of Oakstar's total value.

    C. because as a passive collector of royalties, Oakstar has no meaningful capital expenditures and free cash flow is irrelevant.

8. Using an asset-based approach, the value (net of debt) of Oakstar is *closest* to:

    A. C\$62,250,000.

    B. C\$87,250,000.

    C. C\$199,750,000.

9. The normalized earnings after tax for FAMCO is *closest* to:

    A. US\$32,940,000.

    B. US\$34,260,000.

    C. US\$34,860,000.

10. Using the excess earnings method, the value of FAMCO's intangibles is *closest* to:

    A. US\$144.0 million.

    B. US\$205.7 million.

    C. US\$338.8 million.

11. The guideline transaction that is *most likely* applicable to FAMCO is:

    A. Firm 1.

    B. Firm 2.

    C. Firm 3.

12. The total discount for both control and marketability is *closest* to:

    A. 15%.

    B. 32%.

    C. 35%.

13. Using the build-up method and assuming that no adjustment for industry risk is required, calculate an equity discount rate for a small company, given the following information:

Equity risk premium = 5.0%

Midcap equity risk premium = 3.5%

Small stock risk premium = 4.2%

Income return on long-term bonds = 5.1%

Total return on intermediate-term bonds = 5.3%

Company-specific risk premium = 3.0%

20-Year Treasury bond yield as of the valuation date = 4.5%

The following information relates to questions 14-20

Donald Schmidt is a portfolio manager at FutureTech, an information technology company that is expanding into the food industry. Schmidt meets with Tim Beckett, a FutureTech analyst, to discuss several privately owned companies being investigated for possible acquisition.

Schmidt and Beckett first analyze Dairy Foody, a large, privately owned online food retailer.Beckett observes that the free cash flow growth of Dairy Foody has been quite unstable over time. Schmidt and Beckett discuss the valuation method that is most appropriate to value 100% of Dairy Foody. Schmidt prefers the valuation to reflect market pricing from recent acquisition activity in the food industry, which has been high in recent months.

Schmidt and Beckett then discuss FastDelivery, a family-owned food delivery service. Pro forma financial data for FastDelivery, representing performance mid-economic cycle, are presented in Exhibit 1.

Exhibit 1: FastDelivery: Pro Forma Operating Income after Taxes	
Revenues	$50,000,000
COGS	30,000,000
Gross Profit	20,000,000
SG&A	10,000,000
EBITDA	10,000,000
Depreciation and amortization	3,000,000
EBIT	7,000,000
Pro forma taxes (at 25%)	1,750,000
Operating income after taxes	$5,250,000

Beckett notices two items in FastDelivery's financials that could detract from the reliability of forecasting normalized earnings. Specifically, Beckett notes that in Exhibit 1, SG&A includes the following:

- Management salaries of $5,000,000
- The family's personal expenses of $550,000

Beckett estimates the actual market rate of the management salaries to be $3,500,000.

Schmidt also asks Beckett to calculate the required rate of return on equity for FastDelivery using the build-up method. Beckett collects the following information:

- The risk-free rate is 1%.
- The equity risk premium is 6%.
- The industry risk premium is 2%.
- The small-stock risk premium is 3%.

Schmidt transitions the conversation to Spice World, a privately owned grocery retailer. Schmidt estimates a required rate of return from a selection of guideline public companies. He tells Beckett that the required rate of return needs additional adjustments so that it can be applied to Spice World. First, Schmidt points out that Spice World faces operational and customer concentration risks that do not affect the selected guideline public companies. Second, Schmidt notes that Spice World has fewer employees and a lower level of total assets relative to the guideline public companies.

Having estimated a required rate of return on equity for Spice World, Beckett calculates the company's weighted average cost of capital (WACC) using its existing capital structure, as Schmidt believes that the current debt level is optimal. Beckett utilizes the following information to calculate the WACC for Spice World:

- The cost of equity is 18%.
- The corporate tax rate is 25%.
- The pre-tax cost of debt is 9%.
- The ratio of debt to total capital is 20%.

Schmidt also requests that Beckett value a 15% interest in Food Garden, another grocery retailer. Based on a recent transaction involving a change in control, Beckett estimates the total equity value of Food Garden to be $100,000,000. In arriving at a value for the 15% interest, Beckett concludes that a discount for lack of control (DLOC) of 20% and a discount for lack of marketability (DLOM) of 35% are applicable.

Finally, Beckett and Schmidt discuss LiveLong Foods, a privately owned food preservation company. Schmidt asks Beckett to employ the guideline public company method to value 100% of LiveLong Foods. Beckett observes that a group of comparable public companies has a median market value of invested capital (MVIC) to EBITDA multiple of 10. Beckett notes the following:

- LiveLong Foods' EBITDA is $12,000,000.
- The market value of LiveLong Foods' debt is $6,000,000.
- A combined downward adjustment of 12% for relative risk and growth characteristics should be applied to the median multiple.
- An 18% control premium should also be applied to the median multiple.

14. Given Schmidt's preference, which of the following valuation methods is *most appropriate* to value Dairy Foody?

   A. Excess earnings method

   B. Capitalized cash flow method

   C. Guideline transactions method

15. The normalized operating income for FastDelivery is:

   A. $5,662,500.

   B. $6,375,000.

   C. $6,787,500.

16. Using the build-up method, the required rate of return on equity for FastDelivery

is:

A. 10%.

B. 11%.

C. 12%.

17. Given the observations about Spice World noted by Schmidt, the required rate of return for Spice World should be adjusted to reflect:

A. only a size premium.

B. only a company-specific risk premium.

C. both a size premium and a company-specific risk premium.

18. The WACC for Spice World is *closest* to:

A. 12.15%.

B. 15.75%.

C. 16.20%.

19. Beckett should estimate the value of the 15% equity interest in Food Garden to be:

A. $6,750,000.

B. $7,800,000.

C. $12,750,000.

20. Using the guideline public company method, Beckett should estimate the value of 100% of LiveLong Foods to be:

A. $118,608,000.

B. $121,200,000.

C. $124,608,000.

21. Using the capitalized cash flow method (CCM), calculate the fair market value of 100% of the equity of a hypothetical company, given the following information:

Current year's reported free cash flow to equity = $1,400,000

Current year's normalized free cash flow to equity = $1,800,000

Long-term interest-bearing debt = $2,000,000

Weighted average cost of capital = 15%

Equity discount rate = 18%

Long-term growth rate of FCFE = 5.5%

The following information relates to questions 22-23

You have been asked to value Pacific Corporation, Inc., using an excess earnings method, given the following information:

Working capital balance = $2,000,000

Fair value of fixed assets = $5,500,000

Book value of fixed assets = $4,000,000

Normalized earnings of firm = $1,000,000

Required return on working capital = 5.0%

Required return on fixed assets = 8.0%

Required return on intangible assets = 15.0%

Weighted average cost of capital = 10.0%

Long-term growth rate of residual income = 5.0%

Based on this information:

22. What is the value of Pacific's intangible assets?

23. What is the market value of invested capital?

24. An appraiser has been asked to determine the combined level of valuation discounts for a small equity interest in a private company. The appraiser concluded that an appropriate control premium is 15%. A discount for lack of marketability was estimated at 25%. Given these factors, what is the combined discount?

SOLUTIONS

1. B is correct. Thunder's size and its probable lack of access to public debt markets are potential factors affecting its valuation compared with a public company. Given that the separation of ownership and control at Thunder is similar to that at public companies, however, agency problems are not a distinguishing factor in its valuation.

2. C is correct. The excess earnings method would rarely be applied to value a company's equity, particularly when it is not needed to value intangibles. The asset-based approach is less appropriate because it is infrequently used to estimate the business enterprise value of operating companies. By contrast, the free cash flow method is broadly applicable and readily applied in this case.

3. A is correct. Using Ebinosa's assumptions:

Revenues ($200,000,000 × 1.03 =)		$206,000,000
Gross profit	45%[a]	92,700,000
Selling, general, and administrative expenses	24%[a]	49,440,000
Pro forma EBITDA		43,260,000
Depreciation	2%[a]	4,120,000
Pro forma EBIT		39,140,000
Pro forma taxes on EBIT	35%[b]	13,699,000
Operating income after tax		25,441,000
Plus: Depreciation		4,120,000
Less: Capital expenditures on current sales	125%[c]	5,150,000
Less: Capital expenditures to support future sales	15%[d]	900,000
Less: Working capital requirement	8%[d]	480,000
Free cash flow to the firm		$23,031,000

[a] *Percentage of revenues*
[b] *Percentage of EBIT*
[c] *Percentage of depreciation*
[d] *Percentage of incremental revenues*

4. C is correct. Both statements by Chin are incorrect. If the CAPM is used with public companies with similar operations and similar revenue size, as stated, then the calculation likely captures the small stock premium and should not be added to the estimate. Small stock premiums are associated with build-up models and the expanded CAPM, rather than the CAPM per se. The correct weighted average cost of capital should reflect the risk of Thunder's cash flows, not the risk of the acquirer's cash flows.

5. A is correct. The return on equity is the sum of the risk-free rate, equity risk premium, and the size premium for a total of $4.5 + 5.0 + 2.0 = 11.5\%$. The value of the firm using the CCM is $V = \text{FCFE}_1/(r - g) = 2.5/(0.115 - 0.03) = \$29.41$ million.

6. A strategic buyer seeks to eliminate unnecessary expenses. The strategic buyer would adjust the reported EBITDA by the amount of the officers' excess compensation. A strategic buyer could also eliminate redundant manufacturing costs estimated at £600,000. The pro forma EBITDA a strategic buyer might use in its acquisition analysis is the reported EBITDA of £4,500,000 plus the non-market compensation expense of £500,000 plus the operating synergies (cost savings) of

£600,000. The adjusted EBITDA for the strategic buyer is £4,500,000 + £500,000 + £600,000 = £5,600,000. The financial buyer would also make the adjustment to normalize officers' compensation but would be unable to eliminate redundant manufacturing expenses. Thus, adjusted EBITDA for the financial buyer would be £4,500,000 + £500,000 = £5,000,000.

7. B is correct. Oakstar's primary asset is timberland, the market value of which can be determined from comparable land sales.

8. B is correct. In the absence of market value data for assets and liabilities, the analyst usually must use book value data (the assumption is explicitly made that book values accurately reflect market values as well). Except for timberland, market values for assets are unavailable. Thus, all other assets are assumed to be valued by their book values, which sum to C$500,000 + C$25,000 + C$50,000 + C$750,000 = C$1,325,000. The land's value is determined by the value of C$8,750 per hectare for properties comparable to Oakstar's. Thus, the value of Oakstar's land is C$8,750 × 10,000 = C$87,500,000. Liabilities are assumed to be worth the sum of their book value, or C$1,575,000. Thus, Estimated value = Total assets – Liabilities = C$1,325,000 + C$87,500,000 – C$1,575,000 = C$87,250,000.

9. C is correct. The new interest level is US$2,000,000 instead of US$1,000,000. SG&A expenses are reduced by US$1,600,000 (= US$5,400,000 – US$7,000,000) to US$21,400,000 by salary expense savings. Other than a calculation of a revised provision for taxes, no other changes to the income statement results in normalized earnings before tax of US$58,100,000 and normalized earnings after tax of US$34,860,000.

10. B is correct:

    Return on working capital = 0.08 × US$10,000,000 = US$800,000

    Return on fixed assets = 0.12 × US$45,000,000 = US$5,400,000

    Return on intangibles = US$35,000,000 – US$800,000 – US$5,400,000
    = US$28,800,000

    Value of intangibles using CCM = US$28,800,000/(0.20 – 0.06) = US$205.71 million.

11. C is correct. Firm 3 matches FAMCO in both risk and growth. Firm 1 fails on these factors. In addition, Firm 3 is a better match to FAMCO than Firm 2 because the offer for Firm 3 was a cash offer in normal market conditions, whereas Firm 2 was a stock offer in a boom market and the value does not reflect risk and growth in the immediate future.

12. B is correct. Both discounts apply, and they are multiplicative rather than additive:

    $$1 - (1 - 0.20)(1 - 0.15) = 1 - 0.68$$

13. The build-up method is substantially similar to the extended CAPM except that beta is excluded from the calculation. The equity return requirement is calculated as risk-free rate plus equity risk premium for large-capitalization stocks plus small stock risk premium plus company-specific risk premium: 4.5 + 5.0 + 4.2 + 3.0 = 16.7%. Although practice may vary, in this case, there was no adjustment for industry risk.

14. C is correct. Schmidt and Beckett are valuing 100% of Dairy Foody as part of their acquisition analysis. The guideline transactions method (GTM) uses a mul-

tiple that specifically relates to the sale of entire companies and establishes the value estimate of a business based on pricing multiples derived from the acquisition of control of entire public or private companies. The GTM is appropriate given that Schmidt prefers the valuation to reflect market pricing from recent acquisition activity in the food industry, which has been high in recent months.

A is incorrect because the excess earnings method (EEM) would not likely be used to value 100% of Dairy Foody. Generally, the EEM is used to value intangible assets and very small businesses when other such market approach methods are not feasible, and the EEM is rarely used in pricing entire private businesses. Additionally, Schmidt prefers the valuation to reflect market pricing from recent acquisition activity in the food industry, which has been high in recent months; therefore, the GTM would be more appropriate than the EEM.

B is incorrect because the capitalized cash flow method (CCM) would not likely be used to value 100% of Dairy Foody. The CCM is essentially a stable, growth-free cash flow model that is not a preferable valuation approach when a company is not expected to grow at a constant rate as the method employs a sustainable growth rate to estimate firm value. Dairy Foody has a growth rate that has been quite unstable over time, so the CCM would not be a preferable method to estimate its value. Additionally, the CCM is rarely used for the valuation of public companies, larger private companies, or in the context of acquisitions, but it may be appropriate if market pricing evidence from public companies or transactions is limited. Thus, the CCM would not likely be used to value Dairy Foody because Dairy Foody is a large, privately owned company that is being valued in the context of an acquisition. Finally, Schmidt prefers the valuation to reflect market pricing from recent acquisition activity in the food industry, which has been high in recent months; therefore, the GTM would be more appropriate than the CCM.

15. C is correct. In computing normalized operating income for FastDelivery, SG&A expenses are first reduced by $1,500,000 (from the current $5 million to the market rate of $3.5 million) to reflect the change of management from family members to professional management at the market rate. Second, SG&A should be reduced by an additional $550,000 to remove the family's personal expenses. Based on those adjustments, FastDelivery's pro forma income statement is:

Exhibit 2: FastDelivery: Pro Forma Operating Income after Taxes	
Revenues	$50,000,000
COGS	30,000,000
Gross profit	20,000,000
SG&A	7,950,000
EBITDA	12,050,000
Depreciation and amortization	3,000,000
EBIT	9,050,000
Pro forma taxes (at 25%)	2,262,500
Operating income after taxes	$6,787,500

A is incorrect because it fails to adjust SG&A for the change in management salaries from $5 million to the market rate of $3.5 million:

Exhibit 3: FastDelivery: Pro Forma Operating Income after Taxes

Revenues	$50,000,000
COGS	30,000,000
Gross profit	20,000,000
SG&A	9,450,000
EBITDA	10,550,000
Depreciation and amortization	3,000,000
EBIT	7,550,000
Pro forma taxes (at 25%)	1,887,500
Operating income after taxes	$5,662,500

B is incorrect because it fails to remove the family's personal expenses from SG&A:

Exhibit 4: FastDelivery: Pro Forma Operating Income after Taxes

Revenues	$50,000,000
COGS	30,000,000
Gross profit	20,000,000
SG&A	8,500,000
EBITDA	11,500,000
Depreciation and amortization	3,000,000
EBIT	8,500,000
Pro forma taxes (at 25%)	2,125,000
Operating income after taxes	$6,375,000

16. C is correct. The required rate of return on equity for FastDelivery is 12%:

Risk-free rate	1%
Plus: Small-stock risk premium	3%
Plus: Equity risk premium	6%
Plus: Industry risk premium	2%
Indicated return on equity	12%

A is incorrect because the industry risk premium is excluded from the calculation:

Risk-free rate	1%
Plus : Small-stock risk premium	3%
Plus: Equity risk premium	6%
Indicated return on equity	10%

B is incorrect because the risk-free rate is incorrectly excluded from the calculation:

Equity risk premium	6%
Plus: Small-stock risk premium	3%
Plus: Industry risk premium	2%
Indicated return on equity	11%

17. C is correct. The required return for Spice World should be adjusted to reflect both a size premium and a company-specific risk premium. Spice World is smaller than the guideline public companies, as it has fewer employees and a lower level of total assets. Therefore, the required rate of return should be adjusted to reflect a size premium so that it reflects the level of risk of Spice World. Further, Spice World faces operational and customer concentration risks that do not impact the selected guideline public companies—risks specific to Spice World. These company-specific risks increase the level of risk of Spice World relative to that of the guideline public companies. Consequently, the required return for Spice World should also reflect a company-specific risk premium.

A is incorrect because the required return for Spice World should be adjusted to reflect both a size premium and a company-specific risk premium (not just a size premium). Spice World faces operational and customer concentration risks that do not impact the selected guideline public companies—risks specific to Spice World. These company-specific risks increase the level of risk of Spice World relative to that of the guideline public companies. Consequently, the required return for Spice World should also reflect a company-specific risk premium.

B is incorrect because the required rate of return for Spice World should be adjusted to reflect both a size premium and a company-specific risk premium (not just a company-specific risk premium). Spice World is smaller than the guideline public companies, as it has fewer employees and a lower level of total assets. Therefore, the required return should be adjusted to reflect a size premium so that it reflects the level of risk of Spice World.

18. B is correct. Spice World's WACC is calculated as:

Pre-tax cost of debt	9.00%	
Tax rate complement (1 − tax rate)	× 0.75	
After-tax cost of debt	6.75%	
Weight	× 0.20	
Weighted cost of debt		1.35%
Cost of equity	18.00%	
Weight	× 0.80	
Weighted cost of equity		14.40%
Weighted average cost of capital		15.75%

A is incorrect because Spice World's cost of equity is incorrectly adjusted for taxes:

Pre-tax cost of debt	9%	
Tax rate complement (1 − tax rate)	× 0.75	
After-tax cost of debt	6.75%	
Weight	× 0.20	
Weighted cost of debt		1.35%
Cost of equity	18.0%	
Tax rate complement (1 − tax rate)	× 0.75	

After-tax cost of equity	13.50
Weight	× 0.80
Weighted cost of equity	10.80%
Weighted average cost of capital	12.15%

C is incorrect because Spice World's pre-tax cost of debt, instead of its after-tax cost of debt, is incorrectly used to calculate its weighted cost of debt:

Pre-tax cost of debt	9%
Weight	× 0.20
Weighted cost of debt	1.8%
Cost of equity	18.00%
Weight	× 0.80
Weighted cost of equity	14.40%
Weighted average cost of capital	16.20%

19. B is correct. The lack of control and lack of marketability discounts are applied in sequence. The discounts are multiplicative because the valuation process involves discrete steps—first moving from a controlling to a non-controlling basis, and then moving from a marketable to a non-marketable basis. Therefore, the 15% equity interest in Food Garden is calculated as:

Indicated value of equity in operations	$100,000,000
Interest appraised	×15%
Pro rata value of 15% equity interest	15,000,000
Less: Lack of control discount of 20%	3,000,000
Value assuming ready marketability	12,000,000
Less: Lack of marketability discount of 35%	4,200,000
Indicated value of 15% equity interest	$7,800,000

A is incorrect because the lack of control and marketability discounts are incorrectly added together. Valuation discounts are multiplicative and applied sequentially, not added:

Indicated value of equity in operations	$100,000,000
Interest appraised	×15%
Pro rata value of 15% equity interest	15,000,000
Less: 55%, the sum of the DLOC of 20% and the DLOM of 35%	8,250,000
Indicated value of 15% equity interest	$6,750,000

C is incorrect because the DLOC is incorrectly subtracted from the lack of marketability discount. Valuation discounts are multiplicative and applied sequentially, not subtracted from one another:

Indicated value of equity in operations	$100,000,000
Interest appraised	×15%
Pro rata value of 15% equity interest	15,000,000
Less: 15%, the difference between the DLOM of 35% and the DLOC of 20%	2,250,000

Indicated value of 15% equity interest	$12,750,000

20. A is correct. Using the guideline public company method, the value of LiveLong Foods is calculated in two steps:

First, calculate the pricing multiple for LiveLong Foods:

Initial MVIC to EBITDA from public companies		10.0
Relative risk and growth adjustment for LiveLong Foods	−12%	(1.2)
Multiple before control adjustment		8.8
Control premium adjustment	18%	1.584
Multiple after control adjustment		10.384

Second, calculate the valuation of LiveLong Foods:

Normalized EBITDA	$12,000,000
Pricing multiple	× 10.384
Indicated value of invested capital	$124,608,000
Less: Debt capital	$6,000,000
Indicated value of equity	$118,608,000

B is incorrect because the downward adjustment to LiveLong Foods' pricing multiple and control premium adjustment were incorrectly added together. The valuation adjustments should be applied sequentially, not added:

Initial MVIC to EBITDA from public companies		10.0
6%, the sum of the control premium adjustment and the relative risk and growth adjustment for LiveLong Foods	18% − 12%	0.6
Multiple after adjustment		10.6

Normalized EBITDA	$12,000,000
Pricing multiple	× 10.6
Indicated value of invested capital	$127,200,000
Less: Debt capital	$6,000,000
Indicated value of equity	$121,200,000

C is incorrect because the market value of LiveLong Foods' debt is incorrectly not deducted from the indicated value of invested capital in arriving at the value of LiveLong Foods' equity:

Normalized EBITDA	$12,000,000
Pricing multiple	× 10.384
Indicated value of invested capital	$124,608,000

21. There are FCFF and FCFE variations of the CCM. In this problem, the data permit the application of only the FCFE variation. According to that variation, the estimated value of equity equals the normalized free cash flow to equity estimate for next period divided by the capitalization rate for equity. The capitalization rate is the required rate of return for equity less the long-term growth rate in free

cash flow to equity. Using the current $1.8 million of free cash flow to equity, the 18% equity discount rate, and the long-term growth rate of 5.5% yields a value indication of [($1.8 million)(1.055)]/(0.18 − 0.055) = $1.899 million/0.125 = $15.19 million.

22. The residual income for intangible assets is $460,000 (the normalized earnings of $1,000,000 less the $540,000 required return for working capital and fixed assets). The value of intangible assets can then be calculated using the capitalized cash flow method. The intangibles value is $4,830,000 based on $483,000 of year-ahead residual income available to the intangibles capitalized at 10.0% (15.0% discount rate for intangibles less 5.0% long-term growth rate of residual income).

23. The market value of invested capital is the total of the values of working capital, fixed assets, and intangible assets. This value is $2,000,000 + $5,500,000 + $4,830,000 = $12,330,000.

24. The valuation of a small equity interest in a private company would typically be calculated on a basis that reflects the lack of control and lack of marketability of the interest. The control premium of 15% must first be used to provide an indication of a discount for lack of control (DLOC). A lack of control discount can be calculated using the formula Lack of control discount = 1 − [1/ (1 + Control premium)]. In this case, a lack of control discount of approximately 13% is calculated as 1 − [1/(1 + 15%)]. The discount for lack of marketability (DLOM) was specified. Valuation discounts are applied sequentially and are not added. The formula is (Pro rata control value) × (1 − DLOC) × (1 − DLOM). A combined discount of approximately 35% is calculated as 1 − (1 − 13%) × (1 − 25%) = 0.348, or 34.8%.

Fixed Income

1

The Term Structure and Interest Rate Dynamics

by Thomas S.Y. Ho, PhD, Sang Bin Lee, PhD, and Stephen E. Wilcox, PhD, CFA.

Thomas S.Y. Ho, PhD, is at Thomas Ho Company Ltd (USA). Sang Bin Lee, PhD, is at Hanyang University (South Korea). Stephen E. Wilcox, PhD, CFA, is at Minnesota State University, Mankato (USA).

LEARNING OUTCOMES

Mastery	The candidate should be able to:
☐	describe relationships among spot rates, forward rates, yield to maturity, expected and realized returns on bonds, and the shape of the yield curve
☐	describe how zero-coupon rates (spot rates) may be obtained from the par curve by bootstrapping
☐	describe the assumptions concerning the evolution of spot rates in relation to forward rates implicit in active bond portfolio management
☐	describe the strategy of rolling down the yield curve
☐	explain the swap rate curve and why and how market participants use it in valuation
☐	calculate and interpret the swap spread for a given maturity
☐	describe short-term interest rate spreads used to gauge economy-wide credit risk and liquidity risk
☐	explain traditional theories of the term structure of interest rates and describe the implications of each theory for forward rates and the shape of the yield curve
☐	explain how a bond's exposure to each of the factors driving the yield curve can be measured and how these exposures can be used to manage yield curve risks
☐	explain the maturity structure of yield volatilities and their effect on price volatility
☐	explain how key economic factors are used to establish a view on benchmark rates, spreads, and yield curve changes

1   SPOT RATES, FORWARD RATES, AND THE FORWARD RATE MODEL

☐   describe relationships among spot rates, forward rates, yield to maturity, expected and realized returns on bonds, and the shape of the yield curve

☐   describe how zero-coupon rates (spot rates) may be obtained from the par curve by bootstrapping

Interest rates are both a barometer of the economy and an instrument for its control. The term structure of interest rates—market interest rates at various maturities—is a vital input into the valuation of many financial products. The quantification of interest rate risk is of critical importance to risk managers. Understanding the determinants of interest rates, and thus the drivers of bond returns, is imperative for fixed-income market participants. Here, we explore the tools necessary to understand the term structure and interest rate dynamics—that is, the process by which bond yields and prices evolve over time.

Section 1 explains how spot (or current) rates and forward rates, which are set today for a period starting in the future, are related, as well as how their relationship influences yield curve shape. Section 2 builds upon this foundation to show how forward rates impact the yield-to-maturity and expected bond returns. Section 3 explains how these concepts are put into practice by active fixed-income portfolio managers.

The swap curve is the term structure of interest rates derived from a periodic exchange of payments based on fixed rates versus short-term market reference rates rather than default-risk-free government bonds. Sections 4 and 5 describe the swap curve and its relationship to government yields, known as the swap spread, and explains their use in valuation.

Section 6 describes traditional theories of the term structure of interest rates. These theories outline several qualitative perspectives on economic forces that may affect the shape of the term structure.

Section 7 describes yield curve factor models. The focus is a popular three-factor term structure model in which the yield curve changes are described in terms of three independent movements: level, steepness, and curvature. These factors can be extracted from the variance–covariance matrix of historical interest rate movements.

Section 8 builds on the factor model and describes how to manage the risk of changing rates over different maturities. Section 9 concludes with a discussion of key variables known to influence interest rates, the development of interest rate views based on forecasts of those variables, and common trades tailored to capitalize on an interest rate view. A summary of key points concludes the reading.

Spot Rates and Forward Rates

We first explain the relationships among spot rates, forward rates, yield-to-maturity, expected and realized returns on bonds, and the shape of the yield curve. We then discuss the assumptions made about forward rates in active bond portfolio management.

The price of a risk-free single-unit payment (e.g., \$1, €1, or £1) after N periods is called the **discount factor** with maturity N, denoted by PV_N. The yield-to-maturity of the payment is called a **spot rate**, denoted by Z_N. That is,

$$DF_N = \frac{1}{(1 + Z_N)^N} \tag{1}$$

The N-period discount factor, DF_N, and the N-period spot rate, Z_N, for a range of maturities in years $N > 0$ are called the **discount function** and the **spot yield curve** (or, more simply, **spot curve**), respectively. This spot curve represents the term structure of interest rates. Note that the discount function completely identifies the spot curve and vice versa, because both contain the same set of information about the time value of money.

The spot curve shows, for various maturities, the annualized return on an option-free and default-risk-free **zero-coupon bond** (**zero** for short) with a single payment at maturity. For this reason, spot rates are also referred to as zero-coupon yields or zero rates. The spot rate as a yield concept avoids the need for a reinvestment rate assumption for coupon-paying securities.

As Equation 1 suggests, the spot curve is a benchmark for the time value of money received on a future date as determined by the market supply and demand for funds. It is viewed as the most basic term structure of interest rates because no reinvestment risk is involved; the stated yield equals the actual realized return if the zero is held to maturity. Thus, the yield on a zero-coupon bond maturing in year T is regarded as the most accurate representation of the T-year interest rate.

A **forward rate** is an interest rate determined today for a loan that will be initiated in a future period. The set of forward rates for loans of different maturities with the same future start date is called the **forward curve**. Forward rates and forward curves can be mathematically derived from the current spot curve.

Denote the forward rate of a loan initiated A periods from today with tenor (further maturity) of B periods by $f_{A,B-A}$. Consider a forward contract in which one party, the buyer, commits to pay another party, the seller, a forward contract price $f_{A,B-A}$ at time A for a zero-coupon bond with maturity $B - A$ and unit principal. Because this is an agreement to do something in the future, no money is exchanged at contract initiation. At A, the buyer will pay the seller the contracted forward price and will receive from the seller at time B a payment defined here as a single currency unit.

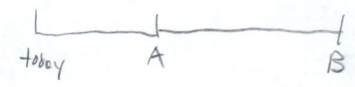

The **forward pricing model** describes the valuation of forward contracts. The no-arbitrage principle, which simply states that tradable securities with identical cash flow payments must have the same price, may be used to derive the model as shown in Equation 2:

$$DF_B = DF_A \times F_{A,B-A} \qquad (2)$$

The discount factors DF_A and DF_B represent the respective prices for period A and a longer period B needed to derive the forward price, $F_{A,B-A}$, a contract which starts in the future at time A and ends at time B. To understand the reasoning behind Equation 2, consider two alternative investments: (1) buying a two-year zero-coupon bond at a cost of $DF_2 = 0.93$ and (2) entering into a one-year forward contract to purchase a one-year zero-coupon bond for $DF_1 = 0.95$. Because the payoffs in two years are the same and the initial costs of the investments must be equal, the no-arbitrage forward price $F_{1,1}$ must equal 0.93/0.95, or 0.9789. Otherwise, any trader could sell the overvalued investment and buy the undervalued investment with the proceeds to generate risk-free profits with zero net investment.

Example 1 should help confirm your understanding of discount factors and forward prices. Please note that the solutions in the examples that follow may be rounded to two or four decimal places.

EXAMPLE 1

Spot and Forward Prices and Rates (1)

Consider a two-year loan beginning in one year ($A = 1$, $B = 3$). The one-year spot rate is $z_1 = z_A = 7\% = 0.07$. The three-year spot rate is $z_3 = z_B = 9\% = 0.09$.

1. Calculate the one-year discount factor: $DF_A = DF_1$.

Solution:

Using Equation 1,

$$DF_1 = \frac{1}{(1 + 0.07)^1} = 0.9346$$

2. Calculate the three-year discount factor: $DF_B = DF_3$.

Solution:

$$DF_3 = \frac{1}{(1 + 0.09)^3} = 0.7722$$

3. Calculate the forward price of a two-year bond to be issued in one year: $F_{A,B-A} = F_{1,3}$.

Solution:

Using Equation 2,

$$0.7722 = 0.9346 \times F_{1,3}.$$

$$F_{1,3} = 0.7722 \div 0.9346 = 0.8262.$$

4. Interpret your answer to Problem 3.

Solution:

The forward contract price of $DF_{1,3} = 0.8262$ is the price agreed on today, to be paid one year from today for a bond with a two-year maturity and a risk-free unit-principal payment (e.g., \$1, €1, or £1) at maturity in three years. As shown in the solution to 3, it is calculated as the three-year discount factor, $DF_3 = 0.7722$, divided by the one-year discount factor, $DF_1 = 0.9346$.

The Forward Rate Model

This section uses the forward rate model to establish that forward rates are above spot rates when the spot curve is upward sloping and below spot rates when the spot curve slopes downward. Exhibit 1 shows these spot versus forward relationships for the US Treasury yield curve in July 2013 versus December 2006, respectively. As we illustrate later, the relationship between spot and forward rates is important for future rate expectations as well as valuing fixed-income instruments.

Exhibit 1: Spot and Forward Curves

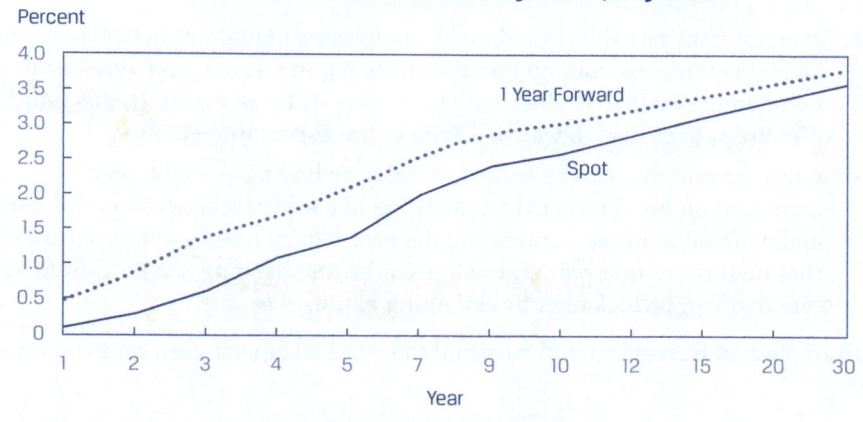

A. Spot vs. Forward US Treasury Yields, July 2013

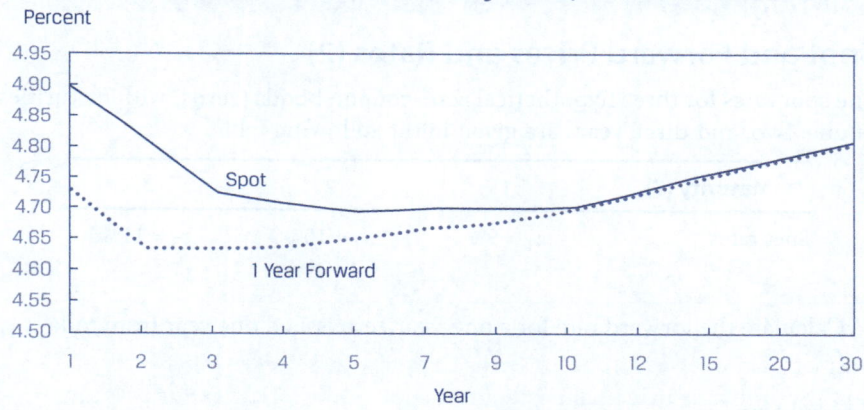

B. Spot vs. Forward US Treasury Yields, December 2006

In contrast to the forward price $F_{A,B-A}$, the forward $rate f_{A,B-A}$ is the discount rate for a risk-free unit-principal payment (e.g., \$1, €1, or £1) B periods from today, valued at time A, such that the present value equals the forward contract price, $DF_{A,B-A}$. Then, by definition,

$$DF_{A,B-A} = \frac{1}{\left(1 + F_{A,B-A}\right)^{B-A}} \qquad (3)$$

By substituting Equation 1 and Equation 3 into Equation 2, the forward pricing model can be expressed in terms of rates as noted by Equation 4, which is the **forward rate model**:

$$\left(1 + z_B\right)^B = \left(1 + z_A\right)^A \left(1 + f_{A,B-A}\right)^{B-A} \qquad (4)$$

Thus, the spot rate for B periods, which is z_B, and the spot rate for A periods, which is z_A, imply a value for the $(B-A)$-period forward rate at A, $f_{A,B-A}$. Equation 4 is important because it shows how forward rates may be extrapolated from spot rates—that is, they are implicit in the spot rates at any given point in time.

Equation 4 suggests two ways to interpret forward rates. For example, suppose $f_{7,1}$, the rate agreed on today for a one-year loan to be made seven years from today, is 3%. Then 3% is the

- reinvestment rate that would make an investor indifferent between buying an eight-year zero-coupon bond or investing in a seven-year zero-coupon bond and at maturity reinvesting the proceeds for one year. In this sense, the forward rate can be viewed as a type of breakeven interest rate.

- one-year rate that can be locked in today by buying an eight-year zero-coupon bond rather than investing in a seven-year zero-coupon bond and, when it matures, reinvesting the proceeds in a zero-coupon instrument that matures in one year. In this sense, the forward rate can be viewed as a rate that can be locked in by extending maturity by one year.

Example 2 addresses forward rates and the relationship between spot and forward rates.

EXAMPLE 2

Spot and Forward Prices and Rates (2)

The spot rates for three hypothetical zero-coupon bonds (zeros) with maturities of one, two, and three years are given in the following table.

Maturity (T)	1	2	3
Spot rates	$z_1 = 9\%$	$z_2 = 10\%$	$z_3 = 11\%$

1. Calculate the forward rate for a one-year zero issued one year from today, $f_{1,1}$.

Solution:

$f_{1,1}$ is calculated as follows (using Equation 4):

$$\left(1 + z_2\right)^2 = \left(1 + z_1\right)^1 \left(1 + f_{1,1}\right)^1$$
$$\left(1 + 0.10\right)^2 = \left(1 + 0.09\right)^1 \left(1 + f_{1,1}\right)^1$$
$$f_{1,1} = \frac{(1.10)^2}{1.09} - 1 = 11.01\%$$

2. Calculate the forward rate for a one-year zero issued two years from today, $f_{2,1}$.

Solution:

$f(2,1)$ is calculated as follows:

$$\left(1 + z_3\right)^3 = \left(1 + z_2\right)^2 \left(1 + f_{2,1}\right)^1$$
$$\left(1 + 0.11\right)^3 = \left(1 + 0.10\right)^2 \left(1 + f_{2,1}\right)^1$$
$$f_{2,1} = \frac{(1.11)^3}{(1.10)^2} - 1 = 13.03\%$$

3. Calculate the forward rate for a two-year zero issued one year from today, $f_{1,2}$.

Solution:

$f_{1,2}$ is calculated as follows:

$$\left(1+z_3\right)^3 = \left(1+z_1\right)^1 \left(1+f_{1,2}\right)^2$$
$$\left(1+0.11\right)^3 = \left(1+0.09\right)^1 \left(1+f_{1,2}\right)^2$$
$$f_{1,2} = \sqrt[2]{\frac{(1.11)^3}{(1.09)^1}} - 1 = 12.01\%$$

4. Based on your answers to 1 and 2, describe the relationship between the spot rates and the implied one-year forward rates.

Solution:

The upward-sloping zero-coupon yield curve is associated with an upward-sloping forward curve (a series of increasing one-year forward rates because 13.03% is greater than 11.01%). This dynamic is explained further in the following discussion.

The relationship between spot rates and one-period forward rates may be demonstrated using the forward rate model and successive substitution, resulting in Equation 5 and Equation 6:

$$\left(1+z_T\right)^T = \left(1+z_1\right) \left(1+f_{2,1}\right) \left(1+f_{3,1}\right) \dots \left(1+f_{T-1,1}\right) \tag{5}$$

$$z_T = \left\{ \left(1+z_1\right) \left(1+f_{2,1}\right) \left(1+f_{3,1}\right) \dots \left(1+f_{T-1,1}\right) \right\}^{\frac{1}{T}} - 1 \tag{6}$$

Equation 6 shows that the spot rate for a security with a maturity of $T > 1$ can be expressed as a geometric mean of the spot rate for a security with a maturity of $T = 1$ and a series of $T - 1$ forward rates.

Equation 6 is critical for active fixed-income portfolio managers. Although the question of whether forward rates are unbiased estimators of market consensus expectations remains open to debate, implied forward rates are generally the best available and most accessible proxy for market expectations of future spot rates. If an active trader can identify a series of short-term bonds whose actual returns exceed today's quoted forward rates, then the total return over her investment horizon would exceed the return on a maturity-matching, buy-and-hold strategy if the yield curve were to remain relatively stable. Later, we will apply this concept to dynamic hedging strategies and the local expectations theory.

Example 3 and Example 4 explore the relationship between spot and forward rates.

EXAMPLE 3

Spot and Forward Prices and Rates (3)

1. Given the data and conclusions for $z_1, f_{1,1}$, and $f_{2,1}$ from Example 2:

$z_1 = 9\%$

$f_{1,1} = 11.01\%$

$$f_{2,1} = 13.03\%$$

Show that the two-year spot rate of $z_2 = 10\%$ and the three-year spot rate of $z_3 = 11\%$ are geometric averages of the one-year spot rate and the forward rates.

Solution:

Using Equation 5,

$$(1 + z_2)^2 = (1 + z_1)(1 + f_{1,1})$$
$$z_2 = \sqrt[2]{(1 + 0.09)(1 + 0.1101)} - 1 \approx 10\%$$

$$(1 + z_3)^3 = (1 + z_1)(1 + f_{1,1})(1 + f_{2,1})$$
$$z_3 = \sqrt[3]{(1 + 0.09)(1 + 0.1101)(1 + 0.1303)} - 1 \approx 11\%$$

We can now consolidate our knowledge of spot and forward rates to explain important relationships between the spot and forward rate curves. The forward rate model (Equation 4) can also be expressed as Equation 7.

$$\left\{ \frac{1 + z_B}{1 + z_A} \right\}^{\frac{A}{B-A}} (1 + z_B) = 1 + f_{A,B-A} \tag{7}$$

To illustrate, suppose $A = 1$, $B = 5$, $z_1 = 2\%$, and $z_5 = 3\%$; the left-hand side of Equation 7 is

$$\left(\frac{1.03}{1.02} \right)^{\frac{1}{4}} (1.03) = (1.0024)(1.03) = 1.0325,$$

so $f_{1,4} = 3.25\%$. Given that the yield curve is upward sloping—so, $z_B > z_A$—Equation 7 implies that the forward rate from A to B is greater than the long-term spot rate: $f_{A,B-A} > z_B$. This is the case in our example, because 3.25% > 3.00%. Conversely, when the yield curve is downward sloping, then $z_B < z_A$ and the forward rate from A to B is lower than the long-term spot rate: $f_{A,B-A} < z_B$. Equation 7 also shows that if the spot curve is flat, all one-period forward rates equal the spot rate. For an upward-sloping yield curve— $z_B > z_A$ —the forward rate rises as time periods increase. For a downward-sloping yield curve— $z_B < z_A$ —the forward rate declines as time periods increase.

EXAMPLE 4

Spot and Forward Prices and Rates (4)

Given the spot rates $z_1 = 9\%$, $z_2 = 10\%$, and $z_3 = 11\%$, as in Example 2 and Example 3:

1. Determine whether the forward rate $f_{1,2}$ is greater than or less than the long-term rate, z_3.

Solution:

The spot rates imply an upward-sloping yield curve, $z_3 > z_2 > z_1$, or in general, $z_B > z_A$. Thus, the forward rate will be greater than the long-term rate, or $f_{A,B-A} > z_B$. Note from Example 2 that $f_{1,2} = 12.01\% > z_3 = 11\%$.

2. Determine whether forward rates rise or fall as the initiation date, A, for the forward rate is later.

Solution:

The spot rates imply an upward-sloping yield curve, $z_3 > z_2 > z_1$. Thus, the forward rates will rise with increasing A. This relationship was shown in Example 2, in which $f_{1,1} = 11.01\%$ and $f_{2,1} = 13.03\%$.

These relationships are illustrated in Exhibit 2 and Exhibit 3 as an extension of Exhibit 1. The spot rates for US Treasuries as of 31 July 2013 constructed using interpolation are the lowest, as shown in the table following the exhibit. Note that the spot curve is upward sloping. The forward curves for the end of July 2014, 2015, 2016, and 2017 are also presented in Exhibit 2. Because the yield curve is upward sloping, these forward curves are all above the spot curve and become successively higher and steeper as the forward period increases, the highest of which is that for July 2017.

Exhibit 2: Historical Example: Upward-Sloping Spot Curve vs. Forward Curves, 31 July 2013

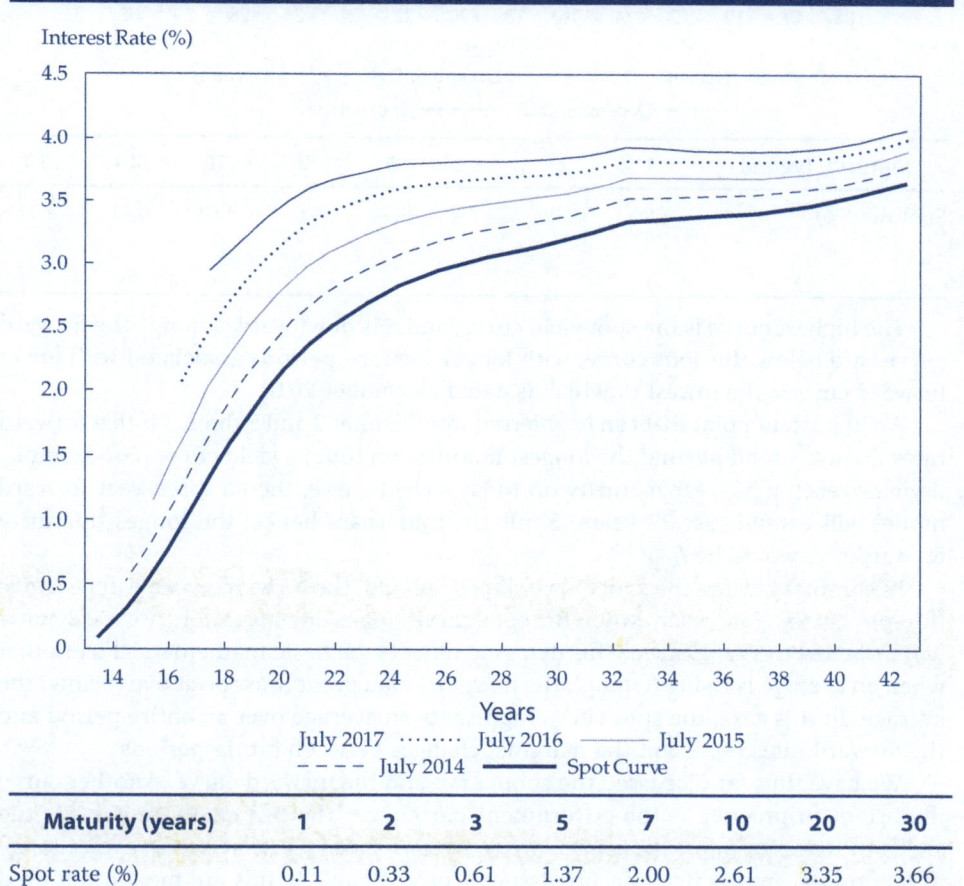

Forward curve: The set of forward rates for loans of different maturities with the same future start date

Maturity (years)	1	2	3	5	7	10	20	30
Spot rate (%)	0.11	0.33	0.61	1.37	2.00	2.61	3.35	3.66

Exhibit 3 shows the opposite case of a downward sloping spot curve based on US Treasury rates as of 31 December 2006. This data also uses interpolation and is somewhat modified to make the yield curve more downward sloping for illustrative purposes. The spot curve and forward curves for the end of December 2007, 2008, 2009, and 2010 are presented in Exhibit 3.

Exhibit 3: Historical Example: Downward-Sloping Spot Curve vs. Forward Curves, 31 December 2006 (modified for illustrative purposes)

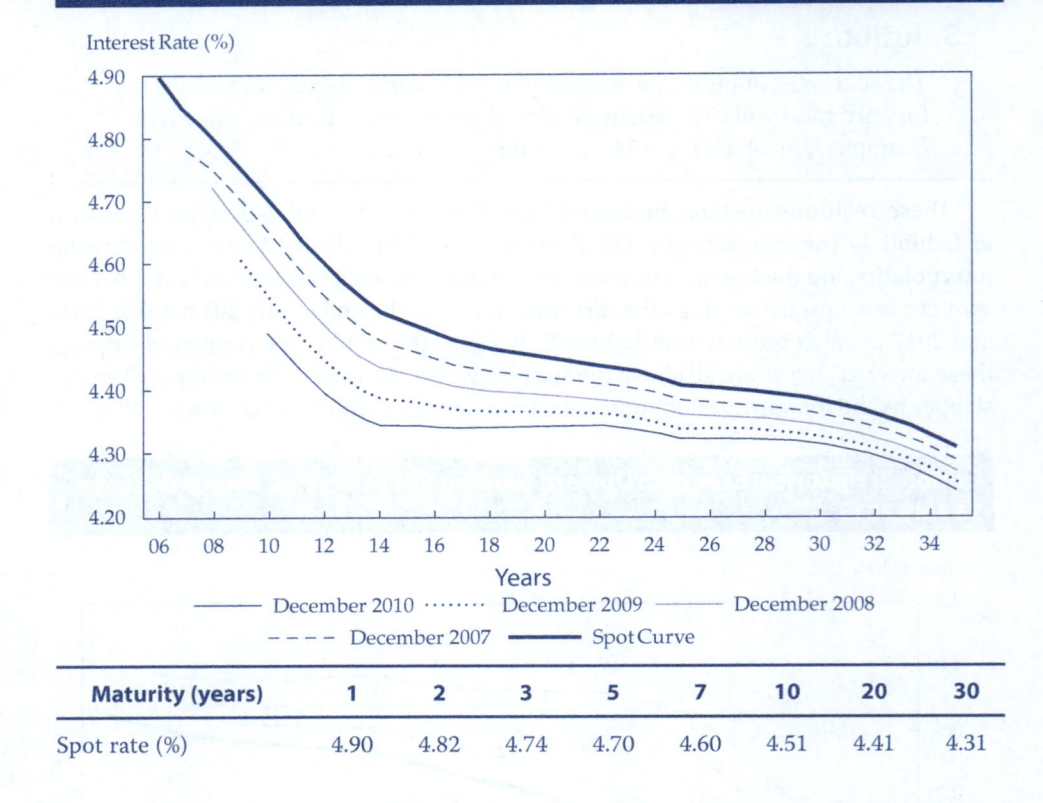

Interest Rate (%)

Maturity (years)	1	2	3	5	7	10	20	30
Spot rate (%)	4.90	4.82	4.74	4.70	4.60	4.51	4.41	4.31

The highest curve is the spot yield curve, and it is downward sloping. The forward curves are below the spot curve, with longer forward periods associated with lower forward curves, the lowest of which is dated December 2010.

An important point that can be inferred from Exhibit 2 and Exhibit 3 is that forward rates do not extend beyond the longest maturity on today's yield curve. For example, if yields reach a 30-year maturity on today's yield curve, then a three-year forward model will extend just 27 years. Similarly, four years hence, the longest-maturity forward rate would be $f_{4,26}$.

In summary, when the spot curve slopes upward, the forward curve will lie above the spot curve. Conversely, when the spot curve slopes downward, the forward curve will lie below the spot curve. This dynamic reflects the basic mathematical truth that when an average is rising (falling), the marginal data point must be above (below) the average. In this case, the spot curve represents an average over an entire period and the forward rates represent the marginal changes between future periods.

We have thus far discussed the spot curve and the forward curve. Another curve important in practice is the government par curve. The **par curve** represents the yields to maturity on coupon-paying government bonds, priced at par, over a range of maturities. In practice, recently issued ("on the run") bonds are most often used to create the par curve, because these securities are most liquid and typically priced at or close to par.

The par curve is important for valuation in that it can be used to construct a zero-coupon yield curve. The process considers a coupon-paying bond as a portfolio of zero-coupon bonds. The zero-coupon rates are determined by using the par yields and solving for the zero-coupon rates one by one, from the shortest to longest maturities using a forward substitution process known as **bootstrapping**.

WHAT IS BOOTSTRAPPING?

Because the practical details of deriving the zero-coupon yield are beyond the scope of this reading, the concept of bootstrapping may be best shown using a numerical illustration. Suppose the following yields are observed for annual coupon sovereign debt:

Par Rates:

One-year par rate = 5%, two-year par rate = 5.97%, three-year par rate = 6.91%, four-year par rate = 7.81%. From these data, we can bootstrap zero-coupon rates.

Zero-Coupon Rates:

Given annual coupons, the one-year zero-coupon rate equals the one-year par rate because it has one cash flow, whereas two-year and longer maturity bonds have coupon payments prior to maturity.

The derivation of zero-coupon rates begins with the two-year maturity. The two-year zero-coupon rate is determined by using $z_1 = 5\%$ and solving for z_2 in the following equation for of one monetary unit of current market value:

$$1 = \frac{0.0597}{(1.05)} + \frac{1 + 0.0597}{(1 + z_2)^2}$$

In the equation, 0.0597 and 1.0597 represent payments from interest and principal and interest, respectively, per unit of principal value. The equation implies that $z_2 = 6\%$. We have bootstrapped the two-year spot rate. Continuing with forward substitution, the three-year zero-coupon rate can be bootstrapped by solving for z_3 using the known values of the one-year and two-year spot rates of 5% and 6%:

$$1 = \frac{0.0691}{(1.05)} + \frac{0.0691}{(1.06)^2} + \frac{1 + 0.0691}{(1 + z_3)^3}$$

Thus, $z_3 = 7\%$. Finally, we solve for the four-year zero-coupon rate, z_4:

$$1 = \frac{0.0781}{(1.05)} + \frac{0.0781}{(1.06)^2} + \frac{0.0781}{(1.07)^3} + \frac{1 + 0.0781}{(1 + z_4)^4}$$

In summary, $z_1 = 5\%$, $z_2 = 6\%$, $z_3 = 7\%$, and $z_4 = 8\%$.

In the preceding discussion, we considered an upward-sloping (spot) yield curve (Exhibit 2) and an inverted or downward-sloping (spot) yield curve (Exhibit 3). In developed markets, yield curves are most commonly upward sloping with diminishing marginal increases in yield for identical changes in maturity; that is, the yield curve "flattens" at longer maturities. Because nominal yields incorporate a premium for expected inflation, an upward-sloping yield curve is generally interpreted as reflecting a market expectation of rising or at least stable future inflation (associated with relatively strong economic growth). The existence of risk premiums (e.g., for the greater interest rate risk of longer-maturity bonds) also contributes to a positive slope.

An inverted yield curve (Exhibit 3) is less common. Such a term structure may reflect a market expectation of declining future inflation rates (because a nominal yield incorporates a premium for expected inflation) from a relatively high current level. Expectations of an economic slowdown may be one reason to anticipate a decline in inflation, and a downward-sloping yield curve is frequently observed before recessions. A flat yield curve typically occurs briefly in the transition from an upward-sloping to a downward-sloping yield curve, or vice versa. A humped yield curve, which is relatively rare, occurs when intermediate-term interest rates are higher than short- and long-term rates.

2   YTM IN RELATION TO SPOT AND FORWARD RATES

☐ | describe the assumptions concerning the evolution of spot rates in relation to forward rates implicit in active bond portfolio management

Yield-to-maturity (YTM) is perhaps the most familiar pricing concept in bond markets. In this section, we clarify how it is related to spot rates and a bond's expected and realized returns.

How is the yield-to-maturity related to spot rates? In bond markets, most bonds outstanding have coupon payments and many have various options, such as a call provision. The YTM of these bonds with maturity T would not be the same as the spot rate at T but should be mathematically related to the spot curve. Because the principle of no arbitrage shows that a bond's value is the sum of the present values of payments discounted by their corresponding spot rates, the YTM of the bond should be some weighted average of spot rates used in the valuation of the bond.

Example 5 addresses the relationship between spot rates and YTM.

EXAMPLE 5

Spot Rate and Yield-to-Maturity

Recall from earlier examples the spot rates $z_1 = 9\%$, $z_2 = 10\%$, and $z_3 = 11\%$. Let y_T be the YTM.

1. Calculate the price of a two-year annual coupon bond using the spot rates. Assume the coupon rate is 6% and the face value is $1,000. Next, state the formula for determining the price of the bond in terms of its YTM. Is z_2 greater than or less than y_2? Why?

Solution:

Using the spot rates,

$$\text{Price} = \frac{\$60}{(1+0.09)^1} + \frac{\$1,060}{(1+0.10)^2} = \$931.08$$

Using the YTM,

$$Price = \frac{\$60}{(1+y_2)} + \frac{\$1,060}{(1+y_2)^2} = \$931.08$$

Note that y_2 is used to discount both the first- and second-year cash flows. Because the bond can have only one price, it follows that $z_1 < y_2 < z_2$ because y_2 is a weighted average of z_1 and z_2 and the yield curve is upward sloping. Using a calculator, one can calculate the YTM as $y_2 = 9.97\%$, which is less than $z_2 = 10\%$ and greater than $z_1 = 9\%$, just as we would expect. Note that y_2 is much closer to z_2 than to z_1 because the bond's largest cash flow occurs in Year 2, thereby giving z_2 a greater weight than z_1 in the determination of y_2.

2. Calculate the price of a three-year annual coupon-paying bond using the spot rates. Assume the coupon rate is 5% and the face value is £100. Next,

write a formula for determining the price of the bond using the YTM. Is z_3 greater or less than y_3? Why?

Solution:

Using the spot rates,

$$\text{Price} = \frac{£5}{(1+0.09)^1} + \frac{£5}{(1+0.10)^2} + \frac{£105}{(1+0.11)^3} = £85.49$$

Using the yield-to-maturity,

$$\text{Price} = \frac{£5}{(1+y_3)} + \frac{£5}{(1+y_3)^2} + \frac{£105}{(1+y_3)^3} = £85.49.$$

Note that y_3 is used to discount all three cash flows. Because the bond can have only one price, y_3 must be a weighted average of $z_1, z_2,$ and z_3. Given that the yield curve is upward sloping in this example, $y_3 < z_3$. Using a calculator to compute YTM, $y_3 = 10.93\%$, which is less than $z_3 = 11\%$ and greater than $z_1 = 9\%$—just as we would expect, because the weighted YTM must lie between the highest and lowest spot rates. Note that y_3 is much closer to z_3 than it is to z_2 or z_1 because the bond's largest cash flow occurs in Year 3, thereby giving z_3 a greater weight than z_1 and z_2 in the determination of y_3.

Investors can expect to earn the yield-to-maturity on a bond only under extremely restrictive assumptions. The YTM is the expected rate of return for a bond held to maturity, assuming that all promised coupon and principal payments are made in full when due and that coupons are reinvested at the original YTM. As interest rates change, the reinvestment of coupons at the original YTM is unlikely. The YTM can provide a poor estimate of expected return if (1) interest rates are volatile, (2) the yield curve is sloped either upward or downward, (3) there is significant risk of default, or (4) the bond has one or more embedded options (e.g., put, call, or conversion). If either (1) or (2) is the case, reinvestment of coupons would not be expected to be at the assumed rate (YTM). Case 3 implies that actual cash flows may differ from those assumed in the YTM calculation, and in Case 4, the exercise of an embedded option would result in a holding period shorter than the bond's original maturity.

The realized return is the actual bond return during an investor's holding period. It is based on actual reinvestment rates and the yield curve at the end of the holding period. If we had perfect foresight, the expected bond return would equal the realized bond return.

To illustrate these concepts, assume that $z_1 = 5\%$, $z_2 = 6\%$, $z_3 = 7\%$, $z_4 = 8\%$, and $z_5 = 9\%$. Consider a five-year annual coupon bond with a coupon rate of 10%. The forward rates extrapolated from the spot rates are $f_{1,1} = 7.0\%, f_{2,1} = 9.0\%, f_{3,1} = 11.1\%,$ and $f_{4,1} = 13.1\%$. The price, determined as a percentage of par, is 105.43.

The yield-to-maturity of 8.62% can be determined by solving

$$105.43 = \frac{10}{(1+y_5)} + \frac{10}{(1+y_5)^2} + \frac{10}{(1+y_5)^3} + \frac{10}{(1+y_5)^4} + \frac{110}{(1+y_5)^5}$$

The yield-to-maturity of 8.62% is the bond's expected return assuming no default, a holding period of five years, and a reinvestment rate of 8.62%. But what if the forward rates are assumed to be the future spot rates?

Using the forward rates as the expected reinvestment rates results in the following expected cash flow at the end of Year 5:

$$10(1 + 0.07)(1 + 0.09)(1 + 0.111)(1 + 0.131) + 10(1 + 0.09)(1 + 0.011)(1 + 0.131)$$
$$+ 10(1 + 0.111)(1 + 0.131) + 10(1 + 0.131) + 110 \approx 162.22$$

Therefore, the expected bond return is $(162.22 - 105.43)/105.43 = 53.87\%$ and the expected annualized rate of return is 9.00% [solve $(1 + x)^5 = 1 + 0.5387$].

From this example, we can see that the expected rate of return is not equal to the YTM even if we make the generally unrealistic assumption that the forward rates are the future spot rates. The YTM is generally a realistic estimate of expected return only if the yield curve is flat. Note that in the foregoing formula, all cash flows were discounted at 8.62% regardless of maturity.

Example 6 will reinforce your understanding of various yield and return concepts.

EXAMPLE 6

Yield and Return Concepts

1. When the spot curve is upward sloping, the forward curve:

   A. lies above the spot curve.

   B. lies below the spot curve.

   C. is coincident with the spot curve.

Solution:

A is correct. Points on a spot curve can be viewed as an average of single-period rates over given maturities, whereas forward rates reflect the marginal changes between future periods.

---

2. Which of the following statements concerning the YTM of a default-risk-free bond is *most* accurate? The YTM of such a bond:

   A. equals the expected return on the bond if the bond is held to maturity.

   B. can be viewed as a weighted average of the spot rates applying to its cash flows.

   C. will be closer to the realized return if the spot curve is upward sloping rather than flat through the life of the bond.

Solution:

B is correct. The YTM is the discount rate that, when applied to a bond's promised cash flows, equates those cash flows to the bond's market price and the fact that the market price should reflect discounting promised cash flows at appropriate spot rates.

---

3. When the spot curve is downward sloping, a later initiation date results in a forward curve that is:

   A. closer to the spot curve.

   B. a greater distance above the spot curve.

   C. a greater distance below the spot curve.

Solution:

C is correct. This answer follows from the forward rate model as expressed in Equation 6. If the spot curve is downward sloping (upward sloping), a later initiation date will result in a forward curve that is a greater distance below (above) the spot curve. See Exhibit 2 and Exhibit 3.

Yield Curve Movement and the Forward Curve

This section establishes several important results concerning forward prices and the spot yield curve to demonstrate the relevance of the forward curve to active bond investors.

The forward contract price remains unchanged as long as future spot rates evolve as predicted by today's forward curve. If a trader expects the future spot rate to be below what is predicted by the prevailing forward rate, the forward contract value is expected to increase and the trader would buy the forward contract. Conversely, if the trader expects the future spot rate to be above that predicted by the existing forward rate, then the forward contract value is expected to decrease and the trader would sell the forward contract.

Using the forward pricing model defined by Equation 2, we can determine the forward contract price that delivers a $(B - A)$-period-maturity bond at time A, $F_{A,B-A}$, using Equation 8 (which is Equation 2 solved for the forward price):

$$F_{A,B-A} = \frac{DF_B}{DF_A} \tag{8}$$

Now suppose that after t periods, the new discount function for some maturity time T period, denoted as DF_T^{new}, is the same as the forward discount function implied by today's discount function, as shown by Equation 9.

$$DF_T^{new} = \frac{DF_{t+T}}{DF_t} \tag{9}$$

Next, after a lapse of t periods, the time to expiration of the contract is $A - t$, and the forward contract price at time t is $F_{A-t,B-A}^{new}$. Equation 8 can be rewritten as Equation 10:

$$F_{A-t,B-A}^{new} = \frac{DF_{B-t}^{new}}{DF_{A-t}^{new}} \tag{10}$$

Substituting Equation 9 into Equation 10 and adjusting for the lapse of time t results in Equation 11:

$$F_{A-t,B-A}^{new} = \frac{DF_{B-t}^{new}}{DF_{A-t}^{new}} = \frac{\frac{DF_B}{DF_t}}{\frac{DF_A}{DF_t}} = \frac{DF_B}{DF_A} = F_{A,B-A} \tag{11}$$

Equation 11 shows that the forward contract price remains unchanged as long as future spot rates are equal to what is predicted by today's forward curve. Therefore, a change in the forward price is the result of a deviation of the spot curve from what is predicted by today's forward curve.

To make these observations concrete, consider a flat yield curve for which the interest rate is 4%. Using Equation 1, the discount factors for the one-year, two-year, and three-year terms are, to four decimal places, as follows:

$$DF_1 = \frac{1}{(1+0.04)} = 0.9615$$

$$DF_2 = \frac{1}{(1+0.04)^2} = 0.9246$$

$$DF_3 = \frac{1}{(1+0.04)^3} = 0.8890$$

Therefore, using Equation 8, the forward contract price that delivers a one-year bond at Year 2 is

$$F_{2,1} = \frac{DF_3}{DF_2} = \frac{0.8890}{0.9246} = 0.9615.$$

Suppose the future discount function at Year 1 is the same as the forward discount function implied by the Year 0 spot curve. The lapse of time is $t = 1$. Using Equation 9, the discount factors for the one-year and two-year terms one year from today are as follows:

$$DF_1^{new} = \frac{DF_2}{DF_1} = \frac{0.9246}{0.9615} = 0.9616$$

$$DF_2^{new} = \frac{DF_3}{DF_1} = \frac{0.8890}{0.9615} = 0.9246$$

Using Equation 10, the price of the forward contract one year from today is

$$F_{2,1}^{new} = \frac{DF_2^{new}}{DF_1^{new}} = \frac{0.9246}{0.9615} = 0.9616.$$

The price of the forward contract is nearly unchanged. This will be the case as long as future discount functions are the same as those based on today's forward curve. From this numerical example, we can see that if the spot rate curve is unchanged, then each bond "rolls down" the curve and earns the current one-period spot rate and subsequent forward rates. Specifically, when one year passes, a three-year bond will return $(0.9246 - 0.8890)/0.8890 = 4\%$, which is equal to the spot rate. Furthermore, if another year passes, the bond will return $(0.9615 - 0.9246)/0.9246 = 4\%$, which is equal to the implied forward rate for a one-year security one year from today.

3   ACTIVE BOND PORTFOLIO MANAGEMENT

☐ | describe the strategy of rolling down the yield curve

One way that active bond portfolio managers attempt to outperform the bond market's return is by anticipating changes in interest rates relative to the projected evolution of spot rates reflected in today's forward curves.

The forward rate model (Equation 4) provides insight into these issues. By rearranging terms in Equation 4 and setting the time horizon to one period, $A = 1$, we obtain

$$\frac{(1+z_B)^B}{(1+f_{A,B-A})^{B-A}} = (1+z_A)^A. \tag{12}$$

The numerator of the left-hand side of Equation 12 is for a bond with an initial maturity of B periods and a remaining maturity of $B - A$ periods after A periods pass. Suppose the prevailing spot yield curve after one period ($A = 1$) is the current forward curve; then, Equation 12 shows that the total return on the bond is the one-period risk-free rate. The following sidebar shows that returns on bonds of varying tenor over a one-year period always equal the one-year rate (the risk-free rate over the one-year period) if the spot rates evolve as implied by the current forward curve at the end of the first year.

WHEN SPOT RATES EVOLVE AS IMPLIED BY THE CURRENT FORWARD CURVE

As in earlier examples, assume the following:

$z_1 = 9\%$

$z_2 = 10\%$

$$z_3 = 11\%$$

$$f_{1,1} = 11.01\%$$

$$f_{1,2} = 12.01\%$$

If the spot curve one year from today reflects the current forward curve, the return on a zero-coupon bond for the one-year holding period is 9%, regardless of the bond's maturity. The following computations assume a par amount of 100 and represent the percentage change in price. Given the rounding of price and the forward rates to the nearest hundredth, the returns all approximate 9%. With no rounding, however, all answers would be precisely 9%.

The return of the one-year zero-coupon bond over the one-year holding period is 9%. The bond is purchased at a price of 91.74 and is worth the par amount of 100 at maturity.

$$\left(100 \div \frac{100}{1+z_1}\right) - 1 = \left(100 \div \frac{100}{1+0.09}\right) - 1 = \frac{100}{91.74} - 1 = 9\%.$$

The return of the two-year zero-coupon bond over the one-year holding period is 9%. The bond is purchased at a price of 82.64. One year from today, the two-year bond has a remaining maturity of one year. Its price one year from today is 90.08, determined as the par amount divided by 1 plus the forward rate for a one-year bond issued one year from today.

$$\left(\frac{100}{\left(1+f_{1,1}\right)} \div \frac{100}{\left(1+z_2\right)^2}\right) - 1 = \left(\frac{100}{(1+0.1101)} \div \frac{100}{(1+0.10)^2}\right) - 1 = \frac{90.08}{82.64} - 1$$

$$= 9\%$$

The return of the three-year zero-coupon bond over the one-year holding period is 9%. The bond is purchased at a price of 73.12. One year from today, the three-year bond has a remaining maturity of two years. Its price one year from today of 79.71 reflects the forward rate for a two-year bond issued one year from today.

$$\left(\frac{100}{\left(1+f_{1,2}\right)^2} \div \frac{100}{\left(1+z_3\right)^3}\right) - 1 = \left(\frac{100}{(1+0.1201)^2} \div \frac{100}{(1+0.11)^3}\right) - 1$$

$$= \frac{79.71}{73.12} - 1 \approx 9\%$$

This numerical example shows that the return of a bond over a one-year period is always the one-year rate (the risk-free rate over the one period) if the spot rates evolve as implied by the current forward curve.

But if the spot curve one year from today differs from today's forward curve, the returns on each bond for the one-year holding period will not all be 9%. To show that the returns on the two-year and three-year bonds over the one-year holding period are not 9%, we assume that the spot rate curve at Year 1 is flat with yields of 10% for all maturities. The return on a one-year zero-coupon bond over the one-year holding period is

$$\left(100 \div \frac{100}{1+0.09}\right) - 1 = 9\%.$$

The return on a two-year zero-coupon bond over the one-year holding period is

$$\left(\frac{100}{1+0.10} \div \frac{100}{(1+0.10)^2}\right) - 1 = 10\%.$$

The return on a three-year zero-coupon bond over the one-year holding period is

$$\left(\frac{100}{(1+0.10)^2} \div \frac{100}{(1+0.11)^3}\right) - 1 = 13.03\%.$$

The bond returns are 9%, 10%, and 13.03%. The returns on the two-year and three-year bonds differ from the one-year risk-free interest rate of 9%.

Equation 12 provides a total return investor with a means to evaluate the cheapness or expensiveness of a bond of a certain maturity. If any of the investor's expected future spot rates is below a quoted forward rate for the same maturity, then (all else being equal) the investor would perceive the bond to be undervalued, in the sense that the market is effectively discounting the bond's payments at a higher rate than the investor and the bond's market price is below the intrinsic value perceived by the investor.

Another example will reinforce the point that if a portfolio manager's projected spot curve is above (below) the forward curve and his expectation turns out to be true, the return will be less (more) than the one-period risk-free interest rate.

For the sake of simplicity, assume a flat yield curve of 8% and that a trader holds a three-year bond paying an 8% annual coupon. Assuming a par value of 100, the current market price is also 100. If today's forward curve turns out to be the spot curve one year from today, the trader will earn an 8% return.

If the trader projects that the spot curve one year from today is above today's forward curve—for example, a flat yield curve of 9%—the trader's expected rate of return is 6.24%, which is less than 8%:

$$\frac{8 + \frac{8}{1 + 0.09} + \frac{108}{(1 + 0.09)^2}}{100} - 1 = 6.24\%$$

If the trader predicts a flat yield curve of 7%, the trader's expected return is 9.81%, which is greater than 8%:

$$\frac{8 + \frac{8}{1 + 0.07} + \frac{108}{(1 + 0.07)^2}}{100} - 1 = 9.81\%$$

As the gap between the projected future spot rate and the forward rate widens, so too will the difference between the trader's expected return and the original YTM of 8%. This logic is the basis for a popular yield curve trade called **rolling down the yield curve**, also referred to as riding the yield curve. As we have noted, when a yield curve is upward sloping, the forward curve is always above the current spot curve. If the trader expects the yield curve to remain static over an investment horizon, then buying bonds with a maturity longer than the investment horizon would provide a total return greater than the return on a maturity-matching strategy. The bond's total return will depend on the spread between the forward rate and the spot rate as well as the maturity of the bond. The longer the bond's maturity, the more sensitive its total return is to the spread. This strategy is shown in Exhibit 4.

- Rolling down the yield curve is appropriate when the yield curve is upward sloping

Exhibit 4: Rolling Down the Yield Curve

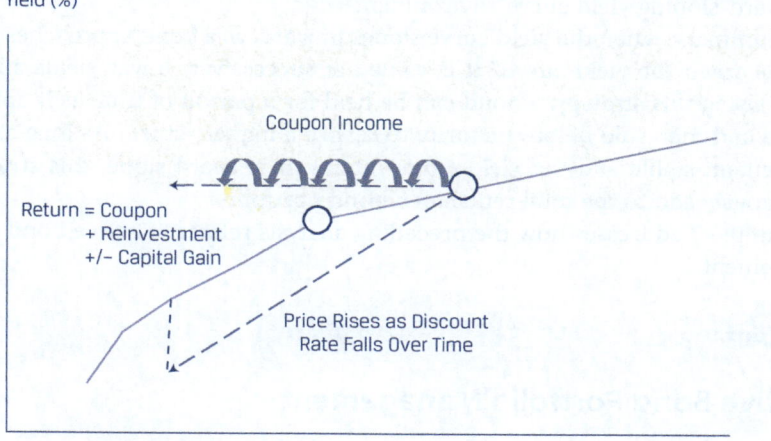

The return on a yield curve rolldown strategy may be demonstrated using a simple example. As stated earlier, the investment return on a fixed-rate (non-defaulted and non-callable) bond return may be defined as follows:

Bond return = Receipt of promised coupons (and principal)

+ Reinvestment of coupon payments

+/– Capital gain/Loss on sale prior to maturity

Say we observe one-, three-, four-, five- and six-year spot rates on annual coupon bonds trading at par of 2%, 4%, 5%, 6%, and 7%, respectively. An investor with a five-year maturity target decides to forgo a matched-maturity 6% five-year bond in favor of the 7%, six-year bond given her expectation of an unchanged yield curve over the next two years. We can compare the annualized return over two years for both bonds, assuming unchanged yields, as follows.

The 6% five-year bond purchased for 100 returns 120.61 in two years [(6 × 1.02) + 6 + 108.49], which consists of the first year's coupon reinvested at the one-year rate, the second annual coupon, and the capital gain on the sale of the 6% bond with three years to maturity at an unchanged three-year yield of 4% [108.49 = 6/1.04 + 6/(1.04)^2 + 106/(1.04)^3]. The annualized rate of return is 9.823% [solve for r, where (120.61/100) = (1 + r)^2].

The 7% six-year bond purchased at par returns 125.03 in two years [(7 × 1.02) + 7 + 110.89] with an annualized return of 11.817%. The excess return of nearly 2% results from both higher coupon income than the five-year matched maturity bond as well as a larger capital gain on the sale of the 7% bond with four years to maturity at an unchanged four-year yield of 5% [110.89 = 7/1.05 + 7/(1.05)^2 + + 7/(1.05)^3 + 107/(1.05)^4].

In the years following the 2008 financial crisis, many central banks acted to keep short-term interest rates very low. As a result, yield curves subsequently had a steep upward slope (see Exhibit 2). For active fixed-income managers, this situation provided an incentive to access short-term funding and invest in long-term bonds. This is just one form of a carry trade, referred to as a maturity spread carry trade, and is subject to significant interest rate risk, such as an unexpected increase in future spot rates (e.g., as a result of a spike in inflation). The maturity spread carry trade, in which the trader borrows short term and lends long term in the same currency, is common in an upward-sloping yield curve environment.

In summary, when the yield curve slopes upward, as a bond approaches maturity or "rolls down the yield curve," it is valued at successively lower yields and higher prices. Using this strategy, a bond can be held for a period of time as it appreciates in price and then sold before maturity to realize a higher return. As long as interest rates remain stable and the yield curve retains an upward slope, this strategy can continuously add to the total return of a bond portfolio.

Example 7 addresses how the preceding analysis relates to active bond portfolio management.

EXAMPLE 7

Active Bond Portfolio Management

1. The "rolling down the yield curve" strategy is executed by buying bonds whose maturities are:

    A. equal to the investor's investment horizon.

    B. longer than the investor's investment horizon.

    C. shorter than the investor's investment horizon.

Solution:

B is correct. A bond with a longer maturity than the investor's investment horizon is purchased but then sold prior to maturity at the end of the investment horizon. If the yield curve is upward sloping and yields do not change, the bond will be valued at successively lower yields and higher prices over time. The bond's total return will exceed that of a bond whose maturity is equal to the investment horizon.

---

2. A bond will be overvalued if the expected spot rate is:

    A. equal to the current forward rate.

    B. lower than the current forward rate.

    C. higher than the current forward rate.

Solution:

C is correct. If the expected discount rate is higher than the forward rate, then the bond will be overvalued. The expected price of the bond is lower than the price obtained from discounting using the forward rate.

---

3. Assume a flat yield curve of 6%. A three-year £100 bond is issued at par paying an annual coupon of 6%. What is the portfolio manager's expected return if he predicts that the yield curve one year from today will be a flat 7%?

    A. 4.19%

    B. 6.00%

    C. 8.83%

Solution:

A is correct. Expected return will be less than the current YTM of 6% if yields increase to 7%. The expected return of 4.19% is computed as follows:

$$\frac{6 + \frac{6}{1 + 0.07} + \frac{106}{(1 + 0.07)^2}}{100} - 1 \approx 4.19\%$$

4. A forward contract price will increase if:

   A. future spot rates evolve as predicted by current forward rates.

   B. future spot rates are lower than what is predicted by current forward rates.

   C. future spot rates are higher than what is predicted by current forward rates.

Solution:

B is correct. The forward rate model can be used to show that a change in the forward contract price requires a deviation of the spot curve from that predicted by today's forward curve. If the future spot rate is lower than what is predicted by the prevailing forward rate, the forward contract price will increase because it is discounted at an interest rate that is lower than the originally anticipated rate.

THE SWAP RATE CURVE

4

☐ | explain the swap rate curve and why and how market participants use it in valuation

Earlier, we described the spot rate curve of default-risk-free bonds as a measure of the time value of money. The swap rate curve, or swap curve for short, is another important representation of the time value of money used in fixed-income markets. Here we will discuss how the swap curve is used in valuation, where the spread of swap rates over government benchmark rates is a proxy for perceived credit risk relative to risk-free debt.

Swap Rate Curve

Interest rate swaps are an integral part of the fixed-income market. These derivative contracts usually involve the net exchange, or swap, of fixed-rate for floating-rate interest payments, and these contracts are an essential tool for investors who use them to hedge, speculate on, or otherwise modify risk. The fixed and floating payments are determined by multiplying the respective rate by a principal (or notional) amount for each interest period over the swap maturity. The rate for the fixed leg of an interest rate swap is known as the **swap rate**. The swap rate is analogous to the YTM on a government bond, which as we saw earlier may be derived from zero rates using bootstrapping. The key difference between the swap rate and the government bond rate is that the swap rate is derived using short-term lending rates rather than default-risk-free rates. Swap floating rates historically referenced short-term survey-based interest rates, such as three- or six-month US dollar Libor (London Interbank Offered Rate) and are slated to transition to transaction-based market reference rates (MRR) based on secured overnight funding transactions. The yield curve of swap rates is called the **swap rate curve** or, more simply, the **swap curve**. Because it is based on so-called **par swaps**, in which the fixed rate is set so that no money is exchanged at contract initiation—the present values of the fixed-rate and benchmark floating-rate legs being equal— the swap curve is a type of par curve. When we refer to the "par curve" here, however, the reference is to the government par yield curve.

The swap market is a highly liquid market for two reasons. First, unlike bonds, a swap does not have multiple borrowers or lenders, only counterparties who exchange cash flows. Such arrangements offer significant flexibility and customization in the swap contract's design. Second, swaps provide one of the most efficient ways to hedge interest rate risk. The Bank for International Settlements (BIS) estimates that the notional amount outstanding on interest rate swaps was nearly $350 trillion as of June 2020.

Many countries do not have a liquid government bond market with maturities longer than one year. The swap curve is a necessary market benchmark for interest rates in these countries. In countries where the private sector is much bigger than the public sector, the swap curve is a far more relevant measure of the time value of money than is the government's cost of borrowing.

Swaps are frequently used as a benchmark in Europe, whereas in Asia, the swap markets and the government bond markets have developed in parallel, and both are used in valuation in credit and loan markets.

Why Do Market Participants Use Swap Rates When Valuing Bonds?

Government spot curves and swap rate curves are the chief reference curves in fixed-income valuation. The choice between them can depend on multiple factors, including the relative liquidity of these two markets. In the United States, where there is both an active Treasury security market and a swap market, the choice of a benchmark for the time value of money often depends on the interest rate exposure profile of the institution using the benchmark. On one hand, wholesale banks frequently use the swap curve to value assets and liabilities because they hedge their balance sheet with swaps. On the other hand, retail banks with little exposure to the swap market are more likely to use the government spot curve as their benchmark.

Let us illustrate how a financial institution uses the swap market for its internal operations. Consider the case of a bank raising funds using a certificate of deposit (CD). Assume the bank can borrow $10 million in the form of a CD that bears interest of 1.5% for a two-year term. Another $10 million CD offers 1.70% for a three-year term. The bank can arrange two swaps: (1) The bank receives 1.50% fixed and pays MRR minus 10 bps with a two-year term and a notional amount of $10 million, and (2) the bank receives 1.70% fixed and pays MRR minus 15 bps with a three-year term and a notional amount of $10 million. After issuing the two CDs and committing to the two swaps, the bank has raised $20 million with an annual funding cost for the first two years of MRR minus 12.5 bps applied to the total notional amount of $20 million. The fixed interest payments received from the counterparty to the swap are paid to the CD investors; in effect, fixed-rate liabilities have been converted to floating-rate liabilities. The margins on the floating rates become the standard by which value is measured in assessing the bank's total funding cost.

By using the swap curve as a benchmark for the time value of money, the investor can adjust the swap spread so that the swap will be fairly priced given the spread. Conversely, given a swap spread, the investor can determine a fair price for the bond. We will use the swap spread in the following section to determine the value of a bond.

How Do Market Participants Use the Swap Curve in Valuation?

Although benchmark swap rates are quoted for specific maturities, swap contracts may be customized by two parties in the over-the-counter market. The fixed payment can be specified by an amortization schedule or involve a coupon with non-standard payment dates. In this section, we will focus on zero-coupon bonds. The yields on these bonds determine the swap curve, which, in turn, can be used to determine bond values.

Each forward date has an associated discount factor that represents the value today of a unit payment that one would hypothetically receive on the forward date expressed as a decimal fraction. For example, if we expect to receive ₩10,000 (10,000 South Korean won) in one year and the current price of the security is ₩9,259.30, then the discount factor for one year will be 0.92593 (= ₩9,259.30/₩10,000). Note that the rate associated with this discount factor is $1/0.92593 - 1 \approx 8.00\%$.

To price a swap using current market rates, as mentioned we must solve for a constant fixed rate that sets the present value of fixed-leg payments equal to the present value of floating-leg payments over the life of the swap. Once established, the fixed cash flows are specified by the coupon rate set at the time of the original agreement. Pricing the floating leg is more complex than pricing the fixed leg because, by definition, its cash flows change with future changes in interest rates. The forward rate for each floating payment date is calculated by using the forward curves.

Let s_T stand for the T-period swap rate. Because the value of a swap at origination is set to zero, the swap rates must satisfy Equation 12. Note that the swap rates can be determined from the spot rates and the spot rates can be determined from the swap rates.

$$\sum_{t=1}^{T} \frac{s_T}{(1+z_t)^t} + \frac{1}{(1+z_T)^T} = 1 \tag{13}$$

equation for solving for a swap rate given a spot rate

The right-hand side of Equation 13 is the value of the floating leg, which is always 1 at origination. The swap rate is determined by equating the value of the fixed leg, on the left-hand side, to the value of the floating leg.

Example 8 addresses the relationship between the swap rate curve and spot curve.

EXAMPLE 8

Determining the Swap Rate Curve

Suppose a government spot curve implies the following discount factors:

$DF_1 = 0.9524$

$DF_2 = 0.8900$

$DF_3 = 0.8163$

$DF_4 = 0.7350$

1. Given this information, determine the swap rate curve.

Solution:

Recall from Equation 1 that $DF_N = \frac{1}{(1+Z_N)^N}$. Therefore,

$$z_N = \left(\frac{1}{DF_N}\right)^{1/N} - 1$$

$$z_1 = \left(\frac{1}{0.9524}\right)^{1/1} - 1 = 5.00\%$$

$$z_2 = \left(\frac{1}{0.8900}\right)^{1/2} - 1 = 6.00\%$$

$$z_3 = \left(\frac{1}{0.8163}\right)^{1/3} - 1 = 7.00\%$$

$$z_4 = \left(\frac{1}{0.7350}\right)^{1/4} - 1 = 8.00\%$$

Using Equation 12, for $N = 1$,

$$\frac{s_1}{(1+z_1)} + \frac{1}{(1+z_1)} = \frac{s_1 + 1}{(1+0.05)} = 1$$

Therefore, $s_1 = 5\%$.

For $T = 2$,

$$\frac{s_2}{(1+z_1)} + \frac{s_2}{(1+z_2)^2} + \frac{1}{(1+z_2)^2} = \frac{s_2}{(1+0.05)} + \frac{s_2 + 1}{(1+0.06)^2} = 1$$

Therefore, $s_2 = 5.97\%$.

For $T = 3$,

$$\frac{s_3}{(1+z_1)} + \frac{s_3}{(1+z_2)^2} + \frac{s_3}{(1+z_3)^3} + \frac{1}{(1+z_3)^3}$$

$$= \frac{s_3}{(1+0.05)} + \frac{s_3}{(1+0.06)^2} + \frac{s_3}{(1+0.07)^3} + \frac{1}{(1+0.07)^3} = 1$$

Therefore, $s_3 = 6.91\%$.

For $T = 4$,

$$\frac{s_4}{(1+z_1)} + \frac{s_4}{(1+z_2)^2} + \frac{s_4}{(1+z_3)^3} + \frac{s_4}{(1+z_4)^4} + \frac{1}{(1+z_4)^4}$$

$$= \frac{s_4}{(1+0.05)} + \frac{s_4}{(1+0.06)^2} + \frac{s_4}{(1+0.07)^3} + \frac{s_4}{(1+0.08)^4} + \frac{1}{(1+0.08)^4} = 1$$

Therefore, $s_4 = 7.81\%$.

Note that the swap rates, spot rates, and discount factors are all mathematically linked together. Having access to data for one of the series allows you to calculate the other two.

5 THE SWAP SPREAD AND SPREADS AS A PRICE QUOTATION CONVENTION

☐   calculate and interpret the swap spread for a given maturity

☐   describe short-term interest rate spreads used to gauge economy-wide credit risk and liquidity risk

The swap spread is a popular way to indicate credit spreads in a market. The **swap spread** is defined as the spread paid by the fixed-rate payer of an interest rate swap over the rate of the "on-the-run" (most recently issued) government security with the same maturity as the swap. The spread captures the yield premium required for credit relative to the benchmark government bond. Because swap rates are built from market rates for short-term risky debt, this spread is a barometer of the market's

[handwritten margin notes: Swap spread: Swap rate - rate on treasury Security]

perceived credit risk relative to default-risk-free rates. This spread typically widens countercyclically, exhibiting greater values during recessions and lower values during economic expansions.

The term "swap spread" is sometimes also used as a reference to a bond's basis point spread over the interest rate swap curve and is a measure of the credit and/or liquidity risk of a bond. Here, a swap spread is an excess yield of swap rates over the yields on government bonds, and we use the terms I-spread, ISPRD, or interpolated spread to refer to bond yields net of the swap rates of the same maturities. In its simplest form, the I-spread can be measured as the difference between the yield-to-maturity of the bond and the swap rate given by a straight-line interpolation of the swap curve.

Often, fixed-income prices will be quoted as a swap rate plus (or minus) a spread, for which the yield is simply the yield on an equal-maturity government bond plus the swap spread. For example, if the fixed rate of a five-year fixed-for-float MRR swap is 2.00% and the five-year Treasury is yielding 1.70%, the swap spread is 2.00% − 1.70% = 0.30%, or 30 bps.

For euro-denominated swaps, the government yield used as a benchmark is most frequently Bunds (German government bonds) with the same maturity. Gilts (UK government bonds) are used as a benchmark in the United Kingdom.

Although the Libor swap curve is being phased out, it has historically been considered to reflect the default risk of A1/A+ rated commercial banks. The transition from Libor to MRR based on secured overnight funding rates will increase the influence of demand and supply conditions in government debt markets on swap rates. Another reason for the popularity of the swap market is that it is led by major financial institutions rather than controlled by governments, so swap rates are more comparable across different countries. The swap market also has more maturities with which to construct a yield curve than do government bond markets. Historically, cash or deposit rates such as Libor have been used for short-maturity yields; interest rate futures such as Eurodollar futures contracts have maturities of up to a year; and swap rates extend to maturities of up to 50 years in US dollars or euro. As the market transitions from Libor, the concept of this spread will be consistent with whichever market-based alternative to Libor emerges.

HISTORY OF THE US SWAP SPREAD SINCE 2008

The fact that governments generally pay less than private entities do in order to borrow suggests that swap spreads should always be positive. However, the 30-year Treasury swap spread turned negative following the collapse of Lehman Brothers Holdings Inc. in September 2008. Strong demand for duration combined with tighter liquidity and greater counterparty risk were widely cited as reasons for this phenomenon. For the period shown, the 30-year Treasury swap spread hit a record low (−62 bps intramonth) during November 2008. The 30-year Treasury swap spread was at or above zero for more than a year before becoming negative once again (see Exhibit 5). A recent study by the Federal Reserve Bank of New York (Boyarchenko, Gupta, Steele, and Yen, 2018) suggests that negative swap spreads have persisted because of increased regulatory capital requirements among swap dealers following the financial crisis.

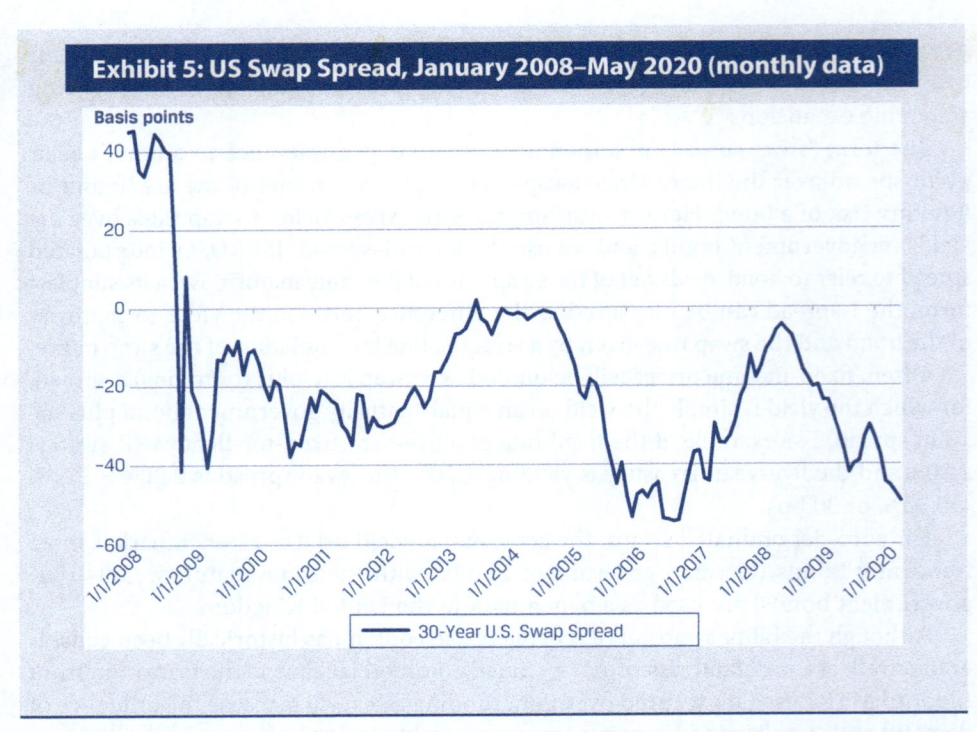

Exhibit 5: US Swap Spread, January 2008–May 2020 (monthly data)

Basis points

— 30-Year U.S. Swap Spread

To illustrate the use of the swap spread in fixed-income pricing, consider a US$1 million investment in GE Capital (GECC) notes with a coupon rate of 1 5/8% (1.625%) that matures on 2 July 2024. Coupons are paid semiannually. The evaluation date is 12 July 2021, so the remaining maturity is 2.97 years [= 2 + (350/360)]. The Treasury rates for two-year and three-year maturities are 0.525% and 0.588%, respectively. By simple interpolation between these two rates, the US Treasury rate for 2.97 years is 0.586% [= 0.525% + (350/360)(0.588% – 0.525%)]. If the swap spread for the same maturity is 0.918%, then the yield-to-maturity on the bond is 1.504% (= 0.918% + 0.586%). Given the yield-to-maturity, the invoice price (price including accrued interest) for US$1 million face value is as follows:

$$\frac{1,000,000\left(\frac{0.01625}{2}\right)}{\left(1+\frac{0.01504}{2}\right)^{\left(1-\frac{10}{180}\right)}} + \frac{1,000,000\left(\frac{0.01625}{2}\right)}{\left(1+\frac{0.01504}{2}\right)^{\left(2-\frac{10}{180}\right)}} + \cdots +$$

$$\frac{1,000,000\left(\frac{0.01625}{2}\right)}{\left(1+\frac{0.01504}{2}\right)^{\left(6-\frac{10}{180}\right)}} + \frac{1,000,000}{\left(1+\frac{0.01504}{2}\right)^{\left(6-\frac{10}{180}\right)}} = \text{US\$1,003,954.12.}$$

The left-hand side sums the present values of the semiannual coupon payments and the final principal payment of US$1,000,000. The accrued interest rate amount is US$451.39 [= 1,000,000 × (0.01625/2)(10/180)]. Therefore, the clean price (price not including accrued interest) is US$1,003,502.73 (= 1,003,954.12 – 451.39).

The swap spread helps an investor to identify the time value, credit, and liquidity components of a bond's YTM. If the bond is default free, then the swap spread could provide an indication of the bond's liquidity, or it could provide evidence of market mispricing. The higher the swap spread, the higher the return that investors require for credit and/or liquidity risks. Another approach introduced in an earlier reading is to calculate a constant yield spread over a government (or interest rate swap) spot curve instead. This spread is known as the zero volatility spread (Z-spread) of a bond over the benchmark rate.

Z-spread: the single rate that, when added to the rates of the spot yield curve, will provide the correct discount rates to price a particular bond.

Spreads as a Price Quotation Convention

Treasury curves and swap curves represent different benchmarks for fixed-income valuation. It is therefore important to distinguish between a bond price quote that uses the bond yield net of a benchmark Treasury yield and one that uses a swap rate.

The Treasury rate can differ from the swap rate for the same term for several reasons. Unlike the cash flows from US Treasury bonds, the cash flows from swaps are subject to greater default risk. Market liquidity for specific maturities may differ. For example, some parts of the term structure of interest rates may be more actively traded with swaps than with Treasury bonds. Finally, arbitrage between these two markets cannot be perfectly executed.

Swap spreads to the Treasury rate (as opposed to **I-spreads**, which are bond rates net of the swap rates of the same maturities) are simply the differences between swap rates and government bond yields of a particular maturity. One problem in defining swap spreads is that, for example, a 10-year swap matures in exactly 10 years, whereas this condition is true for a 10-year government bond only at the time of issuance. By convention, therefore, the 10-year swap spread is defined as the difference between the 10-year swap rate and the 10-year on-the-run government bond. Swap spreads of other maturities are defined similarly.

The curves in Exhibit 6 show the relationship between 10-year Treasury notes and 10-year swap rates. The 10-year swap spread is the 10-year swap rate less the 10-year Treasury note yield. Although positive swap spreads reflecting the difference between MRR-based rates and default-risk-free US government yields were historically the norm, these spreads have narrowed to zero or negative levels since the 2008 financial crisis because of higher swap dealer capital requirements and leverage constraints.

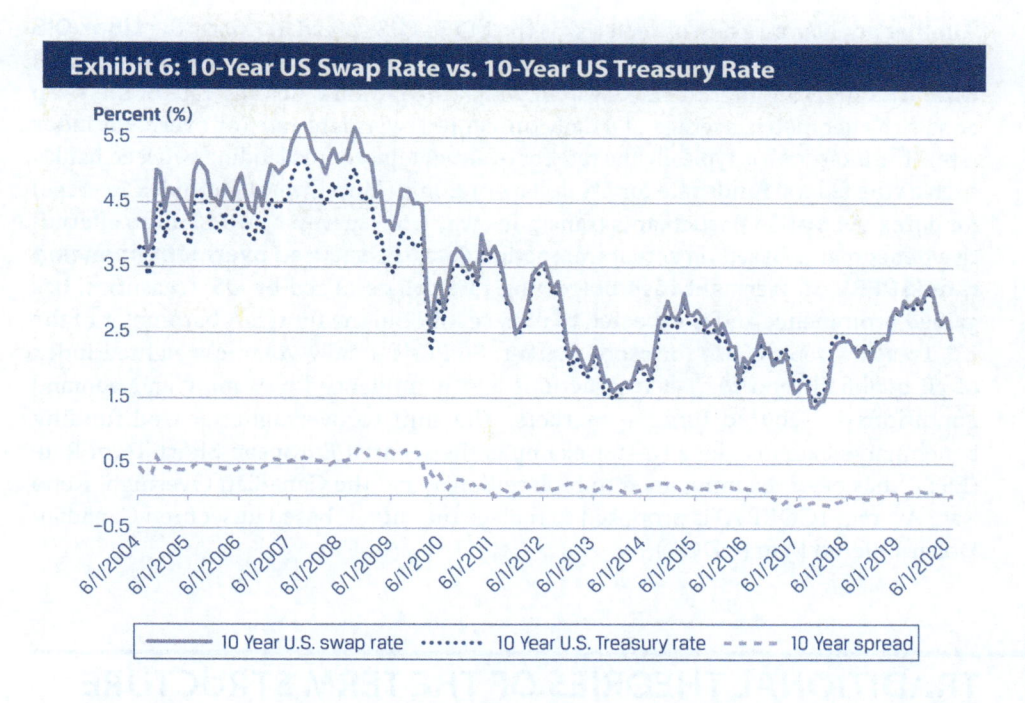

Exhibit 6: 10-Year US Swap Rate vs. 10-Year US Treasury Rate

Legend: 10 Year U.S. swap rate ······· 10 Year U.S. Treasury rate - - - - 10 Year spread

Market participants often use interest rate spreads between short-term government and risky rates as a barometer to evaluate relative credit and liquidity risk. For example, the difference between MRR and the yield on a Treasury bill of the same maturity, or **TED spread**, has historically been a key indicator of perceived credit and liquidity risk. TED is an acronym formed from an abbreviation for the US T-bill (T) and the ticker symbol for the MRR-based Eurodollar futures contract (ED). Exhibit 7 shows the historical TED spread. An increase in the TED spread signals greater perceived credit and liquidity risk, as occurred in early 2020 amid market turmoil related to the COVID-19 pandemic.

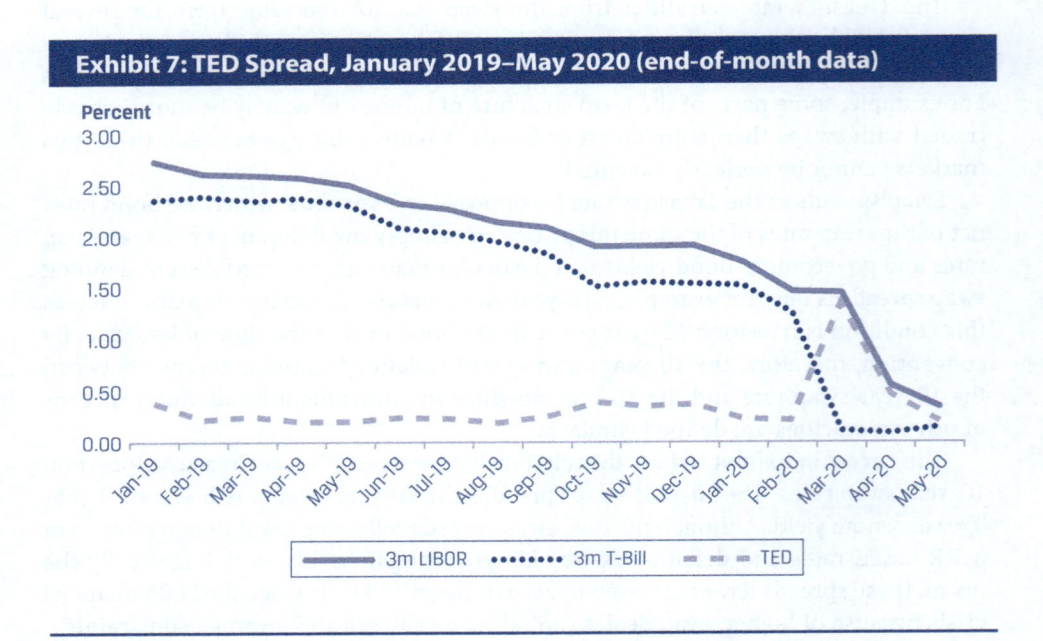

Exhibit 7: TED Spread, January 2019–May 2020 (end-of-month data)

—The MRR-OIS spread is considered an indicator of the risk and liquidity of money market securities.

Another popular measure of such risk is the MRR–OIS spread, formerly the **Libor-OIS spread**, which is the difference between MRR and the **overnight indexed swap (OIS) rate**. An OIS is an interest rate swap in which the periodic floating rate of the swap equals the geometric average of a daily unsecured overnight rate (or overnight index rate). The index rate is typically the rate for overnight unsecured lending between banks, such as the federal funds rate for US dollars or Eonia (Euro OverNight Index Average) for euros. As market participants transition away from survey-based Libor to alternative benchmarks based on actual transaction data, the **secured overnight financing rate (SOFR)**, or overnight cash borrowing rate collateralized by US Treasuries, has gained prominence and is expected to replace Libor in the future. A barometer of the US Treasury repurchase (or repo) market, SOFR is a daily volume-weighted index of all qualified repo market transactions and is influenced by supply and demand conditions in secured funding markets. The shift to overnight secured funding benchmarks extends globally—for example, the secured European Short-Term Rate (ESTR) has been recommended to replace Eonia, and the Canadian Overnight Repo Rate Average (CORRA) is proposed to replace the survey-based unsecured Canadian Dollar Offered Rate (CDOR).

6   TRADITIONAL THEORIES OF THE TERM STRUCTURE OF INTEREST RATES

☐   explain traditional theories of the term structure of interest rates and describe the implications of each theory for forward rates and the shape of the yield curve

This section presents four traditional theories of the underlying economic factors that affect the shape of the yield curve.

Expectations Theory

One branch of traditional term structure theory focuses on interpreting term structure shape in terms of investors' expectations. Historically, the first such theory is known as the **unbiased expectations theory**, also called **pure expectations theory**. It says that the forward rate is an unbiased predictor of the future spot rate; its broadest interpretation is that bonds of any maturity are perfect substitutes for one another. For example, buying a bond with a maturity of five years and holding it for three years has the same expected return as buying a three-year bond or buying a series of three one-year bonds.

The predictions of the unbiased expectations theory are consistent with the assumption of risk neutrality. In a risk-neutral world, investors are unaffected by uncertainty and risk premiums do not exist. Every security is risk free and yields the risk-free rate for that particular maturity. Although such an assumption leads to interesting results, it clearly is in conflict with the large body of evidence showing that investors are risk averse.

A theory that is similar but more rigorous than the unbiased expectations theory is the **local expectations theory**. Rather than asserting that every maturity strategy has the same expected return over a given investment horizon, this theory instead contends that the expected return for every bond over short periods is the risk-free rate. This conclusion results from an assumed no-arbitrage condition in which bond pricing does not allow for traders to earn arbitrage profits.

The primary way that the local expectations theory differs from the unbiased expectations theory is that it can be extended to a world characterized by risk. Although the theory requires that risk premiums be nonexistent for very short holding periods, no such restrictions are placed on longer-term investments. Thus, the theory is applicable to both risk-free as well as risky bonds.

Although the local expectations theory is economically appealing, it is often observed that short-holding-period returns on long-dated bonds in fact exceed those on short-dated bonds. The need for liquidity and the ability to hedge risk essentially ensure that the demand for short-term securities will exceed that for long-term securities. Thus, both the yields and the actual returns for short-dated securities are typically lower than those for long-dated securities.

Liquidity Preference Theory

Whereas expectations theories leave no room for risk aversion, liquidity preference theory attempts to account for it. **Liquidity preference theory** asserts that **liquidity premiums** exist to compensate investors for the added interest rate risk they face when lending long term and that these premiums increase with maturity. Thus, given an expectation of unchanging short-term spot rates, liquidity preference theory predicts an upward-sloping yield curve. The forward rate provides an estimate of the expected spot rate that is biased upward by the amount of the liquidity premium, which invalidates the unbiased expectations theory. The liquidity premium for each consecutive future period should be no smaller than that for the prior period.

For example, the US Treasury offers bonds that mature in 30 years. Most investors, however, have shorter investment horizons than 30 years. For investors to hold these bonds, they would demand a higher return for taking the risk that the yield curve changes and that they must sell the bond prior to maturity at an uncertain price. That incrementally higher return is the liquidity premium. Note that this premium is not to be confused with a yield premium for the lack of liquidity that thinly traded bonds may bear. Rather, it is a premium applying to all long-term bonds, including those with deep markets.

Liquidity preference theory fails to offer a complete explanation of the term structure. Rather, it simply argues for the existence of liquidity premiums. For example, a downward-sloping yield curve could still be consistent with the existence of liquidity premiums if one of the factors underlying the shape of the curve is an expectation of deflation (i.e., a negative rate of inflation resulting from monetary or fiscal policy actions). Expectations of sharply declining spot rates may also result in a downward-sloping yield curve if the expected decline in interest rates is severe enough to offset the effect of the liquidity premiums.

In summary, liquidity preference theory claims that lenders require a liquidity premium as an incentive to lend long term. Thus, forward rates derived from the current yield curve provide an upwardly biased estimate of expected future spot rates. Although downward-sloping or hump-shaped yield curves may sometimes occur, the existence of liquidity premiums implies that the yield curve will typically be upward sloping.

Segmented Markets Theory

Unlike expectations theory and liquidity preference theory, **segmented markets theory** allows for lender and borrower preferences to influence the shape of the yield curve. The result is that yields are not a reflection of expected spot rates or liquidity premiums. Rather, they are solely a function of the supply and demand for funds of a particular maturity. That is, each maturity sector can be thought of as a segmented market in which yield is determined independently from the yields that prevail in other maturity segments.

The theory is consistent with a world in which asset/liability management constraints exist, either regulatory or self-imposed. In such a world, investors might restrict their investment activity to a maturity sector that provides the best match for the maturity of their liabilities. Doing so avoids the risks associated with an asset/liability mismatch.

For example, because life insurers sell long-term liabilities against themselves in the form of life insurance contracts, they tend to be most active as buyers in the long end of the bond market. Similarly, because the liabilities of pension plans are long term, they typically invest in long-term securities. Why would they invest short term given that those returns might decline while the cost of their liabilities stays fixed? In contrast, money market funds would be limited to investing in debt with maturity of one year or less, in general.

In summary, the segmented markets theory assumes that market participants are either unwilling or unable to invest in anything other than securities of their preferred maturity. It follows that the yield of securities of a particular maturity is determined entirely by the supply and demand for funds of that particular maturity.

Preferred Habitat Theory

The **preferred habitat theory** is similar to the segmented markets theory in proposing that many borrowers and lenders have strong preferences for particular maturities, but it does not assert that yields at different maturities are determined independently of each other.

The theory contends, however, that if the expected additional returns to be gained become large enough, institutions will be willing to deviate from their preferred maturities or habitats. For example, if the expected returns on longer-term securities exceed those on short-term securities by a large enough margin, an intermediate-term bond fund might lengthen the maturities of their assets. And if the excess returns expected from buying short-term securities become large enough, life insurance companies might stop limiting themselves to long-term securities and place a larger part of their portfolios in shorter-term investments.

The preferred habitat theory is based on the realistic notion that agents and institutions will accept additional risk in return for additional expected returns. In accepting elements of both the segmented markets theory and the unbiased expectations theory, yet rejecting their extreme polar positions, the preferred habitat theory moves closer to explaining real-world phenomena. In this theory, both market expectations and the institutional factors emphasized in the segmented markets theory influence the term structure of interest rates.

PREFERRED HABITAT AND QE

The term "quantitative easing" (QE) refers to an unconventional monetary policy used by central banks to increase the supply of money in an economy when central bank and/or interbank interest rates are already close to zero. The first of several QE efforts by the US Federal Reserve began in late 2008, following the establishment of a near-zero target range for the federal funds rate. Since then, the Federal Reserve has greatly expanded its holdings of long-term securities via a series of asset purchase programs, with the goal of putting downward pressure on long-term interest rates and thereby making financial conditions even more accommodative. Exhibit 8 presents information regarding the securities held by the Federal Reserve on 20 September 2007 (when all securities held by the Fed were US Treasury issuance) and on 29 October 2014 (when the Federal Reserve ended its third round of QE).

Exhibit 8: Securities Held by the US Federal Reserve

(US$ billions)	20 Sep 2007	29 Oct 2014
Securities held outright	780	4,219
US Treasury	780	2,462
Bills	267	0
Notes and bonds, nominal	472	2,347
Notes and bonds, inflation indexed	36	115
Inflation compensation	5	16
Federal agency	0	40
Mortgage-backed securities	0	1,718

As Exhibit 8 shows, the Federal Reserve's security holdings on 20 September 2007 consisted entirely of US Treasury securities, and about 34% of those holdings were short term in the form of T-bills. On 29 October 2014, only about 58% of the Federal Reserve's security holdings were Treasury securities, and none were T-bills. Furthermore, the Federal Reserve held well over US$1.7 trillion of mortgage-backed securities (MBS), which accounted for 41% of all securities held.

Prior to the QE efforts, the yield on MBS was typically in the 5%–6% range. It declined to less than 2% by the end of 2012. Concepts related to preferred habitat theory could possibly help explain that drop in yield.

The purchase of MBS by the Federal Reserve reduced the supply of these securities that was available for private purchase. Assuming that many MBS investors are either unwilling or unable to withdraw from the MBS market because of their comparative experience and expertise in managing interest rate and repayment risks of MBS versus option-free bonds, MBS investing institutions would have a "preferred habitat" in the MBS market. If they were unable to meet investor demand without bidding more aggressively, these buyers would drive down yields on MBS.

The Federal Reserve's purchase of MBS also resulted in a reduction in MBS yields. If a homeowner prepays on a mortgage, the payment is sent to MBS investors on a pro rata basis. Although investors are uncertain about when such a prepayment will be received, prepayment is more likely in a declining interest rate environment.

Use Example 9 to test your understanding of traditional term structure theories.

EXAMPLE 9

Traditional Term Structure Theories

1. Many fixed-income portfolio managers are limited in or prohibited from high-yield bond investments. When a bond is downgraded from an investment-grade to a high-yield (junk) rating, it is referred to as a *fallen angel*. Because of restrictions, many pension funds sell fallen angels when they are downgraded from investment grade to high yield (junk). This coordinated selling action often results in depressed prices and attractive yields for the fallen angels. Which of the following reasons best explains why fallen angel yields often exceed otherwise identical bonds?

   A. The preferred habitat theory

   B. The segmented markets theory

   C. The local expectations theory

Solution:

B is correct. Market segmentation in this example results from the requirement that some fixed-income fund managers are prohibited or limited in their capacity to hold high-yield bonds. The segmentation results in selling pressure on fallen angels that depresses their prices.

2. The term structure theory in which investors can be induced by relatively attractive yields to hold debt securities whose maturities do not match their investment horizon is *best* described as the:

   A. preferred habitat theory.

   B. segmented markets theory.

   C. unbiased expectations theory.

Solution:

A is correct. Preferred habitat theory asserts that investors are willing to deviate from their preferred maturities if yield differentials encourage the switch. Segmented markets theory is more rigid than preferred habitat in that asset/liability management constraints force investors to buy securities whose horizons match those of their liabilities. The unbiased expectations theory makes no assumptions about maturity preferences. Rather, it contends that forward rates are unbiased predictors of future spot rates.

3. The unbiased expectations theory assumes investors are:

   A. risk averse.

   B. risk neutral.

   C. risk seeking.

Solution:

B is correct. The unbiased expectations theory asserts that different maturity strategies, such as rollover, maturity matching, and riding the yield curve, have the same expected return. By definition, a risk-neutral party is indifferent about choices with equal expected payoffs, even if one choice is riskier. Thus, the predictions of the theory are consistent with the existence of risk-neutral investors.

4. Market evidence shows that forward rates are:

   A. unbiased predictors of future spot rates.

   B. upwardly biased predictors of future spot rates.

   C. downwardly biased predictors of future spot rates.

Solution:

B is correct. The existence of a liquidity premium ensures that the forward rate is an upwardly biased estimate of the future spot rate. Market evidence clearly shows that liquidity premiums exist, and this evidence effectively refutes the predictions of the unbiased expectations theory.

5. Market evidence shows that short holding-period returns on short-maturity bonds *most* often are:

   A. less than those on long-maturity bonds.

   B. about equal to those on long-maturity bonds.

   C. greater than those on long-maturity bonds.

Solution:

A is correct. Although the local expectations theory predicts that the short-run return for all bonds will equal the risk-free rate, most of the evidence refutes that claim. Returns from long-dated bonds are generally higher than those from short-dated bonds, even over relatively short investment horizons. This market evidence is consistent with the risk–expected return trade-off that is central to finance and the uncertainty surrounding future spot rates.

YIELD CURVE FACTOR MODELS

7

☐ | explain how a bond's exposure to each of the factors driving the yield curve can be measured and how these exposures can be used to manage yield curve risks

The effect of yield volatilities on price is an important consideration in fixed-income investment, particularly for risk management and portfolio evaluation. In this section, we describe measuring and managing the interest rate risk of bonds.

A Bond's Exposure to Yield Curve Movement

Shaping risk is defined as the sensitivity of a bond's price to the changing shape of the yield curve. The yield curve's shape changes continually, and yield curve shifts are rarely parallel. For active bond management, a bond investor may want to base trades on a forecasted yield curve shape or may want to hedge the yield curve risk on a bond portfolio using swaps. Shaping risk also affects the value of many options, which is very important because many fixed-income instruments have embedded options.

Exhibit 9 and Exhibit 10 show historical yield curve movements for US and European swap rates from March 2006 until March 2020. The exhibits show the considerable swap yield curve changes over time. In both cases, the pre-financial-crisis March 2006 yield curves represent the highest swap yields and those from March 2020 (amid the COVID-19 pandemic-related market turmoil) the lowest. In the United States, however, the end of quantitative easing and tighter monetary policy resulted in a rebound in swap yields prior to 2020, whereas in Europe, yields remained low or negative because of continued accommodative monetary policy. Note that the vertical axis values of the three exhibits differ, and the horizontal axis is not to scale.

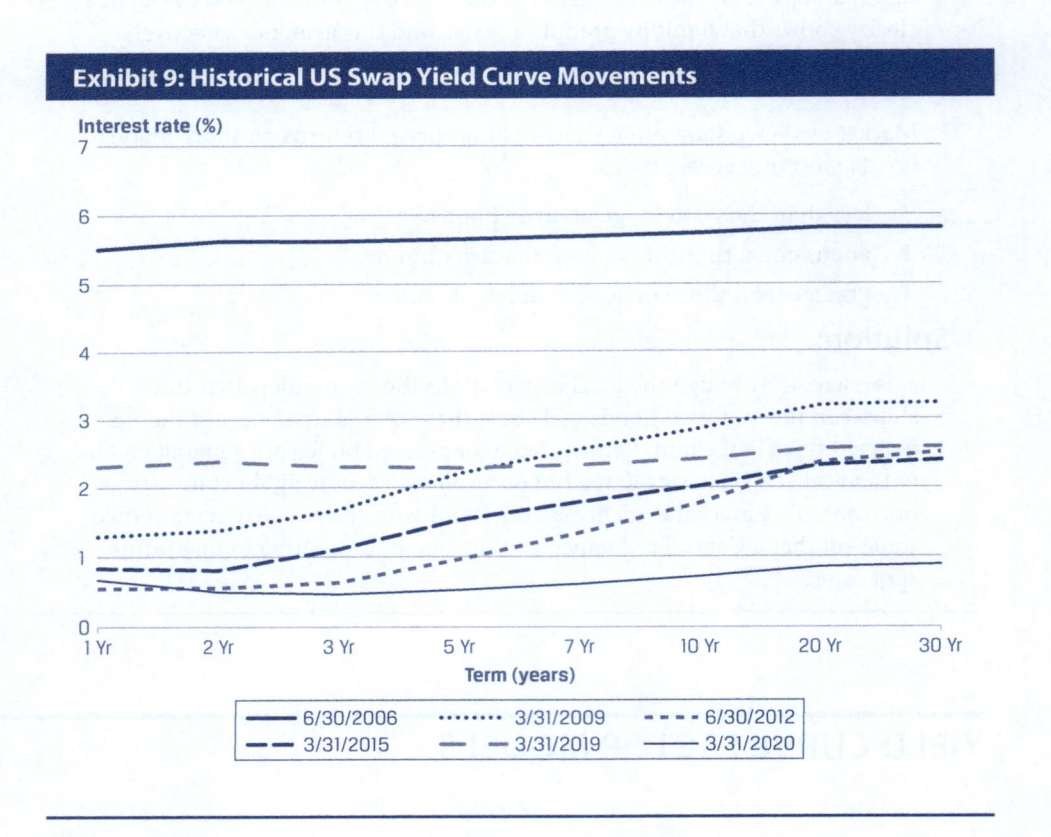

Exhibit 9: Historical US Swap Yield Curve Movements

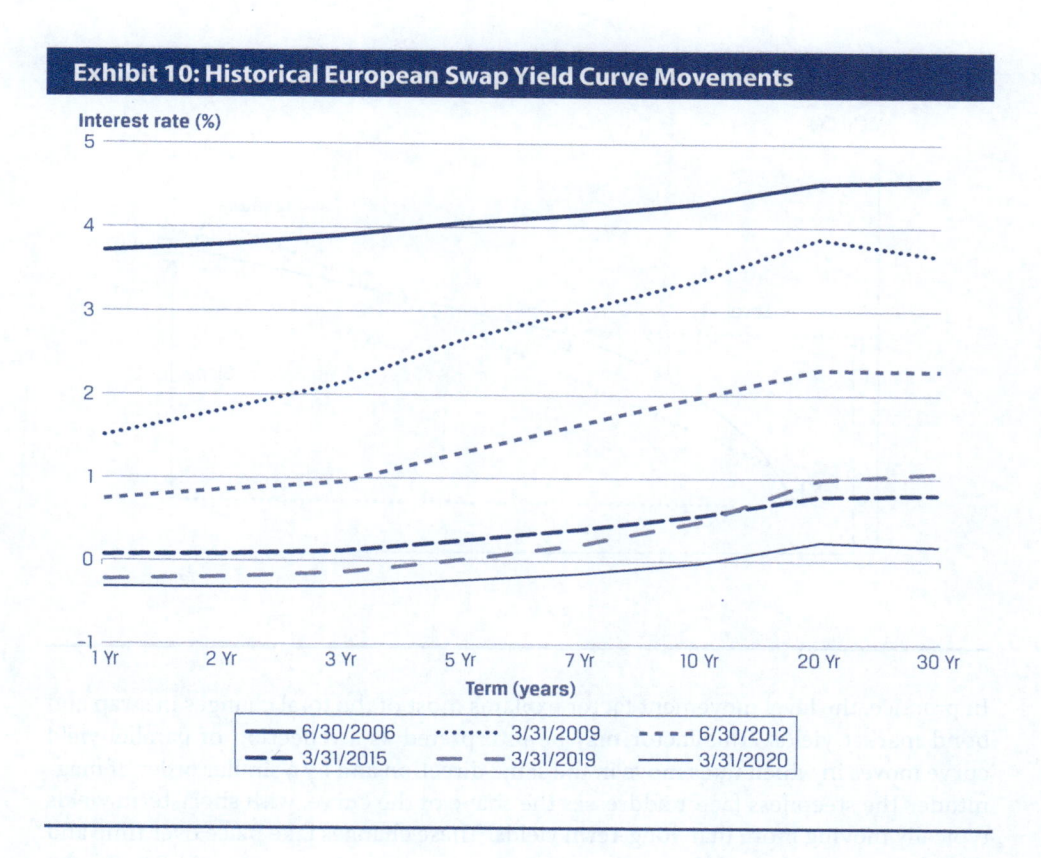

Exhibit 10: Historical European Swap Yield Curve Movements

Legend:
— 6/30/2006 ······ 3/31/2009 – – – 6/30/2012
– – 3/31/2015 — — 3/31/2019 ——— 3/31/2020

Factors Affecting the Shape of the Yield Curve

The previous section showed that the yield curve can take nearly any shape. The challenge for a fixed-income manager is to implement a process to manage the yield curve shape risk in her portfolio. One approach is to find a model that reduces most of the possible yield curve movements to a probabilistic combination of a few standardized yield curve movements. This section presents one of the best-known yield curve factor models.

A **yield curve factor model** is defined as a model or a description of yield curve movements that can be considered realistic when compared with historical data. Research has led to models that can describe these movements with some accuracy. One specific yield curve factor model is the three-factor model of Litterman and Scheinkman (1991), who found that yield curve movements are historically well described by a combination of three independent movements, which they interpreted as **level**, **steepness**, and **curvature**. The level movement refers to an upward or downward shift in the yield curve. The steepness movement refers to a non-parallel shift in the yield curve when either short-term rates change more than long-term rates or long-term rates change more than short-term rates. The curvature movement is a reference to movement in three segments of the yield curve: The short-term and long-term segments rise while the middle-term segment falls, or vice versa. Exhibit 11 illustrates these factors.

Exhibit 11: Primary Yield Curve Factors: Level, Slope, and Curvature

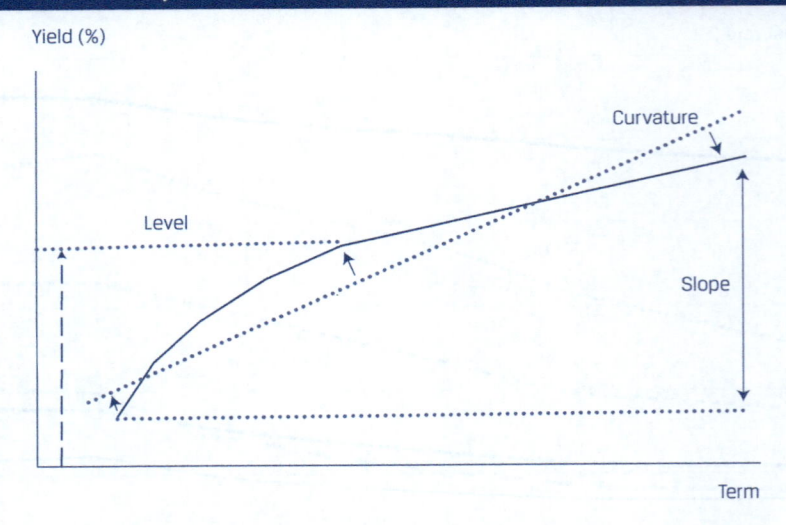

In practice, the level movement factor explains most of the total changes in swap and bond market yields. This factor may be interpreted as a reflection of parallel yield curve moves in which rates move in the same direction and by a similar order of magnitude. The steepness factor addresses the shape of the curve, with short-term yields typically moving more than long-term yields. These changes take place over time and therefore explain less of the total variance in rates than the level factor. Finally, the third factor, curvature, tends to have a negative impact on intermediate yields and a positive impact on short- and long-term yields. This variable explaining the "twist" in the yield curve has the smallest impact of the three.

8   THE MATURITY STRUCTURE OF YIELD CURVE VOLATILITIES

☐ | explain the maturity structure of yield volatilities and their effect on price volatility

Yield Volatility

Quantifying interest rate volatilities is important for fixed income managers for at least two reasons. First, most fixed-income instruments and derivatives have embedded options. Option values, and hence the values of the fixed-income instrument, crucially depend on the level of interest rate volatilities. Second, fixed-income interest rate risk management is clearly an important part of any management process, and such risk management includes controlling the impact of interest rate volatilities on the instrument's price volatility.

The term structure of interest rate volatilities is a representation of the yield volatility of a zero-coupon bond for every maturity of security. This volatility curve (or "vol") or volatility term structure measures yield curve risk.

Interest rate volatility is not the same for all interest rates along the yield curve. On the basis of the typical assumption of a lognormal model, the uncertainty of an interest rate is measured by the annualized standard deviation of the proportional change in a bond yield over a specified interval. For example, if the interval is a one-month period, then the specified interval equals 1/12 years. This measure, called interest rate volatility, is denoted $\sigma(t,T)$, which is the volatility of the rate for a security with maturity T at time t. The term structure of volatilities is given by Equation 14:

$$\sigma(t,T) = \frac{\sigma[\Delta r(t,T)/r(t,T)]}{\sqrt{\Delta t}} \tag{14}$$

In Exhibit 12, to illustrate a term structure of volatility, the data series is deliberately chosen to end before the 2008 financial crisis, which was associated with some unusual volatility magnitudes.

Exhibit 12: Historical Example: US Treasuries, August 2005–December 2007										
Maturity (years)	**0.25**	**0.50**	**1**	**2**	**3**	**5**	**7**	**10**	**20**	**30**
$\sigma(t,T)$	0.3515	0.3173	0.2964	0.2713	0.2577	0.2154	0.1885	0.1621	0.1332	0.1169

For example, the 35.15% standard deviation for the three-month T-bill in Exhibit 12 is based on a monthly standard deviation of 0.1015 = 10.15%, which annualizes as

$$0.1015 \div \sqrt{\tfrac{1}{12}} = 0.3515 = 35.15\%.$$

The volatility term structure typically shows that short-term rates are more volatile than long-term rates. That said, long-term bond *prices* tend to vary more than short-term bond prices given the impact of duration. Research indicates that short-term volatility is most strongly linked to uncertainty regarding monetary policy, whereas long-term volatility is most strongly linked to uncertainty regarding the real economy and inflation. Furthermore, most of the co-movement between short-term and long-term volatilities appears to depend on the ever-changing correlations among these three determinants (monetary policy, the real economy, and inflation). During the period of August 2005–December 2007, long-term volatility was lower than short-term volatility, falling from 35.15% for the 0.25-year rate to 11.69% for the 30-year rate.

Managing Yield Curve Risks Using Key Rate Duration

Yield curve risk—the risk to portfolio value arising from unanticipated changes in the yield curve—can be managed on the basis of several measures of sensitivity to yield curve movements. Management of yield curve risk involves changing the identified exposures to desired values by trades in security or derivative markets (the details fall under the rubric of fixed-income portfolio management and thus are outside the scope of this reading).

One available measure of yield curve sensitivity is effective duration, which measures the sensitivity of a bond's price to a small parallel shift in a benchmark yield curve. Another is based on **key rate duration**, which measures a bond's sensitivity to a small change in a benchmark yield curve at a specific maturity segment. Using one of these last two measures allows identification and management of "shaping risk"—that is, sensitivity to changes in the shape of the benchmark yield curve—in addition to the risk associated with parallel yield curve changes, which is addressed adequately by effective duration.

To make the discussion more concrete, consider a portfolio of 1-year, 5-year, and 10-year zero-coupon bonds with $100 value in each position; total portfolio value is therefore $300. Also consider the hypothetical set of factor movements shown in the following table:

Year	1	5	10
Parallel	1	1	1
Steepness	−1	0	1
Curvature	1	0	1

In the table, a parallel movement or shift means that all the rates shift by an equal amount—in this case, by a unit of 1. A steepness movement means that the yield curve steepens with the long rate shifting up by one unit and the short rate shifting down by one unit. A curvature movement means that both the short rate and the long rate shift up by one unit, whereas the medium-term rate remains unchanged. These movements need to be defined, as they are here, such that none of the movements can be a linear combination of the other two movements. Next, we address the calculation of the various yield curve sensitivity measures.

Because the bonds are zero-coupon bonds, each bond's effective duration is the same as its maturity. The portfolio's effective duration is the weighted sum of the effective duration of each bond position; for this equally weighted portfolio, effective duration is $0.333(1 + 5 + 10) = 5.333$.

To calculate key rate durations, consider various yield curve movements. First, suppose that the one-year rate changes by 100 bps while the other rates remain the same; the sensitivity of the portfolio to that shift is $1/[(300)(0.01)] = 0.3333$. We conclude that the key rate duration of the portfolio ($KeyDur_{Full}$) to the one-year rate, denoted $KeyDur_1$, is 0.3333. Likewise, the key rate durations of the portfolio to the 5-year rate, $KeyDur_5$, and the 10-year rate, $KeyDur_{10}$, are 1.6667 and 3.3333, respectively. Note that the sum of the key rate durations is 5.333, which is the same as the effective duration of the portfolio. This fact can be explained intuitively. Key rate duration measures the portfolio risk exposure to each key rate. If all the key rates move by the same amount, then the yield curve has made a parallel shift, and as a result, the proportional change in value has to be consistent with effective duration. The related model for yield curve risk based on key rate durations ($KeyDur$) is as follows:

$$KeyDur_{Full} = \%\Delta P = \left(\frac{\Delta P}{P}\right) \approx -KeyDur_1\Delta z_1 - KeyDur_5\Delta z_5 - KeyDur_{10}\Delta z_{10}$$
$$= -0.3333\Delta z_1 - 1.6667\Delta z_5 - -3.3333\Delta z_{10}$$

$$(15)$$

Next, we can calculate a measure based on the decomposition of yield curve movements into parallel, steepness, and curvature movements, as described earlier. Define D_L, D_S, and D_C as the sensitivities of portfolio value to small changes in the level, steepness, and curvature factors, respectively. Based on this factor model, Equation 16 shows the proportional change in portfolio value that would result from a small change in the level factor (Δx_L), the steepness factor (Δx_S), and the curvature factor (Δx_C).

$$KeyDur_{Full} = \%\Delta P$$
$$= \left(\frac{\Delta P}{P}\right) \approx -KeyDur_L\Delta x_L - KeyDur_S\Delta z_S - KeyDur_C\Delta z_C \qquad (16)$$

Because $KeyDur_L$ is by definition sensitivity to a parallel shift, the proportional change in the portfolio value per unit shift (the line for a parallel movement in the table) is $5.3333 = (1 + 5 + 10)/[(300)(0.01)]$. The sensitivity for steepness movement can be calculated as follows (see the line for steepness movement in the table). When the steepness makes an upward shift of 100 bps, it would result in a downward shift of 100 bps for the 1-year rate, resulting in a gain of $1, and an upward shift for the 10-year rate, resulting in a loss of $10. The change in value is therefore $(1 - 10)$. $KeyDur_S$ is the negative of the proportional change in price per unit change in this movement and in this case is $3.0 = -(1 - 10)/[(300)(0.01)]$. Considering the line for curvature movement in the table, $KeyDur_C = 3.6667 = (1 + 10)/[(300)(0.01)]$. Thus, for our hypothetical bond portfolio, we can analyze the portfolio's yield curve risk using the following equation:

$$KeyDur_{Full} = \%\Delta P = \left(\frac{\Delta P}{P}\right) \approx -5.3333\Delta x_L - 3.0\Delta z_S - 3.6667\Delta z_C$$

For example, if $\Delta x_L = -0.0050$, $\Delta x_S = 0.002$, and $\Delta x_C = 0.001$, the predicted change in portfolio value would be +1.7%. It can be shown that key rate durations are directly related to level, steepness, and curvature in this example and that one set of sensitivities can be derived from the other. One can use the numerical example to verify that relation by decomposing changes in the term structure into level, slope, and curvature factors:

$$KeyDur_L = KeyDur_1 + KeyDur_5 + KeyDur_{10}$$

$$KeyDur_S = - KeyDur_1 + KeyDur_{10}$$

$$KeyDur_C = KeyDur_1 + KeyDur_{10}$$

Example 10 reviews concepts from this section and the preceding sections.

EXAMPLE 10

Term Structure Dynamics

1. The most important factor in explaining changes in the yield curve has been found to be:

   A. level.

   B. curvature.

   C. steepness.

Solution:

A is correct. Research shows that upward and downward shifts in the yield curve explain more than 75% of the total change in the yield curve.

2. A movement of the yield curve in which the short rate decreases by 150 bps and the long rate decreases by 50 bps would *best* be described as a:

   A. flattening of the yield curve resulting from changes in level and steepness.

   B. steepening of the yield curve resulting from changes in level and steepness.

   C. steepening of the yield curve resulting from changes in steepness and curvature.

Solution:

B is correct. Both the short-term and long-term rates have declined, indicating a change in the level of the yield curve. Short-term rates have declined more than long-term rates, indicating a change in the steepness of the yield curve.

3. The yield curve starts off flat, and then intermediate-maturity yields decrease by 10 bps while short- and long-maturity yields remain constant. This movement is *best* described as involving a change in:

   A. level only.

   B. curvature only.

   C. level and curvature.

   ## Solution:

   B is correct. The curve starts off flat, with identical short, intermediate, and long rates. Both the short-term and long-term rates remained constant, indicating no change in the level of the yield curve. Intermediate rates decreased, however, resulting in curvature.

4. Typically, short-term interest rates:

   A. are less volatile than long-term interest rates.

   B. are more volatile than long-term interest rates.

   C. have about the same volatility as long-term interest rates.

   ## Solution:

   B is correct. A possible explanation is that expectations for long-term inflation and real economic activity affecting longer-term interest rates are slower to change than those related to shorter-term interest rates.

5. Suppose for a given portfolio that key rate changes are considered to be changes in the yield on 1-year, 5-year, and 10-year securities. Estimated key rate durations are $KeyDur_1 = 0.50$, $KeyDur_2 = 0.70$, and $KeyDur_3 = 0.90$. What is the percentage change in the value of the portfolio if a parallel shift in the yield curve results in all yields declining by 50 bps?

   A. −1.05%.

   B. +1.05%.

   C. +2.10%.

   ## Solution:

   B is correct. A decline in interest rates would lead to an increase in bond portfolio value: $-0.50(-0.005) - 0.70(-0.005) - 0.90(-0.005) = 0.0105 = 1.05\%$.

9

DEVELOPING INTEREST RATE VIEWS USING MACROECONOMIC VARIABLES

☐ | explain how key economic factors are used to establish a view on benchmark rates, spreads, and yield curve changes

Interest rate dynamics such as changes in spot versus forward rates and the level, steepness, and curvature of the yield curve are influenced by key economic variables and market events. Implied forward rates serve as market-neutral reference points for fixed income traders. As we illustrated earlier, if today's forward rates are realized in the future, then bond values will simply roll down the yield curve. In practice, active fixed-income market participants establish their own views on future interest rate developments and then position their portfolios in order to capitalize on differences between their own rate view and the market consensus. If their forecast is accurate, the portfolio generates greater returns than it would have otherwise.

This section reviews the key drivers of interest rates before moving on to establishing views and positioning fixed-income portfolios to capitalize on a specific interest rate view.

The term **bond risk premium** refers to the expected excess return of a default-free long-term bond less that of an equivalent short-term bond or the one-period risk-free rate. This premium is also referred to as the term (or duration) premium, and it is usually measured using government bonds to capture uncertainty of default-free rates, whereas credit, liquidity, and other risks may increase the overall risk premium for a specific bond. Unlike *ex post* observed historical returns, the bond risk premium is a forward-looking expectation and must be estimated.

Several macroeconomic factors influence bond pricing and required returns such as inflation, economic growth, and monetary policy, among others.

Research shows that although inflation, GDP, and monetary policy explain most of the variance of bond yields, short- and intermediate-term bond yields are driven mostly by inflation, whereas other factors such as monetary policy are key drivers of long-term yields. Inflation explains about two-thirds of short- and intermediate-term bond yield variation, with the remaining third roughly equally attributable to economic growth and factors including monetary policy. In contrast, monetary policy explains nearly two-thirds of long-term yield variation, and the remaining third is largely attributable to inflation.

Monetary policy impacts the bond risk premium. Central banks such as the European Central Bank control the money supply and influence interest rates through policy tools in order to achieve stable prices and sustainable economic growth. During economic expansions, monetary authorities raise benchmark rates to help control inflation. This action is often consistent with **bearish flattening**, or short-term bond yields rising more than long-term bond yields, resulting in a flatter yield curve. During economic recessions or anticipated recessions, the monetary authority cuts benchmark rates to help stimulate economic activity. The lowering of interest rates is associated with **bullish steepening**, in which short-term rates fall by more than long-term yields, resulting in a steeper term structure. These monetary policy actions lead to procyclical short-term interest rate changes. Exhibit 13 shows these two yield curve changes.

Exhibit 13: Examples of Yield Curve Flattening and Steepening

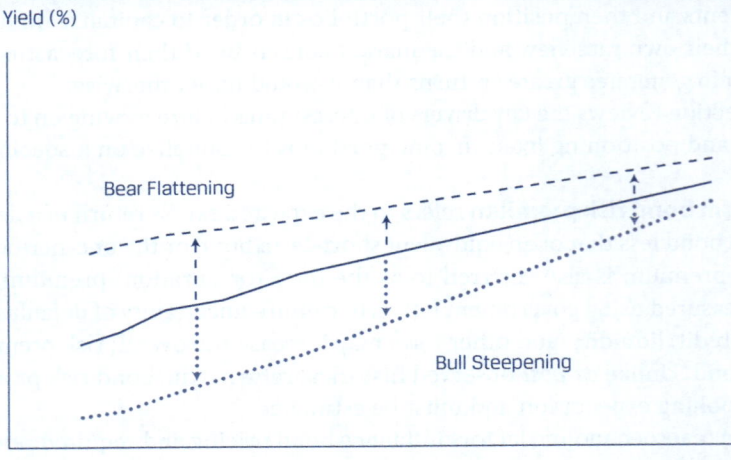

In recent years, central banks have increasingly used their balance sheets for large-sale asset purchases. For example, the Federal Reserve has bought large quantities of US Treasury bonds and mortgage-backed securities. The intended purpose is to stimulate economic activity by increasing the money supply through benchmark bond purchases and driving down the bond risk premium, encouraging capital allocation to incrementally higher-risk assets. Asset purchases impact the term structure by raising demand in a range of maturity segments.

Other factors that influence bond prices, yields, and the bond risk premium include fiscal policy, the maturity structure of debt, and investor demand.

Benchmark government bonds are the means by which nations fund their cumulative (current and past) budget deficits. Greater deficits require more borrowing, which influences both bond supply and required yield. Thus, fiscal supply-side effects affect bond prices and yields by increasing (decreasing) yields when budget deficits rise (fall). In the late 1990s, market participants believed the US government would run fiscal surpluses, leading to a reduction in government bond supply as the Treasury stopped issuing new 30-year bonds for four years. The expected reduction in supply drove long-maturity Treasury yields lower.

Longer government debt maturity structures predict greater excess bond returns. This is effectively a segmented market factor, wherein the greater supply of bonds of long-term maturity increases the yield in that market segment.

Domestic investor demand is a key driver of bond prices, especially among pension funds and insurance companies that use long-dated government bonds to match expected future liabilities. Greater domestic investor demand increases prices and reduces the bond risk premium.

Non-domestic investor demand influences government bond prices and may result either from holding reserves or from actions associated with currency exchange rate management. Non-domestic flows significantly influence bond prices because inflows (outflows) bid up (down) bond prices, lowering (raising) the bond risk premium.

During highly uncertain market periods, investors flock to government bonds in what is termed a **flight to quality**. This term refers to investors' selling off higher-risk asset classes such as stocks and commodities in favor of default-risk-free government bonds. A flight to quality is often associated with **bullish flattening**, in which the yield curve flattens as long-term rates fall by more than short-term rates.

Fixed-income trades based on interest rate forecasts can take a variety of forms, often using bond futures contracts to avoid significant portfolio turnover. Remember that any interest rate view must be evaluated relative to the current short rate and forward curve, because they reflect returns earned by investors rolling down the curve under the current set of implied forward rates.

Investors expecting interest rates to fall will generally extend portfolio duration relative to a benchmark to take advantage of bond price increases from falling rates, whereas investors expecting higher rates will shorten portfolio duration to reduce exposure to falling bond prices.

To capitalize on a steeper curve under which long-term rates rise relative to short-term rates, traders will short long-term bonds and purchase short-term bonds. If on the other hand a trader forecasts curve flattening, whereby short-term rates rise relative to long-term rates, she may capitalize on this trend by purchasing long-term bonds and selling short-term bonds short. In both the expected steepening and flattening trades, the position may be designed as duration neutral in order to insulate from changes in the level of the term structure. Fixed-income investors with long-only investment mandates may alternate between portfolios concentrated in a single maturity, known as a **bullet portfolio**, and those with similar duration that combine short and long maturities, known as a **barbell portfolio**. For example, an investor may seek to capitalize on an expected bullish flattening of the yield curve by shifting from a bullet to a barbell position.

EXAMPLE 11

Building a Rate View Based On Economic Forecasts and Monetary Policy

Morgan Salaz is a fixed income analyst responsible for advising fixed income clients about bond trading opportunities. In the current recessionary environment, the level of government bond yields is low and the term structure is nearly flat. Salaz's firm forecasts that after a brief recession, economic growth will return quickly during the coming 12 months.

1. Which of the following changes to the yield curve is consistent with Salaz's expectation of increasing economic growth over the coming year?

   A. Decrease in the level

   B. Decrease in the term spread of long-term rates over short-term rates

   C. Increase in the term spread of long-term rates over short-term rates

Answer: C is correct. Economic growth forecasts impact long-term rates. The view that economic growth will return to robust levels is consistent with a shift to a positively sloped term structure.

2. Salaz also expects the Federal Reserve to decrease asset purchases of long-term bonds as the economic recovery continues. Which of the following scenarios is consistent with this view? The reduced asset purchases will likely:

   A. amplify the effect of increased economic activity on the term spread.

   B. dampen the effect of increased economic activity on the term spread.

   C. have no effect on the term spread.

Answer: A. Reduced asset purchases constitute a negative shift in demand for longer-term bonds, which raises their yields. The reduced asset purchases of long-maturity bonds would add to the effect of greater economic activity, both of which will increase the term spread.

SUMMARY

- The spot rate for a given maturity can be expressed as a geometric average of the short-term rate and a series of forward rates.
- Forward rates are above (below) spot rates when the spot curve is upward (downward) sloping, whereas forward rates are equal to spot rates when the spot curve is flat.
- If forward rates are realized, then all bonds, regardless of maturity, will have the same one-period realized return, which is the first-period spot rate.
- If the spot rate curve is upward sloping and is unchanged, then each bond "rolls down" the curve and earns the forward rate that rolls out of its pricing (i.e., an N-period zero-coupon bond earns the N-period forward rate as it rolls down to be a $N - 1$ period security). This dynamic implies an expected return in excess of short-maturity bonds (i.e., a **term premium**) for longer-maturity bonds if the yield curve is upward sloping.
- Active bond portfolio management is consistent with the expectation that today's forward curve does not accurately reflect future spot rates.
- The swap curve provides another measure of the time value of money.
- Swaps are an essential tool frequently used by investors to hedge, take a position in, or otherwise modify interest rate risk.
- Bond quote conventions often use measures of spreads. Those quoted spreads can be used to determine a bond's price.
- Swap curves and Treasury curves can differ because of differences in their credit exposures, liquidity, and other supply/demand factors.
- Market participants often use interest rate spreads between short-term government and risky rates as a barometer to evaluate relative credit and liquidity risk.
- The local expectations theory, liquidity preference theory, segmented markets theory, and preferred habitat theory provide traditional explanations for the shape of the yield curve.
- Historical yield curve movements suggest that they can be explained by a linear combination of three principal movements: level, steepness, and curvature.
- The volatility term structure can be measured using historical data and depicts yield curve risk.
- The sensitivity of a bond value to yield curve changes may make use of effective duration, key rate durations, or sensitivities to parallel, steepness, and curvature movements. Using key rate durations or sensitivities to parallel, steepness, and curvature movements allows one to measure and manage shaping risk.

- The term bond risk premium refers to the expected excess return of a default-free long-term bond less that of an equivalent short-term bond or the one-period risk-free rate

- Several macroeconomic factors influence bond pricing and required returns such as inflation, economic growth, and monetary policy, among others.

- During highly uncertain market periods, investors flock to government bonds in a flight to quality that is often associated with bullish flattening, in which long-term rates fall by more than short-term rates.

- Investors expecting rates to fall will generally extend (shorten) portfolio duration to take advantage of expected bond price increases (decreases)

- When investors expect a steeper (flatter) curve under which long-term rates rise (fall) relative to short-term rates, they will sell (buy) long-term bonds and purchase (sell) short-term bonds.

REFERENCES

Boyarchenko, Nina, Pooja Gupta, Nick Steele, Jacqueline Yen. October 2018. "Negative Swap Spreads." Federal Reserve Bank of New York Economic Policy Review24 (2): 1–14.

PRACTICE PROBLEMS

1. Given spot rates for one-, two-, and three-year zero coupon bonds, how many forward rates can be calculated?

2. Give two interpretations for the following forward rate: The two-year forward rate one year from now is 2%.

3. Describe the relationship between forward rates and spot rates if the yield curve is flat.

4. Which forward rate cannot be computed from the one-, two-, three-, and four-year spot rates? The rate for a:

   A. one-year loan beginning in two years

   B. two-year loan beginning in two years

   C. three-year loan beginning in two years

5. Consider spot rates for three zero-coupon bonds: z(1) = 3%, z(2) = 4%, and z(3) = 5%. Which statement is correct? The forward rate for a one-year loan beginning in one year will be:

   A. less than the forward rate for a one-year loan beginning in two years.

   B. greater than the forward rate for a two-year loan beginning in one year.

   C. greater than the forward rate for a one-year loan beginning in two years.

6. If one-period forward rates are decreasing with maturity, the yield curve is *most likely*:

   A. flat.

   B. upward sloping.

   C. downward sloping.

The following information relates to questions 7-17

A one-year zero-coupon bond yields 4.0%. The two- and three-year zero-coupon bonds yield 5.0% and 6.0%, respectively.

7. The rate for a one-year loan beginning in one year is *closest* to:

   A. 4.5%.

   B. 5.0%.

   C. 6.0%.

8. The forward rate for a two-year loan beginning in one year is *closest* to:

   A. 5.0%.

    B. 6.0%.

    C. 7.0%.

9. The forward rate for a one-year loan beginning in two years is *closest* to:

    A. 6.0%.

    B. 7.0%.

    C. 8.0%.

10. The five-year spot rate is not provided here; however, the forward price for a two-year zero-coupon bond beginning in three years is known to be 0.8479. The price today of a five-year zero-coupon bond is *closest* to:

    A. 0.7119.

    B. 0.7835.

    C. 0.9524.

11. The one-year spot rate z_1 is 4%, the forward rate for a one-year loan beginning in one year is 6%, and the forward rate for a one-year loan beginning in two years is 8%. Which of the following rates is *closest* to the three-year spot rate?

    A. 4.0%

    B. 6.0%

    C. 8.0%

12. The one-year spot rate z_1 is 5%, and the forward price for a one-year zero-coupon bond beginning in one year is 0.9346. The spot price of a two-year zero-coupon bond is *closest* to:

    A. 0.87.

    B. 0.89.

    C. 0.93.

13. In a typical interest rate swap contract, the swap rate is *best* describedas the interest rate for the:

    A. fixed-rate leg of the swap.

    B. floating-rate leg of the swap.

    C. difference between the fixed and floating legs of the swap.

14. A two-year fixed-for-floating MRR swap is 1.00%, and the two-year US Treasury bond is yielding 0.63%. The swap spread is *closest* to:

    A. 37 bps.

    B. 100 bps.

    C. 163 bps.

15. The swap spread is quoted as 50 bps. If the five-year US Treasury bond is yielding

2%, the rate paid by the fixed payer in a five-year interest rate swap is *closest* to:

- **A.** 0.50%.
- **B.** 1.50%.
- **C.** 2.50%.

16. If the three-month T-bill rate drops and MRR remains the same, the relevant TED spread:

- **A.** increases.
- **B.** decreases.
- **C.** does not change.

17. Given the yield curve for US Treasury zero-coupon bonds, which spread is *most* helpful pricing a corporate bond? The:

- **A.** Z-spread.
- **B.** TED spread.
- **C.** MRR–OIS spread, formerly the Libor–OIS spread.

The following information relates to questions 18-24

Jane Nguyen is a senior bond trader for an investment bank, and Chris Alexander is a junior bond trader at the bank. Nguyen is responsible for her own trading activities and also for providing assignments to Alexander that will develop his skills and create profitable trade ideas. Exhibit 1 presents the current par and spot rates.

Exhibit 1: Current Par and Spot Rates		
Maturity	**Par Rate**	**Spot Rate**
One year	2.50%	2.50%
Two years	2.99%	3.00%
Three years	3.48%	3.50%
Four years	3.95%	4.00%
Five years	4.37%	

Note: Par and spot rates are based on annual-coupon sovereign bonds.

Nguyen gives Alexander two assignments that involve researching various questions:

Assignment 1   What is the yield-to-maturity of the option-free, default-risk-free bond presented in Exhibit 2? Assume that the bond is held to maturity, and use the rates shown in Exhibit 1.

Exhibit 2: Selected Data for $1,000 Par Bond		
Bond Name	**Maturity (T)**	**Coupon**
Bond Z	Three years	6.00%

Note: Terms are today for a T-year loan.

> Assignment 2   Assuming that the projected spot curve two years from today will be below the current forward curve, is Bond Z fairly valued, undervalued, or overvalued?

After completing his assignments, Alexander asks about Nguyen's current trading activities. Nguyen states that she has a two-year investment horizon and will purchase Bond Z as part of a strategy to ride the yield curve. Exhibit 1 shows Nguyen's yield curve assumptions implied by the spot rates.

18. Based on Exhibit 1, the five-year spot rate is *closest to*:

    A. 4.40%.

    B. 4.45%.

    C. 4.50%.

19. Based on Exhibit 1, the market is *most likely* expecting:

    A. deflation.

    B. inflation.

    C. no risk premiums.

20. Based on Exhibit 1, the forward rate of a one-year loan beginning in three years is *closest to*:

    A. 4.17%.

    B. 4.50%.

    C. 5.51%.

21. Based on Exhibit 1, which of the following forward rates can be computed?

    A. A one-year loan beginning in five years

    B. A three-year loan beginning in three years

    C. A four-year loan beginning in one year

22. For Assignment 1, the yield-to-maturity for Bond Z is *closest* to the:

    A. one-year spot rate.

    B. two-year spot rate.

    C. three-year spot rate.

23. For Assignment 2, Alexander should conclude that Bond Z is currently:

    A. undervalued.

B. fairly valued.

C. overvalued.

24. By choosing to buy Bond Z, Nguyen is *most likely* making which of the following assumptions?

   A. Bond Z will be held to maturity.

   B. The three-year forward curve is above the spot curve.

   C. Future spot rates do not accurately reflect future inflation.

The following information relates to questions 25-29

Laura Mathews recently hired Robert Smith, an investment adviser at Shire Gate Advisers, to assist her in investing. Mathews states that her investment time horizon is short, approximately two years or less. Smith gathers information on spot rates for on-the-run annual-coupon government securities and swap spreads, as presented in Exhibit 1. Shire Gate Advisers recently published a report for its clients stating its belief that, based on the weakness in the financial markets, interest rates will remain stable, the yield curve will not change its level or shape for the next two years, and swap spreads will also remain unchanged.

Exhibit 1: Government Spot Rates and Swap Spreads

	Maturity (years)			
	1	**2**	**3**	**4**
Government spot rate	2.25%	2.70%	3.30%	4.05%
Swap spread	0.25%	0.30%	0.45%	0.70%

Smith decides to examine the following three investment options for Mathews:

Investment 1: Buy a government security that would have an annualized return that is nearly risk free. Smith is considering two possible implementations: a two-year investment or a combination of two one-year investments.

Investment 2: Buy a four-year, zero-coupon corporate bond and then sell it after two years. Smith illustrates the returns from this strategy using the swap rate as a proxy for corporate yields.

Investment 3: Buy a lower-quality, two-year corporate bond with a coupon rate of 4.15% and a Z-spread of 65 bps.

When Smith meets with Mathews to present these choices, Mathews tells him that she is somewhat confused by the various spread measures. She is curious to know whether there is one spread measure that could be used as a good indicator of the risk and liquidity of money market securities during the recent past.

25. In his presentation of Investment 1, Smith could show that under the no-arbitrage principle, the forward price of a one-year government bond to be

issued in one year is *closest* to:

A. 0.9662.

B. 0.9694.

C. 0.9780.

26. In presenting Investment 1, using Shire Gate Advisers' interest rate outlook, Smith could show that riding the yield curve provides a total return that is *most likely*:

A. lower than the return on a maturity-matching strategy.

B. equal to the return on a maturity-matching strategy.

C. higher than the return on a maturity-matching strategy.

27. In presenting Investment 2, Smith should show an annual return *closest* to:

A. 4.31%.

B. 5.42%.

C. 6.53%.

28. The bond in Investment 3 is *most likely* trading at a price of:

A. 100.97.

B. 101.54.

C. 104.09.

29. The *most* appropriate response to Mathews question regarding a spread measure is the:

A. Z-spread.

B. TED spread.

C. MRR–OIS spread, formerly the Libor–OIS spread.

The following information relates to questions 30-40

Liz Tyo is a fund manager for an actively managed global fixed-income fund that buys bonds issued in Countries A, B, and C. She and her assistant are preparing the quarterly markets update. Tyo begins the meeting by distributing the daily rates sheet, which includes the current government spot rates for Countries A, B, and C as shown in Exhibit 1.

Exhibit 1: Today's Government Spot Rates

Maturity	Country A	Country B	Country C
One year	0.40%	−0.22%	14.00%
Two years	0.70	−0.20	12.40
Three years	1.00	−0.12	11.80
Four years	1.30	−0.02	11.00
Five years	1.50	0.13	10.70

Tyo asks her assistant how these spot rates were obtained. The assistant replies, "Spot rates are determined through the process of bootstrapping. It entails backward substitution using par yields to solve for zero-coupon rates one by one, in order from latest to earliest maturities."

Tyo then provides a review of the fund's performance during the last year and comments, "The choice of an appropriate benchmark depends on the country's characteristics. For example, although Countries A and B have both an active government bond market and a swap market, Country C's private sector is much bigger than its public sector, and its government bond market lacks liquidity."

Tyo further points out, "The fund's results were mixed; returns did not benefit from taking on additional risk. We are especially monitoring the riskiness of the corporate bond holdings. For example, our largest holdings consist of three four-year corporate bonds (Bonds 1, 2, and 3) with identical maturities, coupon rates, and other contract terms. These bonds have Z-spreads of 0.55%, 1.52%, and 1.76%, respectively."

Tyo continues, "We also look at risk in terms of the swap spread. We considered historical three-year swap spreads for Country B, which reflect that market's credit and liquidity risks, at three different points in time." Tyo provides the information in Exhibit 2.

Exhibit 2: Selected Historical Three-Year Rates for Country B

Period	Government Bond Yield (%)	Fixed-for-Floating MRR Swap (%)
1 month ago	−0.10	0.16
6 months ago	−0.08	0.01
12 months ago	−0.07	0.71

Tyo then suggests that the firm was able to add return by riding the yield curve. The fund plans to continue to use this strategy but only in markets with an attractive yield curve for this strategy.

She moves on to present her market views on the respective yield curves for a five-year investment horizon.

Country A: "The government yield curve has changed little in terms of its level and shape during the last few years, and I expect this trend to continue. We assume that future spot rates reflect the current forward curve for all maturities."

Country B: "Because of recent economic trends, I expect a reversal in the slope of the current yield curve. We assume that future spot rates will be higher than current forward rates for all maturities."

> **Country C:** "To improve liquidity, Country C's central bank is expected to intervene, leading to a reversal in the slope of the existing yield curve. We assume that future spot rates will be lower than today's forward rates for all maturities."

Tyo's assistant asks, "Assuming investors require liquidity premiums, how can a yield curve slope downward? What does this imply about forward rates?"

Tyo answers, "Even if investors require compensation for holding longer-term bonds, the yield curve can slope downward—for example, if there is an expectation of severe deflation. Regarding forward rates, it can be helpful to understand yield curve dynamics by calculating implied forward rates. To see what I mean, we can use Exhibit 1 to calculate the forward rate for a two-year Country C loan beginning in three years."

30. Did Tyo's assistant accurately describe the process of bootstrapping?

    A. Yes

    B. No, with respect to par yields

    C. No, with respect to backward substitution

31. The swap curve is a better benchmark than the government spot curve for:

    A. Country A.

    B. Country B.

    C. Country C.

32. Based on Exhibit 2, the implied credit and liquidity risks as indicated by the historical three-year swap spreads for Country B were the lowest:

    A. 1 month ago.

    B. 6 months ago.

    C. 12 months ago.

33. Based on Exhibit 1 and Tyo's expectations, which country's term structure is currently best for traders seeking to ride the yield curve?

    A. Country A

    B. Country B

    C. Country C

34. Based on Exhibit 1 and assuming Tyo's market views on yield curve changes are realized, the forward curve of which country will lie below its spot curve?

    A. Country A

    B. Country B

    C. Country C

35. Based on Exhibit 1 and Tyo's expectations for the yield curves, Tyo *most likely* perceives the bonds of which country to be fairly valued?

    A. Country A

B. Country B

C. Country C

36. With respect to their discussion of yield curves, Tyo and her assistant are *most likely* discussing which term structure theory?

   A. Pure expectations theory

   B. Local expectations theory

   C. Liquidity preference theory

37. Tyo's assistant should calculate a forward rate *closest* to:

   A. 9.07%.

   B. 9.58%.

   C. 9.97%.

38. During economic expansions, monetary authorities raise benchmark rates to help control inflation. This action is *most* often consistent with:

   A. bearish flattening.

   B. bullish steepening.

   C. bearish steepening.

39. When government budget deficits fall, fiscal supply-side effects are *most* likely to result in:

   A. higher bond yields.

   B. a steeper yield curve.

   C. lower bond yields.

40. A flight to quality is most often associated with:

   A. a general rise in the level of interest rates.

   B. bullish flattening.

   C. bearish flattening.

The following information relates to questions 41-42

41. Define the yield-to-maturity for a coupon bond.

42. Is it possible for a coupon bond to earn less than the yield-to-maturity if held to maturity?

43. If a bond trader believes that current forward rates overstate future spot rates,

how might she profit from that conclusion?

44. Explain the strategy of rolling down the yield curve.

45. What are the advantages of using the swap curve as a benchmark of interest rates relative to a government bond yield curve?

46. What is the TED spread, and what type of risk does it measure?

47. What is the SOFR rate, and which market conditions does it reflect?

The following information relates to questions 48-51

Rowan Madison is a junior analyst at Cardinal Capital. Sage Winter, a senior portfolio manager and Madison's supervisor, meets with Madison to discuss interest rates and review two bond positions in the firm's fixed-income portfolio.

Winter begins the meeting by asking Madison to state her views on the term structure of interest rates. Madison responds:

"Yields are a reflection of expected spot rates and risk premiums. Investors demand risk premiums for holding long-term bonds, and these risk premiums increase with maturity."

Winter tells Madison that, based on recent changes in spreads, she is concerned about a perceived increase in counterparty risk in the economy and its effect on the portfolio. Madison asks Winter:

"Which spread measure should we use to assess changes in counterparty risk in the economy?"

Winter is also worried about the effect of yield volatility on the portfolio. She asks Madison to identify the economic factors that affect short-term and long-term rate volatility. Madison responds:

"Short-term rate volatility is mostly linked to uncertainty regarding monetary policy, whereas long-term rate volatility is mostly linked to uncertainty regarding the real economy and inflation."

Finally, Winter asks Madison to analyze the interest rate risk portfolio positions in a 5-year and a 20-year bond. Winter requests that the analysis be based on level, slope, and curvature as term structure factors. Madison presents her analysis in Exhibit 1.

Exhibit 1: Three-Factor Model of Term Structure		
	Time to Maturity (years)	
Factor	**5**	**20**
Level	−0.4352%	−0.5128%
Steepness	−0.0515%	−0.3015%
Curvature	0.3963%	0.5227%

Note: Entries indicate how yields would change for a one standard deviation increase in a factor.

Winter asks Madison to perform two analyses:

Analysis 1:   Calculate the expected change in yield on the 20-year bond resulting from a two-standard-deviation increase in the steepness factor.

Analysis 2:   Calculate the expected change in yield on the five-year bond resulting from a one-standard-deviation decrease in the level factor and a one-standard-deviation decrease in the curvature factor.

48. Madison's views on the term structure of interest rates are *most* consistent with the:

  A. local expectations theory.

  B. segmented markets theory.

  C. liquidity preference theory.

49. Is Madison's response regarding the factors that affect short-term and long-term rate volatility correct?

  A. Yes

  B. No, she is incorrect regarding factors linked to long-term rate volatility

  C. No, she is incorrect regarding factors linked to short-term rate volatility

50. Based on Exhibit 1, the results of Analysis 1 should show the yield on the 20-year bond decreasing by:

  A. 0.3015%.

  B. 0.6030%.

  C. 0.8946%.

51. Based on Exhibit 1, the results of Analysis 2 should show the yield on the five-year bond:

  A. decreasing by 0.8315%.

  B. decreasing by 0.0389%.

  C. increasing by 0.0389%.

52. According to the local expectations theory, what would be the difference in the one-month total return if an investor purchased a five-year zero-coupon bond versus a two-year zero-coupon bond?

53. Compare the segmented market and the preferred habitat term structure theories.

The following information relates to questions 54-56

54. List the three factors that have empirically been observed to affect Treasury security returns and explain how each of these factors affects returns on Treasury securities.

55. What has been observed to be the most important factor in affecting Treasury returns?

56. Which measures of yield curve risk can measure shaping risk?

SOLUTIONS

1. Three forward rates can be calculated from the one-, two- and three-year spot rates. The rate on a one-year loan that begins at the end of Year 1 can be calculated using the one- and two-year spot rates; in the following equation, one would solve for $f_{1,1}$:

    $$[1 + z_2]^2 = [1 + z_1]^1[1 + f_{1,1}]^1$$

    The rate on a one-year loan that starts at the end of Year 2 can be calculated from the two- and three-year spot rates. In the following equation, one would solve for $f_{2,1}$:

    $$[1 + z_3]^3 = [1 + z_2]^2[1 + f_{2,1}]^1$$

    Additionally, the rate on a two-year loan that begins at the end of Year 1 can be computed from the one- and three-year spot rates. In the following equation, one would solve for $f_{1,2}$:

    $$[1 + z_3]^3 = [1 + z_1]^1[1 + f_{1,2}]^2$$

2. For the two-year forward rate one year from now of 2%, the two interpretations are as follows:

    - 2% is the rate that will make an investor indifferent between buying a three-year zero-coupon bond or investing in a one-year zero-coupon bond and, when it matures, reinvesting in a zero-coupon bond that matures in two years.

    - 2% is the rate that can be locked in today by buying a three-year zero-coupon bond rather than investing in a one-year zero-coupon bond and, when it matures, reinvesting in a zero-coupon bond that matures in two years.

3. A flat yield curve implies that all spot interest rates are the same. When the spot rate is the same for every maturity, successive applications of the forward rate model will show that all the forward rates will also be the same and equal to the spot rate.

4. C is correct. There is no spot rate information to provide rates for a loan that terminates in five years. That is $f_{2,3}$ is calculated as follows:

    $$f_{2,3} = \sqrt[3]{\frac{[1+z_5]^5}{[1+z_2]^2}} - 1$$

    This equation indicates that in order to calculate the rate for a three-year loan beginning at the end of two years, one needs the five-year spot rate, z_5, and the two-year spot rate, z_2. However, z_5 is not provided.

5. A is correct. The forward rate for a one-year loan beginning in one year, $f_{1,1}$, is $1.04^2/1.03 - 1 = 5\%$. The rate for a one-year loan beginning in two years, $f_{2,1}$, is $1.05^3/1.04^2 - 1 = 7\%$. This confirms that an upward-sloping yield curve is consistent with an upward-sloping forward curve.

6. C is correct. If one-period forward rates are decreasing with maturity, then the forward curve is downward sloping. This turn implies a downward-sloping yield curve where longer-term spot rates z_{B-A} are less than shorter-term spot rates z_A.

7. C is correct. From the forward rate model, we have

    $$[1 + z_2]^2 = [1 + z_1]^1[1 + f_{1,1}]^1$$

    Using the one- and two-year spot rates, we have

    $$(1 + 0.05)^2 = (1 + 0.04)^1[1 + f_{1,1}]^1, \text{ so } \frac{(1+0.05)^2}{(1+0.04)^1} - 1 = f_{1,1} = 6.010\%.$$

8. C is correct. From the forward rate model,

    $$[1 + z_3]^3 = [1 + z_1]^1[1 + f_{1,2}]^2$$

    Using the one- and three-year spot rates, we find

    $$(1 + 0.06)^3 = (1 + 0.04)^1[1 + f_{1,2}]^2, \text{ so } \sqrt{\frac{(1+0.06)^3}{(1+0.04)^1}} - 1 = f_{1,2} = 7.014\%.$$

9. C is correct. From the forward rate model,

    $$[1 + z_3]^3 = [1 + z_2]^2[1 + f_{2,1}]^1$$

    Using the two- and three-year spot rates, we find

    $$(1 + 0.06)^3 = (1 + 0.05)^2[1 + f_{2,1}]^1, \text{ so } \frac{(1+0.06)^3}{(1+0.05)^2} - 1 = f_{2,1} = 8.029\%.$$

10. A is correct. We can convert spot rates to spot prices to find $DF_3 = \frac{1}{(1.06)^3} = 0.8396$.

    The forward pricing model can be used to find the price of the five-year zero as $DF_B = DF_A \times F_{A,B-A}$, so $DF_5 = DF_3 F_{3,2} = 0.8396 \times 0.8479 = 0.7119$.

11. B is correct. Applying the forward rate model, we find

    $$[1 + z_3]^3 = [1 + z_1]^1[1 + f_{1,1}]^1[1 + f_{2,1}]^1$$

    So $[1 + z_3]^3 = (1 + 0.04)^1(1 + 0.06)^1(1 + 0.08)^1, \sqrt[3]{1.1906} - 1 = z_3 = 5.987\%$.

12. B is correct. We can convert spot rates to spot prices and use the forward pricing model, so we have $DF_1 = \frac{1}{(1.05)^1} = 0.9524$.
    The forward pricing model is

    $$DF_B = DF_A \times F_{A,B-A}, \text{ so } DF_2 = DF_1 F_{1,1} = 0.9524 \times 0.9346 = 0.8901.$$

13. A is correct. The swap rate is the interest rate for the fixed-rate leg of an interest rate swap.

14. A is correct. The swap spread = 1.00% − 0.63% = 0.37%, or 37 bps.

15. C is correct. The fixed leg of the five-year fixed-for-floating swap will be equal to the five-year Treasury rate plus the swap spread: 2.0% + 0.5% = 2.5%.

16. A is correct. The TED spread is the difference between the three-month MRR and the three-month Treasury bill rate. If the T-bill rate falls and MRR does not change, the TED spread will increase.

17. A is correct. The Z spread is the single rate that, when added to the rates of the spot yield curve, will provide the correct discount rates to price a particular risky bond.

18. B is correct. The five-year spot rate is determined by using forward substitution and using the known values of the one-year, two-year, three-year, and four-year spot rates, as follows:

$$1 = \frac{0.0437}{1.025} + \frac{0.0437}{(1.03)^2} + \frac{0.0437}{(1.035)^3} + \frac{0.0437}{(1.04)^4} + \frac{1 + 0.0437}{(1 + z_5)^5}$$

$$z_5 = \sqrt[5]{\frac{1.0437}{0.8394}} - 1 = 4.453\%$$

19. B is correct. The spot rates imply an upward-sloping yield curve, $z_3 > z_2 > z_1$. Because nominal yields incorporate a premium for expected inflation, an upward-sloping yield curve is generally interpreted as reflecting a market expectation of increasing, or at least level, future inflation (associated with relatively strong economic growth).

20. C is correct. A one-year loan beginning in three years, or $f_{3,1}$, is calculated as follows:

$$\left[1 + z_{3+1}\right]^{3+1} = \left[1 + z_3\right]^3 \left[1 + f_{3,1}\right]^1$$

$$[1.04]^4 = [1.035]^3 \left[1 + f_{3,1}\right]$$

$$f_{3,1} = \frac{(1.04)^4}{(1.035)^3} - 1 = 5.514\%$$

21. C is correct. Exhibit 1 provides five years of par rates, from which the spot rates for z_1, z_2, z_3, z_4, and z_5 can be derived. Thus the forward rate $f_{1,4}$ can be calculated as follows:

$$f_{1,4} = \sqrt[4]{\frac{\left[1 + z_5\right]^5}{\left[1 + z_1\right]^1}} - 1$$

22. C is correct. The yield-to-maturity, y_3, of Bond Z should be a weighted average of the spot rates used in the valuation of the bond. Because the bond's largest cash flow occurs in Year 3, z_3 will have a greater weight than z_1 and z_2 in determining y_3.
Using the spot rates:

$$\text{Price} = \frac{\$60}{(1.025)^1} + \frac{\$60}{(1.030)^2} + \frac{\$1,060}{(1.035)^3} = \$1,071.16$$

Using the yield-to-maturity:

$$\text{Price} = \frac{\$60}{\left[1 + y(3)\right]^1} + \frac{\$60}{\left[1 + y(3)\right]^2} + \frac{\$1,060}{\left[1 + y(3)\right]^3} = \$1,071.16$$

The computed result is $y_3 = 3.46\%$, which is closest to the three-year spot rate of 3.50%.

23. A is correct. Alexander projects that the spot curve two years from today will be below the current forward curve, which implies that her expected future spot rates beyond two years will be lower than the quoted forward rates. Alexander would perceive Bond Z to be undervalued in the sense that the market is effectively discounting the bond's payments at a higher rate than she would, and the bond's market price is below her estimate of intrinsic value.

24. B is correct. Nguyen's strategy is to ride the yield curve, which is appropriate when the yield curve is upward sloping. The yield curve implied by Exhibit 1 is upward sloping, which implies that the three-year forward curve is above the current spot curve. When the yield curve slopes upward, as a bond approaches maturity or "rolls down the yield curve," the bond is valued at successively lower

yields and higher prices.

25. B is correct. The forward pricing model is based on the no-arbitrage principle and is used to calculate a bond's forward price based on the spot yield curve. The spot curve is constructed by using annualized rates from option-free and default-risk-free zero-coupon bonds.

    Equation 2: $DF_B = DF_A \times F_{A,B-A}$; we need to solve for $F_{1,1}$.

    $DF_1 = 1/(1 + 0.0225)^1$ and $DF_2 = 1/(1 + 0.0270)^2$,

    $F_{1,1} = DF_2/DF_1 = 0.9481/0.9780 = 0.9694$.

26. C is correct. When the spot curve is upward sloping and its level and shape are expected to remain constant over an investment horizon (Shire Gate Advisers' view), buying bonds with a maturity longer than the investment horizon (i.e., riding the yield curve) will provide a total return greater than the return on a maturity-matching strategy.

27. C is correct. The swap spread is a common way to indicate credit spreads in a market. The four-year swap rate (fixed leg of an interest rate swap) can be used as an indication of the four-year corporate yield. Riding the yield curve by purchasing a four-year zero-coupon bond with a yield of 4.75% {i.e., 4.05% + 0.70%, [P_4 = 100/(1 + 0.0475)^4 = 83.058]} and then selling it when it becomes a two-year zero-coupon bond with a yield of 3.00% {i.e., 2.70% + 0.30%, [P_2 = 100/(1 + 0.0300)^2 = 94.260]} produces an annual return of 6.53%: (94.260/83.058)^{0.5} − 1.0 = 0.0653.

28. B is correct. The Z-spread is the constant basis point spread that is added to the default-free spot curve to price a risky bond. A Z-spread of 65 bps for a particular bond would imply adding a fixed spread of 65 bps to maturities along the spot curve to correctly price the bond. Therefore, for the two-year bond, $z_1 = 2.90\%$ (i.e., 2.25% + 0.65%), $z_2 = 3.35\%$ (i.e., 2.70% + 0.65%), and the price of the bond with an annual coupon of 4.15% is as follows:

    $P = 4.15/(1 + 0.029)^1 + 4.15/(1 + 0.0335)^2 + 100/(1 + 0.0335)^2$,

    $P = 101.54$.

29. C is correct. The MRR–OIS spread is considered an indicator of the risk and liquidity of money market securities. This spread measures the difference between MRR and the OIS rate.

30. C is correct. The assistant states that bootstrapping entails *backward* substitution using par yields to solve for zero-coupon rates one by one, in order from latest to earliest maturities. Bootstrapping entails *forward* substitution, however, using par yields to solve for zero-coupon rates one by one, in order from earliest to latest maturities.

31. C is correct. Country C's private sector is much bigger than the public sector, and the government bond market in Country C currently lacks liquidity. Under such circumstances, the swap curve is a more relevant benchmark for interest rates.

32. B is correct. The historical three-year swap spread for Country B was the lowest six months ago. Swap spread is defined as the spread paid by the fixed-rate payer of an interest rate swap over the rate of the "on the run" (most recently issued) government bond security with the same maturity as the swap. The lower (higher) the swap spread, the lower (higher) the return that investors require for credit

and/or liquidity risks.

The fixed rate of the three-year fixed-for-floating Libor swap was 0.01% six months ago, and the three-year government bond yield was –0.08% six months ago. Thus the swap spread six months ago was 0.01% – (–0.08%) = 0.09%.

One month ago, the fixed rate of the three-year fixed-for-floating Libor swap was 0.16%, and the three-year government bond yield was –0.10%. Thus the swap spread one month ago was 0.16% – (–0.10%) = 0.26%.

Twelve months ago, the fixed rate of the three-year fixed-for-floating Libor swap was 0.71%, and the three-year government bond yield was –0.07%. Thus, the swap spread 12 months ago was 0.71% – (–0.07%) = 0.78%.

33. A is correct. Country A's yield curve is upward sloping—a condition for the strategy—and more so than Country B's.

34. B is correct. The yield curve for Country B is currently upward sloping, but Tyo expects a reversal in the slope of the current yield curve. This means she expects the resulting yield curve for Country B to slope downward, which implies that the resulting forward curve would lie below the spot yield curve. The forward curve lies below the spot curve in scenarios in which the spot curve is downward sloping; the forward curve lies above the spot curve in scenarios in which the spot curve is upward sloping.

    A is incorrect because the yield curve for Country A is currently upward sloping and Tyo expects that the yield curve will maintain its shape and level. That expectation implies that the resulting forward curve would be above the spot yield curve.

    C is incorrect because the yield curve for Country C is currently downward sloping and Tyo expects a reversal in the slope of the current yield curve. She thus expects the resulting yield curve for Country C to slope upward, which implies that the resulting forward curve would be above the spot yield curve.

35. A is correct. Tyo's projected spot curve assumes that future spot rates reflect, or will be equal to, the current forward rates for all respective maturities. This assumption implies that the bonds for Country A are fairly valued because the market is effectively discounting the bond's payments at spot rates that match those projected by Tyo.

    B and C are incorrect because Tyo's projected spot curves for the two countries do not match the current forward rates for all respective maturities. In the case of Country B, she expects future spot rates to be higher (than the current forward rates that the market is using to discount the bond's payments). For Country C, she expects future spot rates to be lower (than the current forward rates). Hence, she perceives the Country B bond to be currently overvalued and the Country C bond to be undervalued.

36. C is correct. Liquidity preference theory suggests that liquidity premiums exist to compensate investors for the added interest rate risk that they face when lending long term and that these premiums increase with maturity. Tyo and her assistant are assuming that liquidity premiums exist.

37. A is correct. From the forward rate model, $f_{3,2}$, is found as follows:

$$[1 + z_5]^5 = [1 + z_3]^3[1 + f_{3,2}]^2$$

Using the three-year and five-year spot rates, we find

$(1 + 0.107)^5 = (1 + 0.118)^3[1 + f_{3,2}]^2$, so

$$\sqrt{\frac{(1 + 0.107)^5}{(1 + 0.118)^3}} - 1 = f_{3,2} = 9.07\%$$

38. A is correct. This action is most often consistent with bearish flattening, or short-term bond yields rising more than long-term bond yields resulting in a flatter yield curve.

39. C is correct. When government budget deficits fall, fiscal supply-side effects are most likely to result in lower bond yields.

40. B is correct. A flight to quality is most often associated with bullish flattening, in which the yield curve flattens as long term rates fall by more than short-term rates.

41. The yield-to-maturity of a coupon bond is the expected rate of return on a bond if the bond is held to maturity, there is no default, and the bond and all coupons are reinvested at the original yield-to-maturity.

42. Yes, it is possible. For example, if reinvestment rates for the future coupons are lower than the initial yield-to-maturity, a bondholder may experience lower realized returns.

43. If forward rates are higher than expected future spot rates, the market price of the bond will be lower than the intrinsic value. This dynamic occurs because, everything else held constant, the market is currently discounting the bonds cash flows at a higher rate than the investor's expected future spot rates. The investor can capitalize on this scenario by purchasing the undervalued bond. If expected future spot rates are realized, then bond prices should rise, thus generating gains for the investor.

44. The strategy of rolling down the yield curve is one in which a bond trader attempts to generate a total return over a given investment horizon that exceeds the return to bond with maturity matched to the horizon. The strategy involves buying a bond with maturity more distant than the investment horizon. Assuming an upward-sloping yield curve, if the yield curve does not change level or shape, as the bond approaches maturity (or rolls down the yield curve) it will be priced at successively lower yields. So as long as the bond is held for a period less than maturity, it should generate higher returns because of price gains.

45. Some countries do not have active government bond markets with trading at all maturities. For those countries without a liquid government bond market but with an active swap market, there are typically more points available to construct a swap curve than a government bond yield curve. For those markets, the swap curve may be a superior benchmark.

46. The TED spread is the difference between MRR and the US T-bill rate of matching maturity. It is an indicator of perceived credit and liquidity risk. In particular, because sovereign debt instruments are typically the benchmark for the lowest default risk instruments in a given market, and loans between banks (often at MRR) have some counterparty risk, the TED spread is considered to at least in part reflect default (or counterparty) risk in the banking sector.

47. The secured overnight financing rate (SOFR), or overnight cash borrowing rate collateralized by US Treasuries, is a barometer of the US Treasury repurchase (or repo) market. SOFR is a volume-weighted index of all qualified repo market transactions on a given day and is influenced by supply and demand conditions in secured funding markets.

48. C is correct. Liquidity preference theory asserts that investors demand a risk premium, in the form of a liquidity premium, to compensate them for the added interest rate risk they face when buying long-maturity bonds. The theory also

states that the liquidity premium increases with maturity.

49. A is correct. Madison's response is correct; research indicates that short-term rate volatility is mostly linked to uncertainty regarding monetary policy, whereas long-term rate volatility is mostly linked to uncertainty regarding the real economy and inflation.

50. B is correct. Because the factors in Exhibit 1 have been standardized to have unit standard deviations, a two-standard-deviation increase in the steepness factor will lead to the yield on the 20-year bond decreasing by 0.6030%, calculated as follows:

    Change in 20-year bond yield = $-0.3015\% \times 2 = -0.6030\%$

51. C is correct. Because the factors in Exhibit 1 have been standardized to have unit standard deviations, a one-standard-deviation decrease in both the level factor and the curvature factor will lead to the yield on the five-year bond increasing by 0.0389%, calculated as follows:

    Change in five-year bond yield = $0.4352\% - 0.3963\% = 0.0389\%$

52. The local expectations theory asserts that the total return over a one-month horizon for a five-year zero-coupon bond would be the same as for a two-year zero-coupon bond.

53. Both theories attempt to explain the shape of any yield curve in terms of supply and demand for bonds. In segmented market theory, bond market participants are limited to purchase of maturities that match the timing of their liabilities. In the preferred habitat theory, participants have a preferred maturity for asset purchases, but they may deviate from it if they feel returns in other maturities offer sufficient compensation for leaving their preferred maturity segment.

54. Studies have shown that three factors affect Treasury returns: (1) changes in the level of the yield curve, (2) changes in the slope of the yield curve, and (3) changes in the curvature of the yield curve. Changes in the level refer to upward or downward shifts in the yield curve. For example, an upward shift in the yield curve is likely to result in lower returns across all maturities. Changes in the slope of the yield curve relate to the steepness of the yield curve. Thus, if the yield curve steepens, higher returns for short-maturity bonds and lower returns for long-maturity bonds will likely occur. An example of a change in the curvature of the yield curve is a situation where rates fall at the short and long end of the yield curve while rising for intermediate maturities. In this situation, returns on short and long maturities are likely to rise while declining for intermediate-maturity bonds.

55. Empirically, the most important factor is the change in the level of interest rates.

56. Key rate durations and a measure based on sensitivities to level, slope, and curvature movements can address shaping risk, but effective duration cannot.

The Arbitrage-Free Valuation Framework

by Steven V. Mann, PhD.

Steven V. Mann, PhD, is at the University of South Carolina (USA).

LEARNING OUTCOMES

Mastery	The candidate should be able to:
☐	explain what is meant by arbitrage-free valuation of a fixed-income instrument
☐	calculate the arbitrage-free value of an option-free, fixed-rate coupon bond
☐	describe a binomial interest rate tree framework
☐	describe the process of calibrating a binomial interest rate tree to match a specific term structure
☐	describe the backward induction valuation methodology and calculate the value of a fixed-income instrument given its cash flow at each node
☐	compare pricing using the zero-coupon yield curve with pricing using an arbitrage-free binomial lattice
☐	describe pathwise valuation in a binomial interest rate framework and calculate the value of a fixed-income instrument given its cash flows along each path
☐	describe a Monte Carlo forward-rate simulation and its application
☐	describe term structure models and how they are used

INTRODUCTION

1

☐	explain what is meant by arbitrage-free valuation of a fixed-income instrument

The idea that market prices adjust until there are no arbitrage opportunities forms the basis for valuing fixed-income securities, derivatives, and other financial assets. If both the net proceeds (e.g., buying and selling the same value of an asset) and the risk of an investment are zero, the return on that investment should also be zero.

This reading is designed to equip candidates with a set of bond valuation tools that are consistent with this idea. The remainder of Section 1 further defines the concept of no arbitrage, and Section 2 provides a framework for an arbitrage-free valuation of fixed-income securities. Section 3 introduces the binomial interest rate tree framework based on a lognormal random walk, which is used to value an option-free bond. The binomial tree model is calibrated to the current yield curve in Section 4. This step ensures that the interest rate tree is consistent with pricing using the zero-coupon (i.e., spot) curve as illustrated in Section 5. The reading next turns to an introduction of pathwise valuation, in Section 6. Section 7 describes a Monte Carlo forward-rate simulation and its application. Section 8 goes beyond the lognormal random walk approach to introduce common term structure models. Building on principles established earlier in the reading, these models incorporate assumptions about changes in interest rates and volatility to capture term structure dynamics and are used by practitioners to price and hedge fixed-income securities and derivatives.

The Meaning of Arbitrage-Free Valuation

Arbitrage-free valuation refers to an approach to security valuation that determines security values that are consistent with the absence of an **arbitrage opportunity**, which is an opportunity for trades that earn riskless profits without any net investment of money. In well-functioning markets, prices adjust until there are no arbitrage opportunities, which is the **principle of no arbitrage** that underlies the practical validity of arbitrage-free valuation. This principle itself can be thought of as an implication of the idea that identical assets should sell at the same price.

These concepts will be explained in greater detail shortly, but to indicate how they arise in bond valuation, consider first an imaginary world in which financial assets are free of risk and the benchmark yield curve is flat. In this reading, the terms yield, interest rate, and discount rate will be used interchangeably. A flat yield curve implies that the relevant yield is the same for all cash flows regardless of when the cash flows are delivered in time. Accordingly, the value of a bond is the present value of its certain future cash flows. In discounting those cash flows—determining their present value—investors would use the risk-free interest rate because the cash flows are certain; because the yield curve is assumed to be flat, one risk-free rate would exist and apply to all future cash flows. This is the simplest case of bond valuation one can envision. When we exit this imaginary world and enter more realistic environs, bonds' cash flows are risky (i.e., there is some chance the borrower will default) and the benchmark yield curve is not flat. How would our approach change?

A fundamental principle of valuation is that the value of any financial asset is equal to the present value of its expected future cash flows. This principle holds for any financial asset, from zero-coupon bonds to interest rate swaps. Thus, the valuation of a financial asset involves the following three steps:

Step 1	Estimate the future cash flows.
Step 2	Determine the appropriate discount rate or discount rates that should be used to discount the cash flows.
Step 3	Calculate the present value of the expected future cash flows found in Step 1 by applying the appropriate discount rate or rates determined in Step 2.

The traditional approach to valuing bonds is to discount all cash flows with the same discount rate as if the yield curve were flat. However, a bond is properly thought of as a package or portfolio of zero-coupon bonds, also referred to as zeros or discount instruments. Each zero-coupon bond in such a package can be valued separately at a discount rate that depends on the shape of the yield curve and when its single cash flow is delivered in time. The term structure of these discount rates is referred to as the spot curve. Bond values derived by summing the present values of the individual zeros (cash flows) determined by such a procedure can be shown to be arbitrage free. Ignoring transaction costs for the moment, if the bond's value were much less than the sum of the values of its cash flows individually, a trader would perceive an arbitrage opportunity and buy the bond while selling claims to the individual cash flows and pocketing the excess value. Although the details bear further discussion, the valuation of a bond as a portfolio of zeros based on using the spot curve is an example of arbitrage-free valuation. Regardless of the complexity of the bond, each component must have an arbitrage-free value. A bond with embedded options can be valued in parts as the sum of the arbitrage-free bond without options (that is, a bond with no embedded options) and the arbitrage-free value of each of the options.

The Law of One Price

The central idea of financial economics is that market prices will adjust until there are no opportunities for arbitrage. We will define shortly what is meant by an arbitrage opportunity, but for now think of it as "free money." Prices will adjust until there is no free money to be acquired. Arbitrage opportunities arise from violations of the **law of one price**. The law of one price states that two goods that are perfect substitutes must sell for the same current price in the absence of transaction costs. Two goods that are identical, trading side by side, are priced the same. Otherwise, if it were costless to trade, one would simultaneously buy at the lower price and sell at the higher price. The riskless profit is the difference in the prices. An individual would repeat this transaction without limit until the two prices converge. An implication of these market forces is deceptively straightforward and basic. If you do not put up any of your own money and take no risk, your expected return should be zero.

Arbitrage Opportunity

With this background, let us define arbitrage opportunity more precisely. An arbitrage opportunity is a transaction that involves no cash outlay that results in a riskless profit. There are two types of arbitrage opportunities. The first type of arbitrage opportunity is often called **value additivity**; put simply, the value of the whole equals the sum of the values of the parts. Consider two risk-free investments with payoffs one year from today and the prices today provided in Exhibit 1. Asset A is a simple risk-free zero-coupon bond that pays off one dollar and is priced today at 0.952381 (= 1/1.05). Asset B is a portfolio of 105 units of Asset A that pays off 105 one year from today and is priced today at 97. The portfolio does not equal the sum of the parts. The portfolio (Asset B) is cheaper than buying 105 units of Asset A at a price of 100 and then combining. An astute investor would sell 105 units of Asset A for $105 \times 0.952381 = 100$ while simultaneously buying the portfolio, Asset B, for 97. This position generates a certain 3 today (100 − 97) and generates net 0 one year from today because cash inflow for Asset B matches the amount for the 105 units of Asset A sold. An investor would repeat this trade until the prices are equal.

The second type of arbitrage opportunity is often called **dominance**. A financial asset with a risk-free payoff in the future must have a positive price today. Consider two assets, C and D, that are risk-free zero-coupon bonds. Payoffs in one year and prices today are displayed in Exhibit 1. On careful review, it appears that Asset D is cheap relative to Asset C. If both assets are risk-free, they should have the same discount rate. To make money, sell two units of Asset C at a price of 200 and use the proceeds to purchase one unit of Asset D for 200. The construction of the portfolio involves no net cash outlay today. Although it requires zero dollars to construct today, the portfolio generates 10 one year from today. Asset D will generate a 220 cash inflow, whereas the two units of Asset C sold will produce a cash outflow of 210.

Exhibit 1: Price Today and Payoffs in One Year for Sample Assets		
Asset	Price Today	Payoff in One Year
A	0.952381	1
B	97	105
C	100	105
D	200	220

This existence of both types of arbitrage opportunity is transitory. Investors aware of this mispricing will demand the securities in question in unlimited quantities. Something must change to restore stability. Prices will adjust until there are no arbitrage opportunities.

EXAMPLE 1

Arbitrage Opportunities

1. Which of the following investment alternatives includes an arbitrage opportunity?

   A. **Bond A:** The yield for a 3% annual coupon 10-year bond is 2.5% in New York City. The same bond sells for $104.376 per $100 face value in Chicago.

   B. **Bond B:** The yield for a 3% annual coupon 10-year bond is 3.2% in Hong Kong SAR. The same bond sells for RMB97.220 per RMB100 face value in Shanghai.

Solution:

Bond B is correct. Bond B's arbitrage-free price may be solved for using a financial calculator or Microsoft Excel as $3/1.032 + 3/1.032^2 + \ldots + 103/1.032^{10} = 98.311$, which is higher than the price in Shanghai. Therefore, an arbitrage opportunity exists. Buy bonds in Shanghai for RMB97.220 and sell them in Hong Kong SAR for RMB98.311. You make RMB1.091 per RMB100 of bonds traded.

Bond A's arbitrage-free price is $3/1.025 + 3/1.025^2 + \ldots + 103/1.025^{10} = 104.376$, which matches the price in Chicago. Therefore, no arbitrage opportunity exists in this market.

Implications of Arbitrage-Free Valuation for Fixed-Income Securities

Using the arbitrage-free approach, any fixed-income security should be thought of as a package or portfolio of zero-coupon bonds. Thus, a five-year 2% coupon Treasury issue should be viewed as a package of 11 zero-coupon instruments (10 semiannual coupon payments, 1 of which is made at maturity, and 1 principal value payment at maturity). The market mechanism for US Treasuries that enables this approach is the dealer's ability to separate the bond's individual cash flows and trade them as zero-coupon securities. This process is called **stripping**. In addition, dealers can recombine the appropriate individual zero-coupon securities and reproduce the underlying coupon Treasury. This process is called **reconstitution**. Dealers in sovereign debt markets around the globe are free to engage in the same process.

Arbitrage profits are possible when value additivity does not hold. The arbitrage-free valuation approach does not allow a market participant to realize an arbitrage profit through stripping and reconstitution. By viewing any security as a package of zero-coupon securities, a consistent and coherent valuation framework can be developed. Viewing a security as a package of zero-coupon bonds means that two bonds with the same maturity and different coupon rates are viewed as different packages of zero-coupon bonds and valued accordingly. Moreover, two cash flows with identical risks delivered at the same time will be valued using the same discount rate even though they are attached to two different bonds.

ARBITRAGE-FREE VALUATION FOR AN OPTION-FREE BOND   2

> ☐ | calculate the arbitrage-free value of an option-free, fixed-rate coupon bond

The goal of this section is to develop a method to produce an arbitrage-free value for an option-free bond and to provide a framework—based on interest rate trees—that is rich enough to be applied to the valuation of bonds with embedded options.

For bonds that are option-free, the simplest approach to arbitrage-free valuation involves determining the arbitrage-free value as the sum of the present values of expected future values using the benchmark spot rates. Benchmark securities are liquid, safe securities whose yields serve as building blocks for other interest rates in a country or currency. Sovereign debt is the benchmark in many countries. For example, on-the-run Treasuries serve as benchmark securities in the United States. Par rates derived from the Treasury yield curve can be used to obtain spot rates by means of bootstrapping. Gilts are the benchmark in the United Kingdom, while German bunds serve as the benchmark for euro-denominated bonds. In markets where the sovereign debt market is not sufficiently liquid, the swap curve is a viable alternative.

In this reading, benchmark bonds are assumed to be correctly priced by the market. The valuation model we develop will be constructed to reproduce exactly the prices of the benchmark bonds.

EXAMPLE 2

The Arbitrage-Free Value of an Option-Free Bond

1. The yield-to-maturity ("par rate") for a benchmark one-year annual coupon bond is 2%, for a benchmark two-year annual coupon bond is 3%, and for a benchmark three-year annual coupon bond is 4%. A three-year, 5% annual coupon bond with the same risk and liquidity as the benchmarks is selling for 102.7751 today ($t = 0$) to yield 4%. Is this value correct for the bond given the current term structure?

Solution:

The first step in the solution is to find the correct spot rate (zero-coupon rates) for each year's cash flow. The spot rates may be determined using bootstrapping, which is an iterative process. Using the bond valuation equation below, one can solve iteratively for the spot rates, z_t (rate on a zero-coupon bond of maturity t), given the periodic payment, PMT, on the relevant benchmark bond.

$$100 = \frac{PMT}{(1+z_1)^1} + \frac{PMT}{(1+z_2)^2} + \dots + \frac{PMT+100}{(1+z_N)^N}.$$

A revised equation, which uses the par rate rather than PMT, may also be used to calculate the spot rates. The revised equation is

$$1 = \frac{\text{Par rate}}{(1+z_1)} + \frac{\text{Par rate}}{(1+z_2)^2} + \dots + \frac{\text{Par rate} + 1}{(1+z_N)^N},$$

where par rate is PMT divided by 100 and represents the par rate on the benchmark bond and z_t is the t-period zero-coupon rate.

In this example, the one-year spot rate, z_1, is 2%, which is the same as the one-year par rate. To solve for z_2,

$$1 = \frac{0.03}{(1+z_1)} + \frac{0.03+1}{(1+z_2)^2} = \frac{0.03}{(1+0.02)} + \frac{0.03+1}{(1+z_2)^2}.$$

$$z_2 = 3.015\%.$$

To solve for z_3,

$$1 = \frac{0.04}{(1+z_1)} + \frac{0.04}{(1+z_2)^2} + \frac{0.04+1}{(1+z_3)^3} = \frac{0.04}{(1+0.02)} + \frac{0.04}{(1+0.03015)^2} + \frac{0.04+1}{(1+z_3)^3}.$$

$$z_3 = 4.055\%$$

The spot rates are 2%, 3.015%, and 4.055%. The correct arbitrage-free price for the bond, then, is

$$P_0 = 5/1.02 + 5/1.03015^2 + 105/1.04055^3 = 102.8102.$$

To be arbitrage free, each cash flow of a bond must be discounted by the spot rate for zero-coupon bonds maturing on the same date as the cash flow. Discounting early coupons by the bond's yield-to-maturity gives too much discounting with an upward sloping yield curve and too little discounting for a downward sloping yield curve. The bond is mispriced by 0.0351 per 100 of par value.

For option-free bonds, performing valuation discounting with spot rates produces an arbitrage-free valuation. For bonds that have embedded options, we need a different approach. The challenge one faces when developing a framework for valuing bonds with embedded options is that their expected future cash flows are interest rate dependent. If the bonds are option-free, changes in interest rates have no impact on the size and timing of the bond's cash flows. For bonds with options attached, changes in future interest rates impact the likelihood the option will be exercised and in so doing impact the cash flows. Therefore, to develop a framework that values bonds both without and with embedded options, we must allow interest rates to take on different potential values in the future based on some assumed level of volatility. The vehicle to portray this information is an interest rate "tree" representing possible future interest rates consistent with the assumed volatility. Because the interest rate tree resembles a lattice, these models are often called "lattice models." The interest rate tree performs two functions in the valuation process: (1) Generate the cash flows that are interest rate dependent, and (2) supply the interest rates used to determine the present value of the cash flows. This approach will be used in later readings when considering learning outcome statements involving callable bonds.

An interest rate model seeks to identify the elements or *factors* that are believed to explain the dynamics of interest rates. These factors are random or *stochastic* in nature, so we cannot predict the path of any factor. An interest rate model must, therefore, specify a statistical process that describes the stochastic property of these factors to arrive at a reasonably accurate representation of the behavior of interest rates. What is important to understand is that the interest rate models commonly used are based on how short-term interest rates can evolve (i.e., change) over time. Consequently, these interest rate models are referred to as one-factor models because only one interest rate is being modeled over time. More complex models consider how more than one interest rate changes over time (e.g., the short rate and the long rate) and are referred to as two-factor models.

Our task at hand is to describe the binomial interest rate tree framework. The valuation model we are attempting to build is the binomial lattice model. It is so named because the short interest rate can take on one of two possible values consistent with the volatility assumption and an interest rate model. As we will soon discover, the two possible interest rates next period will be consistent with the following three conditions: (1) an interest rate model that governs the random process of interest rates, (2) the assumed level of interest rate volatility, and (3) the current benchmark yield curve. We take the prices of the benchmark bonds as given so that our model recovers the market values for each benchmark bond. In this way, we tie the model to the current yield curve that reflects the underlying economic reality.

The Binomial Interest Rate Tree

The first step for demonstrating the binomial valuation method is to present the benchmark par curve by using bonds of a country or currency. For simplicity in our illustration, we will use US dollars. The same principles hold with equal force regardless of the country or currency. The benchmark par curve is presented in Exhibit 2. For simplicity, we assume that all bonds have annual coupon payments. Benchmark bonds are conveniently priced at par so the yields-to-maturity and the coupon rates on the bonds are the same. From these par rates, we use the bootstrapping methodology to uncover the underlying spot rates shown in Exhibit 3. Because the par curve is upward sloping, it comes as no surprise that after Year 1 the spot rates are higher than the par rates. In Exhibit 4 we present the one-year implied forward rates derived from the spot curve using no arbitrage. Because the par, spot, and forward curves reflect the same information about interest rates, if one of the three curves is known, it is possible to generate the other two curves. The three curves are identical only if the yield curve is flat.

[Handwritten margin note: — Par curve: represents yields to maturity on coupon-paying government bonds, priced at par, over a range of maturities]

Exhibit 2: Benchmark Par Curve

Maturity (Years)	Par Rate	Bond Price
1	1.00%	100
2	1.20%	100
3	1.25%	100
4	1.40%	100
5	1.80%	100

Exhibit 3: Underlying One-Year Spot Rates of Par Rates

Maturity (Years)	One-Year Spot Rate
1	1.0000%
2	1.2012%
3	1.2515%
4	1.4045%
5	1.8194%

Exhibit 4: One-Year Implied Forward Rates

Maturity (Years)	Forward Rate
Current one-year rate	1.0000%
One-year rate, one year forward	1.4028%
One-year rate, two years forward	1.3521%
One-year rate, three years forward	1.8647%
One-year rate, four years forward	3.4965%

Recall from our earlier discussion that if we value the benchmark bonds using rates derived from these curves, we will recover the market price of par for all five bonds in Exhibit 2. Specifically, par rates represent the single interest applied to all the cash flows that will produce the market prices. Discounting each cash flow separately with the set of spot rates will also give the same answer. Finally, forward rates are the discount rates of a single cash flow over a single period. If we discount each cash flow with the appropriate discount rate for each period, the computed values will match the observed prices.

When we approach the valuation of bonds with cash flows that are interest rate dependent, we must explicitly allow interest rates to change. We accomplish this task by introducing interest rate volatility and generating an interest rate tree later in this reading. An interest rate tree is simply a visual representation of the possible values of interest rates based on an interest rate model and an assumption about interest rate volatility.

A binomial interest rate tree is presented in Exhibit 5. Our goal is to learn how to populate this structure with interest rates. Notice the i's, which represent different potential values the one-year interest rates may take over time. As we move from left to right on the tree, the number of possible interest rates increases. The first is the current time (in years), or formally, Time 0. The interest rate displayed at Time 0 is the discount rate that converts Time 1 payments to Time 0 present values. At the bottom of the graph, time is the unit of measurement. Notice that there is one year between possible interest rates. This is called the "time step," and in our illustration, it matches the frequency of the annual cash flows. The i's in Exhibit 5 are called nodes. The first node is called the root of the tree and is simply the current one-year rate at Time 0. Each node thereafter is represented by a both time element and a rate change component.

Exhibit 5: Binomial Interest Rate Tree

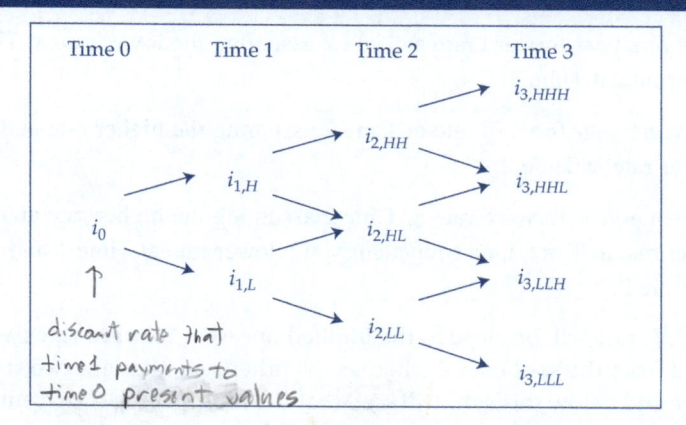

We now turn to the question of how to obtain the two possible values for the one-year interest rate one year from today. Two assumptions are required: an interest rate model and a volatility of interest rates. Recall an interest rate model puts structure on the randomness. We are going to use the lognormal random walk, and the resulting tree structure is often referred to as a lognormal tree. A lognormal model of interest rates insures two appealing properties: (1) non-negativity of interest rates and (2) higher volatility at higher interest rates. At each node, there are two possible rates one year forward at Time 1. We will assume for the time being that each has an equal probability of occurring. The two possible rates we will calculate are going to be higher and lower than the one-year forward rate at Time 1 one year from now.

We denote i_L to be the rate lower than the implied forward rate and i_H to be the higher forward rate. The lognormal random walk posits the following relationship between $i_{1,L}$ and $i_{1,H}$:

$$i_{1,H} = i_{1,L}e^{2\sigma},$$

where σ is the standard deviation and e is Euler's number, the base of natural logarithms, which is a constant 2.7183. The random possibilities each period are (nearly) centered on the forward rates calculated from the benchmark curve. The intuition of this relationship is deceptively quick and simple. Think of the one-year forward implied interest rate from the yield curve as the average of possible values for the one-year rate at Time 1. The lower of the two rates, i_L, is one standard deviation below the mean (one-year implied forward rate), and i_H is one standard deviation above the mean. Thus, the higher and lower values (i_L and i_H) are multiples of each other, and the multiplier is $e^{2\sigma}$. Note that as the standard deviation (i.e., volatility) increases, the multiplier increases, and the two rates will grow farther apart but will still be (nearly) centered on the implied forward rate derived from the spot curve. We will demonstrate this soon.

We use the following notation to describe the tree at Time 1. Let

σ = assumed volatility of the one-year rate,

$i_{1,L}$ = the lower one-year forward rate one year from now at Time 1, and

$i_{1,H}$ = the higher one-year forward rate one year from now at Time 1.

For example, suppose that $i_{1,L}$ is 1.194% and σ is 15% per year; then $i_{1,H}$ = 1.194%($e^{2\times0.15}$) = 1.612%.

At Time 2, there are three possible values for the one-year rate, which we will denote as follows:

$i_{2,LL}$ = one-year forward rate at Time 2 assuming the lower rate at Time 1 and the lower rate at Time 2.

$i_{2,HH}$ = one-year forward rate at Time 2 assuming the higher rate at Time 1 and the higher rate at Time 2.

$i_{2,HL}$ = one-year forward rate at Time 2 assuming the higher rate at Time 1 and the lower rate at Time 2, or equivalently, the lower rate at Time 1 and the higher rate at Time 2.

The middle rate will be close to the implied one-year forward rate two years from now derived from the spot curve, whereas the other two rates are two standard deviations above and below this value. (Recall that the multiplier for adjacent rates on the tree differs by a multiple of e raised to the 2σ.) This type of tree is called a recombining tree because there are two paths to get to the middle rate. This feature of the model results in faster computation because the number of possible outcomes each period grows linearly rather than exponentially.

The relationship between $i_{2,LL}$ and the other two one-year rates is as follows:

$i_{2,HH} = i_{2,LL}(e^{4\sigma})$, and $i_{2,HL} = i_{2,LL}(e^{2\sigma})$.

In a given period, adjacent possible outcomes in the tree are two standard deviations apart. So, for example, if $i_{2,LL}$ is 0.980%, and assuming once again that σ is 15%, we calculate

$i_{2,HH} = 0.980\%(e^{4\times0.15}) = 1.786\%$

and

$i_{2,HL} = 0.980\%(e^{2\times0.15}) = 1.323\%$.

There are four possible values for the one-year forward rate at Time 3. These are represented as follows: $i_{3,HHH}$, $i_{3,HHL}$, $i_{3,LLH}$ and $i_{3,LLL}$. Once again, all the forward rates in the tree are multiples of the lowest possible rates each year. The lowest possible forward rate at Time 3 is $i_{3,LLL}$ and is related to the other three as given below:

$i_{3,HHH} = (e^{6\sigma})i_{3,LLL}$.

$i_{3,HHL} = (e^{4\sigma})i_{3,LLL}$.

$i_{3,LLH} = (e^{2\sigma})i_{3,LLL}$.

Exhibit 6 shows the notation for a four-year binomial interest rate tree. We can simplify the notation by centering the one-year rates on the tree on implied forward rates on the benchmark yield curve, so i_t is the one-year rate t years from now and the centering rate. The subscripts indicate the rates at the end of the year, so in the second year, it is the rate at the end of Time 2 to the end of Time 3. Exhibit 6 uses this uniform notation. Note that adjacent forward rates in the tree are two standard deviations (σ) apart.

adjacent: interest rates in the same column (i.e., same year)

Exhibit 6: Four-Year Binomial Tree

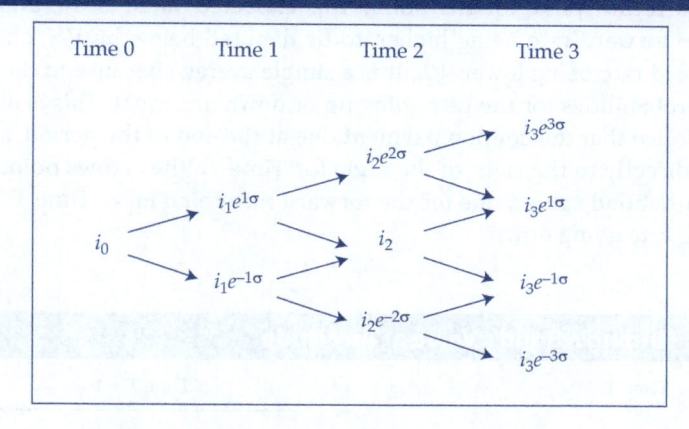

Before we attempt to build an interest rate tree, two additional tools are needed. These tools are introduced in the next two sections.

CREATING A BINOMIAL INTEREST RATE TREE

3

☐ | describe a binomial interest rate tree framework

Recall that variance is a measure of dispersion of a probability distribution. The standard deviation is the square root of the variance and is measured in the same units as the mean. With a simple lognormal distribution, the changes in interest rates are proportional to the level of the one-period interest rates each period. Volatility is measured relative to the current level of rates. It can be shown that for a lognormal distribution the standard deviation of the one-year rate is equal to $i_0\sigma$. For example, if σ is 10% and the one-year rate (i_0) is 2%, then the standard deviation of the one-year rate is 2% × 10% = 0.2%, or 20 bps. As a result, interest rate moves are larger when interest rates are high and are smaller when interest rates are low. One of the characteristics of a lognormal distribution is that negative interest rates are not possible, since as rates approach zero, the absolute change in interest rates becomes smaller and smaller.

There are two methods commonly used to estimate interest rate volatility. The first method uses historical interest rate volatility based on data from the recent past, which is assumed to be indicative of the future. A second method to estimate interest rate volatility is that derived from observed market prices of interest rate derivatives (e.g., swaptions, caps, floors) known as implied volatility.

Determining the Value of a Bond at a Node

To find the value of the bond at a node, we use the backward induction valuation methodology. Barring default, we know that at maturity the bonds will be valued at par. So, we start at maturity, fill in those values, and work back from right to left to find the bond's value at the desired node. Suppose we want to determine the bond's value at the lowest node at Time 1. To find this value, we must first calculate the bond's value at the two nodes to the right of the node we selected. The bond's value at the two nodes immediately to the right must be available.

[Handwritten margin note:] 3 requirements for a binomial interest rate tree:
① Current benchmark interest rates
② interest rate volatility assumption
③ Assumption regarding an interest rate model

A bond's value at any node will depend on the future coupon payment, C, and the expected future value for the bond. This expected value is the average of the value for the forward rate being higher, to be denoted below by VH, and the value for the forward rate being lower, VL. It is a simple average because in the lognormal model the probabilities for the rate going up or down are equal. This is illustrated in Exhibit 7. Notice that the coupon payment due at the end of the period, at Time T + 1, is placed directly to the right of the node for Time T. The arrows point to the two possible future bond values, one for the forward rate going up at Time T + 1 and the other for the rate going down.

Exhibit 7: Finding a Bond's Value at Any Node

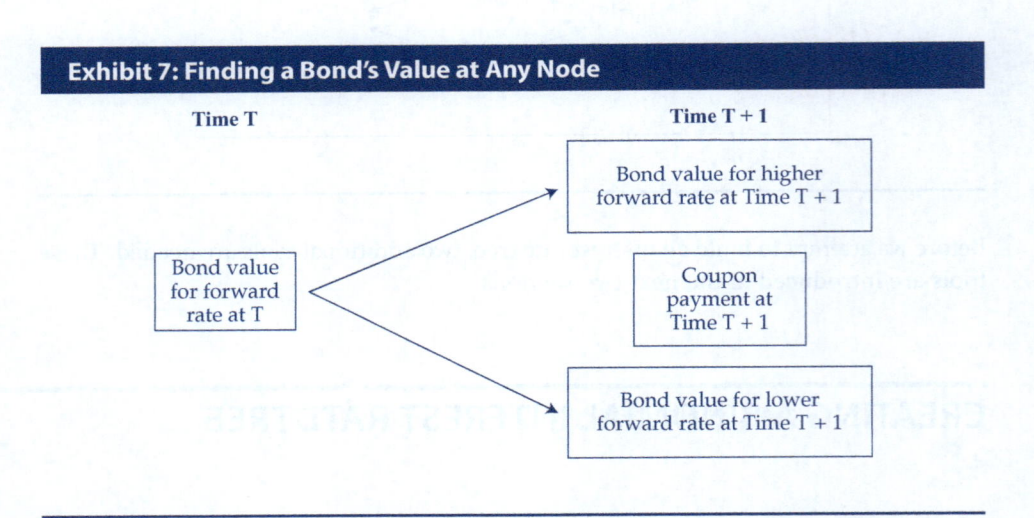

The next step is to determine the present value of the coupon payment and the expected future bond value. The relevant discount rate is the one-year forward rate prevailing at the beginning of the time period, i, at Time T. The bond's value at any node is determined by the following expression:

$$\text{Bond value at a node} = \frac{C + (0.5 \times VH + 0.5 \times VL)}{1 + i}.$$

EXAMPLE 3

Pricing a Bond Using a Binomial Tree

1. Using the interest rate tree in Exhibit 8, find the correct price for a three-year, annual pay bond with a coupon rate of 5%.

Exhibit 8: Three-Year Binomial Interest Rate Tree

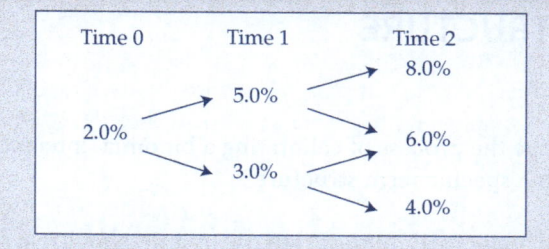

Solution:

Exhibit 9 shows the binomial tree to value the three-year, 5% bond. We start with Time 3. The cash flow is 105, the redemption of par value (100) plus the final coupon payment (5), regardless of the level of the forward rate at Time 2. Using backward induction, we next calculate the present value of the bond as of Time 2 for the three possible forward rates:

$105/1.08 = 97.2222$.

$105/1.06 = 99.0566$.

$105/1.04 = 100.9615$.

Working back to Time 1 requires the use of the general expression above for the value at any node. If the forward rate is 5.0% at Time 1, the bond value is 98.2280:

$$\frac{5 + (0.5 \times 97.2222 + 0.5 \times 99.0566)}{1.05} = 98.2280.$$

If the forward rate instead is 3.0%, the bond value is 101.9506:

$$\frac{5 + (0.5 \times 99.0566 + 0.5 \times 100.9615)}{1.03} = 101.9506.$$

Finally, the value of the bond at Time 0 is 103.0287:

$$\frac{5 + (0.5 \times 98.2280 + 0.5 \times 101.9506)}{1.02} = 103.0287.$$

Exhibit 9: Three-Year Binomial Tree

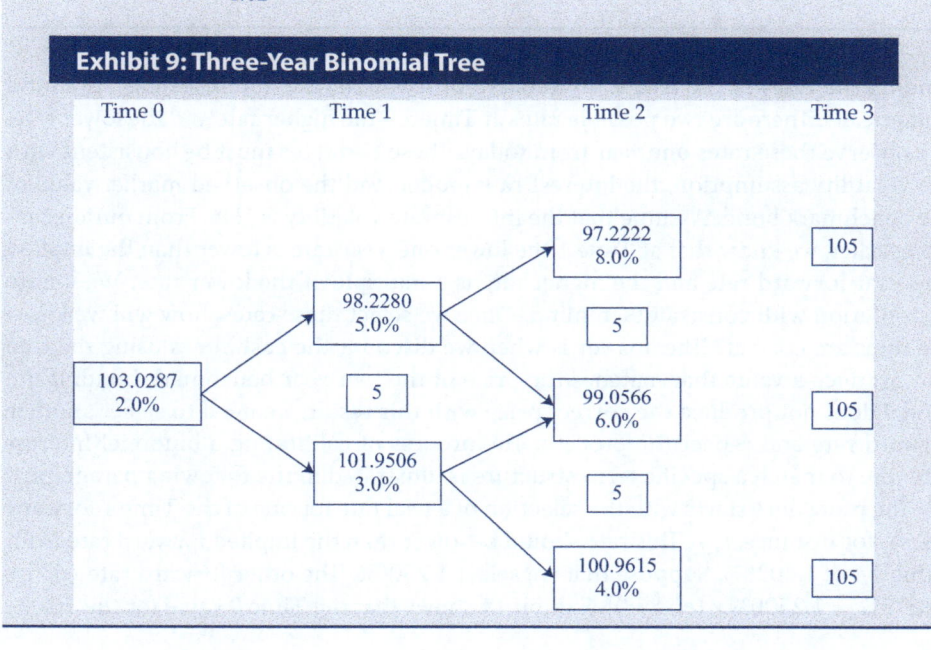

4 CALIBRATING THE BINOMIAL INTEREST RATE TREE TO THE TERM STRUCTURE

☐ | describe the process of calibrating a binomial interest rate tree to match a specific term structure

The construction of a binomial interest rate tree requires multiple steps, but keep in mind what we are trying to accomplish. We assume a process that generates interest rates and volatility. The first step is to describe the calibration of a binomial interest rate tree to match a specific term structure. We do this to ensure that the model is arbitrage free. We fit the interest rate tree to the current yield curve by choosing interest rates such that the model produces the benchmark bond values reported earlier. By doing this, we tie the model to the underlying economic reality.

Recall from Exhibits 2, 3, and 4 the benchmark bond price information and the relevant par, spot, and forward curves. We will assume that volatility, σ, is 15% and construct a four-year tree starting with the two-year bond that carries a coupon rate of 1.20%. A complete four-year binomial interest rate tree is presented in Exhibit 10. We will demonstrate how these rates are determined. The current one-year rate is 1%, i_0.

Exhibit 10: Four-Year Binomial Interest Rate Tree

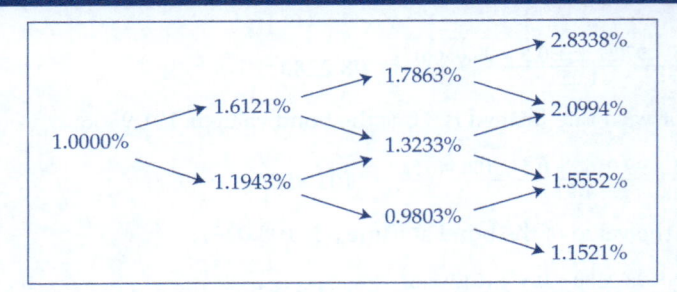

Finding the rates in the tree is an iterative process, and the interest rates are found numerically. There are two possible rates at Time 1—the higher rate and the lower rate. We observe these rates one year from today. These two rates must be consistent with the volatility assumption, the interest rate model, and the observed market value of the benchmark bond. Assume that the interest rate volatility is 15%. From our discussion earlier, we know that at Time 1 the lower one-year rate is lower than the implied one-year forward rate and the higher rate is a multiple of the lower rate. We iterate to a solution with constraints in mind. Once we select these rates, how will we know the rates are correct? The answer is when we discount the cash flows using the tree and produce a value that matches the price of the two-year benchmark bond. If the model does not produce the correct price with this result, we need to select another forward rate and repeat the process. The process of calibrating a binomial interest rate tree to match a specific term structure is illustrated in the following paragraphs.

The procedure starts with the selection of a trial rate for one of the Time 1 forward rates—for instance, $i_{1,L}$. This rate should be lower than the implied forward rate from Exhibit 4 of 1.4028%. Suppose that we select 1.2500%. The other forward rate will be 1.6873% [= 1.2500% × ($e^{2 \times 0.15}$)]. Exhibit 11 shows that the Time 0 value for the 1.20%, two-year bond is 99.9363. The redemption of principal and the final interest payment are placed across from the two nodes for the forward rates. At Time 1, the interest payment due is placed across from the initial rate for Time 0. These are the calculations:

$$101.20/1.016873 = 99.5208.$$

$$101.20/1.012500 = 99.9506.$$

$$\frac{1.20 + (0.5 \times 99.5208 + 0.5 \times 99.9506)}{1.01} = 99.9363.$$

Exhibit 11: Calibrating the Two-Year Binomial Tree

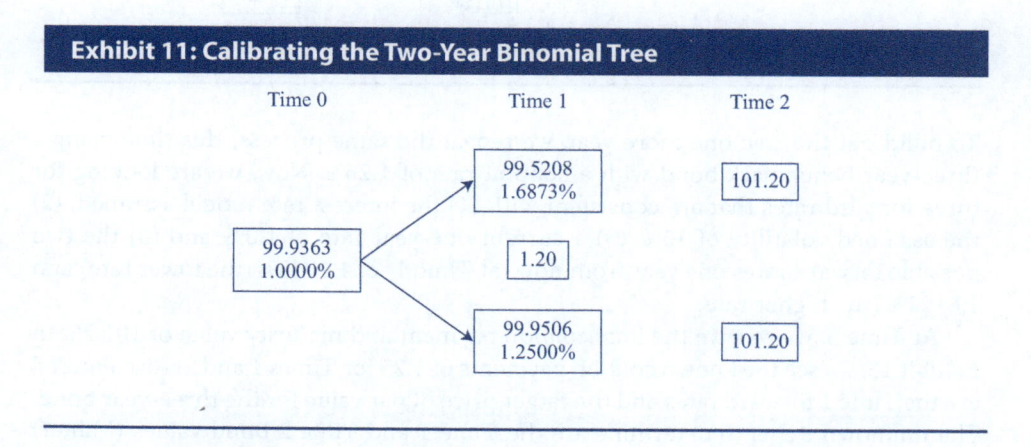

These two trial rates are clearly too high. They need to be lowered somewhat to raise the bond value to attain a Time 0 price for the bond of 100.0000. We could proceed with further trial-and-error search or use an analytic tool, such as Solver in Excel, to carry out this calculation. Essentially, we need to set the cell for the Time 0 bond price to a value of 100.0000 by changing the cell containing the initial lower forward rate for Time 1.

This procedure eventually obtains a value for $i_{1,L}$ of 1.1943%. This is the lower one-year rate. The higher one-year rate is 1.6121% [= 1.1943% $\times$ $(e^{2 \times 0.15})$]. Notice that the average of these two forward rates is 1.4032% [= (1.6121% + 1.1943%)/2], slightly above the implied forward rate of 1.4028% from Exhibit 4. The binomial tree spreads out around the forward rate curve. The average is slightly higher than the implied forward rate because of the assumption of lognormality.

Recall from the information on the benchmark bonds that the two-year bond will pay its maturity value of 100 at Time 2 and an annual coupon payment of 1.20. The bond's value at Time 2 is 101.20. The present value of the coupon payment plus the bond's maturity value if the higher one-year rate is realized, VH, is 99.5944 (= 101.20/1.016121). Alternatively, the present value of the coupon payment plus the bond's maturity value if the lower one-year rate is realized, VL, is 100.0056 (= 101.20/1.011943). These two calculations determine the bond's value one year forward. Effectively, the forward rates move the bond's value from Time 2 to Time 1. Exhibit 12 demonstrates that the arbitrage-free forward rates for Time 1 are 1.6121% and 1.1943%. The value for the bond at Time 0 is 100.0000, confirming the calibration:

$$\frac{1.20 + (0.5 \times 99.5944 + 0.5 \times 100.0056)}{1.010000} = 100.0000.$$

Exhibit 12: Building the Two-Year Binomial Tree

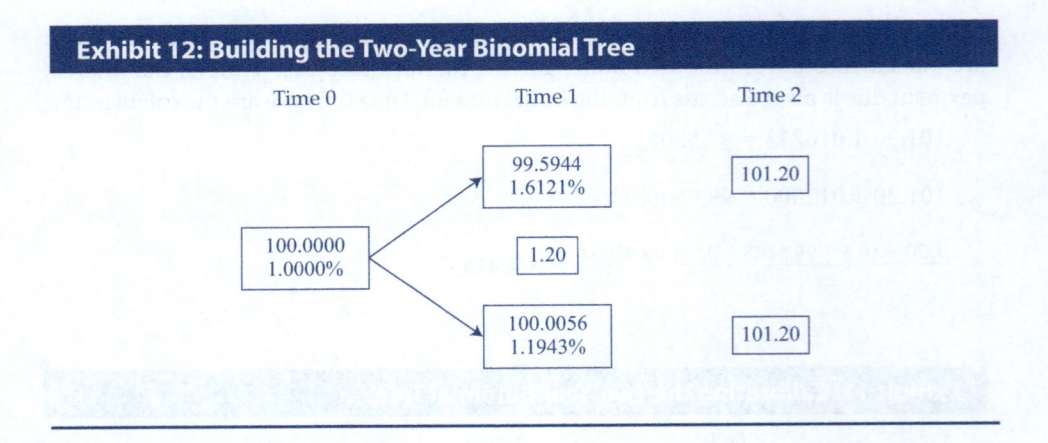

To build out the tree one more year, we repeat the same process, this time using a three-year benchmark bond with a coupon rate of 1.25%. Now, we are looking for three forward rates that are consistent with (1) the interest rate model assumed, (2) the assumed volatility of 15%, (3) a current one-year rate of 1.0%, and (4) the two possible forward rates one year from now (at Time 1) of 1.1943% (the lower rate) and 1.6121% (the higher rate).

At Time 3, we receive the final coupon payment and maturity value of 101.25. In Exhibit 13, we see the known coupon payments of 1.25 for Times 1 and 2. Also entered are the Time 1 forward rates and the target price of par value for the three-year bond. The unknown items to determine are the Time 1 and Time 2 bond values (Value?) and the Time 2 forward rates (?%).

Exhibit 13: Finding the Time 2 Forward Rates

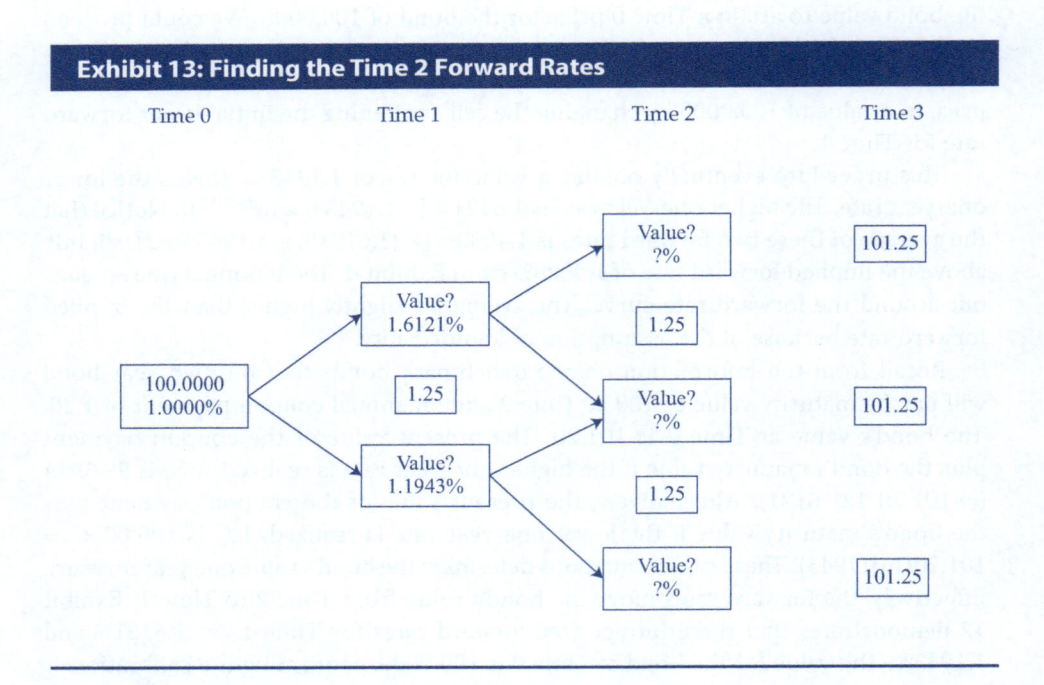

We need to select a trial value for the middle rate, $i_{2,HL}$. A good choice is the implied forward rate of 1.3521%. The trial value for the upper rate, $i_{2,HH}$, would need to be 1.3521% × $(e^{2 \times 0.15})$, and the trial value for the lower rate, $i_{2,LL}$, would need to be 1.3521%/$(e^{2 \times 0.15})$. The middle rate is then changed, changing the others as well, until the value for the 1.25% three-year bond is 100.0000. It turns out that the three forward rates are 1.7863%, 1.3233%, and 0.9803%. To demonstrate that these are the correct values, we simply work backward from the cash flows at Time 3 of the tree in Exhibit 13. The same procedure is used to obtain the values at the other nodes. The completed tree is shown in Exhibit 14.

Exhibit 14: Completed Binomial Tree with Calculated Forward Rates

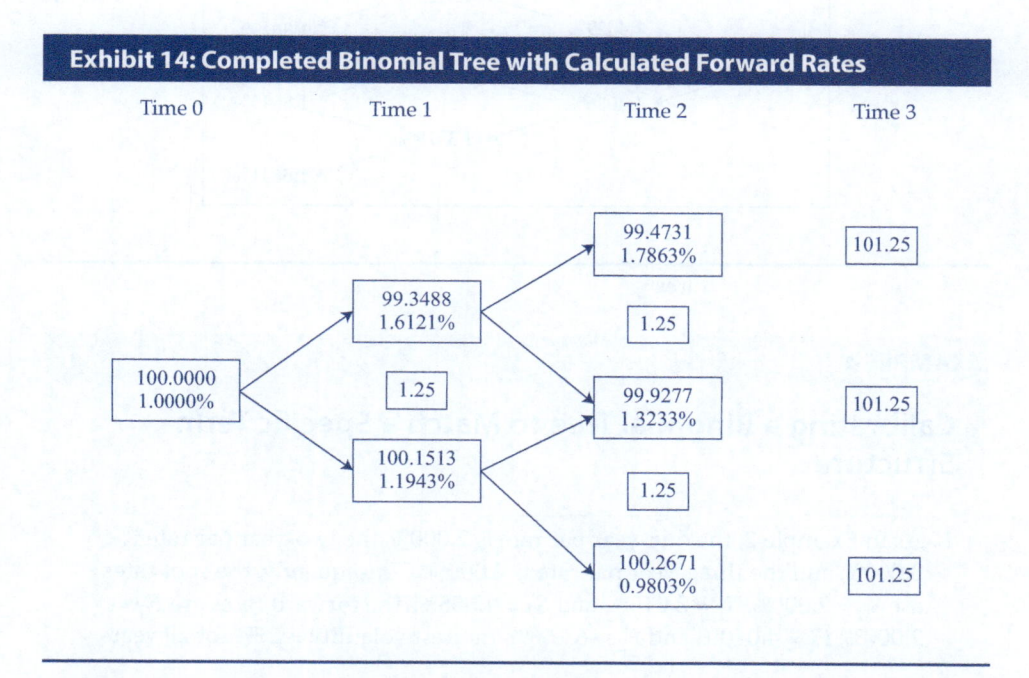

Let us focus on the impact of volatility on the possible forward rates in the tree. If we were to use a higher estimate of volatility—say, 20%—the possible forward rates should spread farther out around the forward curve. If we were to use a lower estimate of volatility—say, 0.01%—the rates should collapse to the implied forward rates from the current yield curve. Exhibit 15 and Exhibit 16 depict the interest rate trees for the volatilities of 20% and 0.01%, respectively, and confirm the expected outcome. Notice that in Exhibit 16 for 0.01% volatility, the Time 1 forward rates are very close to the implied forward rate of 1.4028% shown in Exhibit 4. Likewise, the Time 2 and Time 3 rates are a small range around the forward rates of 1.3521% and 1.8647%, respectively. In fact, if $\sigma = 0$, the binomial tree is simply the implied forward curve.

Exhibit 15: Completed Tree with $\sigma = 20\%$

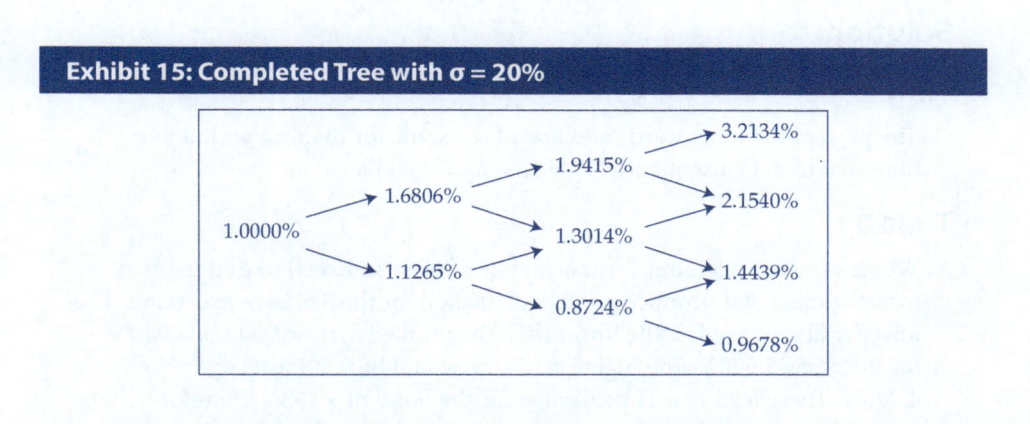

Exhibit 16: Completed Tree with σ = 0.01%

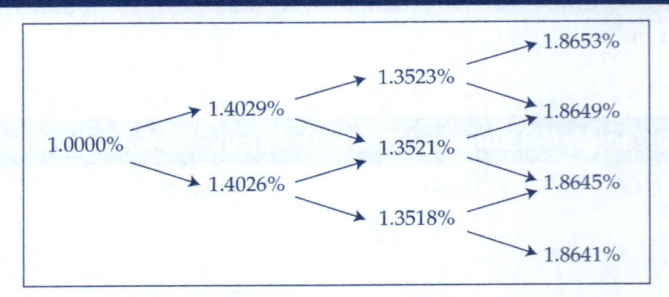

EXAMPLE 4

Calibrating a Binomial Tree to Match a Specific Term Structure

1. As in Example 2, the one-year par rate is 2.000%, the two-year par rate is 3.000%, and the three-year par rate is 4.000%. Consequently, the spot rates are S_0 = 2.000%, S_1 = 3.015%, and S_2 = 4.055%. The forward rates are F_0 = 2.000%, F_1 = 4.040%, and F_2 = 6.166%. Interest volatility is 15% for all years.

Calibrate the binomial tree in Exhibit 17.

Exhibit 17: Binomial Tree to Calibrate

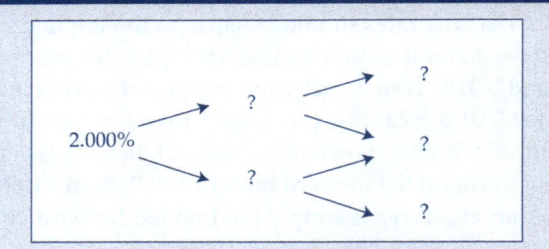

Solution:

Time 0

The par, spot, and forward rates are all the same for the first period in a binomial tree. Consequently, $Y_0 = S_0 = F_0$ = 2.000%.

Time 1

We need to use trial-and-error search (or Solver in Excel) to find the two forward rates that produce a value of 100.000 for the 3%, two-year bond. The lower trial rate needs to be lower than the implied forward rate of 4.040%—for instance, 3.500%. The higher trial rate would be 3.500% × $(e^{2×0.15})$ = 4.725%. These lead to a Time 0 value for the bond of 99.936. Therefore, the next stage in the procedure lowers the trial rates. Finally, the calibrated forward rates are 4.646% and 3.442%. Exhibit 18 shows that these are the correct rates because the value of the bond at Time 0 is 100.000. These are the calculations:

$103/1.04646 = 98.427.$

$103/1.03442 = 99.573.$

$$\frac{3 + (0.5 \times 98.427 + 0.5 \times 99.573)}{1.02} = 100.0000.$$

Exhibit 18: Calibration of Time 1 Forward Rates

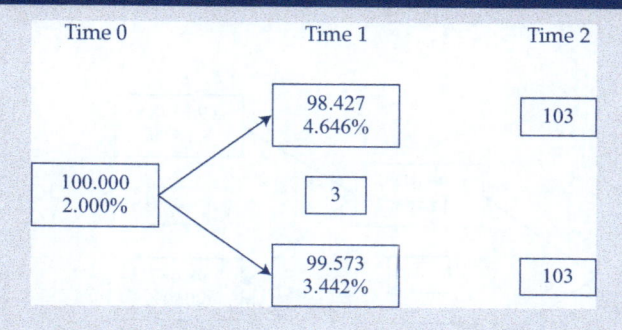

Time 2

The initial trial rate for the middle node for Time 2 is the implied forward rate of 6.166%. The rate for the upper node is 8.323% [= 6.166% × ($e^{2 \times 0.15}$)], and the rate for the lower node is 4.568% [= 6.166%/($e^{2 \times 0.15}$)]. Exhibit 19 shows that these rates for Time 2 and the already calibrated rates for Time 1 lead to a value of 99.898 for the 4% three-year bond as of Time 0. These are not the arbitrage-free rates: The Time 2 rates need to be lowered slightly to get the price up to 100.000.

Exhibit 19: Calibration of Time 2 Forward Rates

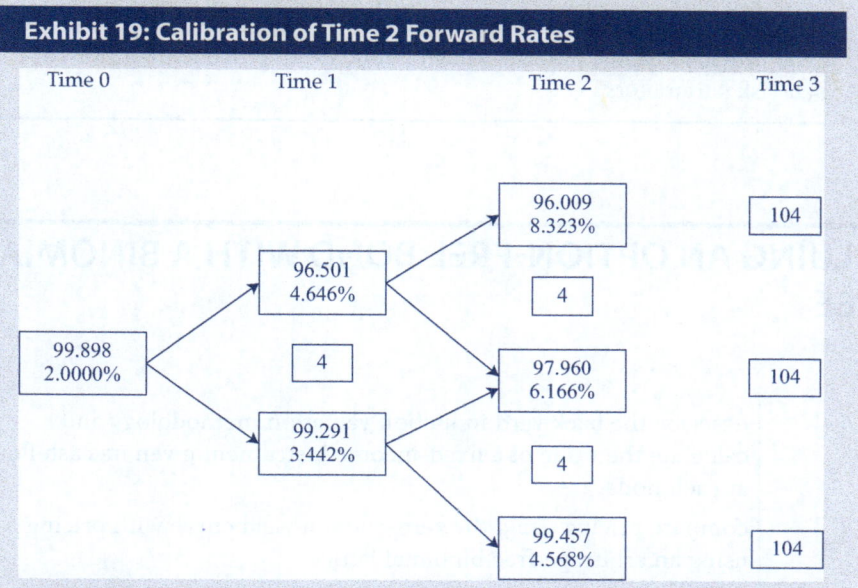

Exhibit 20 displays the completed binomial tree. The calibrated forward rates for Time 2 are 8.167%, 6.050%, and 4.482%. These are the calculations:

$104/1.08167 = 96.148.$

$104/1.06050 = 98.067.$

$104/1.04482 = 99.538.$

$$\frac{4 + (0.5 \times 96.148 + 0.5 \times 98.067)}{1.04646} = 96.618.$$

$$\frac{4 + (0.5 \times 98.067 + 0.5 \times 99.539)}{1.03442} = 99.382.$$

$$\frac{4 + (0.5 \times 96.618 + 0.5 \times 99.382)}{1.02000} = 100.000.$$

Exhibit 20: Completed Binomial Tree

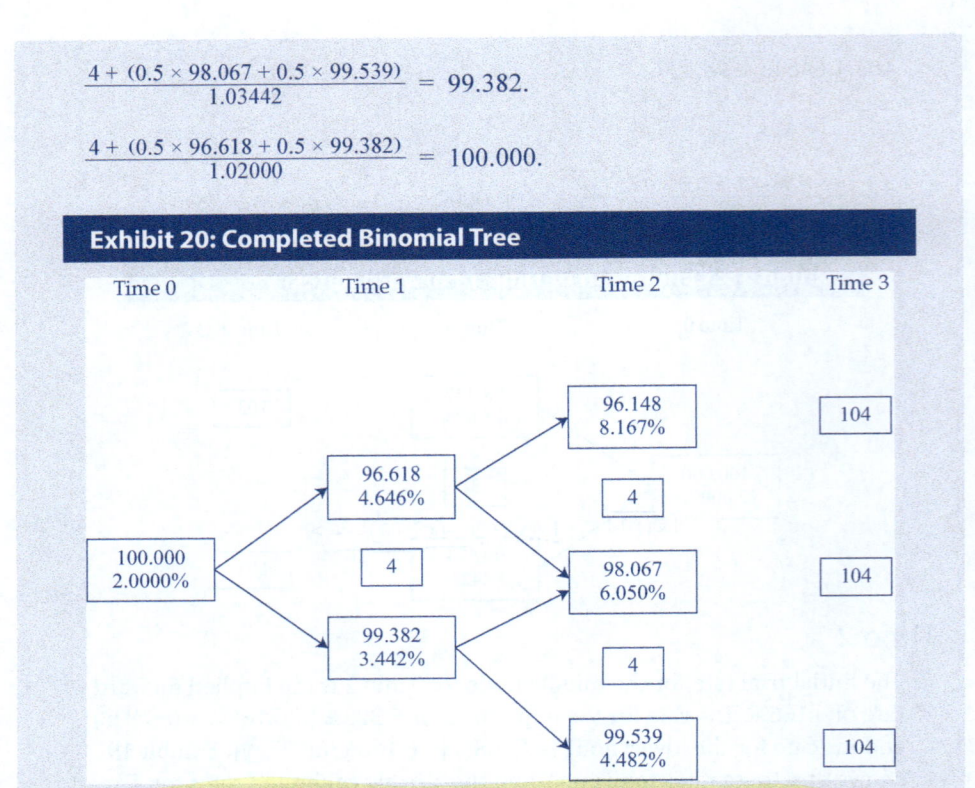

Now that our tree gives the correct prices for the underlying par bonds maturing in one, two, and three years, we say that our tree is calibrated to be arbitrage free. It will price option-free bonds correctly, including prices for the zero-coupon bonds used to find the spot rates, and to the extent that we have chosen an appropriate interest rate process and interest rate volatility, it will provide insights into the value of bonds with embedded options and their risk parameters.

5   VALUING AN OPTION-FREE BOND WITH A BINOMIAL TREE

☐   describe the backward induction valuation methodology and calculate the value of a fixed-income instrument given its cash flow at each node

☐   compare pricing using the zero-coupon yield curve with pricing using an arbitrage-free binomial lattice

Our next task is twofold. First, we calculate the arbitrage-free value of an option-free, fixed-rate coupon bond. Second, we compare the pricing using the zero-coupon yield curve with the pricing using an arbitrage-free binomial lattice. Because these two valuation methods are arbitrage free, these two values must be the same.

Now, consider an option-free bond with four years remaining to maturity and a coupon rate of 2%. Note that this is not a benchmark bond and it carries a higher coupon and price than the four-year benchmark bond, which is priced at par. The value of this bond can be calculated by discounting the cash flow at the spot rates in Exhibit 3 as shown in the following equation:

$$\frac{2}{(1.01)^1} + \frac{2}{(1.012012)^2} + \frac{2}{(1.012515)^3} + \frac{102}{(1.014044)^4} = 102.3254.$$

The binomial interest rate tree should produce the same value as when discounting the cash flows with the spot rates. An option-free bond that is valued by using the binomial interest rate tree should have the same value as when discounting by the spot rates, which is true because the binomial interest rate tree is arbitrage free.

Let us give the tree a test run and use the 2% option-free bond with four years remaining to maturity. Also assume that the issuer's benchmark yield curve is the one given in Exhibit 2; hence the appropriate binomial interest rate tree is the one in Exhibit 10. Exhibit 21 shows the various values in the discounting process and obtains a bond value of 102.3254. The tree produces the same value for the bond as the spot rates produce and is therefore consistent with our standard valuation model.

Exhibit 21: Sample Valuation for an Option-Free Bond using a Binomial Tree

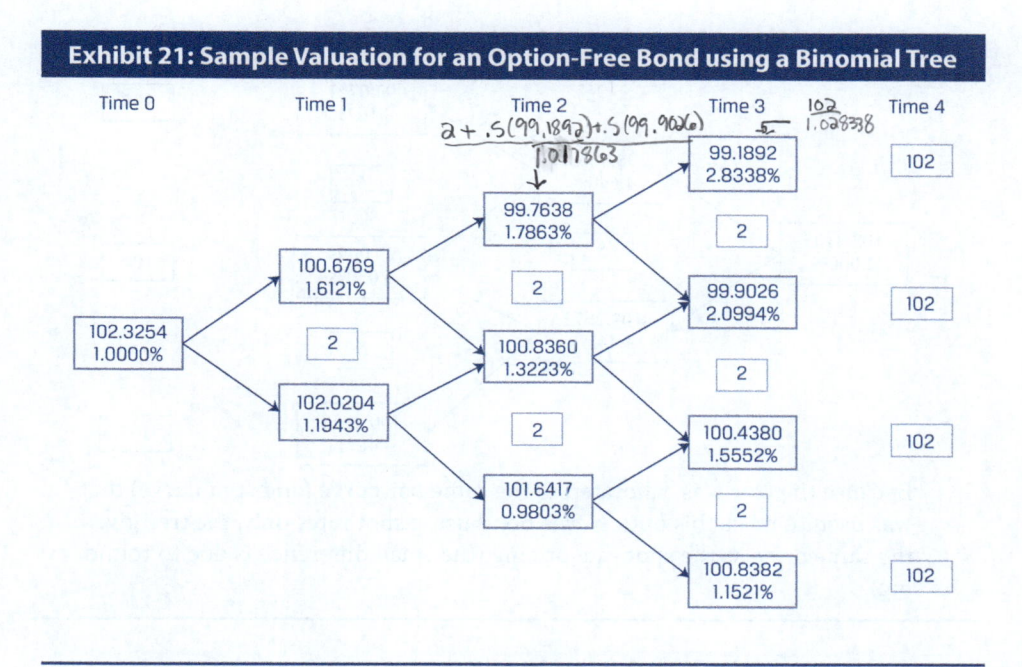

Confirming the Arbitrage-Free Value of a Bond

1. Using the par curve from Example 2 and Example 4, the yield-to-maturity for a one-year annual coupon bond is 2%, for a two-year annual coupon bond is 3%, and for a three-year annual coupon bond is 4%. Because this is the same curve as that used in Example 4, we can use the calibrated tree from that example to price a bond. Let us use a three-year annual coupon bond with a 5% coupon, just as we did in Example 2. We know that if the calibrated tree was built correctly and we perform calculations to value the bond with the tree shown in Exhibit 22, its price should be 102.8105.

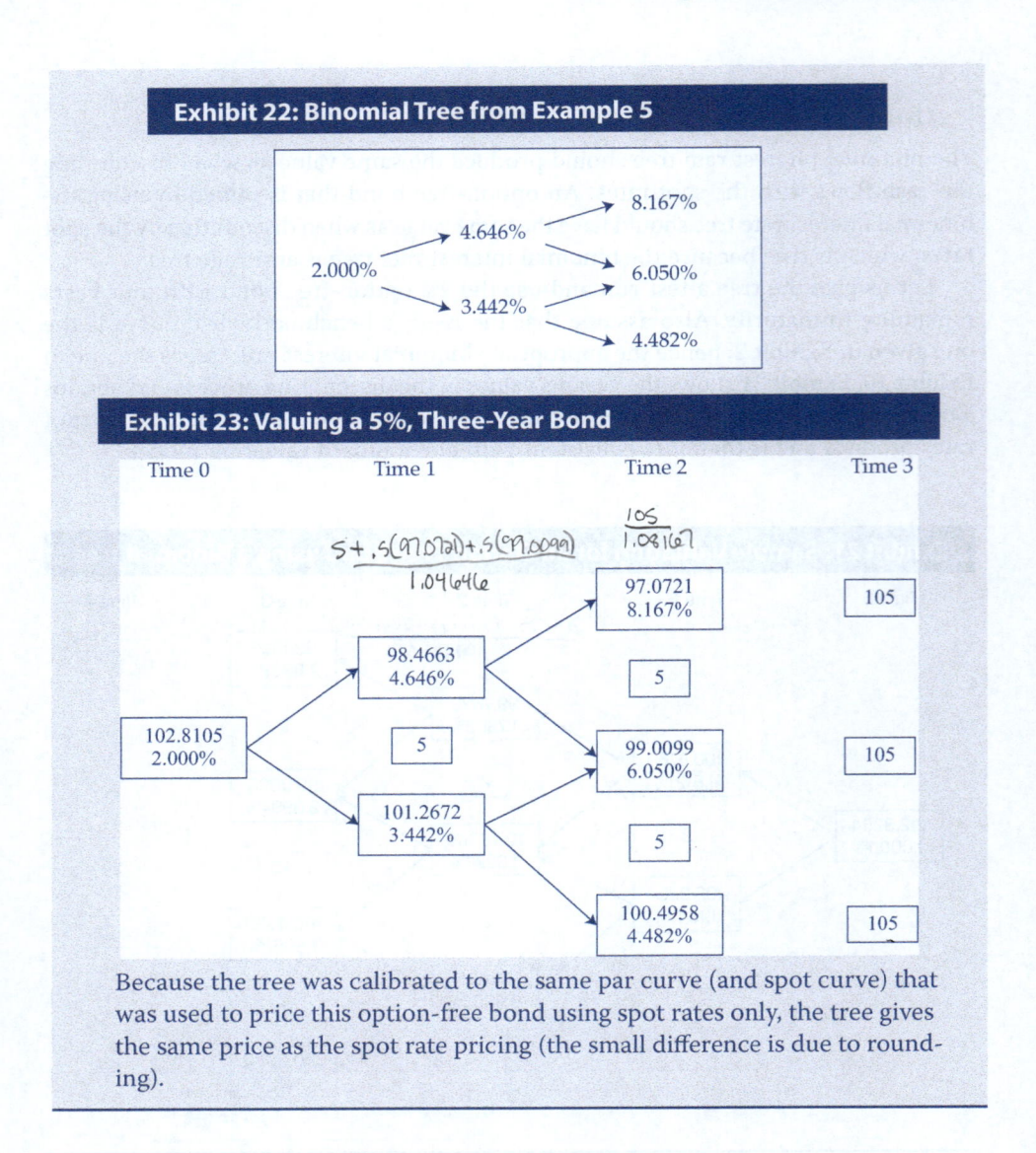

Exhibit 22: Binomial Tree from Example 5

Exhibit 23: Valuing a 5%, Three-Year Bond

Because the tree was calibrated to the same par curve (and spot curve) that was used to price this option-free bond using spot rates only, the tree gives the same price as the spot rate pricing (the small difference is due to rounding).

6

VALUING AN OPTION-FREE BOND WITH PATHWISE VALUATION

☐ describe pathwise valuation in a binomial interest rate framework and calculate the value of a fixed-income instrument given its cash flows along each path

Pathwise valuation is an alternative approach to backward induction in a binomial tree. The binomial interest rate tree specifies all potential rate paths in the model, whereas an interest rate path is the route an interest rate takes from the current time to the security's maturity. Pathwise valuation calculates the present value of a bond for each possible interest rate path and takes the average of these values across paths. We will use the pathwise valuation approach to produce the same value as the backward induction method for an option-free bond. Pathwise valuation involves the following steps: (1) Specify a list of all potential paths through the tree, (2) determine the present value of a bond along each potential path, and (3) calculate the average across all possible paths.

Determining all potential paths is similar to the following experiment. Suppose you are tossing a fair coin and tracking how many ways heads and tails can be combined. We will use a device called Pascal's Triangle, displayed in Exhibit 24. Pascal's Triangle can be built as follows: Start with the number 1 at the top of the triangle. The numbers in the boxes below are the sum of the two numbers above it except that the edges on each side are all 1. The shaded numbers show that 3 is the sum of 2 and 1. Now toss the coin while keeping track of the possible outcomes. The possible groupings are listed in Exhibit 25, where H stands for heads and T stands for tails.

Exhibit 24: Pascal's Triangle

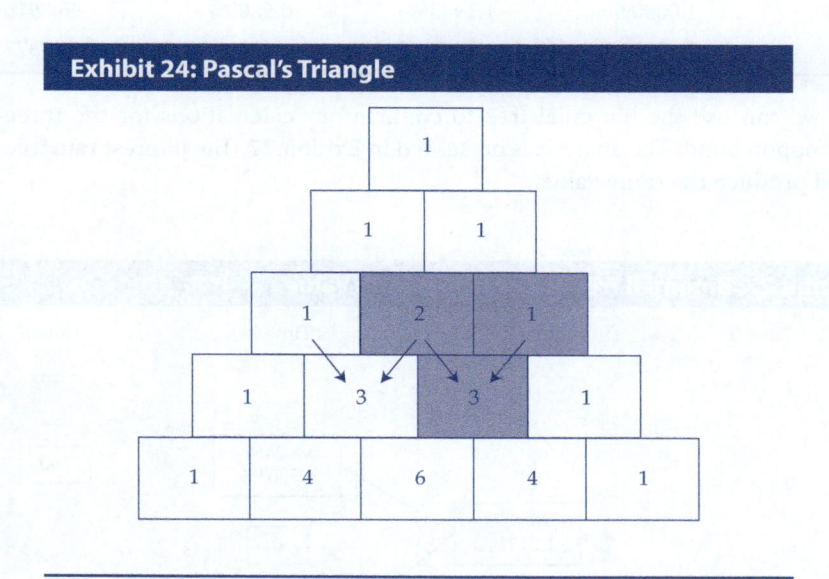

Exhibit 25: Possible Outcomes of Coin Tosses

Number of Tosses	Possible Outcomes	Pascal's Triangle
1	H T	1, 1
2	HH HT TH TT	1,2,1
3	HHH HHT HTH THH HTT THT TTH TTT	1, 3, 3, 1

This experiment mirrors exactly the number of interest rate paths in our binomial interest rate tree. The total number of paths for each period/year can be easily determined by using Pascal's Triangle. Let us work through an example for a three-year zero-coupon bond. From Pascal's Triangle, there are four possible paths to arrive at Year 3: HH, HT, TH, TT. Using the same binomial tree from Exhibit 21, we specify the four paths as well as the possible forward rates along those paths. In Exhibit 26, the last column on the right shows the present value for each path. For example, 100/(1.01000 × 1.016121 × 1.017863) = 95.7291. In the bottom right corner is the average present value across all paths.

Sum the numbers in the third row (from the top) of Pascal's triangle: 1+2+1 = 4

Exhibit 26: Four Interest Rate Paths for a Three-Year Zero-Coupon Bond

Path	Forward Rate Year 1	Forward Rate Year 2	Forward Rate Year 3	Present Value
1	1.0000%	1.6121%	1.7863%	95.7291
2	1.0000%	1.6121%	1.3233%	96.1665
3	1.0000%	1.1943%	1.3233%	96.5636
4	1.0000%	1.1943%	0.9803%	96.8916
				96.3377

Now, we can use the binomial tree to confirm our calculations for the three-year zero-coupon bond. The analysis is presented in Exhibit 27. The interest rate tree does indeed produce the same value.

Exhibit 27: Binomial Tree to Confirm Bond's Value

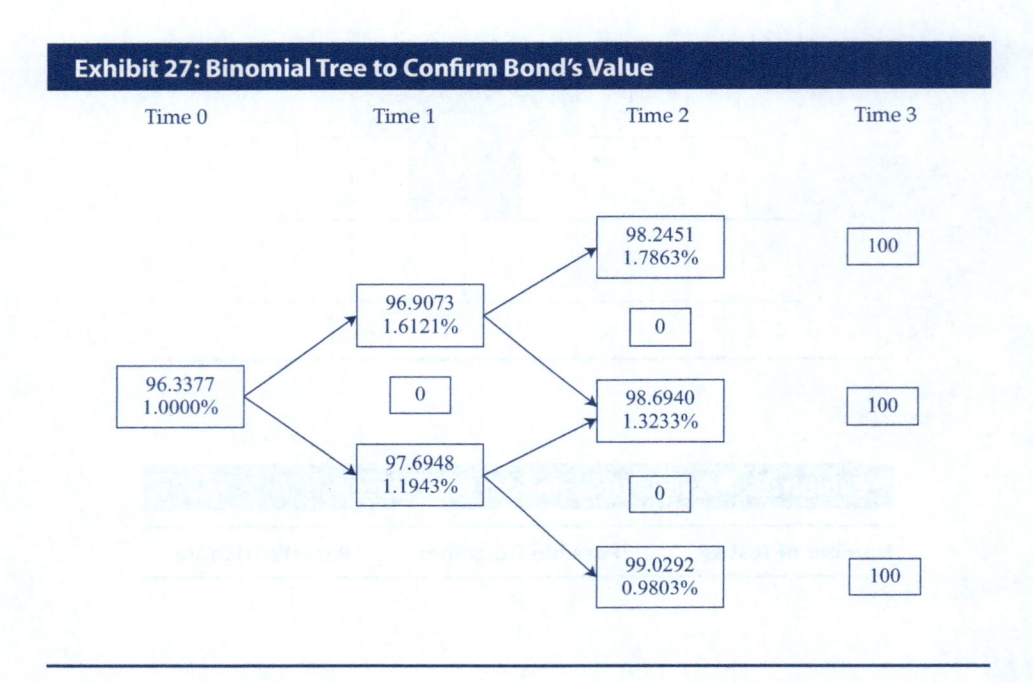

Pathwise Valuation Based on a Binomial Interest Rate Tree

1. Using the par curve from Example 2, Example 4, and Example 5, the yield-to-maturity for a one-year annual coupon bond is 2%, for a two-year annual coupon bond is 3%, and for a three-year annual coupon bond is 4%. We know that if we generate the paths in the tree correctly and discount the cash flows directly, the three-year, 5% annual coupon bond should still be priced at 102.8105, as calculated in Example 5.

There are four paths through the three-year tree. We discount the cash flows along each of the four paths and take their average, as shown in Exhibit 28, Exhibit 29, and Exhibit 30.

Exhibit 28: Cash Flows

Path	Time 0	Time 1	Time 2	Time 3
1	0	5	5	105
2	0	5	5	105
3	0	5	5	105
4	0	5	5	105

Exhibit 29: Discount Rates

Path	Time 0	Time 1	Time 2	Time 3
1	2.000%	4.646%	8.167%	
2	2.000%	4.646%	6.050%	
3	2.000%	3.442%	6.050%	
4	2.000%	3.442%	4.482%	

Exhibit 30: Present Values

Path	Time 0
1	100.5298
2	102.3452
3	103.4794
4	104.8877
Average	**102.8105**

The present values are calculated by discounting the cash flows in Exhibit 28 by the forward rates in Exhibit 29. For example, the present value for the bond along Path 1 is 100.5298:

$$\frac{5}{1.02} + \frac{5}{(1.02)(1.04646)} + \frac{105}{(1.02)(1.04646)(1.08167)} = 100.5298.$$

The present value along Path 3 is 103.4794:

$$\frac{5}{1.02} + \frac{5}{(1.02)(1.03442)} + \frac{105}{(1.02)(1.03442)(1.06050)} = 103.4794.$$

The average for the bond prices using pathwise valuation is 102.8105, which matches the result obtained using backward induction in Exhibit 23.

THE MONTE CARLO METHOD

7

☐ | describe a Monte Carlo forward-rate simulation and its application

The Monte Carlo method is an alternative method for simulating a sufficiently large number of potential interest rate paths to discover how the value of a security is affected. This method involves randomly selecting paths to approximate the results of a complete pathwise valuation. Monte Carlo methods are often used when a security's cash flows are path dependent. Cash flows are path dependent when the cash flow to be received depends on the path followed to reach its current level as well as the current level itself. For example, the valuation of mortgage-backed securities depends to a great extent on the level of prepayments. As mentioned in an earlier reading, prepayments tend to increase when interest rates fall, because borrowers are more likely to pay off mortgage loans and refinance at lower interest rates. Interest rate paths are generated on the basis of some probability distribution and a volatility assumption, and the model is fit to the current benchmark term structure of interest rates. The benchmark term structure is represented by the current spot rate curve such that the average present value across all scenario interest rate paths for each benchmark bond equals its actual market value. By using this approach, the model is rendered arbitrage free, which is equivalent to calibrating the interest rate tree as discussed in Section 3.

Suppose we intend to value with the Monte Carlo method a 30-year bond that has monthly coupon payments (e.g., mortgage-backed securities). The following steps are taken: (1) Simulate numerous (say, 500) paths of one-month interest rates under a volatility assumption and probability distribution, (2) generate spot rates from the simulated future one-month interest rates, (3) determine the cash flow along each interest rate path, (4) calculate the present value for each path, and (5) calculate the average present value across all interest rate paths.

Using the procedure just described, the model will produce benchmark bond values equal to the market prices only by chance. We want to ensure this is the case; otherwise the model will neither fit the current spot curve nor be arbitrage free. A constant is added to all interest rates on all paths such that the average present value for each benchmark bond equals its market value. The constant added to all short interest rates is called a drift term. When this technique is used, the model is said to be drift adjusted.

How many paths are appropriate for the Monte Carlo method? More paths increase the accuracy of the estimate in a statistical sense, but this does not mean the model is closer to the true fundamental value of the security. The Monte Carlo method is only as good as the valuation model used and the accuracy of the inputs.

Yield curve modelers also often include mean reversion in their Monte Carlo estimation. Mean reversion starts with the common-sense notion that history suggests that interest rates almost never get "too high" or "too low." What is meant by "too high" and "too low" is left to the discretion of the modeler. We implement mean reversion by implementing upper and lower bounds on the random process generating future interest rates. Mean reversion has the effect of moving the interest rate toward the implied forward rates from the yield curve.

EXAMPLE 7

The Application of Monte Carlo Simulation to Bond Pricing

---

1. Replace the interest rate paths from Example 6 with randomly generated paths calibrated to the same initial par and spot curves, as shown in Exhibit 31.

Exhibit 31: Discount Rates

Path	Time 0	Time 1	Time 2
1	2.000%	2.500%	4.548%
2	2.000%	3.600%	6.116%
3	2.000%	4.600%	7.766%
4	2.000%	5.500%	3.466%
5	2.000%	3.100%	8.233%
6	2.000%	4.500%	6.116%
7	2.000%	3.800%	5.866%
8	2.000%	4.000%	8.233%

These are forward rates (handwritten annotation pointing to Time 2 row 1)

Exhibit 32: Present Values

Path	Time 0
1	105.7459
2	103.2708
3	100.9104
4	103.8543
5	101.9075
6	102.4236
7	103.3020
8	101.0680
Average	**102.8103**

(handwritten annotation pointing to 105.7459):
$$\frac{5}{1.02} + \frac{5}{(1.02)(1.025)} + \frac{105}{(1.02)(1.025)(1.04548)}$$

Because we continue to get 102.8103, as shown in Exhibit 32, as the price for our three-year, 5% annual coupon bond, we know that the Monte Carlo simulation has been calibrated correctly. The paths are now different enough such that path-dependent securities, such as mortgage-backed securities, can be analyzed in ways that provide insights not possible in binomial trees, because Monte Carlo techniques provide greater flexibility to change parameters over time.

TERM STRUCTURE MODELS

8

☐ | describe term structure models and how they are used

Term structure models provide quantitatively precise descriptions of how interest rates evolve. A model provides a simplified description of a real-world phenomenon on the basis of a set of assumptions. These assumptions cannot be completely accurate in depicting the real world but are necessary for analytical tractability. Despite simplifying assumptions, models explain real-world phenomena sufficiently well to be useful for pricing and hedging.

The binomial tree and Monte Carlo simulation valuation approaches for complex fixed-income instruments described earlier rely on specific assumptions about the underlying asset properties. For example, how do we establish the node values in the binomial trees, and what determines the dispersion in rates from the top to the bottom nodes? This answer comes from term structure models, which make assumptions about the properties of rates over time and then use those properties to "fit," or determine the values of the rates at each node, binomial lattices used for pricing and risk management applications. The following section introduces common term structure models, with an emphasis on the underlying assumptions about the statistical properties of interest rates. Each of the models can be "fit" to lattice models for valuation and risk management applications.

Modeling the future path of interest rates is not only critical for scenario analysis and stress testing individual bonds and bond portfolio values but also important in the valuation of complex fixed-income instruments. A detailed description of these models depends on mathematical and statistical knowledge beyond the scope of this reading, but fixed-income practitioners will often find that these or other term structure models are embedded in many of the desktop tools and data analytics software they may use during their investment industry career. Thus, we provide a broad overview of these models in this reading.

Model Choice

Term structure models go beyond the lognormal random walk approach used earlier to describe the dynamics of the term structure for the purpose of pricing and hedging fixed-income securities and derivatives. All term structure models make simplifying assumptions about the evolution of rates over time. Many different interest rate models that differ in their assumptions exist. Arguably, there are many models, since no one model perfectly captures interest rate dynamics. Modelers face a trade-off between simplicity and accuracy when selecting a term structure model. Practitioners should be aware of the categories of models and their important features (which stem from their assumptions) as well as how those features affect pricing and hedging.

Interest rate factors

The valuation and hedging of fixed-income securities and their derivatives require information across the entire term structure. To develop a term structure model useful for pricing and hedging applications, we focus on modeling the factors that determine the term structure. The simplest class of models use one factor—the short rate, or the one-period rate—as the factor that drives the term structure. Although the use of one factor may seem limiting, because it implies all rates move in the same direction during any short time interval, it does not mean they have to move by the same amounts. Multi-factor models incorporate additional factors, such as the slope of the term structure, with the complexity of the models increasing in the number of factors.

Interest rate process

Term structure models use stochastic processes to describe interest rate dynamics. These stochastic processes have two components: a drift term and an uncertain, or stochastic, term. Although the stochastic processes are continuous time, the models can be "fit" to binomial or trinomial interest rate lattices using a discrete version of the models (integrating over time to obtain rates that span time intervals).

For a one-factor model, the general form of the process describing the short rate's (r) dynamics is

$$dr = \theta_t \, dt + \sigma_t \, dZ.$$

drift term   stochastic term

The drift term, $\theta_t dt$, describes the expected (zero-volatility) rate path. For example, in a one-factor model of the short rate, the drift describes the expected evolution of the short rate over time. The drift term may be constant or mean reverting.

The second term, $\sigma_t dZ$, adds randomness, or volatility, to the process. This dispersion term allows for the pricing of bonds with option features as well as interest rate derivatives and may take a variety of forms. The term Z is a Weiner process that is distributed normally. Given the symmetry of the normal distribution, it is possible and quite common for these models to produce interest rate paths with negative rates.

Within classes of models, such as one-factor no-arbitrage models, the key differences between the various models involve the stochastic difference equation.

Class of model

One class of models uses the arbitrage-free approach combined with assumptions about the statistical properties of interest rates. This class of models is referred to as no-arbitrage term structure models, where no-arbitrage is synonymous with arbitrage free. No-arbitrage term structure models begin with a set of assumptions about the term structure—a factor (or factors) and the stochastic process describing the factor evolution(s)—and take the term structure as given, assuming that both bond prices and the term structure bootstrapped from those prices are correct. The no-arbitrage models are "parameterized," which is the process of determining the values of the variables in the model such that those parameters produce bond prices that match current market prices. These models are used widely in practice and are often favored by practitioners since their pricing results are consistent with market prices.

Equilibrium term structure models seek to describe term structure dynamics using fundamental economic variables that are assumed to affect interest rates. The modeling process imposes restrictions that allow for the derivation of equilibrium prices for bonds and interest rate options.

Although equilibrium models use similar continuous stochastic difference equations to describe interest rate changes, equilibrium model parameters are not forced to values that produce bond prices consistent with current market prices. This property is seen by some market participants as a significant drawback in a static setting, such as pricing and hedging for the current time. However, other practitioners prefer equilibrium models since they capture not just the current market environment as reflected in the term structure but also the possibility of many different future paths. For more dynamic applications, equilibrium models may be preferred.

The best-known equilibrium models are the **Cox-Ingersoll-Ross model** (Cox, Ingersoll, and Ross 1985) and the **Vasicek model** (Vasicek 1977), discussed in the next two sections. Both the Vasicek and Cox–Ingersoll–Ross (CIR) models assume a single factor, the short-term interest rate, r_t. This approach is plausible because empirically, parallel shifts are often found to explain more than 90% of yield changes. In contrast, multifactor models may be able to model the curvature of a yield curve more accurately, but at the cost of greater complexity.

The reason that no-arbitrage models fit the current term structure is their greater number of parameters. These added parameters increase the computational requirements for estimation, which some practitioners find to be undesirable.

Other contrasts are more technical. They include that equilibrium models use real probabilities, whereas arbitrage-free models use so-called risk-neutral probabilities. An excellent example of an equilibrium term structure model is the Cox–Ingersoll–Ross model, discussed next.

[margin note, handwritten:] general equilibrium models

[margin note, handwritten:] – Arbitrage-free models allow for time-varying parameters

Equilibrium Models

This section introduces the Cox–Ingersoll–Ross and Vasicek interest rate models.

The Cox–Ingersoll–Ross model

- Interest rates are mean reverting
- Interest rate variance depends on level of rates

The Cox–Ingersoll–Ross (CIR) model assumes interest rates follow a mean-reverting process. However, the variance of rate changes differs depending on the level of rates. The CIR model uses the following formula to describe the interest rate process:

$$dr_t = k(\theta - r_t)\,dt + \sigma\sqrt{r_t}\,dZ.$$

Note that the drift term has three components. The level of rates at time t is r_t, and θ is the long-run mean rate, so their difference is the distance of the rate from its mean. The drift term equals zero if the rate is at the long-run mean, or $r_t = \theta$. The remaining drift term parameter, k, modulates the speed at which the rate reverts to its mean.

Another important feature of the CIR model is that the random component varies as rates change. In other words, the short-rate volatility is a function of the short rate. Importantly, at low rates, r_t, the term becomes small, which prevents rates from turning negative.

The Vasicek model

- Interest rates are mean reverting
- Interest rate variance is constant
- Interest rates can become negative

Although not developed in the context of a general equilibrium of individuals seeking to optimize consumption and investment decisions, as was the case for the CIR model, the Vasicek model is viewed as an equilibrium term structure model. Similar to the CIR model, the Vasicek model includes mean reversion. The Vasicek model uses the following equation to describe the interest rate process:

$$dr_t = k\left(\theta - r_t\right)dt + \sigma dZ.$$

The Vasicek model has the same drift term as the CIR model and thus tends toward mean reversion in the short rate. The stochastic or volatility term follows a random normal distribution for which the mean is zero and the standard deviation is 1. Unlike the CIR model, interest rates are calculated assuming constant volatility over the period of analysis. As with the CIR model, there is only one stochastic driver of the interest rate process. A key characteristic of the Vasicek model worth noting is that it is theoretically possible for the interest rate to become negative.

Arbitrage-Free Models

We will next illustrate two foundational no-arbitrage term structure models. There are many additional no-arbitrage models, but the basic features are similar, with differences stemming from different assumed interest rate processes.

The Ho–Lee model

- Interest rates are not mean reverting
- Interest rate variance is constant
- Interest rates can become negative

In **arbitrage-free models**, the analysis begins with the current term structure, extrapolated from the market prices of a reference set of financial instruments. A maintained assumption is that the reference bonds are priced correctly. Unlike general equilibrium models, which have only a few parameters and can thus match only a few term structure points, arbitrage-free models allow the parameters to vary deterministically with time, creating a greater number of parameters and thus more points of match. As a result, the market yield curve can be modeled with the accuracy needed for such applications as valuing derivatives and bonds with embedded options.

The first arbitrage-free model was introduced by Ho and Lee (1986). The model is calibrated to market data and uses a binomial lattice approach to generate a distribution of possible future interest rates. In the **Ho–Lee model**, the short rate follows a normal process, as follows:

$$dr_t = \theta_t dt + \sigma dZ.$$

We see that the drift term, θ_t, is time dependent. This time dependency means there is a value for θ_t at each time step, which is critical for the model to produce prices that match market prices.

The Ho–Lee model, similar to the Vasicek model, has constant volatility, and interest rates may become negative because of the symmetry of the normal distribution and the model's use of constant volatility.

The Kalotay–Williams–Fabozzi model

The **Kalotay–Williams–Fabozzi (KWF) model** is analogous to the Ho–Lee model in that it assumes constant drift, no mean reversion, and constant volatility. However, the stochastic differential equation describes the dynamics of the log of the short rate, and as a result, the log of the short rate is distributed normally, meaning the short rate itself is distributed lognormally.

The differential process for the KWF model is

$$d \ln\left(r_t\right) = \theta_t\, dt + \sigma dZ.$$

At first glance, the main implication of modeling the log of the short rate is that it will prevent negative rates. After further analysis, it becomes evident that there are pricing implications where interest rate option values are influenced by the tails of the rate distributions. Exhibit 33 summarizes the key differences between these term structure models.

[handwritten margin notes:]
- Interest rates are not mean reverting
- Interest rate variance is constant
- Describes interest rates as being lognormally distributed, so interest rates cannot be negative

---

Exhibit 33: Term Structure Model Summary

Model	Type	Short Rate	Drift Term	Volatility
CIR	Equilibrium	dr_t	Mean reversion at speed k	Varies with $\sqrt{r}_t$
Vasicek	Equilibrium	dr_t	Mean reversion at speed k	Constant
Ho–Lee	Arbitrage free	dr_t	Time dependent	Constant
KWF	Arbitrage free	$d\ln(r_t)$	Time dependent	Constant

Modern Models

The one-factor models presented thus far are the building blocks on which modern interest rate models rely. Some current models extend those models to include multiple factors, while others use sophisticated approaches that combine observed forward curves with volatilities extracted from interest rate option prices.

The Gauss+ model is a multi-factor interest rate model used extensively in valuation and hedging. The Gauss+ model incorporates short-, medium- and long-term rates. The long-term factor is mean reverting and reflects trends in macroeconomic variables. The medium-term rate also reverts to the long-run rate. The short-term rate does not exhibit a random component, which is consistent with the central bank controlling the short end of the rate curve. This results in a hump-shaped volatility curve across tenors, with medium-term rates being the most volatile.

Although there are many different term structure models, knowledge of the basic assumptions and design of the classic models helps professionals understand and adapt more sophisticated modern models.

Example 8 addresses several basic points about modern term structure models.

EXAMPLE 8

Term Structure Models

1. Which of the following would be expected to provide the *most* accurate modeling with respect to the observed term structure?

    A. CIR model

    B. Ho–Lee model

    C. Vasicek model

Solution:

B is correct. The CIR model and the Vasicek model are examples of equilibrium term structure models, whereas the Ho–Lee model is an example of an arbitrage-free term structure model. A benefit of arbitrage-free term structure models is that they are calibrated to the current term structure. In other words, the starting prices ascribed to securities are those currently found in the market. In contrast, equilibrium term structure models frequently generate term structures that are inconsistent with current market data.

2. Which of the following statements about the Vasicek model is *most* accurate? It has:

    A. a single factor, the long rate.

    B. a single factor, the short rate.

    C. two factors, the short rate and the long rate.

Solution:

B is correct. Use of the Vasicek model requires assumptions for the short-term interest rate, which are usually derived from more general assumptions about the state variables that describe the overall economy. Using the assumed process for the short-term rate, one can determine the yield on longer-term bonds by looking at the expected path of interest rates over time.

3. The CIR model:

    A. assumes interest rates are not mean reverting.

    B. has a drift term that differs from that of the Vasicek model.

    C. assumes interest rate volatility increases with increases in the level of interest rates.

Solution:

C is correct. The drift term of the CIR model is identical to that of the Vasicek model, and both models assume that interest rates are mean reverting. The major difference between the two models is that the CIR model assumes a rise in interest rate volatility as rates increase, while the Vasicek model assumes interest rate volatility is constant.

SUMMARY

This reading presents the principles and tools for arbitrage valuation of fixed-income securities. Much of the discussion centers on the binomial interest rate tree, which can be used extensively to value both option-free bonds and bonds with embedded options. The following are the main points made in the reading:

- A fundamental principle of valuation is that the value of any financial asset is equal to the present value of its expected future cash flows.

- A fixed-income security is a portfolio of zero-coupon bonds, each with its own discount rate that depends on the shape of the yield curve and when the cash flow is delivered in time.

- In well-functioning markets, prices adjust until there are no opportunities for arbitrage, or a transaction that involves no cash outlay yet results in a riskless profit.

- Using the arbitrage-free approach, viewing a security as a package of zero-coupon bonds means that two bonds with the same maturity and different coupon rates are viewed as different packages of zero-coupon bonds and valued accordingly.

- For bonds that are option-free, an arbitrage-free value is simply the present value of expected future values using the benchmark spot rates.

- A binomial interest rate tree permits the short interest rate to take on one of two possible values consistent with the volatility assumption and an interest rate model based on a lognormal random walk.

- An interest rate tree is a visual representation of the possible values of interest rates (forward rates) based on an interest rate model and an assumption about interest rate volatility.

- The possible interest rates for any following period are consistent with the following three assumptions: (1) an interest rate model that governs the random process of interest rates, (2) the assumed level of interest rate volatility, and (3) the current benchmark yield curve.

- From the lognormal distribution, adjacent interest rates on the tree are multiples of e raised to the 2σ power, with the absolute change in interest rates becoming smaller and smaller as rates approach zero.

- We use the backward induction valuation methodology that involves starting at maturity, filling in those values, and working back from right to left to find the bond's value at the desired node.

- The interest rate tree is fit to the current yield curve by choosing interest rates that result in the benchmark bond value. By doing this, the bond value is arbitrage free.

- An option-free bond that is valued by using the binomial interest rate tree should have the same value as when discounting by the spot rates.

- Pathwise valuation calculates the present value of a bond for each possible interest rate path and takes the average of these values across paths.

- The Monte Carlo method is an alternative method for simulating a sufficiently large number of potential interest rate paths in an effort to discover how the value of a security is affected, and it involves randomly selecting paths in an effort to approximate the results of a complete pathwise valuation.

- Term structure models seek to explain the yield curve shape and are used to value bonds (including those with embedded options) and bond-related derivatives. General equilibrium and arbitrage-free models are the two major types of such models.

- Arbitrage-free models are frequently used to value bonds with embedded options. Unlike equilibrium models, arbitrage-free models begin with the observed market prices of a reference set of financial instruments, and the underlying assumption is that the reference set is correctly priced.

PRACTICE PROBLEMS

The following information relates to questions 1-6

Katrina Black, a portfolio manager at Coral Bond Management, Ltd., is conducting a training session with Alex Sun, a junior analyst in the fixed-income department. Black wants to explain to Sun the arbitrage-free valuation framework used by the firm. Black presents Sun with Exhibit 1, showing a fictitious bond being traded on three exchanges, and asks Sun to identify the arbitrage opportunity of the bond. Sun agrees to ignore transaction costs in his analysis.

Exhibit 1: Three-Year, €100 par, 3.00% Coupon, Annual Pay Option-Free Bond		
	Eurex	NYSE Euronext	Frankfurt
Price	€103.7956	€103.7815	€103.7565

Black shows Sun some exhibits that were part of a recent presentation. Exhibit 3 presents most of the data of a binomial lognormal interest rate tree fit to the yield curve shown in Exhibit 2. Exhibit 4 presents most of the data of the implied values for a four-year, option-free, annual pay bond with a 2.5% coupon based on the information in Exhibit 3.

Exhibit 2: Yield-to-Maturity Par Rates for One-, Two-, and Three-Year Annual Pay Option-Free Bonds

One-year	Two-year	Three-year
1.25%	1.50%	1.70%

Exhibit 3: Binomial Interest Rate Tree Fit to the Yield Curve (Volatility = 10%)

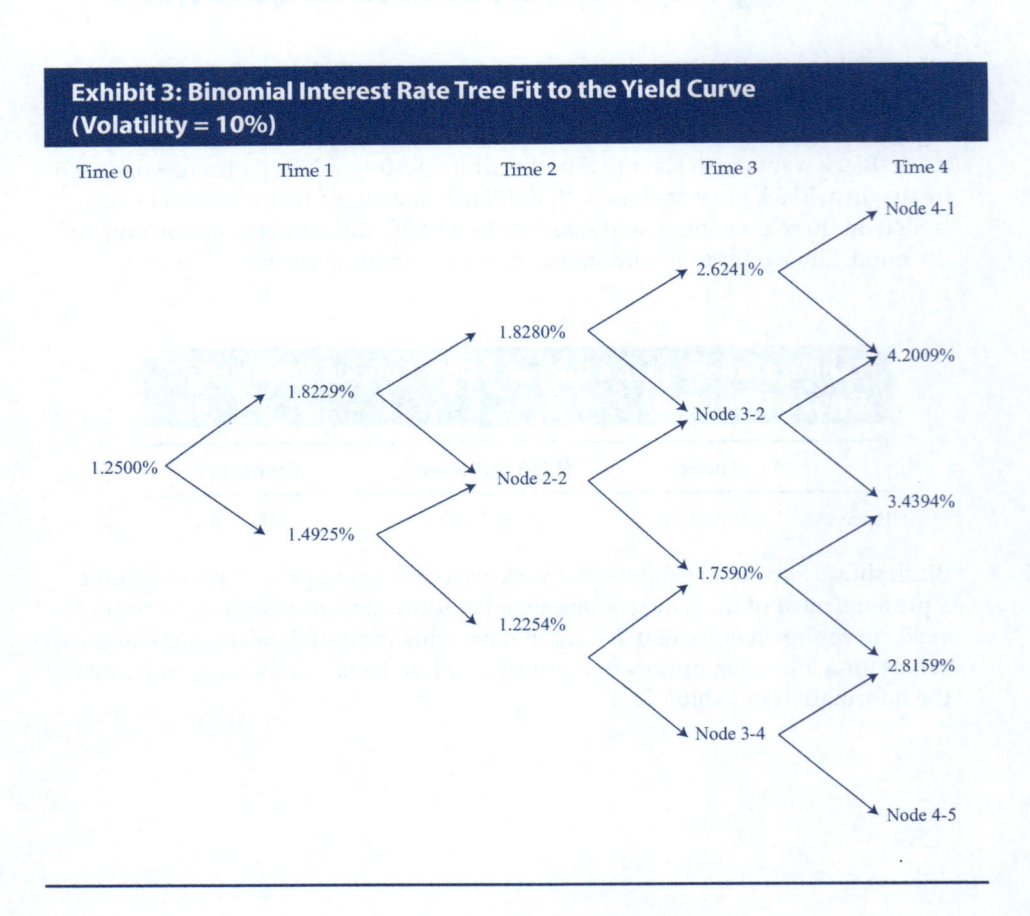

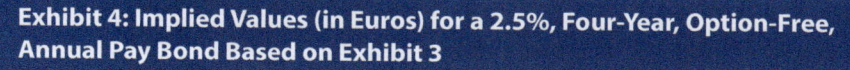

Exhibit 4: Implied Values (in Euros) for a 2.5%, Four-Year, Option-Free, Annual Pay Bond Based on Exhibit 3

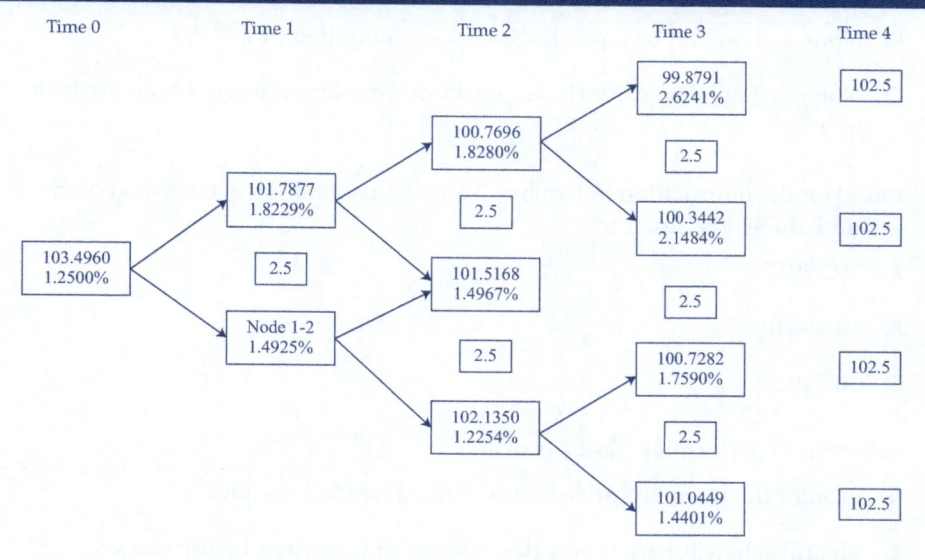

Black asks about the missing data in Exhibits 3 and 4 and directs Sun to complete the following tasks related to those exhibits:

Task 1	Test that the binomial interest tree has been properly calibrated to be arbitrage free.
Task 2	Develop a spreadsheet model to calculate pathwise valuations. To test the accuracy of the spreadsheet, use the data in Exhibit 3 and calculate the value of the bond if it takes a path of lowest rates in Year 1 and Year 2 and the second lowest rate in Year 3.
Task 3	Identify a type of bond where the Monte Carlo calibration method should be used in place of the binomial interest rate method.
Task 4	Update Exhibit 3 to reflect the current volatility, which is now 15%.

1. Based on Exhibit 1, the *best* action that an investor should take to profit from the arbitrage opportunity is to:

   A. buy on Frankfurt, sell on Eurex.

   B. buy on NYSE Euronext, sell on Eurex.

   C. buy on Frankfurt, sell on NYSE Euronext.

2. Based on Exhibits 1 and 2, the exchange that reflects the arbitrage-free price of the bond is:

   A. Eurex.

   B. Frankfurt.

   C. NYSE Euronext.

3. Recall from the reading that each node is represented by both a time element and a rate change component. Which of the following statements about the missing

data in Exhibit 3 is correct?

A. Node 3–2 can be derived from Node 2–2.

B. Node 4–1 should be equal to Node 4–5 multiplied by $e^{0.4}$.

C. Node 2–2 approximates the implied one-year forward rate two years from now.

4. Based on the information in Exhibits 3 and 4, the bond price in euros at Node 1–2 in Exhibit 4 is *closest* to:

A. 102.7917.

B. 104.8640.

C. 105.2917.

5. A benefit of performing Task 1 is that it:

A. enables the model to price bonds with embedded options.

B. identifies benchmark bonds that have been mispriced by the market.

C. allows investors to realize arbitrage profits through stripping and reconstitution.

6. If the assumed volatility is changed as Black requested in Task 4, the forward rates shown in Exhibit 3 will *most likely*:

A. spread out.

B. remain unchanged.

C. converge to the spot rates.

The following information relates to questions 7-10

Betty Tatton is a fixed-income analyst with the hedge fund Sailboat Asset Management (SAM). SAM invests in a variety of global fixed-income strategies, including fixed-income arbitrage. Tatton is responsible for pricing individual investments and analyzing market data to assess the opportunity for arbitrage. She uses two methods to value bonds:

| Method 1 | Discount each year's cash flow separately using the appropriate interest rate curve. |
| Method 2 | Build and use a binomial interest rate tree. |

Tatton compiles pricing data for a list of annual pay bonds (Exhibit 1). Each of the bonds will mature in two years, and Tatton considers the bonds risk-free; both the one-year and two-year benchmark spot rates are 2%. Tatton calculates the arbitrage-free prices and identifies an arbitrage opportunity to recommend to her team.

Exhibit 1: Market Data for Selected Bonds

Asset	Coupon	Market Price
Bond A	1%	98.0584
Bond B	3%	100.9641
Bond C	5%	105.8247

Next, Tatton uses the benchmark yield curve provided in Exhibit 2 to consider arbitrage opportunities of both option-free corporate bonds and corporate bonds with embedded options. The benchmark bonds in Exhibit 2 pay coupons annually, and the bonds are priced at par.

Exhibit 2: Benchmark Par Curve

Maturity (years)	Yield-to-Maturity (YTM)
1	3.0%
2	4.0%
3	5.0%

Tatton then identifies three mispriced three-year annual coupon bonds and compiles data on the bonds (see Exhibit 3).

Exhibit 3: Market Data of Annual Pay Corporate Bonds

Company	Coupon	Market Price	Yield	Embedded Option?
Hutto-Barkley Inc.	3%	94.9984	5.6%	No
Luna y Estrellas Intl.	0%	88.8996	4.0%	Yes
Peaton Scorpio Motors	0%	83.9619	6.0%	No

Lastly, Tatton identifies two mispriced Swiss bonds, Bond X, a three-year bond, and Bond Y, a five-year bond. Both are 6% annual coupon bonds. To calculate the bonds' values, Tatton devises the first three years of the interest rate lognormal tree presented in Exhibit 4 using historical interest rate volatility data. Tatton considers how these data would change if implied volatility, which is higher than historical volatility, were used instead.

Exhibit 4: Interest Rate Tree—Forward Rates Based on Swiss Market

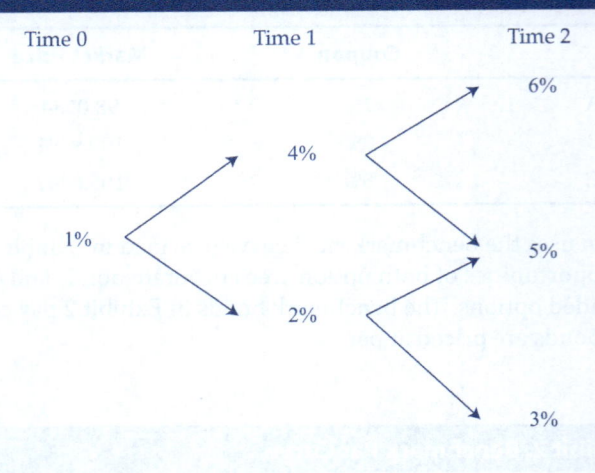

7. Based on Exhibit 1, which of the following bonds *most likely* includes an arbitrage opportunity?

   A. Bond A

   B. Bond B

   C. Bond C

8. Based on Exhibits 2 and 3 and using Method 1, the amount (in absolute terms) by which the Hutto-Barkley Inc. corporate bond is mispriced is *closest* to:

   A. 0.3368 per 100 of par value.

   B. 0.4682 per 100 of par value.

   C. 0.5156 per 100 of par value.

9. Method 1 would *most likely* not be an appropriate valuation technique for the bond issued by:

   A. Hutto-Barkley Inc.

   B. Luna y Estrellas Intl.

   C. Peaton Scorpio Motors.

10. Based on Exhibit 4 and using Method 2, the correct price for Bond X is *closest* to:

   A. 97.2998.

   B. 109.0085.

   C. 115.0085.

The following information relates to questions 11-19

Meredith Alvarez is a junior fixed-income analyst with Canzim Asset Management. Her supervisor, Stephanie Hartson, asks Alvarez to review the asset price and payoff data shown in Exhibit 1 to determine whether an arbitrage opportunity exists.

Exhibit 1: Price and Payoffs for Two Risk-Free Assets

Asset	Price Today	Payoff in One Year
Asset A	$500	$525
Asset B	$1,000	$1,100

Hartson also shows Alvarez data for a bond that trades in three different markets in the same currency. These data appear in Exhibit 2.

Exhibit 2: 2% Coupon, Five-Year Maturity, Annual Pay Bond

	New York	Hong Kong SAR	Mumbai
Yield-to-Maturity	1.9%	2.3%	2.0%

Hartson asks Alvarez to value two bonds (Bond C and Bond D) using the binomial tree in Exhibit 3. Exhibit 4 presents selected data for both bonds.

Exhibit 3: Binomial Interest Rate Tree with Volatility = 25%

Time 0	Time 1	Time 2
		2.7183%
	2.8853%	
1.500%		1.6487%
	1.7500%	
		1.0000%

Exhibit 4: Selected Data on Annual Pay Bonds

Bond	Maturity	Coupon Rate
Bond C	2 years	2.5%
Bond D	3 years	3.0%

Hartson tells Alvarez that she and her peers have been debating various viewpoints regarding the conditions underlying binomial interest rate trees. The following statements were made in the course of the debate.

Statement 1 The only requirements needed to create a binomial interest rate tree are current benchmark interest rates and an assumption about interest rate volatility.

Statement 2 Potential interest rate volatility in a binomial interest rate tree can be estimated using historical interest rate volatility or observed market prices from interest rate derivatives.

Statement 3 A bond value derived from a binomial interest rate tree with a relatively high volatility assumption will be different from the value calculated by discounting the bond's cash flows using current spot rates.

Based on data in Exhibit 5, Hartson asks Alvarez to calibrate a binomial interest rate tree starting with the calculation of implied forward rates shown in Exhibit 6.

Exhibit 5: Selected Data for a Binomial Interest Rate Tree

Maturity	Par Rate	Spot Rate
1	2.5000%	2.5000%
2	3.5000%	3.5177%

Exhibit 6: Calibration of Binomial Interest Rate Tree with Volatility = 25%

Time 0	Time 1
	5.8365%
2.500%	
	Lower one-period forward rate

Hartson mentions pathwise valuations as another method to value bonds using a binomial interest rate tree. Using the binomial interest rate tree in Exhibit 3, Alvarez calculates the possible interest rate paths for Bond D shown in Exhibit 7.

Exhibit 7: Interest Rate Paths for Bond D

Path	Time 0	Time 1	Time 2
1	1.500%	2.8853%	2.7183%
2	1.500	2.8853	1.6487
3	1.500	1.7500	1.6487
4	1.500	1.7500	1.0000

Before leaving for the day, Hartson asks Alvarez about the value of using the Monte Carlo method to simulate a large number of potential interest rate paths to value a bond. Alvarez makes the following statements.

Statement 1 Increasing the number of paths increases the estimate's statistical accuracy.

Statement 2   The bond value derived from a Monte Carlo simulation will be closer to the bond's true fundamental value.

11. Based on Exhibit 1, Alvarez finds that an arbitrage opportunity is:

A. not available.

B. available based on the dominance principle.

C. available based on the value additivity principle.

12. Based on the data in Exhibit 2, the *most* profitable arbitrage opportunity would be to buy the bond in:

A. Mumbai and sell it in Hong Kong SAR.

B. Hong Kong SAR and sell it in New York.

C. New York and sell it in Hong Kong SAR.

13. Based on Exhibits 3 and 4, the value of Bond C at the upper node at Time 1 is *closest* to:

A. 97.1957.

B. 99.6255.

C. 102.1255.

14. Based on Exhibits 3 and 4, the price for Bond D is *closest* to:

A. 97.4785.

B. 103.3230.

C. 106.3230.

15. Which of the various statements regarding binomial interest rate trees is correct?

A. Statement 1

B. Statement 2

C. Statement 3

16. Based on Exhibits 5 and 6, the value of the lower one-period forward rate is *closest to*:

A. 3.5122%.

B. 3.5400%.

C. 4.8037%.

17. Based on Exhibits 4 and 7, the present value of Bond D's cash flows following Path 2 is *closest* to:

A. 97.0322.

B. 102.8607.

   C. 105.8607.

18. Which of the statements regarding Monte Carlo simulation is correct?

   A. Only Statement 4 is correct.

   B. Only Statement 5 is correct.

   C. Both Statement 4 and Statement 5 are correct.

19. Which term structure model can be calibrated to closely fit an observed yield curve?

   A. The Ho–Lee model

   B. The Vasicek model

   C. The Cox–Ingersoll–Ross model

The following information relates to questions 20-21

Keisha Jones is a junior analyst at Sparling Capital. Julie Anderson, a senior partner and Jones's manager, meets with Jones to discuss interest rate models used for the firm's fixed-income portfolio.

Anderson begins the meeting by asking Jones to describe features of equilibrium and arbitrage-free term structure models. Jones responds by making the following statements:

Statement 1   Equilibrium term structure models are factor models that use the observed market prices of a reference set of financial instruments, assumed to be correctly priced, to model the market yield curve.

Statement 2   In contrast, arbitrage-free term structure models seek to describe the dynamics of the term structure by using fundamental economic variables that are assumed to affect interest rates.

Anderson then asks Jones about her preferences concerning term structure models. Jones states:

I prefer arbitrage-free models. Even though equilibrium models require fewer parameters to be estimated relative to arbitrage-free models, arbitrage-free models allow for time-varying parameters. In general, this allowance leads to arbitrage-free models being able to model the market yield curve more precisely than equilibrium models.

20. Which of Jones's statements regarding equilibrium and arbitrage-free term structure models is *incorrect*?

   A. Statement 1 only

   B. Statement 2 only

   C. Both Statement 1 and Statement 2

21. Is Jones correct in describing key differences in equilibrium and arbitrage-free models as they relate to the number of parameters and model accuracy?

    A. Yes

    B. No, she is incorrect about which type of model requires fewer parameter estimates.

    C. No, she is incorrect about which type of model is more precise at modeling market yield curves.

22. Which of the following statements comparing the Ho–Lee and Kalotay–Williams–Fabozzi (KWF) equilibrium term structure models is *correct*?

    A. The Ho–Lee model assumes constant volatility, while the KWF model does not.

    B. The KWF model incorporates the possibility of negative rates, while the Ho–Lee model does not.

    C. The KWF model describes the log of the dynamics of the short rate, while the Ho–Lee model does not.

SOLUTIONS

1. A is correct. This is the same bond being sold at three different prices, so an arbitrage opportunity exists by buying the bond from the exchange where it is priced lowest and immediately selling it on the exchange that has the highest price. Accordingly, an investor would maximize profit from the arbitrage opportunity by buying the bond on the Frankfurt exchange (which has the lowest price, €103.7565) and selling it on the Eurex exchange (which has the highest price, €103.7956) to generate a risk-free profit of €0.0391 (as mentioned, ignoring transaction costs) per €100 par.

   B is incorrect because buying on NYSE Euronext and selling on Eurex would result in a €0.0141 profit per €100 par (€103.7956 − €103.7815 = €0.0141), which is not the maximum arbitrage profit available. A greater profit would be realized if the bond were purchased in Frankfurt and sold on Eurex.

   C is incorrect because buying on Frankfurt and selling on NYSE Euronext would result in an €0.0250 profit per €100 par (€103.7815 − €103.7565 = €0.0250). A greater profit would be realized if the bond were purchased in Frankfurt and sold on Eurex.

2. C is correct. The bond from Exhibit 1 is selling for its calculated value on the NYSE Euronext exchange. The arbitrage-free value of a bond is the present value of its cash flows discounted by the spot rate for zero-coupon bonds maturing on the same date as each cash flow. The value of this bond, 103.7815, is calculated as follows:

	Year 1	Year 2	Year 3	Total PV
Yield-to-maturity	1.2500%	1.500%	1.700%	
Spot rate[1]	1.2500%	1.5019%	1.7049%	
Cash flow	3.00	3.00	103.00	
Present value of payment[2]	2.9630	2.9119	97.9066	103.7815

	Eurex	NYSE Euronext	Frankfurt
Price	€103.7956	€103.7815	€103.7565
Mispricing (per 100 par value)	0.141	0	−0.025

Notes:
(1) Spot rates are calculated using bootstrapping. For example, Year 2 spot rate (z_2): 100 = 1.5/1.0125 + 101.5/$(1 + z_2)^2$; z_2 = 0.015019.
(2) Present value calculated using the formula PV = FV/$(1 + r)^n$, where n = number of years until cash flow, FV = cash flow amount, and r = spot rate.

   A is incorrect because the price on the Eurex exchange, €103.7956, was calculated using the yield-to-maturity rate to discount the cash flows when the spot rates should have been used. C is incorrect because the price on the Frankfurt exchange, €103.7565, uses the Year 3 spot rate to discount all the cash flows.

3. C is correct. Because Node 2–2 is the middle node rate in Year 2, it will be close to the implied one-year forward rate two years from now (as derived from the spot curve). Node 4–1 should be equal to the product of Node 4–5 and $e^{0.8}$. Lastly, Node 3–2 cannot be derived from Node 2–2; it can be derived from any other Year 3 node; for example, Node 3–2 can be derived from Node 3–4 (equal to the product of Node 3–4 and $e^{4\sigma}$).

4. A is correct. The value of a bond at a particular node, in this case Node 1–2, can be derived by determining the present value of the coupon payment and expected future bond values to the right of that node on the tree. In this case, those two nodes are the middle node in Year 2, equal to 101.5168, and the lower node in Year 2, equal to 102.1350. The coupon payment is 2.5. The bond value at Node 1–2 is calculated as follows:

$$\text{Value} = \frac{2.5 + (0.5 \times 101.5168 + 0.5 \times 102.1350)}{1.014925}$$

$$= 102.7917.$$

5. A is correct. Calibrating a binomial interest rate tree to match a specific term structure is important because we can use the known valuation of a benchmark bond from the spot rate pricing to verify the accuracy of the rates shown in the binomial interest rate tree. Once its accuracy is confirmed, the interest rate tree can then be used to value bonds with embedded options. While discounting with spot rates will produce arbitrage-free valuations for option-free bonds, this spot rate method will not work for bonds with embedded options where expected future cash flows are interest-rate dependent (because rate changes impact the likelihood of options being exercised). The interest rate tree allows for the alternative paths that a bond with embedded options might take.

B is incorrect because calibration does not identify mispriced benchmark bonds. In fact, benchmark bonds are employed to prove the accuracy of the binomial interest rate tree, because they are assumed to be correctly priced by the market.

C is incorrect because the calibration of the binomial interest rate tree is designed to produce an arbitrage-free valuation approach and such an approach does not allow a market participant to realize arbitrage profits through stripping and reconstitution.

6. A is correct. Volatility is one of the two key assumptions required to estimate rates for the binomial interest rate tree. Increasing the volatility from 10% to 15% would cause the possible forward rates to spread out on the tree because it increases the exponent in the relationship multiple between nodes ($e^{x\sigma}$, where $x =$ 2 times the number of nodes above the lowest node in a given year in the interest rate tree). Conversely, using a lower estimate of volatility would cause the forward rates to narrow or converge to the implied forward rates from the prevailing yield curve.

B is incorrect because volatility is a key assumption in the binomial interest rate tree model. Any change in volatility will cause a change in the implied forward rates.

C is incorrect because increasing the volatility from 10% to 15% causes the possible forward rates to spread out on the tree, not converge to the implied forward rates from the current yield curve. Rates will converge to the implied forward rates when lower estimates of volatility are assumed.

7. B is correct. Bond B's arbitrage-free price is calculated as follows:

$$\frac{3}{1.02} + \frac{103}{1.02^2} = 101.9416,$$

which is higher than the bond's market price of 100.9641. Therefore, an arbitrage opportunity exists. Since the bond's value (100.9641) is less than the sum of the values of its discounted cash flows individually (101.9416), a trader would perceive an arbitrage opportunity and could buy the bond while selling claims to the individual cash flows (zeros), capturing the excess value. The arbitrage-free prices of Bond A and Bond C are equal to the market prices of the respective bonds, so there is no arbitrage opportunity for these two bonds:

Bond A: $\dfrac{1}{1.02} + \dfrac{101}{1.02^2} = 98.0584.$

Bond C: $\dfrac{5}{1.02} + \dfrac{105}{1.02^2} = 105.8247.$

8. C is correct. The first step in the solution is to find the correct spot rate (zero-coupon rates) for each year's cash flow. The benchmark bonds in Exhibit 2 are conveniently priced at par so the yields-to-maturity and the coupon rates on the bonds are the same. Because the one-year issue has only one cash flow remaining, the YTM equals the spot rate of 3% (or $z_1 = 3\%$). The spot rates for Year 2 (z_2) and Year 3 (z_3) are calculated as follows:

$$100 = \frac{4}{1.0300} + \frac{104}{\left(1 + z_2\right)^2}; \ z_2 = 4.02\%.$$

$$100 = \frac{5}{1.0300} + \frac{5}{(1.0402)^2} + \frac{105}{\left(1 + z_3\right)^3}; \ z_3 = 5.07\%.$$

The correct arbitrage-free price for the Hutto-Barkley Inc. bond is

$$P_0 = \frac{3}{(1.0300)} + \frac{3}{(1.0402)^2} + \frac{103}{(1.0507)^3} = 94.4828.$$

Therefore, the bond is mispriced by 94.9984 − 94.4828 = 0.5156 per 100 of par value.

A is incorrect because the correct spot rates are not calculated and instead the Hutto-Barkley Inc. bond is discounted using the respective YTM for each maturity. Therefore, this leads to an incorrect mispricing of 94.6616 − 94.9984 = −0.3368 per 100 of par value.

B is incorrect because the spot rates are derived using the coupon rate for Year 3 (maturity) instead of using each year's respective coupon rate to employ the bootstrap methodology. This leads to an incorrect mispricing of 94.5302 − 94.9984 = −0.4682 per 100 of par value.

9. B is correct. The Luna y Estrellas Intl. bond contains an embedded option. Method 1 will produce an arbitrage-free valuation for option-free bonds; however, for bonds with embedded options, changes in future interest rates impact the likelihood the option will be exercised and so impact future cash flows. Therefore, to develop a framework that values bonds with embedded options, interest rates must be allowed to take on different potential values in the future based on some assumed level of volatility (Method 2).

A and C are incorrect because the Hutto-Barkley Inc. bond and the Peaton Scorpio Motors bond are both option-free bonds and can be valued using either Method 1 or Method 2 to produce an arbitrage-free valuation.

10. B is correct. This is the binomial tree that obtains a bond value of 109.0085.

Valuing a 6%, Three-Year Bond

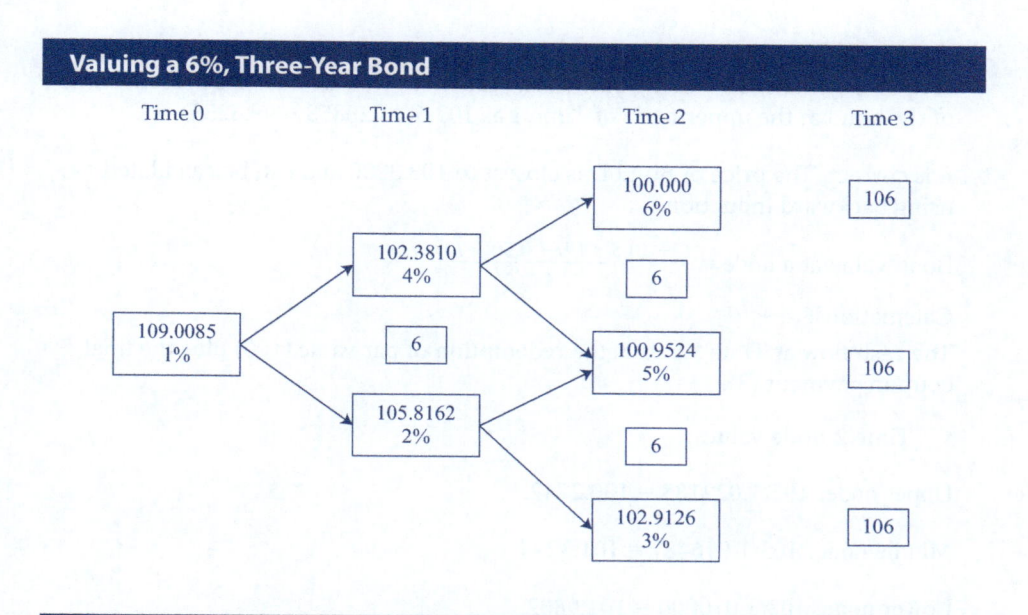

These are the calculations:

$106/1.06 = 100.0000$.

$106/1.05 = 100.9524$.

$106/1.03 = 102.9126$.

$$\frac{6 + (0.5 \times 100.0000 + 0.5 \times 100.9524)}{1.04} = 102.3810.$$

$$\frac{6 + (0.5 \times 100.9524 + 0.5 \times 102.9126)}{1.02} = 105.8162.$$

$$\frac{6 + (0.5 \times 102.3810 + 0.5 \times 105.8162)}{1.01} = 109.0085.$$

A is incorrect because the Time T coupon payment is subtracted from the value in each node calculation for Time T. C is incorrect because it assumes that a coupon is paid at Time 0.

11. B is correct. Based on the dominance principle, an arbitrage opportunity exists. The dominance principle asserts that a financial asset with a risk-free payoff in the future must have a positive price today. Because Asset A and Asset B are both risk-free assets, they should have the same discount rate. Relative to its payoff, Asset A is priced at $500/525, or 0.95238, and Asset B is priced at $1,000/1,100, or 0.90909. Given its higher implied discount rate (10%) and lower corresponding price, Asset B is cheap relative to Asset A, which has a lower implied discount rate (5%) and a higher corresponding price.

    The arbitrage opportunity based on dominance is to sell two units of Asset A for $1,000 and buy one unit of Asset B. There is no cash outlay today, and in one year, the portfolio delivers a net cash inflow of $50 [= $1,100 − (2 × $525)].

12. B is correct. Of the three markets, the New York bond has the lowest yield-to-maturity and, correspondingly, the highest bond price. Similarly, the Hong Kong SAR bond has the highest yield-to-maturity and the lowest bond price of the three markets. Therefore, the most profitable arbitrage trade would be to buy the bond in Hong Kong SAR and sell it in New York.

13. B is correct. The bond value at the upper node at Time 1 is closest to 99.6255.

The cash flow at Time 2 is 102.5, the redemption of par value (100) plus the final coupon payment (2.5). Using backward induction, we calculate the present value of the bond at the upper node of Time 1 as 102.5/1.028853 = 99.6255.

14. B is correct. The price of Bond D is closest to 103.3230 and can be calculated using backward induction.

$$\text{Bond value at a node} = \frac{C + (0.5 \times VH + 0.5 \times VL)}{1 + i}.$$

Calculations:

The cash flow at Time 3 is 103, the redemption of par value (100) plus the final coupon payment (3).

Time 2 node values:

Upper node: 103/1.027183 = 100.2742.

Middle node: 103/1.016487 = 101.3294.

Lower node: 103/1.010000 = 101.9802.

Working back to Time 1 requires the use of the general expression above.

Time 1 node values:

Upper node: $\dfrac{3 + (0.5 \times 100.2742 + 0.5 \times 101.3294)}{1.028853}$ = 100.8908.

Lower node: $\dfrac{3 + (0.5 \times 101.3294 + 0.5 \times 101.9802)}{1.0175}$ = 102.8548.

Time 0 node value:

$\dfrac{3 + (0.5 \times 100.8908 + 0.5 \times 102.8548)}{1.015}$ = 103.3230.

Therefore, the price of the bond is 103.3230.

15. B is correct. Two methods are commonly used to estimate potential interest rate volatility in a binomial interest rate tree. The first method bases estimates on historical interest rate volatility. The second method uses observed market prices of interest rate derivatives.

    Statement 1 is incorrect because there are three requirements to create a binomial interest rate tree, not two. The third requirement is an assumption regarding the interest rate model. Statement 3 is incorrect because the valuation of a bond using spot rates and the valuation of a bond from an interest rate tree will be the same regardless of the volatility assumption used in the model.

16. B is correct. The value of the lower one-period forward rate is closest to 3.5400%. Since the higher one-period forward rate is 5.8365% and interest rate volatility is 25%, the lower rate equals the higher rate multiplied by $e^{-2\sigma}$. This is calculated as $0.058365 \times e^{-0.50} = 0.035400$.

17. B is correct. The present value of Bond D's cash flows following Path 2 is 102.8607 and can be calculated as follows:

$$\frac{3}{1.015} + \frac{3}{(1.015)\,(1.028853)} + \frac{103}{(1.015)\,(1.028853)\,(1.016487)} = 102.8607.$$

18. A is correct. Increasing the number of paths using the Monte Carlo method does increase the estimate's statistical accuracy. It does not, however, provide a value

that is closer to the bond's true fundamental value.

19. A is correct. The Ho–Lee model is arbitrage free and can be calibrated to closely match the observed term structure.

20. C is correct. Both statements are incorrect because Jones incorrectly describes both types of model. Equilibrium term structure models are factor models that seek to describe the dynamics of the term structure by using fundamental economic variables that are assumed to affect interest rates. Arbitrage-free term structure models use observed market prices of a reference set of financial instruments, assumed to be correctly priced, to model the market yield curve.

21. A is correct. Consistent with Jones's statement, equilibrium term structure models require fewer parameters to be estimated relative to arbitrage-free models, and arbitrage-free models allow for time-varying parameters. Consequently, arbitrage-free models can model the market yield curve more precisely than equilibrium models.

22. C is correct. The Kalotay–Williams–Fabozzi equilibrium term structure model is similar to the Ho–Lee model in that it assumes constant drift, no mean reversion, and constant volatility, but the KWF model describes the log of the dynamics of the short rate, while the Ho–Lee model does not.

Valuation and Analysis of Bonds with Embedded Options

by Leslie Abreo, MFE, Ioannis Georgiou, CFA, and Andrew Kalotay, PhD.

Leslie Abreo, MFE, is at ICE Data Analytics LLC (USA). Ioannis Georgiou, CFA, is at Finovex.com (Cyprus). Andrew Kalotay, PhD, is at Andrew Kalotay Advisors, Inc. (USA).

LEARNING OUTCOMES

Mastery	The candidate should be able to:
☐	describe fixed-income securities with embedded options
☐	explain the relationships between the values of a callable or putable bond, the underlying option-free (straight) bond, and the embedded option
☐	describe how the arbitrage-free framework can be used to value a bond with embedded options
☐	explain how interest rate volatility affects the value of a callable or putable bond
☐	explain how changes in the level and shape of the yield curve affect the value of a callable or putable bond
☐	calculate the value of a callable or putable bond from an interest rate tree
☐	explain the calculation and use of option-adjusted spreads
☐	explain how interest rate volatility affects option-adjusted spreads
☐	calculate and interpret effective duration of a callable or putable bond
☐	compare effective durations of callable, putable, and straight bonds
☐	describe the use of one-sided durations and key rate durations to evaluate the interest rate sensitivity of bonds with embedded options
☐	compare effective convexities of callable, putable, and straight bonds
☐	calculate the value of a capped or floored floating-rate bond
☐	describe defining features of a convertible bond

LEARNING OUTCOMES

Mastery	The candidate should be able to:
☐	calculate and interpret the components of a convertible bond's value
☐	describe how a convertible bond is valued in an arbitrage-free framework
☐	compare the risk–return characteristics of a convertible bond with the risk–return characteristics of a straight bond and of the underlying common stock

1   INTRODUCTION

☐	describe fixed-income securities with embedded options

The valuation of a fixed-rate, option-free bond generally requires determining its future cash flows and discounting them at the appropriate rates. Valuation becomes more complicated when a bond has one or more embedded options because the values of embedded options are typically contingent on interest rates.

Understanding how to value and analyze bonds with embedded options is important for practitioners. Issuers of bonds often manage interest rate exposure with embedded options, such as call provisions. Investors in callable bonds must appreciate the risk of being called. The perception of this risk is collectively represented by the premium, in terms of increased coupon or yield, that the market demands for callable bonds relative to otherwise identical option-free bonds. Issuers and investors must also understand how other types of embedded options—such as put provisions, conversion options, caps, and floors—affect bond values and the sensitivity of these bonds to interest rate movements.

We first provide a brief overview of various types of embedded options. We then discuss bonds that include a call or put provision. Taking a building-block approach, we show how the arbitrage-free valuation framework discussed earlier can be applied to the valuation of callable and putable bonds—first in the absence of interest rate volatility, and then when interest rates fluctuate. We also discuss how option-adjusted spreads are used to value risky callable and putable bonds. We then turn to interest rate sensitivity. It highlights the need to use effective duration, including one-sided durations and key rate durations, as well as effective convexity to assess the effect of interest rate movements on the value of callable and putable bonds. We also explain the valuation of capped and floored floating-rate bonds (floaters) and convertible bonds.

Overview of Embedded Options

The term "embedded bond options" or **embedded options** refers to contingency provisions found in the bond's indenture or offering circular. These options represent rights that enable their holders to take advantage of interest rate movements. They can be exercised by the issuer or the bondholder, or they may be exercised automatically depending on the course of interest rates. For example, a call option allows the issuer to benefit from lower interest rates by retiring the bond issue early and refinancing at a lower cost. In contrast, a put option allows the bondholder to benefit from higher interest rates by putting back the bonds to the issuer and reinvesting the proceeds of the retired bond at a higher yield. These options are not independent of the bond and thus cannot be traded separately—hence the adjective "embedded." In this section, we provide a review of familiar embedded options.

Corresponding to every embedded option, or combination of embedded options, is an underlying bond with a specified issuer, issue date, maturity date, principal amount and repayment structure, coupon rate and payment structure, and currency denomination. We also refer to this underlying option-free bond as the **straight bond**. The coupon of an underlying bond can be fixed or floating. Fixed-coupon bonds may have a single rate for the life of the bond, or the rate may step up or step down according to a coupon schedule. The coupons of floaters are reset periodically according to a formula based on a reference rate plus a credit spread—for example, Market reference rate + 100 basis points (bps). Except when we discuss capped and floored floaters, our focus is on fixed-coupon, single-rate bonds, also referred to as fixed-rate bonds.

Simple Embedded Options

Call and put options are standard examples of embedded options. In fact, the vast majority of bonds with embedded options are callable, putable, or both. The call provision is by far the most prevalent type of embedded option.

Call Options

A **callable bond** is a bond that includes an embedded call option. The call option is an issuer option; that is, the right to exercise the option is at the discretion of the bond's issuer. The call provision allows the issuer to redeem the bond issue prior to maturity. Early redemption usually happens when the issuer has the opportunity to replace a high-coupon bond with another bond that has more favorable terms, typically when interest rates have fallen or when the issuer's credit quality has improved.

Until the 1990s, most long-term corporate bonds in the United States were callable after either 5 or 10 years. The initial call price (exercise price) was typically at a premium above par, the premium depended on the coupon, and the call price gradually declined to par a few years prior to maturity. Today, most investment-grade corporate bonds are essentially non-refundable. They may have a "make-whole call," so named because the call price is such that the bondholders are more than "made whole" (compensated) in exchange for surrendering their bonds. The call price is calculated at a narrow spread to a benchmark security—usually an on-the-run sovereign bond, such as Treasuries in the United States or gilts in the United Kingdom. Thus, economical refunding is virtually out of the question. Investors need have no fear of receiving less than their bonds are worth.

Most callable bonds include a call **protection period** during which the issuer cannot call the bond. For example, a 10-year callable bond may have a call protection period of three years, meaning that the first potential call date is three years after the bond's issue date. Call protection periods may be as short as one month or extend to several years. For example, high-yield corporate bonds are often callable a few years after issuance. Holders of such bonds are usually less concerned about early redemption than about possible default. Of course, this perspective can change over the life of the bond—for example, if the issuer's credit quality improves.

Callable bonds include different types of call features. The issuer of a European-style callable bond can exercise the call option only once on the call date. An American-style callable bond is continuously callable at any time starting on the first call date. A Bermudan-style call option can be exercised only on a predetermined schedule on specified dates following the call protection period. These dates are specified in the bond's indenture or offering circular.

With a few exceptions, bonds issued by government-sponsored enterprises in the United States (e.g., Fannie Mae, Freddie Mac, Federal Home Loan Banks, and Federal Farm Credit Banks) are callable. These bonds tend to have relatively short maturities (5–10 years) and very short call protection periods (three months to one year). The call price is almost always at 100% of par, and the call option is often Bermudan style.

Tax-exempt municipal bonds (often called "munis"), a type of non-sovereign (local) government bond issued in the United States, are almost always callable at 100% of par any time after the end of the 10th year. They may also be eligible for advance refunding—a highly specialized topic that is not discussed here.

Although the bonds of US government-sponsored enterprises and municipal issuers account for most of the callable bonds issued and traded globally, bonds that include call provisions are also found in other countries in Asia Pacific, Europe, Canada, and Central and South America. The vast majority of callable bonds are denominated in US dollars or euros because of investors' demand for securities issued in these currencies. Australia, the United Kingdom, Japan, and Norway are examples of countries that have a market for callable bonds denominated in local currency.

Put Options and Extension Options

A **putable bond** is a bond that includes an embedded put option. The put option is an investor option; that is, the right to exercise the option is at the discretion of the bondholder. The put provision allows the bondholders to put back the bonds to the issuer prior to maturity, usually at par. This usually happens when interest rates have risen and higher-yielding bonds are available.

Similar to callable bonds, most putable bonds include protection periods. They can be European or, rarely, Bermudan style, but there are no American-style putable bonds.

Another type of embedded option that resembles a put option is an extension option. At maturity, the holder of an **extendible bond** (sometimes spelled "extendable") has the right to keep the bond for a number of years after maturity, possibly with a different coupon. In this case, the terms of the bond's indenture or offering circular are modified, but the bond remains outstanding. An example of a corporate extendible is an offering from Heathrow Funding Ltd. It pays a 0.50% coupon and matures on 17 May 2024. However, it is extendible to 7 May 2026 as a floating-rate note paying 12-month MRR plus 4.00%. We will discuss the resemblance between a putable and an extendible bond later.

Complex Embedded Options

Although callable and putable bonds are the most common types of bonds with embedded options, there are bonds with other types of options or combinations of options. For instance, some bonds can be both callable and putable. These bonds can be either called by the issuer or put by the bondholders.

Convertible bonds are another type of bond with an embedded option. The conversion option allows bondholders to convert their bonds into the issuer's common stock. Convertible bonds are usually also callable by the issuer; the call provision enables the issuer to take advantage of lower interest rates or to force conversion.

Another layer of complexity is added when the option is contingent on some particular event. An example is the estate put or survivor's option that may be available to retail investors. In the event of the holder's death, this bond can be put at par by the heir(s). Because the estate put comes into play only in the event of the bondholder's death, the value of a bond with an estate put is contingent on the life expectancy of its holder, which is uncertain.

Bonds may contain several interrelated issuer options without any investor option. A prime example is a **sinking fund bond** (sinker). A sinker requires the issuer to set aside funds over time to retire the bond issue, thus reducing credit risk. Such a bond may be callable and may also include options unique to sinking fund bonds, such as an acceleration provision and a delivery option.

SINKING FUND BONDS

The underlying bond has an amortizing structure—for example, a 30-year maturity with level annual principal repayments beginning at the end of the 11th year. In this case, each payment is 5% of the original principal amount. A typical sinking fund bond may include the following options:

- A standard *call option* above par, with declining premiums, starting at the end of Year 10. Thus, the entire bond issue could be called from Year 10 onward.

- An *acceleration provision*, such as a "triple up." Such a provision allows the issuer to repurchase at par three times the mandatory amount, or in this case 15% of the original principal amount, on any scheduled sinking fund date. Assume that the issuer wants to retire the bonds at the end of Year 11. Instead of calling the entire outstanding amount at a premium, it would be more cost effective to "sink" 15% at par and call the rest at a premium. Thus, the acceleration provision provides an additional benefit to the issuer if interest rates decline.

- A *delivery option*, which allows the issuer to satisfy a sinking fund payment by delivering bonds to the bond's trustee in lieu of cash. The bond's trustee is appointed by the issuer but acts in a fiduciary capacity with the bondholders. If the bonds are currently trading below par, say at 90% of par, it is more cost effective for the issuer to buy back bonds from investors to meet the sinking fund requirements than to pay par. The delivery option benefits the issuer if interest rates rise. Of course, the benefit can be materialized only if there is a liquid market for the bonds. Investors can take defensive action by accumulating the bonds and refusing to sell them at a discount.

From the issuer's perspective, the combination of the call option and the delivery option is effectively a "long straddle"—an option strategy involving the purchase of a put option and a call option on the same underlying with the same exercise price and expiration date. At expiration, if the underlying price is above the exercise price, the put option is worthless but the call option is in the money. In contrast, if the underlying price is below the exercise price, the call option is worthless but the put option is in the money. Thus, a long straddle benefits the investor when the underlying price moves up or down. The greater the move up or down (i.e., the greater the volatility), the greater the benefit for the investor. As a consequence, a sinking fund bond benefits the issuer not only if interest rates decline but also if they rise. Determining the combined value of the underlying bond and the three options is quite challenging.

EXAMPLE 1

Types of Embedded Options

1. Investors in putable bonds *most likely* seek to take advantage of:

   A. higher interest rates.

   B. improvements in the issuer's credit rating.

> **C.** movements in the price of the issuer's common stock.
>
> ## Solution:
>
> A is correct. A putable bond offers the bondholder the ability to take advantage of a rise in interest rates by putting back the bond to the issuer and reinvesting the proceeds of the retired bond in a higher-yielding bond.
>
> ---
>
> 2. The conversion option in a convertible bond is a right held by:
>
>   **A.** the issuer.
>   **B.** the bondholders.
>   **C.** the issuer and the bondholders jointly.
>
> ## Solution:
>
> B is correct. A conversion option is a call option that gives the bondholders the right to convert their bonds into the issuer's common stock.

The presence of embedded options affects a bond's value. To quantify this effect, financial theory and financial technology come into play. The following section presents basic valuation and analysis concepts for bonds with embedded options.

2

CALLABLE AND PUTABLE BONDS

- ☐ explain the relationships between the values of a callable or putable bond, the underlying option-free (straight) bond, and the embedded option
- ☐ describe how the arbitrage-free framework can be used to value a bond with embedded options

Under the arbitrage-free framework, the value of a bond with embedded options is equal to the sum of the arbitrage-free values of its parts. We first identify the relationships between the values of a callable or putable bond, the underlying option-free (straight) bond, and the call or put option. We then discuss how to value callable and putable bonds under different risk and interest rate volatility scenarios.

Relationships between the Values of a Callable or Putable Bond, Straight Bond, and Embedded Option

The value of a bond with embedded options is equal to the sum of the arbitrage-free value of the straight bond and the arbitrage-free values of the embedded options.

For a callable bond, the decision to exercise the call option is made by the issuer. Thus, the investor is long the bond but short the call option. From the investor's perspective, therefore, the value of the call option *decreases* the value of the callable bond relative to the value of the straight bond:

Value of callable bond = Value of straight bond − Value of issuer call option.

The value of the straight bond can be obtained by discounting the bond's future cash flows at the appropriate rates. The hard part is valuing the call option because its value is contingent on future interest rates. Specifically, the issuer's decision to call the bond depends on its ability to refinance at a lower cost. In practice, the value of the call option is often calculated as the difference between the value of the straight bond and the value of the callable bond:

Value of issuer call option

= Value of straight bond − Value of callable bond.   (1)

For a putable bond, the decision to exercise the put option is made by the investor. Thus, the investor has a long position in both the bond and the put option. As a consequence, the value of the put option *increases* the value of the putable bond relative to the value of the straight bond.

Value of putable bond = Value of straight bond + Value of investor put option.

It follows that

Value of investor put option

= Value of putable bond − Value of straight bond.   (2)

Although most investment professionals do not need to be experts in bond valuation, they should have a solid understanding of the basic analytical approach, which is presented in the following sections.

Valuation of Default-Free and Option-Free Bonds: A Refresher

An asset's value is the present value of the cash flows the asset is expected to generate in the future. In the case of a default-free and option-free bond, the future cash flows are, by definition, certain. Thus, the question is, at which rates should these cash flows be discounted? The answer is that each cash flow should be discounted at the spot rate corresponding to the cash flow's payment date. Although spot rates might not be directly observable, they can be inferred from readily available information, usually from the market prices of actively traded on-the-run sovereign bonds of various maturities. These prices can be transformed into spot rates, par rates (i.e., coupon rates of hypothetical bonds of various maturities selling at par), or forward rates. Recall from Level I that spot rates, par rates, and forward rates are equivalent ways of conveying the same information; knowing any one of them is sufficient to determine the others.

Suppose we want to value a three-year 4.25% annual coupon bond. Exhibit 1 provides the equivalent forms of a yield curve with maturities of one, two, and three years.

Exhibit 1: Equivalent Forms of a Yield Curve

Maturity (year)	Par Rate (%)	Spot Rate (%)	One-Year Forward Rate (%)	
1	2.500	2.500	0 years from now	2.500
2	3.000	3.008	1 year from now	3.518
3	3.500	3.524	2 years from now	4.564

We start with the par rates provided in the second column of Exhibit 1. Because we are assuming annual coupons and annual compounding, the one-year spot rate is simply the one-year par rate. The hypothetical one-year par bond implied by the given par rate has a single cash flow of 102.500 (principal plus coupon) in Year 1. In order to have a present value of par, this future cash flow must be divided by 1.025. Thus, the one-year spot rate or discount rate is 2.500% (*Note:* All cash flows and values are expressed as a percentage of par).

A two-year 3.000% par bond has two cash flows: 3 in Year 1 and 103 in Year 2. By definition, the sum of the two discounted cash flows must equal 100. We know that the discount rate appropriate for the first cash flow is the one-year spot rate (2.500%). We now solve the following equation to determine the two-year spot rate (z_2):

$$\frac{3}{(1.025)} + \frac{103}{(1+z_2)^2} = 100.$$

We can follow a similar approach to determine the three-year spot rate (z_3):

$$\frac{3.500}{(1.02500)} + \frac{3.500}{(1.03008)^2} + \frac{103.500}{(1+z_3)^3} = 100.$$

The one-year forward rates are determined by using indifference equations. Assume an investor has a two-year horizon. She could invest for two years either at the two-year spot rate or at the one-year spot rate for one year and then reinvest the proceeds at the one-year forward rate one year from now ($F_{1,1}$). The result of investing using either of the two approaches should be the same. Otherwise, there would be an arbitrage opportunity. Thus,

$$(1 + 0.03008)^2 = (1 + 0.02500) \times (1 + F_{1,1}).$$

Similarly, the one-year forward rate two years from now ($F_{2,1}$) can be calculated using the following equation:

$$(1 + 0.03524)^3 = (1 + 0.03008)^2 \times (1 + F_{2,1}).$$

The three-year 4.25% annual coupon bond can now be valued using the spot rates:

$$\frac{4.25}{(1.02500)} + \frac{4.25}{(1.03008)^2} + \frac{104.25}{(1.03524)^3} = 102.114.$$

An equivalent way to value this bond is to discount its cash flows one year at a time using the one-year forward rates:

$$\frac{4.25}{(1.02500)} + \frac{4.25}{(1.02500)\,(1.03518)} + \frac{104.25}{(1.02500)\,(1.03518)\,(1.04564)} = 102.114.$$

Valuation of Default-Free Callable and Putable Bonds in the Absence of Interest Rate Volatility

When valuing bonds with embedded options, the approach relying on one-period forward rates provides a better framework than that relying on the spot rates because we need to know the value of the bond at different points in time in the future to determine whether the embedded option will be exercised at those points in time.

Valuation of a Callable Bond at Zero Volatility

Let us apply this framework to the valuation of a Bermudan-style three-year 4.25% annual coupon bond that is callable at par one year and two years from now. The decision to exercise the call option is made by the issuer. Because the issuer borrowed money, it will exercise the call option when the value of the bond's future cash flows is higher than the call price (exercise price). Exhibit 2 shows how to calculate the value of this callable bond using the one-year forward rates calculated in Exhibit 1.

Exhibit 2: Valuation of a Default-Free Three-Year 4.25% Annual Coupon Bond Callable at Par One Year and Two Years from Now at Zero Volatility

	Today	Year 1	Year 2	Year 3
Cash flow		4.250	4.250	104.250
Discount rate	*not 100.417*	2.500%	3.518%	4.564%
Value of the callable bond	$\frac{100 + 4.250}{1.02500} = 101.707$	$\frac{99.700 + 4.250}{1.03518} = 100.417$ Called at 100	$\frac{104.250}{1.04564} = 99.700$ Not called	

We start by discounting the bond's cash flow at maturity (104.250) to Year 2 using the one-year forward rate two years from now (4.564%). The present value at Year 2 of the bond's future cash flows is 99.700. This value is lower than the call price of 100, so a rational borrower will not call the bond at that point in time. Next, we add the cash flow in Year 2 (4.250) to the present value of the bond's future cash flows at Year 2 (99.700) and discount the sum to Year 1 using the one-year forward rate one year from now (3.518%). The present value at Year 1 of the bond's future cash flows is 100.417. Here, a rational borrower will call the bond at 100 because leaving it outstanding would be more expensive than redeeming it. Last, we add the cash flow in Year 1 (4.250) to the present value of the bond's future cash flows at Year 1 (100.000) then discount the sum to today at 2.500%. The result (101.707) is the value of the callable bond (*Note:* For the purpose of coverage of this topic, all cash flows and values are expressed as a percentage of par).

We can apply Equation 1 to calculate the value of the call option embedded in this callable bond. The value of the straight bond is the value of the default-free and option-free three-year 4.25% annual coupon bond calculated earlier (102.114). Thus,

Value of issuer call option = 102.114 − 101.707 = 0.407.

Recall from the earlier discussion about the relationships between the value of a callable bond, straight bond, and call option that the investor is long the bond and short the call option. Thus, the value of the call option decreases the value of the callable bond relative to that of an otherwise identical option-free bond.

Valuation of a Putable Bond at Zero Volatility

We now apply this framework to the valuation of a Bermudan-style three-year 4.25% annual coupon bond that is putable at par one year and two years from now. The decision to exercise the put option is made by the investor. Because the investor lent money, he will exercise the put option when the value of the bond's future cash flows is lower than the put price (exercise price). Exhibit 3 shows how to calculate the value of the three-year 4.25% annual coupon bond putable at par one year and two years from today.

Exhibit 3: Valuation of a Default-Free Three-Year 4.25% Annual Coupon Bond Putable at Par One Year and Two Years from Now at Zero Volatility

	Today	Year 1	Year 2	Year 3
Cash flow		4.250	4.250	104.250
Discount rate		2.500%	3.518%	4.564%
Value of the putable bond	$\frac{100.707 + 4.250}{1.02500} = 102.397$	$\frac{100 + 4.250}{1.03518} = 100.707$ Not put	$\frac{104.250}{1.04564} = 99.700$ Put at 100	

We can apply Equation 2 to calculate the value of the put option:

Value of investor put option = 102.397 − 102.114 = 0.283.

Because the investor is long the bond and the put option, the value of the put option increases the value of the putable bond relative to that of an otherwise identical option-free bond.

OPTIMAL EXERCISE OF OPTIONS

The holder of an embedded bond option can extinguish (or possibly modify the terms of) the bond. Assuming that the option is currently exercisable, the obvious question is, does it pay to exercise? Assuming that the answer is affirmative, the follow-up question is whether it is better to exercise the option at present or to wait.

Let us consider the first question: Would it be profitable to exercise the option? The answer is usually straightforward: Compare the value of exercising with the value of not exercising. For example, suppose that a bond is currently putable at 100. If the bond's market price is above 100, putting the bond makes no sense because the cash value from selling the bond would exceed 100. In contrast, if the bond's market price is 100, putting the bond should definitely be considered. Note that the market price of the bond cannot be less than 100 because such a situation creates an arbitrage opportunity: Buy the bond below 100 and immediately put it at 100.

The logic of a call decision by the issuer is similar. If a bond's market price is significantly less than the call price, calling is foolish because the bond could be simply repurchased in the market at a lower price. Alternatively, if the price is very close to the call price, calling may make sense.

Assume that we have determined that exercising the option would be profitable. If the option under consideration is European style, it is obvious that it should in fact be exercised: There is no justification for not doing so. But if it is an American-style or Bermudan-style option, the challenge is to determine whether it is better to act now or to wait for a better opportunity. The problem is that although circumstances may become more favorable, they may also get worse. So, option holders must consider the odds and decide to act or wait, depending on their risk preference.

The approach presented here for valuing bonds with embedded options assumes that the option holders, be they issuers or investors, are risk neutral. They exercise if, and only if, the benefit from exercise exceeds the expected benefit from waiting. In reality, option holders may be risk averse and may exercise early even if the option is worth more alive than dead.

EXAMPLE 2

Valuation of Default-Free Callable and Putable Bonds

George Cahill, a portfolio manager, has identified three five-year annual coupon bonds issued by a sovereign government. The three bonds have identical characteristics. The exceptions are that Bond A is an option-free bond; Bond B is callable at par two years and three years from today; and Bond C is also callable at par two years and three years from today as well as putable at par one year from today.

---

1. Relative to the value of Bond A, the value of Bond B is:

   A. lower.

   B. the same.

   C. higher.

Solution:

A is correct. Bond B is a callable bond, and Bond A is the underlying option-free (straight) bond. The call option embedded in Bond B is an issuer option that decreases the bond's value for the investor. If interest rates decline, bond prices usually increase; however, the price appreciation of Bond B will be capped relative to the price appreciation of Bond A because the issuer will call the bond to refinance at a lower cost.

2. Relative to the value of Bond B, the value of Bond C is:

   A. lower.

   B. the same.

   C. higher.

Solution:

C is correct. Relative to Bond B, Bond C includes a put option. A put option is an investor option that increases the bond's value for the investor. Thus, the value of Bond C is higher than that of Bond B.

3. Given an anticipation of rising interest rates, Bond C will be expected to:

   A. be called by the issuer.

   B. be put by the bondholders.

   C. mature without exercise of any of the embedded options.

Solution:

B is correct. As interest rates rise, bond prices decrease. Thus, the bondholders will have an incentive to exercise the put option so that they can reinvest the proceeds of the retired bond at a higher yield.

Exhibit 2 and Exhibit 3 show how callable and putable bonds are valued in the absence of interest rate volatility. In real life, however, interest rates do fluctuate. Thus, the option holder must consider possible evolutions of the yield curve over time.

EFFECT OF INTEREST RATE VOLATILITY

3

☐ explain how interest rate volatility affects the value of a callable or putable bond

☐ explain how changes in the level and shape of the yield curve affect the value of a callable or putable bond

In this section, we discuss the effects of interest rate volatility as well as the level and shape of the yield curve on the value of embedded options.

Interest Rate Volatility

The value of any embedded option, regardless of the type of option, increases with interest rate volatility. The greater the volatility, the more opportunities for the embedded option to be exercised. Thus, it is critical for issuers and investors to understand the effect of interest rate volatility on the value of bonds with embedded options.

The effect of interest rate volatility is represented in an interest rate tree or lattice, as illustrated in Exhibit 4. From each node on the tree starting from today, interest rates could go up or down. From these two states, interest rates could again go up or down. The dispersion between these up and down states anywhere on the tree is determined by the process generating interest rates based on a given yield curve and interest rate volatility assumptions.

Exhibit 4: Building an Interest Rate Tree

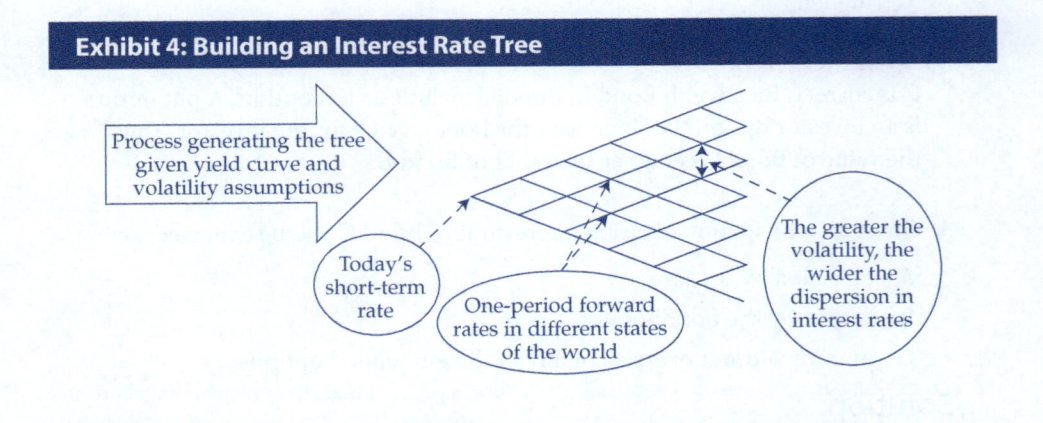

Exhibit 5 and Exhibit 6 show the effect of interest rate volatility on the value of a callable bond and putable bond, respectively.

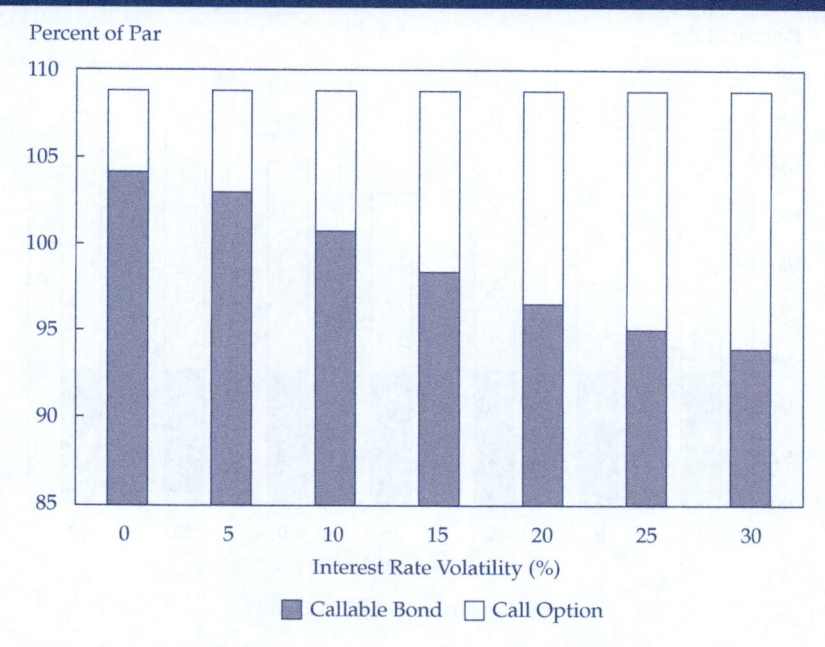

Exhibit 5: Value of a 30-Year 4.50% Bond Callable at Par in 10 Years under Different Volatility Scenarios Assuming a 4% Flat Yield Curve

The stacked bars in Exhibit 5 represent the value of the straight bond, which is unaffected by interest rate volatility. The white component is the value of the call option; taking it away from the value of the straight bond gives the value of the callable bond—the shaded component. All else being equal, the call option increases in value with interest rate volatility. At zero volatility, the value of the call option is 4.60% of par; at 30% volatility, it is 14.78% of par. Thus, as interest rate volatility increases, the value of the callable bond decreases.

Exhibit 6: Value of a 30-Year 3.75% Bond Putable at Par in 10 Years under Different Volatility Scenarios Assuming a 4% Flat Yield Curve

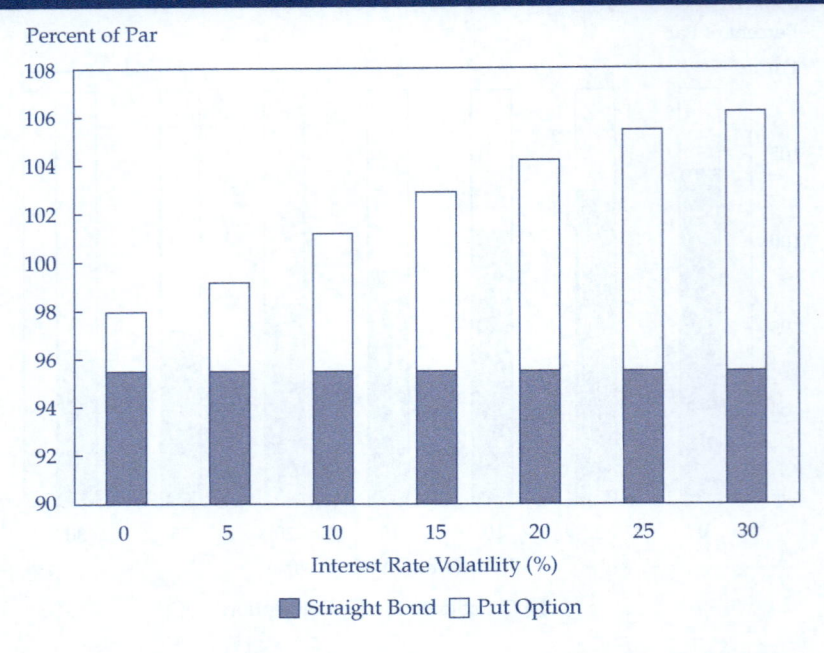

In Exhibit 6, the shaded component is the value of the straight bond, and the white component is the value of the put option; thus, the stacked bars represent the value of the putable bond. All else being equal, the put option increases in value with interest rate volatility. At zero volatility, the value of the put option is 2.30% of par; at 30% volatility, it is 10.54% of par. Thus, as interest rate volatility increases, the value of the putable bond increases.

Level and Shape of the Yield Curve

The value of a callable or putable bond is also affected by changes in the level and shape of the yield curve.

Effect on the Value of a Callable Bond

Exhibit 7 shows the value of the same callable bond as in Exhibit 5 under different flat yield curve levels assuming an interest rate volatility of 15%.

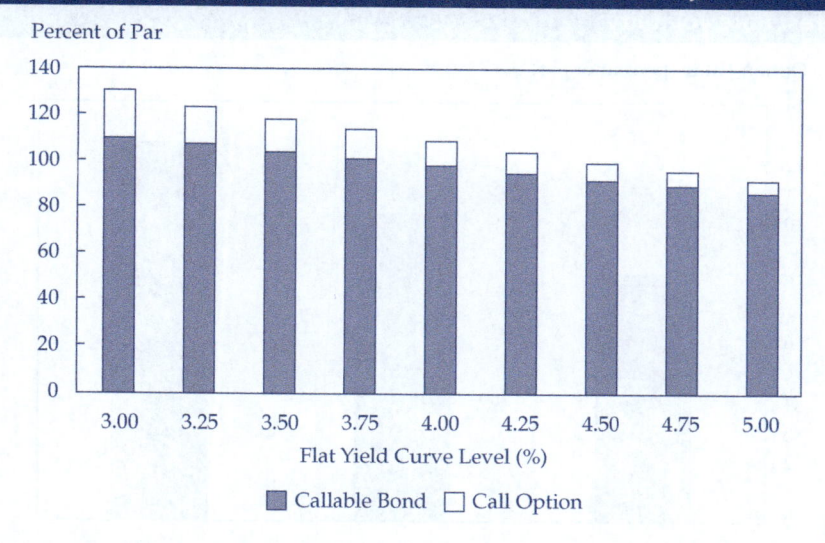

Exhibit 7: Value of a 30-Year 4.50% Bond Callable at Par in 10 Years under Different Flat Yield Curve Levels at 15% Interest Rate Volatility

Percent of Par

Flat Yield Curve Level (%)

■ Callable Bond □ Call Option

Exhibit 7 shows that as interest rates decline, the value of the straight bond rises; however, the rise is partially offset by the increase in the value of the call option. For example, if the yield curve is 5% flat, the value of the straight bond is 92.27% of par and the value of the call option is 5.37% of par; thus, the value of the callable bond is 86.90% of par. If the yield curve declines to 3% flat, the value of the straight bond rises by 40% to 129.54% of par, but the value of the callable bond increases by only 27% to 110.43% of par. Thus, the value of the callable bond rises less rapidly than the value of the straight bond, limiting the upside potential for the investor.

The value of a call option, and thus the value of a callable bond, is also affected by changes in the shape of the yield curve, as illustrated in Exhibit 8.

Exhibit 8: Value of a Call Option Embedded in a 30-Year 4.50% Bond Callable at Par in 10 Years under Different Yield Curve Shapes at 15% Interest Rate Volatility

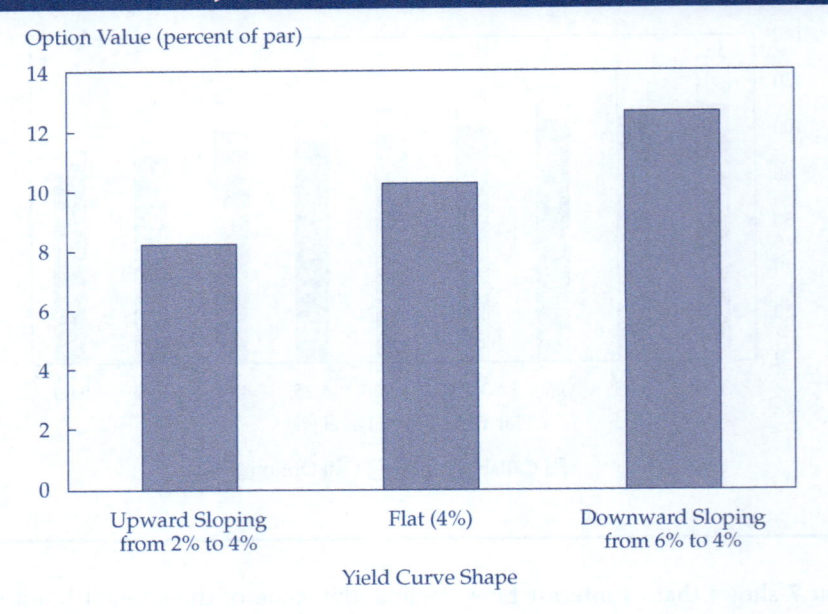

All else being equal, the value of the call option increases as the yield curve flattens. If the yield curve is upward sloping with short-term rates at 2% and long-term rates at 4% (the first bar), the value of the call option represents approximately 8% of par. It rises to approximately 10% of par if the yield curve flattens to 4% (the second bar). The value of the call option increases further if the yield curve actually inverts. Exhibit 8 shows that it exceeds 12% of par if the yield curve is downward sloping with short-term rates at 6% and long-term rates at 4% (the third bar). An inverted yield curve is rare but does happen from time to time.

The intuition to explain the effect of the shape of the yield curve on the value of the call option is as follows. When the yield curve is upward sloping, the one-period forward rates on the interest rate tree are high and opportunities for the issuer to call the bond are fewer. When the yield curve flattens or inverts, many nodes on the tree have lower forward rates that increase the opportunities to call.

Assuming a normal, upward-sloping yield curve at the time of issue, the call option embedded in a callable bond issued at par is out of the money. It would not be called if the arbitrage-free forward rates at zero volatility prevailed. Callable bonds issued at a large premium, as happens frequently in the municipal sector in the United States, are in the money. They will be called if the arbitrage-free forward rates prevail.

Effect on the Value of a Putable Bond

Exhibit 9 and Exhibit 10 show how changes in the level and shape of the yield curve affect the value of the putable bond used in Exhibit 6.

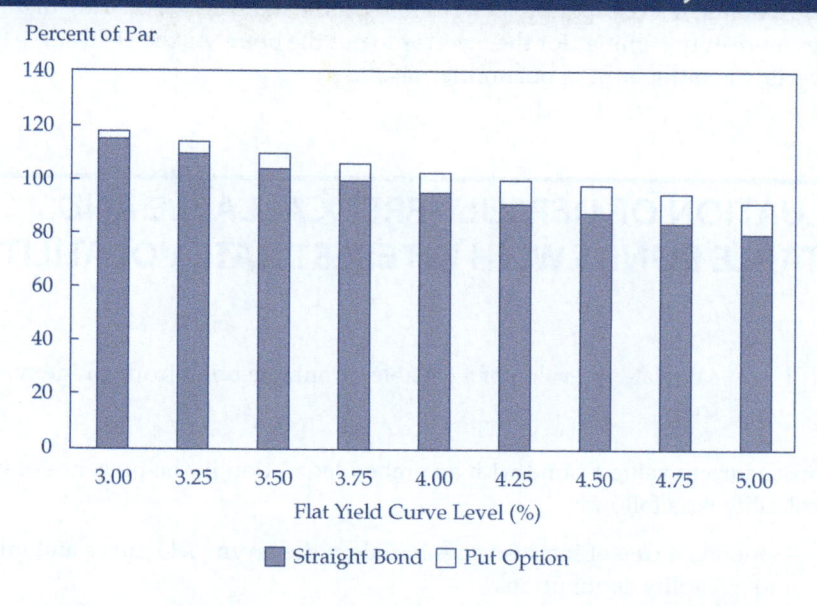

Exhibit 9: Value of a 30-Year 3.75% Bond Putable at Par in 10 Years under Different Flat Yield Curve Levels at 15% Interest Rate Volatility

Exhibit 9 illustrates why the put option is considered a hedge against rising interest rates for investors. As interest rates rise, the value of the straight bond declines; however, the decline is partially offset by the increase in the value of the put option. For example, if the yield curve moves from 3% flat to 5% flat, the value of the straight bond falls by 30% while the fall in the value of the putable bond is limited to 22%.

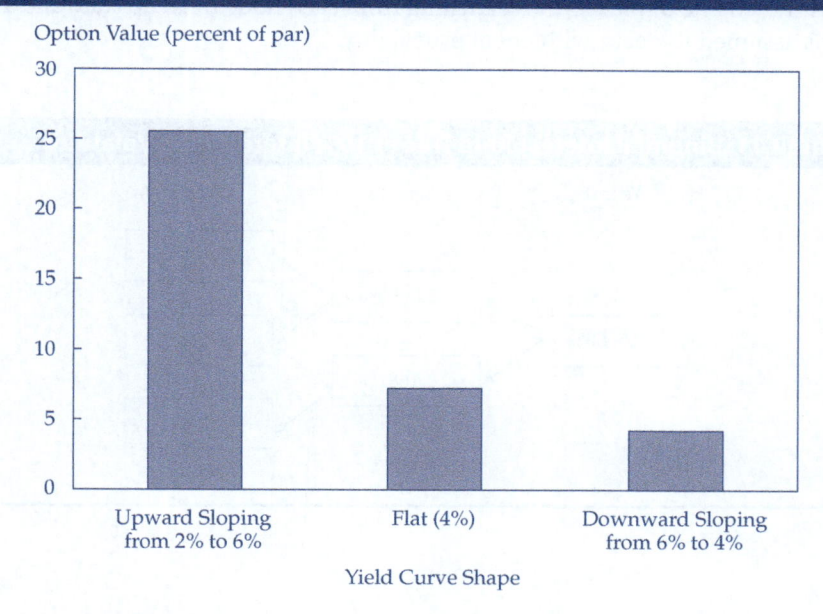

Exhibit 10: Value of the Put Option Embedded in a 30-Year 3.75% Bond Putable at Par in 10 Years under Different Yield Curve Shapes at 15% Interest Rate Volatility

All else being equal, the value of the put option decreases as the yield curve moves from being upward sloping, to flat, to downward sloping. When the yield curve is upward sloping, the one-period forward rates in the interest rate tree are high, which creates more opportunities for the investor to put the bond. As the yield curve flattens or inverts, the number of opportunities declines.

4   VALUATION OF DEFAULT-FREE CALLABLE AND PUTABLE BONDS WITH INTEREST RATE VOLATILITY

☐   calculate the value of a callable or putable bond from an interest rate tree

The procedure to value a bond with an embedded option in the presence of interest rate volatility is as follows:

- Generate a tree of interest rates based on the given yield curve and interest rate volatility assumptions.
- At each node of the tree, determine whether the embedded option will be exercised.
- Apply the backward induction valuation methodology to calculate the bond's present value. This methodology involves starting at maturity and working back from right to left to find the bond's present value.

Let us return to the default-free three-year 4.25% annual coupon bonds discussed earlier to illustrate how to apply this valuation procedure. The bonds' characteristics are identical. The yield curve given in Exhibit 1 remains the same—with one-year, two-year, and three-year par yields of 2.500%, 3.000%, and 3.500%, respectively. But we now assume an interest rate volatility of 10% instead of 0%. The resulting binomial interest rate tree showing the one-year forward rates zero, one, and two years from now is shown in Exhibit 11. The branching from each node to an up state and a down state is assumed to occur with equal probability.

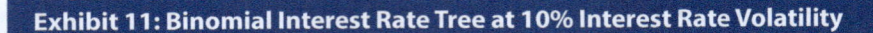

Exhibit 11: Binomial Interest Rate Tree at 10% Interest Rate Volatility

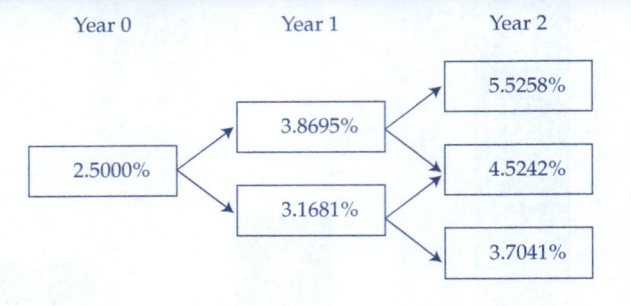

The calibration of a binomial interest rate tree was discussed in earlier coverage of fixed-income concepts. As mentioned before, the one-year par rate, the one-year spot rate, and the one-year forward rate zero years from now are identical (2.500%). Because there is no closed-form solution, the one-year forward rates one year from now in the two states are determined iteratively by meeting the following two constraints:

1. The rate in the up state (R_u) is given by

$$R_u = R_d \times e^{2\sigma\sqrt{t}},$$

   where R_d is the rate in the down state, σ is the interest rate volatility (10% here), and t is the time in years between "time slices" (a year, so here $t = 1$).

2. The discounted value of a two-year par bond (bearing a 3.000% coupon rate in this example) equals 100.

In Exhibit 11 at the one-year time slice, R_d is 3.1681% and R_u is 3.8695%. Having established the rates that correctly value the one-year and two-year par bonds implied by the given par yield curve, we freeze these rates and proceed to iterate the rates in the next time slice to determine the one-year forward rates in the three states two years from now. The same constraints as before apply: (1) Each rate must be related to its neighbor by the factor $e^{2\sigma\sqrt{t}}$, and (2) the rates must discount a three-year par bond (bearing a 3.500% coupon rate in this example) to a value of 100.

Now that we have determined all the one-year forward rates, we can value the three-year 4.25% annual coupon bonds that are either callable or putable at par one year and two years from now.

Valuation of a Callable Bond with Interest Rate Volatility

Exhibit 12 depicts the valuation of a callable bond at 10% volatility.

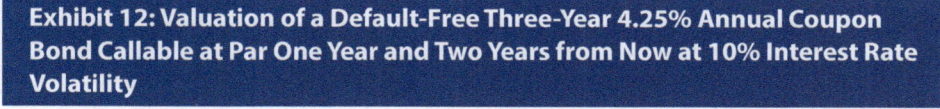

Exhibit 12: Valuation of a Default-Free Three-Year 4.25% Annual Coupon Bond Callable at Par One Year and Two Years from Now at 10% Interest Rate Volatility

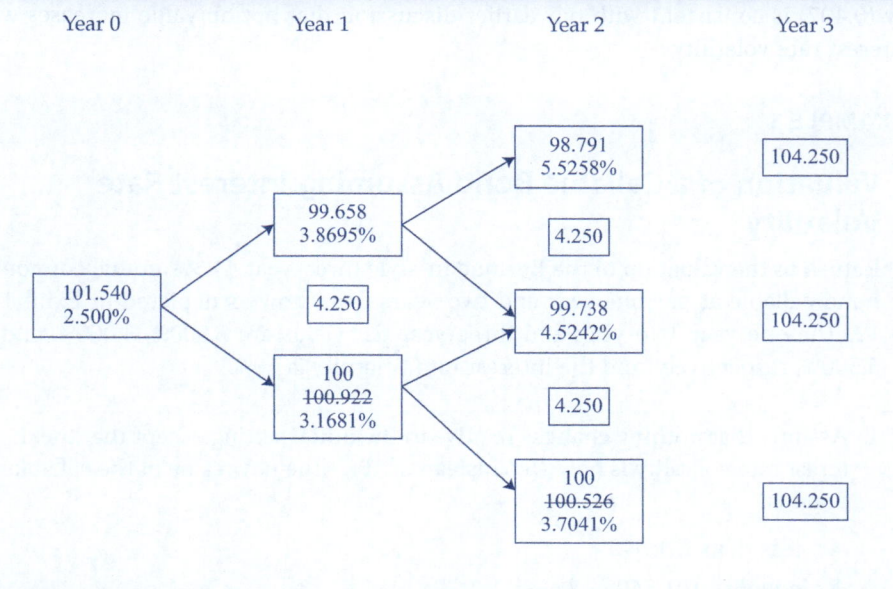

The coupon and principal cash flows are placed directly to the right of the interest rate nodes. The calculated bond values at each node are placed above the interest rate. We start by calculating the bond values at Year 2 by discounting the cash flow for Year 3 with the three possible rates.

$$98.791 = \frac{104.250}{1.055258}$$

$$99.738 = \frac{104.250}{1.045242}$$

$$100.526 = \frac{104.250}{1.037041}$$

Because the bond is callable at par in Year 2, we check each scenario to determine whether the present value of the future cash flows is higher than the call price, in which case the issuer calls the bond. Exercise happens only at the bottom of the tree, where the rate is 3.7041%, and so we reset the value from 100.526 to 100 in that state.

The value in each state of Year 1 is calculated by discounting the values in the two future states emanating from the present state plus the coupon at the appropriate rate in the present state:

$$99.658 = \frac{4.250 + (0.5 \times 98.791 + 0.5 \times 99.738)}{1.038695}.$$

The first term in the numerator is the coupon payment, and the second term is the expected bond value at Year 2. In this model, the probabilities for moving to the higher and lower node are the same (0.5):

$$100.922 = \frac{4.250 + (0.5 \times 99.738 + 0.5 \times 100)}{1.031681}.$$

Notice that the reset value of 100 is used to get the expected bond value. Once again the bond will be callable at the lower node where the interest rate is 3.1681%.

At Year 0, the value of the callable bond is 101.540:

$$101.540 = \frac{4.250 + (0.5 \times 99.658 + 0.5 \times 100)}{1.025000}.$$

The value of the call option, obtained by taking the difference between the value of the straight bond and the value of the callable bond, is now 0.574 (102.114 − 101.540). The fact that the value of the call option is larger at 10% volatility than at 0% volatility (0.407) is consistent with our earlier discussion that option value increases with interest rate volatility.

EXAMPLE 3

Valuation of a Callable Bond Assuming Interest Rate Volatility

Return to the valuation of the Bermudan-style three-year 4.25% annual coupon bond callable at par one year and two years from now as depicted in Exhibit 12. The one-year, two-year, and three-year par yields are 2.500%, 3.000%, and 3.500%, respectively, and the interest rate volatility is 10%.

1. Assume that nothing changes relative to the initial setting except that the interest rate volatility is now 15% instead of 10%. The new value of the callable bond is:

    A. less than 101.540.

    B. equal to 101.540.

    C. more than 101.540.

Handwritten margin note:

— The value of a callable bond (at par) with no call protection period cannot exceed 100, as at that price or higher the bond would be called.

Solution:

A is correct. A higher interest rate volatility increases the value of the call option. Because the value of the call option is subtracted from the value of the straight bond to obtain the value of the callable bond, a higher value for the call option leads to a lower value for the callable bond. Thus, the value of the callable bond at 15% volatility is less than that at 10% volatility—that is, less than 101.540.

---

2. Assume that nothing changes relative to the initial setting except that the bond is now callable at 102 instead of 100. The new value of the callable bond is *closest to*:

   A. 100.000.

   B. 102.000.

   C. 102.114.

Solution:

C is correct. Looking at Exhibit 12, the call price is too high for the call option to be exercised in any scenario. Thus, the value of the call option is zero, and the value of the callable bond is equal to the value of the straight bond—that is, 102.114.

Valuation of a Putable Bond with Interest Rate Volatility

The valuation of the three-year 4.25% annual coupon bond putable at par one year and two years from now at 10% volatility is depicted in Exhibit 13. The procedure for valuing a putable bond is very similar to that described earlier for valuing a callable bond, except that in each state, the bond's value is compared with the put price. The investor puts the bond only when the present value of the bond's future cash flows is lower than the put price. In this case, the value is reset to the put price (100). It happens twice in Year 2, in the states where the interest rates are 5.5258% and 4.5242%. The investor would not exercise the put option in Year 1 because the values for the bond exceed the put price.

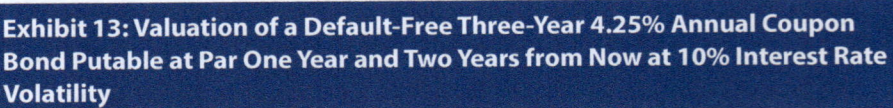

Exhibit 13: Valuation of a Default-Free Three-Year 4.25% Annual Coupon Bond Putable at Par One Year and Two Years from Now at 10% Interest Rate Volatility

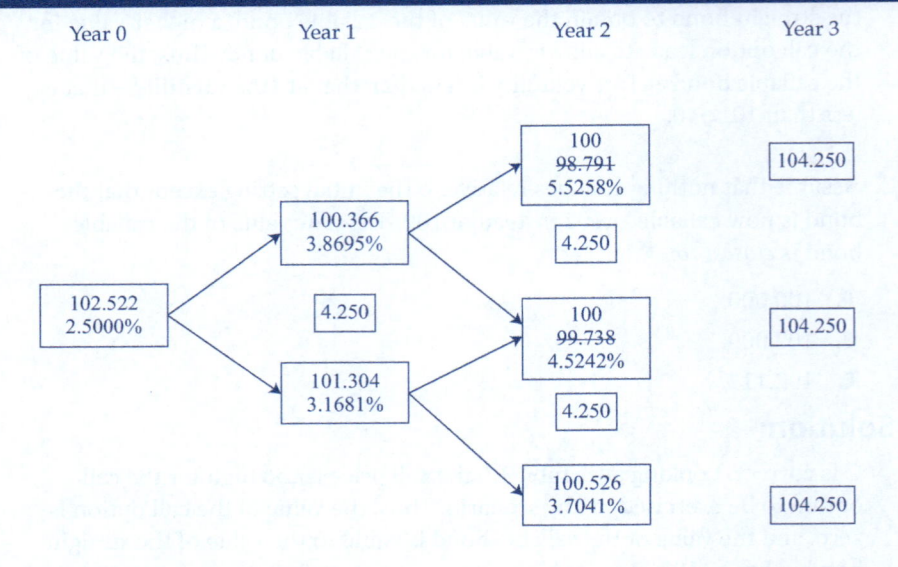

The value of the putable bond is 102.522. The value of the put option, obtained by taking the difference between the value of the putable bond and the value of the straight bond, is now 0.408 (102.522 − 102.114). As expected, the value of the put option is larger at 10% volatility than at 0% volatility (0.283).

2. Assume that nothing changes relative to the initial setting except that the bond is now putable at 95 instead of 100. The new value of the putable bond is *closest to*:

   A. 97.522.

   B. 102.114.

   C. 107.522.

Solution:

B is correct. Looking at Exhibit 13, the put price is too low for the put option to be exercised in any scenario. Thus, the value of the put option is zero, and the value of the putable bond is equal to the value of the straight bond—that is, 102.114.

PUTABLE VS. EXTENDIBLE BONDS

Putable and extendible bonds are equivalent, except that their underlying option-free bonds are different. Consider a three-year 3.30% bond putable in Year 2. Its value should be exactly the same as that of a two-year 3.30% bond extendible by one year. Otherwise, there would be an arbitrage opportunity. Clearly, the cash flows of the two bonds are identical up to Year 2. The cash flows in Year 3 are dependent on the one-year forward rate two years from now. These cash flows will also be the same for both bonds regardless of the level of interest rates at the end of Year 2.

If the one-year forward rate at the end of Year 2 is higher than 3.30%, the putable bond will be put because the bondholder can reinvest the proceeds of the retired bond at a higher yield and the extendible bond will not be extended for the same reason. So, both bonds pay 3.30% for two years and are then redeemed. Alternatively, if the one-year forward rate at the end of Year 2 is lower than 3.30%, the putable bond will not be put because the bondholder would not want to reinvest at a lower yield and the extendible bond will be extended to hold onto the higher interest rate. Thus, both bonds pay 3.30% for three years and are then redeemed.

EXAMPLE 5

Valuation of Bonds with Embedded Options Assuming Interest Rate Volatility

Sidley Brown, a fixed-income associate at KMR Capital, is analyzing the effect of interest rate volatility on the values of callable and putable bonds issued by Weather Analytics (WA). WA is owned by the sovereign government, so its bonds are considered default free. Brown is currently looking at three of WA's bonds and has gathered the following information about them:

Characteristic	Bond X	Bond Y	Bond Z
Time to maturity	Three years from today	Three years from today	Three years from today
Coupon	5.2% annual	Not available	4.8% annual
Type of bond	Callable at par one year and two years from today	Callable at par one year and two years from today	Putable at par two years from today
Price (as a % of par)	Not available	101.325	Not available

The one-year, two-year, and three-year par rates are 4.400%, 4.700%, and 5.000%, respectively. Based on an estimated interest rate volatility of 15%, Brown has constructed the following binomial interest rate tree:

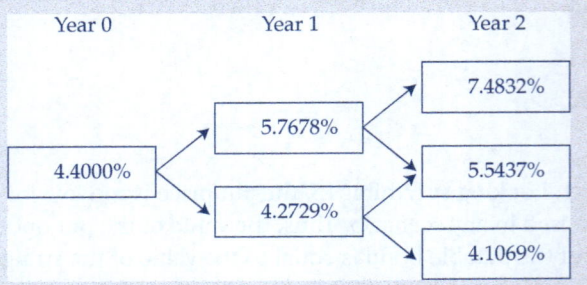

Brown is now analyzing the effect of interest rate volatility on the price of WA's bonds.

1. The price of Bond X is *closest to*:

   A. 96.057% of par.

   B. 99.954% of par.

   C. 100.547% of par.

Solution:

B is correct.

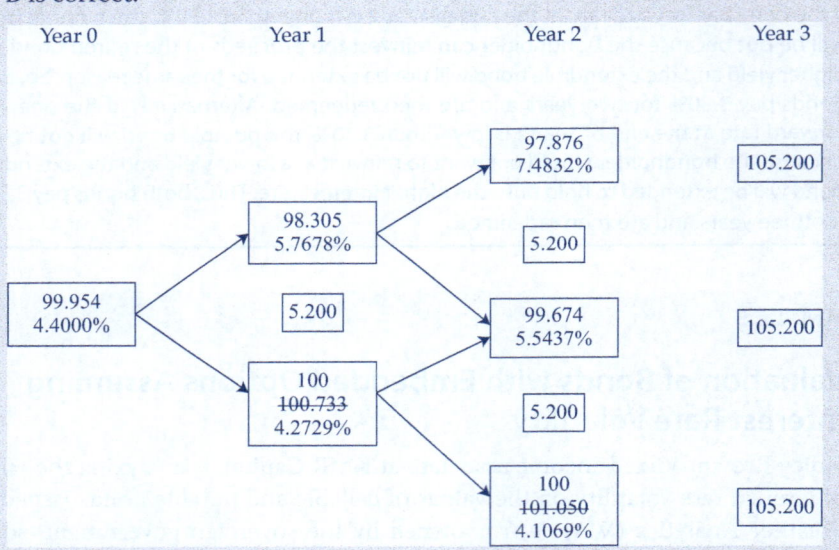

2. The coupon rate of Bond Y is *closest to*:

   A. 4.200%.

   B. 5.000%.

   C. 6.000%.

Solution:

C is correct.

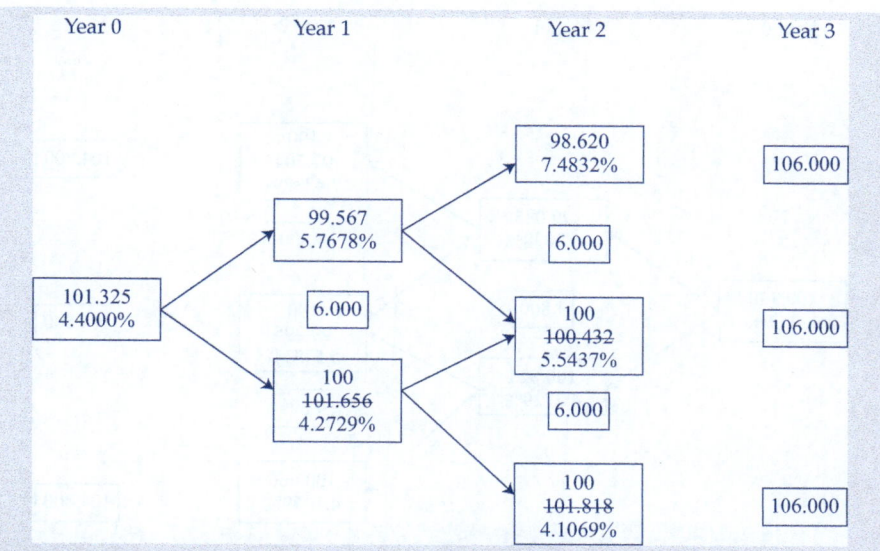

Although the correct answer can be found by using the interest rate tree depicted, it is possible to identify it by realizing that the other two answers are clearly incorrect. The three-year 5% straight bond is worth par given that the three-year par rate is 5%. Because the presence of a call option reduces the price of a callable bond, a three-year 5% bond callable at par can only be worth less than par—and certainly less than 101.325 given the yield curve and interest rate volatility assumptions—so B is incorrect. The value of a bond with a coupon rate of 4% is even less, so A is incorrect. Thus, C must be the correct answer.

3. The price of Bond Z is *closest to*:

   A. 99.638% of par.

   B. 100.340% of par.

   C. 100.778% of par.

Solution:

B is correct.

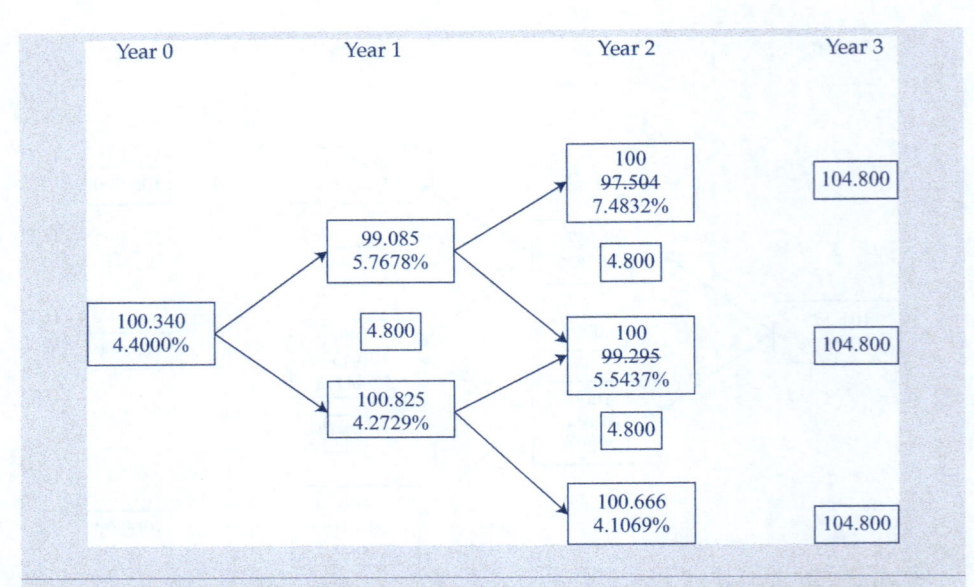

4. Relative to its price at 15% interest rate volatility, the price of Bond X at a lower interest rate volatility will be:

   A. lower.

   B. the same.

   C. higher.

Solution:

C is correct. Bond X is a callable bond. As shown in Equation 1, the value of the call option decreases the value of Bond X relative to the value of the underlying option-free bond. As interest rate volatility decreases, the value of the call option decreases; thus, the value of Bond X increases.

5. Relative to its price at 15% interest rate volatility, the price of Bond Z at a higher interest rate volatility will be:

   A. lower.

   B. the same.

   C. higher.

Solution:

C is correct. Bond Z is a putable bond. As shown in Equation 2, the value of the put option increases the value of Bond Z relative to the value of the underlying option-free bond. As interest rate volatility increases, the value of the put option increases; thus, the value of Bond Z increases.

5 | VALUATION OF RISKY CALLABLE AND PUTABLE BONDS

☐ | explain the calculation and use of option-adjusted spreads

☐ | explain how interest rate volatility affects option-adjusted spreads

Although the approach described earlier for default-free bonds may apply to securities issued by sovereign governments in their local currency, the fact is that most bonds are subject to default. Accordingly, we have to extend the framework to the valuation of risky bonds.

Two distinct approaches to valuing bonds are subject to default risk. The industry-standard approach is to increase the discount rates above the default-free rates to reflect default risk. Higher discount rates imply lower present values, and thus the value of a risky bond will be lower than that of an otherwise identical default-free bond.

The second approach to valuing risky bonds is to make the default probabilities explicit—that is, assigning a probability to each time period going forward. For example, the probability of default in Year 1 may be 1%; the probability of default in Year 2, conditional on surviving Year 1, may be 1.25%; and so on. This approach requires specifying the recovery value given default (e.g., 40% of par). Information about default probabilities and recovery values may be accessible from credit default swaps. This important topic is covered elsewhere.

Option-Adjusted Spread

Depending on available information, two standard approaches are used to construct a suitable yield curve for a risky bond. The more satisfactory but less convenient one is to use an issuer-specific curve, which represents the issuer's borrowing rates over the relevant range of maturities. Unfortunately, most bond professionals do not have access to such a level of detail. A more convenient and relatively satisfactory alternative is to uniformly raise the one-year forward rates derived from the default-free benchmark yield curve by a fixed spread, which is estimated from the market prices of suitable bonds of similar credit quality. This fixed spread is known as the zero-volatility spread, or Z-spread.

To illustrate, we return to the three-year 4.25% option-free bond introduced earlier, but now we assume that it is a risky bond and that the appropriate Z-spread is 100 bps. To calculate the arbitrage-free value of this bond, we have to increase each of the one-year forward rates given in Exhibit 1 by the Z-spread of 100 bps:

$$\frac{4.25}{(1.03500)} + \frac{4.25}{(1.03500)\,(1.04518)} + \frac{104.25}{(1.03500)\,(1.04518)\,(1.05564)} = 99.326.$$

As expected, the value of this risky bond (99.326) is considerably lower than the value of an otherwise identical but default-free bond (102.114).

The same approach can be applied to the interest rate tree when valuing risky bonds with embedded options. In this case, an **option-adjusted spread** (OAS) is used. As depicted in Exhibit 14, the OAS is the constant spread that when added to all the one-period forward rates on the interest rate tree, makes the arbitrage-free value of the bond equal to its market price. Note that the Z-spread for an option-free bond is simply its OAS at zero volatility.

Exhibit 14: Interest Rate Tree and OAS

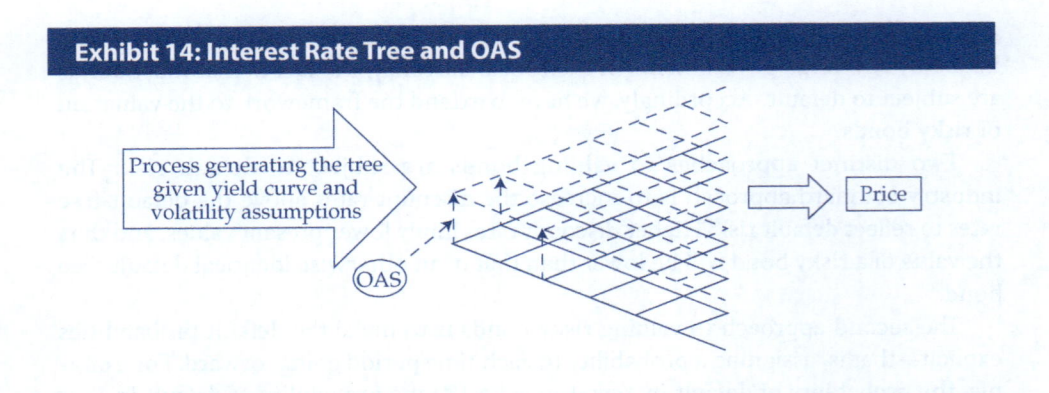

If the bond's price is given, the OAS is determined by trial and error. For example, suppose that the market price of a three-year 4.25% annual coupon bond callable in one year and two years from now (identical to the one valued in Exhibit 12 except that it is risky instead of default-free) is 101.000. To determine the OAS, we try shifting all the one-year forward rates in each state by adding a constant spread. For example, when we add 30 bps to all the one-year forward rates, we obtain a value for the callable bond of 100.973, which is lower than the bond's price. Because of the inverse relationship between a bond's price and its yield, this result means that the discount rates are too high, so we try a slightly lower spread. Adding 28 bps results in a value for the callable bond of 101.010, which is slightly too high. As illustrated in Exhibit 15, the constant spread added uniformly to all the one-period forward rates that justifies the given market price of 101.000 is 28.55 bps; this number is the OAS.

Exhibit 15: OAS of a Risky Three-Year 4.25% Annual Coupon Bond Callable at Par One Year and Two Years from Now at 10% Interest Rate Volatility

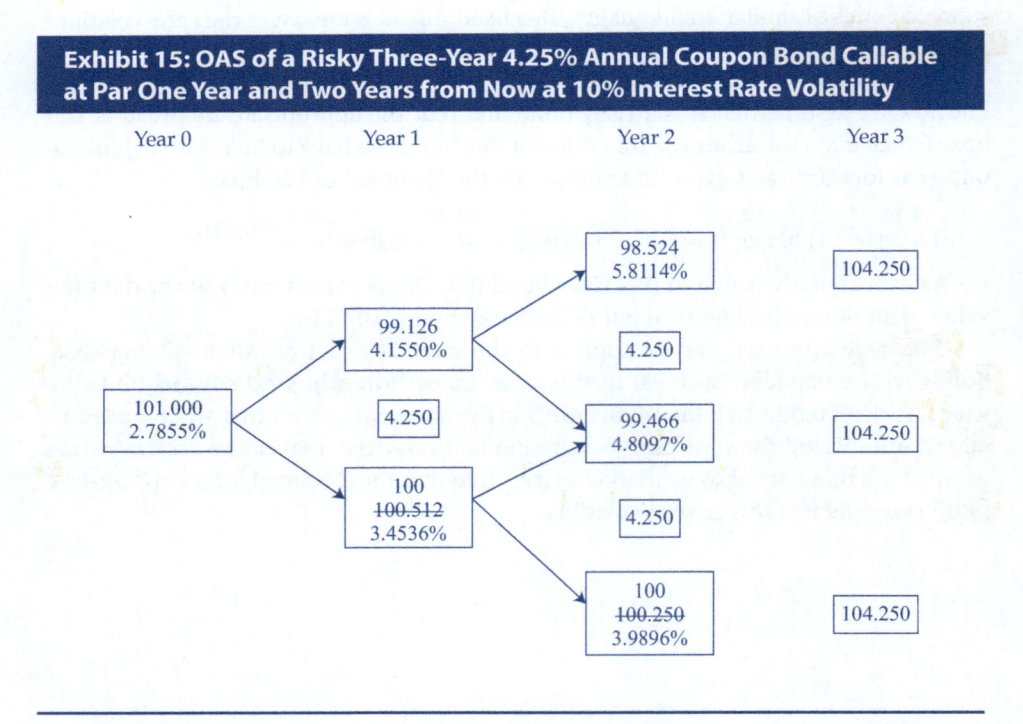

As illustrated in Exhibit 15, the value at each node is adjusted based on whether the call option is exercised. Thus, the OAS removes the amount that results from the option risk, which is why this spread is called "option adjusted."

OAS is often used as a measure of value relative to the benchmark. An OAS lower than that for a bond with similar characteristics and credit quality indicates that the bond is likely overpriced (rich) and should be avoided. A larger OAS than that of a bond with similar characteristics and credit quality means that the bond is likely underpriced (cheap). If the OAS is close to that of a bond with similar characteristics and credit quality, the bond looks fairly priced. In our example, the OAS at 10% volatility is 28.55 bps. This number should be compared with the OAS of bonds with similar characteristics and credit quality to make a judgment about the bond's attractiveness.

Effect of Interest Rate Volatility on Option-Adjusted Spread

The dispersion of interest rates on the tree is volatility dependent, and so is the OAS. Exhibit 16 shows the effect of volatility on the OAS for a callable bond. The bond is a 5% annual coupon bond with 23 years left to maturity, callable in three years, priced at 95% of par, and valued assuming a flat yield curve of 4%.

Exhibit 16: Effect of Interest Rate Volatility on the OAS for a Callable Bond

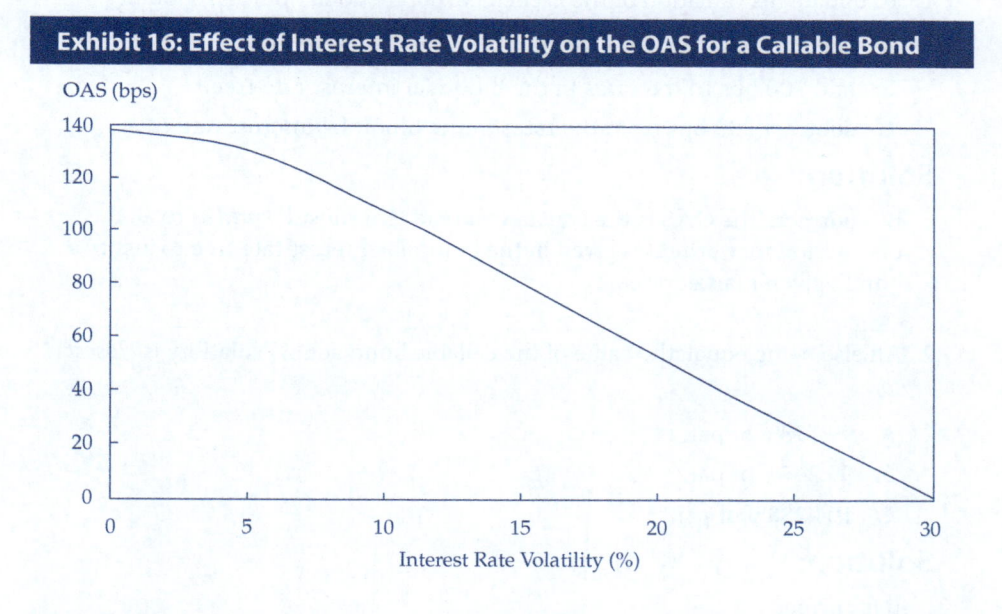

Exhibit 16 shows that as interest rate volatility increases, the OAS for the callable bond decreases. The OAS drops from 138.2 bps at 0% volatility to 1.2 bps at 30% volatility. This exhibit clearly demonstrates the importance of the interest rate volatility assumption. Returning to the example in Exhibit 15, the callable bond may look underpriced at 10% volatility. If an investor assumes a higher volatility, however, the OAS and thus relative cheapness will decrease.

EXAMPLE 6

Option-Adjusted Spread

Robert Jourdan, a portfolio manager, has just valued a 7% annual coupon bond that was issued by a French company and has three years remaining until maturity. The bond is callable at par one year and two years from now. In his valuation, Jourdan used the yield curve based on the on-the-run French government bonds. The one-year, two-year, and three-year par rates are 4.600%, 4.900%, and 5.200%, respectively. Based on an estimated interest rate volatility of 15%, Jourdan constructed the following binomial interest rate tree:

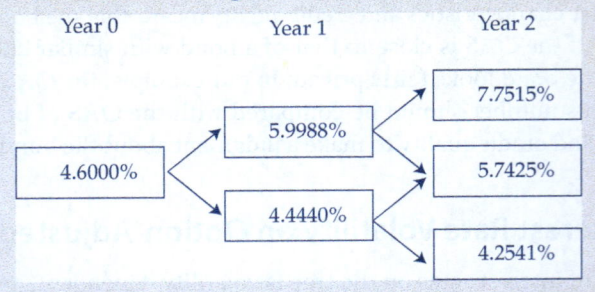

Jourdan valued the callable bond at 102.294% of par. However, Jourdan's colleague points out that because the corporate bond is riskier than French government bonds, the valuation should be performed using an OAS of 200 bps.

1. To update his valuation of the French corporate bond, Jourdan should:

   A. subtract 200 bps from the bond's annual coupon rate.

   B. add 200 bps to the rates in the binomial interest rate tree.

   C. subtract 200 bps from the rates in the binomial interest rate tree.

Solution:

B is correct. The OAS is the constant spread that must be *added* to all the one-period forward rates given in the binomial interest rate tree to justify a bond's given market price.

2. All else being equal, the value of the callable bond at 15% volatility is *closest to*:

   A. 99.198% of par.

   B. 99.247% of par.

   C. 104.288% of par.

Solution:

B is correct.

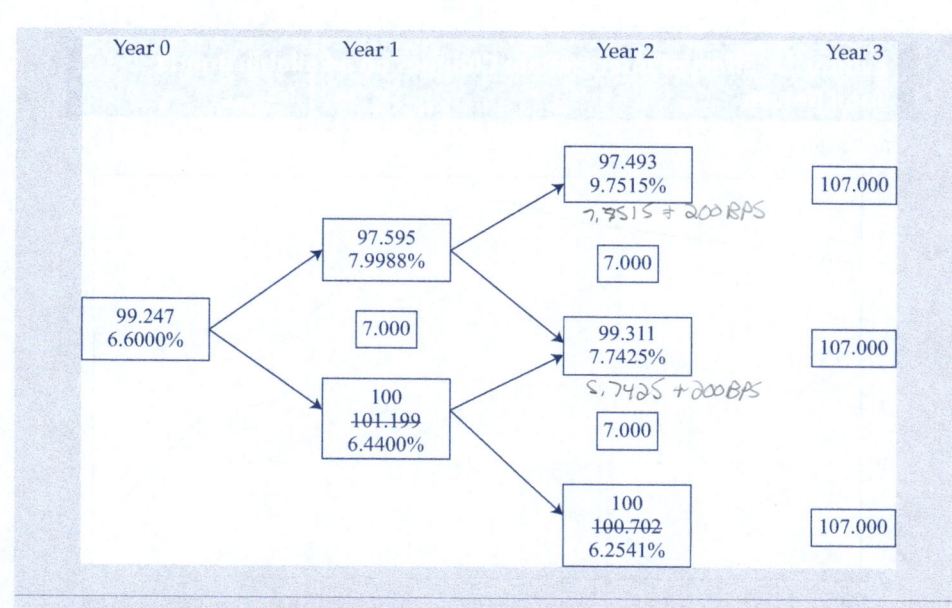

3. Holding the price calculated in the previous question, the OAS for the callable bond at 20% volatility will be:

   A. lower.

   B. the same.

   C. higher.

Solution:

A is correct. If interest rate volatility increases from 15% to 20%, the OAS for the callable bond will decrease.

SCENARIO ANALYSIS OF BONDS WITH OPTIONS

Another application of valuing bonds with embedded options is scenario analysis over a specified investment horizon. In addition to reinvestment of interest and principal, option valuation comes into play in that callable and putable bonds can be redeemed and their proceeds reinvested during the holding period. Making scenario-dependent, optimal option-exercise decisions involves computationally intensive use of OAS technology because the call or put decision must be evaluated considering the evolution of interest rate scenarios during the holding period.

Performance over a specified investment horizon entails a trade-off between reinvestment of cash flows and change in the bond's value. Let us take the example of a 4.5% bond with five years left to maturity and assume that the investment horizon is one year. If the bond is option free, higher interest rates increase the reinvestment income but result in lower principal value at the end of the investment horizon. Because the investment horizon is short, reinvestment income is relatively insignificant and performance will be dominated by the change in the value of the principal. Accordingly, lower interest rates will result in superior performance.

If the bond under consideration is callable, however, it is not at all obvious how the interest rate scenario affects performance. Suppose, for example, that the bond is first callable six months from now and that its current market price is 99.74. Steeply rising interest rates would depress the bond's price, and performance would definitely suffer. But steeply declining interest rates would also be detrimental because the bond would be called and *both interest and principal* would have to be reinvested at lower interest rates. Exhibit 17 shows the return over the one-year investment horizon for the 4.5% bond first callable in six months with five years left to maturity and valued on a 4% flat yield curve.

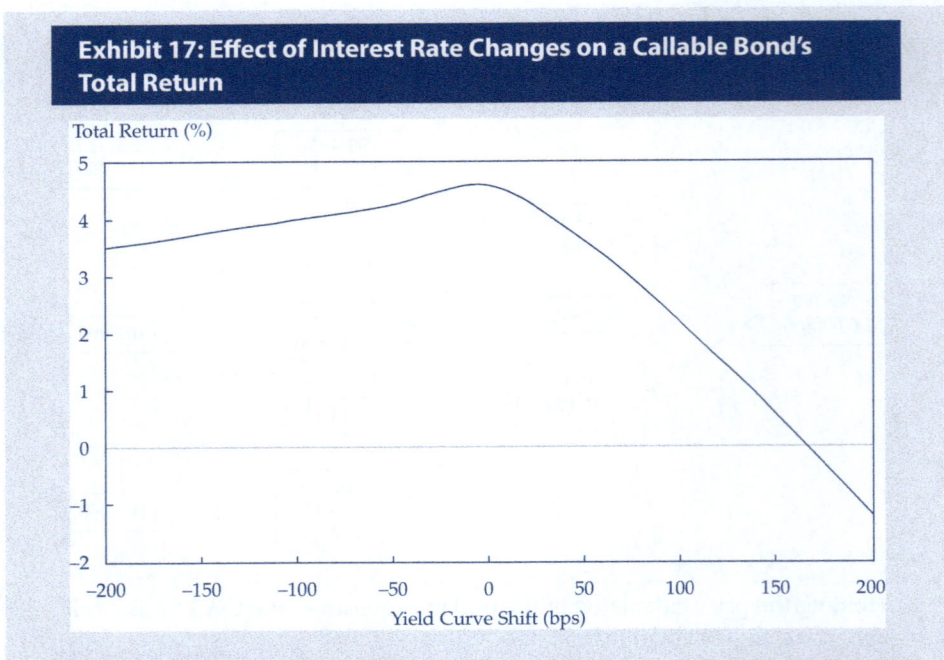

Exhibit 17: Effect of Interest Rate Changes on a Callable Bond's Total Return

Exhibit 17 clearly shows that lower interest rates do not guarantee higher returns for callable bonds. The point to keep in mind is that the bond may be called long before the end of the investment horizon. Assuming that it is called on the horizon date would overestimate performance. Thus, a realistic prediction of option exercise is essential when performing scenario analysis of bonds with embedded options.

6   BONDS WITH EMBEDDED OPTIONS: EFFECTIVE DURATION

☐ | calculate and interpret effective duration of a callable or putable bond
☐ | compare effective durations of callable, putable, and straight bonds

Measuring and managing exposure to interest rate risk are two essential tasks of fixed-income portfolio management. Applications range from hedging a portfolio to asset–liability management of financial institutions. Portfolio managers, whose performance is often measured against a benchmark, also need to monitor the interest rate risk of both their portfolio and the benchmark. In this section, we cover two key measures of interest rate risk: duration and convexity.

Duration

The duration of a bond measures the sensitivity of the bond's full price (including accrued interest) to changes in the bond's yield to maturity (in the case of *yield* duration measures) or to changes in benchmark interest rates (in the case of yield-curve or *curve* duration measures). Yield duration measures, such as modified duration, can be used only for option-free bonds because these measures assume that a bond's expected cash flows do not change when the yield changes. This assumption is in general false for bonds with embedded options because the values of embedded options are typically contingent on interest rates. Thus, for bonds with embedded options, the only appropriate duration measure is the curve duration measure known as effective (or option-adjusted) duration. Because effective duration works for straight bonds as well as for bonds with embedded options, practitioners tend to use it regardless of the type of bond being analyzed.

Effective Duration

Effective duration indicates the sensitivity of the bond's price to a 100 bps parallel shift of the benchmark yield curve—in particular, the government par curve—assuming no change in the bond's credit spread (*Note:* Although it is possible to explore how arbitrary changes in interest rates affect the bond's price, in practice the change is usually specified as a parallel shift of the benchmark yield curve). The formula for calculating a bond's effective duration is

$$\text{EffDur} = \frac{(PV_-) - (PV_+)}{2 \times (\Delta\text{Curve}) \times (PV_0)}, \tag{3}$$

where

ΔCurve = the magnitude of the parallel shift in the benchmark yield curve (in decimal)

PV_- = the full price of the bond when the benchmark yield curve is shifted down by ΔCurve

PV_+ = the full price of the bond when the benchmark yield curve is shifted up by ΔCurve

PV_0 = the current full price of the bond (i.e., with no shift)

How is this formula applied in practice? Without a market price, we would need an issuer-specific yield curve to compute PV_0, PV_-, and PV_+. But practitioners usually have access to the bond's current price and thus use the following procedure:

1. Given a price (PV_0), calculate the implied OAS to the benchmark yield curve at an appropriate interest rate volatility.

2. Shift the benchmark yield curve down, generate a new interest rate tree, and then revalue the bond using the OAS calculated in Step 1. This value is PV_-.

3. Shift the benchmark yield curve up by the same magnitude as in Step 2, generate a new interest rate tree, and then revalue the bond using the OAS calculated in Step 1. This value is PV_+.

4. Calculate the bond's effective duration using Equation 3.

Let us illustrate using the same three-year 4.25% bond callable at par one year and two years from now, the same par yield curve (i.e., one-year, two-year, and three-year par yields of 2.500%, 3.000%, and 3.500%, respectively), and the same interest rate volatility (10%) as before. Also as before, we assume that the bond's current full price is 101.000. We apply the procedure just described:

1. As shown in Exhibit 15, given a price (PV_0) of 101.000, the OAS at 10% volatility is 28.55 bps.

2. We shift the par yield curve down by, say, 30 bps, generate a new interest rate tree, and then revalue the bond at an OAS of 28.55 bps. As shown in Exhibit 18, PV_- is 101.599.

3. We shift the par yield curve up by the same 30 bps, generate a new interest rate tree, and then revalue the bond at an OAS of 28.55 bps. As shown in Exhibit 19, PV_+ is 100.407.

4. Thus,

$$\text{EffDur} = \frac{101.599 - 100.407}{2 \times 0.0030 \times 101.000} = 1.97.$$

An effective duration of 1.97 indicates that a 100 bps increase in interest rate would reduce the value of the three-year 4.25% callable bond by 1.97%.

Exhibit 18: Valuation of a Three-Year 4.25% Annual Coupon Bond Callable at Par One Year and Two Years from Now at 10% Interest Rate Volatility with an OAS of 28.55 bps When Interest Rates Are Shifted Down by 30 bps

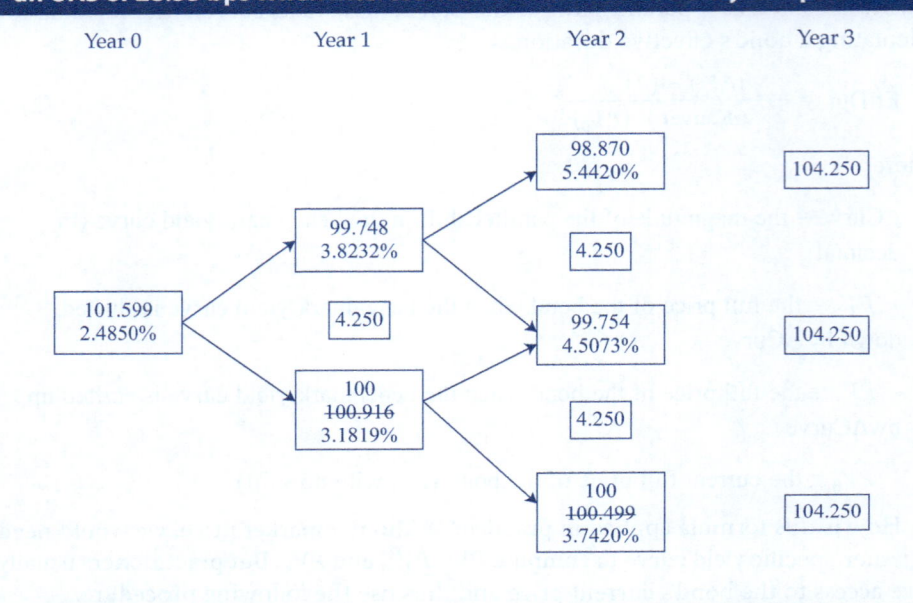

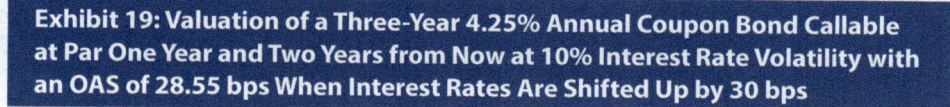

Exhibit 19: Valuation of a Three-Year 4.25% Annual Coupon Bond Callable at Par One Year and Two Years from Now at 10% Interest Rate Volatility with an OAS of 28.55 bps When Interest Rates Are Shifted Up by 30 bps

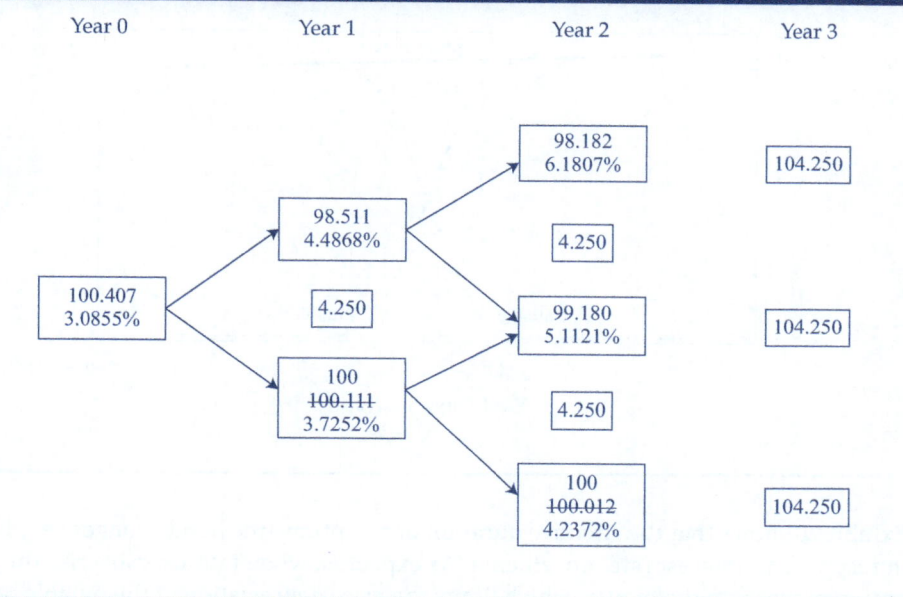

The effective duration of a callable bond cannot exceed that of the straight bond. When interest rates are high relative to the bond's coupon, the call option is out of the money so the bond is unlikely to be called. Thus, the effect of an interest rate change on the price of a callable bond is very similar to that on the price of an otherwise identical option-free bond; the callable and straight bonds have very similar effective durations. In contrast, when interest rates fall, the call option moves into the money. Remember that the call option gives the issuer the right to retire the bond at the call price and thus limits the price appreciation when interest rates decline. As a consequence, the call option reduces the effective duration of the callable bond relative to that of the straight bond.

The effective duration of a putable bond also cannot exceed that of the straight bond. When interest rates are low relative to the bond's coupon, the put option is out of the money so the bond is unlikely to be put. Thus, the effective duration of the putable bond is in this case very similar to that of an otherwise identical option-free bond. In contrast, when interest rates rise, the put option moves into the money and limits the price depreciation because the investor can put the bond and reinvest the proceeds of the retired bond at a higher yield. Thus, the put option reduces the effective duration of the putable bond relative to that of the straight bond.

When the embedded option (call or put) is deep in the money, the effective duration of the bond with an embedded option resembles that of the straight bond maturing on the first exercise date, reflecting the fact that the bond is highly likely to be called or put on that date.

Exhibit 20 compares the effective durations of option-free, callable, and putable bonds. All bonds are 4% annual coupon bonds with a maturity of 10 years. Both the call option and the put option are European-like and exercisable two months from now. The bonds are valued assuming a 4% flat yield curve and an interest rate volatility of 10%.

Exhibit 20: Comparison of the Effective Durations of Option-Free, Callable, and Putable Bonds

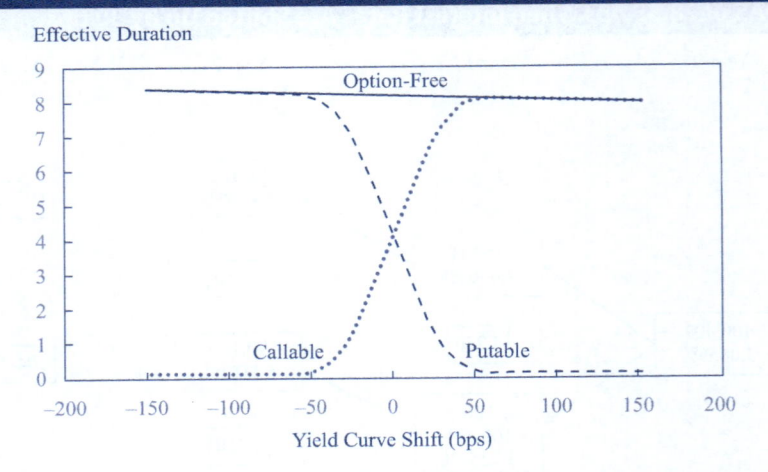

Exhibit 20 shows that the effective duration of an option-free bond changes very little in response to interest rate movements. As expected, when interest rates rise the put option moves into the money, which limits the price depreciation of the putable bond and shortens its effective duration. In contrast, the effective duration of the callable bond shortens when interest rates fall, which is when the call option moves into the money and thus limits the price appreciation of the callable bond.

EFFECTIVE DURATION IN PRACTICE

Effective duration is a concept most practically used in the context of a portfolio. Thus, an understanding of the effective durations of various types of instruments helps manage portfolio duration. In the following table, we show some properties of the effective duration of cash and the common types of bonds:

Type of Bond	Effective Duration
Cash	0
Zero-coupon bond	≈ Maturity
Fixed-rate bond	< Maturity
Callable bond	≤ Duration of straight bond
Putable bond	≤ Duration of straight bond
Floater (MRR flat)	≈ Time (in years) to next reset

In general, a bond's effective duration does not exceed its maturity. There are a few exceptions, however, such as tax-exempt bonds when analyzed on an after-tax basis. Knowing the effective duration of each type of bond is useful when one needs to change portfolio duration. For example, a portfolio manager who wants to shorten the effective duration of a portfolio of fixed-rate bonds can add floaters. For the debt manager of a company or other issuing entity, another way of shortening effective duration is to issue callable bonds. The topic of changing portfolio duration is covered thoroughly in Level III.

[handwritten margin note: —the effective duration of a floating rate bond is close to the time to next reset.]

ONE-SIDED AND KEY RATE DURATION

☐ | describe the use of one-sided durations and key rate durations to evaluate the interest rate sensitivity of bonds with embedded options

Effective durations are normally calculated by averaging the changes resulting from shifting the benchmark yield curve up and down by the same amount. This calculation works well for option-free bonds, but the results can be misleading in the presence of embedded options. The problem is that when the embedded option is in the money, the price of the bond has limited upside potential if the bond is callable or limited downside potential if the bond is putable. Thus, the price sensitivity of bonds with embedded options is not symmetrical to positive and negative changes in interest rates of the same magnitude.

— One-sided up-duration and one-sided down duration will be about equal for option-free bonds

Consider, for example, a 4.5% bond maturing in five years, which is currently callable at 100. On a 4% flat yield curve at 15% volatility, the value of this callable bond is 99.75. If interest rates declined by 30 bps, the price would rise to 100. In fact, no matter how far interest rates decline, the price of the callable bond cannot exceed 100 because no investor will pay more than the price at which the bond can be immediately called. In contrast, the price decline has no limit if interest rates rise. Thus, the average price response to up- and down-shifts of interest rates (effective duration) is not as informative as the price responses to the up-shift (one-sided up-duration) and the down-shift (one-sided down-duration) of interest rates.

Exhibit 21 and Exhibit 22 illustrate why **one-sided durations**—that is, the effective durations when interest rates go up or down—are better at capturing the interest rate sensitivity of a callable or putable bond than the (two-sided) effective durations, particularly when the embedded option is near the money.

Exhibit 21: Durations for a 4.5% Annual Coupon Bond Maturing in Five Years and Immediately Callable at Par on a 4% Flat Yield Curve at 15% Interest Rate Volatility

	At a 4% Flat Yield Curve	Interest Rate up by 30 bps	Interest Rate down by 30 bps
Value of the bond	99.75	99.17	100.00
Duration measure	Effective duration 1.39	One-sided up-duration 1.94	One-sided down-duration 0.84

Exhibit 21 shows that a 30 bps increase in the interest rate has a greater effect on the value of the callable bond than a 30 bps decrease in the interest rate. The fact that the one-sided up-duration is higher than the one-sided down-duration confirms that the callable bond is more sensitive to interest rate rises than to interest rate declines.

Exhibit 22: Durations for a 4.1% Annual Coupon Bond Maturing in Five Years and Immediately Putable at Par on a 4% Flat Yield Curve at 15% Interest Rate Volatility

	At a 4% Flat Yield Curve	Interest Rate up by 30 bps	Interest Rate down by 30 bps
Value of the bond	100.45	100.00	101.81

	At a 4% Flat Yield Curve	Interest Rate up by 30 bps	Interest Rate down by 30 bps
Duration measure	Effective duration 3.00	One-sided up-duration 1.49	One-sided down-duration 4.51

The one-sided durations in Exhibit 22 indicate that the putable bond is more sensitive to interest rate declines than to interest rate rises.

Key Rate Durations

Effective duration is calculated by assuming parallel shifts in the benchmark yield curve. In reality, however, interest rate movements are not as neat. Many portfolio managers and risk managers like to isolate the price responses to changes in the rates of key maturities on the benchmark yield curve. For example, how would the price of a bond be expected to change if only the two-year benchmark rate moved up by 5 bps? The answer is found by using **key rate durations** (also known as partial durations), which reflect the sensitivity of the bond's price to changes in specific maturities on the benchmark yield curve. Thus, key rate durations help portfolio managers and risk managers identify the "shaping risk" for bonds—that is, the bond's sensitivity to changes in the shape of the yield curve (e.g., steepening and flattening).

The valuation procedure and formula applied in the calculation of key rate durations are identical to those used in the calculation of effective duration, but instead of shifting the entire benchmark yield curve, only key points are shifted one at a time. Thus, the effective duration for each maturity point shift is calculated in isolation.

Exhibit 23, Exhibit 24, and Exhibit 25 show the key rate durations for bonds valued at a 4% flat yield curve. Exhibit 23 examines option-free bonds (assuming semi-annual coupons), and Exhibit 24 and Exhibit 25 extend the analysis to callable and putable bonds, respectively.

Exhibit 23: Key Rate Durations of 10-Year Option-Free Bonds Valued at a 4% Flat Yield Curve

Coupon (%)	Price (% of par)	Key Rate Durations				
		Total	2-Year	3-Year	5-Year	10-Year
0	67.30	9.81	−0.07	−0.34	−0.93	11.15
2	83.65	8.83	−0.03	−0.13	−0.37	9.37
4	100.00	8.18	0.00	0.00	0.00	8.18
6	116.35	7.71	0.02	0.10	0.27	7.32
8	132.70	7.35	0.04	0.17	0.47	6.68
10	149.05	7.07	0.05	0.22	0.62	6.18

As shown in Exhibit 23, for option-free bonds not trading at par (the white rows), shifting any par rate has an effect on the value of the bond, but shifting the maturity-matched (10-year in this example) par rate has the greatest effect. This is simply because the largest cash flow of a fixed-rate bond occurs at maturity with the payment of both the final coupon and the principal.

For an option-free bond trading at par (the shaded row), the maturity-matched par rate is the only rate that affects the bond's value. It is a definitional consequence of "par" rates. If the 10-year par rate on a curve is 4%, then a 10-year 4% bond valued on that curve at zero OAS will be worth par regardless of the par rates of the other maturity points on the curve. In other words, shifting any rate other than the 10-year rate on the par yield curve will not change the value of a 10-year bond trading at par. Shifting a par rate up or down at a particular maturity point, however, respectively increases or decreases the *discount rate* at that maturity point. These facts will be useful to remember in the following paragraph.

As illustrated in Exhibit 23, key rate durations can sometimes be negative for maturity points that are shorter than the maturity of the bond being analyzed if the bond is a zero-coupon bond or has a very low coupon. We can explain why this is the case by using the zero-coupon bond (the first row of Exhibit 23). As discussed in the previous paragraph, if we increase the five-year par rate, the value of a 10-year bond trading at par must remain unchanged because the 10-year par rate has not changed. But the five-year zero-coupon rate has increased because of the increase in the five-year par rate. Thus, the value of the five-year coupon of the 10-year bond trading at par will be lower than before the increase. But because the value of the 10-year bond trading at par must remain par, the remaining cash flows, including the cash flow occurring in Year 10, must be discounted at slightly *lower* rates to compensate. This results in a lower 10-year zero-coupon rate, which makes the value of a 10-year zero-coupon bond (whose only cash flow is in Year 10) *rise* in response to an *upward* change in the five-year par rate. Consequently, the five-year key rate duration for a 10-year zero-coupon bond is negative (−0.93).

Unlike for option-free bonds, the key rate durations of bonds with embedded options depend not only on the *time to maturity* but also on the *time to exercise*. Exhibit 24 and Exhibit 25 illustrate this phenomenon for 30-year callable and putable bonds. Both the call option and the put option are European-like exercisable 10 years from now, and the bonds are valued assuming a 4% flat yield curve and a volatility of 15%.

Exhibit 24: Key Rate Durations of 30-Year Bonds Callable in 10 Years Valued at a 4% Flat Yield Curve with 15% Interest Rate Volatility

Coupon (%)	Price (% of par)	Key Rate Durations					
		Total	2-Year	3-Year	5-Year	10-Year	30-Year
2	64.99	19.73	−0.02	−0.08	−0.21	−1.97	22.01
4	94.03	13.18	0.00	0.02	0.05	3.57	9.54
6	114.67	9.11	0.02	0.10	0.29	6.00	2.70
8	132.27	7.74	0.04	0.17	0.48	6.40	0.66
10	148.95	7.14	0.05	0.22	0.62	6.06	0.19

The bond with a coupon of 2% (the first row of Exhibit 24) is unlikely to be called, and thus it behaves more like a 30-year option-free bond, whose effective duration depends primarily on movements in the 30-year par rate. Therefore, the rate that has the highest effect on the value of the callable bond is the maturity-matched (30-year) rate. As the bond's coupon increases, however, so does the likelihood of the bond being called. Thus, the bond's total effective duration shortens, and the rate that has the highest effect on the callable bond's value gradually shifts from the 30-year rate to the 10-year rate. At the very high coupon of 10%, because of the virtual certainty of being called, the callable bond behaves like a 10-year option-free bond; the 30-year key rate duration is negligible (0.19) relative to the 10-year key rate duration (6.06).

Exhibit 25: Key Rate Durations of 30-Year Bonds Putable in 10 Years Valued at a 4% Flat Yield Curve with 15% Interest Rate Volatility

Coupon (%)	Price (% of par)	Key Rate Durations					
		Total	2-Year	3-Year	5-Year	10-Year	30-Year
2	83.89	9.24	−0.03	−0.14	−0.38	8.98	0.81
4	105.97	12.44	0.00	−0.01	−0.05	4.53	7.97
6	136.44	14.75	0.01	0.03	0.08	2.27	12.37
8	169.96	14.90	0.01	0.06	0.16	2.12	12.56
10	204.38	14.65	0.02	0.07	0.21	2.39	11.96

If the 30-year bond putable in 10 years has a high coupon, its price is more sensitive to the 30-year rate because it is unlikely to be put and thus behaves like an otherwise identical option-free bond. The 10% putable bond (the last row of Exhibit 25), for example, is most sensitive to changes in the 30-year rate, as illustrated by a 30-year key rate duration of 11.96. At the other extreme, a low-coupon bond is most sensitive to movements in the 10-year rate. It is almost certain to be put and so behaves like an option-free bond maturing on the put date.

8 EFFECTIVE CONVEXITY

☐ | compare effective convexities of callable, putable, and straight bonds

Duration is an approximation of the expected bond price responses to changes in interest rates because actual changes in bond prices are not linear, particularly for bonds with embedded options. Thus, it is useful to measure **effective convexity**—that is, the sensitivity of duration to changes in interest rates—as well. The formula to calculate a bond's effective convexity is

$$\text{EffCon} = \frac{(PV_-) + (PV_+) - [2 \times (PV_0)]}{(\Delta\text{Curve})^2 \times (PV_0)}, \tag{4}$$

where

ΔCurve = the magnitude of the parallel shift in the benchmark yield curve (in decimal)

PV_- = the full price of the bond when the benchmark yield curve is shifted down by ΔCurve

PV_+ = the full price of the bond when the benchmark yield curve is shifted up by ΔCurve

PV_0 = the current full price of the bond (i.e., with no shift)

Let us return to the three-year 4.25% bond callable at par one year and two years from now. We still use the same par yield curve (i.e., one-year, two-year, and three-year par yields of 2.500%, 3.000%, and 3.500%, respectively) and the same interest rate volatility (10%) as before, but we now assume that the bond's current full price is

100.785 instead of 101.000. Thus, the implied OAS is 40 bps. Given 30 bps shifts in the benchmark yield curve, the resulting PV_- and PV_+ are 101.381 and 100.146, respectively. Using Equation 4, the effective convexity is:

$$\text{EffCon} = \frac{101.381 + 100.146 - 2 \times 100.785}{(0.003)^2 \times 100.785} = -47.41.$$

[Note that there are two different conventions for reporting convexity in practice; "raw" convexity figures, such as in this example, are sometimes scaled (divided) by 100.]

Exhibit 20, shown earlier, displays effective durations but also illustrates the effective convexities of callable and putable bonds. When interest rates are high and the value of the call option is low, the callable and straight bond experience very similar effects from changes in interest rates. They both have positive convexity. However, the effective convexity of the callable bond turns negative when the call option is near the money, as in the example just presented, which indicates that the upside for a callable bond is much smaller than the downside. The reason is because when interest rates decline, the price of the callable bond is capped by the price of the call option if it is near the exercise date.

Conversely, putable bonds always have positive convexity. When the option is near the money, the upside for a putable bond is much larger than the downside because the price of a putable bond is floored by the price of the put option if it is near the exercise date.

Compared side by side, putable bonds have more upside potential than otherwise identical callable bonds when interest rates decline. Putable bonds also have less downside risk than otherwise identical callable bonds when interest rates rise.

EXAMPLE 7

Interest Rate Sensitivity

Erna Smith, a portfolio manager, has two fixed-rate bonds in her portfolio: a callable bond (Bond X) and a putable bond (Bond Y). She wants to examine the interest rate sensitivity of these two bonds to a parallel shift in the benchmark yield curve. Assuming an interest rate volatility of 10%, her valuation software shows how the prices of these bonds change for 30 bps shifts up or down:

	Bond X	Bond Y
Time to maturity	Three years from today	Three years from today
Coupon	3.75% annual	3.75% annual
Type of bond	Callable at par one year from today	Putable at par one year from today
Current price (% of par)	100.594	101.330
Price (% of par) when shifting the benchmark yield curve down by 30 bps	101.194	101.882
Price (% of par) when shifting the benchmark yield curve up by 30 bps	99.860	100.924

1. The effective duration for Bond X is *closest* to:

   A. 0.67.

   B. 2.21.

   C. 4.42.

Solution:

B is correct. The effective duration for Bond X is

$$EffDur = \frac{101.194 - 99.860}{2 \times 0.003 \times 100.594} = 2.21.$$

A is incorrect because the duration of a bond with a single cash flow one year from now is approximately one year, so 0.67 is too low—even assuming that the bond will be called in one year with certainty. C is incorrect because 4.42 exceeds the maturity of Bond X (three years).

2. The effective duration for Bond Y is *closest* to:

   A. 0.48.

   B. 0.96.

   C. 1.58.

Solution:

C is correct. The effective duration for Bond Y is

$$EffDur = \frac{101.882 - 100.924}{2 \times 0.003 \times 101.330} = 1.58.$$

3. When interest rates rise, the effective duration of:

   A. Bond X shortens.

   B. Bond Y shortens.

   C. the underlying option-free (straight) bond corresponding to Bond X lengthens.

Solution:

B is correct. When interest rates rise, a put option moves into the money and the putable bond is more likely to be put. Thus, it behaves like a shorter-maturity bond, and its effective duration shortens. A is incorrect because when interest rates rise, a call option moves out of the money; so, the callable bond is less likely to be called. C is incorrect because the effective duration of an option-free bond goes down as interest rates rise.

4. When the option embedded in Bond Y is in the money, the one-sided durations *most likely* show that the bond is:

   A. more sensitive to a decrease in interest rates.

   B. more sensitive to an increase in interest rates.

   C. equally sensitive to a decrease or to an increase in interest rates.

Solution:

A is correct. If interest rates rise, the investor's ability to put the bond at par limits the price depreciation. In contrast, the increase in the bond's price has no limit when interest rates decline. Thus, the price of a putable bond whose embedded option is in the money is more sensitive to a decrease in interest rates.

5. The price of Bond X is affected:

   A. only by a shift in the one-year par rate.

    B. only by a shift in the three-year par rate.

    C. by all par rate shifts but is most sensitive to shifts in the one-year and three-year par rates.

Solution:

C is correct. The main driver of the call decision is the two-year forward rate one year from now. This rate is most significantly affected by changes in the one-year and three-year par rates.

6. The effective convexity of Bond X:

    A. cannot be negative.

    B. turns negative when the embedded option is near the money.

    C. turns negative when the embedded option moves out of the money.

Solution:

B is correct. The effective convexity of a callable bond turns negative when the call option is near the money because the price response of a callable bond to lower interest rates is capped by the call option. That is, in case of a decline in interest rates, the issuer will call the bonds and refund at lower rates, thus limiting the upside potential for the investor.

7. Which of the following statements is *most* accurate?

    A. Bond Y exhibits negative convexity.

    B. For a given decline in interest rate, Bond X has less upside potential than Bond Y.

    C. The underlying option-free (straight) bond corresponding to Bond Y exhibits negative convexity.

Solution:

B is correct. As interest rates decline, the value of a call option increases whereas the value of a put option decreases. The call option embedded in Bond X limits its price appreciation, but Bond Y has no such cap. Thus, Bond X has less upside potential than Bond Y. A is incorrect because a putable bond always has positive convexity; that is, Bond Y has more upside than downside potential. C is incorrect because an option-free bond exhibits low positive convexity.

CAPPED AND FLOORED FLOATING-RATE BONDS

9

☐ | calculate the value of a capped or floored floating-rate bond

Options in floating-rate bonds (floaters) are exercised automatically depending on the course of interest rates; if the coupon rate rises or falls below the threshold, the cap or floor automatically applies. Similar to callable and putable bonds, capped and floored floaters can be valued by using the arbitrage-free framework.

Valuation of a Capped Floater

The cap provision in a floater prevents the coupon rate from increasing above a specified maximum rate. As a consequence, a **capped floater** protects the issuer against rising interest rates and is thus an issuer option. Because the investor is long the bond but short the embedded option, the value of the cap decreases the value of the capped floater relative to the value of the straight bond:

Value of capped floater

= Value of straight bond − Value of embedded cap. (5)

To illustrate how to value a capped floater, consider a floating-rate bond that has a three-year maturity. The floater's coupon pays the one-year reference rate annually, set in arrears, and is capped at 4.500%. The term "set in arrears" means that the coupon rate is set at the *end* of the coupon period; the payment date and the setting date are one and the same. For simplicity, we assume that the issuer's credit quality closely matches the reference rate swap curve (i.e., there is no credit spread) and that the reference rate swap curve is the same as the par yield curve given in Exhibit 1 (i.e., one-year, two-year, and three-year par yields of 2.500%, 3.000%, and 3.500%, respectively). We also assume that the interest rate volatility is 10%.

The valuation of the capped floater is depicted in Exhibit 26.

Exhibit 26: Valuation of a Three-Year Reference Rate Floater Capped at 4.500% at 10% Interest Rate Volatility

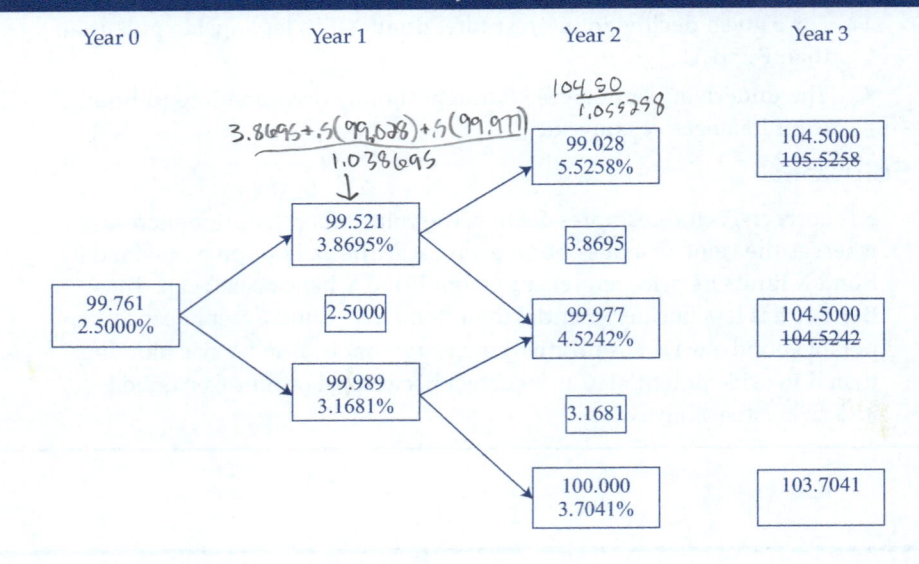

Without a cap, the value of this floater would be 100 because in every scenario, the coupon paid would be equal to the discount rate. But because the coupon rate is capped at 4.500%, which is lower than the highest interest rates in the tree, the value of the capped floater will be lower than the value of the straight bond.

For each scenario, we check whether the cap applies; if it does, the cash flow is adjusted accordingly. For example, at the top of the tree at Year 2, the reference rate (5.5258%) is higher than the 4.500% cap. Thus, the coupon payment at Year 3 is capped at the 4.500 maximum amount, and the cash flow is adjusted downward from the uncapped amount (105.5258) to the capped amount (104.5000). The coupon is also capped when the reference rate is 4.5242% at Year 2.

As expected, the value of the capped floater is lower than 100 (99.761). The value of the cap can be calculated by using Equation 5:

Value of embedded cap = 100 − 99.761 = 0.239.

Valuation of a Floored Floater

The floor provision in a floater prevents the coupon rate from decreasing below a specified minimum rate. As a consequence, a **floored floater** protects the investor against declining interest rates and is thus an investor option. Because the investor is long both the bond and the embedded option, the value of the floor increases the value of the floored floater relative to the value of the straight bond:

Value of floored floater

= Value of straight bond + Value of embedded floor.   (6)

To illustrate how to value a floored floater, we return to the example we used for the capped floater but assume that the embedded option is now a 3.500% floor instead of a 4.500% cap. The other assumptions remain the same. The valuation of the floored floater is depicted in Exhibit 27.

Exhibit 27: Valuation of a Three-Year Reference Rate Floater Floored at 3.500% at 10% Interest Rate Volatility

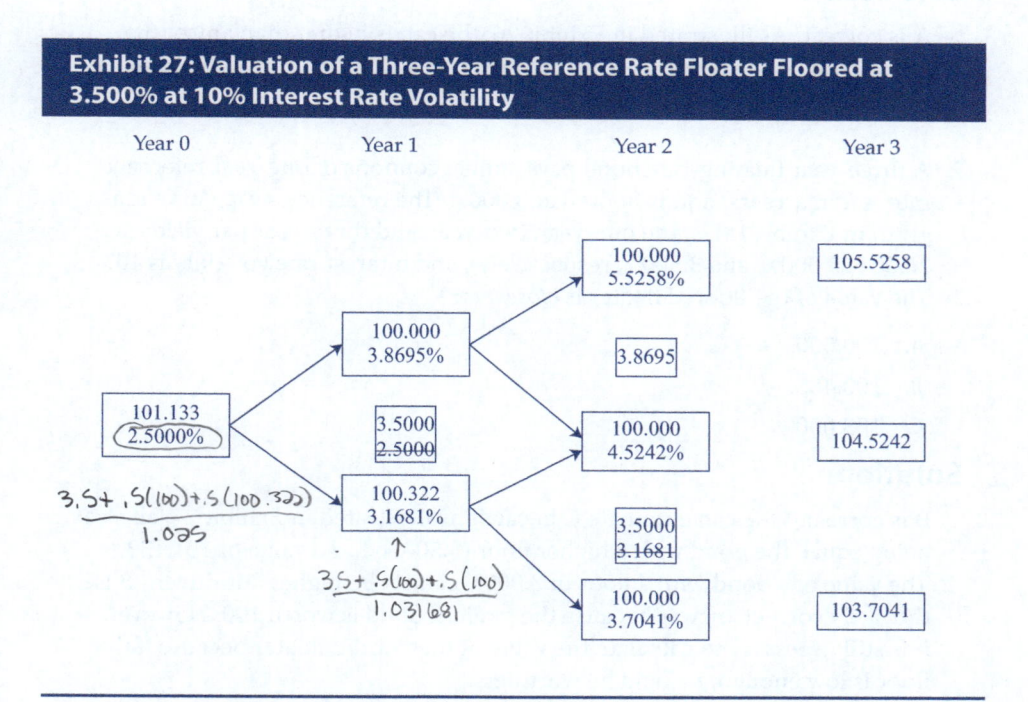

Recall from the discussion about the capped floater that if there were no cap, the value of the floater would be 100 because the coupon paid would equal the discount rate. The same principle applies here: If there were no floor, the value of this floater would be 100. Because the presence of the floor potentially increases the cash flows, however, the value of the floored floater must be equal to or higher than the value of the straight bond.

Exhibit 27 shows that the floor is binding at Year 0 because the reference rate (2.5000%) is less than the cap rate (3.5000%) and at Year 1 at the lower node where the reference rate is 3.1681%. Thus, the corresponding interest payments at Year 1 and 2 are increased to the minimum amount of 3.5000. As a consequence, the value of the floored floater exceeds 100 (101.133). The value of the floor can be calculated by using Equation 6:

Value of embedded floor = 101.133 − 100 = 1.133.

EXAMPLE 8

Valuation of Capped and Floored Floaters

1. A three-year floating rate bond pays annual coupons of one-year reference rate (set in arrears) and is capped at 5.600%. The reference rate swap curve is as given in Exhibit 1 (i.e., the one-year, two-year, and three-year par yields are 2.500%, 3.000%, and 3.500%, respectively), and interest rate volatility is 10%. The value of the capped floater is *closest to*:

   A. 100.000.

   B. 105.600.

   C. 105.921.

Solution:

A is correct. As illustrated in Exhibit 26, the cap is higher than any of the rates at which the floater is reset on the interest rate tree. Thus, the value of the bond is the same as if it had no cap—that is, 100.

---

2. A three-year floating-rate bond pays annual coupons of one-year reference rate (set in arrears) and is floored at 3.000%. The reference swap curve is as given in Exhibit 1 (i.e., the one-year, two-year, and three-year par yields are 2.500%, 3.000%, and 3.500%, respectively), and interest rate volatility is 10%. The value of the floored floater is *closest to*:

   A. 100.000.

   B. 100.488.

   C. 103.000.

Solution:

B is correct. One can eliminate C because as illustrated in Exhibit 27, all else being equal, the bond with a higher floor (3.500%) has a value of 101.133. The value of a bond with a floor of 3.000% cannot be higher. Intuitively, B is the likely correct answer because the straight bond is worth 100. However, it is still necessary to calculate the value of the floored floater because if the floor is low enough, it could be worthless.

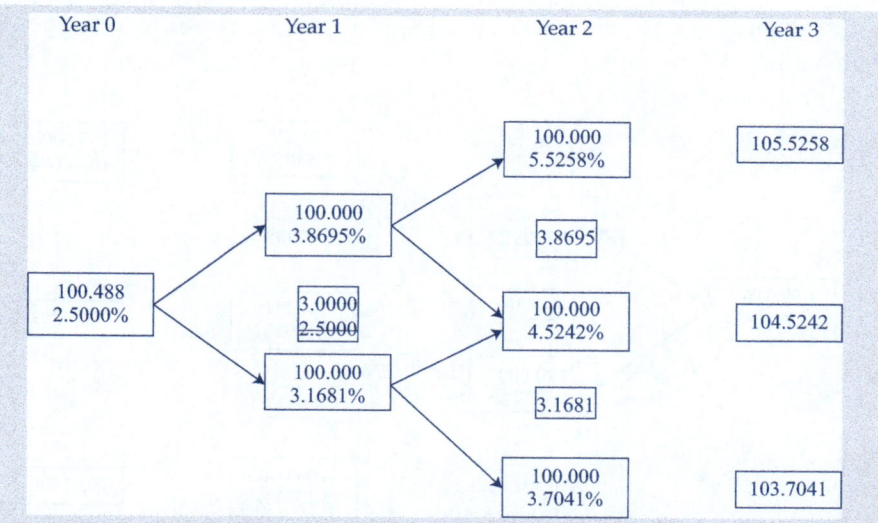

Here, it turns out that the floor adds 0.488 in value to the straight bond. Had the floor been 2.500%, the floored floater and the straight bond would both be worth par.

3. An issuer in the eurozone wants to sell a three-year floating-rate note at par with an annual coupon based on the 12-month Euribor + 300 bps. Because the 12-month Euribor is currently at a historic low and the issuer wants to protect itself against a sudden increase in interest cost, the issuer's advisers recommend increasing the credit spread to 320 bps and capping the coupon at 5.50%. Assuming an interest rate volatility of 8%, the advisers have constructed the following binomial interest rate tree:

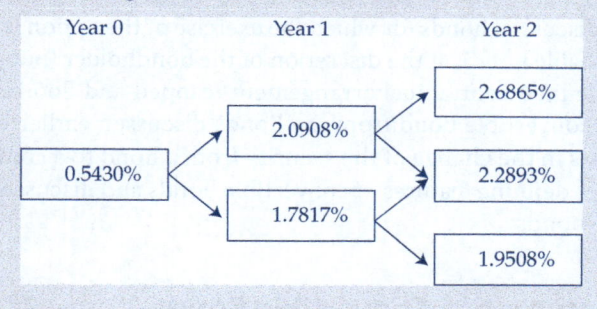

The value of the capped floater is *closest to*:

   A. 92.929.

   B. 99.916.

   C. 109.265.

Solution:

B is correct.

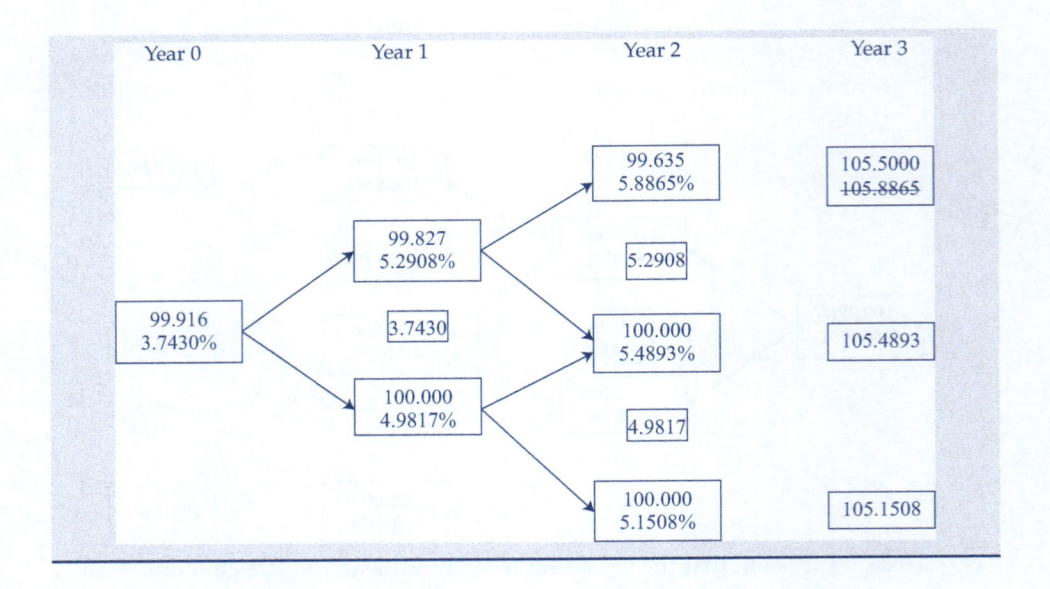

Year 0	Year 1	Year 2	Year 3
		99.635 / 5.8865%	105.5000 / ~~105.8865~~
	99.827 / 5.2908%	5.2908	
99.916 / 3.7430%	3.7430	100.000 / 5.4893%	105.4893
	100.000 / 4.9817%	4.9817	
		100.000 / 5.1508%	105.1508

---

10   CONVERTIBLE BONDS

☐ | describe defining features of a convertible bond
☐ | calculate and interpret the components of a convertible bond's value

So far, we have discussed bonds for which the exercise of the option is at the discretion of the issuer (callable bond), at the discretion of the bondholder (putable bond), or set through a pre-defined contractual arrangement (capped and floored floaters). What distinguishes a convertible bond from the bonds discussed earlier is that exercising the option results in the change of the security from a bond to a common stock. This section describes defining features of convertible bonds and discusses how to analyze and value these bonds.

Defining Features of a Convertible Bond

A **convertible bond** presents the characteristics of an option-free bond and an embedded conversion option, which gives bondholders the right to convert their debt into equity during the **conversion period** at a pre-determined **conversion price**.

Investors usually accept a lower coupon for convertible bonds than for otherwise identical non-convertible bonds because they can participate in the potential upside through the conversion mechanism that allows the bondholders to convert their bonds into shares at a cost lower than market value. The issuer benefits from paying a lower coupon. In case of conversion, an added benefit for the issuer is that it no longer has to repay the debt that was converted into equity.

However, what might appear as a win–win situation for both the issuer and the investors is not a "free lunch" because the issuer's existing shareholders face dilution in case of conversion. In addition, if the underlying share price remains below the conversion price and the bond is not converted, the issuer must repay the debt or refinance it, potentially at a higher cost. If conversion is not achieved, the bondholders will have lost interest income relative to an otherwise identical non-convertible bond that would have been issued with a higher coupon and would have thus offered investors an additional spread.

We will use the information provided in Exhibit 28 to describe the features of a convertible bond and then illustrate how to analyze it. Exhibit 28 is based on a $1 billion convertible bond issued in June 2018 by Twitter, Inc. (TWTR), a company listed on the New York Stock Exchange. Some features of the actual convertible bond, such as the presence of a make-whole call option, have been dropped for simplicity.

Exhibit 28: Twitter, Inc., $1 billion, 0.25% Convertible Bonds Due 15 June 2024

- **Issue Date:** 11 June 2018
- **Ranking:** Senior unsecured
- **Interest:** 0.25% per year. Interest will accrue from 11 June 2018 and will be payable semiannually in arrears on 15 June and 15 December of each year, beginning on 15 December 2018.
- **Issue Price:** 100% of par value
- **Maturity:** 15 June 2024
- **Conversion Rate:** Each bond of par value of $1,000 is convertible to 17.5 shares of common stock.
- **Conversion Price:** $57.14 per share
- **Share Price at Issuance:** $40.10
- (Assumed) **Share Price on 15 June 2019:** $35.14
- (Assumed) **Convertible Bond Price on 15 June 2019:** 95.225% of par value
- **Conversion Premium:** 42.5%

The applicable share price at which the investor can convert the bonds into ordinary (common) shares is called the conversion price. In the Twitter example provided in Exhibit 28, the conversion price is $57.14 per share.

The number of shares of common stock that the bondholder receives from converting the bonds into shares is called the **conversion rate (or ratio)**. In the Twitter example, bondholders who hold $10,000 in par value can convert their bonds into shares and receive 175 shares ($10,000/$57.14). The conversion rate is 17.5 per $1,000 in par value. The conversion may be exercised during a particular period or at set intervals during the life of the bond.

The conversion price in Exhibit 28 is referred to as the *initial* conversion price because it reflects the conversion price *at issuance*. Corporate actions—such as stock splits, bonus share issuances, and rights or warrants issuances—affect a company's share price and may reduce the benefit of conversion for the convertible bondholders. Thus, the terms of issuance of the convertible bond contain detailed information defining how the conversion price and conversion ratio are adjusted should such a corporate action occur during the life of the bond. For example, suppose that Twitter performs a 2:1 stock split to its common shareholders. In this case, the conversion price would be adjusted to $28.57 (i.e., $57.14/2) per share and the conversion rate adjusted to 35 (i.e., 17.5 × 2) shares per $1,000 of nominal value.

As long as the convertible bond is still outstanding and has not been converted, the bondholders receive interest payments (semiannually in the Twitter example). Meanwhile, if the issuer declares and pays dividends, common shareholders receive dividend payments. The terms of issuance may offer no compensation to convertible bondholders for dividends paid out during the life of the bond at one extreme, or they may offer full protection by adjusting the conversion price downward for any dividend payments at the other extreme. Typically, a threshold dividend is defined in the terms of issuance. Annual dividend payments below the threshold dividend have no effect on the conversion price. In contrast, the conversion price is adjusted downward for annual dividend payments above the threshold dividend to offer compensation to convertible bondholders.

Should the issuer be acquired by or merged with another company during the life of the bond, bondholders might no longer be willing to continue lending to the new entity. Change-of-control events are defined in the prospectus or offering circular, and if such an event occurs, convertible bondholders usually have the choice between

- a put option that can be exercised during a specified period following the change-of-control event and that provides full redemption of the nominal value of the bond; or
- an adjusted conversion price that is lower than the initial conversion price. This downward adjustment gives the convertible bondholders the opportunity to convert their bonds into shares earlier and at more advantageous terms—thus allowing them to participate in the announced merger or acquisition as common shareholders.

In addition to a put option in case of a change-of-control event, it is not unusual for a convertible bond to include a put option that convertible bondholders can exercise during specified periods. Put options can be classified as "hard" puts or "soft" puts. In the case of a hard put, the issuer must redeem the convertible bond for cash. In the case of a soft put, the investor has the right to exercise the put but the issuer chooses how the payment will be made. The issuer may redeem the convertible bond for cash, common stock, subordinated notes, or a combination of the three.

It is more frequent for convertible bonds to include a call option that gives the issuer the right to call the bond during a specified period and at specified times. As discussed earlier, the issuer may exercise the call option and redeem the bond early if interest rates are falling or if its credit rating is revised upward—thus enabling the issuance of debt at a lower cost. The issuer may also believe that its share price will increase significantly in the future because of its performance or because of events that will take place in the economy or in its sector. In this case, the issuer may try to maximize the benefit to its existing shareholders relative to convertible bondholders and call the bond. To offer convertible bondholders protection against early repayment, convertible bonds usually have a protection period. Subsequently, they can be called but at a premium, which decreases as the maturity of the bond approaches.

If a convertible bond is callable, the issuer has an incentive to call the bond when the underlying share price increases above the conversion price in order to avoid paying further coupons. Such an event is called **forced conversion** because it forces bondholders to convert their bonds into shares. Otherwise, the redemption value that bondholders would receive from the issuer calling the bond would result in a disadvantageous position and a loss compared with conversion. Even if interest rates have not fallen or the issuer's credit rating has not improved, thus not allowing refinancing at a lower cost, the issuer might still proceed with calling the bond when the underlying share price exceeds the conversion price. Doing so allows the issuer to take advantage of the favorable equity market conditions and force the bondholders to convert their bonds into shares. The forced conversion strengthens the issuer's capital structure and eliminates the risk that a subsequent correction in equity prices prevents conversion and requires redeeming the convertible bonds at maturity.

Analysis of a Convertible Bond

A number of investment metrics and ratios help analyze and value a convertible bond.

Conversion Value

The **conversion value**, or parity value, of a convertible bond indicates the value of the bond if it is converted at the market price of the shares.

Conversion value = Underlying share price × Conversion ratio.

Based on the information provided in Exhibit 28, we can calculate the conversion value for Twitter's convertible bonds at the issuance date and on 15 June 2019 (*Note: The assumed prices actually pertain to 11 April 2019 to simplify the calculation of the straight bond values as there are then five full years to maturity*):

Conversion value at the issuance date = $40.10 × 17.5 = $701.75.

Conversion value on 15 June 2019 = $35.14 × 17.5 = $614.95.

Minimum Value of a Convertible Bond

The minimum value of a convertible bond is equal to the greater of

- the conversion value and
- the value of the underlying option-free bond. Theoretically, the value of the straight bond (straight value) can be estimated by using the market value of a non-convertible bond of the issuer with the same characteristics as the convertible bond but without the conversion option. In practice, such a bond rarely exists. Thus, the straight value is found by using the arbitrage-free framework and by discounting the bond's future cash flows at the appropriate rates.

The minimum value of a convertible bond can also be described as a floor value. It is a *moving* floor, however, because the straight value is not fixed; it changes with fluctuations in interest rates and credit spreads. If interest rates rise, the value of the straight bond falls, making the floor fall. Similarly, if the issuer's credit spread increases—as a result, for example, of a downgrade of its credit rating from investment grade to non-investment grade—the floor value will fall too.

Using the conversion values calculated earlier, the minimum value of Twitter's convertible bonds at the issuance date is

Minimum value at the issuance date = Maximum ($701.75; $1,000)

= $1,000.

The straight value at the issuance date is $1,000 because the issue price is set at 100% of par. But after this date, this value will fluctuate. Thus, to calculate the minimum value of Twitter's convertible bond on 15 June 2019, it is first necessary to calculate the value of the straight bond that day using the arbitrage-free framework. From Exhibit 28, the coupon is 0.25%, paid semiannually. Assuming a 2.5% flat yield curve, the straight value on 15 June 2019 when five years remain until maturity is $894.86 per $1,000 in par value:

$$\frac{\$1.25}{\left(1+\frac{0.025}{2}\right)^1} + \frac{\$1.25}{\left(1+\frac{0.025}{2}\right)^2} + \dots + \frac{\$1,001.25}{\left(1+\frac{0.025}{2}\right)^{10}} = \$894.86.$$

It follows that the minimum value of Twitter's convertible bonds on 15 June 2019 is:

Minimum value = Maximum ($614.95; $894.86) = $894.86.

If the value of the convertible bond were lower than the greater of the conversion value and the straight value, an arbitrage opportunity would ensue. Two scenarios help illustrate this concept. Returning to the Twitter example, suppose that the convertible bond is selling for $850.00 on 15 June 2019—that is, at a price that is lower than the straight value of $894.86. In this scenario, the convertible bond is cheap relative to the straight bond; put another way, the convertible bond offers a higher yield than an otherwise identical non-convertible bond. Thus, investors will find the convertible bond attractive, buy it, and push its price up until the convertible bond price returns to the straight value and the arbitrage opportunity disappears.

Alternatively, assume that on 15 June 2019 the yield on otherwise identical non-convertible bonds is 12.00% instead of 2.50%. Using the arbitrage-free framework, the straight value is $567.59 per $1,000 in par value. Suppose that the convertible bond is selling at this straight value—that is, at a price that is lower than its conversion value of $614.95. In this case, an arbitrageur can buy the convertible bond for $567.59, convert it into 17.5 shares, and sell the shares at $35.14 each or $614.95 in total. The arbitrageur makes a profit equal to the difference between the conversion value and the straight value—that is, $47.36 ($614.95 – $567.59). As more arbitrageurs follow the same strategy, the convertible bond price will increase until it reaches the conversion value and the arbitrage opportunity disappears.

Market Conversion Price, Market Conversion Premium per Share, and Market Conversion Premium Ratio

Many investors do not buy a convertible bond at issuance on the primary market but instead buy such a bond later in its life on the secondary market. The **market conversion premium per share** allows investors to identify the premium or discount payable when buying the convertible bond rather than the underlying common stock:

Market conversion premium per share

$$= \text{Market conversion price} - \text{Underlying share price,}$$

where

$$\text{Market conversion price} = \frac{\text{Convertible bond price}}{\text{Conversion ratio}}.$$

The market conversion price represents the price that investors effectively pay for the underlying common stock if they buy the convertible bond and then convert it into shares. It can be viewed as a break-even price. Once the underlying share price exceeds the market conversion price, any further rise in the underlying share price is certain to increase the value of the convertible bond by at least the same percentage (we will discuss why at a later stage).

Based on the information provided in Exhibit 28,

$$\text{Market conversion price on 15 June 2019} = \frac{\$952.25}{17.5} = \$54.40$$

and

Market conversion premium per share on 15 June 2019

$$= \$54.40 - \$35.14$$

$$= \$19.26.$$

The **market conversion premium ratio** expresses the premium, or discount, investors have to pay as a percentage of the current market price of the shares:

$$\text{Market conversion premium ratio} = \frac{\text{Market conversion premium per share}}{\text{Underlying share price}}.$$

In the Twitter example,

$$\text{Market conversion premium ratio on 15 June 2019} = \frac{\$19.26}{\$35.14}$$

$$= 54.8\%.$$

Why would investors be willing to pay a premium to buy the convertible bond? Recall that the straight value acts as a floor for the convertible bond price. Thus, as the underlying share price falls, the convertible bond price will not fall below the straight value. Viewed in this context, the market conversion premium per share resembles the price of a call option. Investors who buy a call option limit their downside risk to the price of the call option (premium). Similarly, the premium paid when buying a convertible bond allows investors to limit their downside risk to the straight value. There is a fundamental difference, however, between the buyers of a call option and the buyers of a convertible bond. The former know exactly the amount of the downside risk, whereas the latter know only that the most they can lose is the difference between the convertible bond price and the straight value because the straight value is not fixed.

Market conversion discounts per share are rare, but they can theoretically happen given that the convertible bond and the underlying common stock trade in different markets with different types of market participants. For example, highly volatile share prices may result in the market conversion price being lower than the underlying share price.

Downside Risk with a Convertible Bond

Many investors use the straight value as a measure of the downside risk of a convertible bond and calculate the following metric:

$$\text{Premium over straight value} = \frac{\text{Convertible bond price}}{\text{Straight value}} - 1.$$

All else being equal, the higher the premium over straight value, the less attractive the convertible bond. In the Twitter example,

$$Premium\,over\,straight\,value = \frac{\$952.25}{\$894.86}$$

$$= 6.41\%$$

Despite its use in practice, the premium over straight value is a flawed measure of downside risk because, as mentioned earlier, the straight value is not fixed but rather fluctuates with changes in interest rates and credit spreads.

Upside Potential of a Convertible Bond

The upside potential of a convertible bond depends primarily on the prospects of the underlying common stock. Thus, convertible bond investors should be familiar with the techniques used to value and analyze common stocks. These techniques are covered elsewhere.

COMPARISON OF RISK–RETURN CHARACTERISTICS 11

- [ ] describe how a convertible bond is valued in an arbitrage-free framework
- [ ] compare the risk–return characteristics of a convertible bond with the risk–return characteristics of a straight bond and of the underlying common stock

Historically, the valuation of convertible bonds has been challenging because these securities combine characteristics of bonds, stocks, and options—thus requiring an understanding of what affects the value of fixed income, equity, and derivatives. The complexity of convertible bonds has also increased over time as a result of market innovations and additions to the terms and conditions of these securities. For example, there are now contingent convertible bonds and convertible contingent convertible bonds, which are even more complex to value and analyze.

CONTINGENT CONVERTIBLES

Contingent convertible bonds, or "CoCos," pay a higher coupon than otherwise identical non-convertible bonds; however, they usually are deeply subordinated and may be converted into equity or face principal write-downs if regulatory capital ratios are breached. Convertible contingent convertible bonds, or "CoCoCos," combine a traditional convertible bond and a CoCo. They are convertible at the discretion of the investor, thus offering upside potential if the share price increases. They are also converted into equity or face principal write-downs in the event of a regulatory capital breach. CoCos and CoCoCos are usually issued by financial institutions, particularly in Europe.

The fact that many bond's prospectuses or offering circulars frequently provide for an independent financial valuer to determine the conversion price (and, in essence, the value of the convertible bond) under different scenarios is evidence of the complexity associated with valuing convertible bonds. Because of this complexity, convertible bonds in many markets come with selling restrictions. They are typically offered in very high denominations and only to professional or institutional investors. Regulators perceive them as securities that are too risky for retail investors to invest in directly.

As with any fixed-income instrument, convertible bond investors should perform a diligent risk–reward analysis of the issuer, including its ability to service the debt and repay the principal, as well as a review of the bond's terms of issuance (e.g., collateral, credit enhancements, covenants, and contingent provisions). In addition, convertible bond investors must analyze the factors that typically affect bond prices, such as interest rate movements. Because most convertible bonds have lighter covenants than otherwise similar non-convertible bonds and are frequently issued as subordinated securities, the valuation and analysis of some convertible bonds can be complex.

The investment characteristics of a convertible bond depend on the underlying share price, so convertible bond investors must also analyze factors that may affect the issuer's common stock, including dividend payments and the issuer's actions (e.g., acquisitions or disposals, rights issues). Even if the issuer is performing well, adverse market conditions might depress share prices and prevent conversion. Thus, convertible bond investors must also identify and analyze the exogenous reasons that might ultimately have a negative effect on convertible bonds.

Academics and practitioners have developed advanced models to value convertible bonds, but the most commonly used model remains the arbitrage-free framework. A traditional convertible bond can be viewed as a straight bond and a call option on the issuer's common stock, so

Value of convertible bond

= Value of straight bond + Value of call option on the issuer's stock.

Many convertible bonds include a call option that gives the issuer the right to call the bond during a specified period and at specified times. The value of such bonds is

Value of callable convertible bond

= Value of straight bond + Value of call option on the issuer's stock − Value of issuer call option.

Suppose that the callable convertible bond also includes a put option that gives the bondholder the right to require that the issuer repurchase the bond. The value of such a bond is

Value of callable putable convertible bond

= Value of straight bond + Value of call option on the issuer's stock − Value of issuer call option + Value of investor put option.

No matter how many options are embedded into a bond, the valuation procedure remains the same. It relies on generating a tree of interest rates based on the given yield curve and interest rate volatility assumptions, determining at each node of the tree whether the embedded options will be exercised, and then applying the backward induction valuation methodology to calculate the present value of the bond.

Comparison of the Risk–Return Characteristics of a Convertible Bond, the Straight Bond, and the Underlying Common Stock

In its simplest form, a convertible bond can be viewed as a straight bond and a call option on the issuer's common stock. When the underlying share price is well below the conversion price, the convertible bond is described as "busted convertible" and exhibits mostly bond risk–return characteristics. That is, the risk–return characteristics of the convertible bond resemble those of the underlying option-free (straight) bond. In this case, the call option is out of the money, so share price movements do not significantly affect the price of the call option and, thus, the price of the convertible bond. Consequently, the price movement of the convertible bond closely follows that of the straight bond, and such factors as interest rate movements and credit spreads significantly affect the convertible bond price. As the share price approaches zero, the value of the bond will fall to approach the present value of the recovery rate in bankruptcy. The convertible bond exhibits even stronger bond risk–return characteristics when the call option is out of the money and the conversion period is approaching its end because the time value component of the option decreases toward zero, making it highly likely that the conversion option will expire worthless. This scenario is shown in Exhibit 29 on the left.

In contrast, when the underlying share price is above the conversion price, a convertible bond exhibits mostly stock risk–return characteristics (see the right-hand side of Exhibit 29). That is, the risk–return characteristics of the convertible bond resemble those of the underlying common stock. In this case, the call option is in the money, so the price of the call option—and thus the price of the convertible bond—is significantly affected by share price movements but mostly unaffected by factors driving the value of an otherwise identical option-free bond, such as interest rate movements. When the call option is in the money, it is more likely to be exercised by the bondholder and the value of the shares resulting from the conversion is higher than the redemption value of the bond. Such convertible bonds trade at prices that closely follow the conversion value of the convertible bond, and their price exhibits similar movements to that of the underlying stock.

In between the bond and the stock extremes, the call option component increases in value as the underlying share price approaches the conversion price. The return on the convertible bond during such periods increases significantly but at a lower rate than the increase in the underlying share price because the conversion price has not yet been reached. When the share price exceeds the conversion price and goes higher, the change in the convertible bond price converges toward the change in the underlying share price. This is why we noted earlier that when the underlying share price exceeds the market conversion price, any further rise in the underlying share price is certain to increase the value of the convertible bond by at least the same percentage.

The change in the convertible bond price is less than the change in the stock price because the convertible bond has a floor

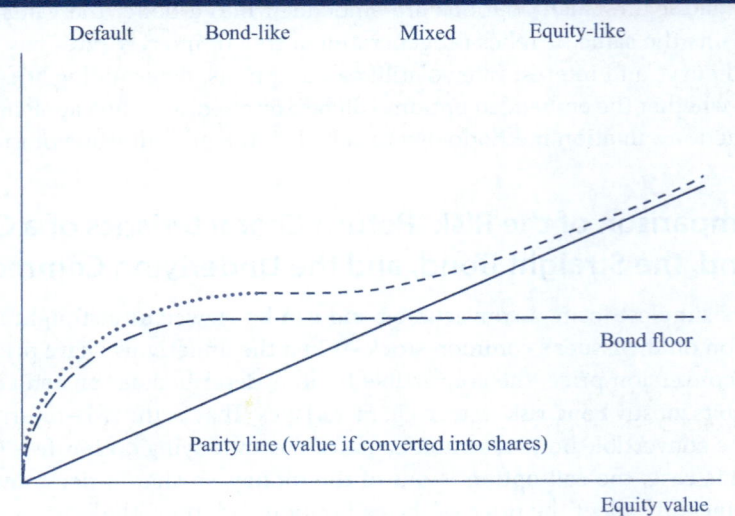

Exhibit 29: Price Behavior of a Convertible Bond and the Underlying Common Stock

Why would an investor not exercise the conversion option when the underlying share price is above the conversion price? The call option on the issuer's common stock may be a European-style option that cannot be exercised now but only at the end of a pre-determined period. Even if the call option is an American-style option, making it possible to convert the bond into equity, it may not be optimal for the convertible bondholder to exercise prior to the expiry of the conversion period. As discussed earlier, it is sometimes better to wait than to exercise an option that is in the money. The investor may also prefer to sell the convertible bond instead of exercising the conversion option.

Except for busted convertibles, the most important factor in the valuation of convertible bonds is the underlying share price. However, it is worth mentioning that large movements in interest rates or in credit spreads may significantly affect the value of convertible bonds. For a convertible bond with a fixed coupon, all else being equal, a significant fall in interest rates would result in an increase in its value and price, whereas a significant rise in interest rates would lead in a decrease in its value and price. Similarly, all else being equal, a significant improvement in the issuer's credit quality would result in an increase in the value and price of its convertible bonds, whereas a deterioration of the issuer's credit quality would lead to a decrease in the value and price of its convertible bonds.

EXAMPLE 9

Valuation of Convertible Bonds

Nick Andrews, a fixed-income investment analyst, has been asked by his supervisor to prepare an analysis of the convertible bond issued by Heavy Element Inc., a chemical industry company, for presentation to the investment committee. Andrews has gathered the following data from the convertible bond's prospectus and market information:

Issuer: Heavy Element Inc.

Issue Date: 15 September 2020

Maturity Date: 15 September 2025

Interest: 3.75% payable annually

Issue Size: $100,000,000

Issue Price: $1,000 at par

Conversion Ratio: 23.26

Convertible Bond Price on 16 September 2022: $1,230

Share Price on 16 September 2022: $52

1. The conversion price is *closest to*:

   A. $19.

   B. $43.

   C. $53.

Solution:

B is correct. The conversion price is equal to the par value of the convertible bond divided by the conversion ratio—that is, $1,000/23.26 = $43 per share.

2. The conversion value on 16 September 2022 is *closest to*:

   A. $24.

   B. $230.

   C. $1,209.

Solution:

C is correct. The conversion value is equal to the underlying share price multiplied by the conversion ratio—that is, $52 × 23.26 = $1,209.

3. The market conversion premium per share on 16 September 2022 is *closest to*:

   A. $0.88.

   B. $2.24.

   C. $9.00.

Solution:

A is correct. The market conversion premium per share is equal to the convertible bond price divided by the conversion ratio, minus the underlying share price—that is, ($1,230/23.26) − $52 = $52.88 − $52 = $0.88.

4. The risk–return characteristics of the convertible bond on 16 September 2022 *most likely* resemble that of:

   A. a busted convertible.

   B. Heavy Element's common stock.

   C. a bond of Heavy Element that is identical to the convertible bond but without the conversion option.

Solution:

B is correct. The underlying share price ($52) is well above the conversion price ($43). Thus, the convertible bond exhibits risk–return characteristics that are similar to those of the underlying common stock. A is incorrect because a busted convertible is a convertible bond for which the underlying common stock trades at a significant discount relative to the conversion price. C is incorrect because it describes a busted convertible.

5. As a result of favorable economic conditions, credit spreads for the chemical industry narrow, resulting in lower interest rates for the debt of such companies as Heavy Element. All else being equal, the price of Heavy Element's convertible bond will *most likely*:

   A. decrease significantly.
   B. not change significantly.
   C. increase significantly.

Solution:

B is correct. The underlying share price ($52) is well above the conversion price ($43). Thus, the convertible bond exhibits mostly stock risk–return characteristics, and its price is mainly driven by the underlying share price. Consequently, the decrease in credit spreads will have little effect on the convertible bond price.

6. Suppose that on 16 September 2022 the convertible bond is available in the secondary market at a price of $1,050. An arbitrageur can make a risk-free profit by:

   A. buying the underlying common stock and shorting the convertible bond.
   B. buying the convertible bond, exercising the conversion option, and selling the shares resulting from the conversion.
   C. shorting the convertible bond and buying a call option on the underlying common stock exercisable at the conversion price on the conversion date.

Solution:

B is correct. The convertible bond price ($1,050) is lower than its minimum value ($1,209). Thus, the arbitrageur can buy the convertible bond for $1,050; convert it into 23.26 shares; and sell the shares at $52 each, or $1,209 in total, making a profit of $159. A and C are incorrect because in both scenarios, the arbitrageur is short the underpriced asset (convertible bond) and long an overpriced asset, resulting in a loss.

7. A few months have passed. Because of chemical spills in lake water at the site of a competing facility, the government has introduced very costly environmental legislation. As a result, share prices of almost all publicly traded chemical companies, including Heavy Element, have decreased sharply. Heavy Element's share price is now $28. Now, the risk–return characteristics of the convertible bond *most likely* resemble that of:

   A. a bond.
   B. a hybrid instrument.

    C. Heavy Element's common stock.

Solution:

A is correct. The underlying share price ($28) is now well below the conversion price ($43), so the convertible bond is a busted convertible and exhibits mostly bond risk–return characteristics. B is incorrect because the underlying share price would have to be close to the conversion price for the risk–return characteristics of the convertible bond to resemble that of a hybrid instrument. C is incorrect because the underlying share price would have to be in excess of the conversion price for the risk–return characteristics of the convertible bond to resemble that of the company's common stock.

SUMMARY

- An embedded option represents a right that can be exercised by the issuer, by the bondholder, or automatically depending on the course of interest rates. It is attached to, or embedded in, an underlying option-free bond called a straight bond.

- Simple embedded option structures include call options, put options, and extension options. Callable and putable bonds can be redeemed prior to maturity, at the discretion of the issuer in the former case and of the bondholder in the latter case. An extendible bond gives the bondholder the right to keep the bond for a number of years after maturity. Putable and extendible bonds are equivalent, except that their underlying option-free bonds are different.

- Complex embedded option structures include bonds with other types of options or combinations of options. For example, a convertible bond includes a conversion option that allows the bondholders to convert their bonds into the issuer's common stock. A bond with an estate put can be put by the heirs of a deceased bondholder. Sinking fund bonds make the issuer set aside funds over time to retire the bond issue and are often callable, may have an acceleration provision, and may also contain a delivery option. Valuing and analyzing bonds with complex embedded option structures is challenging.

- According to the arbitrage-free framework, the value of a bond with an embedded option is equal to the arbitrage-free values of its parts—that is, the arbitrage-free value of the straight bond and the arbitrage-free values of each of the embedded options.

- Because the call option is an issuer option, the value of the call option decreases the value of the callable bond relative to an otherwise identical but non-callable bond. In contrast, because the put option is an investor option, the value of the put option increases the value of the putable bond relative to an otherwise identical but non-putable bond.

- In the absence of default and interest rate volatility, the bond's future cash flows are certain. Thus, the value of a callable or putable bond can be calculated by discounting the bond's future cash flows at the appropriate one-period forward rates, taking into consideration the decision to exercise the option. If a bond is callable, the decision to exercise the option is made by the issuer, which will exercise the call option when the value of the bond's future cash flows is higher than the call price. In contrast, if the bond is putable, the decision to exercise the option is made by the bondholder, who will exercise the put option when the value of the bond's future cash flows is lower than the put price.

- In practice, interest rates fluctuate and interest rate volatility affects the value of embedded options. Thus, when valuing bonds with embedded options, it is important to consider the possible evolution of the yield curve over time.

- Interest rate volatility is modeled using a binomial interest rate tree. The higher the volatility, the lower the value of the callable bond and the higher the value of the putable bond.

- Valuing a bond with embedded options assuming an interest rate volatility requires three steps: (1) Generate a tree of interest rates based on the given yield curve and volatility assumptions; (2) at each node of the tree, determine whether the embedded options will be exercised; and (3) apply the backward induction valuation methodology to calculate the present value of the bond.

- The option-adjusted spread is the single spread added uniformly to the one-period forward rates on the tree to produce a value or price for a bond. OAS is sensitive to interest rate volatility: The higher the volatility, the lower the OAS for a callable bond.

- For bonds with embedded options, the best measure to assess the sensitivity of the bond's price to a parallel shift of the benchmark yield curve is effective duration. The effective duration of a callable or putable bond cannot exceed that of the straight bond.

- When the option is near the money, the convexity of a callable bond is negative, indicating that the upside for a callable bond is much smaller than the downside, whereas the convexity of a putable bond is positive, indicating that the upside for a putable bond is much larger than the downside.

- Because the prices of callable and putable bonds respond asymmetrically to upward and downward interest rate changes of the same magnitude, one-sided durations provide a better indication regarding the interest rate sensitivity of bonds with embedded options than (two-sided) effective duration.

- Key rate durations show the effect of shifting only key points, one at a time, rather than the entire yield curve.

- The arbitrage-free framework can be used to value capped and floored floaters. The cap provision in a floater is an issuer option that prevents the coupon rate from increasing above a specified maximum rate. Thus, the value of a capped floater is equal to or less than the value of the straight bond. In contrast, the floor provision in a floater is an investor option that prevents the coupon from decreasing below a specified minimum rate. Thus, the value of a floored floater is equal to or higher than the value of the straight bond.

- The characteristics of a convertible bond include the conversion price, which is the applicable share price at which the bondholders can convert their bonds into common shares, and the conversion ratio, which reflects the number of shares of common stock that the bondholders receive from converting their bonds into shares. The conversion price is adjusted in case of corporate actions, such as stock splits, bonus share issuances, and rights and warrants issuances. Convertible bondholders may receive compensation when the issuer pays dividends to its common shareholders, and they may be given the opportunity to either put their bonds or convert their bonds into shares earlier and at more advantageous terms in the case of a change of control.

- A number of investment metrics and ratios help analyze and value convertible bonds. The conversion value indicates the value of the bond if it is converted at the market price of the shares. The minimum value of a convertible bond sets a floor value for the convertible bond at the greater of the conversion value or the straight value. This floor is moving, however, because the straight value is not fixed. The market conversion premium represents the price investors effectively pay for the underlying shares if they buy the convertible bond and then convert it into shares. Scaled by the market price of the shares, it represents the premium payable when buying the convertible bond rather than the underlying common stock.

- Because convertible bonds combine characteristics of bonds, stocks, and options, as well as potentially other features, their valuation and analysis are challenging. Convertible bond investors should consider the factors that affect not only bond prices but also the underlying share price.

- The arbitrage-free framework can be used to value convertible bonds, including callable and putable ones. Each component (straight bond, call option of the stock, and call and/or put option on the bond) can be valued separately.

- The risk–return characteristics of a convertible bond depend on the underlying share price relative to the conversion price. When the underlying share price is well below the conversion price, the convertible bond is "busted" and exhibits mostly bond risk–return characteristics. Thus, it is mainly sensitive to interest rate movements. In contrast, when the underlying share price is well above the conversion price, the convertible bond exhibits mostly stock risk–return characteristics. Thus, its price follows similar movements to the price of the underlying stock. In between these two extremes, the convertible bond trades like a hybrid instrument.

PRACTICE PROBLEMS

The following information relates to questions 1-10

Samuel & Sons is a fixed-income specialty firm that offers advisory services to investment management companies. On 1 October 20X0, Steele Ferguson, a senior analyst at Samuel, is reviewing three fixed-rate bonds issued by a local firm, Pro Star, Inc. The three bonds, whose characteristics are given in Exhibit 30, carry the highest credit rating.

Exhibit 1: Fixed-Rate Bonds Issued by Pro Star, Inc.

Bond	Maturity	Coupon	Type of Bond
Bond #1	1 October 20X3	4.40% annual	Option-free
Bond #2	1 October 20X3	4.40% annual	Callable at par on 1 October 20X1 and on 1 October 20X2
Bond #3	1 October 20X3	4.40% annual	Putable at par on 1 October 20X1 and on 1 October 20X2

The one-year, two-year, and three-year par rates are 2.250%, 2.750%, and 3.100%, respectively. Based on an estimated interest rate volatility of 10%, Ferguson constructs the binomial interest rate tree shown in Exhibit 31.

Exhibit 2: Binomial Interest Rate Tree

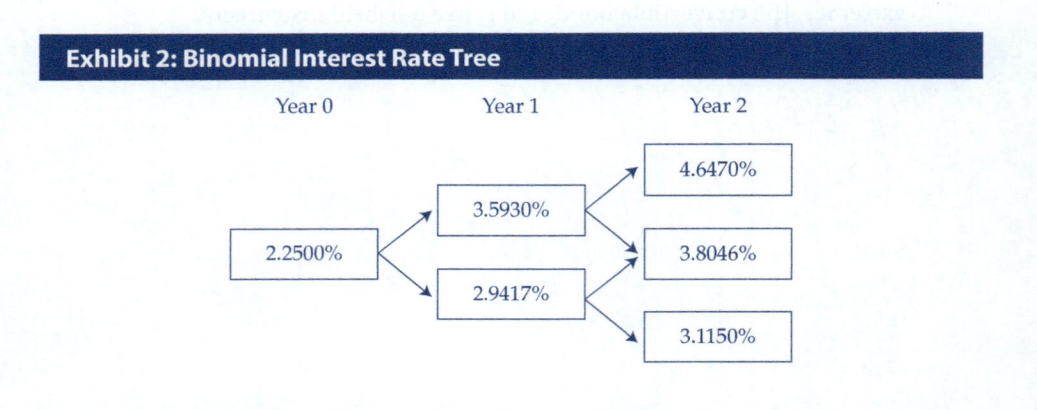

On 19 October 20X0, Ferguson analyzes the convertible bond issued by Pro Star given in Exhibit 32. That day, the option-free value of Pro Star's convertible bond is $1,060 and its stock price $37.50.

Exhibit 3: Convertible Bond Issued by Pro Star, Inc.	
Issue Date:	6 December 20X0
Maturity Date:	6 December 20X4
Coupon Rate:	2%
Issue Price:	$1,000
Conversion Ratio:	31

1. The call feature of Bond #2 is *best* described as:

   A. European style.

   B. American style.

   C. Bermudan style.

2. The bond that would *most likely* protect investors against a significant increase in interest rates is:

   A. Bond #1.

   B. Bond #2.

   C. Bond #3.

3. A fall in interest rates would *most likely* result in:

   A. a decrease in the effective duration of Bond #3.

   B. Bond #3 having more upside potential than Bond #2.

   C. a change in the effective convexity of Bond #3 from positive to negative.

4. The value of Bond #2 is *closest* to:

   A. 102.103% of par.

   B. 103.121% of par.

   C. 103.744% of par.

5. The value of Bond #3 is *closest* to:

   A. 102.103% of par.

   B. 103.688% of par.

   C. 103.744% of par.

6. All else being equal, a rise in interest rates will *most likely* result in the value of the option embedded in Bond #3:

   A. decreasing.

   B. remaining unchanged.

   C. increasing.

7. All else being equal, if Ferguson assumes an interest rate volatility of 15% instead of 10%, the bond that would *most likely* increase in value is:

   A. Bond #1.

   B. Bond #2.

   C. Bond #3.

8. All else being equal, if the shape of the yield curve changes from upward sloping to flattening, the value of the option embedded in Bond #2 will *most likely*:

   A. decrease.

   B. remain unchanged.

   C. increase.

9. The conversion price of the bond in Exhibit 32 is closest to:

   A. $26.67.

   B. $32.26.

   C. $34.19.

10. If the market price of Pro Star's common stock falls from its level on 19 October 20X0, the price of the convertible bond will *most likely*:

   A. fall at the same rate as Pro Star's stock price.

   B. fall but at a slightly lower rate than Pro Star's stock price.

   C. be unaffected until Pro Star's stock price reaches the conversion price.

The following information relates to questions 11-18

John Smith, an investment adviser, meets with Lydia Carter to discuss her pending retirement and potential changes to her investment portfolio. Domestic economic activity has been weakening recently, and Smith's outlook is that equity market values will be lower during the next year. He would like Carter to consider reducing her equity exposure in favor of adding more fixed-income securities to the portfolio.

Government yields have remained low for an extended period, and Smith suggests considering investment-grade corporate bonds to provide additional yield above government debt issues. In light of recent poor employment figures and two consecutive quarters of negative GDP growth, the consensus forecast among economists is that the central bank, at its next meeting this month, will take actions that will lead to lower interest rates.

Smith and Carter review par, spot, and one-year forward rates (Exhibit 1) and four fixed-rate investment-grade bonds issued by Alpha Corporation that are being considered for investment (Exhibit 2).

Exhibit 1: Par, Spot, and One-Year Forward Rates (annual coupon payments)

Maturity (Years)	Par Rate (%)	Spot Rate (%)	One-Year Forward (%)
1	1.0000	1.0000	1.0000
2	1.2000	1.2012	1.4028
3	1.2500	1.2515	1.3522

Exhibit 2: Selected Fixed-Rate Bonds of Alpha Corporation

Bond	Annual Coupon	Type of Bond
Bond 1	1.5500%	Straight bond
Bond 2	1.5500%	Convertible bond: currently trading out of the money
Bond 3	1.5500%	Putable bond: putable at par one year and two years from now
Bond 4	1.5500%	Callable bond: callable at par without any protection periods

Note: All bonds in Exhibit 2 have remaining maturities of exactly three years.

Carter tells Smith that the local news media have been reporting that housing starts, exports, and demand for consumer credit are all relatively strong, even in light of other poor macroeconomic indicators. Smith explains that the divergence in economic data leads him to believe that volatility in interest rates will increase. Smith also states that he recently read a report issued by Brown and Company forecasting that the yield curve could invert within the next six months.

Smith develops a binomial interest rate tree with a 15% interest rate volatility assumption to assess the value of Alpha Corporation's bonds. Exhibit 3 presents the interest rate tree.

Exhibit 3: Binomial Interest Rate Tree for Alpha Corporation with 15% Interest Rate Volatility

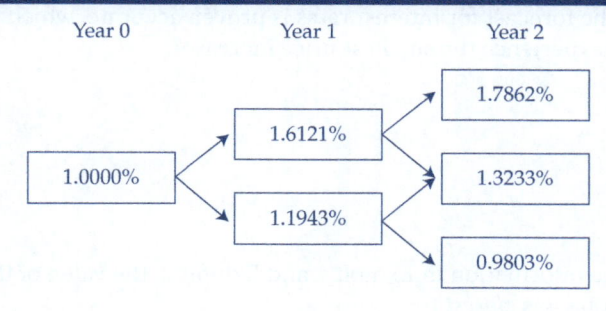

Carter asks Smith about the possibility of analyzing bonds that have lower credit ratings than the investment-grade Alpha bonds. Smith discusses four other corporate bonds with Carter. Exhibit 4 presents selected data on the four bonds.

Exhibit 4: Selected Information on Fixed-Rate Bonds for Beta, Gamma, Delta, and Rho Corporations

Bond	Issuer	Bond Features	Credit Rating
Bond 5	Beta Corporation	Coupon 1.70% Callable in Year 2 OAS of 45 bps	B
Bond 6	Gamma Corporation	Coupon 1.70% Callable in Year 2 OAS of 65 bps	B
Bond 7	Delta Corporation	Coupon 1.70% Callable in Year 2 OAS of 85 bps	B
Bond 8	Rho Corporation	Coupon 1.70% Callable in Year 2 OAS of 105 bps	CCC

Notes: All bonds have remaining maturities of three years. OAS stands for option-adjusted spread.

11. Based on Exhibit 2, and assuming that the forecast for interest rates and Smith's outlook for equity returns are validated, which bond's option is *most likely* to be exercised?

   A. Bond 2

   B. Bond 3

   C. Bond 4

12. Based on Exhibit 2, the current price of Bond 1 is *most likely* greater than the current price of:

   A. Bond 2.

   B. Bond 3.

   C. Bond 4.

13. Assuming the forecast for interest rates is proven accurate, which bond in Exhibit 2 will likely experience the smallest price increase?

   A. Bond 1

   B. Bond 3

   C. Bond 4

14. Based on the information in Exhibit 1 and Exhibit 2, the value of the embedded option in Bond 4 is *closest* to:

   A. nil.

   B. 0.1906.

   C. 0.8789.

15. If Smith's interest rate volatility forecast turns out to be true, which bond in Ex-

hibit 2 is likely to experience the greatest price increase?

A. Bond 2

B. Bond 3

C. Bond 4

16. If the Brown and Company forecast comes true, which of the following is *most* likely to occur? The value of the embedded option in:

A. Bond 3 decreases.

B. Bond 4 decreases.

C. both Bond 3 and Bond 4 increases.

17. Based on Exhibit 2 and Exhibit 3, the market price of Bond 4 is *closest* to:

A. 100.0000.

B. 100.5123.

C. 100.8790.

18. Which of the following conclusions regarding the bonds in Exhibit 4 is correct?

A. Bond 5 is relatively cheaper than Bond 6.

B. Bond 7 is relatively cheaper than Bond 6.

C. Bond 8 is relatively cheaper than Bond 7.

The following information relates to questions 19-27

Rayes Investment Advisers specializes in fixed-income portfolio management. Meg Rayes, the owner of the firm, would like to add bonds with embedded options to the firm's bond portfolio. Rayes has asked Mingfang Hsu, one of the firm's analysts, to assist her in selecting and analyzing bonds for possible inclusion in the firm's bond portfolio.

Hsu first selects two corporate bonds that are callable at par and have the same characteristics in terms of maturity, credit quality, and call dates. Hsu uses the option adjusted spread (OAS) approach to analyze the bonds, assuming an interest rate volatility of 10%. The results of his analysis are presented in Exhibit 1.

Exhibit 1: Summary Results of Hsu's Analysis Using the OAS Approach

Bond	OAS (in bps)
Bond #1	25.5
Bond #2	30.3

Hsu then selects the four bonds issued by RW, Inc., given in Exhibit 2. These bonds all have a maturity of three years and the same credit rating. Bonds #4 and #5 are identical to Bond #3, an option-free bond, except that they each include an embedded option.

Exhibit 2: Bonds Issued by RW, Inc.

Bond	Coupon	Special Provision
Bond #3	4.00% annual	
Bond #4	4.00% annual	Callable at par at the end of years 1 and 2
Bond #5	4.00% annual	Putable at par at the end of years 1 and 2
Bond #6	One-year reference rate annually, set in arrears	

To value and analyze RW's bonds, Hsu uses an estimated interest rate volatility of 15% and constructs the binomial interest rate tree provided in Exhibit 3.

Exhibit 3: Binomial Interest Rate Tree Used to Value RW's Bonds

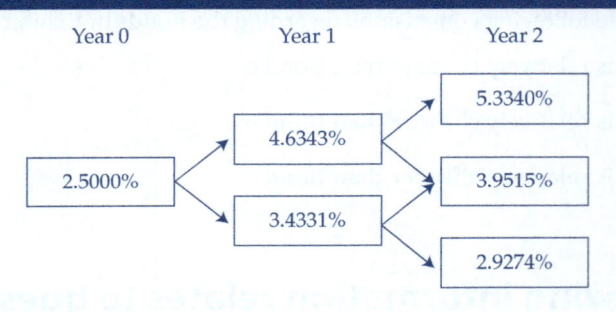

Rayes asks Hsu to determine the sensitivity of Bond #4's price to a 20 bps parallel shift of the benchmark yield curve. The results of Hsu's calculations are shown in Exhibit 40.

Exhibit 4: Summary Results of Hsu's Analysis about the Sensitivity of Bond #4's Price to a Parallel Shift of the Benchmark Yield Curve

	+20 bps	−20 bps
Magnitude of the Parallel Shift in the Benchmark Yield Curve		
Full Price of Bond #4 (% of par)	100.478	101.238

Hsu also selects the two floating-rate bonds issued by Varlep, plc, given in Exhibit 41. These bonds have a maturity of three years and the same credit rating.

Exhibit 5: Floating-Rate Bonds Issued by Varlep, plc	
Bond	**Coupon**
Bond #7	One-year reference rate annually, set in arrears, capped at 5.00%
Bond #8	One-year reference rate annually, set in arrears, floored at 3.50%

To value Varlep's bonds, Hsu constructs the binomial interest rate tree provided in Exhibit 42.

Exhibit 6: Binomial Interest Rate Tree Used to Value Varlep's Bonds

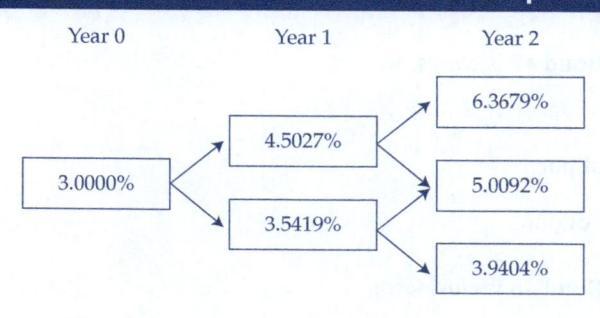

Last, Hsu selects the two bonds issued by Whorton, Inc., given in Exhibit 43. These bonds are close to their maturity date and are identical, except that Bond #9 includes a conversion option. Whorton's common stock is currently trading at $30 per share.

Exhibit 7: Bonds Issued by Whorton, Inc.	
Bond	**Type of Bond**
Bond #9	Convertible bond with a conversion price of $50
Bond #10	Identical to Bond #9 except that it does not include a conversion option

19. Based on Exhibit 1, Rayes would *most likely* conclude that relative to Bond #1, Bond #2 is:

    A. overpriced.

    B. fairly priced.

    C. underpriced.

20. The effective duration of Bond #6 is:

    A. close to 1.

    B. higher than 1 but lower than 3.

    C. higher than 3.

21. In Exhibit 2, the bond whose effective duration might lengthen if interest rates

rise is:

A. Bond #3.

B. Bond #4.

C. Bond #5.

22. The effective duration of Bond #4 is *closest* to:

A. 0.76.

B. 1.88.

C. 3.77.

23. The value of Bond #7 is *closest* to:

A. 99.697% of par.

B. 99.936% of par.

C. 101.153% of par.

24. The value of Bond #8 is *closest* to:

A. 98.116% of par.

B. 100.000% of par.

C. 100.485% of par.

25. The value of Bond #9 is equal to the value of Bond #10:

A. plus the value of a put option on Whorton's common stock.

B. plus the value of a call option on Whorton's common stock.

C. minus the value of a call option on Whorton's common stock.

26. The minimum value of Bond #9 is equal to the *greater* of:

A. the conversion value of Bond #9 and the current value of Bond #10.

B. the current value of Bond #10 and a call option on Whorton's common stock.

C. the conversion value of Bond #9 and a call option on Whorton's common stock.

27. The factor that is currently *least likely* to affect the risk–return characteristics of Bond #9 is:

A. interest rate movements.

B. Whorton's credit spreads.

C. Whorton's common stock price movements.

The following information relates to questions 28-36

Jules Bianchi is a bond analyst for Maneval Investments, Inc. Bianchi gathers data on three corporate bonds, as shown in Exhibit 1.

Exhibit 1: Selected Bond Data

Issuer	Coupon Rate	Price	Bond Description
Ayrault, Inc. (AI)	5.25%	100.200	Callable at par in one year and two years from today
Blum, Inc. (BI)	5.25%	101.300	Option-free
Cresson Enterprises (CE)	5.25%	102.100	Putable at par in one year from today

Note: Each bond has a remaining maturity of three years, annual coupon payments, and a credit rating of BBB.

To assess the interest rate risk of the three bonds, Bianchi constructs two binomial interest rate trees based on a 10% interest rate volatility assumption and a current one-year rate of 4%. Panel A of Exhibit 2 provides an interest rate tree assuming the benchmark yield curve shifts down by 30 bps, and Panel B provides an interest rate tree assuming the benchmark yield curve shifts up by 30 bps. Bianchi determines that the AI bond is currently trading at an option-adjusted spread (OAS) of 13.95 bps relative to the benchmark yield curve.

Exhibit 2: Binomial Interest Rate Trees

Interest Rates Shift Down by 30 bps

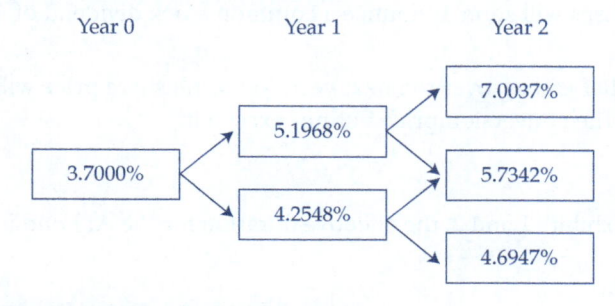

Interest Rates Shift Up by 30 bps

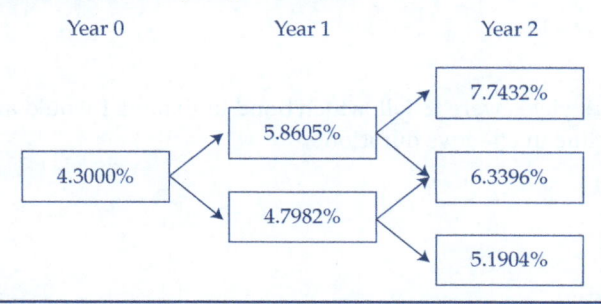

Armand Gillette, a convertible bond analyst, stops by Bianchi's office to discuss two convertible bonds. One is issued by DeLille Enterprises (DE), and the other is issued by Raffarin Incorporated (RI). Selected data for the two bonds are presented in Exhibits 3 and 4.

Exhibit 3: Selected Data for DE Convertible Bond

Issue price	€1,000 at par
Conversion period	13 September 20X5 to 12 September 20X8
Initial conversion price	€10.00 per share
Threshold dividend	€0.50 per share
Change of control conversion price	€8.00 per share
Common stock share price on issue date	€8.70
Share price on 17 September 20X5	€9.10
Convertible bond price on 17 September 20X5	€1,123

Exhibit 4: Selected Data for RI Convertible Bond

Straight bond value	€978
Value of embedded issuer call option	€43
Value of embedded investor put option	€26
Value of embedded call option on issuer's stock	€147
Conversion price	€12.50
Current common stock share price	€11.75

Gillette makes the following comments to Bianchi:

- "The DE bond does not contain any call or put options, but the RI bond contains both an embedded call option and put option. I expect that DeLille Enterprises will soon announce a common stock dividend of €0.70 per share."

- "My belief is that, over the next year, Raffarin's share price will appreciate toward the conversion price but not exceed it."

28. Based on Exhibits 1 and 2, the effective duration for the AI bond is *closest to*:

    A. 1.98.

    B. 2.15.

    C. 2.73.

29. If benchmark yields were to fall, which bond in Exhibit 1 would *most likely* experience a decline in effective duration?

    A. AI bond

    B. BI bond

    C. CE bond

30. Based on Exhibit 1, for the BI bond, one-sided:

　　A. up-duration will be greater than one-sided down-duration.

　　B. down-duration will be greater than one-sided up-duration.

　　C. up-duration and one-sided down-duration will be about equal.

31. Based on Exhibit 1, which key rate duration is the largest for the BI bond?

　　A. One-year key rate duration

　　B. Two-year key rate duration

　　C. Three-year key rate duration

32. Which bond in Exhibit 1 *most likely* has the lowest effective convexity?

　　A. AI bond

　　B. BI bond

　　C. CE bond

33. Based on Exhibit 3, if DeLille Enterprises pays the dividend expected by Gillette, the conversion price of the DE bond will:

　　A. be adjusted downward.

　　B. not be adjusted.

　　C. be adjusted upward.

34. Based on Exhibit 3, the market conversion premium per share for the DE bond on 17 September 20X5 is *closest* to:

　　A. €0.90.

　　B. €2.13.

　　C. €2.53.

35. Based on Exhibit 4, the arbitrage-free value of the RI bond is *closest* to:

　　A. €814.

　　B. €1,056.

　　C. €1,108.

36. Based on Exhibit 4 and Gillette's forecast regarding Raffarin's share price, the return on the RI bond over the next year is *most likely* to be:

　　A. lower than the return on Raffarin's common shares.

　　B. the same as the return on Raffarin's common shares.

　　C. higher than the return on Raffarin's common shares.

SOLUTIONS

1. C is correct. The call option embedded in Bond #2 can be exercised only at two predetermined dates: 1 October 20X1 and 1 October 20X2. Thus, the call feature is Bermudan style.

2. C is correct. The bond that would most likely protect investors against a significant increase in interest rates is the putable bond (i.e., Bond #3). When interest rates have risen and higher-yield bonds are available, a put option allows the bondholders to put back the bonds to the issuer prior to maturity and to reinvest the proceeds of the retired bonds in higher-yielding bonds.

3. B is correct. A fall in interest rates results in a rise in bond values. For a callable bond, such as Bond #2, the upside potential is capped because the issuer is more likely to call the bond. In contrast, the upside potential for a putable bond, such as Bond #3, is uncapped. Thus, a fall in interest rates would result in a putable bond having more upside potential than an otherwise identical callable bond. Note that A is incorrect because the effective duration of a putable bond increases, not decreases, with a fall in interest rates; the bond is less likely to be put and thus behaves more like an option-free bond. C is also incorrect because the effective convexity of a putable bond is always positive. It is the effective convexity of a callable bond that will change from positive to negative if interest rates fall and the call option is near the money.

4. A is correct:

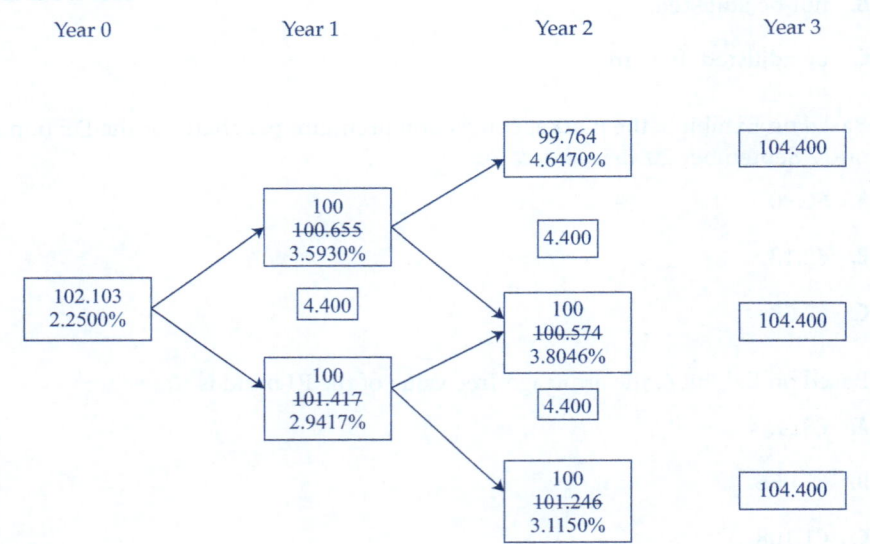

5. C is correct:

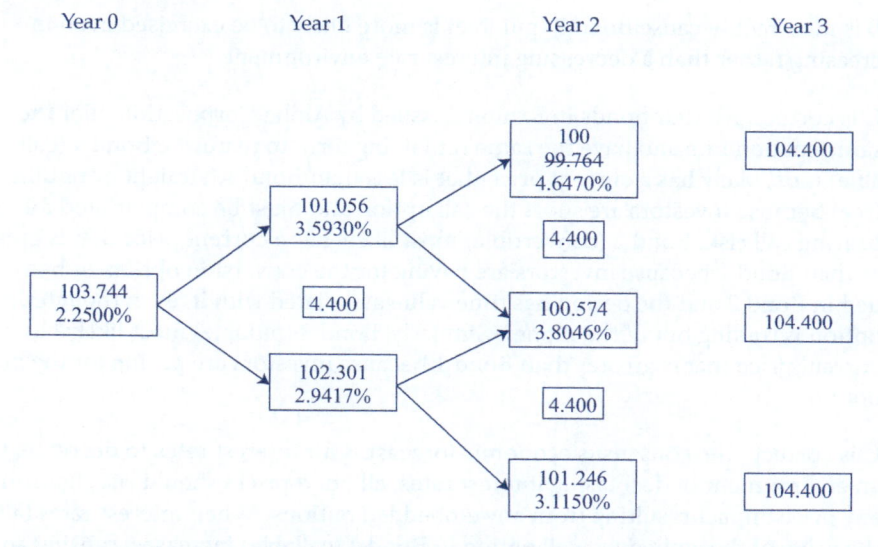

6. C is correct. Bond #3 is a putable bond, and the value of a put option increases as interest rates rise. At higher interest rates, the value of the underlying option-free bond (straight bond) declines, but the decline is offset partially by the increase in the value of the embedded put option, which is more likely to be exercised.

7. C is correct. Regardless of the type of option, an increase in interest rate volatility results in an increase in option value. Because the value of a putable bond is equal to the value of the straight bond *plus* the value of the embedded put option, Bond #3 will increase in value if interest rate volatility increases. Put another way, an increase in interest rate volatility will most likely result in more scenarios where the put option is exercised, which increases the values calculated in the interest rate tree and, thus, the value of the putable bond.

8. C is correct. Bond #2 is a callable bond, and the value of the embedded call option increases as the yield curve flattens. When the yield curve is upward sloping, the one-period forward rates on the interest rate tree are high and opportunities for the issuer to call the bond are fewer. When the yield curve flattens or inverts, many nodes on the tree have lower forward rates, which increase the opportunities to call and, thus, the value of the embedded call option.

9. B is correct. The conversion price of a convertible bond is equal to the par value divided by the conversion ratio—that is, $1,000/31 = $32.26 per share.

10. B is correct. The conversion value of the bond is 31 × $37.50 or $1,162.50, which represents its minimum value. Thus, the convertible bond exhibits mostly stock risk–return characteristics; a fall in the stock price will result in a fall in the convertible bond price. However, the change in the convertible bond price is less than the change in the stock price because the convertible bond has a floor. That floor is the value of the straight (option-free) bond.

11. C is correct. If the central bank takes actions that lead to lower interest rates, the yields on Alpha's bonds are likely to decrease. If the yield to maturity on Bond 4 (callable) falls below the 1.55% coupon rate, the call option will become valuable and Alpha may call the bond because it is in the money.

    A is incorrect because if the equity market declines, the market value of Alpha stock will also likely decrease. Therefore, Bond 2 (convertible) would have a lower conversion value; hence, the conversion option likely would not be exercised. Because Bond 2 is currently trading out of the money, it will likely trade further out of the money once the price of Alpha stock decreases.

B is incorrect because Bond 3 (putable) is more likely to be exercised in an increasing rather than a decreasing interest rate environment.

12. C is correct. All four bonds in Exhibit 2 issued by Alpha Corporation offer the same coupon rate and have the same remaining term to maturity. Bond 4 (callable) most likely has a current price that is less than Bond 1 (straight or option free) because investors are short the call option and must be compensated for bearing call risk. Bond 2 (convertible) most likely has a current price that is greater than Bond 1 because investors are paying for the conversion option embedded in Bond 2 and the option has time value associated with it, even though the option is trading out of the money. Similarly, Bond 3 (putable) most likely has a current price that is greater than Bond 1 because investors are paying for the put option.

13. C is correct. The consensus economic forecast is for interest rates to decrease. In an environment of decreasing interest rates, all bond prices should rise, ignoring any price impact resulting from any embedded options. When interest rates fall, the value of the embedded call option in Bond 4 (callable) increases, causing an opposing effect on price. The put option of putable bonds, by contrast, increases in value when interest rates rise rather than decline.

14. C is correct. Bond 4 is a callable bond. Value of an issuer call option = Value of straight bond − Value of callable bond. The value of the straight bond may be calculated using the spot rates or the one-year forward rates.

    Value of an option-free (straight) bond with a 1.55% coupon using spot rates:

    $$1.55/(1.0100)^1 + 1.55/(1.012012)^2 + 101.55/(1.012515)^3 = 100.8789.$$

    The value of a callable bond (at par) with no call protection period cannot exceed 100, as at that price or higher the bond would be called. The value of the call option = 100.8789 − 100 = 0.8789.

15. B is correct. An increase in interest rate volatility will cause the value of the put and call options embedded in Bond 3 and Bond 4 to increase. Bond 3 (putable) would experience an increase in price because the increased value of the put option increases the bond's value. In contrast, Bond 4 (callable) will experience a price decrease because the increased value of the call option reduces the callable bond's value. Bond 2, an out-of-the-money convertible, will resemble the risk–return characteristics of a straight bond and will thus be unaffected by interest rate volatility.

16. A is correct. All else being equal, the value of a put option decreases as the yield curve moves from being upward sloping to flat to downward sloping (inverted). Alternatively, a call option's value increases as the yield curve flattens and increases further if the yield curve inverts. Therefore, if the yield curve became inverted, the value of the embedded option in Bond 3 (putable) would decrease and the value of the embedded option in Bond 4 (callable) would increase.

17. A is correct. The market price of callable Bond 4 with no protection period cannot exceed 100.

18. B is correct. A bond with a larger option-adjusted spread (OAS) than that of a bond with similar characteristics and credit quality means that the bond is likely underpriced (cheap). Bond 7 (OAS 85 bps) is relatively cheaper than Bond 6 (OAS 65 bps).

    C is incorrect because Bond 8 (CCC) has a lower credit rating than Bond 7 (B) and the OAS alone cannot be used for the relative value comparison. The larger OAS (105 bps) incorporates compensation for the difference between the B and

CCC bond credit ratings. Therefore, there is not enough information to draw a conclusion about relative value.

19. C is correct. The option-adjusted spread (OAS) is the constant spread added to all the one-period forward rates that makes the arbitrage-free value of a risky bond equal to its market price. The OAS approach is often used to assess bond relative values. If two bonds have the same characteristics and credit quality, they should have the same OAS. If this is not the case, the bond with the largest OAS (i.e., Bond #2) is likely to be underpriced (cheap) relative to the bond with the smallest OAS (i.e., Bond #1).

20. A is correct. The effective duration of a floating-rate bond is close to the time to next reset. As the reset for Bond #6 is annual, the effective duration of this bond is close to 1.

21. B is correct. Effective duration indicates the sensitivity of a bond's price to a 100 bps parallel shift of the benchmark yield curve assuming no change in the bond's credit spread. The effective duration of an option-free bond, such as Bond #3, goes down as interest rates rise. As interest rates rise, a call option moves out of the money, which increases the value of the callable bond and lengthens its effective duration. In contrast, as interest rates rise, a put option moves into the money, which limits the price depreciation of the putable bond and shortens its effective duration. Thus, the bond whose effective duration might lengthen if interest rates rise is the callable bond (i.e., Bond #4).

22. B is correct. The effective duration of Bond #4 can be calculated using Equation 3, where ΔCurve is 20 bps, PV_ is 101.238, and PV+ is 100.478. PV$_0$, the current full price of the bond (i.e., with no shift), is not given but can be calculated using Exhibit 3 as follows:

Year 0	Year 1	Year 2	Year 3

Thus, the effective duration of Bond #4 is:

$$\text{EffDur} = \frac{101.238 - 100.478}{2 \times (0.0020) \times (100.873)} = 1.88.$$

23. A is correct:

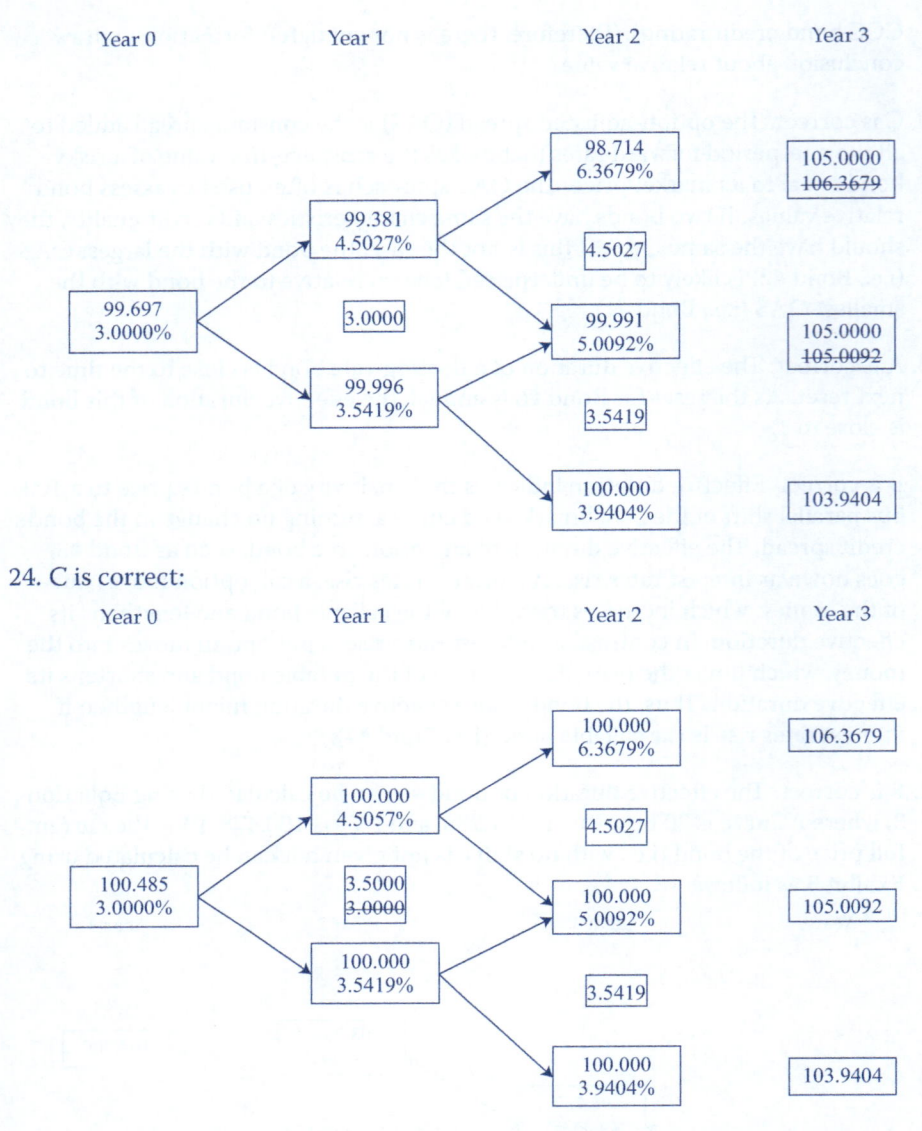

24. C is correct:

25. B is correct. A convertible bond includes a conversion option, which is a call option on the issuer's common stock. This conversion option gives the bondholders the right to convert their debt into equity. Thus, the value of Bond #9, the convertible bond, is equal to the value of Bond #10, the underlying option-free bond (straight bond), plus the value of a call option on Whorton's common stock.

26. A is correct. The minimum value of a convertible bond is equal to the greater of the conversion value of the convertible bond (i.e., Bond #9) and the current value of the straight bond (i.e., Bond #10).

27. C is correct. The risk–return characteristics of a convertible bond depend on the market price of the issuer's common stock (underlying share price) relative to the bond's conversion price. When the underlying share price is well below the conversion price, the convertible bond exhibits mostly bond risk–return characteristics. In this case, the price of the convertible bond is mainly affected by interest rate movements and the issuer's credit spreads. In contrast, when the underlying share price is above the conversion price, the convertible bond exhibits mostly stock risk–return characteristics. In this case, the price of the convertible bond is mainly affected by the issuer's common stock price movements. The underlying share price ($30) is lower than the conversion price of Bond #9 ($50). Thus, Bond #9 exhibits mostly bond risk–return characteristics and is least affected by Whor-

ton's common stock price movements.

28. B is correct. The AI bond's value if interest rates shift down by 30 bps (PV_) is 100.78:

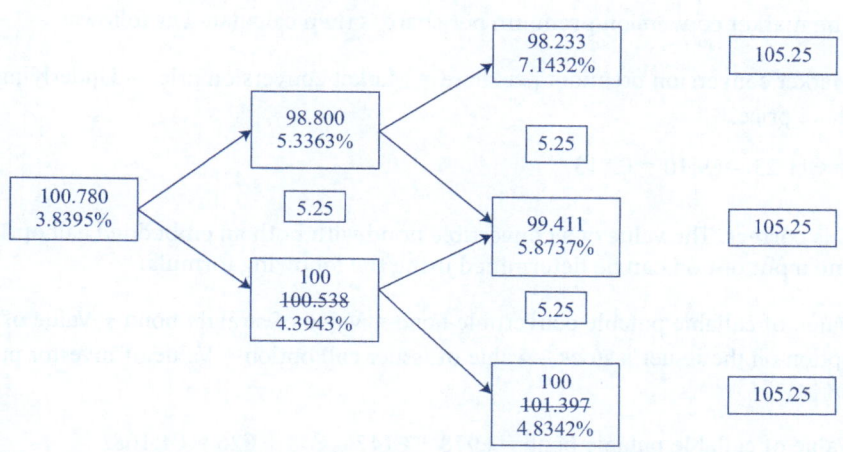

| Year 0 | Year 1 | Year 2 | Year 3 |

The AI bond's value if interest rates shift up by 30 bps (PV₊) is 99.487:

$$\text{EffDur} = \frac{(PV_-) - (PV_+)}{2 \times (\Delta\text{Curve}) \times (PV_0)} = \frac{100.780 - 99.487}{2 \times 0.003 \times 100.200} = 2.15.$$

29. A is correct. The AI bond is a callable bond, and the effective duration of a callable bond decreases when interest rates fall. The reason is because a decline in interest rates may result in the call option moving into the money, which limits the price appreciation of the callable bond. Exhibit 1 also shows that the price of the AI bond is 100.200 and that it is callable at par in one year and two years. Thus, the call option is already in the money and would likely be exercised in response to increases in the AI bond's price.

30. C is correct. The BI bond is an option-free bond, and one-sided up-duration and one-sided down-duration will be about equal for option-free bonds.

31. C is correct. The BI bond is an option-free bond. Its longest key rate duration will be in the year of its maturity because the largest cash flow (payment of both coupon and principal) occurs in that year.

32. A is correct. All else being equal, a callable bond will have lower effective convexity than an option-free bond when the call option is in the money. Similarly, when the call option is in the money, a callable bond will also have lower effective convexity than a putable bond if the put option is out of the money. Exhibit 1 shows that the callable AI bond is currently priced slightly higher than its call price of par value, which means the embedded call option is in the money. The put option embedded in the CE bond is not in the money; the bond is currently priced 2.1% above par value. Thus, at the current price, the putable CE bond is more likely to behave like the option-free BI bond. Consequently, the effective convexity of the AI bond will likely be lower than the option-free BI bond and the putable CE bond.

33. A is correct. The conversion price would be adjusted downward because Gillette's expected dividend payment of €0.70 is greater than the threshold dividend of €0.50.

34. B is correct. The market conversion premium per share is equal to the market conversion price minus the underlying share price. The market conversion price is calculated as follows:

$$\text{Market conversion price} = \frac{\text{Convertible bond price}}{\text{Conversion ratio}}$$

$$= \frac{\text{€}1,123}{\text{€}1,000/\text{€}10 \text{ per share}} = \text{€}11.23 \text{ per share.}$$

The market conversion premium per share is then calculated as follows:

Market conversion premium per share = Market conversion price − Underlying share price.

= €11.23 − €9.10 = €2.13.

35. C is correct. The value of a convertible bond with both an embedded call option and a put option can be determined using the following formula:

Value of callable putable convertible bond = Value of straight bond + Value of call option on the issuer's stock − Value of issuer call option + Value of investor put option.

Value of callable putable bond = €978 + €147 − €43 + €26 = €1,108.

36. A is correct. Over the next year, Gillette believes that Raffarin's share price will continue to increase toward the conversion price but not exceed it. If Gillette's forecast becomes true, the return on the RI bond will increase but at a lower rate than the increase in Raffarin's share price because the conversion price is not expected to be reached.

4

Credit Analysis Models

by James F. Adams, PhD, CFA, and Donald J. Smith, PhD.

James Adams, PhD, CFA, is at New York University (USA). Donald J. Smith, PhD, is at Boston University Questrom School of Business (USA).

LEARNING OUTCOMES

Mastery	The candidate should be able to:
☐	explain expected exposure, the loss given default, the probability of default, and the credit valuation adjustment
☐	explain credit scores and credit ratings
☐	calculate the expected return on a bond given transition in its credit rating
☐	explain structural and reduced-form models of corporate credit risk, including assumptions, strengths, and weaknesses
☐	calculate the value of a bond and its credit spread, given assumptions about the credit risk parameters
☐	interpret changes in a credit spread
☐	explain the determinants of the term structure of credit spreads and interpret a term structure of credit spreads
☐	compare the credit analysis required for securitized debt to the credit analysis of corporate debt

INTRODUCTION

1

Credit analysis plays an important role in the broader fixed-income space. Our coverage will go over important concepts, tools, and applications of credit analysis. We first look at modeling credit risk. The inputs to credit risk modeling are the expected exposure to default loss, the loss given default, and the probability of default. We explain these terms and use a numerical example to illustrate the calculation of the credit valuation adjustment for a corporate bond and its credit spread over a government bond yield taken as a proxy for a default-risk-free rate (or default-free rate).

We then discuss credit scoring and credit ratings. Credit scoring is a measure of credit risk used in retail loan markets, and ratings are used in the wholesale bond market. We explain two types of credit analysis models used in practice—structural models and reduced-form models. Both models are highly mathematical and beyond the scope of our coverage. Therefore, we provide only an overview to highlight the key ideas and the similarities and differences between them. We then use the arbitrage-free framework and a binomial interest rate tree to value risky fixed-rate and floating-rate bonds for different assumptions about interest rate volatility. We also build on the credit risk model to interpret changes in credit spreads that arise from changes in the assumed probability of default, the recovery rate, or the exposure to default loss. We also explain the term structure of credit spreads and finally compare the credit analysis required for securitized debt with the credit analysis of corporate bonds.

2   MODELING CREDIT RISK AND THE CREDIT VALUATION ADJUSTMENT

☐ | explain expected exposure, the loss given default, the probability of default, and the credit valuation adjustment

The difference between the yields to maturity on a corporate bond and a government bond with the same maturity is the most commonly used measure of credit risk. It is called the *credit spread* and is also known in practice as the G-spread. It reveals the compensation to the investor for bearing the default risk of the issuer—the possibility that the issuer fails to make a scheduled payment in full on the due date—and for losses incurred in the event of default.

The terms "default risk" and "credit risk" are sometimes used interchangeably in practice, but we will distinguish between the two in our coverage. Default risk is the narrower term because it addresses the likelihood of an event of default. Credit risk is the broader term because it considers both the default probability and how much is expected to be lost if default occurs. For example, it is possible that the default risk on a collateralized loan is high while the credit risk is low, especially if the value of the collateral is high relative to the amount that is owed.

We assume that the corporate bond and the default-risk-free government bond have the same taxation and liquidity. This is a simplifying assumption, of course. In reality, government bonds typically are more liquid than corporate bonds. Also, differences in liquidity within the universe of corporate bonds are great. Government bonds are available in greater supply than even the most liquid corporates and have demand from a wider set of institutional investors. In addition, government bonds can be used more readily as collateral in repo transactions and for centrally cleared derivatives. Also, there are differences in taxation in some markets. For example, interest income on US corporate bonds is taxable by both the federal and state governments. Government debt, however, is exempt from taxes at the state level. Disregarding tax and liquidity differences allows us to focus on default risk and expected loss as the determining factors for the credit spread.

The first factor to consider in modeling credit risk is the **expected exposure** to default loss. This quantity is the projected amount of money the investor could lose if an event of default occurs, before factoring in possible recovery. Although the most common event of default is nonpayment leading to bankruptcy proceedings, the bond prospectus might identify other events of default, such as the failure to meet a different obligation or the violation of a financial covenant.

Consider a one-year, 4% annual payment corporate bond priced at par value. The expected exposure to default loss at the end of the year is simply 104 (per 100 of par value). Later, we will include multiple time periods and volatility in interest rates. That complicates the calculation of expected exposure because we will need to consider the likelihood that the bond price varies as interest rates vary. In this initial example, the exposure is simply the final coupon payment plus the redemption of principal.

The second factor is the assumed **recovery rate**, which is the percentage of the loss recovered from a bond in default. The recovery rate varies by industry, the degree of seniority in the capital structure, the amount of leverage in the capital structure in total, and whether a particular security is secured or otherwise collateralized. We assume a 40% recovery rate for this corporate bond, which is a common baseline assumption in practice. Given the recovery rate assumption, we can determine the assumed **loss given default** (the amount of loss if a default occurs). This is 62.4 per 100 of par value: $104 \times (1 - 0.40) = 62.4$. A related term is *loss severity*; if the recovery rate is 40%, the assumed loss severity is 60%.

Exhibit 1 illustrates the projected cash flows on the corporate bond. If there is no default, the investor receives 104. If default occurs, the investor receives 41.6: $104 - 62.4 = 41.6$. We assume instantaneous recovery, which surely is another simplifying assumption. In practice, lengthy time delays can occur between the event of default and eventual recovery of cash. Notice that we assume that the recovery rate applies to interest as well as principal. One last note is that in the exhibits that we use, calculations may slightly differ on occasion due to rounding at intermediate steps.

Exhibit 1: A Simple Credit Risk Example

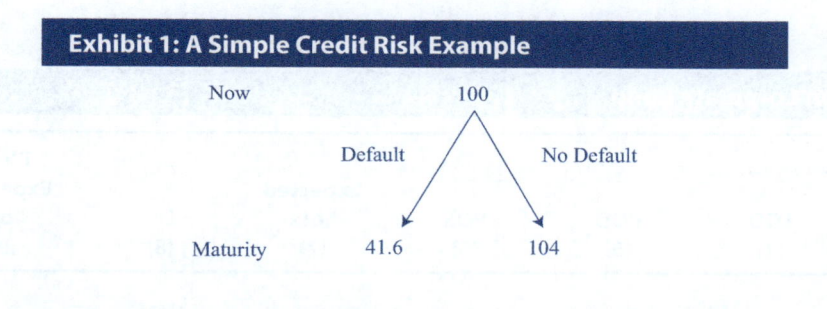

The third factor is the assumed **probability of default**, which is the probability that a bond issuer will not meet its contractual obligations on schedule. It is important in credit risk modeling to distinguish *risk-neutral* probabilities of default and *actual* (or *historical*) default probabilities. "Risk-neutral" follows the usage of the term in option pricing. In the risk-neutral option pricing methodology, the expected value for the payoffs is discounted using the risk-free interest rate. The key point is that in getting the expected value of the option, the risk-neutral probabilities associated with the payoffs need to be used. The same idea applies to valuing corporate bonds.

Suppose that a credit rating agency has collected an extensive dataset on the historical default experience for one-year corporate bonds issued by companies having the same business profile as the issuer in this example. It is observed that 99% of the bonds survive and make the full coupon and principal payment at maturity. Just 1% of the bonds default, resulting in an average recovery rate of 40%. Based on these data, the actual default probability for the corporate bond can reasonably be assumed to be 1%.

If the actual probability of default is used to get the expected future value for the corporate bond, the result is 103.376: $(104 \times 0.99) + (41.6 \times 0.01) = 103.376$. Discounting that amount at an assumed risk-free rate of 3% gives a present value of 100.365: $103.376/1.03 = 100.365$. Note that in risk-neutral valuation, the expected value is discounted using the risk-free rate and not the bond's yield to maturity. The key point is that 100.365 overstates the observed value of the bond, which is 100. The issue is to determine the default probability that does produce a value of 100.

[Handwritten margin notes:]
$P^* = 1.6\% \equiv$ risk-neutral probability
actual default probability = 1%

Denote the risk-neutral default probability to be P^*. The probability of survival is $1 - P^*$. Given that the corporate bond is priced at 100, $P^* = 1.60\%$. This is found as the solution to P^* in

$$100 = \frac{[104 \times (1 - P^*)] + (41.6 \times P^*)}{1.03}.$$

One reason for the difference between actual (or historical) and risk-neutral default probabilities is that actual default probabilities do not include the default risk premium associated with uncertainty over the timing of possible default loss. Another reason is that the observed spread over the yield on a risk-free bond in practice also includes liquidity and tax considerations in addition to credit risk.

To further see the interaction between the credit risk parameters—the expected exposure, the loss given default, and the probability of default—we consider a five-year, zero-coupon corporate bond. Our goal is to determine the fair value for the bond given its credit risk, its yield to maturity, and its spread over a maturity-matching government bond.

Exhibit 2 displays the calculation of the **credit valuation adjustment** (CVA). The CVA is the value of the credit risk in present value terms. In Exhibit 2, LGD stands for the loss given default, POD stands for the probability of default on the given date, POS stands for the probability of survival as of the given date, DF stands for the discount factor, and PV stands for the present value.

Exhibit 2: A Five-Year, Zero-Coupon Corporate Bond

[Handwritten annotations above column headers: "Column 0.4 × (2)" above Recovery; "(2−3)" and "loss given default" above LGD; "probability of default" above POD; "probability of survival" above POS; "(4)×(5)" above Expected Loss; "discount factor" above DF; "(7)×(8)" above PV of Expected Loss]

Date (1)	Exposure (2)	Recovery (3)	LGD (4)	POD (5)	POS (6)	Expected Loss (7)	DF (8)	PV of Expected Loss (9)
0								
1	88.8487	35.5395	53.3092	1.2500%	98.7500%	0.6664	0.970874	0.6470
2	91.5142	36.6057	54.9085	1.2344%	97.5156%	0.6778	0.942596	0.6389
3	94.2596	37.7038	56.5558	1.2189%	96.2967%	0.6894	0.915142	0.6309
4	97.0874	38.8350	58.2524	1.2037%	95.0930%	0.7012	0.888487	0.6230
5	100.0000	40.0000	60.0000	1.1887%	93.9043%	0.7132	0.862609	0.6152
				6.0957%			CVA =	3.1549

[Handwritten annotations within table: beside row 2 POD "0.9875 × 0.0125 → 1.2344%"; beside row 3 POD "0.975156 × 0.0125 → 1.2189%"; beside row 2 POS "0.9875 × 0.9875"; beside row 3 POS "0.9875 × 0.9875 × 0.9875"; above DF column "$\left(\frac{1}{1.03}\right)^t$"; beside DF rows "$\frac{1}{1.03}$", "$\left(\frac{1}{1.03}\right)^2$", "$\left(\frac{1}{1.03}\right)^3$"]

The first step is to get the exposures to default loss. These are shown in Column 2 of Exhibit 2. We assume a flat government bond yield curve at 3.00%. Also, we assume that default occurs only at year-end—on Dates 1, 2, 3, 4, and 5—and that default will not occur on Date 0, the current date. The exposure on Date 5 is 100. For the other dates, we discount using the risk-free rate and the remaining number of years until maturity. For example, exposure at Date 1 is $100/(1.0300)^4 = 88.8487$.

Note that there is no interest rate volatility in this example. In a later section, we will use the arbitrage-free framework to build a binomial interest rate tree for a specified level of volatility. Then, knowing the probability of attaining each node in the tree, we will calculate the *expected exposure* for each date.

Column 3 of Exhibit 2 projects the assumed recovery if default occurs. Here, the recovery rate is a percentage of the exposure. In general, it will be a percentage of the expected exposure, including coupon interest payments, when the model allows for interest rate volatility. We assume for this example that the recovery rate is 40%. The amounts shown in Column 3 are the exposures in Column 2 times 0.40.

Column 4 shows the loss given default. It is the exposure for each date minus the assumed recovery. If the issuer defaults on Date 4, the investor's loss is projected to be 58.2524 (= 97.0874 − 38.8350) per 100 of par value.

The next parameter is the risk-neutral probability of default for each date. In Column 5 of Exhibit 2, we assume that the POD on Date 1 is 1.25%. We use *conditional probabilities of default*, meaning that each year-by-year POD assumes no prior default. These are called hazard rates in statistics. Column 6 reports the probability of survival for each year. The probability of surviving past Date 1 and arriving at Date 2 is 98.75% (= 100% − 1.25%). Therefore, the POD for Date 2 is 1.2344% (= 1.25% × 98.75%), and the POS is 97.5156% (= 98.75% − 1.2344%). The POD for Date 3 is 1.2189% (= 1.25% × 97.5156%), and the POS is 96.2967% (= 97.5156% − 1.2189%). The cumulative probability of default over the five-year lifetime of the corporate bond is 6.0957%, the sum of the PODs in Column 5.

Another method to calculate the POS for each year—a method that is used later in our discussion—is 100% minus the annual default probability raised to the power of the number of years. For example, the probability of the bond surviving until maturity is $(100\% − 1.25\%)^5 = 93.9043\%$. Note that 6.0957% plus 93.9043% equals 100%.

The assumed annual default probability does not need to be the same each year. Later we will show some examples of it changing over the lifetime of the bond.

Column 7 gives the *expected loss* for each date. This is the LGD times the POD. For example, if default occurs on Date 3, the expected loss is 0.6894 per 100 of par value. The exposure is 94.2596. At 40% recovery, the LGD is 56.5558. Assuming no prior default, the POD for that date is 1.2189%. The expected loss of 0.6894 is calculated as 56.5558 times 1.2189%.

Column 8 presents the default-risk-free *discount factors* based on the flat government bond yield curve at 3.00%. The Date 5 discount factor is 0.862609 [$= 1/(1.0300)^5$]. Finally, Column 9 shows the present value of the expected loss for each year. This is the expected loss times the discount factor. The present value of the expected Date 5 loss is 0.6152 per 100 of par value, the expected loss of 0.7132 times 0.862609.

The sum of Column 9 is 3.1549. This amount is known as the credit valuation adjustment. It allows us to calculate the *fair value* of the five-year, zero-coupon corporate bond. If the bond were default free, its price would be 86.2609—that is, the par value of 100 times the Date 5 discount factor. Subtracting the CVA from this amount gives a fair value of 83.1060 (= 86.2609 − 3.1549).

We can now calculate the credit spread on the corporate bond. Given a price of 83.1060, its yield to maturity is 3.77%. The solution for *yield* in this expression is

$$\frac{100}{(1 + \text{Yield})^5} = 83.1060.$$

The yield on the five-year, zero-coupon government bond is 3.00%. Therefore, the credit spread is 77 bps: 3.77% − 3.00% = 0.77%. (Note that an approximation for the credit spread commonly used in practice is the annual default probability times 1 minus the recovery rate. In this case, the approximate credit spread is 0.75% [= 1.25% × (1 − 0.40)].) A key point is that the compensation for credit risk received by the investor can be expressed in two ways: (1) as the CVA of 3.1549 in terms of a present value per 100 of par value on Date 0 and (2) as a credit spread of 77 bps in terms of an annual percentage rate for five years.

Exhibit 3 provides a display of the projected cash flows and annual rates of return depending on when and if default occurs. On Date 0, the five-year, zero-coupon corporate bond is worth its fair value, 83.1060 per 100 of par value. If on Date 1 the issuer defaults, the investor gets the recoverable amount of 35.5395. The annual rate of return is −57.24%, the solution for the internal rate of return (IRR):

$$83.1060 = \frac{35.5395}{1 + \text{IRR}}.$$

$$\text{IRR} = -0.5724.$$

If there is no default, the investor receives the coupon payment on that date, which in this case is zero.

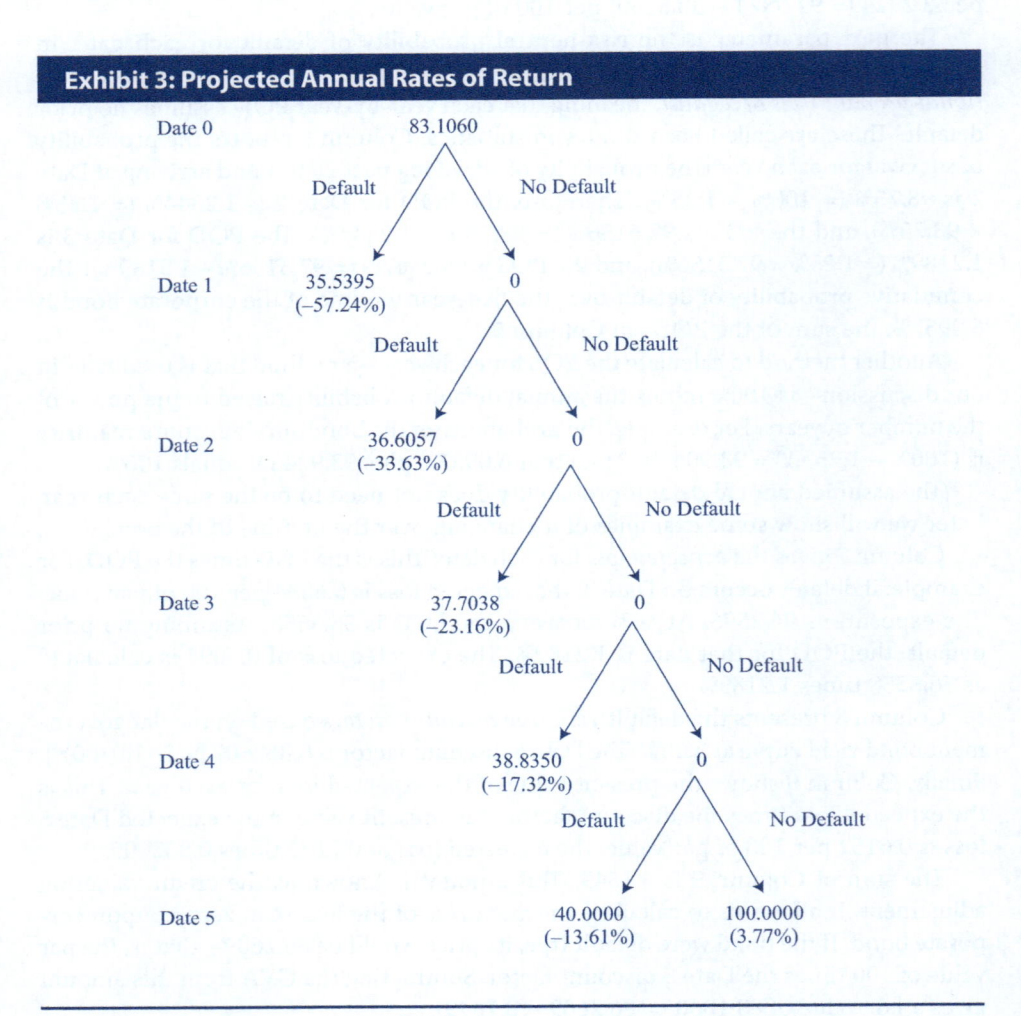

Exhibit 3: Projected Annual Rates of Return

Date 0		83.1060
Date 1	35.5395 (−57.24%)	0
Date 2	36.6057 (−33.63%)	0
Date 3	37.7038 (−23.16%)	0
Date 4	38.8350 (−17.32%)	0
Date 5	40.0000 (−13.61%)	100.0000 (3.77%)

If the issuer defaults on Date 2, the annual rate of return is −33.63%.

$$83.1060 = \frac{0}{(1 + \text{IRR})^1} + \frac{36.6057}{(1 + \text{IRR})^2}.$$
$$\text{IRR} = -0.3363.$$

If the default occurs on the maturity date, the annual rate of return "improves" to −13.61%:

$$83.1060 = \frac{0}{(1 + \text{IRR})^1} + \frac{0}{(1 + \text{IRR})^2} + \frac{0}{(1 + \text{IRR})^3} + \frac{0}{(1 + \text{IRR})^4} + \frac{40.0000}{(1 + \text{IRR})^5}.$$
$$\text{IRR} = -0.1361.$$

If there is no default, which is most likely because the probability of survival to Date 5 is 93.9043%, the realized rate of return is 3.77%. ==This reminds us that a yield to maturity on a risky bond is a measure of return to the investor, assuming no default.==

The key observation from this example is that the investor faces a wide range of outcomes on the bond depending critically on the *timing* of default. This is a source of the default risk premium that typically is built into the pricing of the bond. Stated differently, the probability of default in credit risk models incorporates the likely time of incidence of default events as well as uncertainty over the timing of the events.

Although this is clearly a simple example of a credit risk model, it does serve to illustrate the interaction between the exposure to default loss for each date, the recovery rate, the loss given default, the probability of default, the expected loss, and the present value of expected loss. It can be made more complex and realistic. Here, the initial probability of default (the hazard rate) used to calculate the conditional PODs and the recovery rate is the same for each year, but these parameters could vary year by year. The government bond yield curve is flat, but it could be upward or downward sloping. Then, the discount factors would need to be calculated sequentially by a process known as "bootstrapping." An example of this process is included later.

In this example, we assume an annual default probability and a recovery rate to get the fair value for the risky corporate bond. This could be reversed. Suppose that we observe that the market price for the five-year, zero-coupon bond is 83.1060 and its credit spread is 77 bps. Then, the same table could be used to get—by trial-and-error search—the annual probability of default that is consistent with the bond price and a recovery rate of 40%. That default probability, which is used to calculate the year-by-year PODs, would be 1.25%. Another possibility is to change the assumed recovery rate. Suppose it is 30% of the exposure. Given the observed bond price and credit spread, the default probability would turn out to be 1.0675%. In that case, the lower recovery rate is offset by the lower probability of default. A higher recovery rate would need to be offset by a higher default probability. In general, for a given price and credit spread, the assumed probability of default and the recovery rate are positively correlated.

Analysis of Credit Risk (1)

1. A fixed-income analyst is considering the credit risk over the next year for three corporate bonds currently held in her bond portfolio. Her assessment for the exposure, probability of default, and recovery is summarized in this table:

Corporate Bond	Exposure (per 100 of par value)	Probability of Default	Recovery (per 100 of par value)
A	104	0.75%	40
B	98	0.90%	35
C	92	0.80%	30

Although all three bonds have very similar yields to maturity, the differences in the exposures arise because of differences in their coupon rates.

Based on these assumptions, how would she rank the three bonds, from highest to lowest, in terms of credit risk over the next year?

Solution:

She needs to get the loss given default for each bond and multiply that by the probability of default to get the expected loss. The LGD is the exposure minus the assumed recovery.

Corporate Bond	LGD (per 100 of par value)	POD	Expected Loss
A	64	0.75%	0.480

Corporate Bond	LGD (per 100 of par value)	POD	Expected Loss
B	63	0.90%	0.567
C	62	0.80%	0.496

Based on the expected losses, Bond B has the highest credit risk and Bond A, the lowest. The ranking is B, C, and A. Note that there is not enough information to recommend a trading strategy because the current prices of the bonds are not given.

EXAMPLE 2

Analysis of Credit Risk (2)

1. A fixed-income trader at a hedge fund observes a three-year, 5% annual payment corporate bond trading at 104 per 100 of par value. The research team at the hedge fund determines that the risk-neutral annual probability of default used to calculate the conditional POD for each date for the bond, given a recovery rate of 40%, is 1.50%. The government bond yield curve is flat at 2.50%.

   Based on these assumptions, does the trader deem the corporate bond to be overvalued or undervalued? By how much? If the trader buys the bond at 104, what are the projected annual rates of return?

Solution:

The trader needs to build a table similar to that shown in Exhibit 2; this table is presented in Exhibit 4.

Exhibit 4: CVA Calculation for Example 2

Date	Exposure	Recovery	LGD	POD	POS	Expected Loss	DF	PV of Expected Loss
0								
1	109.8186	43.9274	65.8911	1.5000%	98.5000%	0.9884	0.975610	0.9643
2	107.4390	42.9756	64.4634	1.4775%	97.0225%	0.9524	0.951814	0.9066
3	105.0000	42.0000	63.0000	1.4553%	95.5672%	0.9169	0.928599	0.8514
				4.4328%			CVA =	2.7222

The exposures are the values for the bond plus the coupon payment for each date assuming a yield to maturity of 2.50%. The exposure is 109.8186 for Date 1 when two years to maturity remain:

$$5 + \frac{5}{(1.0250)^1} + \frac{105}{(1.0250)^2} = 109.8186.$$

The assumed recovery for Date 1 is 43.9274 (= 109.8186 × 0.40) for a loss given default of 65.8911 (= 109.8186 − 43.9274). (Note that all calculations are carried out on spreadsheets to preserve precision. The rounded results are reported in the text.) The expected loss is 0.9884 (= 65.8911 × 0.0150).

The discount factor for Date 1 is 0.975610 = $1/(1.0250)^1$. The present value of the expected loss is 0.9643 (= 0.9884 × 0.975610).

The credit valuation adjustment for the bond is 2.7222, the sum of the present values of expected loss. If this five-year, 5% bond were default free, its price would be 107.1401.

$$\frac{5}{(1.0250)^1} + \frac{5}{(1.0250)^2} + \frac{105}{(1.0250)^3} = 107.1401.$$

Therefore, the fair value of the bond given the assumed credit risk parameters is 104.4178 (= 107.1401 − 2.7222). If this three-year, 5% bond were default free, its price would be 107.1401.

The projected annual rates of return for default on Dates 1, 2, and 3 are −57.76%, −33.27%, and −22.23%, respectively. If there is no default, the rate of return is 3.57%, which is the yield to maturity. Note that these rates of return neglect coupon reinvestment risk because internal rate of return calculations implicitly assume reinvestment at the same rate. The calculations are as follows:

$$104 = \frac{43.9274}{(1 + IRR)^1}.$$
$$IRR = -0.5776.$$

$$104 = \frac{5}{(1 + IRR)^1} + \frac{42.9756}{(1 + IRR)^2}.$$
$$IRR = -0.3327.$$

$$104 = \frac{5}{(1 + IRR)^1} + \frac{5}{(1 + IRR)^2} + \frac{42.0000}{(1 + IRR)^3}.$$
$$IRR = -0.2223.$$

$$104 = \frac{5}{(1 + IRR)^1} + \frac{5}{(1 + IRR)^2} + \frac{105}{(1 + IRR)^3}.$$
$$IRR = 0.0357.$$

Environmental, social, and governance (ESG) considerations may also play a role in credit risk assessment. For example, companies responsible for pollution run the risk of fines or other business sanctions, those with poor labor practices risk their reputation and may face customer boycotts or lawsuits, and firms with weak governance are more likely to engage in aggressive or even fraudulent accounting. Estimated probabilities of default and loss given default should incorporate these potential impacts.

Recent years have also seen several types of bond with explicit links to ESG matters. Climate, or green, bonds are typically issued with proceeds earmarked for environmentally beneficial purposes and may come with tax incentives to enhance their attractiveness to investors.

Another category of fixed-income instruments whose special features affect credit risk assessment are catastrophe and pandemic bonds. They resemble an insurance product, rather than a traditional debt instrument. For example, the World Bank issued pandemic bonds in 2017, offering investors high interest payments in return for taking on the risk of losing capital should a pandemic occur, in which case they would pay out aid to poor nations suffering from a serious outbreak of infectious disease. At the time of this writing (July 2020), nearly all the principal from those bonds has been wiped out because caseloads and deaths from COVID-19 have exceeded the bonds' thresholds.

3   CREDIT SCORES AND CREDIT RATINGS

☐   explain credit scores and credit ratings

☐   calculate the expected return on a bond given transition in its credit rating

Credit scores and ratings are used by lenders in deciding to extend credit to a borrower and in determining the terms of the contract. Credit scores are used primarily in the retail lending market for small businesses and individuals. Credit ratings are used in the wholesale market for bonds issued by corporations and government entities, as well as for asset-backed securities (ABS).

Credit scoring methodologies can vary. In some countries, only negative information, such as delinquent payments or outright default, is included. Essentially, everyone has a good credit score until proven otherwise. In other countries, a broader set of information is used to determine the score. A score reflects actual observed factors. In general, credit reporting agencies are national in scope because of differences in legal systems and privacy concerns across countries.

The FICO score, which is the federally registered trademark of the Fair Isaac Corporation, is used in the United States by about 90% of lenders to retail customers. FICO scores are computed using data from consumer credit files collected by three national credit bureaus: Experian, Equifax, and TransUnion. Five primary factors are included in the proprietary algorithm used to get the score:

- 35% for the payment history: This includes the presence or lack of such information as delinquency, bankruptcy, court judgments, repossessions, and foreclosures.

- 30% for the debt burden: This includes credit card debt-to-limit ratios, the number of accounts with positive balances, and the total amount owed.

- 15% for the length of credit history: This includes the average age of accounts on the credit file and the age of the oldest account.

- 10% for the types of credit used: This includes the use of installment payments, consumer finance, and mortgages.

- 10% for recent searches for credit: This includes "hard" credit inquiries when consumers apply for new loans but not "soft" inquiries, such as for employee verification or self-checking one's score.

Fair Isaac Corporation, on its website, notes items that are not included in the FICO credit score: race, color, national origin, sex, marital status, age, salary, occupation, employment history, home address, and child/family support obligations. The company also reports from time to time the distribution across scores, which range from a low of 300 to a perfect score of 850. Exhibit 5 shows the distribution for three particular months: October 2005, before the global financial crisis; April 2009, in the depths of the crisis; and April 2017, well after the crisis. It is evident that the percentage of weak scores increased as economic conditions worsened but has gone down since then. The average FICO score varied from 688 to 687 to 700 during these months.

Exhibit 5: Distribution of FICO Scores

FICO Score	October 2005	April 2009	April 2017
300–499	6.6%	7.3%	4.7%
500–549	8.0%	8.7%	6.8%
550–599	9.0%	9.1%	8.5%
600–649	10.2%	9.5%	10.0%
650–699	12.8%	12.0%	13.2%
700–749	16.4%	15.9%	17.1%
750–799	20.1%	19.3%	19.0%
800–850	16.9%	18.2%	20.7%

Source: Fair Isaac Corporation.

EXAMPLE 3

Credit Scoring

1. Tess Waresmith is a young finance professional who plans to eventually buy a two-family house, live in one unit, and rent the other to help cover the mortgage payments. She is a careful money manager and every year checks her FICO credit score. She is pleased to see that it has improved from 760 last year to 775 this year. Which of these factors can explain the improvement?

   A. She is now one year older and has not had any late payments on credit cards during the year.

   B. Her bank on its own raised her limit on a credit card from $1,000 to $2,500, but she has maintained the same average monthly balance.

   C. She applied for and received a new car loan from her credit union.

   D. She refrained from checking her FICO score monthly, which some of her friends do.

Solution:

Factors A, B, and C help explain the improvement. Going down the list:

   A. Age itself is not a factor used by Fair Isaac to determine the credit score. However, the average age of the accounts is a factor, as is the age of the oldest account. Therefore, other things being equal, the passage of time tends to improve the score. In general, age and credit score are highly correlated.

   B. The credit card debt-to-limit ratio is a component of the debt burden. Having a higher limit for the same average balance reduces the ratio and improves the credit score.

   C. Because the car loan is a new type of credit usage and thus does not have any late payments, it has a positive impact on the score.

   D. Refraining from self-checking one's credit score has no impact. Self-checking is deemed to be a "soft inquiry" and does not factor into the calibration of the FICO score.

Whereas credit scores are the primary measure of credit risk in retail lending, credit ratings are widely used in corporate and sovereign bond markets. The three major global credit rating agencies are Moody's Investors Service, Standard & Poor's, and Fitch Ratings. Each provides quality ratings for issuers as well as specific issues. Similar to credit scores, these are ordinal ratings focusing on the probability of default. The historical corporate default experience by various ratings for 1995 to 2017 is shown in Exhibit 6.

Exhibit 6: Historical Corporate Default Experience by Rating (entries are in %)

A.

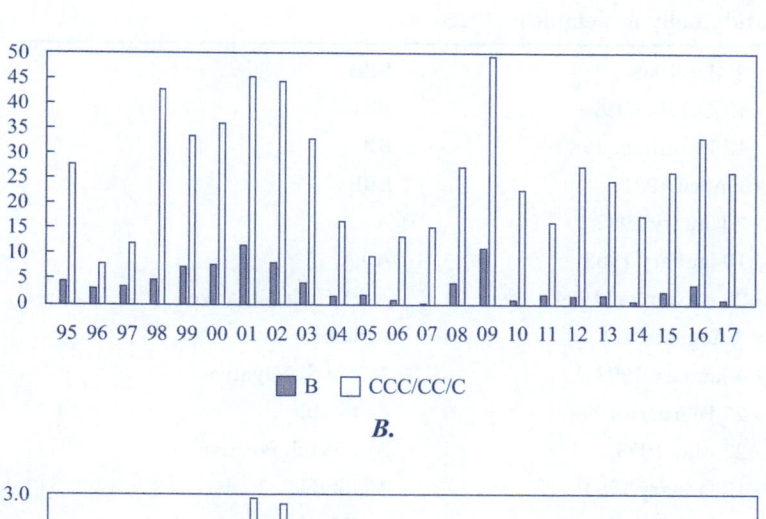

B ☐ CCC/CC/C

B.

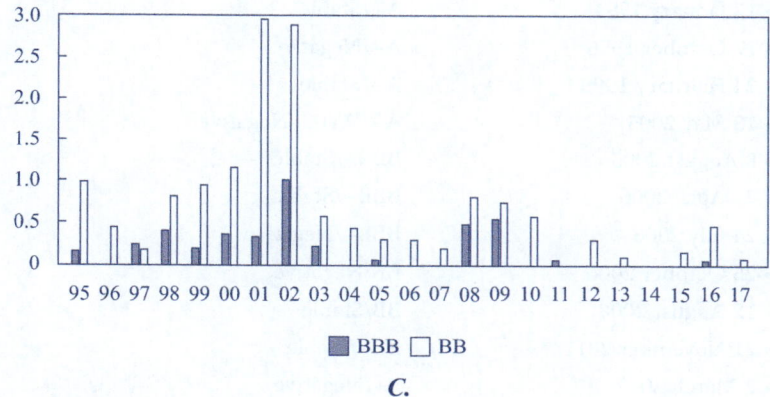

■ BBB ☐ BB

C.

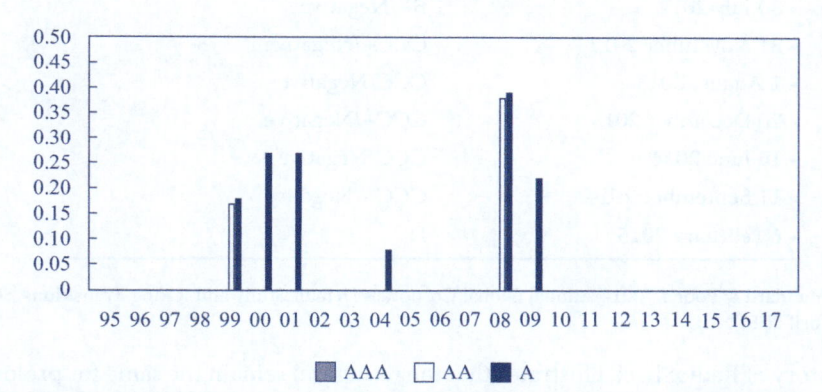

■ AAA ☐ AA ■ A

The credit rating agencies consider the expected loss given default by means of *notching*, which is a rating adjustment methodology (covered earlier in the CFA Program curriculum) to reflect the priority of claim for specific debt issues of that issuer and to reflect any subordination. The issuer rating is typically for senior unsecured debt. The rating on subordinated debt is then adjusted, or "notched," by lowering it one or two levels. This inclusion of loss given default in addition to the probability of default explains why they are called "credit ratings" and not just "default ratings."

In addition to the "letter grade," the rating agencies provide an outlook (positive, stable, or negative) for the issuer as well as when the issuer is under "watch." For example, what follows is the history of Standard & Poor's issuer rating for RadioShack Corporation as it moved from BBB– in 1969 to BB+ in 1978, to AAA in 1983, to BB in 2006, and finally to default in 2015:

• 2 May 1969	BBB–
• 13 October 1978	BB+
• 12 December 1980	BB
• 1 April 1981	BBB+
• 7 January 1982	A
• 10 January 1983	AAA
• 28 November 1984	A+/Watch Negative
• 8 August 1991	A/Stable
• 4 January 1993	A/Watch Negative
• 25 February 1993	A–/Stable
• 27 May 1993	A–/Watch Positive
• 17 January 1994	A–/Stable
• 17 October 1996	A–/Negative
• 24 February 1999	A–/Stable
• 13 May 2005	A–/Watch Negative
• 8 August 2005	BBB+/Stable
• 21 April 2006	BBB–/Stable
• 24 July 2006	BBB–/Negative
• 25 October 2006	BB/Negative
• 12 August 2008	BB/Stable
• 21 November 2011	BB–/Stable
• 2 March 2012	B+/Negative
• 30 July 2012	B–/Negative
• 21 November 2012	CCC+/Negative
• 1 August 2013	CCC/Negative
• 20 December 2013	CCC+/Negative
• 16 June 2014	CCC/Negative
• 11 September 2014	CCC–/Negative
• 6 February 2015	D

Source: Standard & Poor's, "2014 Annual Global Corporate Default Study and Rating Transitions," Table 54 (30 April 2015).

The history of RadioShack illustrates that the rating can remain the same for prolonged periods of time. The company was A+ from 1984 to 1991 and A– from 1993 to 2005. The rating agencies report *transition matrixes* based on their historical experience. Exhibit 7 is a representative example. It shows the probabilities of a particular rating transitioning to a different rating over the course of the following year. An A rated issuer has an 87.50% probability of remaining at that level; a 0.05% probability of moving up to AAA (such as RadioShack did in 1983); a 2.50% probability of moving up to AA; an 8.40% probability of moving down to BBB; 0.75% down to BB; 0.60% to B; 0.12% to CCC, CC, or C; and 0.08% to D, where it is in default.

Exhibit 7: Representative One-Year Corporate Transition Matrix (entries are in %)							
From/To	**AAA**	**AA**	**A**	**BBB**	**BB**	**B**	**CCC, CC, C**	**D**
AAA	**90.00**	9.00	0.60	0.15	0.10	0.10	0.05	0.00
AA	1.50	**88.00**	9.50	0.75	0.15	0.05	0.03	0.02
A	0.05	2.50	**87.50**	8.40	0.75	0.60	0.12	0.08
BBB	0.02	0.30	4.80	**85.50**	6.95	1.75	0.45	0.23
BB	0.01	0.06	0.30	7.75	**79.50**	8.75	2.38	1.25
B	0.00	0.05	0.15	1.40	9.15	**76.60**	8.45	4.20
CCC, CC, C	0.00	0.01	0.12	0.87	1.65	18.50	**49.25**	29.60
Credit Spread	0.60%	0.90%	1.10%	1.50%	3.40%	6.50%	9.50%	

Exhibit 7 also shows representative credit spreads for a 10-year corporate bond. The credit transition matrix and the credit spreads allow a fixed-income analyst to estimate a one-year rate of return given the possibility of credit rating migration but still no default. Assume that an A rated 10-year corporate bond will have a modified duration of 7.2 at the end of the year given stable yields and spreads. For each possible transition, the analyst can calculate the expected percentage price change as the product of the modified duration and the change in the spread:

From A to AAA:	$-7.2 \times (0.60\% - 1.10\%) = +3.60\%$.
From A to AA:	$-7.2 \times (0.90\% - 1.10\%) = +1.44\%$.
From A to BBB:	$-7.2 \times (1.50\% - 1.10\%) = -2.88\%$.
From A to BB:	$-7.2 \times (3.40\% - 1.10\%) = -16.56\%$.
From A to B:	$-7.2 \times (6.50\% - 1.10\%) = -38.88\%$.
From A to CCC, CC, or C:	$-7.2 \times (9.50\% - 1.10\%) = -60.48\%$.

The probabilities of migration now can be used to calculate the expected percentage change in the bond value over the year. The expected percentage change in bond value for an A rated corporate bond is found by multiplying each expected percentage price change for a possible credit transition by its respective transition probability found in the row associated with the A rating and summing the products:

$$(0.0005 \times 3.60\%) + (0.0250 \times 1.44\%) + (0.8750 \times 0\%) + (0.0840 \times -2.88\%) + (0.0075 \times -16.56\%) + (0.0060 \times -38.88\%) + (0.0012 \times -60.48\%)$$

$$= -0.6342\%.$$

Therefore, the expected return on the bond over the next year is its yield to maturity minus 0.6342%, assuming no default. If the bond was not investment grade, the small probability of a transition to default would need to be taken into consideration. Credit spread migration typically reduces the expected return for two reasons. First, the probabilities for change are not symmetrically distributed around the current rating. They are skewed toward a downgrade rather than an upgrade. Second, the increase in the credit spread is much larger for downgrades than the decrease in the spread for upgrades.

EXAMPLE 4

The Impact of Credit Migration on Expected Return

1. Manuel Perello is a wealth manager for several Latin American families who seek to keep a portion of their assets in very high-quality corporate bonds. Mr. Perello explains that the yields to maturity on the bonds should be adjusted for possible *credit spread widening* to measure the expected rate of return over a given time horizon. In his presentation to one of the families, he uses a 10-year, AAA rated corporate bond that would have a modified duration of 7.3 at the end of the year. Using the corporate transition matrix in Exhibit 7, Mr. Perello concludes that the expected return on the bond over the next year can be approximated by the yield to maturity less 32.5 bps to account for a possible credit downgrade even if there is no default. Demonstrate how he arrives at that conclusion.

Solution:

First, calculate the expected percentage price change using the modified duration for the bond and the change in the credit spread:

From AAA to AA:	$-7.3 \times (0.90\% - 0.60\%) = -2.19\%$.
From AAA to A:	$-7.3 \times (1.10\% - 0.60\%) = -3.65\%$.
From AAA to BBB:	$-7.3 \times (1.50\% - 0.60\%) = -6.57\%$.
From AAA to BB:	$-7.3 \times (3.40\% - 0.60\%) = -20.44\%$.
From AAA to B:	$-7.3 \times (6.50\% - 0.60\%) = -43.07\%$.
From AAA to CCC, CC, or C:	$-7.3 \times (9.50\% - 0.60\%) = -64.97\%$.

Second, calculate the expected percentage change in bond value over the year using the probabilities associated with the AAA rating row in the corporate transition matrix:

$$(0.9000 \times 0\%) + (0.0900 \times -2.19\%) + (0.0060 \times -3.65\%) + (0.0015 \times -6.57\%)$$
$$+ (0.0010 \times -20.44\%) + (0.0010 \times -43.07\%) + (0.0005 \times -64.97\%)$$

$$= -0.3249\%.$$

---

4   STRUCTURAL AND REDUCED-FORM CREDIT MODELS

> ☐ | explain structural and reduced-form models of corporate credit risk, including assumptions, strengths, and weaknesses

Credit analysis models fall into two broad categories—structural models and reduced-form models (Fabozzi 2013). Structural models of credit risk date back to the 1970s and the seminal contributions to finance theory by Fischer Black, Myron Scholes, and Robert Merton (Black and Scholes 1973; Merton 1974). Their key insights were that a company defaults on its debt if the value of its assets falls below the amount of its liabilities and that the probability of that event has the features of an option.

Reduced-form varieties emerged in the 1990s (Jarrow and Turnbull 1995; Duffie and Singleton 1999) and avoid a fundamental problem with the structural models. The Black–Scholes–Merton option pricing model explicitly assumes that the assets on which the options are written (i.e., the shares of a company) are actively traded. That assumption is fine for stock options; however, the assets of the company typically do not trade. Reduced-form models get around this problem by not treating default as an endogenous (internal) variable. Instead, the default is an exogenous (external) variable that occurs randomly. Unlike structural models that aim to explain *why* default occurs (i.e., when the asset value falls below the amount of liabilities), reduced-form models aim to explain statistically *when*. This is known as the *default time* and can be modeled using a Poisson stochastic process. The key parameter in this process is the *default intensity*, which is the probability of default over the next time increment. Reduced-form credit risk models are thus also called *intensity-based* and *stochastic default rate* models.

Both types of credit risk model have advantages and disadvantages. Structural models provide insight into the nature of credit risk but can be burdensome to implement. The modeler needs to determine the value of the company, its volatility, and the default barrier that is based on the liabilities of the company. In the model, the company defaults when the value of its assets dips below this default barrier. Although straightforward in theory, it can be difficult in practice because of limitations in available data. Examples of companies hiding debt (Enron Corporation, Tyco International, WorldCom, Parmalat, and Lehman Brothers, to name a few) highlight the challenge to measure the default barrier, especially in times when knowing changes in default probabilities would be most beneficial to investors (Smith 2011).

Reduced-form models have the advantage that the inputs are observable variables, including historical data. The default intensity is estimated using regression analysis on *company-specific* variables (e.g., leverage ratio, net-income-to-assets ratio, and cash-to-assets ratio), and *macroeconomic* variables (e.g., unemployment rate, GDP growth rate, measures of stock market volatility). This flexibility allows the model to directly reflect the business cycle in the credit risk measure.

A disadvantage of reduced-form models is that, unlike structural models, they do not explain the economic reasons for default. Also, reduced-form models assume that default comes as a "surprise" and can occur at any time. In reality, default is rarely a surprise because the issuer usually has been downgraded several times before the final event, as we saw with the RadioShack experience in the previous section.

Exhibit 8 depicts a structural model of default. The vertical axis measures the asset value of the company. It is called a structural model because it depends on the structure of the company's balance sheet—its assets, liabilities, and equity. It also can be called a *company-value* model because the key variable is the asset value of the company. In Exhibit 8, the asset value has been volatile prior to now, time 0, but has remained above the horizontal line that represents the default barrier. If the asset value falls below the barrier, the company defaults on the debt.

Exhibit 8: A Structural Model of Default

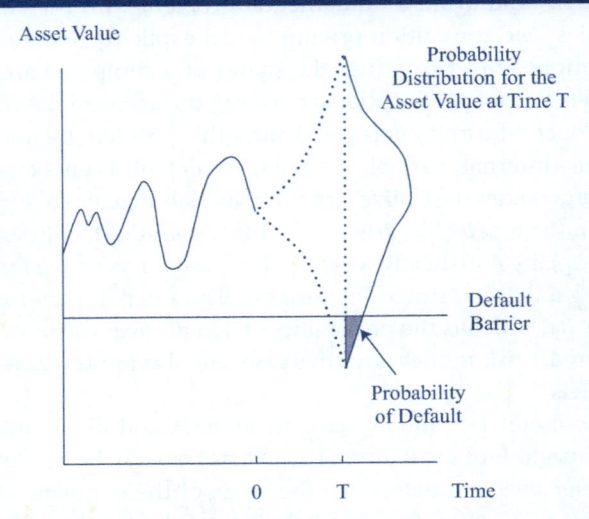

Source: This exhibit is adapted from Duffie and Singleton (2003, p. 54).

There is a probability distribution for the asset value as of some future date, time T. The probability of default is endogenous to this structural model. It is the portion of the probability distribution that lies below the default barrier. This default probability increases with the variance of the future asset value, with greater time to T, and with greater financial leverage. Less debt in the capital structure lowers the horizontal line and reduces the probability of default. These factors indicate that credit risk is linked to option pricing theory.

An important feature of the structural credit models is that they allow interpretation of debt and equity values in terms of options. Let $A(T)$ be the random asset value as of time T. To simplify, we can assume that the debt liabilities are zero-coupon bonds that mature at time T. These bonds have a face value of K, which represents the default barrier in Exhibit 8. The values for debt and equity at time T are denoted $D(T)$ and $E(T)$ and depend on the relationship between $A(T)$ and K:

$$D(T) + E(T) = A(T). \tag{1}$$

$$E(T) = \max[A(T) - K, 0]. \tag{2}$$

$$D(T) = A(T) - \max[A(T) - K, 0]. \tag{3}$$

Equation 1 is the balance sheet identity: The market values of debt and equity at time T equal the asset value. Equation 2 indicates that equity is essentially a purchased call option on the assets of the company whereby the strike price is the face value of the debt. It is a long position in a call option because the value of equity goes up when the asset value goes up. Moreover, like options, equity does not take on negative values. Equation 3 shows that in this formulation, the debtholders own the assets of the company and have written the call option held by the shareholders. We can interpret the premium that the debtholders receive for writing the option as the value of having priority of claim in the event that the asset value falls below K. In that case, the value of equity falls to zero and the debtholders own the remaining assets.

Suppose that at time T, $A(T) > K$ so that the call option is in the money to the shareholders. Then, $E(T) = A(T) - K$ and $D(T) = A(T) - [A(T) - K] = K$. Instead, suppose that $A(T) < K$ so that the call option is out of the money and the debt is in default.

In this case, $E(T) = 0$ and $D(T) = A(T) - 0 = A(T)$. In both situations, as well as when $A(T) = K$, the balance sheet identity holds. Notice that *limited liability* is an inherent assumption in this model. Equity, like options, does not take on negative values.

EXAMPLE 5

An Equivalent Option Interpretation of Debt and Equity

1. Carol Feely is a junior credit analyst at one of the major international credit rating agencies. She understands that in the standard structural models, equity is interpreted as a call option on the asset value of the company. However, she is not comfortable with the assumption that it is the debtholders who implicitly own the assets and write a call option on them. She claims that the model should start with the understanding that the shareholders own the net value of the company, which is $A(T) - K$, and that their limited liability is essentially the value of a long position in a put option at a strike price of K. Furthermore, the debtholders own a "risk-free" bond having a value of K at time T and a short position in the put that is held by the shareholders.

   Demonstrate that Ms. Feely's "embedded put option" interpretation provides the same values for debt and equity at time T as does the more customary call option structural model.

Solution:

A long position in a put option on the asset value at a strike price of K takes the form $\max[K - A(T), 0]$. This put option has intrinsic value to its holder when $K > A(T)$ and is worthless when $K \leq A(T)$. The values for $E(T)$ and $D(T)$ according to Ms. Feely at time T are as follows:

$$E(T) = A(T) - K + \max[K - A(T), 0].$$

$$D(T) = K - \max[K - A(T), 0].$$

If $A(T) > K$ at time T, the put option is out of the money, $E(T) = A(T) - K + 0$ $= A(T) - K$, and $D(T) = K - 0 = K$. If $A(T) < K$, the put is in the money, $E(T)$ $= A(T) - K + [K - A(T)] = 0$, and $D(T) = K - [K - A(T)] = A(T)$. This interpretation indicates that the value of limited liability to shareholders is the value of the put option that they purchase from the debtholders. Ms. Feely is correct in that the same payoffs as the embedded call option interpretation are obtained.

Although credit risk is inherently linked to option pricing, it is the implementation of structural models that has provided practical value to fixed-income analysis. Many credit rating agencies and consultancies, most notably Moody's KMV Corporation, use option pricing methodologies to estimate such credit risk parameters as the probability of default and the loss given default. Building on the classic Black–Scholes–Merton model and later variants, the model builders use historical data on the company's equity price to estimate volatility, which is a key element in option pricing models.

These advantages and disadvantages indicate that the choice of credit risk model depends on how it is to be used and by whom. Structural models require information best known to the managers of the company (and perhaps their commercial bankers and the credit rating agencies). Therefore, they can be used for internal risk management, for banks' internal credit risk measures, and for publicly available credit ratings. Reduced-form models require only information generally available in financial markets, which suggests that they should be used to value risky debt securities and credit derivatives.

5   VALUING RISKY BONDS IN AN ARBITRAGE-FREE FRAMEWORK

☐ calculate the value of a bond and its credit spread, given assumptions about the credit risk parameters

In this section, we use the arbitrage-free framework to analyze the credit risk of a corporate bond in the context of volatile interest rates (based on Smith 2017). Earlier, we solved for the credit valuation adjustment and the credit spread under the assumptions of no interest rate volatility and a flat government bond yield curve. A binomial interest rate tree for benchmark bond yields allows us to calculate the *expected exposure* to default loss. In addition, we have an upward-sloping yield curve for benchmark bonds. We take the risk-neutral probability of default as given, as if it has been determined using a structural or reduced-form credit model. We also assume a recovery rate if default were to occur that conforms to the seniority of the debt issue and the nature of the issuer's assets.

The first step is to build the binomial interest rate tree under the assumption of no arbitrage. Exhibit 9 displays the data on annual payment benchmark government bonds that are used to build the binomial interest rate tree. This is the *par curve* because each bond is priced at par value. The coupon rates are equal to the yields to maturity because the years to maturity are whole numbers (integers) so that there is no accrued interest. The one-year government bond has a negative yield to reflect the conditions seen in some financial markets. Note that the actual one-year security is likely to be a zero-coupon bond priced at a premium, at 100.2506 per 100 of par value: $(100/100.2506) - 1 = -0.0025$. However, on a par curve for which all the bonds are priced at 100, it is shown as having a negative coupon rate.

Exhibit 9: Par Curve for Annual Payment Benchmark Government Bonds, Spot Rates, Discount Factors, and Forward Rates

Maturity	Coupon Rate	Price	Discount Factor	Spot Rate	Forward Rate
1	−0.25%	100	1.002506	−0.2500%	
2	0.75%	100	0.985093	0.7538%	1.7677%
3	1.50%	100	0.955848	1.5166%	3.0596%
4	2.25%	100	0.913225	2.2953%	4.6674%
5	2.75%	100	0.870016	2.8240%	4.9664%

Note: All calculations in this and subsequent exhibits were completed on a spreadsheet; rounded results are reported in the text.

The discount factors and spot rates are bootstrapped using the cash flows on the underlying benchmark bonds in this sequence of equations:

$$100 = (100 - 0.25) \times DF_1.$$

$$DF_1 = 1.002506.$$

$$100 = (0.75 \times 1.002506) + (100.75 \times DF_2).$$

$$DF_2 = 0.985093.$$

$$100 = (1.50 \times 1.002506) + (1.50 \times 0.985093) + (101.50 \times DF_3).$$

$$DF_3 = 0.955848.$$

$$100 = (2.25 \times 1.002506) + (2.25 \times 0.985093) + (2.25 \times 0.955848) + (102.25 \times DF_4).$$

$$DF_4 = 0.913225.$$

$$100 = (2.75 \times 1.002506) + (2.75 \times 0.985093) + (2.75 \times 0.955848) + (2.75 \times 0.913225) + (102.75 \times DF_5).$$

$$DF_5 = 0.870016.$$

The spot (i.e., implied zero-coupon) rates can be calculated from the discount factors; for instance, the two-year spot rate is 0.7538% and the four-year spot rate is 2.2953%:

$$\left(\frac{1}{0.985093}\right)^{1/2} - 1 = 0.007538.$$

$$\left(\frac{1}{0.913225}\right)^{1/4} - 1 = 0.022953.$$

The forward rates are calculated as the ratios of the discount factors. The one-year forward rate two years into the future is 3.0596%: 0.985093/0.955848 − 1 = 0.030596. The one-year forward rate four years into the future is 4.9665%: 0.913225/0.870016 − 1 = 0.049665.

Following the methodology detailed in the "Arbitrage-Free Valuation Framework" topic, we build a binomial interest rate tree for one-year forward rates consistent with the pricing of the benchmark government bonds and an assumption of future interest rate volatility. Here we assume 10% volatility. The resulting binomial interest rate tree is presented in Exhibit 10. Below each rate is the probability of attaining that node in the tree. The current (Date 0) one-year rate of −0.25% will rise to 1.9442% or "fall" to 1.5918% by the end of the year (Date 1) with equal probability. On Date 2, at the end of the second year, the one-year rate will be 3.7026%, 3.0315%, or 2.4820% with probabilities of 0.25, 0.50, and 0.25, respectively. On Date 4, the forward rate will fall within the range of a high of 7.2918% to a low of 3.2764%. For each date, the possible rates are spread out around the forward rates shown in Exhibit 9.

Exhibit 10: One-Year Binomial Interest Rate Tree for 10% Volatility

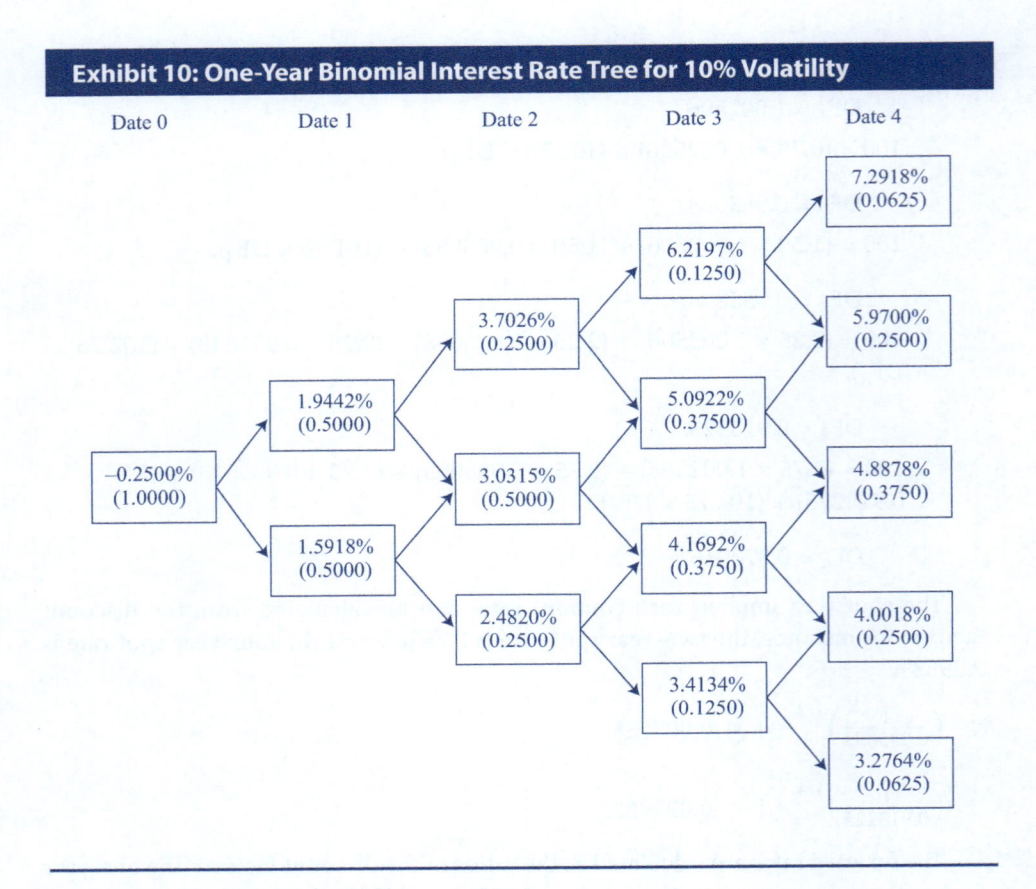

To demonstrate that this is an arbitrage-free binomial interest rate tree, we calculate the Date 0 value of a 2.75% annual payment government bond. We know from Exhibit 9 that this bond is priced at par value. Exhibit 11 shows that the Date 0 value is indeed 100.0000. Notice that the scheduled year-end coupon and principal payments are placed to the right of each forward rate in the tree.

Exhibit 11: Valuation of a 2.75% Annual Payment Government Bond

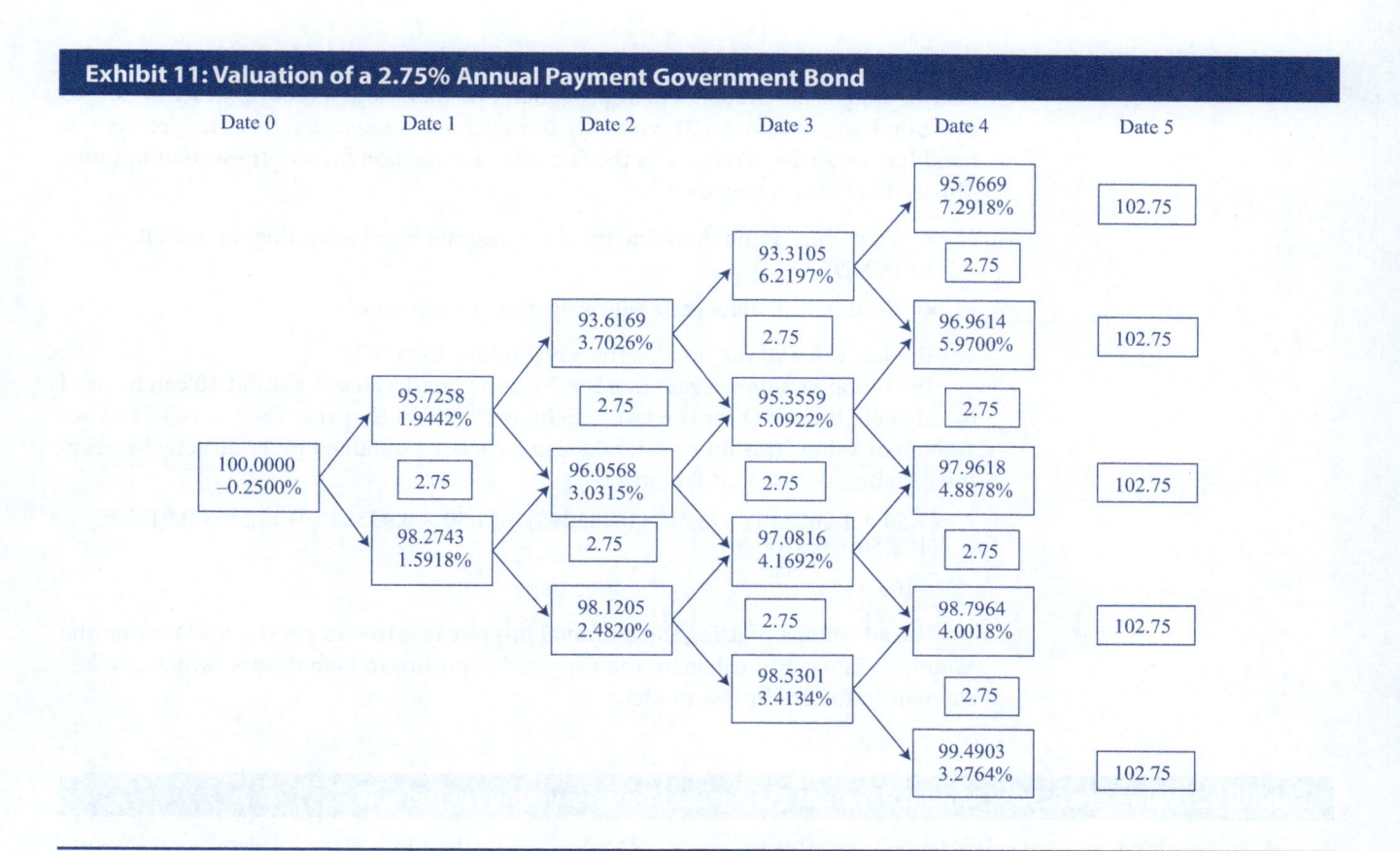

These are the five Date 4 values for the government bond, shown above the interest rate at each node:

$102.75/1.072918 = 95.7669.$

$102.75/1.059700 = 96.9614.$

$102.75/1.048878 = 97.9618.$

$102.75/1.040018 = 98.7964.$

$102.75/1.032764 = 99.4903.$

These are the four Date 3 values:

$$\frac{[(0.5 \times 95.7669) + (0.5 \times 96.9614)] + 2.75}{1.062197} = 93.3105.$$

$$\frac{[(0.5 \times 96.9614) + (0.5 \times 97.9618)] + 2.75}{1.050922} = 95.3559.$$

$$\frac{[(0.5 \times 97.9618) + (0.5 \times 98.7964)] + 2.75}{1.041692} = 97.0816.$$

$$\frac{[(0.5 \times 98.7964) + (0.5 \times 99.4903)] + 2.75}{1.034134} = 98.5301.$$

Continuing with backward induction, the Date 0 value turns out to be 100.0000, confirming that the binomial interest rate tree has been correctly calibrated.

Now consider a five-year, 3.50% annual payment corporate bond. A fixed-income analyst assigns an annual default probability of 1.25% and a recovery rate of 40% to this bond and assumes 10% volatility in benchmark interest rates. The problem at hand for the analyst is to assess the fair value for the bond under these assumptions. This is done in two steps:

- First, determine the value for the corporate bond assuming no default (VND).

- Second, calculate the credit valuation adjustment.

The fair value of the bond is the VND minus the CVA.

The binomial interest rate tree for the benchmark rates in Exhibit 10 can be used to calculate the VND for the bond. Exhibit 12 shows that the VND is 103.5450 per 100 of par value. This number could also have been obtained more directly by using the benchmark discount factors:

$(3.50 \times 1.002506) + (3.50 \times 0.985093) + (3.50 \times 0.955848) + (3.50 \times 0.913225) + (103.50 \times 0.870016)$

$= 103.5450.$

The advantage of using the binomial interest rate tree to get the VND is that the same tree is used to calculate the expected exposure to default loss, which is a key element in the credit risk model.

Exhibit 12: Value of a 3.50% Annual Payment Corporate Bond Assuming No Default

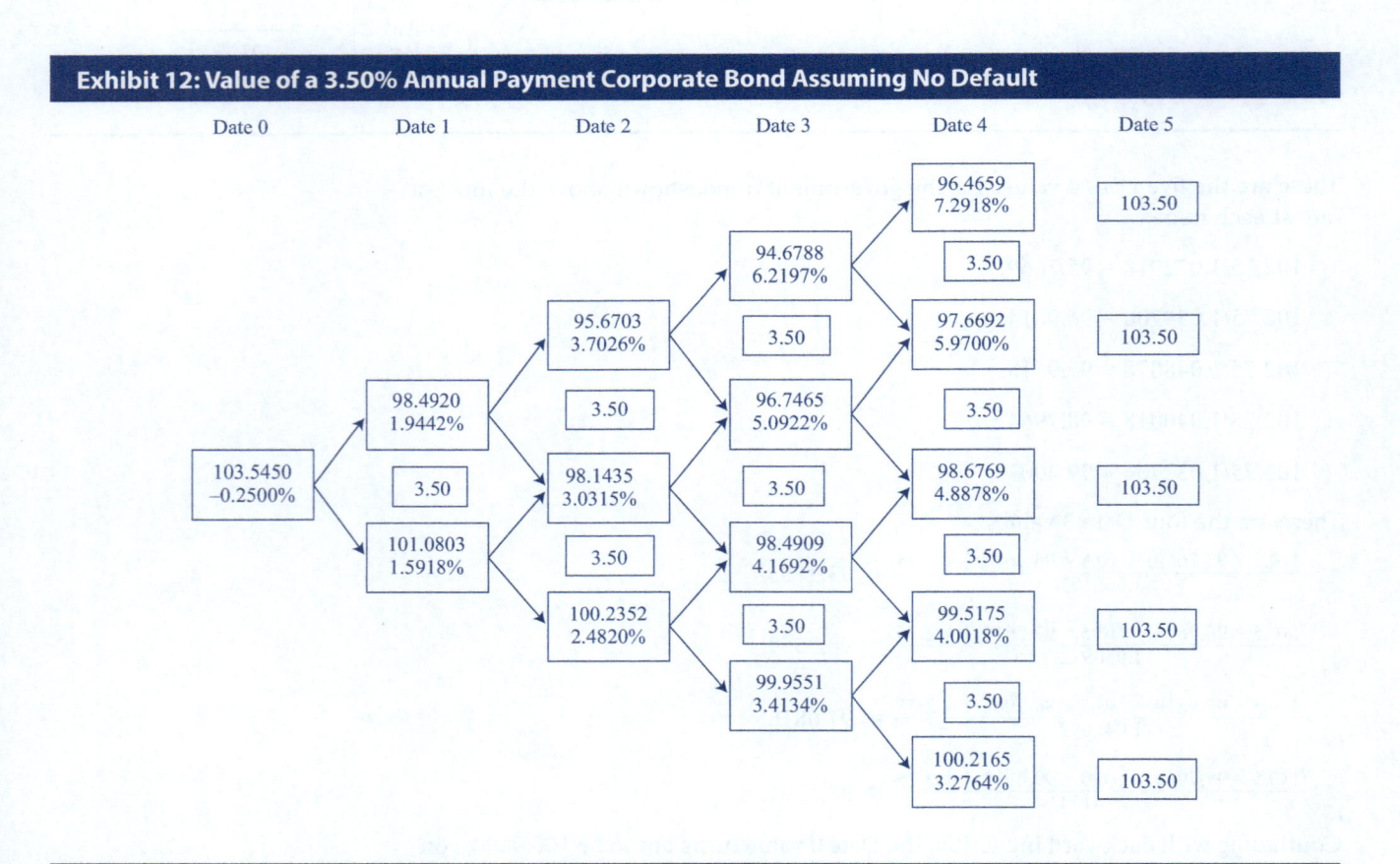

Exhibit 13 shows that the credit valuation adjustment to the value assuming no default is 3.5394 per 100 of par value. The expected exposure for Date 4 is 102.0931, calculated using the bond values at each node, the probability of attaining the node, and the coupon payment:

$$(0.0625 \times 96.4659) + (0.25 \times 97.6692) + (0.375 \times 98.6769) + (0.25 \times 99.5175) +$$
$$(0.0625 \times 100.2165) + 3.50$$
$$= 102.0931.$$

(Note again that all calculations are done on a spreadsheet to maintain precision; only the rounded results are reported in the text.) The loss given default for Date 4 is 61.2559 [= 102.0931 × (1 − 0.40)] because the assumed recovery rate is 40% of the exposure. The probability of default at Date 4 is 1.2037%, assuming no prior default. This is based on the probability of survival into the fourth year. It is calculated as

$$1.25\% \times (100\% - 1.25\%)^3 = 1.2037\%.$$

The probability of survival after Date 3 is $(100\% - 1.25\%)^3$, and the probability of default on Date 4 is 1.25%. The product of the LGD and the POD is the expected loss. The present value of the expected loss, 0.6734, is the contribution to total CVA for Date 4. The sum of the CVAs for each year is the overall CVA.

Exhibit 13: Credit Valuation Adjustment for the 3.50% Annual Payment Corporate Bond

Date	Expected Exposure	LGD	POD	Discount Factor	CVA per Year
0					
1	103.2862	61.9717	1.2500%	1.002506	0.7766
2	101.5481	60.9289	1.2344%	0.985093	0.7409
3	101.0433	60.6260	1.2189%	0.955848	0.7064
4	102.0931	61.2559	1.2037%	0.913225	0.6734
5	103.5000	62.1000	1.1887%	0.870016	0.6422
			6.0957%	CVA =	3.5394

The fixed-income analyst concludes that the fair value of the corporate bond is 100.0056 per 100 of par value: 103.5450 − 3.5394 = 100.0056. Depending on the current market price for the bond, the analyst might recommend a buy or sell decision.

The yield to maturity (YTM) for the corporate bond given a fair value of 100.0056 is 3.4988%:

$$100.0056 = \frac{3.50}{(1+YTM)^1} + \frac{3.50}{(1+YTM)^2} + \frac{3.50}{(1+YTM)^3} + \frac{3.50}{(1+YTM)^4} + \frac{103.50}{(1+YTM)^5}.$$
$$YTM = 0.034988.$$

The five-year par yield for the government bond in Exhibit 9 is 2.75%. Therefore, the credit spread over the benchmark bond is 0.7488% (= 3.4988% − 2.75%). In practice, the credit spread is typically measured against the actual yield on the comparable-maturity government bond, which might be trading at a premium or a discount.

We can say that the credit risk on this corporate bond is captured by a CVA of 3.5394 per 100 in par value as of Date 0 or as an annual spread of 74.88 bps per year for five years. This conclusion, however, assumes that the observed credit spread is based entirely on credit risk. In fact, there usually are liquidity and tax differences between government and corporate bonds. Those differences are neglected in this analysis to focus on credit risk. Stated differently, the liquidity and tax differences are represented in the credit spread.

EXAMPLE 6

Using Credit Analysis in Decision Making

1. Lori Boller is a fixed-income money manager specializing in taking long positions on high-yield corporate bonds that she deems to be undervalued. In particular, she looks for bonds for which the credit spread over government securities appears to indicate too high a probability of default or too low a recovery rate if default were to occur. Currently, she is looking at a three-year, 4.00% annual payment bond that is priced at 104 (per 100 of par value). In her opinion, this bond should be priced to reflect an annual default probability of 2.25% given a recovery rate of 40%. Ms. Boller is comfortable with an assumption of 10% volatility in government bond yields over the next few years. Should she consider buying this bond for her portfolio? Use the government par curve in Exhibit 9 and the binomial interest rate tree in Exhibit 10 in the solution.

Solution:

Ms. Boller needs to calculate the fair value of the three-year, 4% annual payment corporate bond given her assumptions about the credit risk parameters. The results are shown in Exhibit 14.

Exhibit 14: Fair Value of the Three-Year, 4% Annual Payment Corporate Bond

Date	Expected Exposure	LGD	POD	Discount Factor	CVA per Year
0					
1	107.0902	64.2541	2.2500%	1.002506	1.4493
2	104.9120	62.9472	2.1994%	0.985093	1.3638
3	104.0000	62.4000	2.1499%	0.955848	1.2823
			6.5993%	CVA =	4.0954

The VND for the bond is 107.3586. The calculations for the bond values in the binomial interest rate tree are as follows:

$104/1.037026 = 100.2868$.

$104/1.030315 = 100.9400$.

$104/1.024820 = 101.4812$.

$$\frac{(0.5 \times 100.2868) + (0.5 \times 100.9400) + 4}{1.019442} = 102.6183.$$

$$\frac{(0.5 \times 100.9400) + (0.5 \times 101.4812) + 4}{1.015918} = 103.5621.$$

$$\frac{(0.5 \times 102.6183) + (0.5 \times 103.5621) + 4}{0.997500} = 107.3586.$$

The CVA for the bond is 4.0954 given the assumption of an annual default probability of 2.25% and a recovery rate of 40% of the expected exposure. The following are calculations for the Date 1 and Date 2 expected exposures:

$(0.50 \times 102.6183) + (0.50 \times 103.5621) + 4 = 107.0902$.

$(0.25 \times 100.2868) + (0.50 \times 100.9400) + (0.25 \times 101.4812) + 4 = 104.9120$.

The calculations for the LGD are as follows:

$107.0902 \times (1 - 0.40) = 64.2541$.

$104.9120 \times (1 - 0.40) = 62.9472$.

$104 \times (1 - 0.40) = 62.4000$.

The following are calculations for the POD for Date 2 and Date 3:

$2.25\% \times (100\% - 2.25\%) = 2.1994\%$.

$2.25\% \times (100\% - 2.25\%)^2 = 2.1499\%$.

Ms. Boller determines, on the basis of her assumed credit risk parameters, that the fair value for the high-yield corporate bond is 103.2632 (= 107.3586 − 4.0954). Given that the bond is trading at 104, she would likely decline to purchase because in her opinion the bond is overvalued.

A change in the assumed level of interest rate volatility can be shown to have a small impact on the fair value of the corporate bond. Usually the effect of a change in volatility is demonstrated with a bond having an embedded option, such as a callable or putable bond. Here we see an impact of the calculation of CVA on a bond having no embedded options. This is illustrated with Exhibit 15 and Exhibit 16, which use a no-arbitrage binomial interest rate tree for 20% volatility to value the five-year, 3.50% annual payment corporate bond using the same credit risk parameters as in the previous calculations.

Exhibit 15: VND Calculation for the 3.50% Corporate Bond Assuming No Default and 20% Volatility

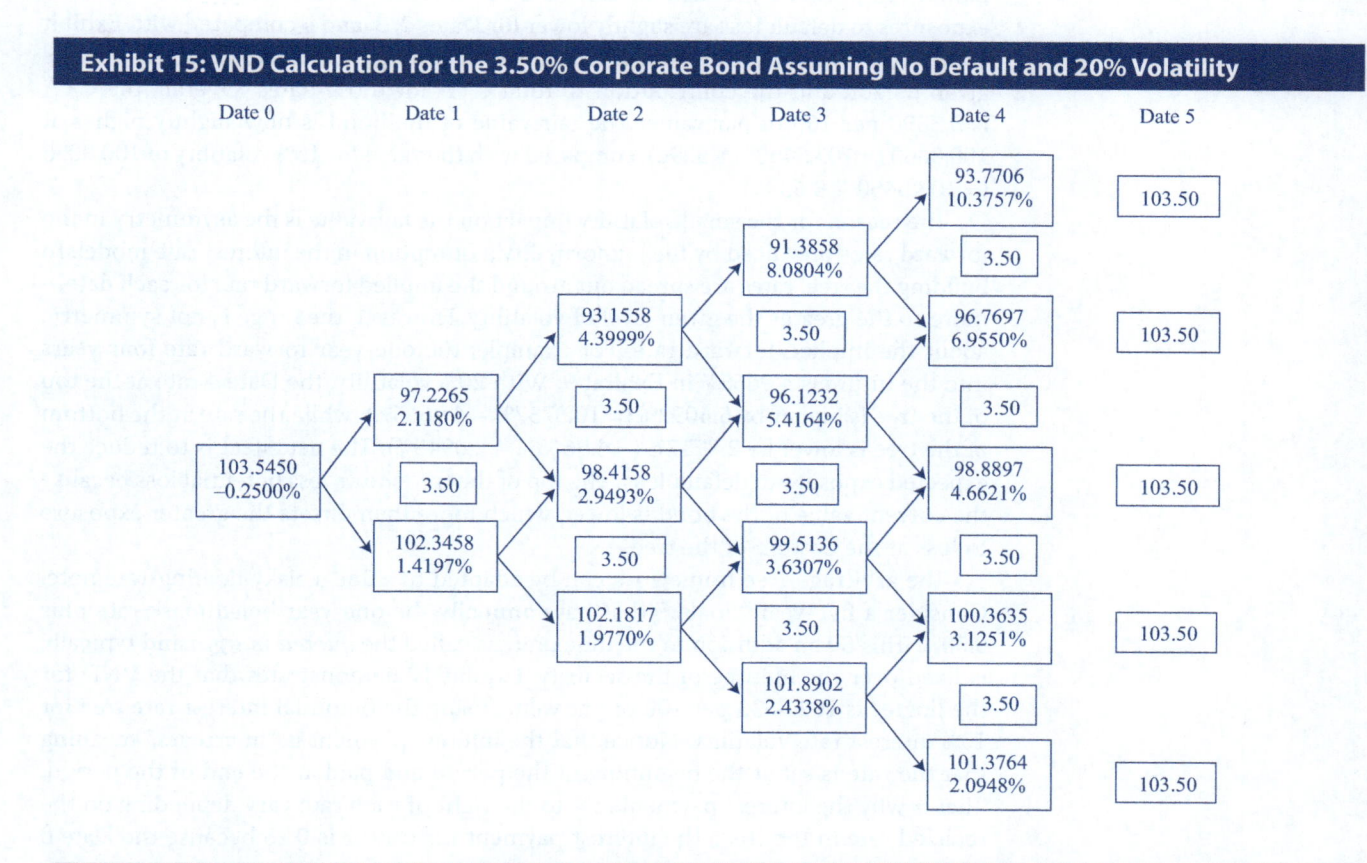

Notice in Exhibit 15 that with 20% volatility, the range in forward rates for each date is now wider. With 10% volatility, the Date 4 rates go from a low of 3.2764% to a high of 7.2918%. Now, with 20% volatility, the range is from 2.0948% to 10.3757%. The key point is that changing all the bond values still results in a VND of 103.5450. This confirms that the tree has been correctly calibrated and that the assumed level of future interest rate volatility has no impact on the value of a default-risk-free government bond. Changes in the fair value of a corporate bond arising from a change in the assumed rate volatility occur only when there are embedded options and, as demonstrated in Exhibit 16, when there is credit risk.

Exhibit 16: CVA Calculation for the 3.50% Corporate Bond Assuming 20% Volatility

Date	Expected Exposure	LGD	POD	Discount Factor	CVA per Year
0					
1	103.2862	61.9717	1.2500%	1.002506	0.7766
2	101.5423	60.9254	1.2344%	0.985093	0.7408
3	101.0233	60.6140	1.2189%	0.955848	0.7062
4	102.0636	61.2382	1.2037%	0.913225	0.6732
5	103.5000	62.1000	1.1887%	0.870016	0.6422
			6.0957%	CVA =	3.5390

Exhibit 16 presents the table to calculate the CVA for 20% volatility. The expected exposures to default loss are slightly lower for Dates 2, 3, and 4 compared with Exhibit 13 for 10% volatility. These small changes feed through the table, reducing the loss given default and the contribution to total CVA for those dates. Overall, the CVA is 3.5390 per 100 of par value. The fair value of the bond is now slightly higher at 100.0060 (= 103.5450 − 3.5390), compared with the value for 10% volatility of 100.0056 (= 103.5450 − 3.5394).

The reason for the small volatility impact on the fair value is the asymmetry in the forward rates produced by the lognormality assumption in the interest rate model. In building the tree, rates are spread out around the implied forward rate for each date—more so the greater the given level of volatility. However, the range is not symmetric about the implied forward rate. For example, the one-year forward rate four years into the future is 4.9665% in Exhibit 9. With 20% volatility, the Date 4 rate at the top of the tree is higher by 5.4092% (= 10.3757% − 4.9665%), while the rate at the bottom of the tree is lower by 2.8717% (= 4.9665% − 2.0948%). The net effect is to reduce the expected exposure to default loss. The top of the tree shows less potential loss because the current value of the bond is lower, which more than offsets the greater exposure to loss at the bottom of the tree.

The arbitrage-free framework can be adapted to value a risky floating-rate note. Consider a five-year "floater" that pays annually the one-year benchmark rate plus 0.50%. This 50 bp addition to the index rate is called the *quoted margin* and typically is fixed over the lifetime of the security. Exhibit 17 demonstrates that the VND for the floater is 102.3633 per 100 of par value, using the binomial interest rate tree for 10% interest rate volatility. Notice that the interest payment is "in arrears," meaning that the rate is set at the beginning of the period and paid at the end of the period. That is why the interest payments set to the right of each rate vary depending on the realized rate in the tree. The interest payment for Date 1 is 0.25 because the Date 0 reference rate is −0.25%: (−0.25% + 0.50%) × 100 = 0.25. The final payment on Date 5 when the floater matures is 105.3878 if the one-year rate is 4.8878% on Date 4: (4.8878% + 0.50%) × 100 + 100 = 105.3878.

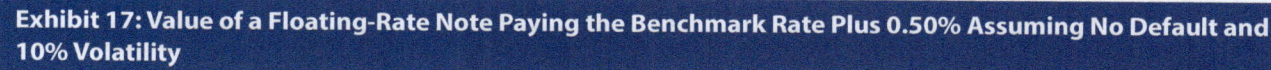

Exhibit 17: Value of a Floating-Rate Note Paying the Benchmark Rate Plus 0.50% Assuming No Default and 10% Volatility

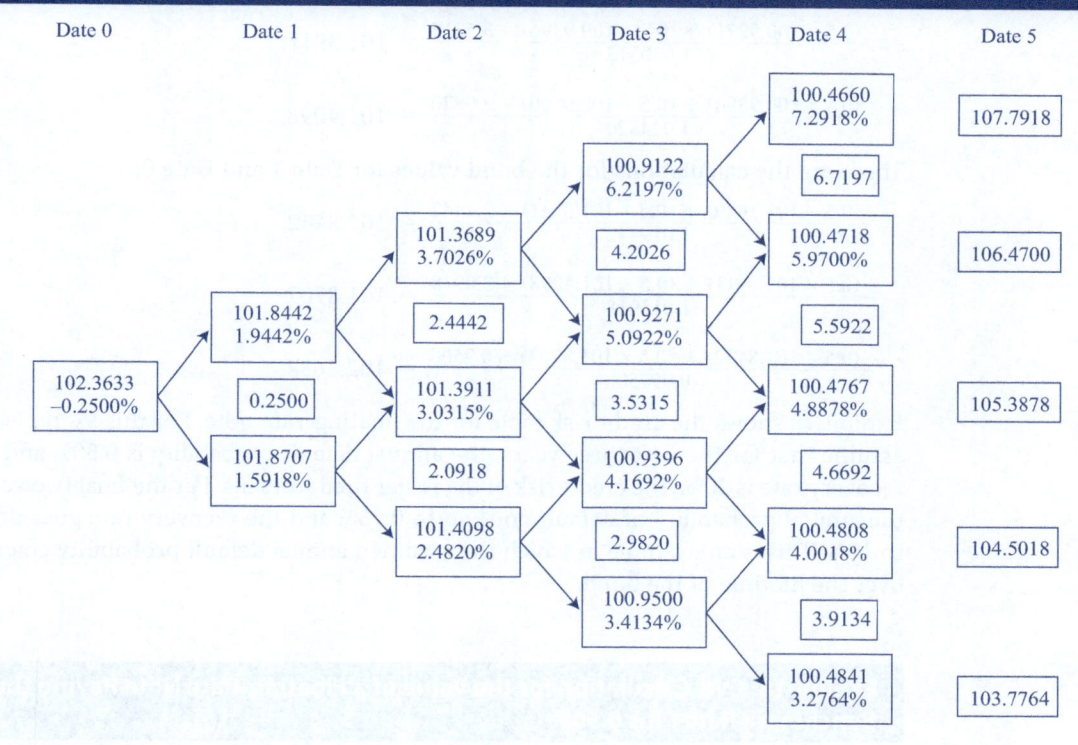

Notice that the bond values for each date are very similar for the various forward rates. That, of course, is the intent of a floating-rate note. The bond values would all be exactly 100.0000 if the note paid the benchmark rate "flat," meaning a quoted margin of zero. The VND of 102.3633 is obtained via backward induction (i.e., beginning at maturity and working backward in time). The following are the calculations for the bond values for Date 4:

107.7918/1.072918 = 100.4660.

106.4700/1.059700 = 100.4718.

105.3878/1.048878 = 100.4767.

104.5018/1.040018 = 100.4808.

103.7764/1.032764 = 100.4841.

These are the calculations for Date 3:

$$\frac{(0.5 \times 100.4660) + (0.5 \times 100.4718) + 6.7197}{1.062197} = 100.9122.$$

$$\frac{(0.50 \times 100.4718) + (0.5 \times 100.4767) + 5.5922}{1.050922} = 100.9271.$$

$$\frac{(0.5 \times 100.4767) + (0.5 \times 100.4808) + 4.6692}{1.041692} = 100.9396.$$

$$\frac{(0.5 \times 100.4808) + (0.5 \times 100.4841) + 3.9134}{1.034134} = 100.9500.$$

These are the calculations for the bond values for Date 2:

$$\frac{(0.5 \times 100.9122) + (0.5 \times 100.9271) + 4.2026}{1.037026} = 101.3689.$$

$$\frac{(0.5 \times 100.9271) + (0.5 \times 100.9396) + 3.5315}{1.030315} = 101.3911.$$

$$\frac{(0.5 \times 100.9396) + (0.5 \times 100.9500) + 2.9820}{1.024820} = 101.4098.$$

These are the calculations for the bond values for Date 1 and Date 0:

$$\frac{(0.5 \times 101.3689) + (0.5 \times 101.3911) + 2.4442}{1.019442} = 101.8442.$$

$$\frac{(0.5 \times 101.3911) + (0.5 \times 101.4098) + 2.0918}{1.015918} = 101.8707.$$

$$\frac{(0.5 \times 101.8442) + (0.5 \times 101.8707) + 0.2500}{0.997500} = 102.3633.$$

Exhibit 18 shows the credit risk table for the floating-rate note. For this example, we assume that for the first three years, the annual default probability is 0.50% and the recovery rate is 20%. The credit risk of the issuer then worsens: For the final two years, the annual probability of default goes up to 0.75% and the recovery rate goes down to 10%. This is an example in which the assumed annual default probability changes over the lifetime of the bond.

Exhibit 18: CVA Calculation for the Value of a Floating-Rate Note Paying the Benchmark Rate Plus 0.50%

Date	Expected Exposure	LGD	POD	Discount Factor	CVA per Year
0					
1	102.1074	81.6859	0.5000%	1.002506	0.4095
2	103.6583	82.9266	0.4975%	0.985093	0.4064
3	104.4947	83.5957	0.4950%	0.955848	0.3955
4	105.6535	95.0881	0.7388%	0.913225	0.6416
5	105.4864	94.9377	0.7333%	0.870016	0.6057
			2.9646%	CVA =	2.4586

Note: Credit risk parameter assumptions: for Dates 1–3, annual default probability = 0.50% and recovery rate = 20%; for Dates 4–5, annual default probability = 0.75% and recovery rate = 10%.

The calculation for the expected exposure recognizes that the bond values for each date follow the probabilities of attaining those rates, whereas possible interest payments use the probabilities for the prior date. For example, the expected exposure to default loss for Date 4 is 105.6535:

$$\begin{bmatrix}(0.0625 \times 100.4660) + (0.25 \times 100.4718) + (0.375 \times 100.4767) \\ + (0.25 \times 100.4808) + (0.0625 \times 100.4841)\end{bmatrix}$$
$$+ [(0.125 \times 6.7197) + (0.375 \times 5.5922) + (0.375 \times 4.6692) + (0.125 \times 3.9134)]$$
$$= 105.6535.$$

The first term in brackets is the expected bond value using the Date 4 probabilities for each of the five possible rates. The second term is the expected interest payment using the Date 3 probabilities for each of the four possible rates.

The expected LGD for Date 2 is 82.9266 [= 103.6583 × (1 – 0.20)]; for Date 4, it is 95.0881 [= 105.6535 × (1 – 0.10)]. The PODs in Exhibit 18 reflect the probability of default for each year. For Date 2, the POD is 0.4975%, conditional on no default on Date 1: 0.50% × (100% – 0.50%) = 0.4975%. For Date 3, the POD is 0.4950%: 0.50% × (100% – 0.50%)^2 = 0.4950%. The probability of survival into the fourth year is 98.5075%: (100% – 0.50%)^3 = 98.5075%. Therefore, the POD for Date 4 increases to 0.7388% because of the assumed worsening credit risk: 0.75% × 98.5075% = 0.7388%. The probability of survival into the fifth year is 97.7687% (= 98.5075% – 0.7388%). The POD for Date 5 is 0.7333% (= 0.75% × 97.7687%). The cumulative probability of default over the lifetime of the floater is 2.9646%.

Given these assumptions about credit risk, the CVA for the floater is 2.4586. The fair value is 99.9047, the VND of 102.3633 minus the CVA. Because the security is priced below par value, its *discount margin* (DM) must be higher than the quoted margin of 0.50%. The discount margin for a floating-rate note is a yield measure commonly used on floating-rate notes in the same manner that the credit spread is used with fixed-rate bonds.

The arbitrage-free framework can be used to determine the DM for this floater by trial-and-error search (or GoalSeek or Solver in Excel). We add a trial DM to benchmark rates that are used to get the bond values at each node in the tree. Then the trial DM is changed until the Date 0 value matches the fair value of 99.9047. Exhibit 19 shows that the DM for this floater is 0.52046%, slightly above the quoted margin because the security is priced at a small discount below par value.

Exhibit 19: The Discount Margin for the Floating-Rate Note Paying the Benchmark Rate Plus 0.50%, Assuming 10% Volatility

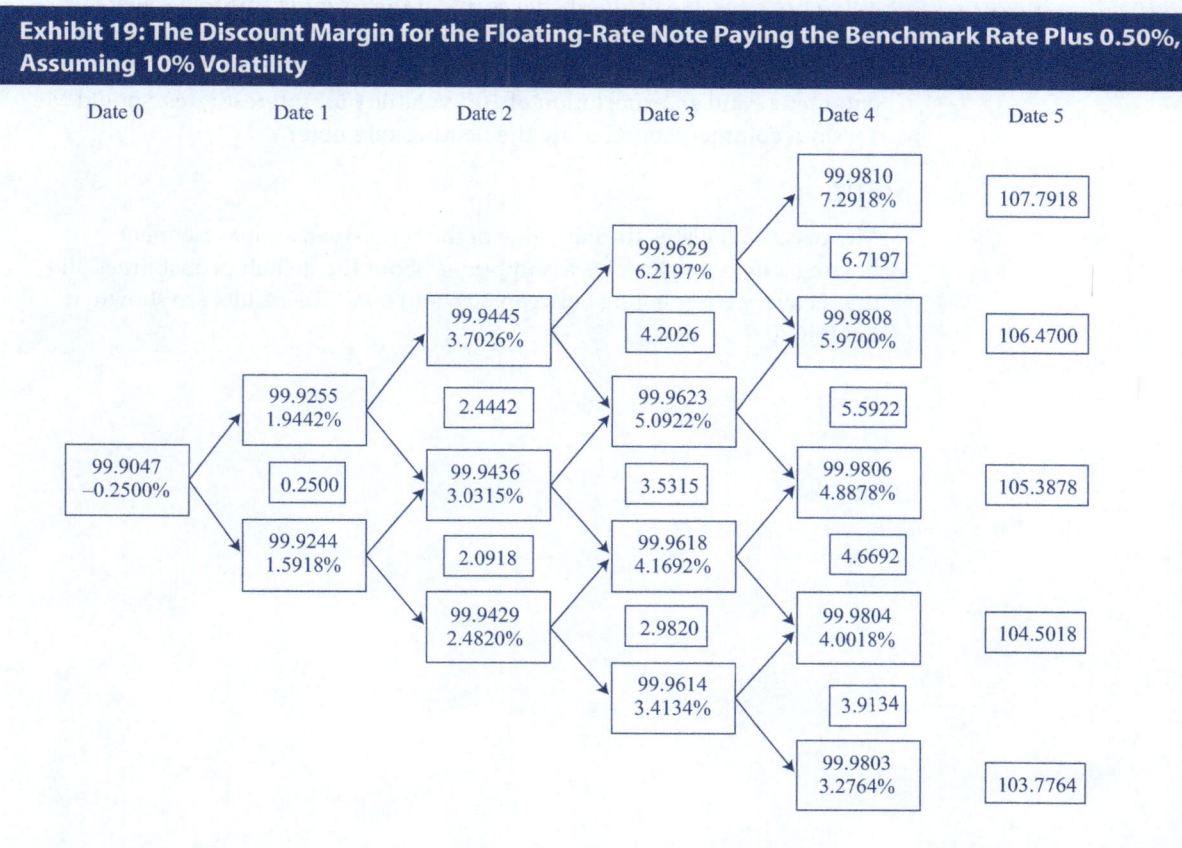

These are the calculations for the bond values for Date 2:

$$\frac{(0.5 \times 99.9629) + (0.5 \times 99.9623) + 4.2026}{1 + 0.037026 + 0.0052046} = 99.9445.$$

$$\frac{(0.5 \times 99.9623) + (0.5 \times 99.9618) + 3.5315}{1 + 0.030315 + 0.0052046} = 99.9436.$$

$$\frac{(0.5 \times 99.9618) + (0.5 \times 99.9614) + 2.9820}{1 + 0.024820 + 0.0052046} = 99.9429.$$

Throughout the binomial interest rate tree, the assumed DM is added to the benchmark rate to factor in credit risk. After a trial-and-error search, a DM of 0.52046% gives the same Date 0 value for the floating-rate note of 99.9047 as is obtained with the VND and CVA models.

EXAMPLE 7

Evaluating a Floating-Rate Note

1. Omar Yassin is an experienced credit analyst at a fixed-income investment firm. His current assignment is to assess potential purchases of distressed high-yield corporate bonds. One intriguing prospect is a three-year, annual payment floating-rate note paying the one-year benchmark rate plus 2.50%. The floater is rated CCC and is priced at 84 per 100 of par value. Based on various research reports on and prices of the issuer's credit default swaps, Mr. Yassin believes the probability of default in the next year is about 30%. If the issuer goes into bankruptcy at any time, he expects the recovery rate to be at least 50%; it could be as high as 60% because of some valuable real estate holdings. He further believes that if the issuer is able to survive this next year, the default probability for the remaining two years will be only about 10% for each year. Based on these assumptions about the credit risk parameters and an expectation of 10% volatility for interest rates, should Mr. Yassin recommend purchasing the floating-rate note?

Solution:

Mr. Yassin calculates the fair value of the three-year, annual payment floating-rate note given his assumptions about the default probabilities and the recovery rate ranging between 50% and 60%. The results are shown in Exhibit 20.

Exhibit 20: Fair Value of the Three-Year, Annual Payment Floating-Rate Note Paying the One-Year Rate Plus 2.50%

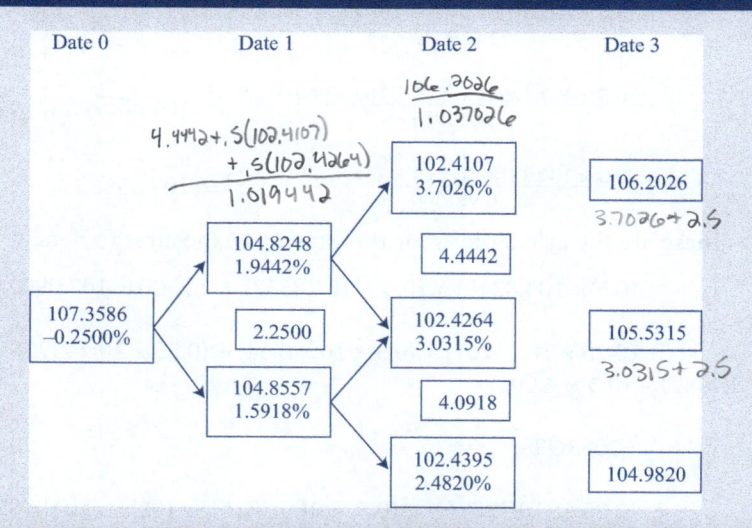

Assumed 50% Recovery Rate

Date	Expected Exposure	LGD	POD	Discount Factor	CVA per Year
0					
1	107.0902	53.5451	30.0000%	1.002506	16.1038
2	106.6938	53.3469	7.0000%	0.985093	3.6786
3	105.5619	52.7810	6.3000%	0.955848	3.1784
			43.3000%	CVA =	22.9608

Fair value = 107.3586 − 22.9608 = 84.3978.

Assumed 60% Recovery Rate

Date	Expected Exposure	LGD	POD	Discount Factor	CVA per Year
0					
1	107.0902	42.8361	30.0000%	1.002506	12.8830
2	106.6938	42.6775	7.0000%	0.985093	2.9429
3	105.5619	42.2248	6.3000%	0.955848	2.5427
			43.3000%	CVA =	18.3686

Fair value = 107.3586 − 18.3686 = 88.9900.

Each projected interest payment in the tree is the benchmark rate at the beginning of the year plus 2.50% times 100. The rate is −0.25% on Date 0; the "in-arrears" interest payment on Date 1 is 2.2500 [= (−0.25% + 2.50%) × 100]. If the rate is 2.4820% on Date 2, the payment at maturity on Date 3 is 104.9820 [= (2.4820% + 2.50%) × 100 + 100].

The VND for the floater is 107.3586. The calculations for the bond values in the binomial interest rate tree are as follows:

106.2026/1.037026 = 102.4107.

105.5315/1.030315 = 102.4264.

$$104.9820/1.024820 = 102.4395.$$

$$\frac{(0.5 \times 102.4107) + (0.5 \times 102.4264) + 4.4442}{1.019442} = 104.8248.$$

$$\frac{(0.5 \times 102.4264) + (0.5 \times 102.4395) + 4.0918}{1.015918} = 104.8557.$$

$$\frac{(0.5 \times 104.8248) + (0.5 \times 104.8557) + 2.2500}{0.997500} = 107.3586.$$

These are the calculations for the expected exposures to default loss:

$$(0.5 \times 104.8248) + (0.5 \times 104.8557) + 2.2500 = 107.0902.$$

$$(0.25 \times 102.4107) + (0.5 \times 102.4264) + (0.25 \times 102.4395) + (0.5 \times 4.4442) + (0.5 \times 4.0918)$$

$$= 106.6938.$$

$$(0.25 \times 106.2026) + (0.5 \times 105.5315) + (0.25 \times 104.9820) = 105.5619.$$

The assumed default probability for the first year is 30%. The POD for Date 2 is 7.00%, which is the probability of survival into the second year, 70%, times the 10% probability of default. The probability of survival into the third year is 63% (= 70% − 7%); the POD for Date 3 is 6.30% (= 10% × 63%).

The decision to consider purchase of the floating-rate note comes down to the assumption about recovery. Exhibit 20 first shows the results for 50% recovery of the expected exposure. The LGD on Date 2 is 53.3469 [= 106.6938 × (1 − 0.50)]. The overall CVA is 22.9608, giving a fair value of 84.3978 (= 107.3586 − 22.9608). Exhibit 20 next shows the results for 60% recovery. With this assumption, the LGD for Date 2 is just 42.6775 [= 106.6938 × (1 − 0.60)]. Stronger recovery reduces the overall CVA to 18.3686. The fair value for the floater is now 88.9900.

Mr. Yassin should recommend purchasing the distressed floating-rate note. Although there is a significant 43.3% probability of default at some point over the three years, the security appears to be fairly priced at 84 given a recovery rate of 50%. At 60% recovery, it is significantly undervalued.

In addition, there is still a 57.7% (= 100% − 43.3%) chance of no default. Exhibit 21 shows the calculation for the discount margin, which is a measure of the return to the investor assuming no default (like a yield to maturity on a fixed-rate bond). Found by a trial-and-error search, the DM is 8.9148%, considerably higher than the quoted margin because the floater is priced at a deep discount.

Exhibit 21: Discount Margin on the Three-Year, Annual Payment Floating-Rate Note Paying the One-Year Rate Plus 2.50%

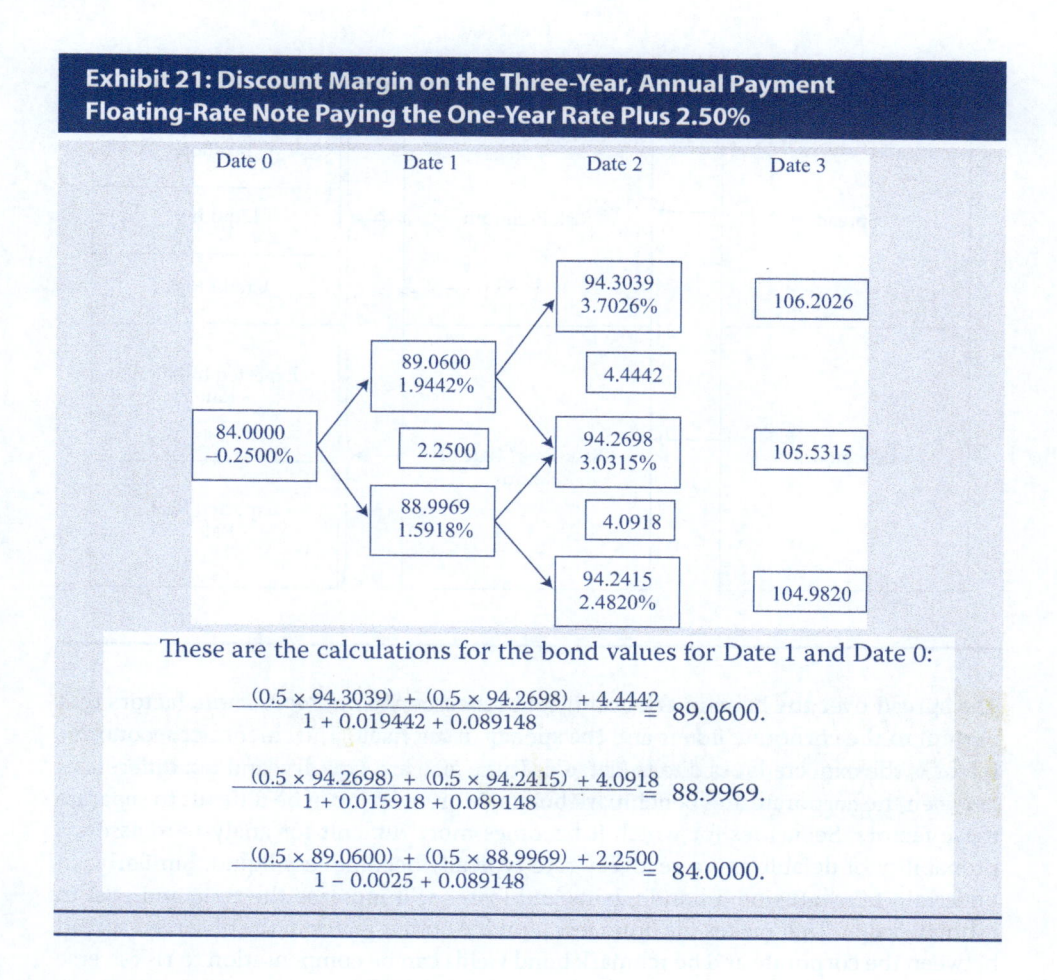

These are the calculations for the bond values for Date 1 and Date 0:

$$\frac{(0.5 \times 94.3039) + (0.5 \times 94.2698) + 4.4442}{1 + 0.019442 + 0.089148} \cong 89.0600.$$

$$\frac{(0.5 \times 94.2698) + (0.5 \times 94.2415) + 4.0918}{1 + 0.015918 + 0.089148} \cong 88.9969.$$

$$\frac{(0.5 \times 89.0600) + (0.5 \times 88.9969) + 2.2500}{1 - 0.0025 + 0.089148} \cong 84.0000.$$

INTERPRETING CHANGES IN CREDIT SPREADS

6

interpret changes in a credit spread

Corporate and benchmark bond yields and the credit spread between them change from day to day. The challenge for a fixed-income analyst is to understand that and be able to explain *why* the yields and spreads change. Exhibit 22 offers a breakdown of the main components of bond yields. Benchmark bond yields, in general, capture the *macroeconomic* factors affecting all debt securities. These are the expected inflation rate and the expected real rate of return. Risk-averse investors in benchmark bonds also might require compensation for uncertainty regarding those variables.

Exhibit 22: Components of a Corporate Bond Yield

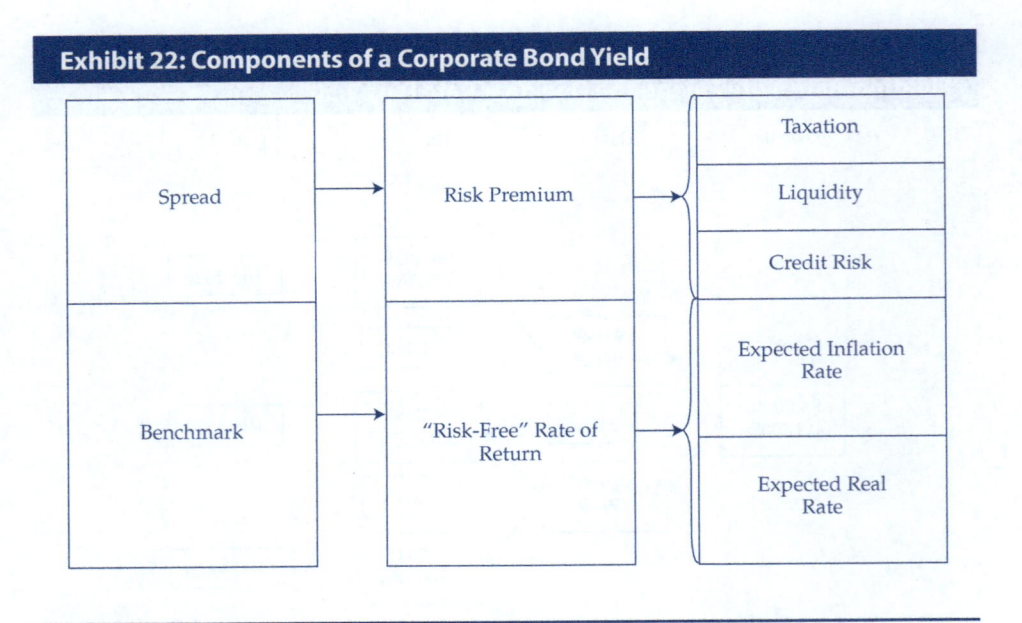

The spread over the benchmark bond yield captures the *microeconomic* factors that pertain to the corporate issuer and the specific issue itself. The chief microeconomic factor is the expected loss due to default. There also are liquidity and tax differences between the corporate and benchmark bonds. Moreover, it can be difficult to separate these factors. Securities for which it becomes more difficult for analysts to assess a probability of default and a recovery rate typically become less liquid. Similarly, an uncertain tax status on a bond's gains and losses will increase the time and cost to estimate value. That makes the bond less liquid. Another factor in the observed spread between the corporate and benchmark bond yields can be compensation to risk-averse investors for uncertainty regarding credit risk, as well as liquidity and tax factors.

Research groups at major banks and consultancies have been working on models to better include counterparty credit risk, funding costs, and liquidity and taxation effects in the valuations of derivatives. First, a value is obtained using benchmark discount factors, in practice, derived from rates on overnight indexed swaps (OIS). These are interest rate swaps that reference an average daily interest rate. For instance, in the United States this daily rate is the effective federal funds rate. Then this OIS value, which is comparable to the VND in the previous section, is adjusted for the other factors. These valuation adjustments collectively are known as the XVA. The credit valuation adjustment is the most developed and most used in practice. Others include a funding valuation adjustment (FVA), a liquidity valuation adjustment (LVA), and a taxation valuation adjustment (TVA). In principle, the same ideas apply to debt securities in that these XVA comprise the observed spread between corporate and benchmark bond yields. For the purposes of our coverage, we focus only on the credit risk component, the CVA.

We can use the arbitrage-free framework and the credit risk model to examine the connections between the default probability, the recovery rate, and the credit spread. To be sure, this is a simple model to illustrate the much more complex models used in practice. These (which are called *XVA engines*) typically use Monte Carlo simulations for thousands of possible paths for interest rates. Our binomial interest rate tree has only 16 paths for the five years; it's a model of the actual model.

Consider again the five-year, 3.50% annual payment corporate bond examined earlier. In Exhibit 12, the value assuming no default was determined to be 103.5450 per 100 of par value. Now let us use the credit risk model to find the probabilities of default that would be consistent with various credit spreads and a recovery rate of 40%. Suppose, as in Exhibit 7, the credit spread for an AAA rated bond is 0.60%. Using trial-and-error search, we find that an annual probability of default of 1.01% produces a 60 bp credit spread. The credit risk table is presented in Exhibit 23. Notice that the expected exposure to default loss and the loss given default are the same as in Exhibit 13. Only the default probabilities and the contributions to total CVA for each year change.

Exhibit 23: CVA Calculation for the 3.50% Corporate Bond Given a Default Probability of 1.01% and a Recovery Rate of 40%

Date	Expected Exposure	LGD	POD	Discount Factor	CVA per Year
0					
1	103.2862	61.9717	1.0100%	1.002506	0.6275
2	101.5481	60.9289	0.9998%	0.985093	0.6001
3	101.0433	60.6260	0.9897%	0.955848	0.5735
4	102.0931	61.2559	0.9797%	0.913225	0.5481
5	103.5000	62.1000	0.9698%	0.870016	0.5240
			4.9490%	CVA =	2.8731

The CVA for the bond is 2.8731 per 100 of par. The fair value is 100.6719 (= 103.5450 − 2.8731). This gives a yield to maturity of 3.35%.

$$100.6719 = \frac{3.50}{(1+YTM)^1} + \frac{3.50}{(1+YTM)^2} + \frac{3.50}{(1+YTM)^3} + \frac{3.50}{(1+YTM)^4} + \frac{103.50}{(1+YTM)^5}.$$

$$YTM = 0.0335.$$

Given that the yield on the five-year benchmark bond is 2.75%, the credit spread is 0.60% (= 3.35% − 2.75%).

We can repeat this exercise for the other credit spreads and ratings shown in Exhibit 7. In each case, trial-and-error search is used to get the initial POD that corresponds to the CVA, the fair value, and the yield to maturity for each assumed spread. The results for the annual and cumulative default probabilities over the five years are shown in Exhibit 24.

Exhibit 24: Default Probabilities Consistent with Given Credit Ratings and Spreads and 40% Recovery

Credit Rating	Credit Spread	Annual Default Probability	Cumulative Default Probability
AAA	0.60%	1.01%	4.95%
AA	0.90%	1.49%	7.23%
A	1.10%	1.83%	8.82%
BBB	1.50%	2.48%	11.80%
BB	3.40%	5.64%	25.19%
B	6.50%	10.97%	44.07%
CCC, CC, C	9.50%	16.50%	59.41%

The default probabilities illustrated in Exhibit 24 might seem high, especially given the historical experience presented in Exhibit 6. Since 1995, no AAA rated company has defaulted; still, we model the likelihood to be over 1% for the first year and almost 5% for the next five years. However, as discussed earlier, these are *risk-neutral* probabilities of default and are higher than the actual probabilities because market prices reflect uncertainty over the timing of possible default. Investors are concerned about credit spread widening, especially if they do not intend to hold the bond to maturity. Credit rating migration from year to year, as illustrated in Exhibit 7, is a concern even for a high-quality investment-grade corporate bond. This is captured in the risk-neutral probability of default. Also, we must remember that observed credit spreads reflect more than just credit risk—there also are liquidity and tax differences. That further explains the difference between risk-neutral and actual default probabilities.

The relationship between the assumed recovery rate and the credit spread can be examined in the context of the credit risk model. Suppose that the five-year, 3.50% annual payment corporate bond has an initial probability of default of 1.83%. In Exhibit 24, we see that for a 40% recovery rate, the credit spread is 1.10%. What if the recovery rate is expected to be only 30%? Exhibit 25 shows the credit risk table for that assumption.

Exhibit 25: CVA Calculation for the 3.50% Corporate Bond Given a Default Probability of 1.83% and a Recovery Rate of 30%

Date	Expected Exposure	LGD	POD	Discount Factor	CVA per Year
0					
1	103.2862	72.3003	1.8300%	1.002506	1.3264
2	101.5481	71.0837	1.7965%	0.985093	1.2580
3	101.0433	70.7303	1.7636%	0.955848	1.1923
4	102.0931	71.4652	1.7314%	0.913225	1.1300
5	103.5000	72.4500	1.6997%	0.870016	1.0714
			8.8212%	CVA =	5.9781

The reduction in the recovery rate from 40% to 30% has an impact on LGD and CVA for each year. The overall CVA is 5.9781 per 100 of par value. The fair value for the bond is 97.5670 (= 103.5450 − 5.9781), and the yield to maturity is 4.05%, giving a credit spread of 1.30% (= 4.05% − 2.75%).

$$97.5670 = \frac{3.50}{(1+YTM)^1} + \frac{3.50}{(1+YTM)^2} + \frac{3.50}{(1+YTM)^3} + \frac{3.50}{(1+YTM)^4} + \frac{103.50}{(1+YTM)^5}.$$

$YTM = 0.0405$.

This example illustrates how a credit rating agency might use "notching" to combine the expected loss given default and the probability of default in setting the rating for a corporate bond. If the issuer were rated single A, associated with a default probability of 1.83% and a recovery rate of 40% on the company's senior unsecured debt, that debt might have a credit spread of 1.10%, comparable to other A rated companies. This particular bond is subordinated, leading analysts at the rating agency to believe that a lower recovery rate assumption of 30% is applicable. That could justify assigning a lower rating of A− or BBB+ on the subordinated debt, along with its 20 bp higher spread.

EXAMPLE 8

Evaluating Changes in Credit Risk Parameters

1. Edward Kapili is a summer intern working on a fixed-income trading desk at a major money-center bank. His supervisor asks him to value a three-year, 3% annual payment corporate bond using a binomial interest rate tree model for 20% volatility and the current par curve for benchmark government bonds. (This is the binomial tree in Exhibit 15.) The assumed annual probability of default is 1.50%, and the recovery rate is 40%.

   The supervisor asks Mr. Kapili if the credit spread over the yield on the three-year benchmark bond, which is 1.50% in Exhibit 9, is likely to go up more if the default probability doubles to 3.00% or if the recovery rate halves to 20%. Mr. Kapili's intuition is that doubling the probability of default has a larger impact on the credit spread. Is his intuition correct?

Solution:

Mr. Kapili first determines the fair value of the three-year, 3% annual payment bond given the assumptions for the original credit risk parameters. The binomial interest rate tree and credit risk table are presented in Exhibit 26.

Exhibit 26: Fair Value of the Three-Year, 3% Annual Payment Corporate Bond Assuming 20% Volatility

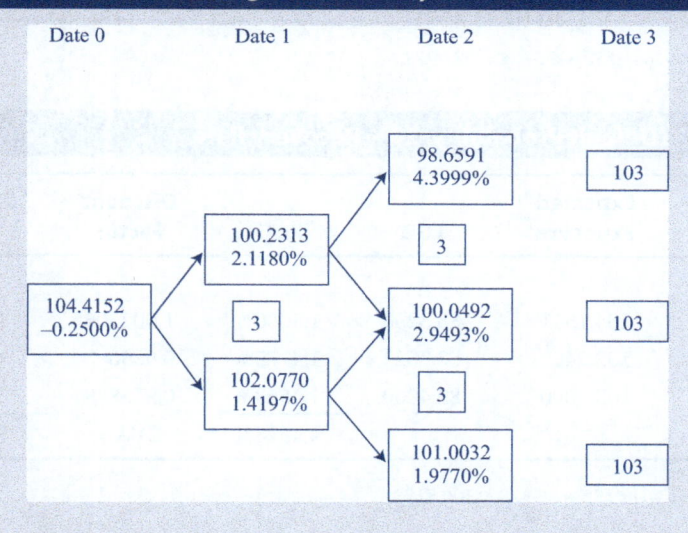

Date	Expected Exposure	LGD	POD	Discount Factor	CVA per Year
0					
1	104.1541	62.4925	1.5000%	1.002506	0.9397
2	102.9402	61.7641	1.4775%	0.985093	0.8990
3	103.0000	61.8000	1.4553%	0.955848	0.8597
			4.4328%	CVA =	2.6984

Fair value = 104.4152 − 2.6984 = 101.7168.

The VND for the bond is 104.4152, the CVA is 2.6984, and the fair value is 101.7168 per 100 of par value. The yield to maturity is 2.40%, and the credit spread is 0.90% (= 2.40% − 1.50%).

$$101.7168 = \frac{3}{(1+YTM)^1} + \frac{3}{(1+YTM)^2} + \frac{103}{(1+YTM)^3}.$$

$$YTM = 0.0240.$$

Next, Mr. Kapili calculates the fair values under the new credit risk parameters, first for doubling the default probability and second for halving the recovery rate. These tables are shown in Exhibit 27.

Exhibit 27: Fair Value Calculations for Doubling the Default Probability and Halving the Recovery Rate

3.00% Default Probability, 40% Recovery Rate

Date	Expected Exposure	LGD	POD	Discount Factor	CVA per Year
0					
1	104.1541	62.4925	3.0000%	1.002506	1.8795
2	102.9402	61.7641	2.9100%	0.985093	1.7705
3	103.0000	61.8000	2.8227%	0.955848	1.6674
			8.7327%	CVA =	5.3174

Fair value = 104.4152 − 5.3174 = 99.0978.

1.50% Default Probability, 20% Recovery Rate

Date	Expected Exposure	LGD	POD	Discount Factor	CVA per Year
0					
1	104.1541	83.3233	1.5000%	1.002506	1.2530
2	102.9402	82.3522	1.4775%	0.985093	1.1986
3	103.0000	82.4000	1.4553%	0.955848	1.1463
			4.4328%	CVA =	3.5978

Fair value = 104.4152 − 3.5978 = 100.8173.

The fair value of the corporate bond falls to 99.0978 when the default probability is raised to 3.00% and the recovery rate stays at 40%. The VND is the same, at 104.4152, and the CVA goes up to 5.3174. The yield to maturity increases to 3.32%, and the credit spread rises to 1.82% (= 3.32% − 1.50%).

$$99.0978 = \frac{3}{(1+YTM)^1} + \frac{3}{(1+YTM)^2} + \frac{103}{(1+YTM)^3}.$$

$$YTM = 0.0332.$$

The fair value of the corporate bond falls to 100.8173 when the recovery rate is reduced by half, to 20%, and the default probability is maintained at 1.50%. The VND is again the same, at 104.4152, and the CVA goes up to 3.5978.

The yield to maturity increases to 2.71%, and the credit spread rises to 1.21% (= 2.71% − 1.50%).

$$100.8173 = \frac{3}{(1+YTM)^1} + \frac{3}{(1+YTM)^2} + \frac{103}{(1+YTM)^3}.$$

$$YTM = 0.0271.$$

Mr. Kapili's intuition is correct: Doubling the default probability has a greater impact on the credit spread than halving the recovery rate.

THE TERM STRUCTURE OF CREDIT SPREADS

7

☐ | explain the determinants of the term structure of credit spreads and interpret a term structure of credit spreads

In the same way that the yield curve is composed of the interest rates on a single government issuer's debt across bond maturities, a credit curve shows the spread over a benchmark security for an issuer for outstanding fixed-income securities with shorter to longer maturities. For example, Exhibit 28 shows the relationship between US Treasury yields of a specific maturity and bonds rated AAA, AA, A, BBB, and BB. The total yields of the bonds are shown in Panel A, and spreads over the benchmark Treasury are shown in Panel B.

Exhibit 28: Composite Yield Graphs

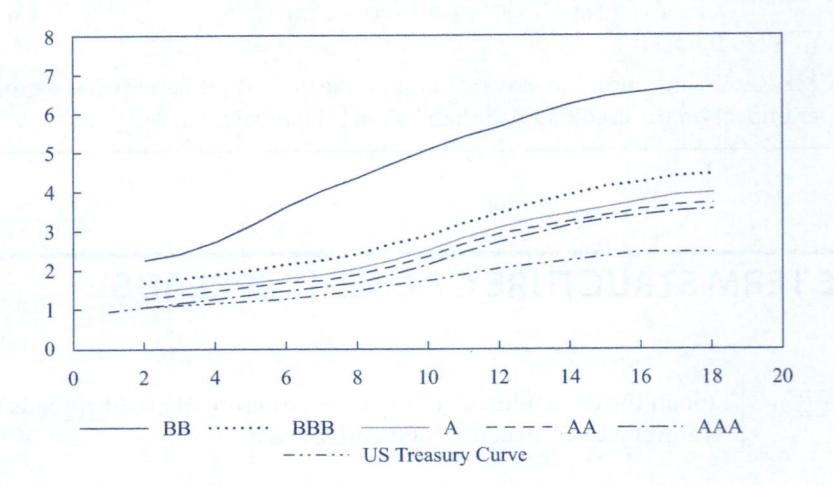

A. Total Yields

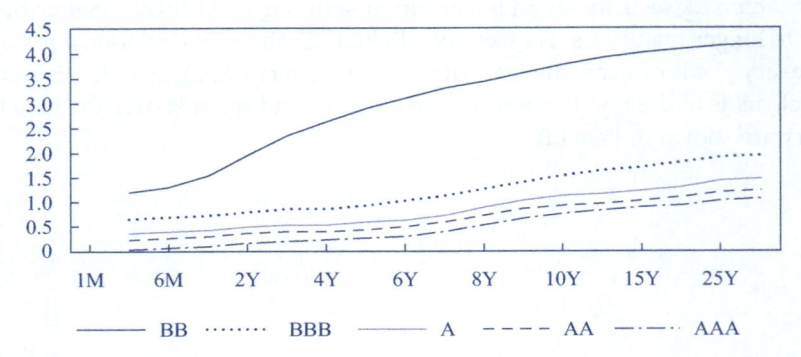

B. Spreads

Source: Bloomberg.

==The term structure of credit spreads is a useful gauge for issuers, underwriters, and investors in measuring the risk–return trade-off for a single issuer or a set of issuers across ratings and/or sectors across maturities.== Issuers often work with their underwriter to consider the terms of a new issuance or a tender for existing debt based on relative credit spreads across maturities. For example, an investment-grade bond portfolio manager might use the existing credit curve for a particular issuer to determine a bid for a new primary debt issuance as well as to inform trading decisions for secondary debt positions. In some cases, investors, issuers, or underwriters might use the credit spread term structure for a particular rating or corporate sector either to derive prospective pricing for a new issuance or to determine fair value spreads for outstanding securities, which is an extension of matrix pricing. A high-yield debt investor might employ the term structure of credit spreads to gauge the risk/reward trade-offs between debt maturities. Given the impact of monetary and fiscal policies on risky debt markets, policymakers have extended their focus from default-risk-free yield curve dynamics to the term structure of credit spreads.

There are several key drivers of the term structure of credit spreads. First, credit quality is a key factor. For investment-grade securities with the highest credit ratings and extremely low spreads, credit spread migration is only possible in one direction given the implied lower bound of zero on credit spreads. As a result, the credit term structure for the most highly rated securities tends to be either flat or slightly upward sloping. Securities with lower credit quality, however, face greater sensitivity to the credit cycle. The greater likelihood of default associated with high-yield securities generally results in a steeper credit spread curve, both in cases where a weaker economy suggests credit spread widening and when an inverted credit spread curve suggests tighter spreads for longer maturities. As a high-yield bond moves further down the credit spectrum into a more distressed scenario, the contractual cash flows through maturity become less certain—with the value of distressed debt converging to a dollar price equal to the recovery rate as default becomes more certain, regardless of the remaining time to maturity. Such a scenario will result in a steeply inverted credit spread term structure. We now review the determinants of that term structure inversion and other implications of this scenario in more detail.

Financial conditions are another critical factor affecting the credit spread term structure. From a macroeconomic perspective, the credit risk of a bond is influenced by expectations for economic growth and inflation. A stronger economic climate is generally associated with higher benchmark yields but lower credit spreads for issuers whose default probability declines during periods of economic growth (cash flows tend to improve and profitability increases under such a scenario). The countercyclical relationship between spreads and benchmark rates is therefore commonly observed across the business cycle.

Market supply and demand dynamics are another critical factor influencing the credit curve term structure. Unlike default-risk-free government securities in developed markets, the relative liquidity of corporate bonds varies widely, with the vast majority of securities not trading on a daily basis. Given that new and most recently issued securities tend to represent the largest proportion of trading volume and are responsible for much of the volatility in credit spreads, the credit curve will be most heavily influenced by the most frequently traded securities. For example, although one might expect the credit curve to steepen for a borrower refinancing near-term maturities with long-term debt, this effect may be partially offset by a tighter bid–offer spread for longer credit maturities. This flattening may also occur within a specific rating or if market participants anticipate significant supply in a particular tenor. Infrequently traded bonds trading with wider bid–offer spreads can also impact the shape of the term structure, so it is important to gauge the size and frequency of trades in bonds across the maturity spectrum to ensure consistency.

Finally, from a microeconomic perspective, company-value model results discussed earlier are another key driver of the credit spread term structure. Under traditional credit analysis, the specific industry or industries within which an issuer operates are considered, as well as key financial ratios, such as cash flow, leverage, and profitability versus sector and ratings peers. This company-specific analysis based on fundamental data has been complemented by more probabilistic, forward-looking structural models for company valuation. These models take stock market valuation, equity volatility, and balance sheet information into account to derive the implied default probability for a company. Holding other factors constant, any microeconomic factor that increases the implied default probability, such as greater equity volatility, will tend to drive a steeper credit spread curve, and the reverse is true with a decline in equity volatility.

Practitioners will frequently employ these tools when analyzing the term structure of credit spreads to determine fair value. For example, the Bloomberg default risk screen (DRSK) shown in Exhibit 29 combines the company-value analysis with fundamental credit ratios for a composite analysis of TransCanada Corporation, a Canadian natural gas transmission and power services company.

Exhibit 29: Default Risk Screen

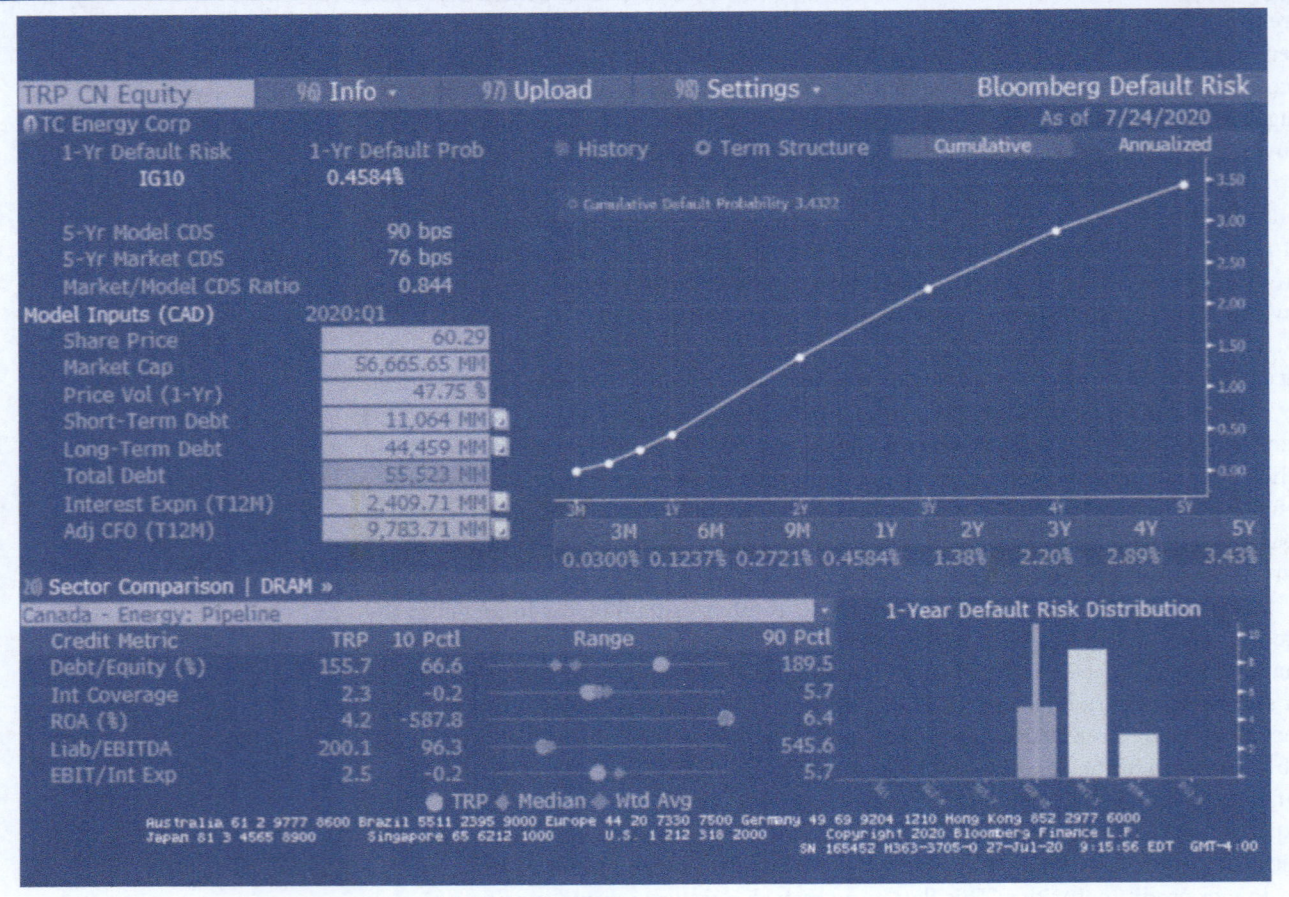

Source: Bloomberg.

Two further considerations are important when analyzing the term structure of credit spreads. The first concerns the appropriate risk-free or benchmark rates used to determine spreads. A frequently traded government security with the nearest maturity to an outstanding corporate bond generally represents the lowest default risk for developed markets, so this is a logical benchmark choice. However, the duration and maturity of the most liquid or on-the-run government bonds rarely match those of corporate bonds trading in the secondary market, so it is often necessary to interpolate between yields of the two government securities with the closest maturity. Because the interpolation may impact the analysis for less liquid maturities, the benchmark swap curve based on interbank rates is often substituted for the government benchmark because of greater swap market liquidity for off-the-run maturities. For example, Exhibit 30 demonstrates the latter methodology on a Bloomberg screen for a composite of BBB rated US industrial corporate issuers versus the benchmark US dollar swap curve, showing a positive-sloped credit spread term structure across maturities.

Exhibit 30: Credit Spreads over Swap Rates

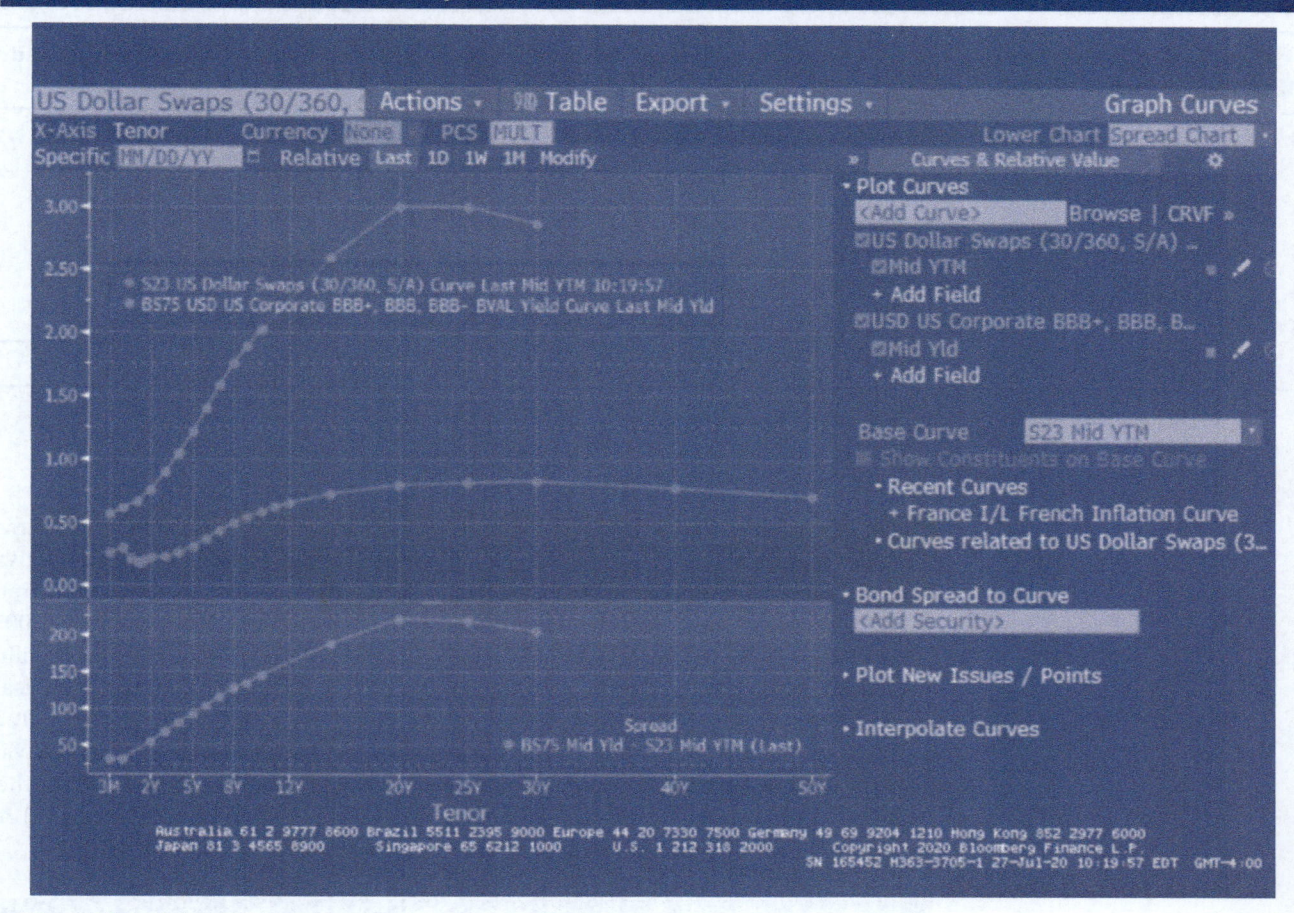

Source: Bloomberg.

The second consideration concerns the all-in spread over the benchmark itself. Term structure analysis should include only bonds with similar credit characteristics, which are typically senior unsecured general obligations of the issuer. Any bonds of the issuer with embedded options, first or second lien provisions, or other unique provisions should be excluded from the analysis. It is also important to note that such securities typically include cross-default provisions so that all securities across the maturity spectrum of a single issuer will be subject to recovery in the event of bankruptcy.

Using the models presented in prior sections, we can demonstrate that the *change* in market expectations of default over time is a key determinant of the shape of the credit curve term structure. This may be shown using a simple extension of the zero-coupon corporate bond example in Exhibit 2 by changing the probability of default. Using a recovery rate of 40% and changing the probability of default from 1.25% to 1.50% raises the credit spread from 77 bps in the original example to 92 bps. These calculations are shown in Exhibit 31.

Exhibit 31: Raising the Default Probability of the Five-Year, Zero-Coupon Corporate Bond

Date	Exposure	Recovery	LGD	POD	POS	Expected Loss	DF	PV of Expected Loss
0								
1	88.8487	35.5395	53.3092	1.5000%	98.5000%	0.7996	0.970874	0.7763
2	91.5142	36.6057	54.9085	1.4775%	97.0225%	0.8113	0.942596	0.7647
3	94.2596	37.7038	56.5558	1.4553%	95.5672%	0.8231	0.915142	0.7532
4	97.0874	38.8350	58.2524	1.4335%	94.1337%	0.8351	0.888487	0.7419
5	100.0000	40.0000	60.0000	1.4120%	92.7217%	0.8472	0.862609	0.7308
				7.2783%			CVA =	3.7670

Fair value = 86.2609 − 3.7670 = 82.4939.
Yield to maturity = 3.9240%.
Credit spread = 3.9240% − 3.00% = 0.9240%.

Flat credit spread curves imply a relatively stable expectation of default over time, whereas an upward-sloping credit curve implies that investors seek greater compensation for assuming issuer default risk over longer periods. For example, we can illustrate this in terms of a credit spread curve by holding the benchmark rate constant at 3.00% across 3-year, 5-year, and 10-year maturities while increasing the default probability over time. Although one could consider an increase in default probability each year, the following example in Exhibit 32 assumes a 1.00% default probability for Years 1, 2, and 3, a 2.00% probability of default in Years 4 and 5, and a 3.00% default probability in Years 6 through 10, with the recovery rate at a constant 40%. (Note that this is another example of the annual default probability changing over the lifetime of the bonds.) As shown in Exhibit 32, the credit spread rises from 62 bps to 86 bps to 132 bps.

Exhibit 32: Increasing the Default Probability for Longer Times to Maturity

Date	Exposure	Recovery	LGD	POD	POS	Expected Loss	DF	PV of Expected Loss
0								
1	94.2596	37.7038	56.5558	1.0000%	99.0000%	0.5656	0.970874	0.5491
2	97.0874	38.8350	58.2524	0.9900%	98.0100%	0.5767	0.942596	0.5436
3	100.0000	40.0000	60.0000	0.9801%	97.0299%	0.5881	0.915142	0.5382
				2.9701%			CVA =	1.6308

Fair value = 91.5142 − 1.6308 = 89.8833.
Yield to maturity = 3.6192%.
Credit spread = 3.6192% − 3.00% = 0.6192%.

Date	Exposure	Recovery	LGD	POD	POS	Expected Loss	DF	PV of Expected Loss
0								
1	88.8487	35.5395	53.3092	1.0000%	99.0000%	0.5331	0.970874	0.5176
2	91.5142	36.6057	54.9085	0.9900%	98.0100%	0.5436	0.942596	0.5124
3	94.2596	37.7038	56.5558	0.9801%	97.0299%	0.5543	0.915142	0.5073
4	97.0874	38.8350	58.2524	1.9406%	95.0893%	1.1304	0.888487	1.0044
5	100.0000	40.0000	60.0000	1.9018%	93.1875%	1.1411	0.862609	0.9843

Date	Exposure	Recovery	LGD	POD	POS	Expected Loss	DF	PV of Expected Loss
				6.8125%			CVA =	3.5259

Fair value = 86.2609 − 3.5259 = 82.7350.
Yield to maturity = 3.8633%.
Credit spread = 3.8633% − 3.00% = 0.8633%.

Date	Exposure	Recovery	LGD	POD	POS	Expected Loss	DF	PV of Expected Loss
0								
1	76.647	30.6567	45.9850	1.0000%	99.0000%	0.4599	0.970874	0.4465
2	78.9409	31.5764	47.3646	0.9900%	98.0100%	0.4689	0.942596	0.4420
3	81.3092	32.5237	48.7855	0.9801%	97.0299%	0.4781	0.915142	0.4376
4	83.7484	33.4994	50.2491	1.9406%	95.0893%	0.9751	0.888487	0.8664
5	86.2609	34.5044	51.7565	1.9018%	93.1875%	0.9843	0.862609	0.8491
6	88.8487	35.5395	53.3092	2.7956%	90.3919%	1.4903	0.837484	1.2481
7	91.5142	36.6057	54.9085	2.7118%	87.6801%	1.4890	0.813092	1.2107
8	94.2596	37.7038	56.5558	2.6304%	85.0497%	1.4876	0.789409	1.1744
9	97.0874	38.8350	58.2524	2.5515%	82.4982%	1.4863	0.766417	1.1391
10	100.0000	40.0000	60.0000	2.4749%	80.0233%	1.4850	0.744094	1.1050
				19.9767%			CVA =	8.9187

Fair value = 74.4094 − 8.9187 = 65.4907.
Yield to maturity = 4.3235%.
Credit spread = 4.3235% − 3.00% = 1.3235%.

Positive-sloped credit spread curves are likely when a high-quality issuer with a strong competitive position in a stable industry has low leverage, strong cash flow, and a high profit margin. This type of issuer tends to exhibit very low short-term credit spreads rising with increasing maturity given greater uncertainty due to the macroeconomic environment, potential adverse changes in the competitive landscape, technological change, or other factors that drive a higher implied probability of default over time. Empirical academic studies also tend to support the view that the credit spread term structure is upward-sloping for investment-grade bond portfolios (Bedendo, Cathcart, and El-Jahel 2007).

Alternatively, high-yield issuers in cyclical industries sometimes face a downward-sloping credit term structure because of issuer- or industry-specific reasons. For example, an ownership change resulting from a leveraged buyout or private equity acquisition may often be accompanied by a significant increase in leverage. In such a case, an inverted credit curve may indicate investor expectations that the new owners will create efficiencies in the restructured organization, leading to improved future cash flow and profitability that will benefit debt investors. Another example of an inverted credit term structure might result when issuers in a historically cyclical industry (such as oil and gas exploration or retail) find themselves at the bottom of an economic cycle, with investor expectations of a recovery in the industry tied to improving credit spreads over time.

That said, it is important to distinguish between scenarios where the contractual cash flows of a risky bond are likely to occur and distressed debt scenarios where investors expect to receive only the recovery rate in a likely bankruptcy scenario. Bonds with a very high likelihood of default tend to trade on a price basis that converges toward the recovery rate rather than on a spread to benchmark rates. This scenario leads to credit spread term structures that may be considered more of an "optical" phenomenon rather than a true reflection of the relative risks and rewards of long-term versus short-term bonds from a single issuer, as illustrated in the following discussion.

To demonstrate this using our zero-coupon bond example, let us shift to a scenario where bondholders with 5-year and 10-year bonds outstanding anticipate an imminent default scenario and both bonds trade at a recovery rate of 40%.

Note that if we solve for the fair value and resulting credit spread over the benchmark yield as in the instances where default probability was 1.25%, we end up with the same VNDs for the 5-year and 10-year bonds, respectively. However, when deriving a credit spread value for both securities assuming recovery in a bankruptcy scenario and cross-default provisions across maturities, the credit valuation adjustment representing the sum of expected losses is simply the difference between the VND and the recovery rate.

For the five-year example, we can thus calculate a VND of 86.2609, a CVA of 46.2609, and a fair value with recovery at 40. This results in a yield of 20.1124% and a credit spread over the government bond of 17.1124%. In the 10-year case, the VND may be shown as 74.4094, a CVA of 34.4094, and a fair value at 40. That gives a yield of 9.5958% and a credit spread of 6.5958%. We end up with a steep and inverted "credit spread" curve.

The interpretation of the credit spread term structure is important for investors seeking to capitalize on a market view that differs from that reflected in the credit curve. For example, if a portfolio manager disagrees with the market's expectation of a high near-term default probability that declines over time, she could sell short-term protection in the credit default swap market and buy longer-term protection. In a scenario where the issuer does not default, the investor retains the premium on protection sold and may either retain or choose to sell back the longer-term credit default swap to realize a gain.

8   CREDIT ANALYSIS FOR SECURITIZED DEBT

☐ | compare the credit analysis required for securitized debt to the credit analysis of corporate debt

Unlike the general obligation nature of most private or sovereign fixed-income securities, securitized debt allows issuers to finance a specific set of assets or receivables (e.g., mortgages, automobile loans, or credit card receivables) rather than an entire balance sheet. Issuers in securitized debt markets are frequently motivated to undertake financing using these more structured securities given their ability to increase debt capacity and reduce the originator's need to maintain regulatory capital or retain residual risk. The isolation of securitized assets generally decreases the relative financing cost for these assets on a stand-alone basis as compared to a general obligation financing of the debt originator. By freeing up capital, an originator is also able to continue to generate income from further originations. Investors, however, seek to benefit from greater diversification, more stable and predictable underlying cash flows, and a return that is greater than that of securities with similar ratings, which provide a reward for accepting the greater complexity associated with collateralized debt. That said, the credit analysis of such structured finance instruments requires a fundamentally different approach compared with other risky bonds given the underlying collateral, the parties associated with the origination or servicing of the portfolio over the life of the security, and the issuing entity, as well as any structural and credit enhancement features typically present in these transactions.

It is important to distinguish first and foremost among the types of securitized debt issued globally, as well as the various forms. In its summary of structured finance asset types shown in Exhibit 33, the German-based rating agency Scope Ratings AG provides its general approach to credit assessment based not only on the underlying time horizon and collateral but also on asset characteristics referred to as granularity and homogeneity.

Exhibit 33: Summary of Asset Types and Characteristics of Core Structured Finance Asset Classes

Deal Type	Underlying Collateral	Risk Horizon	Granularity	Homogeneity	Credit Analysis Approach
Asset-backed CP	Commercial discount credits or credit advances	Short-term	Granular	Homogeneous	Book
Auto ABS	Auto loans or leases	Medium-term	Granular	Homogeneous	Portfolio
CMBS	Commercial mortgages	Typically long-term	Non-granular	Heterogeneous	Loan by loan
Consumer ABS	Consumer loans	Medium-term	Granular	Homogeneous	Portfolio
CRE loans	Commercial real estate loans	Long-term	Non-granular	Heterogeneous	Loan by loan
Credit cards	Credit card balances	Short-term	Granular	Homogeneous	Book
Credit-linked notes/ repackaging	Any financial assets	Typically medium-term	Typically single asset	NA	Pass-through rating/asset by asset
LL CLOs	Leveraged corporate loans	Medium-term	Non-granular	Heterogeneous	Loan by loan
PF CLOs	Project finance debt	Long-term	Non-granular	Heterogeneous	Loan by loan
RMBS	Residential mortgages	Long-term	Granular	Homogeneous	Loan by loan or portfolio
SME ABS	Loans to small- and medium-sized businesses	Typically medium-term	Granular	Mixed	Loan by loan or portfolio
Trade receivables	Commercial credit	Short-term	Typically granular	Homogeneous	Book

Source: Adapted from Scope Ratings AG (2016b, pp. 7–8).

The concept of homogeneity refers to the degree to which underlying debt characteristics within a structured finance instrument are similar across individual obligations. On the one hand, an investor or credit analyst might draw general conclusions about the nature of homogeneous credit card or auto loan obligations given that an individual obligation faces strict eligibility criteria to be included in a specific asset pool. On the other hand, heterogeneous leveraged loan, project finance, or real estate transactions require scrutiny on a loan-by-loan basis given their different characteristics. The granularity of the portfolio refers to the actual number of obligations that make up the overall structured finance instrument. A highly granular portfolio may have hundreds of underlying debtors, suggesting it is appropriate to draw conclusions

[handwritten note:] - A statistics - based approach would work for a static book of loans

about creditworthiness based on portfolio summary statistics rather than investigating each borrower. Alternatively, an asset pool with fewer more-discrete or non-granular investments would warrant analysis of each individual obligation.

The combination of asset type and tenor as well as the relative granularity and homogeneity of the underlying obligations drive the approach to credit analysis for a given instrument type. For example, short-term structured finance vehicles with granular, homogeneous assets tend to be evaluated using a statistics-based approach to the existing book of loans. This changes to a portfolio-based approach for medium-term granular and homogeneous obligations because the portfolio is not static but changes over time. For discrete or non-granular heterogeneous portfolios, a loan-by-loan approach to credit analysis is more appropriate. The following example of a credit card securitization will provide further insight into the process.

Exhibit 34 provides a summary from the prospectus of the Synchrony Credit Card Master Note Trust $750,000,000 Series 2016-1 Asset Backed Notes issued in March 2016. As is spelled out in the prospectus, the Synchrony transaction is backed by credit card receivables having the given credit score distribution presented in the exhibit.

Exhibit 34: A Structured Debt Example, Composition by FICO Credit Score Range

FICO Credit Score Range	Receivables Outstanding	Percentage of Outstanding
Less than or equal to 599	$995,522,016	6.6%
600 to 659	$2,825,520,245	18.7%
660 to 719	$6,037,695,923	39.9%
720 and above	$5,193,614,599	34.4%
No score	$64,390,707	0.4%
Total	**$15,116,743,490**	**100%**

Source: Synchrony Credit Card Master Note Trust $750,000,000 Series 2016-1 Asset Backed Notes Prospectus (p. 93; available at investors.synchronyfinancial.com).

Investors in this type of ABS will base their probability of default on the mean default probability, recovery rate, and variance of a portfolio of borrowers reflecting the distribution of FICO scores within the pool rather than conducting an analysis of individual borrowers. The prospectus provides a broad set of details beyond the FICO scores of borrowers for further in-depth portfolio analysis, including age of the receivables, average outstanding balances, and delinquency rates.

A heterogeneous portfolio of fewer loans, however, requires a fundamentally different approach. In this instance, each obligation within the asset pool may warrant its own analysis to determine whether an individual commercial property or leveraged company is able to meet its financial obligations under the ABS contract. Here the expected default probability and recovery rate on an asset-by-asset basis is the best gauge of how the investment will perform under various scenarios.

A second critical aspect of the credit exposure associated with ABS relates to the origination and servicing of assets over the life of the transaction. The prospectus and other related documents determine the roles and responsibilities of these related parties over the life of an ABS transaction. Upon inception of the transaction, investors rely on the originator/servicer to establish and enforce loan eligibility criteria, secure and maintain proper documentation and records, and maximize timely repayment and contract enforceability in cases of delinquency. Once the asset pool has been identified, investors are also exposed to operational and counterparty risk over the life of an ABS transaction. That is, they remain exposed to the ability of the servicer to effectively manage and service the portfolio over the life of the transaction. For an auto ABS transaction, this may involve the ability to repossess and sell a vehicle at a price close to the residual value in a timely manner in the event that a borrower is unable to pay, while in a commercial real estate transaction, it may involve identifying and replacing a non-performing tenant. Investors in an asset portfolio whose composition changes over time also face exposure to the replacement of obligors over time. In all such instances, not only is the creditworthiness of the servicer important but also of importance is its track record in meeting these servicing obligations, which are frequently gauged by analyzing the performance of more seasoned transactions handled by the same servicer over the credit cycle.

For example, in the case of the Synchrony Credit Card Master Note Trust transaction, Synchrony Financial acts as servicer of the trust and Synchrony Bank, as sub-servicer, is primarily responsible for receiving and processing collections on the receivables. A potential investor might therefore evaluate not only the performance of other debt backed by credit card receivables but also how outstanding notes serviced by Synchrony have performed over time versus its servicing competitors.

Finally, the structure of a collateralized or secured debt transaction is a critical factor in analyzing this type of investment. These structural aspects include both the nature of the obligor itself, which is often a special purpose entity (SPE) whose sole purpose is to acquire a specified pool of assets and issue ABS to finance the SPE, and any structural enhancements of the transaction, which may include overcollateralization, credit tranching (i.e., tiering the claim priorities of ownership or interest), or other characteristics.

A key question related to the issuer is its relationship to the originator—namely, the degree to which the bankruptcy of the obligor is related to that of the originator. The bankruptcy remoteness is typically determined by whether the transfer of the assets from the originator to the SPE may be deemed a true sale, which otherwise allows for the ability to separate risk between the originator and SPE at a later date.

Second, additional credit enhancements are a key structural element to be evaluated in the context of credit risk. Credit enhancements for ABS take on several forms beyond the bankruptcy remoteness of the SPE. For example, ABS transactions frequently have payout or performance triggers that protect investors in the case of adverse credit events. Certain events related to the servicer or seller—such as failure to make deposits or payments or other adverse events—may trigger early repayment ("amortization") of the security. For consumer transactions such as credit card or automotive ABS, the primary protection against a decline in asset quality for investors is additional return built into the transaction that is greater than the expected or historical loss of the asset pool. This additional return is often called the excess spread. Issuers create subordinated tranches of debt that provide added protection to those rated higher and benefit from a greater excess spread cushion over the life of the financing.

Covered bonds, which originated in Germany in the 18th century but have since been adopted by issuers across Europe, Asia, and Australia, have some similarities with these structured finance investments but also have fundamental differences that warrant special consideration. A covered bond is a senior debt obligation of a financial institution that gives recourse to both the originator/issuer and a predetermined underlying collateral pool. Each country or jurisdiction specifies the eligible collateral types and the specific structures permissible in its covered bond market. Covered bonds most frequently have either commercial or residential mortgages meeting specific criteria or public sector debt as underlying collateral.

The dual recourse to the issuing financial institution and the underlying asset pool has been a hallmark of covered bonds since their inception, but it was also reinforced under the European Union Bank Recovery and Resolution Directive (BRRD; see Scope

Ratings AG 2016a). Under the BRRD, covered bonds enjoy unique protection among bank liabilities in the event of restructuring or regulatory intervention. Additionally, the financial institution has the ongoing obligation to maintain sufficient assets in the cover pool to satisfy the claims of covered bondholders at all times, and the obligations of the financial institution with respect to the cover pool are supervised by public or other independent bodies.

Another aspect of covered bonds that needs to be considered in credit analysis is the dynamic nature of the cover pool. In contrast to a static pool of mortgage loans (which expose investors to prepayment risk in the case of US mortgage-backed securities), cover pool sponsors must replace any prepaid or non-performing assets in the cover pool to ensure sufficient cash flows to the maturity of the covered bond.

Analysts should also be aware of various redemption regimes that exist to align the covered bond's cash flows as closely as possible to the original maturity schedule in the event of default of a covered bond's financial sponsor. These include hard-bullet covered bonds; if payments do not occur according to the original schedule, a bond default is triggered and bond payments are accelerated. Another type is soft-bullet covered bonds, which delay the bond default and payment acceleration of bond cash flows until a new final maturity date, which is usually up to a year after the original maturity date. Conditional pass-through covered bonds, in contrast, convert to pass-through securities after the original maturity date if all bond payments have not yet been made.

Credit analysis for covered bonds follows traditional credit analysis in evaluating both the issuer and the cover pool. Given the additional credit enhancements, recovery rates tend to be high and default probabilities low, making covered bonds a relatively safe credit asset. As a result, rating agencies often assign a credit rating to covered bonds that is several notches above that of the issuing financial institution.

SUMMARY

We have covered several important topics in credit analysis. Among the points made are the following:

- Three factors important to modeling credit risk are the expected exposure to default, the recovery rate, and the loss given default.

- These factors permit the calculation of a credit valuation adjustment that is subtracted from the (hypothetical) value of the bond, if it were default risk free, to get the bond's fair value given its credit risk. The credit valuation adjustment is calculated as the sum of the present values of the expected loss for each period in the remaining life of the bond. Expected values are computed using risk-neutral probabilities, and discounting is done at the risk-free rates for the relevant maturities.

- The CVA captures investors' compensation for bearing default risk. The compensation can also be expressed in terms of a credit spread.

- Credit scores and credit ratings are third-party evaluations of creditworthiness used in distinct markets.

- Analysts may use credit ratings and a transition matrix of probabilities to adjust a bond's yield to maturity to reflect the probabilities of credit migration. Credit spread migration typically reduces expected return.

- Credit analysis models fall into two broad categories: structural models and reduced-form models.

- Structural models are based on an option perspective of the positions of the stakeholders of the company. Bondholders are viewed as owning the assets of the company; shareholders have call options on those assets.

- Reduced-form models seek to predict *when* a default may occur, but they do not explain the *why* as structural models do. Reduced-form models, unlike structural models, are based only on observable variables.

- When interest rates are assumed to be volatile, the credit risk of a bond can be estimated in an arbitrage-free valuation framework.

- The discount margin for floating-rate notes is similar to the credit spread for fixed-coupon bonds. The discount margin can also be calculated using an arbitrage-free valuation framework.

- Arbitrage-free valuation can be applied to judge the sensitivity of the credit spread to changes in credit risk parameters.

- The term structure of credit spreads depends on macro and micro factors.

- As it concerns macro factors, the credit spread curve tends to become steeper and to widen in conditions of weak economic activity. Market supply and demand dynamics are important. The most frequently traded securities tend to determine the shape of this curve.

- Issuer- or industry-specific factors, such as the chance of a future leverage-decreasing event, can cause the credit spread curve to flatten or invert.

- When a bond is very likely to default, it often trades close to its recovery value at various maturities; moreover, the credit spread curve is less informative about the relationship between credit risk and maturity.

- For securitized debt, the characteristics of the asset portfolio themselves suggest the best approach for a credit analyst to take when deciding among investments. Important considerations include the relative concentration of assets and their similarity or heterogeneity as it concerns credit risk.

REFERENCES

Bedendo, Mascia, Lara Cathcart, Lina El-Jahel. 2007. "The Slope of the Term Structure of Credit Spreads: An Empirical Investigation." Journal of Financial Research30 (2): 237–57. 10.1111/j.1 475-6803.2007.00212.x

Black, Fisher, Myron Scholes. 1973. "The Pricing of Options and Corporate Liabilities." Journal of Political Economy81:637–54. 10.1086/260062

Duffie, Darrell, Kenneth J. Singleton. 1999. "Modeling the Term Structure of Defaultable Bonds." Review of Financial Studies12:687–720. 10.1093/rfs/12.4.687

Duffie, Darrell, Kenneth J. Singleton. 2003. Credit Risk: Pricing, Measurement, and Management. Princeton University Press.

Fabozzi, Frank J. 2013. Bond Markets, Analysis, and Strategies. 8th ed., Pearson.

Jarrow, Robert, Stuart Turnbull. 1995. "Pricing Derivatives on Financial Securities Subject to Default Risk." Journal of Finance50:53–85. 10.1111/j.1540-6261.1995.tb05167.x

Merton, Robert. 1974. "On the Pricing of Corporate Debt: The Risk Structure of Interest Rates." Journal of Finance29:449–70.

Scope Ratings AG2016a. "Covered Bond Rating Methodology" (22 July): www.scoperatings. com.

Scope Ratings AG2016b. "General Structured Finance Rating Methodology" (31 August): www. scoperatings.com.

Smith, Donald J. 2011. "Hidden Debt: From Enron's Commodity Prepays to Lehman's Repo 105s." Financial Analysts Journal67 (5): 15–22. 10.2469/faj.v67.n5.2

Smith, Donald J. 2017. Valuation in a World of CVA, DVA, and FVA: A Tutorial on Debt Securities and Interest Rate Derivatives. World Scientific Publishing Company. 10.1142/10511

PRACTICE PROBLEMS

The following information relates to questions 1-8

Lena Liecken is a senior bond analyst at Taurus Investment Management. Kristel Kreming, a junior analyst, works for Liecken in helping conduct fixed-income research for the firm's portfolio managers. Liecken and Kreming meet to discuss several bond positions held in the firm's portfolios.

Bonds I and II both have a maturity of one year, an annual coupon rate of 5%, and a market price equal to par value. The risk-free rate is 3%. Historical default experiences of bonds comparable to Bonds I and II are presented in Exhibit 1.

Exhibit 1: Credit Risk Information for Comparable Bonds

Bond	Recovery Rate	Percentage of Bonds That Survive and Make Full Payment
I	40%	98%
II	35%	99%

Bond III is a zero-coupon bond with three years to maturity. Liecken evaluates similar bonds and estimates a recovery rate of 38% and a risk-neutral default probability of 2%, assuming conditional probabilities of default. Kreming creates Exhibit 2 to compute Bond III's credit valuation adjustment. She assumes a flat yield curve at 3%, with exposure, recovery, and loss given default values expressed per 100 of par value.

Exhibit 2: Analysis of Bond III

Date	Exposure	Recovery	Loss Given Default	Probability of Default	Probability of Survival	Expected Loss	Present Value of Expected Loss
0							
1	94.2596	35.8186	58.4410	2.0000%	98.0000%	1.1688	1.1348
2	97.0874	36.8932	60.1942	1.9600%	96.0400%	1.1798	1.1121
3	100.0000	38.0000	62.0000	1.9208%	94.1192%	1.1909	1.0898
Sum				5.8808%		3.5395	3.3367

Bond IV is an AA rated bond that matures in five years, has a coupon rate of 6%, and a modified duration of 4.2. Liecken is concerned about whether this bond will be downgraded to an A rating, but she does not expect the bond to default during the next year. Kreming constructs a partial transition matrix, which is presented in Exhibit 3, and suggests using a model to predict the rating change of Bond IV using leverage ratios, return on assets, and macroeconomic variables.

Exhibit 3: Partial One-Year Corporate Transition Matrix (entries in %)			
From/To	AAA	AA	A
AAA	92.00	6.00	1.00
AA	2.00	89.00	8.00
A	0.05	1.00	85.00
Credit Spread (%)	0.50	1.00	1.75

Kreming calculates the risk-neutral probabilities, compares them with the actual default probabilities of bonds evaluated over the past 10 years, and observes that the actual and risk-neutral probabilities differ. She makes two observations regarding the comparison of these probabilities:

Observation 1   Actual default probabilities include the default risk premium associated with the uncertainty in the timing of the possible default loss.

Observation 2   The observed spread over the yield on a risk-free bond in practice includes liquidity and tax considerations, in addition to credit risk.

1. The expected exposure to default loss for Bond I is:

   A. less than the expected exposure for Bond II.

   B. the same as the expected exposure for Bond II.

   C. greater than the expected exposure for Bond II.

2. Based on Exhibit 1, the loss given default for Bond II is:

   A. less than that for Bond I.

   B. the same as that for Bond I.

   C. greater than that for Bond I.

3. Based on Exhibit 1, the expected future value of Bond I at maturity is *closest* to:

   A. 98.80.

   B. 103.74.

   C. 105.00.

4. Based on Exhibit 1, the risk-neutral default probability for Bond I is *closest* to:

   A. 2.000%.

   B. 3.175%.

   C. 4.762%.

5. Based on Exhibit 2, the credit valuation adjustment for Bond III is *closest* to:

   A. 3.3367.

    B. 3.5395.

    C. 5.8808.

6. Based on Exhibit 3, if Bond IV's credit rating changes during the next year to an A rating, its expected price change would be *closest* to:

    A. −8.00%.

    B. −7.35%.

    C. −3.15%.

7. Kreming's suggested model for Bond IV is a:

    A. structural model.

    B. reduced-form model.

    C. term structure model.

8. Which of Kreming's observations regarding actual and risk-neutral default probabilities is correct?

    A. Only Observation 1

    B. Only Observation 2

    C. Both Observation 1 and Observation 2

The following information relates to questions 9-23

Daniela Ibarra is a senior analyst in the fixed-income department of a large wealth management firm. Marten Koning is a junior analyst in the same department, and David Lok is a member of the credit research team.

The firm invests in a variety of bonds. Ibarra is presently analyzing a set of bonds with some similar characteristics, such as four years until maturity and a par value of €1,000. Exhibit 1 includes details of these bonds.

Exhibit 1: A Brief Description of the Bonds Being Analyzed

Bond	Description
B1	A zero-coupon, four-year corporate bond with a par value of €1,000. The wealth management firm's research team has estimated that the risk-neutral probability of default for each date for the bond is 1.50%, and the recovery rate is 30%.
B2	A bond similar to B1, except that it has a fixed annual coupon rate of 6% paid annually.
B3	A bond similar to B2 but rated AA.
B4	A bond similar to B2 but the coupon rate is the one-year benchmark rate plus 4%.

Ibarra asks Koning to assist her with analyzing the bonds. She wants him to perform the analysis with the assumptions that there is no interest rate volatility and that the government bond yield curve is flat at 3%.

Ibarra performs the analysis assuming an upward-sloping yield curve and volatile interest rates. Exhibit 2 provides the data on annual payment benchmark government bonds.

She uses these data to construct a binomial interest rate tree based on an assumption of future interest rate volatility of 20%.

Exhibit 2: Par Curve for Annual Payment Benchmark Government Bonds

Maturity	Coupon Rate	Price	Discount Factor	Spot Rate	Forward Rate
1	−0.25%	€100	1.002506	−0.2500%	
2	0.75%	€100	0.985093	0.7538%	1.7677%
3	1.50%	€100	0.955848	1.5166%	3.0596%
4	2.25%	€100	0.913225	2.2953%	4.6674%

Answer the first five questions based on the assumptions made by Marten Koning, the junior analyst. Answer the subsequent questions based on the assumptions made by Daniela Ibarra, the senior analyst.

Note: All calculations in this problem set are carried out on spreadsheets to preserve precision. The rounded results are reported in the solutions.

9. The market price of Bond B1 is €875. The bond is:

   A. fairly valued.

   B. overvalued.

   C. undervalued.

10. Koning realizes that an increase in the recovery rate would lead to an increase in the bond's fair value, whereas an increase in the probability of default would lead to a decrease in the bond's fair value. He is not sure, however, which effect would be greater. So, he increases both the recovery rate and the probability of default by 25% of their existing estimates and recomputes the bond's fair value. The recomputed fair value is closest to:

    A. €843.14.

    B. €848.00.

    C. €855.91.

11. The fair value of Bond B2 is closest to:

    A. €1,069.34.

    B. €1,111.51.

    C. €1,153.68.

12. The market price of Bond B2 is €1,090. If the bond is purchased at this price and there is a default on Date 3, the rate of return to the bond buyer would be closest to:

    A. −28.38%.

B. −41.72%.

C. −69.49%.

13. Bond B3 will have a modified duration of 2.75 at the end of the year. Based on the representative one-year corporate transition matrix in Exhibit 3 and assuming no default, how should the analyst adjust the bond's yield to maturity to assess the expected return on the bond over the next year?

Exhibit 3: Representative One-Year Corporate Transition Matrix (entries are in %)

From/To	AAA	AA	A	BBB	BB	B	CCC, CC, C	D
AAA	**90.00**	9.00	0.60	0.15	0.10	0.10	0.05	0.00
AA	1.50	**88.00**	9.50	0.75	0.15	0.05	0.03	0.02
A	0.05	2.50	**87.50**	8.40	0.75	0.60	0.12	0.08
BBB	0.02	0.30	4.80	**85.50**	6.95	1.75	0.45	0.23
BB	0.01	0.06	0.30	7.75	**79.50**	8.75	2.38	1.25
B	0.00	0.05	0.15	1.40	9.15	**76.60**	8.45	4.20
CCC, CC, C	0.00	0.01	0.12	0.87	1.65	18.50	**49.25**	29.60
Credit Spread	0.60%	0.90%	1.10%	1.50%	3.40%	6.50%	9.50%	

A. Add 7.7 bps to YTM.

B. Subtract 7.7 bps from YTM.

C. Subtract 9.0 bps from YTM.

14. David Lok has estimated the probability of default of Bond B1 to be 1.50%. He is presenting the approach the research team used to estimate the probability of default. Which of the following statements is Lok likely to make in his presentation if the team used a reduced-form credit model?

A. Option pricing methodologies were used, with the volatility of the underlying asset estimated based on historical data on the firm's stock price.

B. Regression analysis was used, with the independent variables including both firm-specific variables, such as the debt ratio and return on assets, and macroeconomic variables, such as the rate of inflation and the unemployment rate.

C. The default barrier was first estimated, followed by the estimation of the probability of default as the portion of the probability distribution that lies below the default barrier.

15. In the presentation, Lok is asked why the research team chose to use a reduced-form credit model instead of a structural model. Which statement is he likely to make in reply?

A. Structural models are outdated, having been developed in the 1970s; reduced-form models are more modern, having been developed in the 1990s.

B. Structural models are overly complex because they require the use of option pricing models, whereas reduced-form models use regression analysis.

C. Structural models require "inside" information known to company management, whereas reduced-form models can use publicly available data on the firm.

16. As previously mentioned, Ibarra is considering a future interest rate volatility of 20% and an upward-sloping yield curve, as shown in Exhibit 2. Based on her analysis, the fair value of Bond B2 is closest to:

   A. €1,101.24.

   B. €1,141.76.

   C. €1,144.63.

17. Ibarra wants to know the credit spread of Bond B2 over a theoretical comparable-maturity government bond with the same coupon rate as this bond. The foregoing credit spread is closest to:

   A. 108 bps.

   B. 101 bps.

   C. 225 bps.

18. Ibarra is interested in analyzing how a simultaneous decrease in the recovery rate and the probability of default would affect the fair value of Bond B2. She decreases both the recovery rate and the probability of default by 25% of their existing estimates and recomputes the bond's fair value. The recomputed fair value is closest to:

   A. €1,096.59.

   B. €1,108.40.

   C. €1,111.91.

19. The wealth management firm has an existing position in Bond B4. The market price of B4, a floating-rate note, is €1,070. Senior management has asked Ibarra to make a recommendation regarding the existing position. Based on the assumptions used to calculate the estimated fair value only, her recommendation should be to:

   A. add to the existing position.

   B. hold the existing position.

   C. reduce the existing position.

20. The issuer of the floating-rate note, B4, is in the energy industry. Ibarra believes that oil prices are likely to increase significantly in the next year, which will lead to an improvement in the firm's financial health and a decline in the probability of default from 1.50% in Year 1 to 0.50% in Years 2, 3, and 4. Based on these expectations, which of the following statements is correct?

   A. The CVA will decrease to €22.99.

   B. The note's fair value will increase to €1,177.26.

C. The value of the FRN, assuming no default, will increase to €1,173.55.

21. The floating-rate note, B4, is currently rated BBB by Standard & Poor's and Fitch Ratings (and Baa by Moody's Investors Service). Based on the research department assumption about the probability of default in Question 10 and her own assumption in Question 11, which action does Ibarra *most likely* expect from the credit rating agencies?

    A. Downgrade from BBB to BB.

    B. Upgrade from BBB to AAA.

    C. Place the issuer on watch with a positive outlook.

22. During the presentation about how the research team estimates the probability of default for a particular bond issuer, Lok is asked for his thoughts on the shape of the term structure of credit spreads. Which statement is he most likely to include in his response?

    A. The term structure of credit spreads typically is flat or slightly upward sloping for high-quality investment-grade bonds. High-yield bonds are more sensitive to the credit cycle, however, and can have a more upwardly sloped term structure of credit spreads than investment-grade bonds or even an inverted curve.

    B. The term structure of credit spreads for corporate bonds is always upward sloping—more so the weaker the credit quality because probabilities of default are positively correlated with the time to maturity.

    C. There is no consistent pattern for the term structure of credit spreads. The shape of the credit term structure depends entirely on industry factors.

23. The final question for Lok is about covered bonds. The person asking says, "I've heard about them but don't know what they are." Which statement is Lok most likely to make to describe a covered bond?

    A. A covered bond is issued in a non-domestic currency. The currency risk is then fully hedged using a currency swap or a package of foreign exchange forward contracts.

    B. A covered bond is issued with an attached credit default swap. It essentially is a "risk-free" government bond.

    C. A covered bond is a senior debt obligation giving recourse to the issuer as well as a predetermined underlying collateral pool, often commercial or residential mortgages.

The following information relates to questions 24-30

Anna Lebedeva is a fixed-income portfolio manager. Paulina Kowalski, a junior analyst, and Lebedeva meet to review several positions in Lebedeva's portfolio.

Lebedeva begins the meeting by discussing credit rating migration. Kowalski asks Lebedeva about the typical impact of credit rating migration on the expected return on a bond. Lebedeva asks Kowalski to estimate the expected return over the next year on a bond issued by Entre Corp. The BBB rated bond has a yield to maturity of 5.50% and a modified duration of 7.54. Kowalski calculates the expected return on the bond over the next year given the partial credit transition and credit spread data in Exhibit 1. She assumes that market spreads and yields will remain stable over the year.

Exhibit 1: One-Year Transition Matrix for BBB Rated Bonds and Credit Spreads

	AAA	AA	A	BBB	BB	B	CCC, CC, C
Probability (%)	0.02	0.30	4.80	85.73	6.95	1.75	0.45
Credit spread	0.60%	0.90%	1.10%	1.50%	3.40%	6.50%	9.50%

Lebedeva next asks Kowalski to analyze a three-year bond, issued by VraiRive S.A., using an arbitrage-free framework. The bond's coupon rate is 5%, with interest paid annually and a par value of 100. In her analysis, she makes the following three assumptions:

- The annual interest rate volatility is 10%.
- The recovery rate is one-third of the exposure each period.
- The annual probability of default each year is 2.00%.

Selected information on benchmark government bonds for the VraiRive bond is presented in Exhibit 2, and the relevant binomial interest rate tree is presented in Exhibit 3.

Exhibit 2: Par Curve Rates for Annual Payment Benchmark Government Bonds

Maturity	Coupon Rate	Price	Discount Factor	Spot Rate	Forward Rate
1	3.00%	100	0.970874	3.0000%	3.0000%
2	4.20%	100	0.920560	4.2255%	5.4656%
3	5.00%	100	0.862314	5.0618%	6.7547%

Exhibit 3: One-Year Binomial Interest Rate Tree for 10% Volatility (risk-neutral probabilities in parentheses)

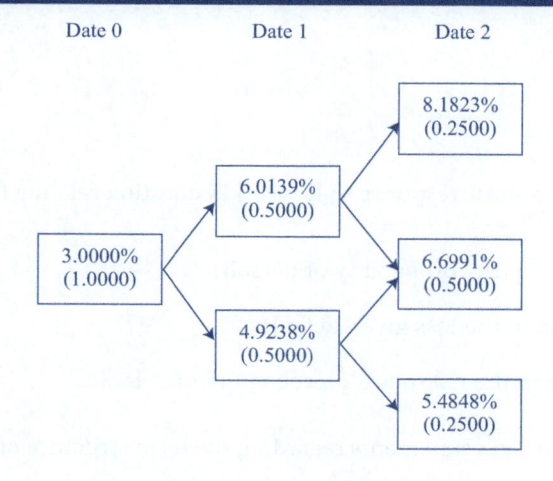

Kowalski estimates the value of the VraiRive bond assuming no default(VND) as well as the fair value of the bond. She then estimates the bond's yield to maturity and the bond's credit spread over the benchmark in Exhibit 2. Kowalski asks Lebedeva, "What might cause the bond's credit spread to decrease?"

Lebedeva and Kowalski next discuss the drivers of the term structure of credit spreads. Kowalski tells Lebedeva the following:

| Statement 1 | The credit term structure for the most highly rated securities tends to be either flat or slightly upward sloping. |
| Statement 2 | The credit term structure for lower-rated securities is often steeper, and credit spreads widen with expectations of strong economic growth. |

Next, Kowalski analyzes the outstanding bonds of DLL Corporation, a high-quality issuer with a strong, competitive position. Her focus is to determine the rationale for a positive-sloped credit spread term structure.

Lebedeva ends the meeting by asking Kowalski to recommend a credit analysis approach for a securitized asset-backed security (ABS) held in the portfolio. This non-static asset pool is made up of many medium-term auto loans that are homogeneous, and each loan is small relative to the total value of the pool.

24. The *most appropriate* response to Kowalski's question regarding credit rating migration is that it has:

    A. a negative impact.

    B. no impact.

    C. a positive impact.

25. Based on Exhibit 1, the one-year expected return on the Entre Corp. bond is *closest* to:

    A. 3.73%.

    B. 5.50%.

    C. 7.27%.

26. Based on Kowalski's assumptions and Exhibits 2 and 3, the credit spread on the VraiRive bond is *closest* to:

    A. 0.6949%.

    B. 0.9388%.

    C. 1.4082%.

27. The *most appropriate* response to Kowalski's question relating to the credit spread is:

    A. an increase in the probability of default.

    B. an increase in the loss given default.

    C. a decrease in the risk-neutral probability of default.

28. Which of Kowalski's statements regarding the term structure of credit spreads is correct?

    A. Only Statement 1

    B. Only Statement 2

    C. Both Statement 1 and Statement 2

29. DLL's credit spread term structure is *most* consistent with the firm having:

    A. low leverage.

    B. weak cash flow.

    C. a low profit margin.

30. Given the description of the asset pool of the ABS, Kowalski should recommend a:

    A. loan-by-loan approach.

    B. portfolio-based approach.

    C. statistics-based approach.

SOLUTIONS

1. B is correct. The expected exposure is the projected amount of money that an investor could lose if an event of default occurs, before factoring in possible recovery. The expected exposure for both Bond I and Bond II is 100 + 5 = 105.

2. C is correct. The loss given default is a positive function of the expected exposure to default loss and a negative function of the recovery rate. Because Bond II has a lower recovery rate than Bond I and the same expected exposure to default loss (100 + 5 = 105), it will have a higher loss given default than Bond I will have. The loss given default for Bond I is 105 × (1 – 0.40) = 63.00. The loss given default for Bond II is 105 × (1 – 0.35) = 68.25.

3. B is correct. In the event of no default, the investor is expected to receive 105. In the event of a default, the investor is expected to receive 105 – [105 × (1 – 0.40)] = 42. The expected future value of the bond is, therefore, the weighted average of the no-default and default amounts, or (105 × 0.98) + (42 × 0.02) = 103.74.

4. B is correct. The risk-neutral default probability, P^*, is calculated using the current price, the expected receipt at maturity with no default (that is, 100 + 5 = 105), the expected receipt at maturity in the event of a default (that is, 0.40 × 105 = 42), and the risk-free rate of interest (0.03):

$$100 = \frac{[105 \times (1 - P^*)] + (42 \times P^*)}{1.03}.$$

Solving for P^* gives 0.031746, or 3.1746%.

5. A is correct. The CVA is the sum of the present value of expected losses on the bond, which from Exhibit 2 is 3.3367.

6. C is correct. The expected percentage price change is the product of the negative of the modified duration and the difference between the credit spread in the new rating and the old rating:

Expected percentage price change = –4.2 × (0.0175 – 0.01) = –0.0315, or –3.15%.

7. B is correct. A reduced-form model in credit risk analysis uses historical variables, such as financial ratios and macroeconomic variables, to estimate the default intensity. A structural model for credit risk analysis, in contrast, uses option pricing and relies on a traded market for the issuer's equity.

8. B is correct. Observation 1 is incorrect, but Observation 2 is correct. The actual default probabilities do not include the default risk premium associated with the uncertainty in the timing of the possible default loss. The observed spread over the yield on a risk-free bond in practice does include liquidity and tax considerations, in addition to credit risk.

9. B is correct. The following table shows that the credit valuation adjustment (CVA) for the bond is €36.49, the sum of the present values of expected loss. The steps taken to complete the table are as follows.

| Step 1 | Exposure at date T is $\dfrac{€1,000}{(1 + r)^{4-T}}$, where r is 3%. That is, exposure is computed by discounting the face value of the bond using the risk-free rate and the number of years until maturity. |

Step 2   Recovery = Exposure × Recovery rate.

Step 3   Loss given default (LGD) = Exposure – Recovery.

Step 4   Probability of default (POD) on Date 1 is 1.50%. The probability of survival (POS) on Date 1 is 98.50%.

For subsequent dates, POD is calculated as the annual default probability multiplied by the previous date's POS.

For example, to determine the Date 2 POD (1.4775%), the annual default probability (1.50%) is multiplied by the Date 1 POS (98.50%).

Step 1   POS in Dates 2–4 = POS in the previous year – POD.

That is, POS in year T = POS in year $(T - 1)$ – POD in year T.

POS can also be determined by subtracting the annual default probability from 100% and raising it to the power of the number of years:

$(100\% - 1.5000\%)^1 = 98.5000\%$.

$(100\% - 1.5000\%)^2 = 97.0225\%$.

$(100\% - 1.5000\%)^3 = 95.5672\%$.

$(100\% - 1.5000\%)^4 = 94.1337\%$.

Step 2   Expected loss = LGD × POD.

Step 3   Discount factor (DF) for date T is $\dfrac{1}{(1 + r)^T}$, where r is 3%.

Step 4   PV of expected loss = Expected loss × DF.

Date	Exposure	Recovery	LGD	POD	POS	Expected Loss	DF	PV of Expected Loss
0								
1	€915.14	€274.54	€640.60	1.5000%	98.5000%	€9.61	0.970874	€9.33
2	€942.60	€282.78	€659.82	1.4775%	97.0225%	€9.75	0.942596	€9.19
3	€970.87	€291.26	€679.61	1.4553%	95.5672%	€9.89	0.915142	€9.05
4	€1,000.00	€300.00	€700.00	1.4335%	94.1337%	€10.03	0.888487	€8.92
							CVA =	€36.49

The value of the bond if it were default free would be 1,000 × DF for Date 4 = €888.49.

Fair value of the bond considering CVA = €888.49 – CVA = €888.49 – €36.49 = €852.00.

Because the market price of the bond (€875) is greater than the fair value of €852, B is correct.

A is incorrect because the market price of the bond differs from its fair value. C is incorrect because although the bond's value if the bond were default free is greater than the market price, the bond has a risk of default, and CVA lowers its fair value to below the market price.

10. B is correct. The recovery rate to be used now in the computation of fair value is 30% × 1.25 = 37.5%, whereas the default probability to be used is 1.50% × 1.25 =

1.875%.

Using the steps outlined in the solution to Question 1, the following table is prepared, which shows that the bond's CVA increases to 40.49. Thus, Koning concludes that a change in the probability of default has a greater effect on fair value than a similar change in the recovery rate. The steps taken to complete the table are the same as those in the previous problem. There are no changes in exposures and discount factors in this table.

Date	Exposure	Recovery	LGD	POD	POS	Expected Loss	DF	PV of Expected Loss
0								
1	€915.14	€343.18	€571.96	1.8750%	98.1250%	€10.72	0.970874	€10.41
2	€942.60	€353.47	€589.12	1.8398%	96.2852%	€10.84	0.942596	€10.22
3	€970.87	€364.08	€606.80	1.8053%	94.4798%	€10.95	0.915142	€10.03
4	€1,000.00	€375.00	€625.00	1.7715%	92.7083%	€11.07	0.888487	€9.84
							CVA =	€40.49

Changes in the default probability and recovery rates do not affect the value of the default-free bond. So, it is the same as in the previous question: €888.49.

Fair value of the bond considering CVA = €888.49 − CVA = €888.49 − €40.49 = €848.00

11. A is correct. The following table shows that the CVA for the bond is €42.17, the sum of the present values of expected loss. The steps taken to complete the table are as follows.

Step 1   Exposure at Date 4 is €1,000 + Coupon amount = €1,000 + €60 = €1,060. Exposure at a date T prior to that is the coupon on date T + PV at date T of subsequent coupons + PV of €1,000 to be received at Date 4. For example, exposure at Date 2 is

$$€60 + \frac{€60}{1+0.03} + \frac{€60}{(1+0.03)^2} + \frac{€1,000}{(1+0.03)^2} = €60 + \frac{€60}{1+0.03} + \frac{€1,060}{(1+0.03)^2}.$$
$$= €1,117.40.$$

Steps 2 through 8 are the same as those in the solution to Question 1.

Date	Exposure	Recovery	LGD	POD	POS	Expected Loss	DF	PV of Expected Loss
0								
1	€1,144.86	€343.46	€801.40	1.5000%	98.5000%	€12.02	0.970874	€11.67
2	€1,117.40	€335.22	€782.18	1.4775%	97.0225%	€11.56	0.942596	€10.89
3	€1,089.13	€326.74	€762.39	1.4553%	95.5672%	€11.10	0.915142	€10.15
4	€1,060.00	€318.00	€742.00	1.4335%	94.1337%	€10.64	0.888487	€9.45
							CVA =	€42.17

The value of the bond if it were default free would be €60 × DF_1 + €60 × DF_2 + €60 × DF_3 + €1,060 × DF_4 = €1,111.51.

Fair value of the bond considering CVA = €1,111.51 − €42.17 = €1,069.34.

12. A is correct. If default occurs on Date 3, the rate of return can be obtained by solving the following equation for internal rate of return (IRR):

$$\text{€}1,090 = \frac{\text{€}60}{1 + \text{IRR}} + \frac{\text{€}60}{(1 + \text{IRR})^2} + \frac{\text{€}326.74}{(1 + \text{IRR})^3}.$$

In this equation, €60 is the amount of coupon received at Dates 1 and 2 prior to default at Date 3. The amount €326.74 is the recovery at Time 3 (from the CVA table in the solution to the previous question). The solution to the foregoing equation can be obtained using the cash flow IRR function on your calculator.

13. B is correct. For each possible transition, the expected percentage price change, computed as the product of the modified duration and the change in the spread as shown in Exhibit 3 (relating to question 5), is calculated as follows:

From AA to AAA: −2.75 × (0.60% − 0.90%) = +0.83%.

From AA to A: −2.75 × (1.10% − 0.90%) = −0.55%.

From AA to BBB: −2.75 × (1.50% − 0.90%) = −1.65%.

From AA to BB: −2.75 × (3.40% − 0.90%) = −6.88%.

From AA to B: −2.75 × (6.50% − 0.90%) = −15.40%.

From AA to C: −2.75 × (9.50% − 0.90%) = −23.65%.

The expected percentage change in the value of the AA rated bond is computed by multiplying each expected percentage price change for a possible credit transition by its respective transition probability given in Exhibit 3 and summing the products:

(0.0150 × 0.83%) + (0.8800 × 0%) + (0.0950 × −0.55%) + (0.0075 × −1.65%) + (0.0015 × −6.88%) + (0.0005 × −15.40%) + (0.0003 × −23.65%)

= −0.0774%.

Therefore, the expected return on the bond over the next year is its YTM minus 0.0774%, assuming no default.

14. B is correct. Statement B is correct because a reduced-form credit model involves regression analysis using information generally available in the financial markets, such as the measures mentioned in the statement.

Statement A is incorrect because it is consistent with the use of a structural model and not a reduced-form model. It is a structural model that is based on the premise that a firm defaults on its debt if the value of its assets falls below its liabilities and that the probability of that event has the characteristics of an option.

Statement C is incorrect because it is consistent with the use of a structural model and not a reduced-form model. A structural model involves the estimation of a default barrier, and default occurs if the value of firm's assets falls below the default barrier.

15. C is correct. Structural models require information best known to the managers of the company. Reduced-form models require information only generally available in financial markets.

A is incorrect because although it is literally true, when the models were developed is immaterial. Structural models are currently used in practice by commercial banks and credit rating agencies.

B is incorrect because computer technology facilitates valuation using option pricing models as well as regression analysis.

16. A is correct. The following tree shows the valuation assuming no default of Bond B2, which pays a 6% annual coupon.

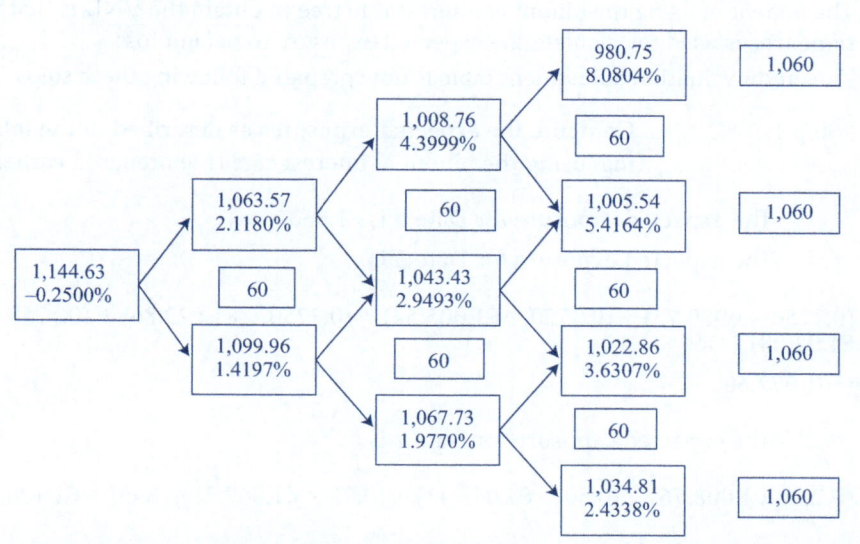

The scheduled year-end coupon and principal payments are placed to the right of each forward rate in the tree. For example, the Date 4 values are the principal plus the coupon of 60. The following are the four Date 3 values for the bond, shown above the interest rate at each node:

€1,060/1.080804 = €980.75.

€1,060/1.054164 = €1,005.54.

€1,060/1.036307 = €1,022.86.

€1,060/1.024338 = €1,034.81.

These are the three Date 2 values:

$$\frac{(0.5 \times €980.75) + (0.5 \times €1,005.54) + €60}{1.043999} = €1,008.76.$$

$$\frac{(0.5 \times €1,005.54) + (0.5 \times €1,022.86) + €60}{1.029493} = €1,043.43.$$

$$\frac{(0.5 \times €1,022.86) + (0.5 \times €1,034.81) + €60}{1.019770} = €1,067.73.$$

These are the two Date 1 values:

$$\frac{(0.5 \times €1,008.76) + (0.5 \times €1,043.43) + €60}{1.021180} = €1,063.57.$$

$$\frac{(0.5 \times €1,043.43) + (0.5 \times €1,067.73) + €60}{1.014197} = €1,099.96.$$

This is the Date 0 value:

$$\frac{(0.5 \times €1,063.57) + (0.5 \times €1,099.96) + €60}{0.997500} = €1,144.63.$$

So, the value of the bond assuming no default is 1,144.63. This value could also have been obtained more directly using the benchmark discount factors from Exhibit 2:

$$€60 \times 1.002506 + €60 \times 0.985093 + €60 \times 0.955848 + €1,060 \times 0.913225$$
$$= €1,144.63.$$

The benefit of using the binomial interest rate tree to obtain the VND is that the same tree is used to calculate the expected exposure to default loss.

The credit valuation adjustment table is now prepared following these steps:

Step 1	Compute the expected exposures as described in the following, using the binomial interest rate tree prepared earlier.

The expected exposure for Date 4 is €1,060.

The expected exposure for Date 3 is

$$(0.1250 \times €980.75) + (0.3750 \times €1,005.54) + (0.3750 \times €1,022.86) + (0.1250 \times €1,034.81) + 60$$
$$= €1,072.60.$$

The expected exposure for Date 2 is

$$(0.25 \times €1,008.76) + (0.50 \times €1,043.43) + (0.25 \times €1,067.73) + €60 = €1,100.84.$$

The expected exposure for Date 1 is

$$(0.50 \times €1,063.57) + (0.50 \times €1,099.96) + 60 = €1,141.76.$$

Step 2	LGD = Exposure × (1 − Recovery rate).
Step 3	The initial default probability is 1.50%. For subsequent dates, POD is calculated as the default probability multiplied by the previous date's POS.

For example, to determine the Date 2 POD (1.4775%), the default probability (1.5000%) is multiplied by the Date 1 POS (98.5000%).

Step 4	POS is determined by subtracting the default probability from 100% and raising it to the power of the number of years:

$$(100\% - 1.5000\%)^1 = 98.5000\%.$$

$$(100\% - 1.5000\%)^2 = 97.0225\%.$$

$$(100\% - 1.5000\%)^3 = 95.5672\%.$$

$$(100\% - 1.5000\%)^4 = 94.1337\%.$$

Step 5	Expected loss = LGD × POD.
Step 6	Discount factors in year T are obtained from Exhibit 2.
Step 7	PV of expected loss = Expected loss × DF.

Date	Exposure	LGD	POD	POS	Expected Loss	DF	PV of Expected Loss
0							
1	€1,141.76	€799.23	1.5000%	98.5000%	€11.99	1.002506	€12.02
2	€1,100.84	€770.58	1.4775%	97.0225%	€11.39	0.985093	€11.22

Date	Exposure	LGD	POD	POS	Expected Loss	DF	PV of Expected Loss
3	€1,072.60	€750.82	1.4553%	95.5672%	€10.93	0.955848	€10.44
4	€1,060.00	€742.00	1.4335%	94.1337%	€10.64	0.913225	€9.71
						CVA =	€43.39

Fair value of the bond considering CVA = €1,144.63 − CVA = €1,144.63 − €43.39 = €1,101.24.

17. A is correct. The corporate bond's fair value is computed in the solution to Question 8 as €1,101.24. The YTM can be obtained by solving the following equation for IRR:

$$€1,101.24 = \frac{€60}{1+IRR} + \frac{€60}{(1+IRR)^2} + \frac{€60}{(1+IRR)^3} + \frac{€1,060}{(1+IRR)^4}.$$

The solution to this equation is 3.26%.

Valuation of a four-year, 6% coupon bond under no default is computed in the solution to Question 8 as 1,144.63. So, the YTM of a theoretical comparable-maturity government bond with the same coupon rate as the corporate bond, B2, can be obtained by solving the following equation for IRR:

$$€1,144.63 = \frac{€60}{1+IRR} + \frac{€60}{(1+IRR)^2} + \frac{€60}{(1+IRR)^3} + \frac{€1,060}{(1+IRR)^4}.$$

The solution to this equation is 2.18%. So, the credit spread that the analyst wants to compute is 3.26% − 2.18% = 1.08%, or 108 bps.

B is incorrect because it is the spread over the four-year government par bond that has a YTM of 2.25% in Exhibit 2: 3.26% − 2.25% = 1.01%, or 101 bps. Although this spread is commonly used in practice, the analyst is interested in finding the spread over a theoretical 6% coupon government bond.

C is incorrect because it is the YTM of the coupon four-year government bond in Exhibit 2.

18. B is correct. The recovery rate to be used now in the computation of fair value is 30% × 0.75 = 22.500%, whereas the default probability to be used is 1.50% × 0.75 = 1.125%.

The tree that shows the valuation assuming no default of Bond B2 in the solution to Question 8 will not be affected by the foregoing changes. Accordingly, VND remains €1,144.63.

Following the steps outlined in the solution to Question 8, the following table is prepared, which shows that the CVA for the bond decreases to €36.23. Thus, Ibarra concludes that a decrease in the probability of default has a greater effect on fair value than a similar decrease in the recovery rate. The steps taken to complete the table are the same as those in Question 8. There are no changes in exposures or discount factors in this table.

Date	Exposure	LGD	POD	POS	Expected Loss	DF	PV of Expected Loss
0							
1	€1,141.76	€884.87	1.1250%	98.8750%	€9.95	1.002506	€9.98
2	€1,100.84	€853.15	1.1123%	97.7627%	€9.49	0.985093	€9.35
3	€1,072.60	€831.26	1.0998%	96.6628%	€9.14	0.955848	€8.74
4	€1,060.00	€821.50	1.0875%	95.5754%	€8.93	0.913225	€8.16
						CVA =	€36.23

Fair value of the bond considering CVA = €1,144.63 − CVA = €1,144.63 − €36.23 = €1,108.40.

19. A is correct. The following tree shows the valuation assuming no default of the floating-rate note (FRN), B4, which has a quoted margin of 4%.

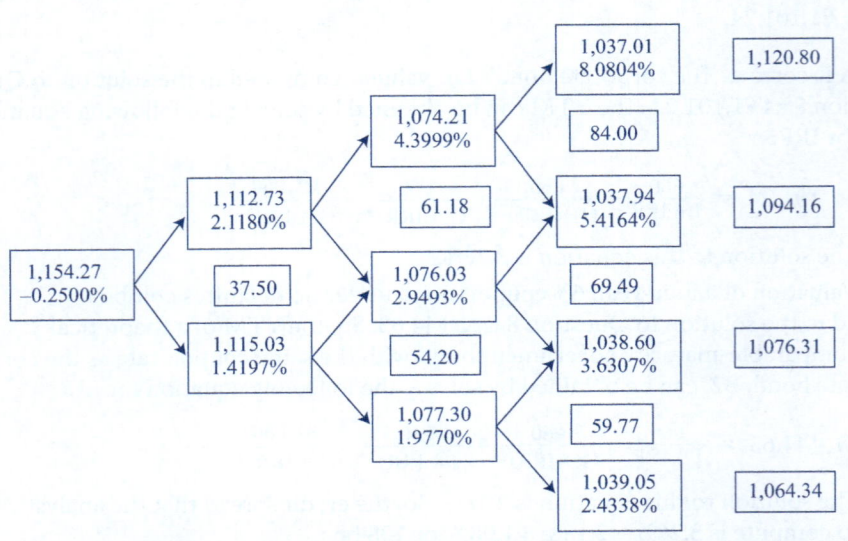

The scheduled year-end coupon and principal payments are placed to the right of each forward rate in the tree. For example, the four Date 4 values are the principal plus the coupon.

€1,000 × (1 + 0.080804 + 0.04) = €1,120.80.

€1,000 × (1 + 0.054164 + 0.04) = €1,094.16.

€1,000 × (1 + 0.036307 + 0.04) = €1,076.31.

€1,000 × (1 + 0.024338 + 0.04) = €1,064.34.

The following are the four Date 3 bond values for the note, shown above the interest rate at each node:

€1,120.80/1.080804 = €1,037.01.

€1,094.16/1.054164 = €1,037.94.

€1,076.31/1.036307 = €1,038.60.

€1,064.34/1.024338 = €1,039.05.

The three Date 3 coupon amounts are computed based on the interest rate at Date 2 plus the quoted margin of 4%:

€1,000 × (0.043999 + 0.04) = €84.00.

€1,000 × (0.029493 + 0.04) = €69.49.

€1,000 × (0.019770 + 0.04) = €59.77.

There are three Date 2 bond values:

$$\frac{(0.5 \times €1,037.01) + (0.5 \times €1,037.94) + €84.00}{1.043999} = €1,074.21.$$

$$\frac{(0.5 \times €1,037.94) + (0.5 \times €1,038.60) + €69.49}{1.029493} = €1,076.03.$$

$$\frac{(0.5 \times €1,038.60) + (0.5 \times €1,039.05) + €59.77}{1.019770} = €1,077.30.$$

The two Date 2 coupon amounts are computed based on the interest rate at Date 1 plus the quoted margin of 4%:

$$€1,000 \times (0.021180 + 0.04) = €61.18.$$

$$€1,000 \times (0.014197 + 0.04) = €54.20.$$

The Date 1 coupon amount is computed based on the interest rate at date 0 plus the quoted margin of 4%:

$$€1,000 \times (-0.0025 + 0.04) = €37.50.$$

These are the calculations for the bond values for Date 1 and Date 0:

$$\frac{(0.5 \times €1,074.21) + (0.5 \times €1,076.03) + €61.18}{1.021180} = €1,112.73.$$

$$\frac{(0.5 \times €1,076.06) + (0.5 \times €1,077.30) + €54.20}{1.014197} = €1,115.0.$$

Then, the VND is calculated as follows:

$$\frac{(0.5 \times €1,112.73) + (0.5 \times €1,115.03) + €37.50}{0.9975} = €1,154.27.$$

The expected exposures are then computed using the binomial interest rate tree prepared earlier. For example, the expected exposure for Date 4 is computed as follows:

$$(0.125 \times €1,120.80) + (0.375 \times €1,094.16) + (0.375 \times €1,076.31) + (0.125 \times €1,064.34)$$

$$= €1,087.07.$$

Similarly, the expected exposure for Date 3 is computed as follows:

$$(0.125 \times €1,037.01) + (0.375 \times €1,037.94) + (0.375 \times €1,038.60) + (0.125 \times €1,039.05) + (0.250 \times €84) + (0.500 \times €69.49) + (0.250 \times €59.77)$$

$$= €1,108.90.$$

The expected exposures for Dates 2 and 1 are computed similarly, and the credit valuation adjustment table is completed following Steps 2–7 outlined in the solution to Question 8.

Date	Exposure	LGD	POD	POS	Expected Loss	DF	PV of Expected Loss
0							
1	€1,151.38	€805.97	1.5000%	98.5000%	€12.09	1.002506	€12.12
2	€1,133.58	€793.51	1.4775%	97.0225%	€11.72	0.985093	€11.55
3	€1,108.90	€776.23	1.4553%	95.5672%	€11.30	0.955848	€10.80
4	€1,087.07	€760.95	1.4335%	94.1337%	€10.91	0.913225	€9.96
						CVA =	€44.43

Fair value of the FRN considering CVA = €1,154.27 − CVA = €1,154.27 − €44.43 = €1,109.84.

Because the market price of €1,070 is less than the estimated fair value, the analyst should recommend adding to existing positions in the FRN.

B and C are incorrect because the FRN is perceived to be undervalued in the market.

20. A is correct. The changing probability of default will not affect the binomial tree prepared in the solution to Question 11. The Date 1 value remains €1,154.27, which is also the VND. The expected exposures, loss given default, and discount factors are also unaffected by the changing probability of default. The following is the completed credit valuation adjustment table.

Date	Exposure	LGD	POD	POS	Expected Loss	DF	PV of Expected Loss
0							
1	€1,151.38	€805.97	1.5000%	98.5000%	€12.09	1.002506	€12.12
2	€1,133.58	€793.51	0.4925%	98.0075%	€3.91	0.985093	€3.85
3	€1,108.90	€776.23	0.4900%	97.5175%	€3.80	0.955848	€3.64
4	€1,087.07	€760.95	0.4876%	97.0299%	€3.71	0.913225	€3.39
						CVA =	€22.99

Thus, CVA decreases to €22.99.

21. C is correct. The credit rating agencies typically make incremental changes, as seen in a transition matrix provided in Exhibit 3. Ibarra believes the bond is undervalued, because her assessment of the probability of default and the recovery rate is more optimistic than that of the agencies. Therefore, she most likely expects the credit rating agencies to put the issuer on a positive watch.

A is incorrect because the bond is perceived to be undervalued, not overvalued. Ibarra is not expecting a credit downgrade.

B is incorrect because it is not the *most likely* expectation. The rating agencies rarely change an issuer's rating from BBB all the way to AAA. In Exhibit 3 (relating to question 5) the probability of a BBB rated issuer going from BBB to AAA is 0.02%, whereas to go from BBB to A it is 4.80%.

22. A is correct.

B is incorrect because, although generally true for investment-grade bonds, the statement neglects the fact that high-yield issuers sometimes face a downward-sloping credit term structure. Credit term structures are not *always* upward sloping.

C is incorrect because there is a consistent pattern for the term structure of credit spreads: Typically, it is upwardly sloped because greater time to maturity is associated with higher projected probabilities of default and lower recovery rates.

23. C is correct. A covered bond is a senior debt obligation of a financial institution that gives recourse to the originator/issuer as well as a predetermined underlying collateral pool. Each country or jurisdiction specifies the eligible collateral types as well as the specific structures permissible in the covered bond market. Covered bonds usually have either commercial or residential mortgages meeting specific criteria or public sector exposures as underlying collateral.

A is incorrect. The term "covered" is used in foreign exchange analysis, for instance, "covered interest rate parity." In the context of securitized debt, a covered bond is secured by specific assets in addition to the overall balance sheet of the issuer.

B is incorrect because a covered bond does not involve a credit default swap. In addition, an issuer is not likely to sell a credit default swap on its own liability.

24. A is correct. Credit spread migration typically reduces the expected return for two reasons. First, the probabilities for rating changes are not symmetrically distributed around the current rating; they are skewed toward a downgrade rather than an upgrade. Second, the increase in the credit spread is much larger for downgrades than is the decrease in the spread for upgrades.

25. A is correct. The expected return on the Entre Corp. bond over the next year is its yield to maturity plus the expected percentage price change in the bond over the next year. In the following table, for each possible transition, the expected percentage price change is the product of the bond's modified duration of 7.54, multiplied by –1, and the change in the spread, weighted by the given probability:

Expected percentage price change = (0.0002 × 6.786%) + (0.0030 × 4.524%) + (0.0480 × 3.016%) + (0.8573 × 0.000%) + (0.0695 × –14.326%) + (0.0175 × –37.700%) + (0.0045 × –60.320%) = –1.76715%.

So, the expected return on the Entre Corp. bond is its yield to maturity plus the expected percentage price change due to credit migration:

Expected return = 5.50% – 1.77% = 3.73%.

	Expected % Price Change (1)	Probability (2)	Expected % Price Change × Probability (1 × 2)
From BBB to AAA	–7.54 × (0.60% – 1.50%) = 6.786%	0.0002	0.00136
From BBB to AA	–7.54 × (0.90% – 1.50%) = 4.524%	0.0030	0.01357
From BBB to A	–7.54 × (1.10% – 1.50%) = 3.016%	0.0480	0.14477
From BBB to BB	–7.54 × (3.40% – 1.50%) = –14.326%	0.0695	–0.99566
From BBB to B	–7.54 × (6.50% – 1.50%) = –37.700%	0.0175	–0.65975
From BBB to CCC, CC, or C	–7.54 × (9.50% – 1.50%) = –60.320%	0.0045	–0.27144
		Total:	–1.76715

26. C is correct. The credit spread can be calculated in three steps:

Step 1   Estimate the value of the three-year VraiRive bond assuming no default. Based on Kowalski's assumptions and Exhibits 2 and 3, the value of the three-year VraiRive bond assuming no default is 100.0000.

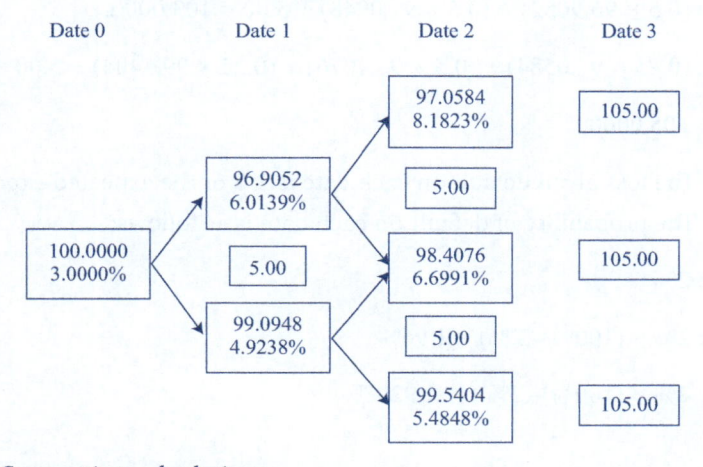

Supporting calculations:

The bond value in each node is the value of next period's cash flows discounted by the forward rate. For the three nodes on Date 2, the bond values are as follows:

$105/1.081823 = 97.0584$.

$105/1.066991 = 98.4076$.

$105/1.054848 = 99.5404$.

For the two nodes on Date 1, the two bond values are as follows:

$[(0.5 \times 97.0584) + (0.5 \times 98.4076) + 5.00]/1.060139 = 96.9052$.

$[(0.5 \times 98.4076) + (0.5 \times 99.5404) + 5.00]/1.049238 = 99.0948$.

Finally, for the node on Date 0, the bond value is

$[(0.5 \times 96.9052) + (0.5 \times 99.0948) + 5.00]/1.030000 = 100.0000$.

Therefore, the VND for the VraiRive bond is 100.0000.

Step 2   Calculate the credit valuation adjustment, and then subtract the CVA from the VND from Step 1 to establish the fair value of the bond. The CVA equals the sum of the present values of each year's expected loss and is calculated as follows:

Date	Expected Exposure	Loss Given Default	Probability of Default	Discount Factor	Present Value of Expected Loss
1	103.0000	68.6667	2.0000%	0.970874	1.3333
2	103.3535	68.9023	1.9600%	0.920560	1.2432
3	105.0000	70.0000	1.9208%	0.862314	1.1594
				CVA =	3.7360

Supporting calculations:

The expected exposures at each date are the bond values at each node, weighted by their risk-neutral probabilities, plus the coupon payment:

Date 1: $(0.5 \times 96.9052) + (0.5 \times 99.0948) + 5.00 = 103.0000$.

Date 2: $(0.25 \times 97.0584) + (0.5 \times 98.4076) + (0.25 \times 99.5404) + 5.00 = 103.3535$.

Date 3: 105.0000

The loss given default on each date is 2/3 of the expected exposure.

The probability of default on each date is as follows:

Date 1: 2%

Date 2: $2\% \times (100\% - 2\%) = 1.96\%$.

Date 3: $2\% \times (100\% - 2\%)^2 = 1.9208\%$.

The discount factor on each date is 1/(1 + spot rate for the date) raised to the correct power.

Finally, the credit valuation adjustment each year is the product of the LGD times the POD times the discount factor, as shown in the last column of the table. The sum of the three annual CVAs is 3.7360.

So, the fair value of the VraiRive bond is the VND less the CVA, or VND − CVA = 100 − 3.7360 = 96.2640.

Step 3   Based on the fair value from Step 2, calculate the yield to maturity of the bond, and solve for the credit spread by subtracting the yield to maturity on the benchmark bond from the yield to maturity on the VraiRive bond. The credit spread is equal to the yield to maturity on the VraiRive bond minus the yield to maturity on the three-year benchmark bond (which is 5.0000%). Based on its fair value of 96.2640, the VraiRive bond's yield to maturity is

$$96.2640 = \frac{5}{(1 + \text{YTM})} + \frac{5}{(1 + \text{YTM})^2} + \frac{105}{(1 + \text{YTM})^3}.$$

Solving for YTM, the yield to maturity is 6.4082%. Therefore, the credit spread on the VraiRive bond is 6.4082% − 5.0000% = 1.4082%.

27. C is correct. A decrease in the risk-neutral probability of default would decrease the credit valuation adjustment and decrease the credit spread. In contrast, increasing the bond's loss-given-default assumption and increasing the probability-of-default assumption would increase the credit valuation adjustment and decrease the fair value of the bond (and increase the yield to maturity and the credit spread over its benchmark).

28. A is correct. For investment-grade bonds with the highest credit ratings, credit spreads are extremely low, and credit migration is possible only in one direction given the implied lower bound of zero on credit spreads. As a result, the credit term structure for the most highly rated securities tends to be either flat or slightly upward sloping. Securities with lower credit quality, however, face greater sensitivity to the credit cycle. Credit spreads would decrease, not increase, with the expectation of economic growth. There is a countercyclical relationship between credit spreads and benchmark rates over the business cycle. A strong economic climate is associated with higher benchmark yields but lower credit spreads because the probability of issuers defaulting declines in such good times.

29. A is correct. Positive-sloped credit spread curves may arise when a high-quality issuer with a strong competitive position in a stable industry has low leverage, strong cash flow, and a high profit margin. This type of issuer tends to exhibit very low short-term credit spreads that rise with increasing maturity given greater uncertainty due to the macroeconomic environment, potential adverse changes in the competitive landscape, technological change, or other factors that drive a higher implied probability of default over time. Empirical academic studies also tend to support the view that the credit spread term structure is upward sloping for investment-grade bond portfolios.

30. B is correct. The auto ABS is granular, with many small loans relative to the size of the total portfolio. The auto loans are also homogeneous. These characteristics support using the portfolio-based approach. A loan-by-loan approach would be inefficient because of the large number of basically similar loans; this approach is best for a portfolio of discrete, large loans that are heterogeneous. A statistics-based approach would work for a static book of loans, whereas the auto loan portfolio would be dynamic and would change over time.

Credit Default Swaps

by Brian Rose, and Don M. Chance, PhD, CFA.

Brian Rose (USA). Don M. Chance, PhD, CFA, is at Louisiana State University (USA).

LEARNING OUTCOMES

Mastery	The candidate should be able to:
☐	describe credit default swaps (CDS), single-name and index CDS, and the parameters that define a given CDS product
☐	describe credit events and settlement protocols with respect to CDS
☐	explain the principles underlying and factors that influence the market's pricing of CDS
☐	describe the use of CDS to manage credit exposures and to express views regarding changes in the shape and/or level of the credit curve
☐	describe the use of CDS to take advantage of valuation disparities among separate markets, such as bonds, loans, equities, and equity-linked instruments

INTRODUCTION

1

Derivative instruments in which the underlying is a measure of a borrower's credit quality are widely used and well established in a number of countries. We explore basic definitions of such instruments, explain the main concepts, cover elements of valuation and pricing, and discuss applications.

BASIC DEFINITIONS AND CONCEPTS

2

☐	describe credit default swaps (CDS), single-name and index CDS, and the parameters that define a given CDS product

A **credit derivative** is a derivative instrument in which the underlying is a measure of a borrower's credit quality. Four types of credit derivatives are (1) total return swaps, (2) credit spread options, (3) credit-linked notes, and (4) credit default swaps, or CDS. CDS are the most liquid of the four and, as such, are the topic we focus on. In a CDS, one party makes payments to the other and receives in return the promise of compensation if a third party defaults.

In any derivative, the payoff is based on (derived from) the performance of an underlying instrument, rate, or asset that we call the "underlying." For a CDS, the underlying is the credit quality of a borrower. At its most fundamental level, a CDS provides compensation equal to expected recovery when a credit event occurs, but it also changes in value to reflect changes in the market's perception of a borrower's credit quality well in advance of default. The value of a CDS will rise and fall as opinions change about the likelihood and severity of a potential default. The actual event of default might never occur, but a decline in the price of a bond when investors perceive an increase in the likelihood of default is a mark-to-market loss to the bondholder. The most common credit events include bankruptcy, failure to pay, and restructuring. Another type of credit event which may be encountered in sovereign and municipal government bond markets is a moratorium or, more drastically, a repudiation of debt in which the governmental authority declares a moratorium on payments due under the terms of the obligation or challenges the validity of the entire debt obligation. (Other, less common credit events are also defined in the International Swaps and Derivatives Association's Credit Derivatives Definitions, but we will not consider them here.) Credit default swaps are designed to protect creditors against credit events such as these. The industry has expended great effort to provide clear guidance on what credit events are covered by a CDS contract. As with all efforts to write a perfect contract, however, no such device exists and disputes do occasionally arise. We will take a look at these issues later.

In addition to hedging credit risk, investors use CDS to

- leverage their portfolios,
- access maturity exposures not available in the cash market,
- access credit risk while limiting interest rate risk, and
- improve the liquidity of their portfolios given the illiquidity in the corporate bond market.

In addition, the CDS market has increased transparency and insight into the actual cost of credit risk. The higher relative liquidity and relative sophistication of CDS investors allow for more accurate price discovery and facilitate trading during liquidity events when the cash market for bonds becomes illiquid. While many of the applications listed above are beyond the scope of this reading, a basic understanding of this important fixed-income tool is necessary for all investment professionals.

Let's now define a **credit default swap**:

> *A credit default swap is a derivative contract between two parties, a credit protection buyer and credit protection seller, in which the buyer makes a series of cash payments to the seller and receives a promise of compensation for credit losses resulting from a credit event in an underlying.*

In a CDS contract there are two counterparties, the **credit protection buyer** and the **credit protection seller**. The buyer agrees to make a series of periodic payments to the seller over the life of the contract (which are determined and fixed at contract initiation) and receives in return a promise that if default occurs, the protection seller will compensate the protection buyer. If default occurs, the periodic payments made by the protection buyer to the protection seller terminate. Exhibit 1 shows the structure of payment flows.

Exhibit 1: Payment Structure of a CDS

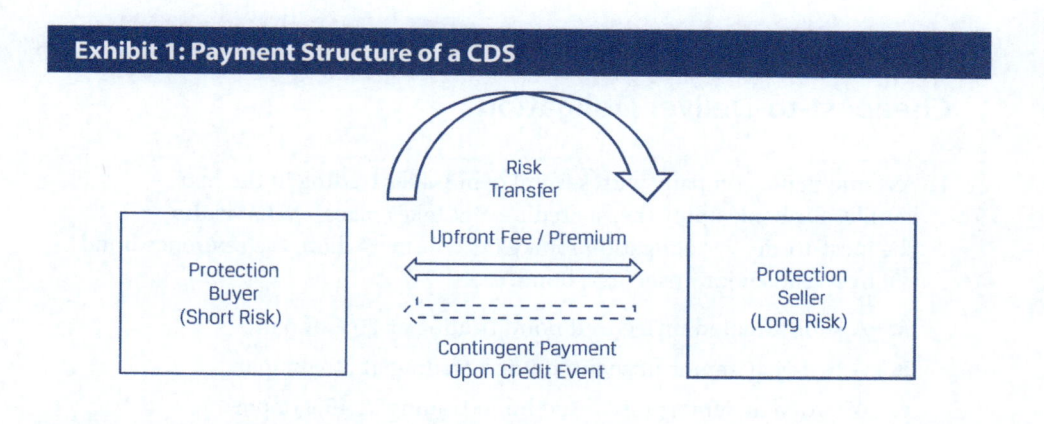

Credit default swaps are somewhat similar to put options. Put options effectively enable the option holder to sell (put) the underlying security to the option seller if the underlying performs poorly relative to the exercise price. Similarly, in the event of a credit event on the underlying security, the buyer of credit protection receives a payment from the credit protection seller equal to the par or notional value of the security less the expected recovery value. If the credit quality of the underlying deteriorates but there is no outright credit event, the credit protection buyer is compensated only if the contract is unwound. How that compensation occurs and how much protection it provides are some points we will discuss.

A CDS does not eliminate credit risk. The definition of a default in the swap contract may not perfectly align with a traditional default event, so the magnitude of the change in value of the contract may differ from the change in value of the underlying. In addition, the credit protection buyer assumes counterparty risk with respect to the credit protection seller. Although there are no guarantees that the credit protection seller will not default, as was seen with several large financial institutions in the financial crisis that started in 2007, most credit protection sellers are relatively high-quality borrowers. If they were not, they could not be active sellers of credit protection.

The majority of CDS are written on debt issued by corporate borrowers, which will be our focus in this reading. But note that CDS can also be written on the debt of sovereign governments and state and local governments. In addition, CDS can be written on portfolios of loans, mortgages, or debt securities.

Types of CDS

There are three types of CDS: single-name CDS, index CDS, and tranche CDS. Other CDS-related instruments, such as options on CDS (or CDS swaptions) are beyond the scope of this discussion. A CDS on one specific borrower is called a **single-name CDS**. The borrower is called the **reference entity**, and the contract specifies a **reference obligation**, a particular debt instrument issued by the borrower. Only a small subset of issuers, typically with large outstanding liquid debt, have single-name CDS. The designated instrument is usually a senior unsecured obligation, but the reference obligation is not the only instrument covered by the CDS. Any debt obligation issued by the borrower that is ranked equal to or higher than the reference obligation with respect to the priority of claims is covered. The payoff of the CDS is determined by the **cheapest-to-deliver** obligation, which is the debt instrument that can be purchased and delivered at the lowest cost but has the same seniority as the reference obligation.

EXAMPLE 1

Cheapest-to-Deliver Obligation

1. Assume that a company with several debt issues trading in the market files for bankruptcy (i.e., a credit event takes place). What is the cheapest-to-deliver obligation for a CDS contract where the reference bond is a five-year senior unsecured bond?

   A. A subordinated unsecured bond trading at 20% of par

   B. A five-year senior unsecured bond trading at 50% of par

   C. A two-year senior unsecured bond trading at 45% of par

Solution:

C is correct. The cheapest-to-deliver, or lowest-priced, instrument is the two-year senior unsecured bond trading at 45% of par. Although the bond in A trades at a lower dollar price, it is subordinated and, therefore, does not qualify for coverage under the CDS. Note that even though the CDS holder holds the five-year bonds, he will receive payment on the CDS based on the cheapest-to-deliver obligation, not the specific obligation he holds.

A second type of credit default swap, an **index CDS**, involves a portfolio of single-name CDS. This type of instrument allows participants to take positions on the credit risk of a combination of companies, in much the same way that investors can trade index or exchange-traded funds that are combinations of the equities of companies. The two most commonly traded CDS index products are the North American indexes (CDS) and the European, Asian, and Australian indexes (iTraxx). Correlation of defaults is a strong determinant of a portfolio's behavior. For index CDS, this concept takes the form of a factor called **credit correlation**, and it is a key determinant of the value of an index CDS. Analyzing the effects of those correlations is a highly specialized subject, but be aware that much effort is placed on modeling how defaults by certain companies are connected to defaults by other companies. The more correlated the defaults, the more costly it is to purchase protection for a combination of the companies. In contrast, for a diverse combination of companies whose defaults have low correlations, it will be much less expensive to purchase protection.

A third type of CDS is the **tranche CDS**, which covers a combination of borrowers but only up to pre-specified levels of losses—much in the same manner that asset-backed securities are divided into tranches, each covering particular levels of losses. Coverage of tranche CDS is beyond the scope of this reading.

---

3   IMPORTANT FEATURES OF CDS MARKETS

☐ | describe credit events and settlement protocols with respect to CDS

As we will describe in more detail later, the CDS market is large, global, and well organized. The unofficial industry governing body is the International Swaps and Derivatives Association (ISDA), which publishes industry-supported conventions that facilitate the functioning of the market. Parties to CDS contracts generally agree that their contracts will conform to ISDA specifications. These terms are specified in a document called the **ISDA Master Agreement**, which the parties to a CDS sign.

In Europe, the standard CDS contract is called the Standard Europe Contract, and in the United States and Canada, it is called the Standard North American Contract. Other standardized contracts exist for Asia, Australia, Latin America, and a few other specific countries.

Each CDS contract specifies a **notional amount**, or "notional" for short, which is the amount of protection being purchased. The notional amount can be thought of as the *size* of the contract. It is important to understand that the total notional amount of CDS can exceed the amount of debt outstanding of the reference entity. As we will discuss later, the credit protection buyer does not have to be an actual creditor holding exposure (i.e., owning a loan, bond, or other debt instrument). It can be simply a party that believes that there will be a change in the credit quality of the reference entity.

As with all derivatives, the CDS contract has an expiration or maturity date, and coverage is provided up to that date. The typical maturity range is 1 to 10 years, with 5 years being the most common and actively traded maturity, but the two parties can negotiate any maturity. Maturity dates are typically the 20th day of March, June, September, or December. The March and September maturity dates are the most liquid, as these are when the index CDS contracts roll.

The buyer of a CDS pays a periodic premium to the seller, referred to as the **CDS spread**, which is a return over a market reference rate required to protect against credit risk. It is sometimes referred to as a credit spread. Conceptually, it is the same as the credit spread on a bond, the compensation for bearing credit risk.

An important advancement in the development of CDS has been in establishing standard annual coupon rates on CDS contracts. (Note that the reference bond will make payments that are referred to collectively as the coupon while a CDS on the reference bond will have its own coupon rate.) Formerly, the coupon rate on the CDS was set at the credit spread. If a CDS required a rate of 4% to compensate the protection seller for the assumption of credit risk, the protection buyer made quarterly payments amounting to 4% annually. Now CDS coupon rates are standardized, with the most common coupons being either 1% or 5%. The 1% rate typically is used for a CDS on an investment-grade company or index, and the 5% rate is used for a CDS on a high-yield company or index. Obviously, either standardized rate might not be the appropriate rate to compensate the seller. Clearly, not all investment-grade companies have equivalent credit risk, and not all high-yield companies have equivalent credit risk. In effect, the standard rate may be too high or too low. This discrepancy is accounted for by an **upfront payment**, commonly called the **upfront premium**. The differential between the credit spread and the standard rate is converted to a present value basis. Thus, a credit spread greater than the standard rate would result in a cash payment from the protection buyer to the protection seller. Similarly, a credit spread less than the standard rate would result in a cash payment from the protection seller to the protection buyer.

Regardless of whether either party makes an upfront payment, the reference entity's credit quality could change during the life of the contract, thereby resulting in changes in the value of the CDS. These changes are reflected in the price of the CDS in the market. Consider a high-yield company with a 5% credit spread and a CDS coupon of 5%. Therefore, there is no upfront payment. The protection buyer simply agrees to make payments equal to 5% of the notional over the life of the CDS. Now suppose that at some later date, the reference entity experiences a decrease in its credit quality. The credit protection buyer is thus paying 5% for risk that now merits a rate higher than 5%. The coverage and cost of protection are the same, but the risk being covered is greater. The value of the CDS to the credit protection buyer has, therefore, increased, and if desired, she could unwind the position to capture the gain. The credit protection seller has experienced a loss in value of the instrument because he is receiving 5% to cover a risk that is higher than it was when the contract was initiated. It should be apparent that absent any other exposure to the reference entity, if the credit quality of the reference entity decreases, the credit protection buyer gains and the credit protection seller loses. The market value of the CDS reflects these gains and losses.

The terminology in CDS markets can be confusing. In equity and fixed-income markets, we think of buyers as being long and sellers as being short. In the CDS market, however, that is not always true. In single-name CDS, the *buyer* of credit protection is *short credit exposure* and the *seller* of credit protection is *long credit exposure*. This is consistent with the fact that in the financial world, "shorts" are said to benefit when things go badly. When credit quality deteriorates, the credit protection buyer benefits, and when it improves, the credit protection seller benefits. To make things even more confusing, though, the opposite is true in CDS index positions: The *buyer* of a CDX is *long* credit exposure and the seller of a CDX is *short* credit exposure. To minimize the confusion, we use the terms *credit protection seller* and *credit protection buyer* throughout our discussion. .

Credit and Succession Events

The **credit event** is what defines default by the reference entity—that is, the event that triggers a payment from the credit protection seller to the credit protection buyer. This event must be unambiguous: Did it occur, or did it not? For the market to function well, the answer to this question must be clear.

As previously mentioned, the most common credit events include bankruptcy, failure to pay, and restructuring. **Bankruptcy** is a declaration provided for by a country's laws that typically involves the establishment of a legal procedure that forces creditors to defer their claims. Bankruptcy essentially creates a temporary fence around the company through which the creditors cannot pass. During the bankruptcy process, the defaulting party works with its creditors and the court to attempt to establish a plan for repaying the debt. If that plan fails, there is likely to be a full liquidation of the company, at which time the court determines the payouts to the various creditors. Until liquidation occurs, the company normally continues to operate. Many companies do not liquidate and are able to emerge from bankruptcy. A bankruptcy filing by the reference entity is universally regarded as a credit event in CDS contracts.

Another credit event recognized in standard CDS contracts is **failure to pay**, which occurs when a borrower does not make a scheduled payment of principal or interest on an outstanding obligation after a grace period, without a formal bankruptcy filing. (Failure to pay credit events are defined in the CDS contract. ISDA contracts define failure to pay events uniformly, but the same is not true for bespoke CDS.) The third type of event, **restructuring**, refers to a number of possible events, including reduction or deferral of principal or interest, change in seniority or priority of an obligation, or change in the currency in which principal or interest is scheduled to be paid. To qualify as a credit event, the restructuring must be either involuntary or coercive. An involuntary credit event is one that is forced on the borrower by the creditors. A coercive credit event is one that is forced on the creditors by the borrower. Debt restructuring is not a credit event in the United States; issuers generally restructure under *bankruptcy*, which *is* a credit event. Restructuring is a credit event in other countries where the use of bankruptcy court to reorganize is less common. The Greek debt crisis is a good example of a restructuring that triggered a credit event.

Determination of whether a credit event occurs is done by a 15-member group within the ISDA called the Determinations Committee (DC). Each region of the world has a Determinations Committee, which consists of 10 CDS dealer (sell-side) banks and 5 non-bank (buy-side) end users. To declare a credit event, there must be a supermajority vote of 12 members.

[Handwritten margin note: - A credit event (failure to pay) occurs when a borrower does not make a scheduled payment of principal or interest on any outstanding obligations after a grace period, even without a formal bankruptcy filing.]

The Determinations Committees also play a role in determining whether a **succession event** occurred. A succession event arises when there is a change in the corporate structure of the reference entity, such as through a merger, a divestiture, a spinoff, or any similar action in which ultimate responsibility for the debt in question becomes unclear. For example, if a company acquires all of the shares of a target company, it ordinarily assumes the target company's debt as well. Many mergers, however, are more complicated and can involve only partial acquisition of shares. Spinoffs and divestitures can also involve some uncertainty about who is responsible for certain debts. When such a question arises, it becomes critical for CDS holders. The question is ordinarily submitted to a Determinations Committee, and its resolution often involves complex legal interpretations of contract provisions and country laws. If a succession event is declared, the CDS contract is modified to reflect the DC's interpretation of whoever it believes becomes the obligor for the original debt. Ultimately, the CDS contract could be split among multiple entities.

[handwritten margin note: DC: determinations Committee]

Settlement Protocols

If the DC declares that a credit event has occurred, the two parties to a CDS have the right, but not the obligation, to settle. **Settlement** typically occurs 30 days after declaration of the credit event by the DC. CDS can be settled by **physical settlement** or by **cash settlement**. The former is less common and involves actual delivery of the debt instrument in exchange for a payment by the credit protection seller of the notional amount of the contract. In cash settlement, the credit protection seller pays cash to the credit protection buyer. Determining the amount of that payment is a critical factor because opinions can differ about how much money has actually been lost. The payment should essentially be the loss that the credit protection buyer has incurred, but determining that amount is not straightforward. Default on a debt does not mean that the creditor will lose the entire amount owed. A portion of the loss could be recovered. The percentage of the loss recovered is called the **recovery rate** (RR). (In most models, the recovery rate applies only to the principal.) The complement is called the **loss given default** (LGD), which is essentially an estimate of the expected credit loss. The **payout amount** is determined as the loss given default multiplied by the notional.

Loss given default = 1 − Recovery rate (%).

Payout amount = LGD × Notional.

Actual recovery can be a very long process, however, and can occur much later than the payoff date of the CDS. To determine an appropriate LGD, the industry conducts an auction in which major banks and dealers submit bids and offers for the cheapest-to-deliver defaulted debt. This process identifies the market's expectation for the recovery rate and the complementary LGD, and the CDS parties agree to accept the outcome of the auction, even though the actual recovery rate can ultimately be quite different, which is an important point if the CDS protection buyer also holds the underlying debt.

EXAMPLE 2

Settlement Preference

A French company files for bankruptcy, triggering various CDS contracts. It has two series of senior bonds outstanding: Bond A trades at 30% of par, and Bond B trades at 40% of par. Investor X owns €10 million of Bond A and owns €10 million of CDS protection. Investor Y owns €10 million of Bond B and owns €10 million of CDS protection.

1. Determine the recovery rate for both CDS contracts.

Solution:

Bond A is the cheapest-to-deliver obligation, trading at 30% of par, so the recovery rate for both CDS contracts is 30%.

2. Explain whether Investor X would prefer to cash settle or physically settle her CDS contract or whether she is indifferent.

Solution:

Investor X has no preference between settlement methods. She can cash settle for €7 million [(1 − 30%) × €10 million] and sell her bond for €3 million, for total proceeds of €10 million. Alternatively, she can physically deliver her entire €10 million face amount of bonds to the counterparty in exchange for €10 million in cash.

3. Explain whether Investor Y would prefer to cash settle or physically settle his CDS contract or whether he is indifferent.

Solution:

Investor Y would prefer a cash settlement because he owns Bond B, which is worth more than the cheapest-to-deliver obligation. He will receive the same €7 million payout on his CDS contract but can sell Bond B for €4 million, for total proceeds of €11 million. If he were to physically settle his contract, he would receive only €10 million, the face amount of his bond.

CDS Index Products

So far, we have mostly been focusing on single-name CDS. As noted, there are also index CDS products. A company called Markit has been instrumental in producing CDS indexes. Of course, a CDS index is not in itself a traded instrument any more than a stock index is a traded product. As with the major stock indexes, however, the industry has created traded instruments based on the Markit indexes. These instruments are CDS that generate a payoff based on any default that occurs on any entity covered by the index.

The Markit indexes are classified by region and further classified (or divided) by credit quality. The two most commonly traded regions are North America and Europe. North American indexes are identified by the symbol CDX, and European, Asian, and Australian indexes are identified as iTraxx. Within each geographic category are investment-grade and high-yield indexes. The former are identified as CDX IG and iTraxx Main, each comprising 125 entities. The latter are identified as CDX HY, consisting of 100 entities, and iTraxx Crossover, consisting of up to 75 high-yield entities. Investment-grade index CDS are typically quoted in terms of spreads, whereas high-yield index CDS are quoted in terms of prices. Both types of products use standardized coupons. All CDS indexes are equally weighted. Thus, if there are 125 entities, the settlement on one entity is 1/125 of the notional. (Note that some confusion might arise from quoting certain CDS as prices and some as spreads, but keep in mind that the bond market quotes bonds often as prices and sometimes as yields. For example, a Treasury bond can be described as having a price of 120 or a yield of 2.68%. Both terms, combined with the other characteristics of the bond, imply the same concept.)

Markit updates the components of each index every six months by creating new series while retaining the old series. The latest-created series is called the **on-the-run** series, whereas the older series are called **off-the-run** series. When an investor moves from one series to a new one, the move is called a **roll**. When an entity within an index defaults, that entity is removed from the index and settled as a single-name CDS based on its relative proportion in the index. The index then moves forward with a smaller notional.

Index CDS are typically used to take positions on the credit risk of the sectors covered by the indexes as well as to protect bond portfolios that consist of or are similar to the components of the indexes. (An important reminder: When you *buy* a CDS index position, you are *long the credit exposure*, but when you *buy* a single-name CDS position, you have *bought credit protection*. To avoid confusion, we do not talk about buying and selling CDS herein but focus on the desired exposure, using the terms *buy protection* and *sell protection*.)

Standardization is generally undertaken to increase trading volume, which is somewhat limited in the single-name market with so many highly diverse entities. With CDS indexes on standardized portfolios based on the credit risk of well-identified companies, market participants have responded by trading them in large volumes. Indeed, index CDS are typically more liquid than single-name CDS, with average daily trading volume several times that of single-name CDS.

EXAMPLE 3

Hedging and Exposure Using Index CDS

Assume that an investor sells $500 million of protection using the CDX IG index, which has 125 reference entities. Concerned about the creditworthiness of a few of the components, the investor hedges a portion of the credit risk in each. For Company A, he purchases $3 million of single-name CDS protection, and Company A subsequently defaults.

1. What is the investor's net notional exposure to Company A?

Solution:

The investor is long $4 million notional credit exposure ($500 million/125) through the index CDS and is short $3 million notional credit exposure through the single-name CDS. His net notional credit exposure is $1 million.

2. What proportion of his exposure to Company A has he hedged?

Solution:

He has hedged 75% of his exposure ($3 million out of $4 million).

3. What is the remaining notional on his index CDS trade?

Solution:

His index CDS has $496 million remaining notional credit exposure ($500 million original notional minus the $4 million notional related to Company A, which is no longer in the index).

Market Characteristics

Credit default swaps trade in the over-the-counter market. To better understand this market, we will first review how credit derivatives and specifically CDS were started.

As financial intermediaries, banks draw funds from savings-surplus sectors, primarily consumers, and channel them to savings-deficit sectors, primarily businesses. Corporate lending is a core element of banking. When a bank makes a corporate loan, it assumes two primary risks. One is that the borrower will not repay principal and interest, and the other is that interest rates will change such that the return the bank is earning on its outstanding loans is less than the rate available on comparable instruments in the marketplace. The former is called **credit risk** or **default risk**, and the latter is called **interest rate risk**. There are many ways to manage interest rate risk. Until around the mid-1990s, credit risk was largely managed using traditional methods—such as analysis of the borrower, its industry, and the macroeconomy—as well as control methods, such as credit limits, monitoring, and collateral. In effect, the only defenses against credit risk were to not make a loan, to lend but require collateral (the value of which is also at risk), or to lend and closely monitor the borrower, hoping that any problems could be foreseen and dealt with before a default occurred.

Around 1995, credit derivatives were created to provide a new and potentially more effective method of managing credit risk. They allow credit risk to be transferred from the lender to another party. In so doing, they facilitate the separation of interest rate risk from credit risk. Banks can then provide their most important service—lending—knowing that the credit risk can be transferred to another party if so desired. This ability to easily transfer credit risk allows banks to greatly expand their loan business. Given that lending is such a large and vital component of any economy, credit derivatives facilitate economic growth and have expanded to cover, and indeed are primarily focused on, the short-, intermediate-, and long-term bond markets. In fact, credit derivatives are more effective in the bond market, in which terms and conditions are far more standard, than in the bank loan market. Of the four types of credit derivatives, credit default swaps have clearly established themselves as the most widely used instrument. Indeed, in today's markets CDS are nearly the only credit derivative used to any great extent. CDS transactions are executed in the over-the-counter market by phone, instant message, or the Bloomberg message service. Trade information is reported to the **Depository Trust and Clearinghouse Corporation**, which is a US-headquartered entity providing post-trade clearing, settlement, and information services for many kinds of securities. Regulations require the central clearing of many CDS contracts, meaning that parties will send their contracts through clearinghouses that collect and distribute payments and impose margin requirements, as well as mark positions to market. Central clearing of CDS has risen dramatically since 2010. Currently, slightly more than half of all CDS are centrally cleared, up from just 10% in 2010.

The CDS market today is considerably smaller than it was prior to the 2008 financial crisis. The Bank for International Settlements reported that as of December 2019, the gross notional amount of CDS was about $7.6 trillion with a market value of $199 billion. (For comparison, the notional amounts for interest rate contracts—forward rate agreements, swaps, options—as of December 2019 was about $449 trillion.) As of December 2007, CDS gross notional was $57.9 trillion, nearly 8 times larger.

More than 90% of all CDS market activity is now derived from trading in five major CDS indexes: iTraxx Europe, iTraxx Europe Crossover, iTraxx Europe Senior Financials, CDX IG, and CDS HY.

BASICS OF VALUATION AND PRICING

4

explain the principles underlying and factors that influence the market's pricing of CDS

Derivatives are typically priced by solving for the cost of a position that fully offsets the underlying exposure and earns the risk-free rate. In the context of CDS, this "price" is the CDS spread or upfront payment for a particular coupon rate under the contract. Although CDS are referred to as "swaps," they in fact resemble options because of the contingent nature of the payment made by the protection seller to the protection buyer if a credit event occurs as established by the ISDA Determinations Committee as outlined above.

Unlike conventional derivative instruments, the CDS settlement amount under a credit event as declared by the ISDA Determinations Committee is far less clear than for derivatives whose underlying involves actively traded assets, such as equities, interest rates, or currencies. Credit does not "trade" in the traditional sense but, rather, exists implicitly within the bond and loan market. The unique debt structure and composition of each CDS reference entity adds to the complexity of establishing the basis between a CDS contract and a specific outstanding bond or loan.

The details of credit derivative models are beyond the scope of this reading, but it is important for investment industry analysts to have a thorough understanding of the factors that determine CDS pricing.

Basic Pricing Concepts

In our earlier coverage of credit strategies, we established that the credit valuation adjustment (CVA) may be thought of as the present value of credit risk for a loan, bond, or derivative obligation. In principle, the CVA should, therefore, be a reasonable approximation for the CDS hedge position outlined previously that would leave an investor with a risk-free rate of return. Exhibit 2 summarizes the CVA calculation for a financial exposure.

Exhibit 2: Credit Valuation Adjustment

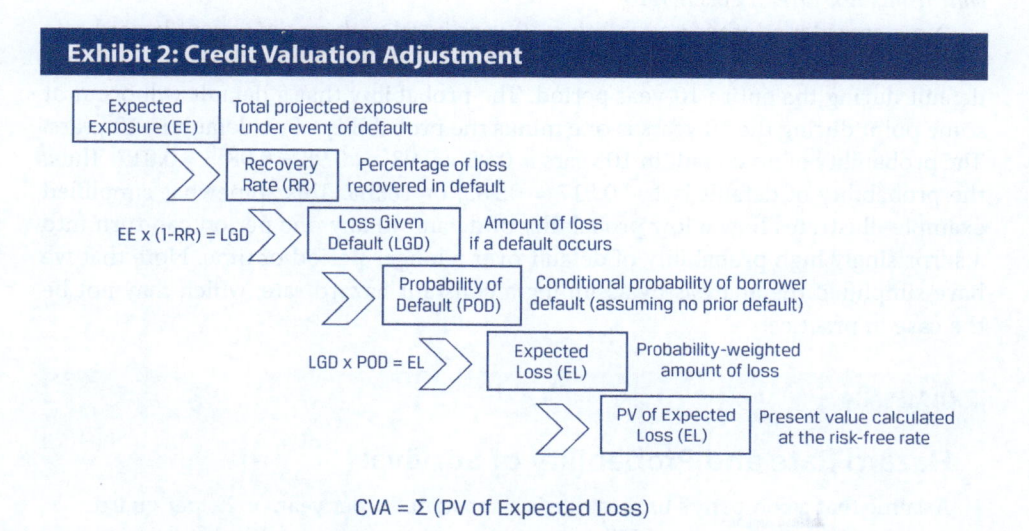

CVA = Σ (PV of Expected Loss)

CVA is a function of expected exposure (EE), recovery rate, loss given default, the **probability of default** (POD) to arrive at an expected loss (EL), and a discount factor to arrive at the present value of expected loss.

Considering each of these CVA components in turn, the expected exposure reflects the notional value of the underlying CDS contract. Recall that the recovery rate is the percentage of loss recovered from a bond in default, whereas the loss given default is a function of the loss severity multiplied by the exposure amount.

The probability of default is a key element of CDS pricing that may be illustrated using a simple example. Consider a one-period CDS swap with no upfront payment where we ignore the time value of money and assume that default is possible only at maturity. The fair price of CDS protection for this period for a given borrower may be estimated as

$$\text{CDS spread} \approx (1 - RR) \times POD.$$

For example, if the probability of default is 2% and the recovery rate is 60%, the estimated CDS spread for the period would be 80 bps for the period. Assuming a $100 notional contract value and a period of a year, the CDS contract fair value would be (the present value of) $0.80.

It is important to note that the POD is a conditional probability over time. That is, assuming a two-period case, the probability of default in Period 2 is contingent on "surviving" to (i.e., not defaulting by) the end of Period 1. Note that we simplify the analysis by assuming discrete times of potential default versus the continuous time assumption common in CDS pricing models.

For example, consider a two-year, 5%, $1,000 loan with one interest payment of $50 due in one year and final interest and principal of $1,050 due in two years. Assume further that we estimate a 2% chance of defaulting on the first payment and a 4% chance of defaulting on the second payment. To calculate the POD over the life of the loan, we first determine the **probability of survival** (POS) for Period 1. The POS is 0.98 (100% minus the 2% POD at T_1) multiplied by 0.96 (100% minus the 4% POD at T_2), approximately 94.08%. Thus, the POD over the life of the loan is 100% − 94.08% = 5.92%.

This conditional probability of default is also known as the **hazard rate**, as described in an earlier reading. The hazard rate is the probability that an event will occur *given that it has not already occurred.*

Now consider another possibility, a 10-year bond with an equivalent hazard rate of 2% each year. Suppose we want to know the probability that the borrower will not default during the entire 10-year period. The probability that a default will occur at some point during the 10 years is one minus the probability of no default in 10 years. The probability of no default in 10 years is $0.98 \times 0.98 \ldots 0.98 = 0.98^{10} = 0.817$. Thus, the probability of default is $1 - 0.817 = 0.183$, or 18.3%. This somewhat simplified example illustrates how a low probability of default in any one period can turn into a surprisingly high probability of default over a longer period of time. Note that we have simplified the analysis by assuming a constant hazard rate, which may not be the case in practice.

EXAMPLE 4

Hazard Rate and Probability of Survival

Assume that a company's hazard rate is a constant 8% per year, or 2% per quarter. An investor sells five-year CDS protection on the company with the premiums paid quarterly over the next five years.

1. What is the probability of survival for the first quarter?

Solution:

The probability of survival for the first quarter is 98% (100% minus the 2% hazard rate).

2. What is the conditional probability of survival for the second quarter?

Solution:

The conditional probability of survival for the second quarter is also 98%, because the hazard rate is constant at 2%. In other words, *conditional on the company having survived the first quarter,* there is a 2% probability of default in the second quarter.

3. What is the probability of survival through the second quarter?

Solution:

The probability of survival through the second quarter is 96.04%. The probability of survival through the first quarter is 98%, and the conditional probability of survival through the second quarter is also 98%. The probability of survival through the second quarter is thus 98% × 98% = 96.04%. Alternatively, 1 − 96.04% = 3.96% is the probability of default sometime during the first two quarters.

Understanding the concept of pricing a CDS is facilitated by recognizing that there are essentially two sides, or legs, of a contract. There is the **protection leg**, which is the contingent payment that the credit protection seller may have to make to the credit protection buyer, and the **premium leg**, which is the series of payments the credit protection buyer promises to make to the credit protection seller. Exhibit 3 provides an illustration of the process.

Exhibit 3: Determination of CDS Protection vs. Premium Legs

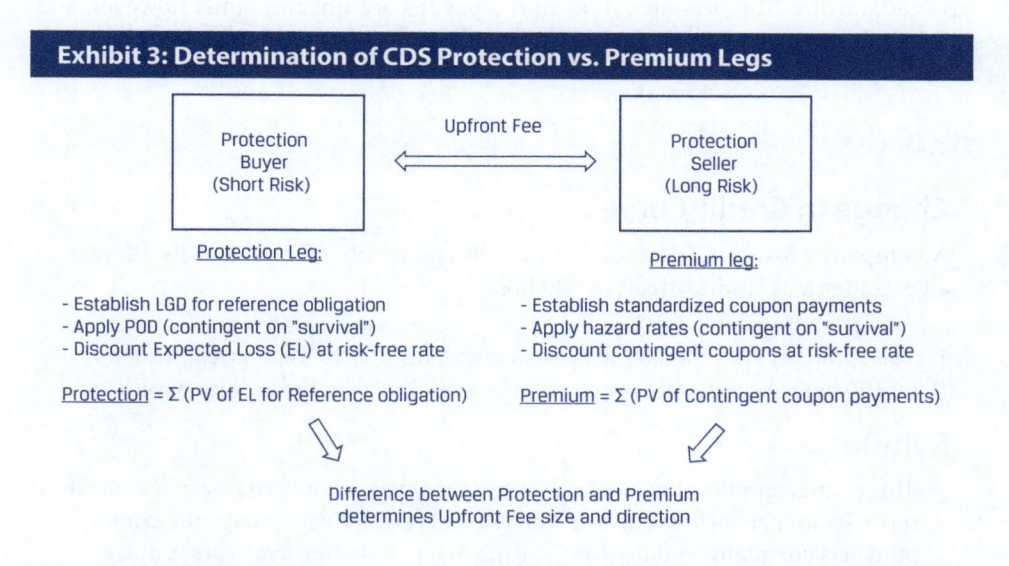

Exhibit 3 shows the upfront payment as the difference in value of the protection and premium legs. The party with a claim on the greater present value must pay the difference at the initiation date of the contract:

Upfront payment = PV (Protection leg) – PV (Premium leg).

If the result is greater (less) than zero, the protection buyer (seller) pays the protection seller (buyer). Actual CDS pricing and valuation models are more mathematically complex but are based on this conceptual framework.

The Credit Curve and CDS Pricing Conventions

The credit spread of a debt instrument is the rate in excess of a market reference rate that investors expect to receive to justify holding the instrument. The reference rate may itself contain some credit risk, as it reflects the rate at which commercial banks lend to one another. The credit spread can be expressed roughly as the probability of default multiplied by the loss given default, with LGD in terms of a percentage. The credit spreads for a range of maturities of a company's debt make up its **credit curve**. The credit curve is somewhat analogous to the term structure of interest rates, which is the set of rates on default-free debt over a range of maturities, but the credit curve applies to non-government borrowers and incorporates credit risk into each rate.

The CDS market for a given borrower is integrated with the credit curve of that borrower. In fact, given the evolution and high degree of efficiency of the CDS market, the credit curve is essentially determined by the CDS rates. The curve is affected by a number of factors, a key one of which is the set of aforementioned hazard rates. A constant hazard rate will tend to flatten the credit curve. Upward-sloping credit curves imply a greater likelihood of default in later years, whereas downward-sloping credit curves imply a greater probability of default in the earlier years. Downward-sloping curves are less common and often a result of severe near-term stress in the financial markets. The credit curve would not be completely flat even if the hazard rates are constant, because of discounting. For example, a company issuing 5- and 10-year zero-coupon bonds could have equally likely probabilities of default and hence equal expected payoffs. The present values of the payoffs are not the same, however, and so the discount rates that equate the present value to the expected payoffs will not be the same.

EXAMPLE 5

Change in Credit Curve

A company's 5-year CDS trades at a credit spread of 300 bps, and its 10-year CDS trades at a credit spread of 500 bps.

---

1. The company's 5-year spread is unchanged, but the 10-year spread widens by 100 bps. Describe the implication of this change in the credit curve.

Solution:

This change implies that although the company is not any riskier in the short term, its longer-term creditworthiness is less attractive. Perhaps the company has adequate liquidity for the time being, but after five years it must begin repaying debt or it will be expected to have cash flow difficulties.

2. The company's 10-year spread is unchanged, but the 5-year spread widens by 500 bps. Describe the implication of this change in the credit curve.

Solution:

This change implies that the company's near-term credit risk is now much greater. In fact, the probability of default will decrease if the company can survive for the next five years. Perhaps the company has run into liquidity issues that must be resolved soon, and if not resolved, the company will default.

CDS Pricing Conventions

With corporate bonds, we typically refer to their values in terms of prices or spreads. The spread is a more informative measure than price. A high-yield bond can be offered with a coupon equal to its yield and, therefore, a price of par value. An investment-grade bond with the same maturity can likewise be offered with a coupon equal to its yield, and therefore, its price is at par. These two bonds would have identical prices at the offering date, and their prices might even be close through much of their lives, but they are quite different bonds. Focusing on their prices would, therefore, provide little information. Their spreads are much more informative. With a market reference rate or the risk-free rate as a benchmark, investors can get a sense for the amount of credit risk implied by their prices, maturities, and coupons. The same is true for CDS. Although CDS have their own prices, their spreads are far more informative.

The reference entity will not necessarily have outstanding debt with credit spreads matching the 1% or 5% standardized coupons conventionally used in CDS contracts. Therefore, the present value of the promised payments from the credit protection buyer to the credit protection seller will most likely be different than the present value of the coupons on the reference entity's debt. The present value difference is the upfront premium paid from one party to the other.

Present value of credit spread = Upfront premium + Present value of fixed coupon.

A good rough approximation used in the industry is that the upfront premium is

Upfront premium ≈ (Credit spread – Fixed coupon) × Duration.

The upfront premium must ultimately be converted to a price, which is done by subtracting the percentage premium from 100.

Upfront premium % = 100 – Price of CDS in currency per 100 par.

Note that the duration used here is effective duration, since the cash flows arising from the coupon leg of the CDS are uncertain because they are contingent on the reference entity not defaulting.

EXAMPLE 6

Premiums and Credit Spreads

1. Assume a high-yield company's 10-year credit spread is 600 bps and the duration of the CDS is 8 years. What is the approximate upfront premium required to buy 10-year CDS protection? Assume high-yield companies have 5% coupons on their CDS.

Solution:

To buy 10-year CDS protection, an investor would have to pay a 500 bp coupon plus the present value of the difference between that coupon and the current market spread (600 bps). In this case, the upfront premium would be approximately 100 bps × 8 (duration), or 8% of the notional.

2. Imagine an investor sold five-year protection on an investment-grade company and had to pay a 2% upfront premium to the buyer of protection. Assume the duration of the CDS to be four years. What are the company's credit spreads and the price of the CDS per 100 par?

Solution:

The value of the upfront premium is equal to the premium (−2%) divided by the duration (4), or −50 bps. The sign of the upfront premium is negative because the seller is paying the premium rather than receiving it. The credit spread is equal to the fixed coupon (100 bps) plus the upfront premium, amortized over the duration of the CDS (−50 bps), or 50 bps. As a reminder, because the company's credit spread is less than the fixed coupon, the protection seller must pay the upfront premium to the protection buyer. The price in currency would be 100 minus the upfront premium, but the latter is negative, so the price is 100 − (−2) = 102.

Valuation Changes in CDS during Their Lives

As with any traded financial instrument, a CDS has a value that fluctuates during its lifetime. That value is determined in the competitive marketplace. Market participants constantly assess the current credit quality of the reference entity to determine its current value and (implied) credit spread. Clearly, many factors can change over the life of the CDS. By definition, the duration shortens through time. Likewise, the probability of default, the expected loss given default, and the shape of the credit curve will all change as new information is received. The exact valuation procedure of the CDS is precisely the same as it is when the CDS is first issued and simply incorporates the new inputs. The new market value of the CDS reflects gains and losses to the two parties.

Consider the following example of a five-year CDS with a fixed 1% coupon. The credit spread on the reference entity is 2.5%. In promising to pay 1% coupons to receive coverage on a company whose risk justifies 2.5% coupons, the present value of the protection leg exceeds the present value of the payment leg. The difference is the upfront premium, which will be paid by the credit protection buyer to the credit protection seller. During the life of the CDS, assume that the credit quality of the reference entity improves, such that the credit spread is now 2.1%. Now, consider a newly created CDS with the same remaining maturity and 1% coupon. The present value of the payment leg would still be less than the present value of the protection leg, but the difference would be less than it was when the original CDS was created because the risk is now less. Logically, it should be apparent that for the original transaction, the seller has gained and the buyer has lost. The difference between the original upfront premium and the new value is the seller's gain and buyer's loss. A rough approximation of the change in value of the CDS for a given change in spread is as follows:

Profit for the buyer of protection ≈ Change in spread in bps × Duration × Notional.

Alternatively, we might be interested in the CDS percentage price change, which is obtained as

% Change in CDS price = Change in spread in bps × Duration.

The percentage change in the price of a bond is approximately the change in its yield multiplied by its modified duration. For the CDS, the change in yield is analogous to the change in spread, measured in basis points. The duration of the CDS is analogous to the duration of the bond on which the CDS is written.

EXAMPLE 7

Profit and Loss from Change in Credit Spread

An investor buys $10 million of five-year protection, and the CDS contract has a duration of four years. The company's credit spread was originally 500 bps and widens to 800 bps.

1. Does the investor (credit protection buyer) benefit or lose from the change in credit spread?

Solution:

The investor owns protection and is therefore short the credit exposure. As the credit spread widens (the credit quality of the underlying deteriorates), the value of the credit protection she owns increases.

2. Estimate the CDS price change and estimated profit to the investor.

Solution:

The percentage price change is estimated as the change in spread (300 bps) multiplied by the duration (4), or 12%. The profit to the investor is 12% times the notional ($10 million), or $1.2 million.

Monetizing Gains and Losses

As with any financial instrument, changes in the price of a CDS give rise to opportunities to unwind the position and either capture a gain or realize a loss. This process is called **monetizing** a gain or loss. Keep in mind that the protection seller is effectively long the reference entity. He has entered into a contract to insure the debt of the reference entity, for which he receives a series of promised payments and possibly an upfront premium. He clearly benefits if the reference entity's credit quality improves because he continues to receive the same compensation but bears less risk. Using the opposite argument, the credit protection buyer benefits from a deterioration of the reference entity's credit quality. Thus, the credit protection seller is more or less long the company's bonds and the credit protection buyer is more or less short the company's bonds. As the company's credit quality changes through time, the market value of the CDS changes, giving rise to gains and losses for the CDS counterparties. The counterparties can realize those gains and losses by entering into new offsetting contracts, effectively selling their CDS positions to other parties.

Going back to the example in the previous section where the credit quality of the reference entity improved—the credit spread on the reference entity declined from 2.5% to 2.1%. The implied upfront premium on a new CDS that matches the terms of the original CDS with adjusted maturity is now the market value of the original CDS. The premium on the new CDS is smaller than that on the original CDS.

Now, suppose that the protection buyer in the original transaction wants to unwind her position. She would then enter into a new CDS as a protection seller and receive the newly calculated upfront premium. As we noted, this value is less than what he paid originally. Likewise, the protection seller in the original transaction could offset his position by entering into a new CDS as a protection buyer. He would pay an upfront premium that is less than what he originally received. The original protection buyer monetizes a loss, and the seller monetizes a gain. The transaction to unwind the CDS does not need to be done with the same original party, although doing so offers some advantages. Central clearing of CDS transactions facilitates the unwind transaction.

At this point, we have identified two ways of realizing a profit or loss on a CDS. One is to effectively exercise the CDS in response to a default. The other is to unwind the position by entering into a new offsetting CDS in the market. A third, less common method occurs if there is no default. A party can simply hold the position until expiration, at which time the credit protection seller has captured all of the premiums and has not been forced to make any payments, and the seller's obligation for any further payments is terminated. The spread of the CDS will go to zero, in much the same manner as a bond converges toward par as it approaches maturity.

The CDS seller clearly gains, having been paid to bear the risk of default that is becoming increasingly unlikely, and the CDS buyer loses. The buyer loses on the CDS because it paid premiums to receive protection in the event of a default, which did not occur. Although the CDS position itself is a loss, the buyer's overall position is not necessarily a loss. If the buyer is a creditor of the reference entity, the premium "loss" is no different than a homeowner's insurance premium payment on his house; he wouldn't consider that payment a loss simply because his house did not burn down.

5   APPLICATIONS OF CDS

☐ | describe the use of CDS to manage credit exposures and to express views regarding changes in the shape and/or level of the credit curve

Credit default swaps, as demonstrated, facilitate the transfer of credit risk. As simple as that concept seems, there are many different circumstances under which CDS are used. In this section, we consider some applications of this instrument.

Any derivative instrument has two general uses. One is to exploit an expected movement in the underlying. The derivative typically requires less capital and is usually an easier instrument in which to create a short economic exposure as compared with the underlying. The derivatives market can also be more efficient, meaning that it can react to information more rapidly and have more liquidity than the market for the underlying. Thus, information or an expectation of movement in the underlying can often be exploited much more efficiently with the derivative than with the underlying directly.

The other trading opportunity facilitated by derivatives is in valuation differences between the derivative and the underlying. If the derivative is mispriced relative to the underlying, one can take the appropriate position in the derivative and an offsetting position in the underlying. If the valuation assessment is correct and other investors come to the same conclusion, the values of the derivative and underlying will converge, and the investor will earn a return that is essentially free of risk because the risk of the underlying has been hedged away by holding offsetting positions in the derivative and the underlying. Whether this happens as planned depends on both the efficiency of the market and the quality of the valuation model. Differences can also exist between the derivative and other derivatives on the same underlying.

These two general types of uses are also the major applications of CDS. We will refer to them as managing credit exposures, meaning the taking on or shedding of credit risk in light of changing expectations and/or valuation disparities. With valuation disparities, the focus is on differences in the pricing of credit risk in the CDS market relative to that of the underlying bonds.

Managing Credit Exposures

The most basic application of a CDS is to increase or decrease credit exposure. The most obvious such application is for a lender to buy protection to reduce its credit exposure to a borrower. For the seller of protection, the trade adds credit exposure. A lender's justification for using a CDS seems obvious. The lender may have assumed too much credit risk but does not want to sell the bond or loan because there can be significant transaction costs, because later it may want the bond or loan back, or because the market for the bond or loan is relatively illiquid. If the risk is temporary, it is almost always easier to temporarily reduce risk by using a CDS. Beyond financial institutions, any organization exposed to credit risk is potentially a candidate for using CDS.

The justification for selling credit protection is somewhat less obvious. The seller can be a CDS dealer, whose objective is to profit from making markets in CDS. A dealer typically attempts to manage its exposure by either diversifying its credit risks or hedging the risk by entering into a transaction with yet another party, such as by shorting the debt or equity of the reference entity, often accompanied by investment of the funds in a repurchase agreement, or repo. If the dealer manages the risk effectively, the risk assumed in selling the CDS is essentially offset when the payment for assuming the risk exceeds the cost of removing the risk. Achieving this outcome successfully requires sophisticated credit risk modeling.

Although dealers make up a large percentage of protection sellers, not all sellers are dealers. Consider that any bondholder is a buyer of credit and interest rate risk. If the bondholder wants only credit risk, it can obtain it by selling protection, which would require far less capital and incur potentially lower overall transaction costs than buying the bond. Moreover, the CDS can be more liquid than the bond, so the position can be unwound much more easily.

As noted, it is apparent why a party making a loan might want credit protection. Consider, however, that a party with no exposure to the reference entity might also purchase credit protection. Such a position is called a **naked credit default swap**, and it has resulted in some controversy in regulatory and political circles. In buying protection without owning the underlying, the investor is taking a position that the entity's credit quality will deteriorate, whereas the seller of protection without owning the underlying is taking the position that the entity's credit quality will improve or that the CDS was overpriced.

Some regulators and politicians believe it is inappropriate for a party with no exposure to a borrower to speculate that the borrower's financial condition will deteriorate. This controversy accelerated during the financial crisis of 2008–2009 because many investors bought protection without owning the underlying and benefited from the crisis.

The counterargument, however, is that elsewhere in the financial markets, such bets are made all of the time in the form of long puts, short futures, and short sales of stocks and bonds. These instruments are generally accepted as a means of protecting oneself against poor performance in the financial markets. Credit protection is also a means of protecting oneself against poor performance. In addition, proponents of naked CDS argue that they bring liquidity to the credit market, potentially providing more stability, not less. Nonetheless, naked CDS trading is banned in Europe for sovereign debt, although it is generally permitted otherwise.

CDS trading strategies, with or without naked exposure, can take several forms. An investor can choose to be long or short the credit exposure, as we have previously discussed. Alternatively, the party can be a credit protection seller on one reference entity and a credit protection buyer on a different entity. This is called a **long/short credit trade**. This transaction is a bet that the credit position of one entity will improve relative to that of another. The two entities might be related in some way or might produce substitute goods. For example, one might take a position that because of competition and changes in the luxury car industry, the credit quality of Daimler will improve and that of BMW will weaken, so selling protection on Daimler and buying protection on BMW would be appropriate. Similarly, an investor may undertake a long/short trade based on other factors, such as environmental, social, and governance (ESG) considerations. For instance, an investor may be concerned about a company's poor ESG-related practices and policies relative to another company. In this case, the investor could buy protection using the CDS of a company with weak ESG practices and policies and sell protection using the CDS of a company with strong ESG practices and policies. Example 8 provides a case study of ESG considerations in a long/short ESG trade.

EXAMPLE 8

Long/Short Trade with ESG Considerations

Overview

An analyst is evaluating two US apparel companies: Atelier and Trapp. Atelier is a large company that focuses on high-end apparel brands. It is profitable despite a high cost structure. Trapp is smaller and less profitable than Atelier. Trapp focuses on less expensive brands and strives to keep costs low. Both companies purchase their merchandise from suppliers all over the world. The analyst recognizes that apparel companies must maintain adequate oversight over their suppliers to control the risks of reputational damage and inventory disruptions. Supplier issues are particularly relevant for Atelier and Trapp following a recent fire that occurred at the factory of Global Textiles, a major supplier to both companies. The fire resulted in multiple casualties and unfavorable news headlines.

The analyst notices a significant difference in the way Atelier and Trapp approach ESG considerations. After the fire at its supplier, Atelier signed an "Accord on Fire and Building Safety," which is a legally binding agreement between global apparel manufacturers, retailers, and trade unions in the country where the fire occurred. After signing the accord, Atelier made a concerted effort to fix and enhance machinery in factories of its suppliers. Its objective was to improve workplace safety—notably, to reduce lost employee time due to factory incidents and the rate of factory accidents and fatalities.

Investors view Atelier's corporate governance system favorably because management interests and stakeholder interests are strongly aligned. Atelier's board of directors includes a high percentage of independent directors and is notably diverse. In contrast, Trapp's founder is the majority owner of the company and serves as CEO and chairman of the board of directors. Furthermore, Trapp's board is composed mainly of individuals who have minimal industry expertise. As a consequence, Trapp's board was unprepared to adequately respond to the Global Textiles fire. Given the lack of independence and expertise of Trapp's board, investors consider Trapp's corporate governance system to be poor. Because of its emphasis on low costs and reflecting its less experienced board, Trapp chose not to sign the accord.

Implications for CDS

Single-name CDS on both Atelier and Trapp are actively traded in the market, although Trapp's CDS is less liquid. Before the Global Textiles fire, five-year CDS for Trapp traded at a spread of 250 bps, compared to a spread of 150 bps for the five-year CDS for Atelier. The difference in spreads reflects Trapp's lower trading liquidity, perceived lower creditworthiness (primarily reflecting its smaller size and lower profitability), and hence higher default risk relative to Atelier.

After the Global Textiles fire, spreads on the CDS for all companies in the apparel sector widened considerably. Credit spreads for the five-year CDS on Atelier widened by 60 bps (to 210 bps), and credit spreads for the five-year CDS on Trapp widened by 75 bps (to 325 bps). The analyst believes that over the longer term, the implications of the fire at Global Textiles will be even more adverse for Trapp relative to Atelier. The analyst's view largely reflects Trapp's higher ESG-related risks, especially the perceived weaker safety in its factories and its weaker corporate governance system. In particular, the analyst believes that spreads of Trapp's CDS will remain wider than their pre-fire level of 250 bps, but Atelier's CDS spreads will return to their pre-fire level of 150 bps.

1. Describe how the analyst can use CDS to exploit the potential opportunity.

Solution

The analyst can try to exploit the potential opportunity by buying protection (shorting the credit) on Trapp using five-year CDS and selling protection (going long the credit) on Atelier using five-year CDS. This trade would reflect both the anticipated continuing adverse spreads for Trapp relative to the pre-fire level and the return of spreads for Atelier to their lower pre-fire levels. For example, assume Atelier's five-year CDS spread returns to 150 bps from 210 bps, but Trapp's five-year CDS spread narrows to just 300 bps from 325 bps. The difference in spreads between the two companies' CDS would have widened from 115 bps (325 bps – 210 bps) right after the factory fire occurred to 150 bps (300 bps – 150 bps). This 35 bp difference in spread would represent profit (excluding trading costs) to the analyst from the long/short trade.

Similar to a long/short trade involving individual entities (companies), an investor might also create a long/short trade using CDS indexes. For example, if the investor anticipates a weakening economy, she could buy protection using a high-yield CDS index and sell protection using an investment-grade CDS index. As high-yield spreads widen relative to investment-grade spreads, the trade would realize a profit. As another example, a trader expecting a strengthening in the Asian economy relative to the European economy could buy protection using a European CDS index and sell protection using an Asian CDS index. As Asia spreads narrow relative to European spreads, the trade would realize a profit.

Another type of long/short trade, called a **curve trade**, involves buying single-name or index protection at one maturity and selling protection on the same reference entity at a different maturity. Consider two CDS maturities, which we will call the short-term and the long-term to keep things simple. We will assume the more common situation of an upward-sloping credit curve, meaning that long-term CDS rates (and credit spreads) are higher than short-term rates. If the curve changes shape, it becomes either steeper or flatter. A steeper (flatter) curve means that long-term credit risk increases (decreases) relative to short-term credit risk. An investor who believes that long-term credit risk will increase relative to short-term credit risk (credit curve steepening) can buy protection by buying a long-term single-name CDS or selling a long-term CDS index and sell protection by selling a short-term single-name CDS or buying a short-term CDS index. In the short run, a curve-steepening trade is bullish. It implies that the short-term outlook for the reference entity is better than the long-term outlook. In the short run, a curve-flattening trade is bearish. It implies that the short-run outlook for the reference entity looks worse than the long-run outlook and reflects the expectation of near-term problems for the reference entity.

EXAMPLE 9

Curve Trading

An investor owns some intermediate-term bonds issued by a company and has become concerned about the risk of a near-term default, although he is not very concerned about a default in the long term. The company's two-year CDS currently trades at 350 bps, and the four-year CDS is at 600 bps.

1. Describe a potential curve trade that the investor could use to hedge the default risk.

Solution:

The investor anticipates a flattening credit curve for the reference company, with spreads rising at the shorter end of the curve. Thus, he would buy credit protection on the two year (buy the two-year single-name CDS) while selling credit protection further out on the curve (sell the four-year single-name CDS).

2. Explain why an investor may prefer to use a curve trade as a hedge against the company's default risk rather than simply buying protection on the reference entity.

Solution:

The long/short trade reduces the cost of buying near-term credit protection, with the cost of the credit protection offset by the premium received from selling protection further out on the curve. This works only as long as the investor's expectations about the relative risk of near- and longer-term default hold true.

Of course, there can be changes to the credit curve that take the form of simple shifts in the general level of the curve, whereby all spreads go up or down by roughly equal amounts. As with long-duration bonds relative to short-duration bonds, the values of longer-term CDS will move more than those of shorter-term CDS. As an example, a trader who believes that all spreads will go up will want to be a buyer of credit protection but will realize that longer-term CDS will move more than short-term CDS. Thus, she might want to buy protection at the longer part of the curve and hedge by selling protection at the shorter part of the curve. She will balance the sizes of the positions so that the volatility of the position she believes will gain in value will be more than that of the other position. If more risk is desired, she might choose to trade only the more volatile leg.

VALUATION DIFFERENCES AND BASIS TRADING

6

☐ | describe the use of CDS to take advantage of valuation disparities among separate markets, such as bonds, loans, equities, and equity-linked instruments

Different investors will have different assessments of the price of credit risk. Such differences of opinion will lead to valuation disparities. Clearly, there can be only one appropriate price at which credit risk can be eliminated, but that price is not easy to determine. The party that has the best estimate of the appropriate price of credit risk can capitalize on its knowledge or ability at the expense of another party. Any such comparative advantage can be captured by trading the CDS against either the reference entity's debt or equity or derivatives on its debt or equity, but such trading is critically dependent on the accuracy of models that isolate the credit risk component of the return. The details of those models are left to CDS specialists, but it is important for candidates to understand the basic ideas.

The yield on the bond issued by the reference entity to a CDS contains a factor that reflects the credit risk. In principle, the amount of yield attributable to credit risk on the bond should be the same as the credit spread on a CDS. It is, after all, the compensation paid to the party assuming the credit risk, regardless of whether that risk is borne by a bondholder or a CDS seller. But there may be a difference in the credit risk compensation in the bond market and CDS market. This differential pricing can arise from mere differences of opinions, differences in models used by participants in the two markets, differences in liquidity in the two markets, and supply and demand conditions in the repo market, which is a primary source of financing for bond purchases. A difference in the credit spreads in these two markets is the foundation of a strategy known as a **basis trade**.

The general idea behind most basis trades is that any such mispricing is likely to be temporary and the spreads should return to equivalence when the market recognizes the disparity. For example, suppose the bond market implies a 5% credit risk premium whereas the CDS market implies a 4% credit risk premium. The trader does not know which is correct but believes these two rates will eventually converge. From the perspective of the CDS, its risk premium is too low relative to the bond credit risk premium. From the perspective of the bond, its risk premium is too high relative to the CDS market, which means its price is too low. So, the CDS market could be pricing in too little credit risk, and/or the bond market could be pricing in too much credit risk. Either market could be correct; it does not matter. The investor would buy the bond at a price that appears to overestimate its credit risk and, at the same time, buy credit protection at what appears to be an unjustifiably low premium, simultaneously hedging interest rate risk exposure with a duration strategy or interest rate derivatives. The risk is balanced because the default potential on the bond is protected by the CDS. If convergence occurs, the trade would capture the 1% differential in the two markets.

To determine the profit potential of such a trade, it is necessary to decompose the bond yield into the risk-free rate plus the funding spread plus the credit spread. The risk-free rate plus the funding spread is essentially the market reference rate. The credit spread is then the excess of the yield over the market reference rate and can be compared with the credit spread in the CDS market. If the spread is higher in the bond market than in the CDS market, it is said to be a negative basis. If the spread is higher in the CDS market than in the bond market, it is said to be a positive basis. Note that in practice, the above decomposition can be complicated by the existence of embedded options, such as with callable and convertible bonds or when the bond is not selling near par. Those factors would need to be accounted for in the calculations.

EXAMPLE 10

Bonds vs. Credit Default Swaps

An investor wants to be long the credit risk of a given company. The company's bond currently yields 6% and matures in five years. A comparable five-year CDS contract has a credit spread of 3.25%. The investor can borrow at MRR, which is currently 2.5%.

---

1. Calculate the bond's credit spread.

Solution:

The bond's credit spread is equal to the yield (6%) minus the market reference rate (2.5%). Therefore, the bond's credit spread is currently 3.5%.

---

2. Identify a basis trade that would exploit the current situation.

Solution:

The bond and CDS markets imply different credit spreads. Credit risk is cheap in the CDS market (3.25%) relative to the bond market (3.5%). The investor should buy protection in the CDS market at 3.25% and go long the bond, with its 3.5% credit spread, netting 25 bps.

Another type of trade using CDS can occur within the instruments issued by a single entity. Credit risk is an element of virtually every unsecured debt instrument or the capital leases issued by a company. Each of these instruments is priced to reflect the appropriate credit risk. Investors can use the CDS market to first determine whether any of these instruments is incorrectly priced relative to the CDS and then buy the cheaper one and sell the more expensive one. Again, there is the assumption that the market will adjust. This type of trading is much more complex, however, because priority of claims means that not all of the instruments pay off equally if default occurs.

EXAMPLE 11

Using CDS to Trade on a Leveraged Buyout

An investor believes that a company will undergo a leveraged buyout (LBO) transaction, whereby it will issue large amounts of debt and use the proceeds to repurchase all of the publicly traded equity, leaving the company owned by management and a few insiders.

1. Why might the CDS spread change?

Solution:

Taking on the additional debt will almost surely increase the probability of default, thereby increasing the CDS spread.

2. What equity-versus-credit trade might an investor execute in anticipation of such a corporate action?

Solution:

The investor might consider buying the stock and buying credit protection. Both legs will profit if the LBO occurs because the stock price will rise as the company repurchases all outstanding equity and the CDS price will rise as its spread widens to reflect the increased probability of default.

CDS indexes also create an opportunity for a type of arbitrage trade. If the cost of the index is not equivalent to the aggregate cost of the index components, an investor might go long the cheaper instrument and short the more expensive instrument. There is the implicit assumption that convergence will occur. If it does, the investor gains the benefit while basically having neutralized the risk. Transaction costs in this type of arbitrage trade can be quite significant and nullify the profit potential for all but the largest investors.

SUMMARY

- A credit default swap (CDS) is a contract between two parties in which one party purchases protection from another party against losses from the default of a borrower for a defined period of time.

- A CDS is written on the debt of a third party, called the reference entity, whose relevant debt is called the reference obligation, typically a senior unsecured bond.

- A CDS written on a particular reference obligation normally provides coverage for all obligations of the reference entity that have equal or higher seniority.

- The two parties to the CDS are the credit protection buyer, who is said to be short the reference entity's credit, and the credit protection seller, who is said to be long the reference entity's credit.

- The CDS pays off upon occurrence of a credit event, which includes bankruptcy, failure to pay, and, in some countries, involuntary restructuring.

- Settlement of a CDS can occur through a cash payment from the credit protection seller to the credit protection buyer as determined by the cheapest-to-deliver obligation of the reference entity or by physical delivery of the reference obligation from the protection buyer to the protection seller in exchange for the CDS notional.

- A cash settlement payoff is determined by an auction of the reference entity's debt, which gives the market's assessment of the likely recovery rate. The credit protection buyer must accept the outcome of the auction even though the ultimate recovery rate could differ.

- CDS can be constructed on a single entity or as indexes containing multiple entities. Bespoke CDS or baskets of CDS are also common.

- The fixed payments made from CDS buyer to CDS seller are customarily set at a fixed annual rate of 1% for investment-grade debt or 5% for high-yield debt.

- Valuation of a CDS is determined by estimating the present value of the payment leg, which is the series of payments made from the protection buyer to the protection seller, and the present value of the protection leg, which is the payment from the protection seller to the protection buyer in event of default. If the present value of the payment leg is greater than the present value of the protection leg, the protection buyer pays an upfront premium to the seller. If the present value of the protection leg is greater than the present value of the payment leg, the seller pays an upfront premium to the buyer.

- An important determinant of the value of the expected payments is the hazard rate, the probability of default given that default has not already occurred.

- CDS prices are often quoted in terms of credit spreads, the implied number of basis points that the credit protection seller receives from the credit protection buyer to justify providing the protection.

- Credit spreads are often expressed in terms of a credit curve, which expresses the relationship between the credit spreads on bonds of different maturities for the same borrower.

- CDS change in value over their lives as the credit quality of the reference entity changes, which leads to gains and losses for the counterparties, even though default may not have occurred or may never occur. CDS spreads approach zero as the CDS approaches maturity.

- Either party can monetize an accumulated gain or loss by entering into an offsetting position that matches the terms of the original CDS.

- CDS are used to increase or decrease credit exposures or to capitalize on different assessments of the cost of credit among different instruments tied to the reference entity, such as debt, equity, and derivatives of debt and equity.

PRACTICE PROBLEMS

The following information relates to questions 1–6

UNAB Corporation

On 1 January 20X2, Deem Advisors purchased a $10 million six-year senior unsecured bond issued by UNAB Corporation. Six months later (1 July 20X2), concerned about the portfolio's credit exposure to UNAB, Doris Morrison, the chief investment officer at Deem Advisors, buys $10 million protection on UNAB with a standardized coupon rate of 5%. The reference obligation of the CDS is the UNAB bond owned by Deem Advisors. UNAB adheres to the ISDA CDS protocols.

On 1 January 20X3, Morrison asks Bill Watt, a derivatives analyst, to assess the current credit quality of UNAB bonds and the value of Deem Advisors' CDS on UNAB debt. Watt gathers the following information on UNAB's debt issues currently trading in the market:

  Bond 1: A two-year senior unsecured bond trading at 40% of par

  Bond 2: A five-year senior unsecured bond trading at 50% of par

  Bond 3: A five-year subordinated unsecured bond trading at 20% of par

With respect to the credit quality of UNAB, Watt makes the following statement:

"There is severe near-term stress in the financial markets, andUNAB's credit curve clearly reflects the difficult environment."

On 1 July 20X3, UNAB fails to make a scheduled interest payment on the outstanding subordinated unsecured obligation after a grace period; however, the company does not file for bankruptcy. Morrison asks Watt to determine if UNAB experienced a credit event and, if so, to recommend a settlement preference.

Kand Corporation

Morrison is considering purchasing protection on Kand Corporation debt to hedge the portfolio's position in Kand. She instructs Watt to determine if an upfront payment would be required and, if so, the amount of the premium. Watt presents the information for the CDS in Exhibit 1.

Exhibit 1: Summary Data for 10-year CDS on Kand Corporation	
Credit spread	700 bps
Duration	7 years
Coupon rate	5%

Morrison purchases 10-year protection on Kand Corporation debt. Two months later the credit spread for Kand Corporation has increased by 200 bps. Morrison asks Watt to close out the firm's CDS position on Kand Corporation by entering into a new, offsetting contract.

Tollunt Corporation

Deem Advisors' chief credit analyst recently reported that Tollunt Corporation's five-year bond is currently yielding 7% and a comparable CDS contract has a credit spread of 4.25%. Since the current market reference rate is 2.5%, Watt has recommended executing a basis trade to take advantage of the pricing of Tollunt's bonds and CDS. The basis trade would consist of purchasing both the bond and the CDS contract.

1. If UNAB experienced a credit event on 1 July, Watt should recommend that Deem Advisors:

   A. prefer a cash settlement.

   B. prefer a physical settlement.

   C. be indifferent between a cash or a physical settlement.

2. According to Watt's statement, the shape of UNAB's credit curve is *most likely*:

   A. flat.

   B. upward-sloping.

   C. downward-sloping.

3. Should Watt conclude that UNAB experienced a credit event?

   A. Yes

   B. No, because UNAB did not file for bankruptcy

   C. No, because the failure to pay occurred on a subordinated unsecured bond

4. Based on Exhibit 1, the upfront premium as a percent of the notional for the CDS protection on Kand Corporation would be *closest* to:

   A. 2.0%.

   B. 9.8%.

   C. 14.0%.

5. If Deem Advisors enters into a new offsetting contract two months after purchasing protection on Kand Corporation, this action will *most likely* result in:

   A. a loss on the CDS position.

   B. a profit on the CDS position.

   C. neither a loss nor a profit on the CDS position.

6. If convergence occurs in the bond and CDS markets for Tollunt Corporation, a basis trade will capture a profit *closest* to:

   A. 0.25%.

   B. 1.75%.

   C. 2.75%.

The following information relates to questions 7-14

John Smith, a fixed-income portfolio manager at a €10 billion sovereign wealth fund (the Fund), meets with Sofia Chan, a derivatives strategist with Shire Gate Securities (SGS), to discuss investment opportunities for the Fund. Chan notes that SGS adheres to ISDA (International Swaps and Derivatives Association) protocols for credit default swap (CDS) transactions and that any contract must conform to ISDA specifications. Before the Fund can engage in trading CDS products with SGS, the Fund must satisfy compliance requirements.

Smith explains to Chan that fixed-income derivatives strategies are being contemplated for both hedging and trading purposes. Given the size and diversified nature of the Fund, Smith asks Chan to recommend a type of CDS that would allow the Fund to simultaneously fully hedge multiple fixed-income exposures.

Smith and Chan discuss opportunities to add trading profits to the Fund. Smith asks Chan to determine the probability of default associated with a five-year investment-grade bond issued by Orion Industrial. Selected data on the Orion Industrial bond are presented in Exhibit 1.

Exhibit 1: Selected Data on Orion Industrial Five-Year Bond

Year	Hazard Rate
1	0.22%
2	0.35%
3	0.50%
4	0.65%
5	0.80%

Chan explains that a single-name CDS can also be used to add profit to the Fund over time. Chan describes a hypothetical trade in which the Fund sells £6 million of five-year CDS protection on Orion, where the CDS contract has a duration of 3.9 years. Chan assumes that the Fund closes the position six months later, after Orion's credit spread narrowed from 150 bps to 100 bps.

Chan discusses the mechanics of a long/short trade. In order to structure a number of potential trades, Chan and Smith exchange their respective views on individual companies and global economies. Chan and Smith agree on the following outlooks.

> **Outlook 1:** The European economy will weaken.
>
> **Outlook 2:** The US economy will strengthen relative to that of Canada.
>
> **Outlook 3:** The credit quality of electric car manufacturers will improve relative to that of traditional car manufacturers.

Chan believes US macroeconomic data are improving and that the general economy will strengthen in the short term. Chan suggests that a curve trade could be used by the Fund to capitalize on her short-term view of a steepening of the US credit curve.

Another short-term trading opportunity that Smith and Chan discuss involves the merger and acquisition market. SGS believes that Delta Corporation may make an unsolicited bid at a premium to the market price for all of the publicly traded shares of Zega, Inc. Zega's market capitalization and capital structure are comparable to Delta's; both firms are highly levered. It is anticipated that Delta will issue new equity along with 5- and 10-year senior unsecured debt to fund the acquisition, which will significantly increase its debt ratio.

7. To satisfy the compliance requirements referenced by Chan, the Fund is *most likely* required to:

    A. set a notional amount.

    B. post an upfront payment.

    C. sign an ISDA master agreement.

8. Which type of CDS should Chan recommend to Smith?

    A. CDS index

    B. Tranche CDS

    C. Single-name CDS

9. Based on Exhibit 1, the probability of Orion defaulting on the bond during the first three years is *closest* to:

    A. 1.07%.

    B. 2.50%.

    C. 3.85%.

10. To close the position on the hypothetical Orion trade, the Fund:

    A. sells protection at a higher premium than it paid at the start of the trade.

    B. buys protection at a lower premium than it received at the start of the trade.

    C. buys protection at a higher premium than it received at the start of the trade.

11. The hypothetical Orion trade generated an approximate:

    A. loss of £117,000.

    B. gain of £117,000.

    C. gain of £234,000.

12. Based on the three economic outlook statements, a profitable long/short trade would be to:

    A. sell protection using a Canadian CDX IG and buy protection using a US CDX IG.

    B. buy protection using an iTraxx Crossover and sell protection using an iTraxx Main.

    C. buy protection using an electric car CDS and sell protection using a traditional car CDS.

13. The curve trade that would *best* capitalize on Chan's view of the US credit curve

is to:

   A. buy protection using a 20-year CDX and buy protection using a 2-year CDX.

   B. buy protection using a 20-year CDX and sell protection using a 2-year CDX.

   C. sell protection using a 20-year CDX and buy protection using a 2-year CDX.

14. A profitable equity-versus-credit trade involving Delta and Zega is to:

   A. short Zega shares and buy protection on Delta using the 10-year CDS.

   B. go long Zega shares and buy protection on Delta using 5-year CDS.

   C. go long Delta shares and buy protection on Delta using 5-year CDS.

SOLUTIONS

1. A is correct. Deem Advisors would prefer a cash settlement. Deem Advisors owns Bond 2 (trading at 50% of par), which is worth more than the cheapest-to-deliver obligation (Bond 1, also a senior secured bond, trading at 40% of par). Based on the price of this cheapest-to-deliver security, the estimated recovery rate is 40%. Thus, Deem Advisors can cash settle for $6 million [= (1 − 40%) × $10 million] on its CDS contract and sell the bond it owns, Bond 2, for $5 million, for total proceeds of $11 million. If Deem Advisors were to physically settle the contract, only $10 million would be received, the face amount of the bonds, and it would deliver Bond 2.

   B is incorrect because if Deem Advisors were to physically settle the contract, it would receive only $10 million, which is less than the $11 million that could be obtained from a cash settlement. C is incorrect because Deem Advisors would not be indifferent between settlement protocols as the firm would receive $1 million more with a cash settlement in comparison to a physical settlement.

2. C is correct. A downward-sloping credit curve implies a greater probability of default in the earlier years than in the later years. Downward-sloping curves are less common and often are the result of severe near-term stress in the financial markets.

   A is incorrect because a flat credit curve implies a constant hazard rate (conditional probability of default). B is incorrect because an upward-sloping credit curve implies a greater probability of default in later years.

3. A is correct. UNAB experienced a credit event when it failed to make the scheduled coupon payment on the outstanding subordinated unsecured obligation. Failure to pay, a credit event, occurs when a borrower does not make a scheduled payment of principal or interest on outstanding obligations after a grace period, even without a formal bankruptcy filing.

   B is incorrect because a credit event can occur without filing for bankruptcy. The three most common credit events are bankruptcy, failure to pay, and restructuring.

   C is incorrect because a credit event (failure to pay) occurs when a borrower does not make a scheduled payment of principal or interest on *any* outstanding obligations after a grace period, even without a formal bankruptcy filing.

4. C is correct. An approximation for the upfront premium is (Credit spread − Fixed coupon rate) × Duration of the CDS. To buy 10-year CDS protection, Deem Advisors would have to pay an approximate upfront premium of 1,400 bps [(700 − 500) × 7], or 14% of the notional.

   A is incorrect because 200 bps, or 2%, is derived by taking the simple difference between the credit spread and the fixed coupon rate (700 − 500), ignoring the duration component of the calculation. B is incorrect because 980 bps, or 9.8%, is the result of dividing the credit spread by the fixed coupon rate and multiplying by the duration of the CDS [(700/500) × 7].

5. B is correct. Deem Advisors purchased protection and therefore is economically short and benefits from an increase in the company's spread. Since putting on the protection, the credit spread increased by 200 bps, and Deem Advisors realizes the profit by entering into a new, offsetting contract (sells protection to another party at a higher premium).

   A is incorrect because a decrease (not increase) in the spread would result in a loss for the credit protection buyer. C is incorrect because Deem Advisors, the credit protection buyer, would profit from an increase in the company's credit spread, not break even.

6. A is correct. A difference in credit spreads in the bond market and CDS market is the foundation of the basis trade strategy. If the spread is higher in the bond market than in the CDS market, it is said to be a negative basis. In this case, the bond credit spread is currently 4.50% (bond yield minus MRR) and the comparable CDS contract has a credit spread of 4.25%. The credit risk is cheap in the CDS market relative to the bond market. Since the protection and the bond were both purchased, if convergence occurs, the trade will capture the 0.25% differential in the two markets (4.50% − 4.25%).

   B is incorrect because the bond market implies a 4.50% credit risk premium (bond yield minus the market reference rate) and the CDS market implies a 4.25% credit risk premium. Convergence of the bond market credit risk premium and the CDS credit risk premium would result in capturing the differential, 0.25%. The 1.75% is derived by incorrectly subtracting MRR from the credit spread on the CDS (= 4.25% − 2.50%).

   C is incorrect because convergence of the bond market credit risk premium and the CDS credit risk premium would result in capturing the differential, 0.25%. The 2.75% is derived incorrectly by subtracting the credit spread on the CDS from the current bond yield (= 7.00% − 4.25%).

7. C is correct. Parties to CDS contracts generally agree that their contracts will conform to ISDA specifications. These terms are specified in the ISDA master agreement, which the parties to a CDS sign before any transactions are made. Therefore, to satisfy the compliance requirements referenced by Chan, the sovereign wealth fund must sign an ISDA master agreement with SGS.

8. A is correct. A CDS index (e.g., CDX and iTraxx) would allow the Fund to simultaneously fully hedge multiple fixed-income exposures. A tranche CDS will also hedge multiple exposures, but it would only partially hedge those exposures.

9. A is correct. Based on Exhibit 1, the probability of survival for the first year is 99.78% (100% minus the 0.22% hazard rate). Similarly, the probability of survival for the second and third years is 99.65% (100% minus the 0.35% hazard rate) and 99.50% (100% minus the 0.50% hazard rate), respectively. Therefore, the probability of survival of the Orion bond through the first three years is equal to 0.9978 × 0.9965 × 0.9950 = 0.9893, and the probability of default sometime during the first three years is 1 − 0.9893, or 1.07%.

10. B is correct. The trade assumes that £6 million of five-year CDS protection on Orion is initially sold, so the Fund received the premium. Because the credit spread of the Orion CDS narrowed from 150 bps to 100 bps, the CDS position will realize a financial gain. This financial gain is equal to the difference between the upfront premium received on the original CDS position and the upfront premium to be paid on a new, offsetting CDS position. To close the position and monetize this gain, the Fund should unwind the position by buying protection for a lower premium (relative to the original premium collected).

11. B is correct. The gain on the hypothetical Orion trade is £117,000, calculated as follows.

    Approximate profit = Change in credit spread (in bps) × Duration × Notional amount.

    Approximate profit = (150 bps − 100 bps) × 3.9 × £6 million.

    Approximate profit = 0.005 × 3.9 × £6 million.

    = £117,000.

    The Fund gains because it sold protection at a spread of 150 bps and closed out the position by buying protection at a lower spread of 100 bps.

12. B is correct. Based on Outlook 1, Chan and Smith anticipate that Europe's economy will weaken. In order to profit from this forecast, one would buy protection using a high-yield CDS index (e.g., iTraxx Crossover) and sell protection using an investment-grade CDS index (e.g., iTraxx Main).

13. B is correct. To take advantage of Chan's view of the US credit curve steepening in the short term, a curve trade will entail shorting (buying protection using) a long-term (20-year) CDX and going long (selling protection using) a short-term (2-year) CDX. A steeper curve means that long-term credit risk increases relative to short-term credit risk.

14. B is correct. The shares of Zega can be sold at a higher price as a result of the unsolicited bid in the market. If Delta Corporation issues significantly more debt, there is a higher probability that it may default. If the Fund sells protection on Delta now, the trade will realize a profit as credit spreads widen. An equity-versus-credit trade would be to go long (buy) the Zega shares and buy protection on Delta.

Glossary

Abnormal earnings   See *residual income*.

Abnormal return   The amount by which a security's actual return differs from its expected return, given the security's risk and the market's return.

Absolute convergence   The idea that developing countries, regardless of their particular characteristics, will eventually catch up with the developed countries and match them in per capita output.

Absolute valuation model   A model that specifies an asset's intrinsic value.

Absolute version of PPP   An extension of the law of one price whereby the prices of goods and services will not differ internationally once exchange rates are considered.

Accounting estimates   Estimates used in calculating the value of assets or liabilities and in the amount of revenue and expense to allocate to a period. Examples of accounting estimates include, among others, the useful lives of depreciable assets, the salvage value of depreciable assets, product returns, warranty costs, and the amount of uncollectible receivables.

Accumulated benefit obligation   The actuarial present value of benefits (whether vested or non-vested) attributed, generally by the pension benefit formula, to employee service rendered before a specified date and based on employee service and compensation (if applicable) before that date. The accumulated benefit obligation differs from the projected benefit obligation in that it includes no assumption about future compensation levels.

Accuracy   The percentage of correctly predicted classes out of total predictions. It is an overall performance metric in classification problems.

Acquisition   When one company, the acquirer, purchases from the seller most or all of another company's (the target) shares to gain control of either an entire company, a segment of another company, or a specific group of assets in exchange for cash, stock, or the assumption of liabilities, alone or in combination. Once an acquisition is complete, the acquirer and target merge into a single entity and consolidate management, operations, and resources.

Activation function   A functional part of a neural network's node that transforms the total net input received into the final output of the node. The activation function operates like a light dimmer switch that decreases or increases the strength of the input.

Active factor risk   The contribution to active risk squared resulting from the portfolio's different-than-benchmark exposures relative to factors specified in the risk model.

Active return   The return on a portfolio minus the return on the portfolio's benchmark.

Active risk   The standard deviation of active returns.

Active risk squared   The variance of active returns; active risk raised to the second power.

Active share   A measure of how similar a portfolio is to its benchmark. A manager who precisely replicates the benchmark will have an active share of zero; a manager with no holdings in common with the benchmark will have an active share of one.

Active specific risk   The contribution to active risk squared resulting from the portfolio's active weights on individual assets as those weights interact with assets' residual risk.

Adjusted funds from operations (AFFO)   Funds from operations adjusted to remove any non-cash rent reported under straight-line rent accounting and to subtract maintenance-type capital expenditures and leasing costs, including leasing agents' commissions and tenants' improvement allowances.

Adjusted present value   As an approach to valuing a company, the sum of the value of the company, assuming no use of debt, and the net present value of any effects of debt on company value.

Adjusted R^2   Goodness-of-fit measure that adjusts the coefficient of determination, R^2, for the number of independent variables in the model.

Administrative regulations or administrative law   Rules issued by government agencies or other regulators.

Advanced set   An arrangement in which the reference interest rate is set at the time the money is deposited.

Advanced settled   An arrangement in which a forward rate agreement (FRA) expires and settles at the same time, at the FRA expiration date.

Agency issues   Conflicts of interest that arise when the agent in an agency relationship has goals and incentives that differ from the principal to whom the agent owes a fiduciary duty. Also called *agency problems* or *principal–agent problems*.

Agglomerative clustering   A bottom-up hierarchical clustering method that begins with each observation being treated as its own cluster. The algorithm finds the two closest clusters, based on some measure of distance (similarity), and combines them into one new larger cluster. This process is repeated iteratively until all observations are clumped into a single large cluster.

Akaike's information criterion (AIC)   A statistic used to compare sets of independent variables for explaining a dependent variable. It is preferred for finding the model that is best suited for prediction.

Allowance for loan losses   A balance sheet account; it is a contra asset account to loans.

Alpha   The return on an asset in excess of the asset's required rate of return; the risk-adjusted return.

American Depositary Receipt   A negotiable certificate issued by a depositary bank that represents ownership in a non-US company's deposited equity (i.e., equity held in custody by the depositary bank in the company's home market).

Analysis of variance (ANOVA)   The analysis that breaks the total variability of a dataset (such as observations on the dependent variable in a regression) into components representing different sources of variation.

Application programming interface (API)   A set of well-defined methods of communication between various software components and typically used for accessing external data.

Arbitrage   1) The simultaneous purchase of an undervalued asset or portfolio and sale of an overvalued but equivalent asset or portfolio, in order to obtain a riskless profit on the price differential. Taking advantage of a market inefficiency in a risk-free manner. 2) The condition in a financial market in which equivalent assets or combinations of assets sell for two different prices, creating an opportunity to profit at no risk with no commitment of money. In a well-functioning financial market, few arbitrage opportunities are possible. 3) A risk-free operation that earns an expected positive net profit but requires no net investment of money.

Arbitrage-free models Term structure models that project future interest rate paths that emanate from the existing term structure. Resulting prices are based on a no-arbitrage condition.

Arbitrage-free valuation An approach to valuation that determines security values consistent with the absence of any opportunity to earn riskless profits without any net investment of money.

Arbitrage opportunity An opportunity to conduct an arbitrage; an opportunity to earn an expected positive net profit without risk and with no net investment of money.

Arbitrage portfolio The portfolio that exploits an arbitrage opportunity.

Ask price The price at which a trader will sell a specified quantity of a security. Also called *ask*, *offer price*, or *offer*.

Asset-based approach Approach that values a private company based on the values of the underlying assets of the entity less the value of any related liabilities.

Asset-based valuation An approach to valuing natural resource companies that estimates company value on the basis of the market value of the natural resources the company controls.

At market contract When a forward contract is established, the forward price is negotiated so that the market value of the forward contract on the initiation date is zero.

Authorized participants (APs) A special group of institutional investors who are authorized by the ETF issuer to participate in the creation/redemption process. APs are large broker/dealers, often market makers.

Autocorrelations The correlations of a time series with its own past values.

Autoregressive model (AR) A time series regressed on its own past values in which the independent variable is a lagged value of the dependent variable.

Backtesting The process that approximates the real-life investment process, using historical data, to assess whether an investment strategy would have produced desirable results.

Backward propagation The process of adjusting weights in a neural network, to reduce total error of the network, by moving backward through the network's layers.

Backwardation A condition in the futures markets in which the spot price exceeds the futures price, the forward curve is downward sloping, and the convenience yield is high.

Bag-of-words (BOW) A collection of a distinct set of tokens from all the texts in a sample dataset. BOW does not capture the position or sequence of words present in the text.

Balance sheet restructuring Altering the composition of the balance sheet by either shifting the asset composition, changing the capital structure, or both.

Bankruptcy A declaration provided for by a country's laws that typically involves the establishment of a legal procedure that forces creditors to defer their claims.

Barbell portfolio Fixed-income portfolio that combines short and long maturities.

Base error Model error due to randomness in the data.

Basic earnings per share (EPS) Net earnings available to common shareholders (i.e., net income minus preferred dividends) divided by the weighted average number of common shares outstanding during the period.

Basis The difference between the spot price and the futures price. As the maturity date of the futures contract nears, the basis converges toward zero.

Basis trade A trade based on the pricing of credit in the bond market versus the price of the same credit in the CDS market. To execute a basis trade, go long the "underpriced" credit and short the "overpriced" credit. A profit is realized as the implied credit prices converge.

Bearish flattening Term structure shift in which short-term bond yields rise more than long-term bond yields, resulting in a flatter yield curve.

Benchmark value of the multiple In using the method of comparables, the value of a price multiple for the comparison asset; when we have comparison assets (a group), the mean or median value of the multiple for the group of assets.

Best ask The offer to sell with the lowest ask price. Also called *best offer* or *inside ask*.

Best bid The highest bid in the market.

Best offer The lowest offer (ask price) in the market.

Bias error Describes the degree to which a model fits the training data. Algorithms with erroneous assumptions produce high bias error with poor approximation, causing underfitting and high in-sample error.

Bid price In a price quotation, the price at which the party making the quotation is willing to buy a specified quantity of an asset or security.

Bid–ask spread The ask price minus the bid price.

Bill-and-hold basis Sales on a bill-and-hold basis involve selling products but not delivering those products until a later date.

Blockage factor An illiquidity discount that occurs when an investor sells a large amount of stock relative to its trading volume (assuming it is not large enough to constitute a controlling ownership).

Bond indenture A legal contract specifying the terms of a bond issue.

Bond risk premium The expected excess return of a default-free long-term bond less that of an equivalent short-term bond.

Bond yield plus risk premium (BYPRP) approach An estimate of the cost of common equity that is produced by summing the before-tax cost of debt and a risk premium that captures the additional yield on a company's stock relative to its bonds.

Bonus issue of shares A type of dividend in which a company distributes additional shares of its common stock to shareholders instead of cash.

Book value The net amount shown for an asset or liability on the balance sheet; book value may also refer to the company's excess of total assets over total liabilities. Also called *carrying value*.

Book value of equity Shareholders' equity (total assets minus total liabilities) minus the value of preferred stock; common shareholders' equity.

Book value per share The amount of book value (also called carrying value) of common equity per share of common stock, calculated by dividing the book value of shareholders' equity by the number of shares of common stock outstanding.

Bootstrap aggregating (or bagging) A technique whereby the original training dataset is used to generate n new training datasets or bags of data. Each new bag of data is generated by random sampling with replacement from the initial training set.

Bootstrapping The use of a forward substitution process to determine zero-coupon rates by using the par yields and solving for the zero-coupon rates one by one, from the shortest to longest maturities.

Bottom-up approach With respect to forecasting, an approach that usually begins at the level of the individual company or a unit within the company.

Breakup value The value derived using a sum-of-the-parts valuation.

Breusch–Godfrey (BG) test A test used to detect autocorrelated residuals up to a predesignated order of the lagged residuals.

Breusch–Pagan (BP) test A test for the presence of heteroskedasticity in a regression.

Bullet portfolio A fixed-income portfolio concentrated in a single maturity.

Bullish flattening Term structure change in which the yield curve flattens in response to a greater decline in long-term rates than short-term rates.

Bullish steepening Term structure change in which short-term rates fall by more than long-term yields, resulting in a steeper term structure.

Buy-side analysts Analysts who work for investment management firms, trusts, bank trust departments, and similar institutions.

Buyback A transaction in which a company buys back its own shares. Unlike stock dividends and stock splits, share repurchases use corporate cash.

CDS spread A periodic premium paid by the buyer to the seller that serves as a return over a market reference rate required to protect against credit risk.

Callable bond A bond containing an embedded call option that gives the issuer the right to buy the bond back from the investor at specified prices on pre-determined dates.

Canceled shares Shares that were issued, subsequently repurchased by the company, and then retired (cannot be reissued).

Capital asset pricing model (CAPM) A single factor model such that excess returns on a stock are a function of the returns on a market index.

Capital charge The company's total cost of capital in money terms.

Capital deepening An increase in the capital-to-labor ratio.

Capitalization of earnings method In the context of private company valuation, a valuation model based on an assumption of a constant growth rate of free cash flow to the firm or a constant growth rate of free cash flow to equity.

Capitalization rate The divisor in the expression for the value of perpetuity. In the context of real estate, it is the divisor in the direct capitalization method of estimating value. The cap rate equals net operating income divided by value.

Capitalized cash flow method In the context of private company valuation, a valuation model based on an assumption of a constant growth rate of free cash flow to the firm or a constant growth rate of free cash flow to equity. Also called *capitalized cash flow model*.

Capitalized income method In the context of private company valuation, a valuation model based on an assumption of a constant growth rate of free cash flow to the firm or a constant growth rate of free cash flow to equity.

Capped floater Floating-rate bond with a cap provision that prevents the coupon rate from increasing above a specified maximum rate. It protects the issuer against rising interest rates.

Carry arbitrage model A no-arbitrage approach in which the underlying instrument is either bought or sold along with an opposite position in a forward contract.

Carry benefits Benefits that arise from owning certain underlyings; for example, dividends, foreign interest, and bond coupon payments.

Carry costs Costs that arise from owning certain underlyings. They are generally a function of the physical characteristics of the underlying asset and also the interest forgone on the funds tied up in the asset.

Cash available for distribution See *adjusted funds from operations*.

Cash-generating unit The smallest identifiable group of assets that generates cash inflows that are largely independent of the cash inflows of other assets or groups of assets.

Cash settlement A procedure used in certain derivative transactions that specifies that the long and short parties settle the derivative's difference in value between them by making a cash payment.

Catalyst An event or piece of information that causes the marketplace to re-evaluate the prospects of a company.

Ceiling analysis A systematic process of evaluating different components in the pipeline of model building. It helps to understand what part of the pipeline can potentially improve in performance by further tuning.

Centroid The center of a cluster formed using the k-means clustering algorithm.

Chain rule of forecasting A forecasting process in which the next period's value as predicted by the forecasting equation is substituted into the right-hand side of the equation to give a predicted value two periods ahead.

Cheapest-to-deliver The debt instrument that can be purchased and delivered at the lowest cost yet has the same seniority as the reference obligation.

Classification and regression tree A supervised machine learning technique that can be applied to predict either a categorical target variable, producing a classification tree, or a continuous target variable, producing a regression tree. CART is commonly applied to binary classification or regression.

Clean surplus relation The relationship between earnings, dividends, and book value in which ending book value is equal to the beginning book value plus earnings less dividends, apart from ownership transactions.

Club convergence The idea that only rich and middle-income countries sharing a set of favorable attributes (i.e., are members of the "club") will converge to the income level of the richest countries.

Cluster A subset of observations from a dataset such that all the observations within the same cluster are deemed "similar."

Clustering The sorting of observations into groups (clusters) such that observations in the same cluster are more similar to each other than they are to observations in other clusters.

Cobb–Douglas production function A function of the form $Y = K^{\alpha} L^{1-\alpha}$ relating output (Y) to labor (L) and capital (K) inputs.

Coefficient of determination The percentage of the variation of the dependent variable that is explained by the independent variables. Also referred to as the R-squared or R^2.

Cointegrated Describes two time series that have a long-term financial or economic relationship such that they do not diverge from each other without bound in the long run.

Collateral return The component of the total return on a commodity futures position attributable to the yield for the bonds or cash used to maintain the futures position. Also called *collateral yield*.

Collection frequency (CF) The number of times a given word appears in the whole corpus (i.e., collection of sentences) divided by the total number of words in the corpus.

Commercial real estate properties Income-producing real estate properties; properties purchased with the intent to let, lease, or rent (in other words, produce income).

Commodity swap A type of swap involving the exchange of payments over multiple dates as determined by specified reference prices or indexes relating to commodities.

Company fundamental factors Factors related to the company's internal performance, such as factors relating to earnings growth, earnings variability, earnings momentum, and financial leverage.

Company share-related factors Valuation measures and other factors related to share price or the trading characteristics of the shares, such as earnings yield, dividend yield, and book-to-market value.

Comparables Assets used as benchmarks when applying the method of comparables to value an asset. Also called *comps, guideline assets,* or *guideline companies*.

Compiled financial statements Financial statements that are not accompanied by an auditor's opinion letter.

Complexity A term referring to the number of features, parameters, or branches in a model and to whether the model is linear or non-linear (non-linear is more complex).

Composite variable A variable that combines two or more variables that are statistically strongly related to each other.

Comprehensive income All changes in equity other than contributions by, and distributions to, owners; income under clean surplus accounting; includes all changes in equity during a period except those resulting from investments by owners and distributions to owners. Comprehensive income equals net income plus other comprehensive income.

Comps Assets used as benchmarks when applying the method of comparables to value an asset.

Concentrated ownership Ownership structure consisting of an individual shareholder or a group (controlling shareholders) with the ability to exercise control over the corporation.

Conditional convergence The idea that convergence of per capita income is conditional on the countries having the same savings rate, population growth rate, and production function.

Conditional heteroskedasticity A condition in which the variance of residuals of a regression are correlated with the value of the independent variables.

Conditional VaR (CVaR) The weighted average of all loss outcomes in the statistical (i.e., return) distribution that exceed the VaR loss. Thus, CVaR is a more comprehensive measure of tail loss than VaR is. Sometimes referred to as the *expected tail loss* or *expected shortfall*.

Confirmation bias A belief perseverance bias in which people tend to look for and notice what confirms their beliefs, to ignore or undervalue what contradicts their beliefs, and to misinterpret information as support for their beliefs.

Confusion matrix A grid used for error analysis in classification problems, it presents values for four evaluation metrics including true positive (TP), false positive (FP), true negative (TN), and false negative (FN).

Conglomerate discount When an issuer is trading at a valuation lower than the sum of its parts, which is generally the result of diseconomies of scale or scope or the result of the capital markets having overlooked the business and its prospects.

Constant dividend payout ratio policy A policy in which a constant percentage of net income is paid out in dividends.

Constant returns to scale The condition that if all inputs into the production process are increased by a given percentage, then output rises by that same percentage.

Contango A condition in the futures markets in which the spot price is lower than the futures price, the forward curve is upward sloping, and there is little or no convenience yield.

Contingent consideration Potential future payments to the seller that are contingent on the achievement of certain agreed-on occurrences.

Continuing earnings Earnings excluding nonrecurring components. Also referred to as *core earnings, persistent earnings,* or *underlying earnings*.

Continuing residual income Residual income after the forecast horizon.

Continuing value The analyst's estimate of a stock's value at a particular point in the future.

Control premium An increment or premium to value associated with a controlling ownership interest in a company.

Convergence The tendency for differences in output per capita across countries to diminish over time. In technical analysis, the term describes the case when an indicator moves in the same manner as the security being analyzed.

Conversion period For a convertible bond, the period during which bondholders have the right to convert their bonds into shares.

Conversion price For a convertible bond, the price per share at which the bond can be converted into shares.

Conversion rate (or ratio) For a convertible bond, the number of shares of common stock that a bondholder receives from converting the bond into shares.

Conversion value For a convertible bond, the value of the bond if it is converted at the market price of the shares. Also called *parity value*.

Convertible bond Bond that gives the bondholder the right to exchange the bond for a specified number of common shares in the issuing company.

Convexity A measure of how interest rate sensitivity changes with a change in interest rates.

Cook's distance A metric for identifying influential data points. Also known as Cook's D (D_i).

Core earnings Earnings excluding nonrecurring components. Also referred to as *continuing earnings, persistent earnings,* or *underlying earnings*.

Core real estate investment style Investing in high-quality, well-leased, core property types with low leverage (no more than 30% of asset value) in the largest markets with strong, diversified economies. It is a conservative strategy designed to avoid real estate–specific risks, including leasing, development, and speculation in favor of steady returns. Hotel properties are excluded from the core categories because of the higher cash flow volatility resulting from single-night leases and the greater importance of property operations, brand, and marketing.

Corpus A collection of text data in any form, including list, matrix, or data table forms.

Cost approach An approach that values a private company based on the values of the underlying assets of the entity less the value of any related liabilities. In the context of real estate, this approach estimates the value of a property based on what it would cost to buy the land and construct a new property on the site that has the same utility or functionality as the property being appraised.

Cost of carry model A model that relates the forward price of an asset to the spot price by considering the cost of carry (also referred to as future-spot parity model).

Cost of debt The required return on debt financing to a company, such as when it issues a bond, takes out a bank loan, or leases an asset through a finance lease.

Cost of equity The return required by equity investors to compensate for both the time value of money and the risk. Also referred to as the required rate of return on common stock or the required return on equity.

Cost restructuring Actions to reduce costs by improving operational efficiency and profitability, often to raise margins to a historical level or to those of comparable industry peers.

Country risk premium (CRP) The additional return required by investors to compensate for the risk associated with investing in a foreign country relative to the investor's domestic market.

Country risk rating (CRR) The rating of a country based on many risk factors, including economic prosperity, political risk, and ESG risk.

Covariance stationary Describes a time series when its expected value and variance are constant and finite in all periods and when its covariance with itself for a fixed number of periods in the past or future is constant and finite in all periods.

Covered bonds A senior debt obligation of a financial institution that gives recourse to the originator/issuer and a predetermined underlying collateral pool.

Covered interest rate parity The relationship among the spot exchange rate, the forward exchange rate, and the interest rates in two currencies that ensures that the return on a hedged (i.e., covered) foreign risk-free investment is the same as the return on a domestic risk-free investment. Also called *interest rate parity*.

Cox-Ingersoll-Ross model A general equilibrium term structure model that assumes interest rates are mean reverting and interest rate volatility is directly related to the level of interest rates.

Creation basket The list of securities (and share amounts) the authorized participant (AP) must deliver to the ETF manager in exchange for ETF shares. The creation basket is published each business day.

Creation units Large blocks of ETF shares transacted between the authorized participant (AP) and the ETF manager that are usually but not always equal to 50,000 shares of the ETF.

Creation/redemption The process in which ETF shares are created or redeemed by authorized participants transacting with the ETF issuer.

Credit correlation The correlation of credit (or default) risks of the underlying single-name CDS contained in an index CDS.

Credit curve The credit spreads for a range of maturities of a company's debt.

Credit default swap A derivative contract between two parties in which the buyer makes a series of cash payments to the seller and receives a promise of compensation for credit losses resulting from the default.

Credit derivative A derivative instrument in which the underlying is a measure of the credit quality of a borrower.

Credit event An event that defines a payout in a credit derivative. Events are usually defined as bankruptcy, failure to pay an obligation, or an involuntary debt restructuring.

Credit protection buyer One party to a credit default swap; the buyer makes a series of cash payments to the seller and receives a promise of compensation for credit losses resulting from the default.

Credit protection seller One party to a credit default swap; the seller makes a promise to pay compensation for credit losses resulting from the default.

Credit risk The risk of loss caused by a counterparty's or debtor's failure to make a promised payment. Also called *default risk*.

Credit spread The compensation for the risk inherent in a company's debt security.

Credit valuation adjustment The value of the credit risk of a bond in present value terms.

Cross-validation A technique for estimating out-of-sample error directly by determining the error in validation samples.

Cumulative preferred stock Preferred stock that requires that the dividends be paid in full to preferred stock owners for any missed dividends prior to any payment of dividends to common stock owners.

Current exchange rate For accounting purposes, the spot exchange rate on the balance sheet date.

Current rate method Approach to translating foreign currency financial statements for consolidation in which all assets and liabilities are translated at the current exchange rate. The current rate method is the prevalent method of translation.

Curvature One of the three factors (the other two are level and steepness) that empirically explain most of the changes in the shape of the yield curve. A shock to the curvature factor affects mid-maturity interest rates, resulting in the term structure becoming either more or less hump-shaped.

Curve trade Buying a CDS of one maturity and selling a CDS on the same reference entity with a different maturity.

Customer concentration risk The risk associated with sales dependent on a few customers.

Cyclical businesses Businesses with high sensitivity to business- or industry-cycle influences.

Data preparation (cleansing) The process of examining, identifying, and mitigating (i.e., cleansing) errors in raw data.

Data snooping The practice of determining a model by extensive searching through a dataset for statistically significant patterns.

Data wrangling (preprocessing) This task performs transformations and critical processing steps on cleansed data to make the data ready for ML model training (i.e., preprocessing), and includes dealing with outliers, extracting useful variables from existing data points, and scaling the data.

Deep learning Machine learning using neural networks with many hidden layers.

Deep neural networks Neural networks with many hidden layers—at least 2 but potentially more than 20—that have proven successful across a wide range of artificial intelligence applications.

Default risk See *credit risk*.

Defined benefit pension plans Plans in which the company promises to pay a certain annual amount (defined benefit) to the employee after retirement. The company bears the investment risk of the plan assets.

Defined contribution pension plans Individual accounts to which an employee and typically the employer makes contributions during their working years and expect to draw on the accumulated funds at retirement. The employee bears the investment and inflation risk of the plan assets.

Delay costs Implicit trading costs that arise from the inability to complete desired trades immediately. Also called *slippage*.

Delta The relationship between the option price and the underlying price, which reflects the sensitivity of the price of the option to changes in the price of the underlying. Delta is a good approximation of how an option price will change for a small change in the stock.

Dendrogram A type of tree diagram used for visualizing a hierarchical cluster analysis; it highlights the hierarchical relationships among the clusters.

Depository Trust and Clearinghouse Corporation A US-headquartered entity providing post-trade clearing, settlement, and information services.

Diluted earnings per share (Diluted EPS)Net income, minus preferred dividends, divided by the weighted average number of common shares outstanding considering all dilutive securities (e.g., convertible debt and options); the EPS that would result if all dilutive securities were converted into common shares.

Dilution A reduction in proportional ownership interest as a result of the issuance of new shares.

Dimension reduction A set of techniques for reducing the number of features in a dataset while retaining variation across observations to preserve the information contained in that variation.

Diminishing marginal productivity When each additional unit of an input, keeping the other inputs unchanged, increases output by a smaller increment.

Direct capitalization method In the context of real estate, this method estimates the value of an income-producing property based on the level and quality of its net operating income.

Discount To reduce the value of a future payment in allowance for how far away it is in time; to calculate the present value of some future amount. Also, the amount by which an instrument is priced below its face value.

Discount factor The price equivalent of a zero rate. Also may be stated as the present value of a currency unit on a future date.

Discount for lack of control An amount or percentage deducted from the pro rata share of 100% of the value of an equity interest in a business to reflect the absence of some or all of the powers of control.

Discount for lack of marketability An amount of percentage deducted from the value of an ownership interest to reflect the relative absence of marketability.

Discount function Discount factors for the range of all possible maturities. The spot curve can be derived from the discount function and vice versa.

Discounted abnormal earnings model A model of stock valuation that views intrinsic value of stock as the sum of book value per share plus the present value of the stock's expected future residual income per share.

Discounted cash flow (DCF) method Income approach that values an asset based on estimates of future cash flows discounted to present value by using a discount rate reflective of the risks associated with the cash flows. In the context of real estate, this method estimates the value of an income-producing property based on discounting future projected cash flows.

Discounted cash flow method Income approach that values an asset based on estimates of future cash flows discounted to present value by using a discount rate reflective of the risks associated with the cash flows. In the context of real estate, this method estimates the value of an income-producing property based on discounting future projected cash flows.

Discounted cash flow model A model of intrinsic value that views the value of an asset as the present value of the asset's expected future cash flows.

Dispersed ownership Ownership structure consisting of many shareholders, none of which has the ability to individually exercise control over the corporation.

Divestiture When a seller sells a company, segment of a company, or group of assets to an acquirer. Once complete, control of the target is transferred to the acquirer.

Dividend A distribution paid to shareholders based on the number of shares owned.

Dividend coverage ratio The ratio of net income to dividends.

Dividend discount model (DDM) A present value model of stock value that views the intrinsic value of a stock as present value of the stock's expected future dividends.

Dividend discount model (DDM) The model of the value of stock that is the present value of all future dividends, discounted at the required return on equity.

Dividend displacement of earnings The concept that dividends paid now displace earnings in all future periods.

Dividend imputation tax system A taxation system that effectively assures corporate profits distributed as dividends are taxed just once and at the shareholder's tax rate.

Dividend index point A measure of the quantity of dividends attributable to a particular index.

Dividend payout ratio The ratio of cash dividends paid to earnings for a period.

Dividend policy The strategy a company follows with regard to the amount and timing of dividend payments.

Dividend rate The annualized amount of the most recent dividend.

Dividend recapitalization Restructuring the mix of debt and equity, typically shifting the capital structure from equity to debt through debt-financed share repurchases. The objective is to reduce the issuer's weighted average cost of capital by replacing expensive equity with cheaper debt by purchasing equity from shareholders using newly issued debt.

Dividend yield Annual dividends per share divided by share price.

Divisive clustering A top-down hierarchical clustering method that starts with all observations belonging to a single large cluster. The observations are then divided into two clusters based on some measure of distance (similarity). The algorithm then progressively partitions the intermediate clusters into smaller ones until each cluster contains only one observation.

Document frequency (DF) The number of documents (texts) that contain a particular token divided by the total number of documents. It is the simplest feature selection method and often performs well when many thousands of tokens are present.

Document term matrix (DTM) A matrix where each row belongs to a document (or text file), and each column represents a token (or term). The number of rows is equal to the number of documents (or text files) in a sample text dataset. The number of columns is equal to the number of tokens from the BOW built using all the documents in the sample dataset. The cells typically contain the counts of the number of times a token is present in each document.

Dominance An arbitrage opportunity when a financial asset with a risk-free payoff in the future must have a positive price today.

Double taxation system Corporate earnings are taxed twice when paid out as dividends. First, corporate pretax earnings are taxed regardless of whether they will be distributed as dividends or retained at the corporate level. Second, dividends are taxed again at the individual shareholder level.

Downstream A transaction between two related companies, an investor company (or a parent company) and an associate company (or a subsidiary) such that the investor company records a profit on its income statement. An example is a sale of inventory by the investor company to the associate or by a parent to a subsidiary company.

Dual-class shares Shares that grant one share class superior or even sole voting rights, whereas the other share class has inferior or no voting rights.

Due diligence Investigation and analysis in support of an investment action, decision, or recommendation.

Dummy variable An independent variable that takes on a value of either 1 or 0, depending on a specified condition. Also known as an *indicator variable*.

Duration A measure of the approximate sensitivity of a security to a change in interest rates (i.e., a measure of interest rate risk).

Durbin–Watson (DW) test A test for the presence of first-order serial correlation.

Dutch disease A situation in which currency appreciation driven by strong export demand for resources makes other segments of the economy (particularly manufacturing) globally uncompetitive.

ESG integration An ESG investment approach that focuses on systematic consideration of material ESG factors in asset allocation, security selection, and portfolio construction decisions for the purpose of achieving the product's stated investment objectives. Used interchangeably with **ESG investing**.

Earnings surprise The portion of a company's earnings that is unanticipated by investors and, according to the efficient market hypothesis, merits a price adjustment.

Earnings yield EPS divided by price; the reciprocal of the P/E.

Economic profit Equal to accounting profit less the implicit opportunity costs not included in total accounting costs; the difference between total revenue (TR) and total cost (TC). Also called *abnormal profit* or *supernormal profit*.

Economic sectors Large industry groupings.

Economic value added (EVA*) A commercial implementation of the residual income concept; the computation of EVA* is the net operating profit after taxes minus the cost of capital, where these inputs are adjusted for a number of items.

Economies of scale A situation in which average costs per unit of good or service produced fall as volume rises. In reference to mergers, the savings achieved through the consolidation of operations and elimination of duplicate resources.

Edwards–Bell–Ohlson model A model of stock valuation that views intrinsic value of stock as the sum of book value per share plus the present value of the stock's expected future residual income per share.

Effective convexity A *curve convexity* statistic that measures the secondary effect of a change in a benchmark yield curve on a bond's price.

Effective duration Sensitivity of the bond's price to a 100 bps parallel shift of the benchmark yield curve, assuming no change in the bond's credit spread.

Effective spread Two times the difference between the execution price and the midpoint of the market quote at the time an order is entered.

Eigenvalue A measure that gives the proportion of total variance in the initial dataset that is explained by each eigenvector.

Eigenvector A vector that defines new mutually uncorrelated composite variables that are linear combinations of the original features.

Embedded options Contingency provisions found in a bond's indenture or offering circular representing rights that enable their holders to take advantage of interest rate movements. They can be exercised by the issuer, by the bondholder, or automatically depending on the course of interest rates.

Ensemble learning A technique of combining the predictions from a collection of models to achieve a more accurate prediction.

Ensemble method The method of combining multiple learning algorithms, as in ensemble learning.

Enterprise value Total company value (the market value of debt, common equity, and preferred equity) minus the value of cash and investments.

Enterprise value multiple A valuation multiple that relates the total market value of all sources of a company's capital (net of cash) to a measure of fundamental value for the entire company (such as a pre-interest earnings measure).

Equity charge The estimated cost of equity capital in money terms.

Equity investment A company purchasing another company's equity but less than 50% of its shares. The two companies maintain their independence, but the investor company has investment exposure to the investee and, in some cases depending on the size of the investment, can have representation on the investee's board of directors to influence operations.

Equity REITs REITs that own, operate, and/or selectively develop income-producing real estate.

Equity risk premium (ERP) Compensation for bearing market risk.

Equity swap A swap transaction in which at least one cash flow is tied to the return on an equity portfolio position, often an equity index.

Error autocorrelations The autocorrelations of the error term.

***Ex ante* tracking error** A measure of the degree to which the performance of a given investment portfolio might be expected to deviate from its benchmark; also known as *relative VaR*.

***Ex ante* version of PPP**   The hypothesis that expected changes in the spot exchange rate are equal to expected differences in national inflation rates. An extension of relative purchasing power parity to expected future changes in the exchange rate.

Ex-dividend   Trading ex-dividend refers to shares that no longer carry the right to the next dividend payment.

Ex-dividend date   The first date that a share trades without (i.e., "ex") the right to receive the declared dividend for the period.

Excess earnings method   Income approach that estimates the value of all intangible assets of the business by capitalizing future earnings in excess of the estimated return requirements associated with working capital and fixed assets.

Exercise date   The date when employees actually exercise stock options and convert them to stock.

Exercise value   The value of an option if it were exercised. Also sometimes called *intrinsic value.*

Expanded CAPM   An adaptation of the CAPM that adds to the CAPM a premium for small size and company-specific risk.

Expectations approach   A procedure for obtaining the value of an option derived from discounting at the risk-free rate its expected future payoff based on risk neutral probabilities.

Expected exposure   The projected amount of money an investor could lose if an event of default occurs, before factoring in possible recovery.

Expected shortfall   The average loss conditional on exceeding the VaR cutoff; sometimes referred to as *conditional VaR* or *expected tail loss.*

Expected tail loss   See *expected shortfall.*

Exploratory data analysis (EDA)   The preliminary step in data exploration, where graphs, charts, and other visualizations (heat maps and word clouds) as well as quantitative methods (descriptive statistics and central tendency measures) are used to observe and summarize data.

Exposure to foreign exchange risk   The risk of a change in value of an asset or liability denominated in a foreign currency due to a change in exchange rates.

Extendible bond   Bond with an embedded option that gives the bondholder the right to keep the bond for a number of years after maturity, possibly with a different coupon.

Extra dividend   A dividend paid by a company that does not pay dividends on a regular schedule, or a dividend that supplements regular cash dividends with an extra payment.

F1 score   The harmonic mean of precision and recall. F1 score is a more appropriate overall performance metric (than accuracy) when there is unequal class distribution in the dataset and it is necessary to measure the equilibrium of precision and recall.

FX carry trade   An investment strategy that involves taking long positions in high-yield currencies and short positions in low-yield currencies.

Factor   A common or underlying element with which several variables are correlated.

Factor betas   An asset's sensitivity to a particular factor; a measure of the response of return to each unit of increase in a factor, holding all other factors constant.

Factor portfolio   See *pure factor portfolio.*

Factor price   The expected return in excess of the risk-free rate for a portfolio with a sensitivity of 1 to one factor and a sensitivity of 0 to all other factors.

Factor risk premium   The expected return in excess of the risk-free rate for a portfolio with a sensitivity of 1 to one factor and a sensitivity of 0 to all other factors. Also called *factor price.*

Factor risk premiums   The expected return in excess of the risk-free rate for a portfolio with a sensitivity of 1 to one factor and a sensitivity of 0 to all other factors. Also called factor price.

Failure to pay   When a borrower does not make a scheduled payment of principal or interest on any outstanding obligations after a grace period.

Fair market value   The price, expressed in terms of cash equivalents, at which a property (asset) would change hands between a hypothetical willing and able buyer and a hypothetical willing and able seller, acting at "arm's length" in an open and unrestricted market, when neither is under compulsion to buy or sell and when both have reasonable knowledge of the relevant facts. Fair market value is most often used in a tax reporting context in the United States.

Fair value   The amount at which an asset could be exchanged, or a liability settled, between knowledgeable, willing parties in an arm's-length transaction; the price that would be received to sell an asset or paid to transfer a liability in an orderly transaction between market participants.

Fama–French models   Factor models that explain the drivers of returns related to three, four, or five factors.

Feature engineering   A process of creating new features by changing or transforming existing features.

Feature selection   A process whereby only pertinent features from the dataset are selected for model training. Selecting fewer features decreases model complexity and training time.

Features   The independent variables (X's) in a labeled dataset.

Finance (or capital) lease   A lease that is viewed as a financing arrangement.

Financial contagion   A situation in which financial shocks spread from their place of origin to other locales. In essence, a faltering economy infects other, healthier economies.

Financial leverage   The use of fixed sources of capital, such as debt, relative to sources without fixed costs, such as equity.

Financial transaction   A purchase involving a buyer having essentially no material synergies with the target (e.g., the purchase of a private company by a company in an unrelated industry or by a private equity firm would typically be a financial transaction).

First-differencing   A transformation that subtracts the value of the time series in period $t - 1$ from its value in period t.

First-order serial correlation   The correlation of residuals with residuals adjacent in time.

Fitting curve   A curve which shows in- and out-of-sample error rates (E_{in} and E_{out}) on the y-axis plotted against model complexity on the x-axis.

Fixed price tender offer   Offer made by a company to repurchase a specific number of shares at a fixed price that is typically at a premium to the current market price.

Fixed-rate perpetual preferred stock   Nonconvertible, noncallable preferred stock that has a fixed dividend rate and no maturity date.

Flight to quality   During times of market stress, investors sell higher-risk asset classes such as stocks and commodities in favor of default-risk-free government bonds.

Float   Amounts collected as premium and not yet paid out as benefits.

Floored floater Floating-rate bond with a floor provision that prevents the coupon rate from decreasing below a specified minimum rate. It protects the investor against declining interest rates.

Flotation cost Fees charged to companies by investment bankers and other costs associated with raising new capital.

Forced conversion For a convertible bond, when the issuer calls the bond and forces bondholders to convert their bonds into shares, which typically happens when the underlying share price increases above the conversion price.

Foreign currency transactions Transactions that are denominated in a currency other than a company's functional currency.

Forward curve A series of forward rates, each having the same time frame.

Forward dividend yield A dividend yield based on the anticipated dividend during the next 12 months.

Forward-looking estimates Estimates based on current and expectations. Also referred to as ex ante estimates.

Forward P/E A P/E calculated on the basis of a forecast of EPS; a stock's current price divided by next year's expected earnings.

Forward price Represents the price agreed upon in a forward contract to be exchanged at the contract's maturity date, T. This price is shown in equations as $F_0(T)$.

Forward pricing model The model that describes the valuation of forward contracts.

Forward propagation The process of adjusting weights in a neural network, to reduce total error of the network, by moving forward through the network's layers.

Forward rate An interest rate determined today for a loan that will be initiated in a future period.

Forward rate agreement An over-the-counter forward contract in which the underlying is an interest rate on a deposit. A forward rate agreement (FRA) calls for one party to make a fixed interest payment and the other to make an interest payment at a rate to be determined at contract expiration.

Forward rate model The forward pricing model expressed in terms of spot and forward interest rates.

Forward rate parity The proposition that the forward exchange rate is an unbiased predictor of the future spot exchange rate.

Forward value The monetary value of an existing forward contract.

Franchising An owner of an asset and associated intellectual property divests the asset and licenses intellectual property to a third-party operator (franchisee) in exchange for royalties. Franchisees operate under the constraints of a franchise agreement.

Franking credit A tax credit received by shareholders for the taxes that a corporation paid on its distributed earnings.

Free cash flow method Income approach that values an asset based on estimates of future cash flows discounted to present value by using a discount rate reflective of the risks associated with the cash flows.

Free cash flow to equity The cash flow available to a company's common shareholders after all operating expenses, interest, and principal payments have been made and necessary investments in working and fixed capital have been made.

Free cash flow to equity model A model of stock valuation that views a stock's intrinsic value as the present value of expected future free cash flows to equity.

Free cash flow to the firm The cash flow available to the company's suppliers of capital after all operating expenses (including taxes) have been paid and necessary investments in working and fixed capital have been made.

Free cash flow to the firm model A model of stock valuation that views the value of a firm as the present value of expected future free cash flows to the firm.

Frequency analysis The process of quantifying how important tokens are in a sentence and in the corpus as a whole. It helps in filtering unnecessary tokens (or features).

Functional currency The currency of the primary economic environment in which an entity operates.

Fundamental factor models A multifactor model in which the factors are attributes of stocks or companies that are important in explaining cross-sectional differences in stock prices.

Fundamentals Economic characteristics of a business, such as profitability, financial strength, and risk.

Funds available for distribution (FAD) See *adjusted funds from operations*.

Funds from operations (FFO) Net income (computed in accordance with generally accepted accounting principles) *plus* (1) gains and losses from sales of properties and (2) depreciation and amortization.

Futures price The pre-agreed price at which a futures contract buyer (seller) agrees to pay (receive) for the underlying at the maturity date of the futures contract.

Futures value The monetary value of an existing futures contract.

Gamma A numerical measure of how sensitive an option's delta (the sensitivity of the derivative's price) is to a change in the value of the underlying.

General linear *F*-test A test statistic used to assess the goodness of fit for an entire regression model, so it tests all independent variables in the model.

Generalize When a model retains its explanatory power when predicting out-of-sample (i.e., using new data).

Global CAPM (GCAPM) A single-factor model with a global index representing the single factor.

Going-concern assumption The assumption that the business will maintain its business activities into the foreseeable future.

Going-concern value A business's value under a going-concern assumption.

Goodwill An intangible asset that represents the excess of the purchase price of an acquired company over the value of the net identifiable assets acquired.

Gordon growth model A DDM that assumes dividends grow at a constant rate into the future.

Grant date The day that stock options are granted to employees.

Green bond Bonds in which the proceeds are designated by issuers to fund a specific project or portfolio of projects that have environmental or climate benefits.

Greenmail The purchase of the accumulated shares of a hostile investor by a company that is targeted for takeover by that investor, usually at a substantial premium over market price.

Greenwashing The risk that a green bond's proceeds are not actually used for a beneficial environmental or climate-related project.

Grid search A method of systematically training a model by using various combinations of hyperparameter values, cross validating each model, and determining which combination of hyperparameter values ensures the best model performance.

Gross domestic product The market value of all final goods and services produced within the economy during a given period (output definition) or, equivalently, the aggregate income earned by all households, all companies, and the government within the economy during a given period (income definition).

Gross lease A lease under which the tenant pays a gross rent to the landlord, who is responsible for all operating costs, utilities, maintenance expenses, and real estate taxes relating to the property.

Ground truth The known outcome (i.e., target variable) of each observation in a labelled dataset.

Growth accounting equation The production function written in the form of growth rates. For the basic Cobb–Douglas production function, it states that the growth rate of output equals the rate of technological change plus α multiplied by the growth rate of capital plus $(1 - \alpha)$ multiplied by the growth rate of labor.

Growth capital expenditures Capital expenditures needed for expansion.

Guideline assets Assets used as benchmarks when applying the method of comparables to value an asset.

Guideline companies Assets used as benchmarks when applying the method of comparables to value an asset.

Guideline public companies Public-company comparables for the company being valued.

Guideline public company method A variation of the market approach; establishes a value estimate based on the observed multiples from trading activity in the shares of public companies viewed as reasonably comparable to the subject private company.

Guideline transactions method A variation of the market approach; establishes a value estimate based on pricing multiples derived from the acquisition of control of entire public or private companies that were acquired.

Harmonic mean A type of weighted mean computed as the reciprocal of the arithmetic average of the reciprocals.

Hazard rate The probability that an event will occur, given that it has not already occurred.

Hedonic index Unlike a repeat-sales index, a hedonic index does not require repeat sales of the same property. It requires only one sale. The way it controls for the fact that different properties are selling each quarter is to include variables in the regression that control for differences in the characteristics of the property, such as size, age, quality of construction, and location.

Heteroskedastic When the variance of the residuals differs across observations in a regression.

Heteroskedasticity The property of having a nonconstant variance; refers to an error term with the property that its variance differs across observations.

Hierarchical clustering An iterative unsupervised learning procedure used for building a hierarchy of clusters.

High-leverage point An observation of an independent variable that has an extreme value and is potentially influential.

Highest and best use The concept that the best use of a vacant site is the use that would result in the highest value for the land. Presumably, the developer that could earn the highest

risk-adjusted profit based on time, effort, construction and development cost, leasing, and exit value would be the one to pay the highest price for the land.

Historical exchange rates For accounting purposes, the exchange rates that existed when the assets and liabilities were initially recorded.

Historical scenario analysis A technique for exploring the performance and risk of investment strategies in different structural regimes.

Historical simulation A simulation method that uses past return data and a random number generator that picks observations from the historical series to simulate an asset's future returns.

Historical simulation method The application of historical price changes to the current portfolio.

Historical stress testing The process that tests how investment strategies would perform under some of the most negative (i.e., adverse) combinations of events and scenarios.

Ho–Lee model The first arbitrage-free term structure model. The model is calibrated to market data and uses a binomial lattice approach to generate a distribution of possible future interest rates.

Holdout samples Data samples that are not used to train a model.

Homoskedasticity The property of having a constant variance; refers to an error term that is constant across observations.

Horizontal ownership Companies with mutual business interests (e.g., key customers or suppliers) that have cross-holding share arrangements with each other.

Human capital An implied asset; the net present value of an investor's future expected labor income weighted by the probability of surviving to each future age. Also called *net employment capital*.

Hybrid approach With respect to forecasting, an approach that combines elements of both top-down and bottom-up analyses.

Hyperparameter A parameter whose value must be set by the researcher before learning begins.

iNAVs "Indicated" net asset values are intraday "fair value" estimates of an ETF share based on its creation basket.

ISDA Master Agreement A standard or "master" agreement published by the International Swaps and Derivatives Association. The master agreement establishes the terms for each party involved in the transaction.

I-spreads Shortened form of "interpolated spreads" and a reference to a linearly interpolated yield.

Idiosyncratic risk premium (IRP) The additional return required for bearing company-specific risks.

Illiquidity discount A reduction or discount to value that reflects the lack of depth of trading or liquidity in that asset's market.

Impairment Diminishment in value as a result of carrying (book) value exceeding fair value and/or recoverable value.

Impairment of capital rule A legal restriction that dividends cannot exceed retained earnings.

Implementation shortfall (IS) The difference between the return for a notional or paper portfolio, where all transactions are assumed to take place at the manager's decision price, and the portfolio's actual return, which reflects realized transactions, including all fees and costs.

Implied volatility The standard deviation that causes an option pricing model to give the current option price.

In-sample forecast errors The residuals from a fitted time-series model within the sample period used to fit the model.

Income approach A valuation approach that values an asset as the present discounted value of the income expected from it. In the context of real estate, this approach estimates the value of a property based on an expected rate of return. The estimated value is the present value of the expected future income from the property, including proceeds from resale at the end of a typical investment holding period.

Incremental borrowing rate (IBR) The rate of interest that the lessee would have to pay to borrow using a collateralized loan over the same term as a lease.

Incremental VaR (IVaR) A measure of the incremental effect of an asset on the VaR of a portfolio by measuring the difference between the portfolio's VaR while including a specified asset and the portfolio's VaR with that asset eliminated.

Indenture A written contract between a lender and borrower that specifies the terms of the loan, such as interest rate, interest payment schedule, or maturity.

Independent board directors Directors with no material relationship with the company with regard to employment, ownership, or remuneration.

Independent regulators Regulators recognized and granted authority by a government body or agency. They are not government agencies per se and typically do not rely on government funding.

Index CDS A type of credit default swap that involves a combination of borrowers.

Industry risk premium (IP) The additional return that is required to bear industry-specific risk.

Industry shocks Unexpected changes to an industry from regulations or the legal environment, technology, or changes in the growth rate of the industry.

Industry structure An industry's underlying economic and technical characteristics.

Influence plot A visual that shows, for all observations, studentized residuals on the y-axis, leverage on the x-axis, and Cook's D as circles whose size is proportional to the degree of influence of the given observation.

Influential observation An observation in a statistical analysis whose inclusion may significantly alter regression results.

Information gain A metric which quantifies the amount of information that the feature holds about the response. Information gain can be regarded as a form of non-linear correlation between Y and X.

Information ratio (IR) Mean active return divided by active risk; or alpha divided by the standard deviation of diversifiable risk.

Informational frictions Forces that restrict availability, quality, and/or flow of information and its use.

Inside ask See *best ask*.

Inside bid See *best bid*.

Inside spread The spread between the best bid price and the best ask price. Also called the *market bid-ask spread*, *inside bid-ask spread*, or *market spread*.

Insiders Corporate managers and board directors who are also shareholders of a company.

Intangible assets Assets without a physical form, such as patents and trademarks.

Inter-temporal rate of substitution The ratio of the marginal utility of consumption s periods in the future (the numerator) to the marginal utility of consumption today (the denominator).

Interaction term A term that combines two or more variables and represents their joint influence on the dependent variable.

Intercept dummy An indicator variable that allows a single regression model to estimate two lines of best fit, each with differing intercepts, depending on whether the dummy takes a value of 1 or 0.

Interest rate risk The risk that interest rates will rise and therefore the market value of current portfolio holdings will fall so that their current yields to maturity then match comparable instruments in the marketplace.

Interlocking directorates Corporate structure in which individuals serve on the board of directors of multiple corporations.

International CAPM (ICAPM) A two-factor model with a global index and a wealth-weighted currency index.

International Fisher effect The proposition that nominal interest rate differentials across currencies are determined by expected inflation differentials.

Intrinsic value The amount gained (per unit) by an option buyer if an option is exercised at any given point in time. May be referred to as the exercise value of the option.

Inverse price ratio The reciprocal of a price multiple—for example, in the case of a P/E, the "earnings yield" E/P (where P is share price and E is earnings per share).

Investment value The value to a specific buyer, taking account of potential synergies based on the investor's requirements and expectations.

Joint test of hypotheses The test of hypotheses that specify values for two or more independent variables in the hypotheses.

Joint venture Two or more companies form and control a new, separate company to achieve a business objective. Each participant contributes assets, employees, know-how, or other resources to the joint venture company. The participants maintain their independence otherwise and continue to do business apart from the joint venture, but they share in the joint venture's profits or losses.

Judicial law Interpretations of courts.

Justified price multiple The estimated fair value of the price multiple, usually based on forecasted fundamentals or comparables.

Justified (fundamental) P/E The price-to-earnings ratio that is fair, warranted, or justified on the basis of forecasted fundamentals.

K-fold cross-validation A technique in which data (excluding test sample and fresh data) are shuffled randomly and then are divided into k equal sub-samples, with $k - 1$ samples used as training samples and one sample, the kth, used as a validation sample.

K-means A clustering algorithm that repeatedly partitions observations into a fixed number, k, of non-overlapping clusters.

K-nearest neighbor A supervised learning technique that classifies a new observation by finding similarities ("nearness") between this new observation and the existing data.

Kalotay–Williams–Fabozzi (KWF) model An arbitrage-free term structure model that describes the dynamics of the log of the short rate and assumes constant drift, no mean reversion, and constant volatility.

Key rate durations Sensitivity of a bond's price to changes in specific maturities on the benchmark yield curve. Also called *partial durations*.

kth-order autocorrelation   The correlation between observations in a time series separated by k periods.

LASSO   Least absolute shrinkage and selection operator is a type of penalized regression which involves minimizing the sum of the absolute values of the regression coefficients. LASSO can also be used for regularization in neural networks.

Labeled dataset   A dataset that contains matched sets of observed inputs or features (X's) and the associated output or target (Y).

Labor force   Everyone of working age (ages 16 to 64) who either is employed or is available for work but not working.

Labor force participation rate   The percentage of the working age population that is in the labor force.

Labor productivity   The quantity of goods and services (real GDP) that a worker can produce in one hour of work.

Labor productivity growth accounting equation   States that potential GDP growth equals the growth rate of the labor input plus the growth rate of labor productivity.

Lack of marketability discount   An extra return to investors to compensate for lack of a public market or lack of marketability.

Latency   The elapsed time between the occurrence of an event and a subsequent action that depends on that event.

Law of one price   A principle that states that if two investments have the same or equivalent future cash flows regardless of what will happen in the future, then these two investments should have the same current price.

Leading dividend yield   Forecasted dividends per share over the next year divided by current stock price.

Leading P/E   A P/E calculated on the basis of a forecast of EPS; a stock's current price divided by next year's expected earnings.

Learning curve   A curve that plots the accuracy rate (= 1 − error rate) in the validation or test samples (i.e., out-of-sample) against the amount of data in the training sample, which is thus useful for describing under- and overfitting as a function of bias and variance errors.

Learning rate   A parameter that affects the magnitude of adjustments in the weights in a neural network.

Level   One of the three factors (the other two are steepness and curvature) that empirically explain most yield curve shape changes. A shock to the level factor changes the yield for all maturities by an almost identical amount.

Leverage   A measure for identifying a potentially influential high-leverage point.

Leveraged buyout (LBO)   An acquirer (typically an investment fund specializing in LBOs) uses a significant amount of debt to finance the acquisition of a target and then pursues restructuring actions, with the goal of exiting the target with a sale or public listing.

Libor–OIS spread   The difference between Libor and the overnight indexed swap rate.

Likelihood ratio (LR) test   A method to assess the fit of logistic regression models and is based on the log-likelihood metric that describes the model's fit to the data.

Limit order book   The book or list of limit orders to buy and sell that pertains to a security.

Linear classifier   A binary classifier that makes its classification decision based on a linear combination of the features of each data point.

Linear trend   A trend in which the dependent variable changes at a constant rate with time.

Liquidating dividend   A dividend that is a return of capital rather than a distribution from earnings or retained earnings.

Liquidation value   The value of a company if the company were dissolved and its assets sold individually.

Liquidity preference theory   A term structure theory that asserts liquidity premiums exist to compensate investors for the added interest rate risk they face when lending long term.

Liquidity premium   An extra return that compensates investors for the risk of loss relative to an investment's fair value if the investment needs to be converted to cash quickly.

Local currency   The currency of the country where a company is located.

Local expectations theory   A term structure theory that contends the return for all bonds over short periods is the risk-free rate.

Log-linear model   With reference to time-series models, a model in which the growth rate of the time series as a function of time is constant.

Log odds   The natural log of the odds of an event or characteristic happening. Also known as the *logit function*.

Logistic regression (logit)   A regression in which the dependent variable uses a logistic transformation of the event probability.

Logistic transformation   The log of the probability of an occurrence of an event or characteristic divided by the probability of the event or characteristic not occurring.

Long/short credit trade   A credit protection seller with respect to one entity combined with a credit protection buyer with respect to another entity.

Look-ahead bias   A bias caused by using information that was unavailable on the test date.

Lookback period   The time period used to gather a historical data set.

Loss given default   The amount that will be lost if a default occurs.

Macroeconomic factor model   A multifactor model in which the factors are surprises in macroeconomic variables that significantly explain equity returns.

Macroeconomic factors   Factors related to the economy, such as the inflation rate, industrial production, or economic sector membership.

Maintenance capital expenditures   Capital expenditures needed to maintain operations at the current level.

Majority shareholders   Shareholders that own more than 50% of a corporation's shares.

Majority-vote classifier   A classifier that assigns to a new data point the predicted label with the most votes (i.e., occurrences).

Marginal VaR (MVaR)   A measure of the effect of a small change in a position size on portfolio VaR.

Market approach   Valuation approach that values an asset based on pricing multiples from sales of assets viewed as similar to the subject asset.

Market conditions   Interest rates, inflation rates, and other economic characteristics that comprise the macroeconomic environment.

Market conversion premium per share   For a convertible bond, the difference between the market conversion price and the underlying share price, which allows investors to identify the premium or discount payable when buying a convertible bond rather than the underlying common stock.

Market conversion premium ratio For a convertible bond, the market conversion premium per share expressed as a percentage of the current market price of the shares.

Market efficiency A finance perspective on capital markets that deals with the relationship of price to intrinsic value. The traditional efficient markets formulation asserts that an asset's price is the best available estimate of its intrinsic value. The rational efficient markets formulation asserts that investors should expect to be rewarded for the costs of information gathering and analysis by higher gross returns.

Market fragmentation Trading the same instrument in multiple venues.

Market impact The effect of the trade on transaction prices. Also called *price impact*.

Market model A regression model with the return on a stock as the dependent variable and the returns on a market index as the independent variable.

Market value of invested capital The market value of debt and equity.

Mature growth rate The earnings growth rate in a company's mature phase; an earnings growth rate that can be sustained long term.

Maximum drawdown The worst cumulative loss ever sustained by an asset or portfolio. More specifically, maximum drawdown is the difference between an asset's or a portfolio's maximum cumulative return and its subsequent lowest cumulative return.

Maximum likelihood estimation (MLE) A method that estimates values for the intercept and slope coefficients in a logistic regression that make the data in the regression sample most likely.

Mean reversion The tendency of a time series to fall when its level is above its mean and rise when its level is below its mean; a mean-reverting time series tends to return to its long-term mean.

Metadata Data that describes and gives information about other data.

Method based on forecasted fundamentals An approach to using price multiples that relates a price multiple to forecasts of fundamentals through a discounted cash flow model.

Method of comparables An approach to valuation that involves using a price multiple to evaluate whether an asset is relatively fairly valued, relatively undervalued, or relatively overvalued when compared to a benchmark value of the multiple.

Midquote price The average, or midpoint, of the prevailing bid and ask prices.

Minority interest The proportion of the ownership of a subsidiary not held by the parent (controlling) company.

Minority shareholders Particular shareholders or a block of shareholders holding a small proportion of a company's outstanding shares, resulting in a limited ability to exercise control in voting activities.

Mispricing Any departure of the market price of an asset from the asset's estimated intrinsic value.

Model specification The set of independent variables included in a model and the model's functional form.

Molodovsky effect The observation that P/Es tend to be high on depressed EPS at the bottom of a business cycle and tend to be low on unusually high EPS at the top of a business cycle.

Momentum indicators Valuation indicators that relate either price or a fundamental (such as earnings) to the time series of their own past values (or in some cases to their expected value).

Monetary assets and liabilities Assets and liabilities with value equal to the amount of currency contracted for, a fixed amount of currency. Examples are cash, accounts receivable, accounts payable, bonds payable, and mortgages payable. Inventory is not a monetary asset. Most liabilities are monetary.

Monetary/non-monetary method Approach to translating foreign currency financial statements for consolidation in which monetary assets and liabilities are translated at the current exchange rate. Non-monetary assets and liabilities are translated at historical exchange rates (the exchange rates that existed when the assets and liabilities were acquired).

Monetizing Unwinding a position to either capture a gain or realize a loss.

Monte Carlo simulation A technique that uses the inverse transformation method for converting a randomly generated uniformly distributed number into a simulated value of a random variable of a desired distribution. Each key decision variable in a Monte Carlo simulation requires an assumed statistical distribution; this assumption facilitates incorporating non-normality, fat tails, and tail dependence as well as solving high-dimensionality problems.

Mortgage A loan with real estate serving as collateral for the loan.

Multicollinearity When two or more independent variables are highly correlated with one another or are approximately linearly related.

Multiple linear regression Modeling and estimation method that uses two or more independent variables to describe the variation of the dependent variable. Also referred to as *multiple regression*.

Mutual information Measures how much information is contributed by a token to a class of texts. MI will be 0 if the token's distribution in all text classes is the same. MI approaches 1 as the token in any one class tends to occur more often in only that particular class of text.

N-grams A representation of word sequences. The length of a sequence varies from 1 to n. When one word is used, it is a unigram; a two-word sequence is a bigram; and a 3-word sequence is a trigram; and so on.

n-Period moving average The average of the current and immediately prior $n - 1$ values of a time series.

NTM P/E Next 12-month P/E: current market price divided by an estimated next 12-month EPS.

Naked credit default swap A position where the owner of the CDS does not have a position in the underlying credit.

Name entity recognition An algorithm that analyzes individual tokens and their surrounding semantics while referring to its dictionary to tag an object class to the token.

Negative serial correlation A situation in which residuals are negatively related to other residuals.

Nested models Models in which one regression model has a subset of the independent variables of another regression model.

Net asset balance sheet exposure When assets translated at the current exchange rate are greater in amount than liabilities translated at the current exchange rate. Assets exposed to translation gains or losses exceed the exposed liabilities.

Net asset value per share (NAVPS) Net asset value divided by the number of shares outstanding.

Net lease A lease under which the tenant pays a net rent to the landlord and an additional amount based on the tenant's pro rata share of the operating costs, utilities, maintenance expenses, and real estate taxes relating to the property.

Net liability balance sheet exposure When liabilities translated at the current exchange rate are greater assets translated at the current exchange rate. Liabilities exposed to translation gains or losses exceed the exposed assets.

Net operating income (NOI) Gross rental revenue minus operating costs but before deducting depreciation, corporate overhead, and interest expense. In the context of real estate, a measure of the income from the property after deducting operating expenses for such items as property taxes, insurance, maintenance, utilities, repairs, and insurance but before deducting any costs associated with financing and before deducting federal income taxes. It is similar to EBITDA in a financial reporting context.

Net regulatory burden The private costs of regulation less the private benefits of regulation.

Network externalities The impact that users of a good, a service, or a technology have on other users of that product; it can be positive (e.g., a critical mass of users makes a product more useful) or negative (e.g., congestion makes the product less useful).

Neural networks Computer programs based on how our own brains learn and process information.

No-arbitrage approach A procedure for obtaining the value of an option based on the creation of a portfolio that replicates the payoffs of the option and deriving the option value from the value of the replicating portfolio.

No-growth company A company without positive expected net present value projects.

No-growth value per share The value per share of a no-growth company, equal to the expected level amount of earnings divided by the stock's required rate of return.

Non-cash rent An amount equal to the difference between the average contractual rent over a lease term (the straight-line rent) and the cash rent actually paid during a period. This figure is one of the deductions made from FFO to calculate AFFO.

Non-convergence trap A situation in which a country remains relatively poor, or even falls further behind, because it fails to implement necessary institutional reforms and/or adopt leading technologies.

Non-monetary assets and liabilities Assets and liabilities that are not monetary assets and liabilities. Non-monetary assets include inventory, fixed assets, and intangibles, and non-monetary liabilities include deferred revenue.

Non-renewable resources Finite resources that are depleted once they are consumed; oil and coal are examples.

Non-residential properties Commercial real estate properties other than multi-family properties, farmland, and timberland.

Nonearning assets Cash and investments (specifically cash, cash equivalents, and short-term investments).

Normal EPS The EPS that a business could achieve currently under mid-cyclical conditions. Also called *normalized EPS*.

Normal Q-Q plot A visual used to compare the distribution of the residuals from a regression to a theoretical normal distribution.

Normalized EPS The EPS that a business could achieve currently under mid-cyclical conditions. Also called *normal EPS*.

Normalized earnings The expected level of mid-cycle earnings for a company in the absence of any unusual or temporary factors that affect profitability (either positively or negatively).

Normalized P/E P/E based on normalized EPS data.

Notional amount The amount of protection being purchased in a CDS.

Off-the-run A series of securities or indexes that were issued/created prior to the most recently issued/created series.

Offshoring Refers to relocating operations from one country to another, mainly to reduce costs through lower labor costs or to achieve economies of scale through centralization, but still maintaining operations within the corporation.

Omitted variable bias Bias resulting from the omission of an important independent variable from a regression model.

On-the-run The most recently issued and most actively traded sovereign securities.

One hot encoding The process by which categorical variables are converted into binary form (0 or 1) for machine reading. It is one of the most common methods for handling categorical features in text data.

One-sided durations Effective durations when interest rates go up or down, which are better at capturing the interest rate sensitivity of bonds with embedded options that do not react symmetrically to positive and negative changes in interest rates of the same magnitude.

One-tier board Board structure consisting of a single board of directors, composed of executive (internal) and non-executive (external) directors.

Opportunity cost Reflects the foregone opportunity of investing in a different asset. It is typically denoted by the risk-free rate of interest, r.

Option-adjusted spread (OAS) Constant spread that, when added to all the one-period forward rates on the interest rate tree, makes the arbitrage-free value of the bond equal to its market price.

Orderly liquidation value The estimated gross amount of money that could be realized from the liquidation sale of an asset or assets, given a reasonable amount of time to find a purchaser or purchasers.

Other comprehensive income Items of comprehensive income that are not reported on the income statement; comprehensive income minus net income.

Other post-employment benefits Promises by the company to pay benefits in the future, such as life insurance premiums and all or part of health care insurance for its retirees.

Out-of-sample forecast errors The differences between actual and predicted values of time series outside the sample period used to fit the model.

Outlier An observation that has an extreme value of the dependent variable and is potentially influential.

Outsourcing Shifting internal business services to a subcontractor that can offer services at lower costs by scaling to serve many clients.

Overfitting Situation in which the model has too many independent variables relative to the number of observations in the sample, such that the coefficients on the independent variables represent noise rather than relationships with the dependent variable.

Overnight indexed swap (OIS) rate   An interest rate swap in which the periodic floating rate of the swap equals the geometric average of a daily unsecured overnight rate (or overnight index rate).

PEG ratio   The P/E-to-growth ratio, calculated as the stock's P/E divided by the expected earnings growth rate.

Pairs trading   An approach to trading that uses pairs of closely related stocks, buying the relatively undervalued stock and selling short the relatively overvalued stock.

Par curve   A sequence of yields-to-maturity such that each bond is priced at par value. The bonds are assumed to have the same currency, credit risk, liquidity, tax status, and annual yields stated for the same periodicity.

Par swap   A swap in which the fixed rate is set so that no money is exchanged at contract initiation.

Parametric method   A method of estimating VaR that uses the historical mean, standard deviation, and correlation of security price movements to estimate the portfolio VaR. Generally assumes a normal distribution but can be adapted to non-normal distributions with the addition of skewness and kurtosis. Sometimes called the *variance–covariance method* or the *analytical method*.

Partial regression coefficient   Coefficient that describes the effect of a one-unit change in the independent variable on the dependent variable, holding all other independent variables constant. Also known as *partial slope coefficient*.

Parts of speech   An algorithm that uses language structure and dictionaries to tag every token in the text with a corresponding part of speech (i.e., noun, verb, adjective, proper noun, etc.).

Payout amount   The loss given default times the notional.

Payout policy   The principles by which a company distributes cash to common shareholders by means of cash dividends and/or share repurchases.

Payouts   Cash dividends and the value of shares repurchased in any given year.

Penalized regression   A regression that includes a constraint such that the regression coefficients are chosen to minimize the sum of squared residuals *plus* a penalty term that increases in size with the number of included features.

Pension obligation   The present value of future benefits earned by employees for service provided to date.

Perfect capital markets   Markets in which, by assumption, there are no taxes, transaction costs, or bankruptcy costs and in which all investors have equal ("symmetric") information.

Perpetuity   A perpetual annuity, or a set of never-ending level sequential cash flows, with the first cash flow occurring one period from now.

Persistent earnings   Earnings excluding nonrecurring components. Also referred to as *core earnings, continuing earnings,* or *underlying earnings*.

Physical settlement   Involves actual delivery of the debt instrument in exchange for a payment by the credit protection seller of the notional amount of the contract.

Point-in-time data   Data consisting of the exact information available to market participants as of a given point in time. Point-in-time data is used to address look-ahead bias.

Portfolio balance approach   A theory of exchange rate determination that emphasizes the portfolio investment decisions of global investors and the requirement that global investors willingly hold all outstanding securities denominated in each currency at prevailing prices and exchange rates.

Positive serial correlation   A situation in which residuals are positively related to other residuals.

Potential GDP   The maximum amount of output an economy can sustainably produce without inducing an increase in the inflation rate. The output level that corresponds to full employment with consistent wage and price expectations.

Precision   In error analysis for classification problems it is ratio of correctly predicted positive classes to all predicted positive classes. Precision is useful in situations where the cost of false positives (FP), or Type I error, is high.

Preferred habitat theory   A term structure theory that contends that investors have maturity preferences and require yield incentives before they will buy bonds outside of their preferred maturities.

Premise of value   The status of a company in the sense of whether it is assumed to be a going concern or not.

Premium leg   The series of payments the credit protection buyer promises to make to the credit protection seller.

Premiums   Amounts paid by the purchaser of insurance products.

Present value model   A model of intrinsic value that views the value of an asset as the present value of the asset's expected future cash flows.

Present value of growth opportunities   The difference between the actual value per share and the no-growth value per share. Also called *value of growth*.

Presentation currency   The currency in which financial statement amounts are presented.

Price improvement   When trade execution prices are better than quoted prices.

Price momentum   A valuation indicator based on past price movement.

Price multiples   The ratio of a stock's market price to some measure of value per share.

Price-to-earnings ratio   (P/E) The ratio of share price to earnings per share.

Priced risk   Risk for which investors demand compensation for bearing (e.g., equity risk, company-specific factors, macroeconomic factors).

Principal components analysis (PCA)   An unsupervised ML technique used to transform highly correlated features of data into a few main, uncorrelated composite variables.

Principle of no arbitrage   In well-functioning markets, prices will adjust until there are no arbitrage opportunities.

Prior transaction method   A variation of the market approach; considers actual transactions in the stock of the subject private company.

Private market value   The value derived using a sum-of-the-parts valuation.

Pro forma financial statements   Financial statements that include the effect of a corporate restructuring.

Probability of default   The likelihood that a borrower defaults or fails to meet its obligation to make full and timely payments of principal and interest.

Probability of survival   The probability that a bond issuer will meet its contractual obligations on schedule.

Procedural law   The body of law that focuses on the protection and enforcement of the substantive laws.

Projection error   The vertical (perpendicular) distance between a data point and a given principal component.

Prospective P/E   A P/E calculated on the basis of a forecast of EPS; a stock's current price divided by next year's expected earnings.

Protection leg The contingent payment that the credit protection seller may have to make to the credit protection buyer.

Protection period Period during which a bond's issuer cannot call the bond.

Provision for loan losses An income statement expense account that increases the amount of the allowance for loan losses.

Prudential supervision Regulation and monitoring of the safety and soundness of financial institutions to promote financial stability, reduce system-wide risks, and protect customers of financial institutions.

Pruning A regularization technique used in CART to reduce the size of the classification or regression tree—by pruning, or removing, sections of the tree that provide little classifying power.

Purchasing power gain A gain in value caused by changes in price levels. Monetary liabilities experience purchasing power gains during periods of inflation.

Purchasing power loss A loss in value caused by changes in price levels. Monetary assets experience purchasing power loss during periods of inflation.

Purchasing power parity (PPP) The idea that exchange rates move to equalize the purchasing power of different currencies.

Pure expectations theory A term structure theory that contends the forward rate is an unbiased predictor of the future spot rate. Also called the *unbiased expectations theory*.

Pure factor portfolio A portfolio with sensitivity of 1 to the factor in question and a sensitivity of 0 to all other factors.

Putable bond Bond that includes an embedded put option, which gives the bondholder the right to put back the bonds to the issuer prior to maturity, typically when interest rates have risen and higher-yielding bonds are available.

Qualitative dependent variable A dependent variable that is discrete (binary). Also known as a *categorical dependent variable*.

Quality of earnings analysis The investigation of issues relating to the accuracy of reported accounting results as reflections of economic performance. Quality of earnings analysis is broadly understood to include not only earnings management but also balance sheet management.

Random forest classifier A collection of a large number of decision trees trained via a bagging method.

Random walk A time series in which the value of the series in one period is the value of the series in the previous period plus an unpredictable random error.

Rate implicit in the lease (RIIL) The discount rate that equates the present value of the lease payment with the fair value of the leased asset, considering also the lessor's direct costs and the present value of the leased asset's residual value.

Rational efficient markets formulation See *market efficiency*.

Readme files Text files provided with raw data that contain information related to a data file. They are useful for understanding the data and how they can be interpreted correctly.

Real estate investment trusts (REITs) Tax-advantaged entities (companies or trusts) that own, operate, and—to a limited extent—develop income-producing real estate property.

Real estate operating companies (REOCs) Regular taxable real estate ownership companies that operate in the real estate industry in countries that do not have a tax-advantaged REIT regime in place or that are engage in real estate activities of a kind and to an extent that do not fit in their country's REIT framework.

Real interest rate parity The proposition that real interest rates will converge to the same level across different markets.

Real options Options that relate to investment decisions such as the option to time the start of a project, the option to adjust its scale, or the option to abandon a project that has begun.

Rebalance return A return from rebalancing the component weights of an index.

Recall Also known as *sensitivity*, in error analysis for classification problems it is the ratio of correctly predicted positive classes to all actual positive classes. Recall is useful in situations where the cost of false negatives (FN), or Type II error, is high.

Recency bias The behavioral tendency to place more relevance on recent events.

Reconstitution When dealers recombine appropriate individual zero-coupon securities and reproduce an underlying coupon Treasury.

Recovery rate The percentage of the loss recovered.

Redemption basket The list of securities (and share amounts) the authorized participant (AP) receives when it redeems ETF shares back to the ETF manager. The redemption basket is published each business day.

Reference entity The borrower (debt issuer) covered by a single-name CDS.

Reference obligation A particular debt instrument issued by the borrower that is the designated instrument being covered.

Regime With reference to a time series, the underlying model generating the times series.

Regular expression (regex) A series of texts that contains characters in a particular order. Regex is used to search for patterns of interest in a given text.

Regularization A term that describes methods for reducing statistical variability in high-dimensional data estimation problems.

Regulatory arbitrage Entities identify and use some aspect of regulations that allows them to exploit differences in economic substance and regulatory interpretation or in foreign and domestic regulatory regimes to their (the entities') advantage.

Regulatory burden The costs of regulation for the regulated entity.

Regulatory capture Theory that regulation often arises to enhance the interests of the regulated.

Regulatory competition Regulators may compete to provide a regulatory environment designed to attract certain entities.

Reinforcement learning Machine learning in which a computer learns from interacting with itself or data generated by the same algorithm.

Relative-strength indicators Valuation indicators that compare a stock's performance during a period either to its own past performance or to the performance of some group of stocks.

Relative VaR See *ex ante tracking error*.

Relative valuation models A model that specifies an asset's value relative to the value of another asset.

Relative version of PPP The hypothesis that changes in (nominal) exchange rates over time are equal to national inflation rate differentials.

Renewable resources Resources that can be replenished, such as a forest.

Rental price of capital The cost per unit of time to rent a unit of capital.

Reorganization A court-supervised restructuring process available in some jurisdictions for companies facing insolvency from burdensome debt levels. A bankruptcy court assumes control of the company and oversees an orderly negotiation process between the company and its creditors for asset sales, conversion of debt to equity, refinancing, and so on.

Repeat sales index As the name implies, this type of index relies on repeat sales of the same property. In general, the idea supporting this type of index is that because it is the same property that sold twice, the change in value between the two sale dates indicates how market conditions have changed over time.

Replacement cost In the context of real estate, the value of a building assuming it was built today using current construction costs and standards.

Reporting unit For financial reporting under US GAAP, an operating segment or one level below an operating segment (referred to as a component).

Required rate of return on equity The minimum rate of return required by an investor to invest in an asset, given the asset's riskiness. Also known as the required return on equity.

Residential properties Properties that provide housing for individuals or families. Single-family properties may be owner-occupied or rental properties, whereas multi-family properties are rental properties even if the owner or manager occupies one of the units.

Residual autocorrelations The sample autocorrelations of the residuals.

Residual income Earnings for a given period, minus a deduction for common shareholders' opportunity cost in generating the earnings. Also called *economic profit* or *abnormal earnings*.

Residual income method Income approach that estimates the value of all intangible assets of the business by capitalizing future earnings in excess of the estimated return requirements associated with working capital and fixed assets.

Residual income model (RIM) A model of stock valuation that views intrinsic value of stock as the sum of book value per share plus the present value of the stock's expected future residual income per share. Also called *discounted abnormal earnings model* or *Edwards–Bell–Ohlson model*.

Restricted model A regression model with a subset of the complete set of independent variables.

Restructuring Reorganizing the capital structure of a firm.

Return on invested capital A measure of the profitability of a company relative to the amount of capital invested by the equity- and debtholders.

Reverse carry arbitrage A strategy involving the short sale of the underlying and an offsetting opposite position in the derivative.

Reverse stock split A reduction in the number of shares outstanding with a corresponding increase in share price, but no change to the company's underlying fundamentals.

Reverse stress testing A risk management approach in which the user identifies key risk exposures in the portfolio and subjects those exposures to extreme market movements.

Reviewed financial statements A type of non-audited financial statements; typically provide an opinion letter with representations and assurances by the reviewing accountant that are less than those in audited financial statements.

Rho The change in a given derivative instrument for a given small change in the risk-free interest rate, holding everything else constant. Rho measures the sensitivity of the option to the risk-free interest rate.

Risk-based models Models of the return on equity that identify risk factors or drivers and sensitivities of the return to these factors.

Risk budgeting The establishment of objectives for individuals, groups, or divisions of an organization that takes into account the allocation of an acceptable level of risk.

Risk decomposition The process of converting a set of holdings in a portfolio into a set of exposures to risk factors.

Risk factors Variables or characteristics with which individual asset returns are correlated. Sometimes referred to simply as *factors*.

Risk-free rate The minimum rate of return expected on a security that has no default risk.

Risk parity A portfolio allocation scheme that weights stocks or factors based on an equal risk contribution.

Robust standard errors Method for correcting residuals for conditional heteroskedasticity. Also known as *heteroskedasticity-consistent standard errors* or *White-corrected standard errors*.

Roll When an investor moves its investment position from an older series to the most current series.

Roll return The component of the return on a commodity futures contract attributable to rolling long futures positions forward through time. Also called *roll yield*.

Rolling down the yield curve A maturity trading strategy that involves buying bonds with a maturity longer than the intended investment horizon. Also called *riding the yield curve*.

Rolling windows A backtesting method that uses a rolling-window (or walk-forward) framework, rebalances the portfolio after each period, and then tracks performance over time. As new information arrives each period, the investment manager optimizes (revises and tunes) the model and readjusts stock positions.

Root mean squared error (RMSE) The square root of the average squared forecast error; used to compare the out-of-sample forecasting performance of forecasting models.

Sale-leaseback A situation in which a company sells the building it owns and occupies to a real estate investor and the company then signs a long-term lease with the buyer to continue to occupy the building. At the end of the lease, use of the property reverts to the landlord.

Sales comparison approach In the context of real estate, this approach estimates value based on what similar or comparable properties (comparables) transacted for in the current market.

Sales risk The uncertainty regarding the price and number of units sold of a company's products.

Scaled earnings surprise Unexpected earnings divided by the standard deviation of analysts' earnings forecasts.

Scaling The process of adjusting the range of a feature by shifting and changing the scale of the data. Two of the most common ways of scaling are normalization and standardization.

Scatterplot matrix A visualization technique that shows the scatterplots between different sets of variables, often with the histogram for each variable on the diagonal. Also referred to as a *pairs plot*.

Scenario analysis A technique for exploring the performance and risk of investment strategies in different structural regimes.

Schwarz's Bayesian information criterion (BIC or SBC) A statistic used to compare sets of independent variables for explaining a dependent variable. It is preferred for finding the model with the best goodness of fit.

Scree plots A plot that shows the proportion of total variance in the data explained by each principal component.

Screening The application of a set of criteria to reduce a set of potential investments to a smaller set having certain desired characteristics.

Seasonality A characteristic of a time series in which the data experience regular and predictable periodic changes; for example, fan sales are highest during the summer months.

Secured overnight financing rate (SOFR) A daily volume-weighted index of rates on qualified cash borrowings collateralized by US Treasuries that is expected to replace Libor as a floating reference rate for swaps.

Security selection risk See *active specific risk*.

Segmented markets theory A term structure theory that contends yields are solely a function of the supply and demand for funds of a particular maturity.

Self-regulating organizations (SROs) Self-regulating bodies that are given recognition and authority, including enforcement power, by a government body or agency.

Self-regulatory bodies Private, non-governmental organizations that both represent and regulate their members. Some self-regulating organizations are also independent regulators.

Sell-side analysts Analysts who work at brokerages.

Sensitivity analysis Analysis that shows the range of possible outcomes as specific assumptions are changed.

Sentence length The number of characters, including spaces, in a sentence.

Serial correlation A condition found most often in time series in which residuals are correlated across observations. Also known as *autocorrelation*.

Serial-correlation consistent standard errors Method for correcting serial correlation. Also known as *serial correlation and heteroskedasticity adjusted standard errors*, *Newey–West standard errors*, and *robust standard errors*.

Service period For employee stock options, usually the period between the grant date and the vesting date.

Settled in arrears An arrangement in which the interest payment is made (i.e., settlement occurs) at the maturity of the underlying instrument.

Settlement The closing date at which the counterparties of a derivative contract exchange payment for the underlying as required by the contract.

Shadow banking Lending by financial institutions that are not regulated as banks.

Shaping risk The sensitivity of a bond's price to the changing shape of the yield curve.

Share repurchase A transaction in which a company buys back its own shares. Unlike stock dividends and stock splits, share repurchases use corporate cash.

Shareholder activism Strategies used by shareholders to attempt to compel a company to act in a desired manner.

Shareholders' equity Total assets minus total liabilities.

Simulation A technique for exploring how a target variable (e.g. portfolio returns) would perform in a hypothetical environment specified by the user, rather than a historical setting.

Single-name CDS Credit default swap on one specific borrower.

Sinking fund bond A bond that requires the issuer to set aside funds over time to retire the bond issue, thus reducing credit risk.

Size premium (SP) Additional return compensation for bearing the additional risk associated with smaller companies.

Slope dummy An indicator variable that allows a single regression model to estimate two lines of best fit, each with differing slopes, depending on whether the dummy takes a value of 1 or 0.

Soft margin classification An adaptation in the support vector machine algorithm which adds a penalty to the objective function for observations in the training set that are misclassified.

Sovereign yield spread The spread between the yield on a foreign country's sovereign bond and a similar-maturity domestic sovereign bond.

Special dividend A dividend paid by a company that does not pay dividends on a regular schedule, or a dividend that supplements regular cash dividends with an extra payment.

Specific-company risk premium (SCRP) Additional return required by investors for bearing non-diversifiable company-specific risk.

Spin off When a company separates a distinct part of its business into a new, independent company. The term is used to describe both the transaction and the separated component, while the company that conducts the transaction and formerly owned the spin off is known as the parent.

Split-rate tax system In reference to corporate taxes, a split-rate system taxes earnings to be distributed as dividends at a different rate than earnings to be retained. Corporate profits distributed as dividends are taxed at a lower rate than those retained in the business.

Spot curve A sequence of yields-to-maturity on zero-coupon bonds. Sometimes called *zero* or *strip curve* (because coupon payments are "stripped" off the bonds).

Spot price The current price of an asset or security. For commodities, the current price to deliver a physical commodity to a specific location or purchase and transport it away from a designated location.

Spot rate The interest rate that is determined today for a risk-free, single-unit payment at a specified future date.

Spot yield curve The term structure of spot rates for loans made today.

Stabilized NOI In the context of real estate, the expected NOI when a renovation is complete.

Stable dividend policy A policy in which regular dividends are paid that reflect long-run expected earnings. In contrast to a constant dividend payout ratio policy, a stable dividend policy does not reflect short-term volatility in earnings.

Standardized beta With reference to fundamental factor models, the value of the attribute for an asset minus the average value of the attribute across all stocks, divided by the standard deviation of the attribute across all stocks.

Standardized unexpected earnings Unexpected earnings per share divided by the standard deviation of unexpected earnings per share over a specified prior time period.

Statistical factor model A multifactor model in which statistical methods are applied to a set of historical returns to determine portfolios that best explain either historical return covariances or variances.

Statutes Laws enacted by legislative bodies.

Steady-state rate of growth The constant growth rate of output (or output per capita) that can or will be sustained indefinitely once it is reached. Key ratios, such as the capital–output ratio, are constant on the steady-state growth path.

Steepness The difference between long-term and short-term yields that constitutes one of the three factors (the other two are level and curvature) that empirically explain most of the changes in the shape of the yield curve.

Stock dividend A type of dividend in which a company distributes additional shares of its common stock to shareholders instead of cash.

Stop-loss limit Constraint used in risk management that requires a reduction in the size of a portfolio, or its complete liquidation, when a loss of a particular size occurs in a specified period.

Straight bond An underlying option-free bond with a specified issuer, issue date, maturity date, principal amount and repayment structure, coupon rate and payment structure, and currency denomination.

Straight debt Debt with no embedded options.

Straight-line rent The average annual rent under a multi-year lease agreement that contains contractual increases in rent during the life of the lease.

Straight-line rent adjustment See *non-cash rent*.

Straight voting A shareholder voting process in which shareholders receive one vote for each share owned.

Stranded assets Assets that are obsolete or not economically viable.

Strategic transaction A purchase involving a buyer that would benefit from certain synergies associated with owning the target firm.

Stress tests A risk management technique that assesses the portfolio's response to extreme market movements.

Stripping A dealer's ability to separate a bond's individual cash flows and trade them as zero-coupon securities.

Studentized residual A *t*-distributed statistic that is used to detect outliers.

Substantive law The body of law that focuses on the rights and responsibilities of entities and relationships among entities.

Succession event A change of corporate structure of the reference entity, such as through a merger, a divestiture, a spinoff, or any similar action, in which ultimate responsibility for the debt in question is unclear.

Sum-of-the-parts valuation A valuation that sums the estimated values of each of a company's businesses as if each business were an independent going concern.

Summation operator A functional part of a neural network's node that multiplies each input value received by a weight and sums the weighted values to form the total net input, which is then passed to the activation function.

Supernormal growth Above-average or abnormally high growth rate in earnings per share.

Supervised learning A machine learning approach that makes use of labeled training data.

Support vector machine A linear classifier that determines the hyperplane that optimally separates the observations into two sets of data points.

Survivorship bias The exclusion of poorly performing or defunct companies from an index or database, biasing the index or database toward financially healthy companies.

Sustainable growth rate The rate of dividend (and earnings) growth that can be sustained over time for a given level of return on equity, keeping the capital structure constant and without issuing additional common stock.

Swap curve The term structure of swap rates.

Swap rate The fixed rate to be paid by the fixed-rate payer specified in a swap contract.

Swap rate curve The term structure of swap rates.

Swap spread The difference between the fixed rate on an interest rate swap and the rate on a Treasury note with equivalent maturity; it reflects the general level of credit risk in the market.

Synergies The combination of two companies being more valuable than the sum of the parts. Generally, synergies take the form of lower costs ("cost synergies") or increased revenues ("revenue synergies") through combinations that generate lower costs or higher revenues, respectively.

Systematic risk Risk that affects the entire market or economy; it cannot be avoided and is inherent in the overall market. Systematic risk is also known as non-diversifiable or market risk.

Systemic risk Refers to risks supervisory authorities believe are likely to have broad impact across the financial market infrastructure and affect a wide swath of market participants.

TED spread A measure of perceived credit risk determined as the difference between Libor and the T-bill yield of matching maturity.

Tail risk The risk that losses in extreme events could be greater than would be expected for a portfolio of assets with a normal distribution.

Takeover premium The amount by which the per-share takeover price exceeds the unaffected price expressed as a percentage of the unaffected price. It reflects the amount shareholders require to relinquish their control of the company to the acquirer.

Tangible assets Identifiable, physical assets such as property, plant, and equipment.

Tangible book value per share Common shareholders' equity minus intangible assets reported on the balance sheet, divided by the number of shares outstanding.

Target In machine learning, the dependent variable (Y) in a labeled dataset; the company in a merger or acquisition that is being acquired.

Target capital structure A company's chosen proportions of debt and equity.

Target payout ratio A strategic corporate goal representing the long-term proportion of earnings that the company intends to distribute to shareholders as dividends.

Taxable REIT subsidiaries Subsidiaries that pay income taxes on earnings from non-REIT-qualifying activities like merchant development or third-party property management.

Technical indicators Momentum indicators based on price.

Temporal method A variation of the monetary/non-monetary translation method that requires not only monetary assets and liabilities, but also non-monetary assets and liabilities that are measured at their current value on the balance sheet date to be translated at the current exchange rate. Assets and liabilities are translated at rates consistent with the timing of their measurement value. This method is typically used when the functional currency is other than the local currency.

Term frequency (TF)   Ratio of the number of times a given token occurs in all the texts in the dataset to the total number of tokens in the dataset.

Term premium   The additional return required by lenders to invest in a bond to maturity net of the expected return from continually reinvesting at the short-term rate over that same time horizon.

Terminal price multiples   The price multiple for a stock assumed to hold at a stated future time.

Terminal share price   The share price at a particular point in the future.

Terminal value of the stock   The analyst's estimate of a stock's value at a particular point in the future. Also called *continuing value of the stock*.

Test sample   A data sample that is used to test a model's ability to predict well on new data.

Theta   The change in a derivative instrument for a given small change in calendar time, holding everything else constant. Specifically, the theta calculation assumes nothing changes except calendar time. Theta also reflects the rate at which an option's time value decays.

Time series   A set of observations on a variable's outcomes in different time periods.

Tobin's *q*   The ratio of the market value of debt and equity to the replacement cost of total assets.

Token   The equivalent of a word (or sometimes a character).

Tokenization   The process of representing ownership rights to physical assets on a blockchain or distributed ledger.

Top-down approach   With respect to forecasting, an approach that usually begins at the level of the overall economy. Forecasts are then made at more narrowly defined levels, such as sector, industry, and market for a specific product.

Total factor productivity (TFP)   A multiplicative scale factor that reflects the general level of productivity or technology in the economy. Changes in total factor productivity generate proportional changes in output for any input combination.

Total invested capital   The sum of market value of common equity, book value of preferred equity, and face value of debt.

Tracking error   The standard deviation of the differences between a portfolio's returns and its benchmark's returns; a synonym of *active risk*. Also called *tracking risk*.

Tracking risk   The standard deviation of the differences between a portfolio's returns and its benchmarks returns. Also called *tracking error*.

Trailing dividend yield   The reciprocal of current market price divided by the most recent annualized dividend.

Trailing P/E   A stock's current market price divided by the most recent four quarters of EPS (or the most recent two semi-annual periods for companies that report interim data semi-annually). Also called *current P/E*.

Training sample   A data sample that is used to train a model.

Tranche CDS   A type of credit default swap that covers a combination of borrowers but only up to pre-specified levels of losses.

Transaction exposure   The risk of a change in value between the transaction date and the settlement date of an asset of liability denominated in a foreign currency.

Treasury shares/stock   Shares that were issued and subsequently repurchased by the company.

Trend   A long-term pattern of movement in a particular direction.

Triangular arbitrage   An arbitrage transaction involving three currencies that attempts to exploit inconsistencies among pairwise exchange rates.

Trimming   Also called truncation, it is the process of removing extreme values and outliers from a dataset.

Triple-net leases   Leases that require each tenant to pay its share of the following three operating expenses: common area maintenance and repair expenses; property taxes; and building insurance costs. Also known as *NNN leases*.

Two-tier board   Board structure consisting of a supervisory board that oversees a management board.

Unbiased expectations theory   A term structure theory that contends the forward rate is an unbiased predictor of the future spot rate. Also called the *pure expectations theory*.

Unconditional heteroskedasticity   When heteroskedasticity of the error variance is not correlated with the regression's independent variables.

Uncovered interest rate parity   The proposition that the expected return on an uncovered (i.e., unhedged) foreign currency (risk-free) investment should equal the return on a comparable domestic currency investment.

Underlying earnings   Earnings excluding nonrecurring components. Also referred to as *continuing earnings, core earnings,* or *persistent earnings*.

Unexpected earnings   The difference between reported EPS and expected EPS. Also referred to as an *earnings surprise*.

Unit root   A time series that is not covariance stationary is said to have a unit root.

Unrestricted model   A regression model with the complete set of independent variables.

Unsupervised learning   A machine learning approach that does not make use of labeled training data.

Upfront payment   The difference between the credit spread and the standard rate paid by the protection buyer if the standard rate is insufficient to compensate the protection seller. Also called *upfront premium*.

Upfront premium   See *upfront payment*.

Upstream   A transaction between two related companies, an investor company (or a parent company) and an associate company (or a subsidiary company) such that the associate company records a profit on its income statement. An example is a sale of inventory by the associate to the investor company or by a subsidiary to a parent company.

Validation sample   A data sample that is used to validate and tune a model.

Valuation   The process of determining the value of an asset or service either on the basis of variables perceived to be related to future investment returns or on the basis of comparisons with closely similar assets.

Value additivity   An arbitrage opportunity when the value of the whole equals the sum of the values of the parts.

Value at risk (VaR)   The minimum loss that would be expected a certain percentage of the time over a certain period of time given the assumed market conditions.

Value of growth   The difference between the actual value per share and the no-growth value per share.

Variance error   Describes how much a model's results change in response to new data from validation and test samples. Unstable models pick up noise and produce high variance error, causing overfitting and high out-of-sample error.

Variance inflation factor (VIF)   A statistic that quantifies the degree of multicollinearity in a model.

Vasicek model A partial equilibrium term structure model that assumes interest rates are mean reverting and interest rate volatility is constant.

Vega The change in a given derivative instrument for a given small change in volatility, holding everything else constant. A sensitivity measure for options that reflects the effect of volatility.

Venture capital investors Private equity investors in development-stage companies.

Vertical ownership Ownership structure in which a company or group that has a controlling interest in two or more holding companies, which in turn have controlling interests in various operating companies.

Vested benefit obligation The actuarial present value of vested benefits.

Vesting date The date that employees can first exercise stock options.

Visibility The extent to which a company's operations are predictable with substantial confidence.

Voting caps Legal restrictions on the voting rights of large share positions.

Web spidering (scraping or crawling) programs Programs that extract raw content from a source, typically web pages.

Weighted average cost of capital (WACC) A weighted average of the after-tax required rates of return on a company's common stock, preferred stock, and long-term debt, where the weights are the fraction of each source of financing in the company's target capital structure.

Weighted harmonic mean See *harmonic mean*.

Winsorization The process of replacing extreme values and outliers in a dataset with the maximum (for large value outliers) and minimum (for small value outliers) values of data points that are not outliers.

Write-down A reduction in the value of an asset as stated in the balance sheet.

Yield curve factor model A model or a description of yield curve movements that can be considered realistic when compared with historical data.

Zero A bond that does not pay a coupon but is priced at a discount and pays its full face value at maturity.

Zero-coupon bond A bond that does not pay interest during its life. It is issued at a discount to par value and redeemed at par. Also called *pure discount bond*.